ONLY BY EXPERIENCE

ONLY BY EXPERIENCE

AN ANTHOLOGY OF SLAVE NARRATIVES

a *Broadview Anthology of American Literature* edition

General Editors, *The Broadview Anthology of American Literature*:

Derrick R. Spires, Cornell University
Rachel Greenwald Smith, Saint Louis University
Christina Roberts, Seattle University
Joseph Rezek, Boston University
Justine S. Murison, University of Illinois, Urbana-Champaign
Laura L. Mielke, University of Kansas
Christopher Looby, University of California, Los Angeles
Rodrigo Lazo, University of California, Irvine
Alisha Knight, Washington College
Hsuan L. Hsu, University of California, Davis
Michael Everton, Simon Fraser University
Christine Bold, University of Guelph

broadview press

BROADVIEW PRESS – www.broadviewpress.com
Peterborough, Ontario, Canada

Founded in 1985, Broadview Press remains a wholly independent publishing house. Broadview's focus is on academic publishing: our titles are accessible to university and college students as well as scholars and general readers. With over 800 titles in print, Broadview has become a leading international publisher in the humanities, with world-wide distribution. Broadview is committed to environmentally responsible publishing and fair business practices.

Library and Archives Canada Cataloguing in Publication

Title: Only by experience : an anthology of slave narratives / general editors, The Broadview anthology of American literature: Derrick R. Spires, Cornell University [and eleven others].
Names: Spires, Derrick Ramon, editor.
Description: Series statement: A Broadview anthology of American literature edition | Includes bibliographical references.
Identifiers: Canadiana (print) 20230228100 | Canadiana (ebook) 20230228135 | ISBN 9781554816415 (softcover) | ISBN 9781770489097 (PDF) | ISBN 9781460408414 (EPUB)
Subjects: LCSH: Slave narratives. | LCSH: Enslaved persons' writings. | LCSH: Enslaved persons—Biography. | LCGFT: Slave narratives. | LCGFT: Autobiographies.
Classification: LCC HT869 .O55 2023 | DDC 306.3/620922—dc23

Broadview Press handles its own distribution in North America:
PO Box 1243, Peterborough, Ontario K9J 7H5, Canada
555 Riverwalk Parkway, Tonawanda, NY 14150, USA
Tel: (705) 743-8990; Fax: (705) 743-8353
email: customerservice@broadviewpress.com

For all territories outside of North America, distribution is handled by Eurospan Group.

Broadview Press acknowledges the financial support of the Government of Canada for our publishing activities.

Canada

Developmental Editors: Laura Buzzard, Nora Ruddock, Maxwell Uphaus
Cover Designer: Lisa Brawn
Typesetter: Alexandria Stuart

PRINTED IN CANADA

I want to add my testimony to that of abler pens to convince the people of the Free States what Slavery really is. Only by experience can anyone realize how deep, and dark, and foul is that pit of abominations.

—Harriet Jacobs

Contents

Preface

Only by Experience and *The Broadview Anthology of American Literature*

The publication in 2022 of the first two volumes of the full *Broadview Anthology of American Literature*—and the publication of the first volume of that anthology's Concise Edition in 2023—has been met with near-universal acclaim. The anthology "will be a gift to classrooms for years to come," Lara Langer Cohen of Swarthmore College has written; the Broadview "should be the new gold standard for scholars and teachers alike," in the view of Michael D'Alessandro of Duke University; John Hay of UNLV has echoed that thought, writing that the anthology "constitutes a new standard for the teaching of American literature"; Hester Blum of Penn State has commented on the degree to which her "classes will be greatly enriched by its capacious vision."

The Broadview Anthology of American Literature's publication has been met as well with numerous requests that the publishers make the material presented in the anthology volumes accessible in as many ways as possible, to accommodate the needs of as wide a variety of courses as possible. Hence the publication of a series of *Broadview Anthology of American Literature* editions, beginning with ten volumes in 2023. Nine of those ten are composed of works by individual authors, including an edition of Susanna Rowson's *Slaves in Algiers; or, A Struggle for Freedom*, an edition of Emily Dickinson's *Selected Poems and Letters*, editions of selected work by Frederick Douglass and Martin R. Delany, and an edition of selections from Herman Melville's *Moby-Dick*. The present, more wide-ranging volume is issued in response to requests that we make *The Broadview Anthology of American Literature*'s unusually broad selection of slave narratives available in a form designed for use in the many courses, in History as well as in English departments, that focus on the history and literature of slavery in America, and on the slave narrative genre in particular.

With one significant exception, the material included in this volume has all been drawn from *The Broadview Anthology of American Literature*. The exception is *The History of Mary Prince, A West African Slave, Related by Herself*, which—together with accompanying contextual material, including excerpts from Ashton Warner's narrative—has been drawn from *The Broadview Anthology of British Literature* (an anthology that follows the same editorial principles as its American counterpart). The inclusion of Mary Prince and Ashton

Warner—as well as of James Albert Ukawsaw Gronniosaw, Olaudah Equiano, and Briton Hammon—is designed to facilitate discussion of slave narratives in a transatlantic context. The inclusion of Hammon's narrative, written by someone who may or may not have actually been enslaved, is designed as well to facilitate wide-ranging discussions of the slave narrative genre—discussions to which many of the other texts in the volume are of obvious relevance. How and where did the genre originate? What are its characteristics? How did it develop? How far can or should it be said to extend?

In one other instance, we have also included in these pages material that is not currently included in either *The Broadview Anthology of American Literature* or *The Broadview Anthology of British Literature*. *The Broadview Anthology of American Literature* includes very substantial selections from Harriet Jacobs's *Incidents in the Life of a Slave Girl, Written by Herself*, but omits a number of chapters. In response to several requests, we have in the present anthology included Jacobs's narrative in its entirety.

The anthology's title is borrowed from a paragraph in Jacobs's preface, in which she discusses her motivation for writing her narrative. As she declares, she has written of her experiences not "to draw attention" to herself or to "excite sympathy" for her "own sufferings," but rather to provide a sense to those who have not experienced it of "what slavery really is." "Only by experience," Jacobs writes—or, she implies, by reading direct, personal accounts of such experience—"can anyone realize how deep, and dark, and foul is that pit of abominations."

The sheer amount of work involved in creating comprehensive new anthologies is enormous—and so too is the amount of expertise that must be called on. With our experience from *The Broadview Anthology of British Literature* very much in mind, we decided when we embarked on *The Broadview Anthology of American Literature* to involve a large number of contributors in the process, and to encourage a high degree of collaboration at every level. First and foremost have been the distinguished academics who serve as General Editors, and who have throughout taken the lead in the process of making selections for the anthology. But in all there have been hundreds of people involved at various stages in advising, researching, drafting headnotes or annotations, reviewing material, editing material, and carrying out the work of designing and typesetting the texts and other materials. That approach allowed us to prepare a large anthology of high quality with unusual speed—but we have throughout remained acutely aware of the importance of maintaining a high degree of consistency. Material has been reviewed and revised in-house at Broadview, by outside editors, and by a variety of academics with an extraordinarily diverse range of backgrounds and academic specialities, as well as by members of the group of General Editors for the project as a whole. The aim has been not only to ensure accuracy but also to make sure that the same standards are applied throughout the anthology to matters such as extent and coverage in author introductions, level of annotation, tone of writing, and student accessibility.

Editorial Procedures, Conventions, and Apparatus

The in-house set of editorial guidelines for *The Broadview Anthology of American Literature* now runs to over 40 pages, covering everything from conventions for the spacing of marginal notes, to the use of small caps for the abbreviations CE and BCE, to the approach we have adopted to references in author headnotes to name changes. Perhaps the most important core principle in the headnotes for each author and in annotations throughout the anthology is to endeavor to provide a sufficient amount of information to enable students to read and interpret these texts, but without making evaluative judgments or imposing particular interpretations. In practice that is all a good deal more challenging than it sounds; it is often extremely difficult to describe why a particular author is considered to be important without using language that verges on the interpretive or the evaluative. But it is a fine line that we have all agreed is worth trying to walk; we hope that readers will find that the anthology achieves an appropriate balance.

Author Headnotes: We aim throughout to be factual in the information we provide in author headnotes, and not to direct students' response with a particular evaluative or interpretive emphasis. But at the same time, we aim to engage student interest by making clear the degree to which and the ways in which a particular author's works have provoked a deep response or excited controversy, whether in their own day or in more recent times. Of necessity we provide something by way of conventional biographies of the authors—an overview of each author's life and works. But we strive as well in each case to provide what might be called a biography of the texts themselves: a summary of the reception history for key works, and an indication of why—in their own day, in our era, and in the intervening decades—the works have been considered worthy of attention and engagement (or, in some cases, have been unjustly neglected).

Annotation: It is also often difficult to make judgments as to where it is appropriate to provide an explanatory annotation for a word or phrase. Our policy has been to annotate where we believe that most undergraduates are likely to have difficulty understanding the denotative meaning. (We have made it a practice not to provide notes discussing connotative meanings.) But in practice the vocabularies of undergraduates at any given level may vary enormously, both from institution to institution and within any given college or university class. Where a word might not be known to many students but is not extraordinarily unusual or obscure, we will leave it to students unfamiliar with the word to look up its meaning. In the other direction, we make it a practice to annotate seemingly familiar words where they are being used in a text in ways that many undergraduates may not be familiar with; if a child is described as having grown up in "mean circumstances," we will gloss *mean* as *humble, impoverished*. On the whole, we provide somewhat more annotation than do most anthologies, and somewhat less interpretation. Again, we hope that readers will find that the anthology has struck an appropriate balance.

Spelling and Punctuation: The level of capitalization in many eighteenth- and early nineteenth-century texts can be a distraction for students coming for the first time to the literature of these periods—as can the ways in which such texts are often punctuated. Spelling and punctuation in the great majority of texts included in the anthology have accordingly been lightly modernized; however, we aim as well to provide readers with some sense of the historical development of the language. To that end we have included examples of texts in their original form—in some cases through the use of pages shown in facsimile, in others by providing short passages in original spelling and punctuation.

We use modern conventions of American spelling and punctuation in all material newly prepared for the anthology (author headnotes, annotations, etc.). We have not, however, "Americanized" all spellings in the texts themselves; texts from earlier periods of course use spellings that we would now categorize as British rather than American, which have been retained.

The Ethics and Politics of Annotation, Capitalization, etc.: Many anthologies have traditionally allowed many offensive words or phrases (racist, sexist, anti-Semitic, anti-Muslim, anti-gay, etc.) either to pass entirely without comment, or to be glossed with apologist comments that leave the impression that such terms were excusable in the past, and may even be unobjectionable in the present. Most obviously, many anthologies print "the n-word" where it appears in various texts without remarking on its presence. Our view is that, where such terms appear, they should generally be annotated, with a footnote making clear the degree to which such terms are highly offensive—and saying something as well about the history of their use. Like other Broadview anthologies, this volume endeavors, first, not to allow such words and phrases to pass without comment; and second, to gloss without glossing over.

Issues of ethics and politics often arise as well over debated points of present-day usage. Some of these—such as the decision whether or not to use "slave"—involve word choice. Our policy has been to avoid the use of this noun wherever possible; "enslaved people" may be somewhat more wordy than "slaves," but it has the advantage of emphasizing the essential humanity of those being referred to. We have, however, retained the compound "slave narrative," on the grounds that it denotes a now-well-established genre of writing.

Other issues involve capitalization. As is the case with many other issues in the often-fraught history of racial and ethnic terminology, there may here be reasonable arguments that point in somewhat different directions. After much discussion, we have chosen not to capitalize "black" in these pages (except, of course, where it is capitalized in the literary texts themselves); though many respected media outlets have in recent years made it a policy to capitalize "black," our view is that the capitalization of "black" may be taken to implicitly encourage the highly questionable assumption that a single, monolithic "black" ethnicity or culture exists.

Texts: Each author entry concludes with a note on the text(s), addressing issues regarding different versions and source texts. In some cases, we have also used footnotes to clarify textual issues.

We make it a practice to include the date when the work was first made public, whether through publication in print or, in the case of oratory, when the speech was first delivered. Where that date is known to differ substantially from the date of composition, a note to this effect is included in parentheses.

Note on the Cover

The quilt featured on this anthology's cover was the work of two enslaved sisters, Ellen Morton Littlejohn and Margaret Morton Bibb, both of whom were born into slavery on a Kentucky plantation; they crafted this quilt, the main design motif of which is known as a "Star of Bethlehem" pattern, sometime between about 1837 and 1850. The Jamaican writer Jacqueline Bishop has eloquently described the significance of such quilts for African Americans and other members of the African diaspora, in terms that also readily apply to the ways in which the writers of slave narratives created powerful literary art out of their own experiences of loss, dispersal, survival, and resilience: "Spectacular quilts. Bold in colour, composition and design. ... I loved the piecing of things together, of trying to make something whole out of pieces, of something old taking on new life, of one thing becoming another; of making so much beauty out of the scraps of life."

⌘ ⌘ ⌘

Timeline: Transatlantic Slavery and Black Writing in English, 1444–1865

1444	Portuguese traders transport 235 enslaved people from Africa to Portugal, initiating the Atlantic slave trade
c. 1500	Spain and Portugal begin establishing colonies in Central America, the Caribbean, and South America; other European countries, including England and France, follow suit over the next two centuries. Increasingly, captives are shipped to these colonies from Africa and enslaved, joining and/or replacing enslaved Indigenous people
1525	First voyage of a slave ship directly from Africa to the Americas
1526	A Spanish expedition to present-day South Carolina includes enslaved Africans; the Africans' rebellion prevents the Spanish from establishing a colony, and they abandon it a year later
1565	Permanent Spanish settlement founded at St. Augustine, Florida; Spanish colonists bring with them approximately 50 enslaved Africans
1619	"20. and odd" enslaved persons from the African Kingdom of Ndongo, or "Angola," arrive in Virginia aboard a privateer ship flying the Dutch flag—the first recorded black people to be enslaved in the British North American colonies that would later form the United States
1641	Massachusetts becomes the first British colony to legalize slavery
1708	South Carolina becomes the first British colony with a black majority
1720–80	Peak years of the slave trade to British North America
c. 1746	LUCY TERRY composes "Bars Fight," the earliest known surviving poem by an African American (pub. 1854)
1760	BRITON HAMMON, *A Narrative of the Uncommon Sufferings, and Surprizing Deliverance of Briton Hammon, A Negro Man*

1772 *Somerset v. Stewart*, an English court case in which the judiciary freed James Somerset, an enslaved man, and ruled that he could not be compelled by his enslaver to leave England; the case had limited practical impact but was a watershed moment in the burgeoning abolition movement

1772 JAMES GRONNIOSAW, *A Narrative of the Most Remarkable Particulars in the Life of James Albert Ukawsaw Gronniosaw, an African Prince, as Related by Himself*

1773 PHILLIS WHEATLEY, *Poems on Various Subjects*—the first published volume of poetry by an African American

1775 America's first abolitionist society founded

1777 Vermont becomes the first of the Thirteen Colonies to abolish slavery

1782 IGNATIUS SANCHO, *The Letters of the Late Ignatius Sancho, an African* (posthumous)

1785 JOHN MARRANT, *A Narrative of the Lord's Wonderful Dealings with John Marrant, a Black*

1787 The Society for the Abolition of the Slave Trade founded in Britain

1787 Free African Society founded in America by Absalom Jones and Richard Allen

1787 OTTOBAH CUGOANO, *Thoughts and Sentiments on the Evil and Wicked Traffic of the Slavery and Commerce of the Human Species*

1789 OLAUDAH EQUIANO, *The Interesting Narrative of the Life of Olaudah Equiano*

1791–1804 Haitian Revolution, which establishes Haiti as an independent nation and ends slavery there

1793 British colony of Upper Canada implements gradual abolition of slavery

1793 U.S. Congress passes first Fugitive Slave Act

1793 DAVID GEORGE, *An Account of the Life of Mr. David George*

1794 French Republic (established during the French Revolution) bans slavery in French colonies; slavery is later reinstated by Napoleon in 1802

1795   First Naturalization Act restricts U.S. citizenship to free white people

1798   VENTURE SMITH, *A Narrative of the Life and Adventures of Venture, A Native of Africa*

1807   Britain passes Act for the Abolition of the Slave Trade and U.S. Congress passes Act Prohibiting Importation of Slaves; both acts ban the international slave trade but not slavery itself, which continues through internal trades

1808–26   Spanish American wars of independence end Spanish control of Latin American colonies except for Cuba and Puerto Rico; some of the new nations abolish slavery soon after achieving independence, while others retain slavery as late as the 1850s (and the Portuguese colony of Brazil retains it until 1888)

1810   BOYREREAU BRINCH, *The Blind African Slave, or Memoirs of Boyrereau Brinch, Nick-named Jeffrey Brace*

1819   Attorney General of Upper Canada confirms that formerly enslaved people who have fled the United States and entered Upper Canada are "protected by the laws of England" and cannot be forced to return

1822   The West African colony (later independent nation) of Liberia is established by the American Colonization Society as a place to which free African Americans can "return"

1827   *Freedom's Journal* founded—the first African American-published newspaper in the United States

1829   DAVID WALKER, *An Appeal to the Coloured Citizens of the World*

1829   Slavery abolished in Mexico

1831   Nat Turner leads a rebellion of the enslaved in Virginia; 55 white people are killed, and roughly 200 black people are killed in retaliation

1831   WILLIAM LLOYD GARRISON begins publishing *The Liberator*

1831   MARY PRINCE, *The History of Mary Prince, A West African Slave, Related by Herself*

1831–32   The Baptist War, a rebellion of enslaved people in the British colony of Jamaica, is quickly suppressed, but the extremity of the violence involved pushes the British Empire toward abolition

1833   American Anti-Slavery Society founded

1833   British Slavery Abolition Act outlaws slavery in most British possessions; it begins to take effect in 1834 and provides for the gradual emancipation of enslaved people, as well as monetary compensation for their enslavers

1839   *Amistad* Rebellion

1840   The first World Anti-Slavery Convention is held in London

1843   National Convention of Colored Citizens held in Buffalo, New York

1845   FREDERICK DOUGLASS, *Narrative of the Life of Frederick Douglass*

1847   WILLIAM WELLS BROWN, *Narrative of William W. Brown, a Fugitive Slave*

1848   French government abolishes slavery in all its colonies

1849   Harriet Tubman escapes to freedom

1849   JOSIAH HENSON, *The Life of Josiah Henson, Formerly a Slave, Now an Inhabitant of Canada, as Narrated by Himself*

1850   U.S. Congress passes second Fugitive Slave Act

1850   SOJOURNER TRUTH, *The Narrative of Sojourner Truth, A Northern Slave*

1852   FREDERICK DOUGLASS, "What to the Slave Is the Fourth of July?"

1852   HARRIET BEECHER STOWE, *Uncle Tom's Cabin*

1852   MARY ANN SHADD CARY, *A Plea for Emigration*

1853   SOLOMON NORTHUP, *Twelve Years a Slave*

1853   WILLIAM WELLS BROWN, *Clotel*

1854   FRANCES ELLEN WATKINS HARPER, *Poems on Miscellaneous Subjects*

1854   Republican Party formed in the United States in opposition to slavery's westward expansion

1855   FREDERICK DOUGLASS, *My Bondage and My Freedom*

1856   *The Narratives of Fugitive Slaves in Canada*

1857   *Dred Scott v. Sandford*, in which the U.S. Supreme Court rules that black people "are not included, and were not intended to be included, under the word 'citizens' in the Constitution"

1859   HARRIET WILSON, *Our Nig, or Sketches from the Life of a Free Black*

1859   John Brown leads raid on Harpers Ferry

1860   WILLIAM AND ELLEN CRAFT, *Running a Thousand Miles for Freedom*

1860–61 Eleven southern states variously secede from the Union and form the Confederate States of America

1861   HARRIET JACOBS, *Incidents in the Life of a Slave Girl, Written by Herself*

1861–65 American Civil War

1863   Emancipation Proclamation issued by Abraham Lincoln

1865   Thirteenth Amendment abolishes slavery in the United States

1865   The Ku Klux Klan is formed

James Albert Ukawsaw Gronniosaw
c. 1705 – 1775

James Albert Ukawsaw Gronniosaw was the first black author to be published in Great Britain. His autobiography, *A Narrative of the Most Remarkable Particulars in the Life of James Albert Ukawsaw Gronniosaw, an African Prince, as Related by Himself*, dictated to an unknown female amanuensis and first published in 1772, is thought to be the second slave narrative ever published, after Briton Hammon's in 1760. His work established tropes that became widespread in subsequent slave narratives—most notable among them the trope of the "talking book" that seems to have originated with Gronniosaw's description of hearing a ship's captain reading from the Bible, and then later putting his ear against the book and being dismayed to find that it would not speak to him; scholars have traced at least four appearances of the same trope in later slave narratives. Overall, though, Gronniosaw's work is largely an outlier in the tradition of slave narratives—a work that complicates the history of the genre rather than fitting neatly within it.

Gronniosaw's *Narrative* conforms to very few of what have since become the established conventions of the slave narrative; perhaps most significantly, it does not overtly express an antislavery viewpoint. Indeed, the *Narrative* reads less as slave narrative than as a spiritual autobiography, in which Gronniosaw chronicles his conversion and his progress as a Christian. Gronniosaw identifies John Bunyan, whose *Pilgrim's Progress* was one of the shaping texts of the eighteenth century, as an important influence, and Ottobah Cugoano, in his 1787 work, *Thoughts and Sentiments on the Evil and Wicked Traffic of the Slavery and Commerce of the Human Species*, fairly concluded that Gronniosaw "would not have given [up] his faith in the Christian religion in exchange for all the kingdoms of Africa, if they could have been given to him, in place of his poverty, for it."

Gronniosaw was likely born in or around 1705 in Bornu, an empire in what is now northeastern Nigeria. He relates that he was the youngest of six children and the grandson of the king. While Gronniosaw implies that he grew up in a pagan culture in which celestial bodies were "the objects of our worship," the area was in fact very largely Muslim. As scholars have pointed out, this background renders highly questionable Gronniosaw's presentation of himself as unusual within his culture for possessing an innate sense of monotheism—for believing, in his own words, "that there was some great man of power which resided above the sun, moon, and stars."

Scholars have not, however, questioned Gronniosaw's account of how, as a teenager, he was lured from his home and into enslavement by a merchant from the Gold Coast (modern-day Ghana). After narrowly avoiding execution there at the hands of a rival king (who had assumed he was his grandfather's spy), Gronniosaw was sold and enslaved, first by the captain of a Dutch ship and later by a man named Vanhorn in New York, who then sold him to a "Mr. Freelandhouse"—since identified as Theodorus Jacobus Frelinghuysen, an influential evangelical Dutch Reformed minister in New Jersey. Gronniosaw was enslaved by the Frelinghuysen family for about twenty years. During this time, he was sent to school and he learned to read; Frelinghuysen is said to have taken "great pains" to give Gronniosaw a religious education. Freed and left a small sum of money in Frelinghuysen's will, Gronniosaw chose to remain with the family until Mrs. Frelinghuysen and all five of their sons died, all within a few years of each other. He later left America and traveled to the Caribbean, working as a cook on board a privateer for some time during the Seven Years' War. By the early 1760s he had settled permanently in England.

In London, Gronniosaw met a widow named Betty who worked as a weaver; the white Englishwoman and the black African American were married in or around 1763. Gronniosaw recounts in his *Narrative* the death in infancy of their daughter; baptism records indicate that the couple had four other children together: Mary, Edward, Samuel, and James Albert. The family was impoverished and continually reliant on the charity of others for food and for employment; it is out of these circumstances that Gronniosaw's *Narrative* seems to have emerged.

Gronniosaw dedicated the *Narrative* to his patroness, Selina Hastings, Countess of Huntingdon. Hastings was a wealthy, influential, and well-connected Calvinist who donated much of her fortune to further Calvinist causes through the establishment of chapels and schools. Gronniosaw would have been first introduced to Calvinism by the Frelinghuysen family. Through them he became acquainted with the Reverend George Whitefield, another close associate of Countess Hastings (Whitefield left his Georgia orphanage, plantation, and enslaved people to her in his will). It is likely that Benjamin Fawcett, the minister at Kidderminster who baptized Gronniosaw's children, established the connection between Hastings and Gronniosaw.

While Hastings paid for the publication of Gronniosaw's *Narrative*, her cousin Walter Shirley's preface to the work indicates that "Albert and his distressed family" were to receive "the sole profits arising from the sale of it." As Hastings's beneficiary, Gronniosaw may well have felt bound by her vested interest in enslavement (and by the widespread Calvinist view that the institution of slavery had the virtue of ensuring that enslaved Africans were exposed to Christianity) to refrain from any condemnation of slavery.

The first edition of Gronniosaw's *Narrative* was published in Bath and sold for sixpence. It was evidently intended primarily as a religious tract, and was distributed mainly in Calvinist strongholds in Britain. By 1800 the *Narrative* had been reprinted ten times, translated into Welsh, and published serially in America.

An obituary published in the *Chester Chronicle* indicates that Gronniosaw died and was buried in Chester, Cheshire, England at age 70 on 28 September 1775, just three years after the publication of his *Narrative*. The obituary calls him "an African prince, of Zoara" who "left the country in the early part of his life, with a view to acquire proper notions of the Divine Being, and of the worship due to Him," and notes that he "published a narrative of his life."

Note on the Text

The text presented here is based chiefly on the original Bath edition, which was probably published in December 1772 (though a publication year of 1770 is sometimes erroneously given; the title page of the first edition does not include a date). Spelling and puctuation have been modernized in accordance with the practices of this anthology.

⌘⌘⌘

A Narrative of the Most Remarkable Particulars in the Life of James Albert Ukawsaw Gronniosaw, an African Prince, as Related by Himself

I will bring the blind by a way that they know not; I will lead them in paths that they have not known. I will make darkness light before them and crooked things straight. These things will I do unto them and not forsake them.
Isaiah 42.16

To the Right Honourable the Countess of Huntingdon,

This narrative of my life and of God's wonderful dealings with me is, through her ladyship's permission, most humbly dedicated by her ladyship's most obliged and obedient servant,

James Albert

THE PREFACE
TO THE READER

This account of the life and spiritual experience of James Albert was taken from his own mouth and committed to paper by the elegant pen of a young lady of the town of Leominster,[1] for her own private satisfaction and without any intention at first that it should be made public. But she has now been prevailed on to commit it to the press, both with a view to serve Albert and his distressed family, who have the sole profits arising from the sale of it, and likewise, as it is apprehended, this little history contains matter well worth the notice and attention of every Christian reader.

Perhaps we have here, in some degree, a solution of that question that has perplexed the minds of so many serious persons, viz., in what manner will God deal with those benighted[2] parts of the world where the gospel of Jesus Christ hath never reached? Now it appears, from the experience of this remarkable person, that God does not save without the knowledge of the truth; but, with respect to those whom he hath foreknown, though born under every outward disadvantage and in regions of the grossest darkness and ignorance, he most amazingly acts upon and influences their minds, and, in the course of wisely

---

1   *Leominster*   Town in Herefordshire, England.
2   *benighted*   Unenlightened.

and most wonderfully appointed providences, he brings them to the means of spiritual information, gradually opens to their view the light of his truth, and gives them full possession and enjoyment of the inestimable blessings of his gospel. Who can doubt but that the suggestion so forcibly pressed upon the mind of Albert (when a boy) that there was a being superior to the sun, moon, and stars (the objects of African idolatry) come from the Father of lights[1] and was, with respect to him, the first fruit of the display of gospel glory? His long and perilous journey to the coast of Guinea, where he was sold for a slave and so brought into a Christian land; shall we consider this as the alone effect of a curious and inquisitive disposition? Shall we, in accounting for it, refer to nothing higher than mere chance and accidental circumstances? Whatever infidels and Deists may think, I trust the Christian reader will easily discern an all-wise and omnipotent appointment and direction in these movements. He belonged to the redeemer of lost sinners; he was the purchase of his cross, and therefore the Lord undertook to bring him by a way that he knew not, out of darkness into his marvellous light, that he might lead him to a saving heart-acquaintance and union with the triune[2] God in Christ reconciling the world unto himself and not imputing their trespasses. As his call was very extraordinary, so there are certain particulars exceedingly remarkable in his experience. God has put singular honour upon him in the exercise of his faith and patience, which, in the most distressing and pitiable trials and calamities, have been found to the praise and glory of God. How deeply must it affect a tender heart not only to be reduced to the last extremity himself, but to have his wife and children perishing for want before his eyes! Yet his faith did not fail him; he put his trust in the Lord, and he was delivered. And at this instant, though born in an exalted station of life and now under the pressure of various afflicting providences, I am persuaded (for I know the man) he would rather embrace the dunghill, having Christ in his heart, than give up his spiritual possessions and enjoyment to fill the throne of princes. It perhaps may not be amiss to observe that James Albert left his native country (as near as I can guess from certain circumstances) when he was about 15 years old. He now appears to be turned of sixty, has a good natural understanding, is well acquainted with the scriptures and the things of God, has an amiable and tender disposition, and his character can be well attested not only at Kidderminster,[3] the place of his residence, but likewise by many creditable persons in London and other places. Reader, recommending this narrative to your perusal and him who is the subject of it to your charitable regard,

---

1 *Father of lights* See James 1.17: "Every good gift and every perfect gift is from above, and cometh down from the Father of lights, with whom is no variableness, neither shadow of turning."
2 *triune* Three in one; a reference to the Holy Trinity.
3 *Kidderminster* Town in Worcestershire, England to the southwest of Birmingham.

I am your faithful and obedient servant,
For Christ's sake,
W. Shirley[1]

AN ACCOUNT OF JAMES ALBERT, ETC.

I was born in the city Bournou; my mother was the eldest daughter of the reigning king there, of which Bournou[2] is the chief city. I was the youngest of six children and particularly loved by my mother, and my grandfather almost doted on me.

I had, from my infancy, a curious turn of mind; [I] was more grave and reserved in my disposition than either of my brothers and sisters. I often teased them with questions they could not answer, for which reason they disliked me as they supposed that I was either foolish or insane. 'Twas certain that I was, at times, very unhappy in myself, it being strongly impressed on my mind that there was some great man of power which resided above the sun, moon, and stars, the objects of our worship. My dear indulgent mother would bear more with me than any of my friends beside. I often raised my hand to heaven and asked her who lived there. [I] was much dissatisfied when she told me the sun, moon, and stars, being persuaded, in my own mind, that there must be some superior power. I was frequently lost in wonder at the works of the creation, was afraid and uneasy and restless, but could not tell for what. I wanted to be informed of things that no person could tell me and was always dissatisfied. These wonderful impressions begun in my childhood and followed me continually till I left my parents, which affords me matter of admiration and thankfulness.

To this moment, I grew more and more uneasy every day, insomuch that one Saturday (which is the day on which we keep our Sabbath), I laboured under anxieties and fears that cannot be expressed; and, what is more extraordinary, I could not give a reason for it. I rose, as our custom is, about three o'clock (as we are obliged to be at our place of worship an hour before the sunrise). We say nothing in our worship, but continue on our knees with our hands held up, observing a strict silence till the sun is at a certain height, which I suppose to be about 10 or 11 o'clock in England, when, at a certain sign made by the priest, we get up (our duty being over) and disperse to our different houses. Our place of meeting is under a large palm tree. We divide ourselves into many congregations, as it is impossible for the same tree to

---

1   *W. Shirley*   The Reverend Walter Shirley (1725–1785), a Calvinistic Methodist clergy member from Leicestershire.
2   *Bournou*   Bornu, a former kingdom in modern-day northeast Nigeria.

cover the inhabitants of the whole city, though they are extremely large, high, and majestic. The beauty and usefulness of them are not to be described; they supply the inhabitants of the country with meat, drink, and clothes.[1] The body of the palm tree is very large. At a certain season of the year, they tap it and bring vessels to receive the wine of which they draw great quantities, the quality of which is very delicious. The leaves of this tree are of a silky nature; they are large and soft. When they are dried and pulled to pieces, it has much the same appearance as the English flax, and the inhabitants of Bournou manufacture it for clothing, etc. This tree likewise produces a plant or substance which has the appearance of a cabbage and very like it, in taste almost the same; it grows between the branches. Also, the palm tree produces a nut, something like a cocoa, which contains a kernel, in which is a large quantity of milk very pleasant to the taste. The shell is of a hard substance and of a very beautiful appearance and serves for basins, bowls, etc.

I hope this digression will be forgiven. I was going to observe that after the duty of our Sabbath was over (on the day in which I was more distressed and afflicted than ever), we were all on our way home as usual when a remarkable black cloud arose and covered the sun. Then followed very heavy rain and thunder more dreadful than ever I had heard: the heavens roared, and the earth trembled at it. I was highly affected and cast down, insomuch that I wept sadly and could not follow my relations and friends home. I was obliged to stop and felt as if my legs were tied; they seemed to shake under me. So I stood still, being in great fear of the man of power that I was persuaded in myself lived above. One of my young companions (who entertained a particular friendship for me and I for him) came back to see for me. He asked me why I stood still in such very hard rain. I only said to him that my legs were weak, and I could not come faster. He was much affected to see me cry and took me by the hand and said he would lead me home, which he did. My mother was greatly alarmed at my tarrying out in such terrible weather; she asked me many questions, such as what I did so for and if I was well. "My dear mother," says I. "Pray tell me, who is the great man of power that makes the thunder?" She said there was no power but the sun, moon, and stars, that they made all our country. I then enquired how all our people came. She answered me, "From one another," and so carried me to many generations back. "Then," says I, "who made the first man? And who made the first cow and the first lion, and where does the fly come from, as no one can make him?" My mother seemed in great trouble; she was apprehensive that my senses were impaired or that I

---

1 [Gronniosaw's note] It is a generally received opinion, in England, that the natives of Africa go entirely unclothed; but this supposition is very unjust: they have a kind of dress so as to appear decent, though it is very slight and thin.

was foolish. My father came in and, seeing her in grief, asked the cause. But when she related our conversation to him, he was exceedingly angry with me and told me he would punish me severely if ever I was so troublesome again, so that I resolved never to say anything more to him. But I grew very unhappy in myself. My relations and acquaintances endeavoured by all the means they could think on to divert me, by taking me to ride upon goats (which is much the custom of our country) and to shoot with a bow and arrow. But I experienced no satisfaction at all in any of these things, nor could I be easy by any means whatever. My parents were very unhappy to see me so dejected and melancholy.

About this time, there came a merchant from the Gold Coast[1] (the third city in Guinea); he traded with the inhabitants of our country in ivory, etc. He took great notice of my unhappy situation and enquired into the cause. He expressed vast concern for me and said if my parents would part with me for a little while and let him take me home with him, it would be of more service to me than anything they could do for me. He told me that if I would go with him, I should see houses with wings to them walk upon the water, and should also see the white folks, and that he had many sons of my age, which should be my companions. And he added to all this that he would bring me safe back again soon. I was highly pleased with the account of this strange place and was very desirous of going. I seemed sensible of a secret impulse upon my mind, which I could not resist, that seemed to tell me I must go. When my dear mother saw that I was willing to leave them, she spoke to my father and grandfather and the rest of my relations, who all agreed that I should accompany the merchant to the Gold Coast. I was the more willing, as my brothers and sisters despised me and looked on me with contempt on the account of my unhappy disposition, and even my servants slighted me and disregarded all I said to them. I had one sister who was always exceeding fond of me, and I loved her entirely. Her name was Logwy; she was quite white and fair with fine light hair, though my father and mother were black. I was truly concerned to leave my beloved sister, and she cried most sadly to part with me, wringing her hands and discovered every sign of grief that can be imagined. Indeed, if I could have known when I left my friends and country that I should never return to them again, my misery on that occasion would have been inexpressible. All my relations were sorry to part with me; my dear mother came with me upon a camel more than three hundred miles. The first of our journey lay chiefly through woods. At night we secured ourselves from the wild beasts by making fires all around us. We and our camels kept within the circle, or we must have been torn to pieces by the lions and other wild

---

1   *Gold Coast*   Region on the Gulf of Guinea named for its chief export; modern-day Ghana.

creatures that roared terribly as soon as night came on and continued to do so till morning. There can be little said in favour of the country through which we passed, only a valley of marble that we came through which is unspeakably beautiful. On each side of this valley are exceedingly high and almost inaccessible mountains. Some of these pieces of marble are of prodigious length and breadth, but of different sizes and colour and shaped in a variety of forms in a wonderful manner. It is most of it veined with gold mixed with striking and beautiful colours so that when the sun darts upon it, it is as pleasing a sight as can be imagined. The merchant that brought me from Bournou was in partnership with another gentleman who accompanied us; he was very unwilling that he should take me from home, as, he said, he foresaw many difficulties that would attend my going with them. He endeavoured to prevail on the merchant to throw me into a very deep pit that was in the valley, but he refused to listen to him and said he was resolved to take care of me. But the other was greatly dissatisfied, and, when we came to a river, which we were obliged to pass through, he purposed throwing me in and drowning me, but the merchant would not consent to it, so that I was preserved.

We travelled till about four o'clock every day and then began to make preparations for night by cutting down large quantities of wood to make fires to preserve us from the wild beasts. I had a very unhappy and discontented journey, being in continual fear that the people I was with would murder me. I often reflected with extreme regret on the kind friends I had left, and the idea of my dear mother frequently drew tears from my eyes. I cannot recollect how long we were in going from Bournou to the Gold Coast, but as there is no shipping nearer to Bournou than that city, it was tedious in travelling so far by land, being upwards of a thousand miles. I was heartily rejoiced when we arrived at the end of our journey. I now vainly imagined that all my troubles and inquietudes would terminate here; but could I have looked into futurity, I should have perceived that I had much more to suffer than I had before experienced, and that they had as yet but barely commenced.

I was now more than a thousand miles from home, without a friend or any means to procure one. Soon after I came to the merchant's house, I heard the drums beat remarkably loud and the trumpets blow—the persons accustomed to this employ are obliged to go upon a very high structure appointed for that purpose, that the sound might be heard at a great distance. They are higher than the steeples are in England. I was mightily pleased with sounds so entirely new to me and was very inquisitive to know the cause of this rejoicing and asked many questions concerning it. I was answered that it was meant as a compliment to me, because I was grandson to the King of Bournou.

This account gave me a secret pleasure, but I was not suffered long to enjoy this satisfaction, for in the evening of the same day, two of the merchant's sons (boys about my own age) came running to me and told me that the next day I was to die, for the king intended to behead me. I replied that I was sure it could not be true, for that I came there to play with them, and to see houses walk upon the water with wings to them, and the white folks. But I was soon informed that their king imagined that I was sent by my father as a spy and would make such discoveries at my return home that would enable them to make war with the greater advantage to ourselves, and for these reasons he had resolved I should never return to my native country. When I heard this, I suffered misery that cannot be described. I wished a thousand times that I had never left my friends and country. But still the Almighty was pleased to work miracles for me.

The morning I was to die, I was washed, and all my gold ornaments made bright and shining, and then carried to the palace, where the king was to behead me himself (as is the custom of the place). He was seated upon a throne at the top of an exceeding large yard, or court, which you must go through to enter the palace; it is as wide and spacious as a large field in England. I had a lane of life-guards[1] to go through; I guessed it to be about three hundred paces.

I was conducted by my friend, the merchant, about halfway up, then he durst proceed no further. I went up to the king alone—I went with an undaunted courage, and it pleased God to melt the heart of the king, who sat with his scimitar[2] in his hand ready to behead me; yet, being himself so affected, he dropped it out of his hand and took me upon his knee and wept over me. I put my right hand round his neck and pressed him to my heart. He sat me down and blessed me, and added that he would not kill me, and that I should not go home, but be sold for a slave, so then I was conducted back again to the merchant's house.

The next day he took me on board a French brig,[3] but the captain did not choose to buy me; he said I was too small, so the merchant took me home with him again.

The partner, whom I have spoken of as my enemy, was very angry to see me return and again purposed putting an end to my life, for he represented to the other that I should bring them into troubles and difficulties and that I was so little that no person would buy me.

The merchant's resolution began to waver, and I was indeed afraid that I should be put to death; but however, he said he would try me once more.

A few days after, a Dutch ship came into the harbour, and they carried me onboard in hopes that the captain would purchase me. As they went, I heard

---

1 *life-guards* Soldiers acting as bodyguards.
2 *scimitar* Short, curved sword.
3 *brig* Two-masted ship.

them agree that if they could not sell me then, they would throw me overboard. I was in extreme agonies when I heard this, and as soon as ever I saw the Dutch captain, I ran to him and put my arms round him and said, "Father, save me," (for I knew that if he did not buy me, I should be treated very ill or possibly murdered). And though he did not understand my language, yet it pleased the Almighty to influence him in my behalf, and he bought me for two yards of check,[1] which is of more value there than in England.

When I left my dear mother, I had a large quantity of gold about me, as is the custom of our country. It was made into rings, and they were linked into one another and formed into a kind of chain, and so put round my neck and arms and legs, and a large piece hanging at one ear almost in the shape of a pear. I found all this troublesome and was glad when my new master took it from me—I was now washed and clothed in the Dutch or English manner. My master grew very fond of me, and I loved him exceedingly. I watched every look, was always ready when he wanted me, and endeavoured to convince him, by every action, that my only pleasure was to serve him well. I have since thought that he must have been a serious man; his actions corresponded very well with such a character. He used to read prayers in public to the ship's crew every Sabbath day, and when first I saw him read, I was never so surprised in my whole life as when I saw the book talk to my master, for I thought it did, as I observed him to look upon it and move his lips. I wished it would do so to me. As soon as my master had done reading, I followed him to the place where he put the book, being mightily delighted with it, and when nobody saw me, I opened it and put my ear down close upon it in great hope that it would say something to me, but was very sorry and greatly disappointed when I found it would not speak. This thought immediately presented itself to me: that everybody and everything despised me because I was black.

I was exceedingly seasick at first, but when I became more accustomed to the sea, it wore off. My master's ship was bound for Barbados. When we came there, he thought fit to speak of me to several gentlemen of his acquaintance, and one of them expressed a particular desire to see me. He had a great mind to buy me, but the captain could not immediately be prevailed on to part with me; but however, as the gentleman seemed very solicitous, he at length let me go, and I was sold for fifty dollars (four and sixpenny pieces in English). My new master's name was Vanhorn, a young gentleman; his home was in New England in the city of New York, to which place he took me with him. He dressed me in his livery[2] and was very good to me. My chief business was to wait at table and tea and clean knives, and I had a very easy place; but

---

1 *check* Checkered fabric.
2 *livery* Uniform.

the servants used to curse and swear surprisingly, which I learned faster than anything; 'twas almost the first English I could speak. If any of them affronted me, I was sure to call upon God to damn them immediately; but I was broke of it all at once, occasioned by the correction of an old black servant that lived in the family. One day, I had just cleaned the knives for dinner when one of the maids took one to cut bread and butter with. I was very angry with her and called upon God to damn her, when this old black man told me I must not say so. I asked him why. He replied there was a wicked man called the Devil that lived in hell and would take all that said these words and put them in the fire and burn them. This terrified me greatly, and I was entirely broke of swearing. Soon after this, as I was placing the china for tea, my mistress came into the room just as the maid had been cleaning it; the girl had unfortunately sprinkled the wainscot[1] with the mop, at which my mistress was angry. The girl very foolishly answered her again, which made her worse, and she called upon God to damn her. I was vastly concerned to hear this, as she was a fine young lady and very good to me, insomuch that I could not help speaking to her. "Madam," says I, "you must not say so," "Why?" says she. "Because there is a black man called the Devil that lives in hell, and he will put you in the fire and burn you, and I shall be very sorry for that." "Who told you this?" replied my lady. "Old Ned," says I. "Very well," was all her answer; but she told my master of it, and he ordered that Old Ned should be tied up and whipped, and was never suffered to come into the kitchen with the rest of the servants afterwards. My mistress was not angry with me, but rather diverted with my simplicity and, by way of talk, she repeated what I had said to many of her acquaintance that visited her. Among the rest, Mr. Freelandhouse, a very gracious, good minister heard it, and he took a great deal of notice of me and desired my master to part with me to him. He would not hear of it at first, but, being greatly persuaded, he let me go, and Mr. Freelandhouse gave £50 for me. He took me home with him and made me kneel down and put my two hands together and prayed for me, and every night and morning he did the same. I could not make out what it was for, nor the meaning of it, nor what they spoke to when they talked—I thought it comical, but I liked it very well. After I had been a little while with my new master, I grew more familiar and asked him the meaning of prayer (I could hardly speak English to be understood). He took great pains with me and made me understand that he prayed to God, who lived in Heaven, that he was my father and best friend. I told him that this must be a mistake, that my father lived at Bournou, and I wanted very much to see him, and likewise my dear mother and sister, and I wished he would be so good as to send me home to them; and I added

---

1 wainscot Wood paneling on the lower part of a wall.

all I could think of to induce him to convey me back. I appeared in great trouble, and my good master was so much affected that the tears ran down his face. He told me that God was a great and good spirit, that he created all the world and every person and thing in it, in Ethiopia, Africa, and America, and everywhere. I was delighted when I heard this. There, says I, I always thought so when I lived at home! Now if I had wings like an eagle, I would fly to tell my dear mother that God is greater than the sun, moon, and stars, and that they were made by him.

I was exceedingly pleased with this information of my master's because it corresponded so well with my own opinion. I thought now if I could but get home, I should be wiser than all my countryfolks, my grandfather, or father, or mother, or any of them. But though I was somewhat enlightened by this information of my master's, yet I had no other knowledge of God but that he was a good spirit and created everybody and everything. I never was sensible in myself, nor had anyone ever told me that he would punish the wicked and love the just. I was only glad that I had been told there was a God because I had always thought so.

My dear kind master grew very fond of me, as was his lady; she put me to school, but I was uneasy at that and did not like to go. But my master and mistress requested me to learn in the gentlest terms and persuaded me to attend my school without any anger at all that, at last, I came to like it better and learned to read pretty well. My schoolmaster was a good man; his name was Vanosdore and very indulgent to me. I was in this state when, one Sunday, I heard my master preach from these words out of the Revelations chap. i v. 7: "Behold, he cometh in the clouds; and every eye shall see him, and they that pierced him." These words affected me excessively; I was in great agonies because I thought my master directed them to me only, and I fancied that he observed me with unusual earnestness—I was farther confirmed in this belief as I looked round the church and could see no one person beside myself in such grief and distress as I was. I began to think that my master hated me and was very desirous to go home to my own country, for I thought that if God did come (as he said), he would be sure to be most angry with me, as I did not know what he was, nor had ever heard of him before.

I went home in great trouble but said nothing to anybody. I was somewhat afraid of my master; I thought he disliked me. The next text I heard him preach from was Heb. xii 14: "Follow peace with all men, and holiness, without which no man shall see the Lord." He preached the law so severely that it made me tremble. He said that God would judge the whole world: Ethiopia, Asia, and Africa, and everywhere. I was now excessively perplexed and undetermined what to do, as I had now reason to believe my situation would be equally bad to go as to stay. I kept these thoughts to myself and said nothing to any person whatever.

I should have complained to my good mistress of this great trouble of mind, but she had been a little strange to me for several days before this happened, occasioned by a story told of me by one of the maids. The servants were all jealous and envied me the regard and favour shown me by my master and mistress, and the Devil, being always ready and diligent in wickedness, had influenced this girl to make a lie on me. This happened about hay harvest, and one day, when I was unloading the wagon to put the hay into the barn, she watched an opportunity, in my absence, to take the fork out of the stick and hide it. When I came again to my work and could not find it, I was a good deal vexed, but I concluded it was dropped somewhere among the hay, so I went and bought another with my own money. When the girl saw that I had another, she was so malicious that she told my mistress I was very unfaithful and not the person she took me for, and that she knew I had, without my master's permission, ordered many things in his name that he must pay for, and as a proof of my carelessness produced the fork she had taken out of the stick and said she had found it out of doors. My lady, not knowing the truth of these things, was a little shy to me till she mentioned it, and then I soon cleared myself and convinced her that these accusations were false.

I continued in a most unhappy state for many days. My good mistress insisted on knowing what was the matter. When I made known my situation, she gave me John Bunyan on *The Holy War*[1] to read; I found his experience similar to my own, which gave me reason to suppose he must be a bad man, as I was convinced of my own corrupt nature and the misery of my own heart. And as he acknowledged that he was likewise in the same condition, I experienced no relief at all in reading his work, but rather the reverse. I took the book to my lady and informed her I did not like it at all; it was concerning a wicked man as bad as myself, and I did not choose to read it, and I desired her to give me another, wrote by a better man that was holy and without sin. She assured me that John Bunyan was a good man, but she could not convince me; I thought him to be too much like myself to be upright, as his experience seemed to answer with my own.

I am very sensible that nothing but the great power and unspeakable mercies of the Lord could relieve my soul from the heavy burden it laboured under at that time. A few days after, my master gave me Baxter's *Call to the Unconverted*.[2] This was no relief to me neither; on the contrary, it occasioned as much distress in me as the other had before done, as it invited all to come

---

1 *The Holy War* John Bunyan's 1682 allegorical novel in which the city of Mansoul ("man's soul") rejects the rule of Shaddai (God), allowing the tyrannical reign of Diabolus (the Devil) until Shaddai's son Emmanuel (Christ) redeems it.

2 *Call to the Unconverted* 1658 evangelical tract by puritan minister and theologian Richard Baxter (1615–91).

to Christ, and I found myself so wicked and miserable that I could not come. This consideration threw me into agonies that cannot be described, insomuch that I even attempted to put an end to my life—I took one of the large case knives[1] and went into the stable with an intent to destroy myself; and as I endeavoured with all my strength to force the knife into my side, it bent double. I was instantly struck with horror at the thought of my own rashness, and my conscience told me that had I succeeded in this attempt, I should probably have gone to hell.

I could find no relief, nor the least shadow of comfort; the extreme distress of my mind so affected my health that I continued very ill for three days and nights and would admit of no means to be taken for my recovery, though my lady was very kind and sent many things to me. But I rejected every means of relief and wished to die. I would not go into my own bed, but lay in the stable upon straw. I felt all the horrors of a troubled conscience, so hard to be born, and saw all the vengeance of God ready to overtake me. I was sensible that there was no way for me to be saved unless I came to Christ, and I could not come to him: I thought that it was impossible he should receive such a sinner as me.

The last night that I continued in this place, in the midst of my distress these words were brought home upon my mind: "Behold the Lamb of God."[2] I was something comforted at this and began to grow easier and wished for day that I might find these words in my bible. I rose very early the following morning and went to my schoolmaster, Mr. Vanosdore, and communicated the situation of my mind to him. He was greatly rejoiced to find me enquiring the way to Zion and blessed the Lord who had worked so wonderfully for me, a poor heathen. I was more familiar with this good gentleman than with my master or any other person and found myself more at liberty to talk to him: he encouraged me greatly and prayed with me frequently, and I was always benefited by his discourse.

About a quarter of a mile from my master's house stood a large, remarkably fine oak tree in the midst of a wood. I often used to be employed there in cutting down trees (a work I was very fond of); I seldom failed going to this place every day—sometimes twice a day if I could be spared. It was the highest pleasure I ever experienced to sit under this oak, for there I used to pour out all my complaints to the Lord, and when I had any particular grievance, I used to go there and talk to the tree and tell my sorrows, as if it had been to a friend.

---

1   *case knives*   Knives constructed according to the same principle as the modern pocket-knife, with one or more blades folding out of the handle (which doubles as a sheath).

2   *Behold the Lamb of God*   Cf. John 1.29: "The next day John seeth Jesus coming unto him, and saith, Behold the Lamb of God, which taketh away the sin of the world," and John 1.36: "And looking upon Jesus as he walked, he saith, Behold the Lamb of God!"

Here I often lamented my own wicked heart and undone state and found more comfort and consolation than I ever was sensible of before. Whenever I was treated with ridicule or contempt, I used to come here and find peace. I now began to relish the book my master gave me, Baxter's *Call to the Unconverted*, and took great delight in it. I was always glad to be employed in cutting wood; 'twas a great part of my business, and I followed it with delight, as I was then quite alone, and my heart lifted up to God, and I was enabled to pray continually, and blessed forever be his holy name, he faithfully answered my prayers. I can never be thankful enough to Almighty God for the many comfortable opportunities I experienced there.

It is possible the circumstance I am going to relate will not gain credit with many, but this I know, that the joy and comfort it conveyed to me cannot be expressed and only conceived by those who have experienced the like.

I was one day in a most delightful frame of mind: my heart so overflowed with love and gratitude to the author of all my comforts. I was so drawn out of myself and so filled and awed by the presence of God that I saw (or thought I saw) light inexpressible dart down from heaven upon me and shone around me for the space of a minute. I continued on my knees, and joy unspeakable took possession of my soul. The peace and serenity which filled my mind after this was wonderful and cannot be told. I would not have changed situations or been anyone but myself for the whole world. I blessed God for my poverty, that I had no worldly riches or grandeur to draw my heart from him. I wished at that time, if it had been possible for me, to have continued on that spot forever. I felt an unwillingness in myself to have anything more to do with the world or to mix with society again. I seemed to possess a full assurance that my sins were forgiven me. I went home all my way rejoicing, and this text of scripture came full upon my mind: "And I will make an everlasting covenant with them, that I will not turn away from them, to do them good; but I will put my fear in their hearts that they shall not depart from me."[1] The first opportunity that presented itself, I went to my old schoolmaster and made known to him the happy state of my soul, who joined with me in praise to God for his mercy to me, the vilest of sinners. I was now perfectly easy and had hardly a wish to make beyond what I possessed, when my temporal comforts were all blasted by the death of my dear and worthy master Mr. Freelandhouse, who was taken from this world rather suddenly: he had but a short illness and died of a fever. I held his hand in mine when he departed; he told me he had given me my freedom. I was at liberty to go where I would. He added that he had always prayed for me and hoped I should be kept unto the end. My master left me by his will ten pounds and my freedom.

---

1 *And ... me* Jeremiah 32.40.

I found that if he had lived, 'twas his intention to take me with him to Holland, as he had often mentioned me to some friends of his there that were desirous to see me; but I chose to continue with my mistress, who was as good to me as if she had been my mother.

The loss of Mr. Freelandhouse distressed me greatly, but I was rendered still more unhappy by the clouded and perplexed situation of my mind; the great enemy of my soul, being ready to torment me, would present my own misery to me in such striking light and distress me with doubts, fears, and such a deep sense of my own unworthiness that after all the comfort and encouragement I had received, I was often tempted to believe I should be a castaway at last. The more I saw of the beauty and glory of God, the more I was humbled under a sense of my own vileness. I often repaired to my old place of prayer; I seldom came away without consolation. One day, this scripture was wonderfully applied to my mind: "And ye are complete in him, which is the head of all principalities and power."[1] The Lord was pleased to comfort me by the application of many gracious promises at times when I was ready to sink under my trouble. "Wherefore he is able also to save them to the uttermost that come unto God by him, seeing he ever liveth to make intercession for them."[2] Hebrews x ver. 14: "For by one offering he hath perfected for ever them that are sanctified."

My kind, indulgent mistress lived but two years after my master. Her death was a great affliction to me. She left five sons, all gracious young men and ministers of the gospel. I continued with them all, one after another, till they died; they lived but four years after their parents. When it pleased God to take them to himself, I was left quite destitute, without a friend in the world. But I, who had so often experienced the goodness of God, trusted in him to do what he pleased with me. In this helpless condition, I went in the wood to prayer as usual, and though the snow was a considerable height, I was not sensible of cold or any other inconveniency. At times, indeed, when I saw the world frowning round me, I was tempted to think that the Lord had forsaken me. I found great relief from the contemplation of these words in Isaiah xlix v. 16: "Behold, I have graven thee on the palms of my hands; thy walls are continually before me." And very many comfortable promises were sweetly applied to me. The lxxxix Psalm and 34th verse: "My covenant will I not break, nor alter the thing that is gone out of my lips." Hebrews chap. xvi v. 17, 18. Philippians chap. i v. 6,[3] and several more.

---

1   *And ... power*   Colossians 2.10.

2   *Wherefore ... them*   Hebrews 7.25.

3   *Philippians chap. i v. 6*   "Being confident of this very thing, that he which hath begun a good work in you will perform it until the day of Jesus Christ."

As I had now left all my dear and valued friends, every place in the world was alike to me. I had for a great while entertained a desire to come to England. I imagined that all the inhabitants of this island were holy, because all those that had visited my master from thence were good (Mr. Whitefield[1] was his particular friend), and the authors of the books that had been given me were all English. But above all places in the world, I wished to see Kidderminster, for I could not but think that on the spot where Mr. Baxter had lived and preached, the people must be all righteous.

The situation of my affairs required that I should tarry a little longer in New York, as I was something in debt and was embarrassed how to pay it. About this time, a young gentleman that was a particular acquaintance of one of my young master's pretended to be a friend to me and promised to pay my debts, which was three pounds, and he assured me he would never expect the money again. But in less than a month, he came and demanded it; and when I assured him I had nothing to pay, he threatened to sell me. Though I knew he had no right to do that, yet as I had no friend in the world to go to, it alarmed me greatly. At length he purposed my going a-privateering, that I might by these means be enabled to pay him, to which I agreed. Our captain's name was ———. I went in character of cook to him. Near St. Domingo, we came up to five French ships, merchantmen.[2] We had a very smart engagement that continued from eight in the morning till three in the afternoon, when victory declared on our side. Soon after this, we were met by three English ships, which joined us and that encouraged us to attack a fleet of 36 ships. We boarded the three first and then followed the others and had the same success with twelve, but the rest escaped us. There was a great deal of bloodshed, and I was near death several times, but the Lord preserved me.

I met with many enemies and much persecution among the sailors; one of them was particularly unkind to me and studied ways to vex and tease me. I can't help mentioning one circumstance that hurt me more than all the rest, which was that he snatched a book out of my hand that I was very fond of and used frequently to amuse myself with and threw it into the sea. But what is remarkable, he was the first that was killed in our engagement. I don't pretend to say that this happened because he was not my friend, but I thought 'twas a very awful providence to see how the enemies of the Lord are cut off.

Our captain was a cruel, hard-hearted man. I was excessively sorry for the prisoners we took in general, but the pitiable case of one young gentleman grieved me to the heart. He appeared very amiable, was strikingly handsome.

---

1   *Mr. Whitefield*   The influential evangelist George Whitefield spent some time in New York during his 1739–41 preaching tour of the American colonies.

2   *St. Domingo*   Spanish colony on the island of Hispaniola; modern-day Dominican Republic; *merchantmen*   Cargo ships.

Our captain took four thousand pounds from him, but that did not satisfy him, as he imagined he was possessed of more and had somewhere concealed it, so that the captain threatened him with death, at which he appeared in the deepest distress and took the buckles out of his shoes and untied his hair, which was very fine and long and in which several very valuable rings were fastened. He came into the cabin to me and in the most obliging terms imaginable asked for something to eat and drink, which, when I gave him, he was so thankful and pretty in his manner that my heart bled for him, and I heartily wished that I could have spoken in any language in which the ship's crew would not have understood me that I might have let him know his danger: for I heard the captain say he was resolved upon his death, and he put his barbarous design into execution, for he took him on shore with one of the sailors, and there they shot him.

This circumstance affected me exceedingly; I could not put him out of my mind a long while. When we returned to New York, the captain divided the prize money[1] among us that we had taken. When I was called upon to receive my part, I waited upon Mr. —— (the gentleman that paid my debt and was the occasion of my going abroad) to know if he chose to go with me to receive my money or if I should bring him what I owed. He chose to go with me, and when the captain laid my money on the table ('twas an hundred and thirty-five pounds), I desired Mr. —— to take what I was indebted to him, and he swept it all into his handkerchief and would never be prevailed on to give a farthing of money, nor anything at all beside. And he likewise secured a hogshead[2] of sugar, which was my due from the same ship. The captain was very angry with him for this piece of cruelty to me, as was every other person that heard it. But I have reason to believe (as he was one of the principal merchants in the city) that he transacted business for him and on that account did not choose to quarrel with him.

At this time, a very worthy gentleman, a wine merchant, his name Dunscum, took me under his protection and would have recovered my money for me if I had chose it, but I told him to let it alone, that I would rather be quiet. I believed that it would not prosper with him; and so it happened, for by a series of losses and misfortunes he became poor and was soon after drowned as he was on a party of pleasure. The vessel was driven out to sea and struck against a rock by which means every soul perished.

I was very much distressed when I heard it and felt greatly for his family, who were reduced to very low circumstances. I never knew how to set a proper value on money. If I had but a little meat and drink to supply the present

---

1 *prize money* Money awarded to ships' crews for the capture of enemy vessels.
2 *hogshead* Large cask.

necessaries of life, I never wished for more; and when I had any, I always gave it if ever I saw an object in distress. If it was not for my dear wife and children, I should pay as little regard to money now as I did at that time. I continued some time with Mr. Dunscum as his servant; he was very kind to me. But I had a vast inclination to visit England and wished continually that it would please Providence to make a clear way for me to see this island. I entertained a notion that if I could get to England, I should never more experience either cruelty or ingratitude, so that I was very desirous to get among Christians. I knew Mr. Whitefield very well. I had heard him preach often at New York. In this disposition, I listed in the twenty-eighth Regiment of Foot, who were designed for Martinico in the late war.[1] We went in Admiral Pocock's[2] fleet from New York to Barbados; from thence to Martinico. When that was taken, we proceeded to the Havana, and took that place likewise.[3] There I got discharged.

I was then worth about thirty pounds, but I never regarded money in the least, nor would I tarry to receive my prize money lest I should lose my chance of going to England. I went with the Spanish prisoners to Spain and came to Old England with the English prisoners. I cannot describe my joy when we were within sight of Portsmouth. But I was astonished when we landed to hear the inhabitants of that place curse and swear and otherwise profane. I expected to find nothing but goodness, gentleness, and meekness in this Christian land; I then suffered great perplexities of mind.

I enquired if any serious Christian people resided there; the woman I made this enquiry of answered me in the affirmative and added that she was one of them. I was heartily glad to hear her say so. I thought I could give her my whole heart; she kept a public house. I deposited with her all the money that I had not an immediate occasion for, as I thought it would be safer with her. It was 25 guineas,[4] but 6 of them I desired her to lay out to the best advantage to buy me some shirts, hat, and some other necessaries. I made her a present of a very handsome large looking glass[5] that I brought with me from Martinico in order to recompense her for the trouble I had given her. I must do this woman the justice to acknowledge that she did lay out some little for my use, but the 19 guineas and part of the 6 with my watch she would not return, but denied that I ever gave it her.

---

1 *Martinico* Martinique, one of the Lesser Antilles islands in the Caribbean Sea; *the late war* The Seven Years' War (1756–63). The 28th Regiment of Foot aided in the British invasion of French-held Martinique in January and February 1762.

2 *Admiral Pocock* British naval officer Admiral Sir George Pocock (1706–92).

3 *Havana ... likewise* British forces took control of Havana in 1762, and the island of Cuba briefly became a British possession; the British traded it for much of Florida in the treaty of 1763.

4 *guineas* Gold coins valued at twenty-one shillings, equivalent to just over one pound sterling.

5 *looking glass* Mirror.

I soon perceived that I was got among bad people who defrauded me of my money and watch, and that all my promised happiness was blasted. I had no friend but God, and I prayed to him earnestly. I could scarcely believe it possible that the place where so many eminent Christians had lived and preached could abound with so much wickedness and deceit. I thought it worse than Sodom[1] (considering the great advantages they have). I cried like a child and that almost continually; at length God heard my prayers and raised me a friend indeed.

This publican had a brother who lived on Portsmouth Common; his wife was a very serious good woman. When she heard of the treatment I had met with, she came and enquired into my real situation and was greatly troubled at the ill-usage I had received and took me home to her own house. I began now to rejoice, and my prayer was turned into praise. She made use of all the arguments in her power to prevail on her who had wronged me to return my watch and money, but it was to no purpose, as she had given me no receipt and I had nothing to show for it; I could not demand it. My good friend was excessively angry with her and obliged her to give me back four guineas, which she said she gave me out of charity, though in fact it was my own, and much more. She would have employed some rougher means to oblige her to give up my money, but I would not suffer her. "Let it go," says I. "My God is in heaven." Still, I did not mind my loss in the least; all that grieved me was that I had been disappointed in finding some Christian friends with whom I hoped to enjoy a little sweet and comfortable society.

I thought the best method that I could take now was to go to London and find out Mr. Whitefield, who was the only living soul I knew in England, and get him to direct me to some way or other to procure a living without being troublesome to any person. I took leave of my Christian friend at Portsmouth and went in the stage[2] to London. A creditable tradesman in the city, who went up with me in the stage, offered to show me the way to Mr. Whitefield's Tabernacle. Knowing that I was a perfect stranger, I thought it very kind and accepted his offer, but he obliged me to give him half a crown for going with me and likewise insisted on my giving him five shillings more for conducting me to Dr. Gifford's[3] meeting.

I began now to entertain a very different idea of the inhabitants of England than what I had figured to myself before I came amongst them. Mr. Whitefield received me very friendly, was heartily glad to see me, and directed me to a proper place to board and lodge in Petticoat Lane[4] till he could think

---

1 *Sodom* Biblical city that epitomized wickedness and debauchery.
2 *stage* Stagecoach, used for mail and passenger transport.
3 *half a crown* Silver coin worth two and a half shillings; *Dr. Gifford* Baptist minister Andrew Gifford (1700–84).
4 *Petticoat Lane* Market street in Spitalfields in London's East End.

of some way to settle me in, and paid for my lodging and all my expenses. The morning after I came to my new lodging, as I was at breakfast with the gentlewoman of the house, I heard the noise of some looms over our heads. I enquired what it was; she told me a person was weaving silk. I expressed a great desire to see it and asked if I might. She told me she would go up with me; she was sure I should be very welcome. She was as good as her word, and as soon as we entered the room, the person that was weaving looked about and smiled upon us, and I loved her from that moment. She asked me many questions, and I in turn talked a great deal to her. I found she was a member of Mr. Allen's[1] meeting, and I begun to entertain a good opinion of her, though I was almost afraid to indulge this inclination, lest she should prove like all the rest I had met with at Portsmouth, etc. and which had almost given me a dislike to all white women. But after a short acquaintance, I had the happiness to find she was very different and quite sincere, and I was not without hope that she entertained some esteem for me. We often went together to hear Dr. Gifford, and as I had always a propensity to relieve every object in distress as far as I was able, I used to give to all that complained to me sometimes half a guinea at a time, as I did not understand the real value of it. This gracious, good woman took great pains to correct and advise me in that and many other respects.

After I had been in London about six weeks, I was recommended to the notice of some of my late master Mr. Freelandhouse's acquaintance, who had heard him speak frequently of me. I was much persuaded by them to go to Holland. My master lived there before he bought me and used to speak of me so respectfully among his friends there that it raised in them a curiosity to see me, particularly the gentlemen engaged in the ministry, who expressed a desire to hear my experience and examine me. I found that it was my good old master's design that I should have gone if he had lived, for which reason I resolved upon going to Holland and informed my dear friend Mr. Whitefield of my intention. He was much averse to my going at first, but after I gave him my reasons appeared very well satisfied. I likewise informed my Betty (the good woman that I have mentioned above) of my determination to go to Holland, and I told her that I believed she was to be my wife: that if it was the Lord's will, I desired it, but not else. She made me very little answer, but has since told me she did not think it at that time.

I embarked at Tower Wharf at four o'clock in the morning and arrived at Amsterdam the next day by three o'clock in the afternoon. I had several letters of recommendation to my old master's friends, who received me very graciously. Indeed, one of the chief ministers was particularly good to me; he

---

1 *Mr. Allen* John Allen (c. 1741–80s), Calvinist minister of the Particular Baptist Church in Petticoat Lane.

kept me at his house a long while and took great pleasure in asking questions, which I answered with delight, being always ready to say, "Come unto me all ye that fear God, and I will tell what he hath done for my soul."[1] I cannot but admire the footsteps of Providence, astonished that I should be so wonderfully preserved! Though the grandson of a king, I have wanted bread and should have been glad of the hardest crust I ever saw. I, who at home was surrounded and guarded by slaves, so that no indifferent person might approach me, and clothed with gold, have been inhumanly threatened with death and frequently wanted clothing to defend me from the inclemency of the weather; yet, I never murmured, nor was I discontented. I am willing, and even desirous, to be counted as nothing, a stranger in the world and a pilgrim here, for "I know that my redeemer liveth,"[2] and I'm thankful for every trial and trouble that I've met with, as I am not without hope that they have been all sanctified to me.

The Calvinist ministers desired to hear my experience from myself, which proposal I was very well pleased with. So I stood before 38 ministers every Thursday for seven weeks together, and they were all very well satisfied and persuaded I was what I pretended to be. They wrote down my experience as I spoke it, and the Lord Almighty was with me at that time in a remarkable manner and gave me words and enabled me to answer them; so great was his mercy to take me in hand, a poor blind heathen.

At this time, a very rich merchant at Amsterdam offered to take me into his family in the capacity of his butler, and I very willingly accepted it. He was a gracious, worthy gentleman and very good to me. He treated me more like a friend than a servant. I tarried there a twelvemonth but was not thoroughly contented; I wanted to see my wife (that is now), and for that reason I wished to return to England. I wrote to her once in my absence, but she did not answer my letter, and I must acknowledge if she had, it would have given me a less opinion of her. My master and mistress persuaded me much not to leave them, and likewise their two sons who entertained a good opinion of me, and if I had found my Betty married on my arrival in England, I should have returned to them again immediately.

My lady purposed my marrying her maid; she was an agreeable young woman, had saved a good deal of money, but I could not fancy her, though she was willing to accept of me, but I told her my inclinations were engaged in England, and I could think of no other person. On my return home, I found my Betty disengaged. She had refused several offers in my absence and told her sister that, she thought, if ever she married, I was to be her husband.

---

1 *Come ... soul* Psalm 66.16.
2 *I know that my redeemer liveth* Job 19.25.

Soon after I came home, I waited on Doctor Gifford, who took me into his family and was exceedingly good to me. The character of this pious, worthy gentleman is well known; my praise can be of no use or signification at all. I hope I shall ever gratefully remember the many favours I have received from him. Soon after I came to Doctor Gifford, I expressed a desire to be admitted into their church and sit down with them; they told me I must first be baptized, so I gave in my experience before the church, with which they were very well satisfied, and I was baptized by Doctor Gifford with some others. I then made known my intentions of being married, but I found there were many objections against it because the person I had fixed on was poor. She was a widow; her husband had left her in debt and with a child, so that they persuaded me against it out of real regard to me. But I had promised and was resolved to have her; as I knew her to be a gracious woman, her poverty was no objection to me, as they had nothing else to say against her. When my friends found that they could not alter my opinion respecting her, they wrote to Mr. Allen, the minister she attended, to persuade her to leave me, but he replied that he would not interfere at all, that we might do as we would. I was resolved that all my wife's little debt should be paid before we were married, so that I sold almost everything I had, and with all the money I could raise cleared all that she owed, and I never did anything with a better will in all my life, because I firmly believed that we should be very happy together; and so it proved, for she was given me from the Lord. And I have found her a blessed partner, and we have never repented, though we have gone through many great troubles and difficulties.

My wife got a very good living by weaving and could do extremely well; but just at that time, there was great disturbance among the weavers so that I was afraid to let my wife work, lest they should insist on my joining the rioters, which I could not think of, and, possibly, if I had refused to do so, they would have knocked me on the head. So that by these means my wife could get no employ, neither had I work enough to maintain my family. We had not yet been married a year before all these misfortunes overtook us.

Just at this time, a gentleman that seemed much concerned for us advised me to go into Essex[1] with him and promised to get me employed. I accepted his kind proposal, and he spoke to a friend of his, a Quaker, a gentleman of large fortune, who resided a little way out of the town of Colchester;[2] his name was Handbarrar. He ordered his steward[3] to set me to work.

There were several employed in the same way with myself. I was very thankful and contented, though my wages were but small. I was allowed but eight

---

1 *Essex* County northeast of London.
2 *Quaker* Member of the Society of Friends, a Protestant denomination; Quakers dressed plainly and sought to avoid worldly vanities; *Colchester* Town in the county of Essex.
3 *steward* Primary servant in charge of fellow servants and household affairs.

pence a day and found myself in victuals; but after I had been in this situation for a fortnight,[1] my master, being told that a black was at work for him, had an inclination to see me. He was pleased to talk to me for some time and at last enquired what wages I had; when I told him, he declared it was too little and immediately ordered his steward to let me have eighteen pence a day, which he constantly gave me after, and I then did extremely well.

I did not bring my wife with me. I came first alone, and it was my design, if things answered according to our wishes, to send for her—I was now thinking to desire her to come to me when I received a letter to inform me she was just brought to bed and in want of many necessaries. This news was a great trial to me and a fresh affliction; but my God, faithful and abundant in mercy, forsook me not in this trouble. As I could not read English, I was obliged to apply to someone to read the letter I received, relative to my wife. I was directed by the good providence of God to a worthy young gentleman, a Quaker, and friend of my master. I desired he would take the trouble to read my letter for me, which he readily complied with and was greatly moved and affected at the contents, insomuch that he said he would undertake to make a gathering for me, which he did and was the first to contribute to it himself. The money was sent that evening to London by a person who happened to be going there; nor was this all the goodness that I experienced from these kind friends, for as soon as my wife came about and was fit to travel, they sent for her to me and were at the whole expense of her coming. So evidently has the love and mercy of God appeared through every trouble that ever I experienced. We went on very comfortably all the summer. We lived in a little cottage near Mr. Handbarrar's house; but when the winter came on, I was discharged as he had no further occasion for me. And now the prospect began to darken upon us again. We thought it most advisable to move our habitation a little nearer to the town, as the house we lived in was very cold and wet and ready to tumble down.

The boundless goodness of God to me has been so very great, that, with the most humble gratitude, I desire to prostrate myself before him, for I have been wonderfully supported in every affliction. My God never left me. I perceived light still through the thickest darkness.

My dear wife and I were now both unemployed; we could get nothing to do. The winter proved remarkably severe, and we were reduced to the greatest distress imaginable. I was always very shy of asking for anything. I could never beg, neither did I choose to make known our wants to any person for fear of offending, as we were entire strangers. But our last bit of bread was gone, and I was obliged to think of something to do for our support. I did not mind for myself at all, but to see my dear wife and children in want pierced me to the

---

1   *victuals* Food and provisions; *fortnight* Two weeks.

heart. I now blamed myself for bringing her from London, as doubtless, had we continued there, we might have found friends to keep us from starving. The snow was at this season remarkably deep so that we could see no prospect of being relieved. In this melancholy situation, not knowing what step to pursue, I resolved to make my case known to a gentleman's gardener that lived near us and entreat him to employ me. But when I came to him, my courage failed me, and I was ashamed to make known our real situation. I endeavoured all I could to prevail on him to set me to work, but to no purpose: he assured me it was not in his power. But just as I was about to leave him, he asked me if I would accept of some carrots. I took them with great thankfulness and carried them home. He gave me four; they were very large and fine. We had nothing to make fire with, so consequently could not boil them, but was glad to have them to eat raw. Our youngest child was quite an infant, so that my wife was obliged to chew it and fed her in that manner for several days. We allowed ourselves but one every day, lest they should not last till we could get some other supply. I was unwilling to eat at all myself, nor would I take any the last day that we continued in this situation, as I could not bear the thought that my dear wife and children would be in want of every means of support. We lived in this manner till our carrots were all gone, then my wife began to lament because of our poor babies. But I comforted her all I could, still hoping and believing that my God would not let us die, but that it would please him to relieve us, which he did by almost a miracle.

We went to bed as usual, before it was quite dark (as we had neither fire nor candle), but had not been there long before some person knocked at the door and enquired if James Albert lived there. I answered in the affirmative and rose immediately; as soon as I opened the door, I found it was the servant of an eminent attorney who resided at Colchester. He asked me how it was with me, if I was not almost starved? I burst out a-crying and told him I was indeed. He said his master supposed so and that he wanted to speak with me, and I must return with him. This gentleman's name was Daniel; he was a sincere, good Christian. He used to stand and talk with me frequently when I worked in the road for Mr. Handbarrar and would have employed me himself if I had wanted work. When I came to his house, he told me that he had thought a good deal about me of late and was apprehensive that I must be in want and could not be satisfied till he sent to enquire after me. I made known my distress to him, at which he was greatly affected and generously gave me a guinea and promised to be kind to me in future. I could not help exclaiming, "O the boundless mercies of my God!" I prayed unto him, and he has heard me; I trusted in him, and he has heard me. Where shall I begin to praise him, or how shall I love him enough?

I went immediately and bought some bread and cheese and coal and carried it home. My dear wife was rejoiced to see me return with something to eat. She instantly got up and dressed our babies while I made a fire, and the first nobility in the land never made a more comfortable meal. We did not forget to thank the Lord for all his goodness to us. Soon after this, as the spring came on, Mr. Peter Daniel employed me in helping to pull down a house and rebuilding it. I had then very good work and full employ. He sent for my wife and children to Colchester and provided us a house where we lived very comfortably. I hope I shall always gratefully acknowledge his kindness to myself and family. I worked at this house for more than a year till it was finished, and after that I was employed by several successively and was never so happy as when I had something to do. But perceiving the winter coming on and work rather slack, I was apprehensive that we should again be in want or become troublesome to our friends.

I had at this time an offer made me of going to Norwich[1] and having constant employ. My wife seemed pleased with this proposal, as she supposed she might get work there in the weaving manufactory, being the business she was brought up to and more likely to succeed there than any other place; and we thought, as we had an opportunity of moving to a town where we could both be employed, it was most advisable to do so, and that probably we might settle there for our lives. When this step was resolved on, I went first alone to see how it would answer, which I very much repented after, for it was not in my power immediately to send my wife any supply, as I fell into the hands of a master that was neither kind nor considerate; and she was reduced to great distress so that she was obliged to sell the few goods that we had, and when I sent for her was under the disagreeable necessity of parting with our bed.

When she came to Norwich, I hired a room ready furnished. I experienced a great deal of difference in the carriage[2] of my master from what I had been accustomed to from some of my other masters. He was very irregular in his payments to me. My wife hired a loom and wove all the leisure time she had, and we began to do very well till we were overtaken by fresh misfortunes. Our three poor children fell ill of the smallpox; this was a great trial to us, but still I was persuaded in myself we should not be forsaken. And I did all in my power to keep my dear partner's spirits from sinking. Her whole attention now was taken up with the children as she could mind nothing else, and all I could get was but little to support a family in such a situation, beside paying for the hire of our room, which I was obliged to omit doing for several weeks. But the woman to whom we were indebted would not excuse us, though I promised

---

1   *Norwich* City in Norfolk, a county in the east of England.
2   *carriage* Behavior.

she should have the very first money we could get after my children came about; but she would not be satisfied and had the cruelty to threaten us that if we did not pay her immediately, she would turn us all into the street.

The apprehension of this plunged me in the deepest distress, considering the situation of my poor babies: if they had been in health, I should have been less sensible of this misfortune. But my God, still faithful to his promise, raised me a friend. Mr. Henry Gurdney, a Quaker, a gracious gentleman, heard of our distress; he sent a servant of his own to the woman we hired the room of, paid our rent, and bought all the goods with my wife's loom and gave it us all.

Some other gentlemen, hearing of his design, were pleased to assist him in these generous acts, for which we never can be thankful enough. After this, my children soon came about; we began to do pretty well again. My dear wife worked hard and constant when she could get work, but it was upon a disagreeable footing as her employ was so uncertain: sometimes she could get nothing to do, and at other times, when the weavers of Norwich had orders from London, they were so excessively hurried that the people they employed were often obliged to work on the Sabbath day; but this my wife would never do, and it was matter of uneasiness to us that we could not get our living in a regular manner, though we were both diligent, industrious, and willing to work. I was far from being happy in my master; he did not use me well. I could scarcely ever get my money from him, but I continued patient till it pleased God to alter my situation.

My worthy friend Mr. Gurdney advised me to follow the employ of chopping chaff[1] and bought me an instrument for that purpose. There were but few people in the town that made this their business beside myself, so that I did very well indeed, and we became easy and happy. But we did not continue long in this comfortable state. Many of the inferior people were envious and ill-natured and set up the same employ and worked under price on purpose to get my business from me, and they succeeded so well that I could hardly get anything to do and became again unfortunate. Nor did this misfortune come alone, for just at this time, we lost one of our little girls who died of a fever. This circumstance occasioned us new troubles, for the Baptist minister refused to bury her because we were not their members. The parson of the parish denied us because she had never been baptized. I applied to the Quakers but met with no success; this was one of the greatest trials I ever met with, as we did not know what to do with our poor baby. At length I resolved to dig a grave in the garden behind the house and bury her there, when the parson of the parish sent for me to tell me he would bury the child, but did not choose

---

1   *chaff*   Seed casings from grains such as wheat.

to read the burial service over her. I told him I did not mind whether he would or not, as the child could not hear it.

We met with a great deal of ill treatment after this and found it very difficult to live. We could scarcely get work to do and were obliged to pawn our clothes. We were ready to sink under our troubles when I purposed to my wife to go to Kidderminster and try if we could do there. I had always an inclination for that place, and now more than ever as I had heard Mr. Fawcet mentioned in the most respectful manner as a pious worthy gentleman, and I had seen his name in a favourite book of mine, Baxter's *Saints' Everlasting Rest*;[1] and as the manufactory of Kidderminster seemed to promise my wife some employment, she readily came into my way of thinking.

I left her once more and set out for Kidderminster in order to judge if the situation would suit us. As soon as I came there, I waited immediately on Mr. Fawcet, who was pleased to receive me very kindly and recommended me to Mr. Watson, who employed me in twisting silk and worsted[2] together. I continued here about a fortnight, and when I thought it would answer our expectation, I returned to Norwich to fetch my wife; she was then near her time and too much indisposed. So we were obliged to tarry until she was brought to bed, and as soon as she could conveniently travel, we came to Kidderminster, but we brought nothing with us as we were obliged to sell all we had to pay our debts and the expenses of my wife's illness, etc.

Such is our situation at present. My wife, by hard labour at the loom, does everything that can be expected from her towards the maintenance of our family, and God is pleased to incline the hearts of his people at times to yield us their charitable assistance, being myself through age and infirmity able to contribute but little to their support. As pilgrims, and very poor pilgrims, we are travelling through many difficulties towards our heavenly home and waiting patiently for his gracious call, when the Lord shall deliver us out of the evils of this present world and bring us to the everlasting glories of the world to come. To him be praise for ever and ever, amen.

—1772

---

1 *Mr. Fawcet … Rest*   Benjamin Fawcett (1715–80), an English minister who published abridged versions of many of Richard Baxter's works, including *The Saints' Everlasting Rest* (1650), a devotional book on Heaven that was originally more than 800,000 words long.
2 *worsted*   Type of woolen fabric.

Briton Hammon
fl. c. 1760

On Christmas Day 1747, Massachusetts "servant" Briton Hammon embarked, with the permission of his "Master" John Winslow, on a sea voyage to Jamaica, little knowing that what should have been a half-year engagement would turn into thirteen years of captivity and displacement on both sides of the Atlantic before he could return to his home in the British colonies. Within a month of Hammon's homecoming, a pamphlet titled *A Narrative of the Uncommon Sufferings and Surprising Deliverance of Briton Hammon, A Negro Man* (1760) appeared in Boston. It purported to be a dramatic account of faith, divine Providence, and the "barbarous" savagery of Hammon's Indigenous captors. Yet to modern readers, this text is far more than a conventional—and conventionally xenophobic—captivity narrative. As the first black-authored text published in North America, and thus the first published written work in the canon of African American literature, Briton Hammon's *Narrative* is a work of unquestionable historical importance. It is also a work of very considerable interest as literature. Hammon's ambiguous social status, and his confession that the text omits "a great many things," complicate matters considerably—as do the ways in which race was constructed in the early Atlantic world. These factors call into question any simple or literal interpretations of Hammon's account of captivity, or of his "deliverance."

In June 1748, following a successful harvest in the Caribbean, the ship on which Hammon was employed was cast away off the coast of Florida, where the entire crew—aside from Hammon himself—were subsequently killed by a group of Indigenous Floridians. (Though Hammon's *Narrative* does not attempt to specify this group, some modern historians have speculated that they were of the Calusa people, whose population had, by the 1700s, been severely depleted through slaving raids encouraged by the English.) The *Narrative* goes on to describe Hammon's series of sufferings as a captive first of the Floridians and next of the Spanish in colonial Cuba; it recounts as well his later years aboard a number of English trading vessels and Royal Navy warships during the Seven Years' War, before his eventual reunion with John Winslow in London.

The account of these events in the *Narrative* is the only record we have of Hammon's life, though various conjectures have been made in recent decades on the basis of a handful of documents and census records in which his name appears. The *Narrative* itself tells us remarkably little about Hammon's life or status before and after his Atlantic adventures. Most notably, it is left unclear whether Hammon—whose race is only mentioned in the title of the work—was an enslaved person, an indentured servant, or a free employee to John Winslow. (The loose usage of the terms "master" and "servant" during the eighteenth century does not rule out any of these possibilities.) While there is increasing historical consensus that Hammon was probably enslaved (with some historians pointing out that the unambiguous term "slave" was often evaded in the slaveholding North), there continues to be disagreement as to the circumstances that led Winslow to allow Hammon to temporarily leave his service in the first place.

Likewise, the circumstances surrounding the creation and publication of Hammon's *Narrative* are almost completely obscure. Readers have generally assumed that the text, like the texts of many African American captivity narratives later in the century, would have been written by a white amanuensis based on Hammon's retelling, though again, this is conjecture. What we do know is that Hammon's *Narrative* was printed by eminent Boston publishers John Green and Joseph Russell in 1760, and that earlier that year another text had been printed by Green & Russell's frequent associates Fowle & Draper, bearing a remarkably similar title: *A Plain Narrative of the Uncommon Sufferings, and Remarkable Deliverance of Thomas Brown, of Charlestown, in New England.*

These and other circumstances surrounding Hammon's text bring to the fore questions about literary genre in the eighteenth-century literary world, as well as questions about interpretation and about black literary history as a whole. It seems at times clear that the *Narrative* falls into the genre of the captivity narrative, an extraordinarily popular and also highly homogeneous genre in both Britain and the colonial Americas; captivity narratives were often deeply spiritual in tone and almost always centered on the literal and psychological resistance of the (usually white) captives to the culture of their Indigenous captors. Throughout his own tale, the Protestant Hammon emphasizes God's role in saving him from both the pagan Native Americans and the Catholic Spanish, and the text ends with impassioned praise of God's Providence in finally reuniting him with his "good Master" Winslow. Yet the degree to which the *Narrative*'s language reflects Hammon's private experience, rather than simply reflecting the literary and social conventions of the era, remains in doubt. Can Hammon's *Narrative* be considered a captivity narrative in the traditional sense, if he was never free to begin with? To what degree might the captivity narrative genre have provided Hammon with a language for thinking through enslavement? If Hammon's exact status is unclear, to what degree does that fact complicate the relationship of this text to earlier and later texts in the literature of slavery? Readers have been wrestling with such questions since Hammon's text was rediscovered by African American bibliographer

Dorothy Porter in the mid-twentieth century; there is scant evidence for a wide readership of the text before this point.

It is accepted that in 1762 Hammon married Hannah, an African American woman and member of Plymouth's First Church, with whom he had one child. For many years this was all that was known of Hammon's life after his return to New England. More recent research, however, has revealed that Hammon probably changed his name to Nichols some time in the late 1770s, after the family with whom he and his master were living when Winslow died in 1774. Briton Nichols is listed as having fought for the Continental Army in the American Revolutionary War, as did many members of the white Nichols family (Winslow's surviving descendants remained staunch Loyalists). In later census records, Briton Nichols is described as a free husband and father. This information may further complicate interpretations of an intriguing text that provides a unique perspective on the lives of enslaved and free people of African descent in eighteenth-century America.

Note on the Text

The text of the work presented below is based on the 1760 edition of *A Narrative of the Uncommon Sufferings and Surprizing Deliverance of Briton Hamon, A Negro Man,—Servant to General Winslow, Of Marshfield, in New-England; Who returned to* Boston, *after having been absent almost Thirteen Years.* Spelling and punctuation have been modernized in accordance with the practices of this anthology.

⌘ ⌘ ⌘

NARRATIVE
Of the
UNCOMMON SUFFERINGS,
AND
Surprizing DELIVERANCE
OF
Briton Hammon,
A Negro Man,---- Servant to
GENERAL WINSLOW,
Of *Marshfield,* in NEW-ENGLAND ;

Who returned to *Boston,* after having been absent almost Thirteen Years.

CONTAINING

An Account of the many Hardships he underwent from the Time he left his Master's House, in the Year 1747, to the Time of his Return to *Boston.*—How he was Cast away in the Capes of *Florida* ;—the horrid Cruelty and inhuman Barbarity of the *Indians* in murdering the whole Ship's Crew ;—the Manner of his being carry'd by them into Captivity. Also, An Account of his being Confined Four Years and Seven Months in a close Dungeon,—And the remarkable Manner in which he met with his *good old Master* in *London* ; who returned to *New-England,* a Passenger, in the same Ship.

BOSTON, Printed and Sold by GREEN & RUSSELL, in Queen-Street. 1760.

A Narrative of the Uncommon Sufferings and Surprising Deliverance of Briton Hammon, A Negro Man

To the reader,

As my capacities and condition of life are very low, it cannot be expected that I should make those remarks on the sufferings I have met with, or the kind Providence of a good God for my preservation, as one in a higher station; but shall leave that to the reader as he goes along, and so I shall only relate matters of fact as they occur to my mind.

On Monday, 25th day of December, 1747, with the leave of my Master, I went from Marshfield,[1] with an intention to go a voyage to sea, and the next day, the 26th, got to Plymouth, where I immediately shipped myself on board of a sloop,[2] Capt. John Howland, Master,[3] bound to Jamaica and the Bay.[4] We sailed from Plymouth in a short time, and after a pleasant passage of about thirty days arrived at Jamaica. We was detained at Jamaica only five days, from whence we sailed for the Bay, where we arrived safe in ten days. We loaded our vessel with logwood,[5] and sailed from the Bay the 25th day of May following, and the 15th day of June, we were cast away[6] on Cape Florida, about five leagues from the shore. Being now destitute of every help, we knew not what to do or what course to take in this our sad condition. The Captain was advised, intreated, and begged on, by every person on board, to heave over[board] but only twenty ton of the wood, and we should get clear—which if he had done, might have saved his vessel and cargo, and not only so, but his own life, as well as the lives of the mate and nine hands,[7] as I shall presently relate.

After being upon this reef two days, the Captain ordered the boat[8] to be hoisted out, and then asked who were willing to tarry[9] on board? The whole crew was for going on shore at this time, but as the boat would not carry

---

1 *Marshfield* Town in Plymouth County, Massachusetts.
2 *sloop* Small sailing ship.
3 *Capt. John Howland, Master* Throughout the text Hammon frequently follows the mention of a ship with the name of its captain, common practice in writing of this era.
4 *the Bay* The Bay of Capeche, in the Gulf of Mexico.
5 *logwood* Tree native to Mexico and Central America, extensively harvested during this period for its use as a dye.
6 *cast away* Ran aground.
7 *hands* Members of the ship's crew.
8 *boat* I.e., the lifeboat.
9 *tarry* Wait.

twelve persons at once, and to prevent any uneasiness, the Captain, a passenger, and one hand tarried on board, while the mate, with seven hands besides myself, were ordered to go on shore in the boat, which as soon as we had reached, one half were to be landed, and the other four to return to the sloop, to fetch the Captain and the others on shore. The Captain ordered us to take with us our arms,[1] ammunition, provisions and necessaries for cooking, as also a sail to make a tent of, to shelter us from the weather. After having left the sloop, we stood towards the shore, and being within two leagues of the same, we espied a number of canoes, which we at first took to be rocks, but soon found our mistake, for we perceived they moved towards us. We presently saw an English colour[2] hoisted in one of the canoes, at the sight of which we were not a little rejoiced, but on our advancing yet nearer, we found them, to our very great surprise, to be Indians, of which there were sixty. Being now so near them [that] we could not possibly make our escape, they soon came up with and boarded us, took away all our arms, ammunition, and provision. The whole number of canoes (being about twenty) then made for the sloop, except two which they left to guard us, who ordered us to follow on with them; the eighteen which made for the sloop went so much faster than we that they got on board above three hours before we came alongside, and had killed Captain Howland, the passenger and the other hand. We came to the larboard[3] side of the sloop, and they ordered us round to the starboard, and as we were passing round the bow,[4] we saw the whole number of Indians advancing forward and loading their guns, upon which the mate said, "*my lads, we are all dead men*," and before we had got round, they discharged their small arms upon us, and killed three of our hands, viz.[5] Reuben Young of Cape Cod, Mate; Joseph Little; and Lemuel Doty of Plymouth, upon which I immediately jumped overboard, choosing rather to be drowned than to be killed by those barbarous and inhuman savages. In three or four minutes after, I heard another volley, which dispatched[6] the other five, viz. John Nowland, and Nathaniel Rich, both belonging to Plymouth; and Elkanah Collymore, and James Webb, strangers;[7] and Moses Newmock, Mulatto.[8] As soon as they

---

1   *arms*   Weapons.
2   *colour*   Flag.
3   *larboard*   Port or left side of a ship; the right side is known as the starboard.
4   *bow*   Front end of a ship.
5   *viz.*   Abbreviation of the Latin videlicet, meaning "namely," or "that is to say."
6   *dispatched*   Killed.
7   *strangers*   Foreigners.
8   *Mulatto*   Term, now considered offensive, that was commonly used in the eighteenth century in Britain and North America to classify individuals of mixed racial background; while "mulatto" generally meant a person with one white and one black parent, the term was often used rather loosely and might refer more to a person's physical appearance than to his or her actual known ancestry.

had killed the whole of the people, one of the canoes paddled after me, and soon came up with me, hauled me into the canoe, and beat me most terribly with a cutlass. After that they tied me down; then this canoe stood for[1] the sloop again and as soon as she came alongside, the Indians on board the sloop betook themselves to their canoes, then set the vessel on fire, making a prodigious shouting and hallowing[2] like so many devils. As soon as the vessel was burnt down to the water's edge, the Indians stood for the shore, together with our boat, on board of which they put five hands. After we came to the shore, they led me to their huts, where I expected nothing but immediate death, and as they spoke broken English, were often telling me, while coming from the sloop to the shore, that they intended to roast me alive. But the Providence of God ordered it otherwise, for He appeared for my help in this mount of difficulty, and they were better to me than my fears, and soon unbound me, but set a guard over me every night. They kept me with them about five weeks, during which time they used me pretty well, and gave me boiled corn, which was what they often eat themselves.

The Way I made my Escape from these Villains was this; A Spanish Schooner arriving there from St. Augustine,[3] the Master of which, whose Name was Romond, asked the Indians to let me go on board his Vessel, which they granted, and the Captain[4] knowing me very well, weigh'd Anchor and carry'd me off to the Havanna,[5] and after being there four Days the Indians came after me, and insisted on having me again, as I was their Prisoner;—They made Application to the Governor,[6] and demanded me again from him; in answer to which the Governor told them, that as they had put the whole Crew to Death, they should not have me again, and so paid them Ten Dollars for me, adding, that he would not have them kill any Person hereafter, but take as many of them as they could, of those that should be cast away, and bring them to him, for which he would pay them Ten Dollars a-head. At the Havanna I lived with the Governor in the Castle about a Twelve-month, Where I was walking thro' the Street, I met with a Press-Gang[7] who immediately prest

---

1   *stood for*   Steered towards.
2   *hallowing*   Hallooing; shouting.
3   *St. Augustine*   Then the capital of Spanish Florida.
4   [Hammon's note]   The way I came to know this gentleman was, by his being taken last war by an English privateer, and brought into Jamaica, while I was there. [*last war*   The War of Jenkins' Ear (1739–48), a conflict between Britain and Spain fought primarily in the Caribbean. Hammon's master, John Winslow, had led an attack on Cartagena in 1740.]
5   *the Havanna*   Capital of Spanish Cuba.
6   *the Governor*   I.e., the Governor of Cuba, Francisco Cajigal de la Vega (1691–1777).
7   *Press-Gang*   Group authorized to seize men (generally, though not always, those appearing to be of "seafaring habits") off the streets and force them into military or naval service;   *Press*   Impress; compel into service.

me, and put me into Goal,[1] and with a Number of others I was confin'd till next Morning, when we were all brought out, and ask'd who would go on board the King's Ships, four of which having been lately built, were bound to Old-Spain, and on my refusing to serve on board, they put me in a close[2] Dungeon, where I was confin'd *Four Years and seven months*; during which time I often made application to the Governor, by Persons who came to see the Prisoners, but they never acquainted him with it, nor did he know all this Time what became of me, which was the means of[3] my being confin'd there so long. But kind Providence so order'd it, that after I had been in this Place so long as the Time mention'd above the Captain of a Merchantman,[4] belonging to Boston, having sprung a Leak was obliged to put into the Havanna to refit, and while he was at Dinner at Mrs. Betty Howard's, she told the Captain of my deplorable Condition, and said she would be glad, if he could by some means or other relieve me; The Captain told Mrs. Howard he would use his best Endeavours for my Relief and Enlargement.[5]

Accordingly, after dinner, [the Captain] came to the prison and asked the keeper if he might see me; upon his request I was brought out of the dungeon, and after the Captain had interrogated me, [he] told me he would intercede with the Governor for my relief out of that miserable place, which he did, and the next day the Governor sent an order to release me. I lived with the Governor about a year after I was delivered from the dungeon, in which time I endeavoured three times to make my escape, the last of which proved effectual. The first time I got on board of Captain Marsh, an English twenty-gun ship, with a number of others, and lay on board concealed that night; and the next day the ship being under sail, I thought myself safe, and so made my appearance upon deck, but as soon as we were discovered the Captain ordered the boat out, and sent us all on shore. I entreated the Captain to let me, in particular,[6] tarry on board, begging and crying to him to commiserate my unhappy condition, and added that I had been confined almost five years in a close dungeon, but the Captain would not hearken to any entreaties, for fear of having the Governor's displeasure, and so I was obliged to go on shore.

After being on shore another twelvemonth, I endeavoured to make my escape the second time by trying to get on board of a sloop bound to Jamaica, and as I was going from the city to the sloop, was unhappily taken by the guard, and ordered back to the castle, and there confined. However, in a short

---

1   *Goal*   Gaol; jail.
2   *close*   Narrow; enclosed.
3   *means of*   Reason for.
4   *Merchantman*   Merchant vessel.
5   *Enlargement*   Release.
6   *in particular*   I.e., as an exception from the others.

time I was set at liberty, and ordered with a number of others to carry the[1] Bishop from the castle through the country to confirm the old people,[2] baptize children, etc., for which he receives large sums of money. I was employed in this service about seven months, during which time I lived very well, and then returned to the castle again, where I had my liberty to walk about the city, and do work for myself. The *Beaver*, an English Man of War,[3] then lay in the harbour, and having been informed by some of the ship's crew that she was to sail in a few days, I had nothing now to do but to seek an opportunity how I should make my escape.

Accordingly, one Sunday night the Lieutenant of the ship with a number of the barge crew were in a tavern, and Mrs. Howard, who had before been a friend to me, interceded with the Lieutenant to carry me on board. The Lieutenant said he would with all his heart, and immediately I went on board in the barge. The next day the Spaniards came alongside the *Beaver* and demanded me again, with a number of others who had made their escape from them and got on board the ship, but just before I did; but the Captain, who was a true Englishman, refused them, and said he could not answer it, to deliver up any Englishmen under English colours. In a few days we set sail for Jamaica, where we arrived safe, after a short and pleasant passage.

After being at Jamaica a short time we sailed for London, as convoy to a fleet of merchantmen, who all arrived safe in the Downs.[4] I was turned over to another ship, the *Arcenceil*, and there remained about a month. From this ship I went on board the *Sandwich* of 90 guns; on board the *Sandwich* I tarried six weeks, and then was ordered on board the *Hercules*, Capt. John Porter, a 74-gun ship. We sailed on a cruise, and met with a French 84-gun ship, and had a very smart engagement[5] in which about seventy of our hands were killed and wounded. The Captain lost his leg in the engagement, and I was wounded in the head by a small shot. We should have[6] taken this ship, if they had not cut away the most of our rigging; however, in about three hours after, a 64-gun ship came up with and took her. I was discharged from the *Hercules* the 12th day of May 1759 (having been on board of that ship three months), on account of my being disabled in the arm and rendered incapable of service, after being

---

1   [Hammon's note] He is carried (by way of respect) in a large two-arm chair; the chair is lined with crimson velvet, and supported by eight persons.

2   *confirm the old people* I.e., administer the Catholic sacrament of confirmation. (It is usually administered around the age of thirteen; it is unclear whether "old" here refers to young people who have come of age, or older Catholics who never received the rite during their youth.)

3   *Man of War* Warship.

4   *the Downs* Anchorage off the coast of Kent in the English Channel.

5   [Hammon's note] A particular account of this engagement has been published in the Boston newspapers. [*smart engagement* Fierce battle.]

6   *should have* Would have.

honourably paid the wages due to me. I was put into the Greenwich Hospital, where I stayed and soon recovered. I then shipped myself a cook[1] on board *Captain Martyn*, an armed ship in the King's service. I was on board this ship almost two months, and after being paid my wages was discharged in the month of October. After my discharge from *Captain Martyn*, I was taken sick in London of a fever, and was confined about six weeks, where I expended all my money and [was] left in very poor circumstances; and unhappy for me I knew nothing of my good Master's[2] being in London at this my very difficult time. After I got well of my sickness, I shipped myself on board of a large ship bound to Guinea,[3] and being in a public house[4] one evening, I overheard a number of persons talking about rigging a vessel bound to New England. I asked them to what part of New England this vessel was bound? [and] they told me, to Boston; and having asked them who was Commander? they told me, Captain Watt. In a few minutes after this the mate of the ship came in, and I asked him if Captain Watt did not want a cook, who told me he did, and that the Captain would be in in a few minutes; and in about half an hour the Captain came in, and then I shipped myself at once, after begging off from the ship bound to Guinea. I worked on board Captain Watt's ship almost three months before she sailed, and one day, being at work in the hold,[5] I overheard some persons on board mention the name of Winslow, at the name of which I was very inquisitive, and having asked what Winslow they were talking about, they told me it was General Winslow, and that he was one of the passengers. I asked them what General Winslow? for I never knew my good Master by that title before; but after enquiring more particularly I found it must be Master, and in a few days' time the truth was joyfully verified by a happy sight of his person, which so overcome me that I could not speak to him for some time. My good Master was exceeding glad to see me, telling me that I was like one arose from the dead, for he thought I had been dead a great many years, having heard nothing of me for almost thirteen years.

I think I have not deviated from truth, in any particular of this my narrative, and though I have omitted a great many things, yet what is wrote may suffice to convince the reader, that I have been most grievously afflicted, and yet through the Divine Goodness, as miraculously preserved, and delivered out of many dangers; of which I desire to retain a grateful remembrance, as long as I live in the world.

---

1   *shipped myself a cook*   I.e., was hired as a ship's cook.
2   *my good Master*   I.e., John Winslow.
3   *Guinea*   At this period the name Guinea was often used to refer to West Africa as a whole; in this instance, the ship was probably headed there to buy enslaved people for trade.
4   *public house*   Pub.
5   *hold*   Inner chamber of a ship in which cargo is held.

And now, that in the Providence of that God who delivered his servant David out of the paw of the lion and out of the paw of the bear,[1] I am freed from a long and dreadful captivity, among worse savages than they; and am returned to my own native land, to show how great things the Lord hath done for me. I would call upon all men, and say, O Magnify the Lord with me, and let us exalt his name together! O that men would praise the Lord for His goodness, and for his wonderful works to the children of men![2]

—1760

---

1 *who delivered … bear* See 1 Samuel 17.37: "David said moreover, The Lord that delivered me out of the paw of the lion, and out of the paw of the bear, he will deliver me out of the hand of this Philistine."
2 *children of men* See Psalm 90.3: "Thou turnest man to destruction; and sayest, Return, ye children of men."

Boyrereau Brinch
c. 1742 – 1827

Boyrereau Brinch's memoir suggests that he experienced a happy childhood in West Africa in a place he called Bow-woo (probably in what is now Mali) before his abduction into slavery. After a brief period as an enslaved sailor, Brinch was taken to Connecticut and sold numerous times before eventually obtaining his freedom by serving in the Revolutionary War (1775–83). He moved to Vermont, where he became a farmer and prominent abolitionist. Brinch, though literate, was blind in the last decades of his life, and he dictated his biography to Benjamin Prentiss, a white lawyer who acted as both his editor and scribe, and who appears to have been at least as close to poverty as Brinch himself. Prentiss and Brinch hoped to earn some money from their venture as well as to increase awareness of the harms of slavery, but their book garnered almost no interest; by the 1810s the abolitionist movement had focused its attention on the South and was far less interested in the stories of enslaved people in the North. Twenty-first-century readers, however, have found much of historical and literary interest in Brinch's vivid and penetrating descriptions of places and events from his West African homeland to the battles of the American Revolution. The following excerpts begin with the infamous Middle Passage and the process of "slave-breaking" that enslaved people often endured before they were considered fit for sale. The selection concludes with a brief account of some of the people Brinch was sold to in Connecticut, providing some sense of the range of experiences that enslaved people might have in the North.

Note on the Text

The text of the excerpts presented below is based on the 1810 first edition of *The Blind African Slave*. Spelling and punctuation have been modernized in accordance with the practices of this anthology.

⌘ ⌘ ⌘

from *The Blind African Slave, or Memoirs of Boyrereau Brinch, Nicknamed Jeffrey Brace*

from CHAPTER 4

... As soon as we had fairly got under way, and about bidding adieu to the African coast forever, the captain and many of the officers made choice of such of the young women as they chose to sleep with them in their hammocks, whom they liberated from chains and introduced into their several[1] apartments. After the officers had provided themselves with mistresses of color, they made arrangements for the keeping and feeding the slaves. We were fastened in rows, as before observed, so that we could set upon our rumps or lie upon our backs, as was most convenient, and as our exercises were not much, we, it was concluded, could do with little food; our allowance was put at two scanty meals per day, which consisted of about six ounces of boiled rice and Indian corn each meal, with the addition of about one gill of fresh water. While in this situation, the ship's crew had been butchering a goat, and threw some meat, which fell near me, but a boy caught [it] too quick for me, and swallowed it as soon as a hound would have done. I thought it was my right as it fell before me, and therefore clenched him, but one of my comrades interfered and, admonishing us, said it was extremely wrong for us to contend, as we had no parents or friends to take our parts, and could only bring disgrace upon ourselves. We desisted and mutually exchanged forgiveness. ...

In this situation upon the boisterous deep, where each gale wafted us to a returnless distance from our families and friends, almost famished with hunger and thirst, to add horror to the scene, the sailors who were not provided with mistresses would force[2] the women before the eyes of their husbands. A sailor one day forced the wife of a slave by the name of Blay, before his face. Blay, whose blood boiled with wrath and indignation, said to his comrades in chains, "Let us rise and take them, and force them to conduct us back to our native country again; there is more of us than of them, and who is there among us who had not rather die honorably than live ignominious slaves?" The interpreter happened to overhear him, and gave information against him. Poor Blay was taken to the gunwale and received 80 lashes, and was then put

---

1 *several* Various.
2 *force* Rape.

in chains with a double weight of iron. At this treatment, well may we cry out with Ezekiel—"Behold their abomination in the sight of the Lord."[1]

After a voyage of about five months, the vessel arrived at Barbados, in the West Indies, in the year of our Lord, one thousand seven hundred and fifty-nine, or one thousand seven hundred and sixty, with the slaves who had not either died with disease, mourned themselves to death, or starved. Many of the children actually died with hunger, pent up in the same ship where midnight and beastly intoxication bloated the miserable owner. The cries of the innocent African boy, destitute of the protection of a parent, if they reached the ears, could not penetrate the heart of a christian so as to cause him to bestow a morsel of bread upon his infant captive, even enough to save his life.

The slaves, consisting of about three hundred in number, including women and children, were carefully taken out of the ship and put into a large prison, or rather house of subjection. In this house we were all, above twelve years of age, chained together, and sat in large circles round the room, and put to picking oakum.[2] A slave by the name of Syneyo, from the town of Yellow-Bonga,[3] taken in the manner formerly described, and who was one of the judges in that place,[4] refused to work. He rose up, and in his native language, made the following speech to the captain, which was repeated to him by the interpreter:

"Sir, we will sooner suffer death than submit to such abominable degradation. The brow of our great father, the sun, frowns with indignation on beholding the majesty of human nature abused, as we are, and rendered more brutal than the ravenous wild beasts, as ye are. Feel like mortal man, and what I say may prevent your spirit from being blotted out forever. You came to our country; you and your friends were treated with hospitality; we washed and anointed your feet; we gave you the best of our wines to drink, our most delicious food to eat; we entertained you with every amusement our country could afford. We prayed for you, burnt incense and offered up sacrifices for you; we gave you presents of gold, ivory, corn[5] and rice, with many other valuable things; and what return did you make us? You invited us to see your ship; we were credulous, even vigilance was asleep; you traitorously gave us opiates, which caused us to sleep; you bound us captives and bore us away to this

---

1   *Behold their ... the Lord*   See Ezekiel 8, in which Ezekiel is shown a vision of the people of Israel committing a series of "abominations."
2   *picking oakum*   Unraveling old tarry ropes to extricate oakum, a tarred fiber used largely as a sealant for wooden ships. Picking oakum was a tedious, painful task often assigned to prisoners as a form of punishment.
3   *Yellow-Bonga*   Town Brinch describes as being about 280 miles south of his home, Bow-woo.
4   *in that place*   I.e., in his home of Yellow-Bonga.
5   *corn*   Grain.

DESCRIPTION OF A SLAVE SHIP.

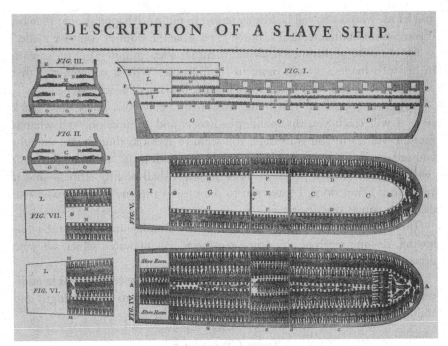

Illustration of a slave ship, 1789. This image, showing how enslaved people were held on the British slave ship *Brooks*, was widely circulated by abolitionists; this particular version appeared in a London broadside. The accompanying description noted that, without sufficient room to lie on their backs, "the men ... were placed, as is usual in full ships, on their sides, or on each other."

place; you and your myrmidons[1] ravished our wives and daughters, whipped us with many stripes, starved our children to death, and suffered[2] others to die unnoticed. And now you hold us in bondage and oblige us to work unceasingly. Is this the reward of friendship, hospitality and protection? Are you a christian people? Then do unto us as we have done unto you; strip us of these chains, and conduct us back to our own shores. If christianity will not move you to perform so just an act, look at those little fatherless children, whom you kidnapped from their parents—hear their cries, behold their sufferings, think of the bewailing of their bereft parents, look across the great waters to that village where you were almost idolized—view the distresses your conduct has brought upon it, and if you have one spark of human sensibility, or even the least shade of humanity, if you are what you profess to be, a christian; repent

---

1 *myrmidons* Subordinates who follow commands—especially unethical commands—without question.
2 *suffered* Allowed.

and let us, whom you call heathens, return to our once happy shores; thereby, if you cannot obliterate, heal as much as possible the wounds you have made."

On the close of this speech, all was silent for a few minutes; but the captain in his turn made a speech more to the purpose. With a countenance that would terrify a crocodile and a voice like the braying of a jack-ass, he said:

"Oh you impudent, rebellious, treasonable, cowardly, saucy, low, black slave, I will teach you discipline, obedience, and submission, and what is more, I will learn[1] you your duty. You seem to speak as though you thought yourself equal to white people, you Ethiopian black brute, you shall have but twelve kernels of corn per day—your breakfast shall be fifty stripes—and if your work is not done, I leave you to the care of this my overseer, who will deal with you as you deserve."

This order was strictly complied with. From Monday until Wednesday following, no one received any other allowance, except water, which we were driven to, in drove,[2] and obliged to lie down and drink.

From Wednesday until Saturday, we had each one ounce of biscuit in addition. All began to be subdued and to work according to their strength and abilities.

from Chapter 5

… We … suffered for food in a manner and to a degree of which even a faint description would be considered as fabulous, therefore I forbear to disclose it. Thus I remained for about three months from the time I was taken from the ship, starved, whipped and tortured in the most shameful manner, obliged to work unceasingly, in order I suppose that the clement, benevolent and charitable white man should be satisfied that the heathen spirit of an African boy of noble birth should be sufficiently subdued, rendered tame, docile and submissive; and all for my good that I should thereby become a tame, profitable and honest slave. The natural man must be obliterated and degraded, that even the thought of liberty must never be suffered to contaminate itself in a negro's mind; and the odious thing, equality, should be taught by European discipline never to raise its head. …

[Brinch is sold to a frigate captain and forced to fight in the Seven Years' War (1756–63); he is then taken to Connecticut and sold again, to a profoundly cruel Puritan living in Milford, a small town near New Haven. This new enslaver is so abusive that another Milford resident, Samuel Eals, feels compelled to rescue Brinch and give him an opportunity to recover from the starvation and physical injury he has been subjected to.]

---

1 *learn* Teach.
2 *drove* Herd.

from CHAPTER 8

... Mr. Samuel Eals used me very well while I remained with him; but as soon as I was able to work, I was sold to one Peter Pridon, son of the old priest Pridon, of Old Milford. I lived with him about two months and got five severe whippings for crying nights. From Pridon I was bartered away for some old horses to one Gibbs, who was a man of very inferior talents, possessing great pride and ostentation, always at work and in a hurry. He had the longest nose and chin I ever saw attached to a man's face, thin lips, and a voice that was less pleasing than the ravens. With this man I stayed about three months, and to describe the particular management of his family would only mortify those who live in the same way at the present time. I have thought he took a peculiar delight in whipping me, as I uniformly received about four whippings per day. If I was awkward, cried too much, or was lazy, it was sure to purchase me a good drubbing.[1] Sometimes I got a flogging for freezing my feet while I was foddering[2] and cutting the ice out of the watering place. And one day, while I was getting corn up stairs, I designedly pushed his boy downstairs, for while I had the basket upon my shoulder he began whipping me & chirping to me, as would a driver to his horse. For this I was knocked downstairs, basket, corn and all shared the same fate; and to complete my punishment, the next morning I received fifty lashes with a horse-whip. Next I was sold to Phineas Baldwin of the town of Old Milford. I continued with him until summer, or rather spring, when I went to live with his son Phineas, who had two small children to tend. In his nursery I was engaged until the last of May, when I was sold to Jones Green, of the same place. Green did not whip me but about twice in a week, except now and then a kicking. From Green I was transferred to one Murrier, a tanner, where I remained until September, at which time the widow Mary Stiles, of Woodbury, Connecticut, bought me. This was a glorious era in my life, as widow Stiles was one of the finest women in the world; she possessed every christian virtue. ...

When this lady died I descended like real estate, in fee simple[3] to her son Benjamin Stiles, Esq. About four years after her death, her two sons, Benjamin and David, were drafted to fight in the revolution. I also entered the banners of freedom. Alas! Poor African slave, to liberate freemen, my tyrants. ...
—1810

---

1   *drubbing*   Beating.
2   *foddering*   Feeding animals.
3   *fee simple*   Term usually used in reference to land; it indicates that the land's owner possesses it entirely (as opposed to, for example, leasing it) and can sell or use it as desired.

Venture Smith
c. 1729 – 1805

When he dictated the story of his life to an amanuensis in the late 1790s, Venture Smith was a prosperous farmer, sailor, and landowner, and in many ways a respected member of his Connecticut community. Yet Smith was, as the title of his autobiography describes him, "A Native of Africa," and had experienced the cruelties of American slavery firsthand, having spent twenty-six years of his life enslaved. The text that resulted from his narration, *A Narrative of the Life and Adventures of Venture, A Native of Africa* (1798), is among the most distinctive memoirs of slavery published before the Civil War, both for its literary qualities and for its subject's unique path to self-made freedom. Advertised upon publication as a lesson in morality for both black and white audiences, the *Narrative* demonstrates the diversity of early African American literature and contributes today to our understanding of the complexity of race relations in eighteenth-century America.

The *Narrative* describes Smith's remarkable journey from princedom in West Africa to enslavement in colonial New England, and ultimately to freedom and financial prosperity in Connecticut. Named Broteer Furro at birth, Smith's father was Saungm Furro, prince of what the *Narrative* refers to as the Tribe of Dukandarra. Kidnapped as a child by African slave traders under the command of "some white nation," Broteer was forced to witness the brutal murder of his father before being trafficked to the coast of what is now Ghana, where he was purchased by Rhode Island farmer Robinson Mumford, who proceeded to give him the name "Venture" (because he was purchased with Mumford's "own private venture"). After enduring the harrowing ordeal of the Middle Passage aboard Mumford's ship, the *Charming Susannah* (during which many of the enslaved people died of smallpox), most of Venture's fellow Africans were sold into plantation slavery in Barbados—a near death sentence, due to the extraordinarily harsh conditions they were subjected to there.

Venture, however, was taken back with Mumford to his property in Rhode Island, where he was trained into household slavery. His enslavement would continue for the next two-and-a-half decades in various locations in colonial Rhode Island, Long Island, and Connecticut, during which he married Marget, a fellow enslaved person, joined a failed escape attempt, and was himself sold to different enslavers three further times, resulting in a temporary separation from his wife and their youngest daughter. It was under his fourth and final enslaver, Colonel Oliver Smith, that Venture undertook the drawn-out task of "redeeming" himself—purchasing his own way out of slavery—by selling his labor during his spare hours. Venture took his new last name from

Colonel Smith—who had priced Venture's freedom at the exorbitant fee of seventy-two pounds. Over the course of the next two decades, Smith worked tirelessly, primarily as a woodcutter, eventually securing the freedom of his two children, his pregnant wife, and several other enslaved men.

By the time of his *Narrative*'s publication, Smith was a landowner of above-average means, owning well over 100 acres of land in Connecticut. Despite his apparent social respectability, however, it is worth noting that Smith was repeatedly cheated in his business endeavors, and that he was often prevented on account of his race from seeking full reparations for these losses, a fact he occasionally reflects upon in his *Narrative* with bitterness. It is unclear what exactly motivated Smith, at the age of nearly seventy, to have his auto-biography recorded and published, though it appears he was encouraged in the endeavor by several community and family members. Most scholars today accept the local tradition that his amanuensis was Elisa Niles, a white Connecticut schoolteacher and Revolutionary War veteran; nothing more is known about Niles's relationship to Smith.

A Narrative of the Life and Adventures of Venture, A Native of Africa, was pub-lished in Connecticut in 1798 by Charles Holt, publisher of the *New London Bee*, where he promoted Smith as "a negro remarkable for size, strength, industry, fidelity, and frugality." Holt may have seen Smith's story of self-made success as fitting into his own moral publishing agenda; among the works he wrote and printed were numerous tracts on temperance and industry, and his 1798 printings also included an edition of *The Life of Dr. Benjamin Franklin*. We do not know for certain the degree to which either Smith, Niles, or Holt were familiar with the developing tradition of the slave narrative, or with other autobiographical texts by African and African American authors—such as those by Olaudah Equiano and John Marrant—but certainly Smith's own *Narrative* occupies a distinctive place in that genre. Most notably, Smith's *Nar-rative* is almost (though not entirely) void of Christian religious references; in a burgeoning literary tradition saturated with many deeply spiritual texts, this was a significant absence.

Smith's *Narrative* was never a best seller, and was out of print even in Con-necticut for a good deal of the nineteenth century. Yet aspects of Venture Smith's story appear to have remained alive in his community long after his death. In 1896—almost 100 years after its original publication—a new edi-tion of the *Narrative* was published with an appendix entitled "Traditions of Venture!" Quite aside from being a model of frugal morality or indeed a representative of antislavery resistance, Smith had become, according to this appendix, a figure of local legend. The appendix collects numerous folkloric stories regarding Smith's large stature and impressive physical feats, as well as descriptions of his numerous descendants; it does not comment on Smith's enslavement, aside from remarking that Colonel Oliver Smith "generously permitted" Venture to purchase his freedom.

Smith died in 1805, at the age of approximately seventy-seven. An account of his burial is given in the 1896 edition of the *Narrative*: "His heavy body was conveyed … to the cemetery adjoining the First Congregational Church in East Haddam, for burial, by four strong men fittingly chosen. The two in front were white, proving the respect he had won, while two of his own race assisted in the rear." Smith was seldom mentioned in studies of slavery or of the abolitionist movement until late in the twentieth century. Since at least 2006, when the graves of Smith and Marget were excavated as part of a heavily publicized project led by their descendants, his *Narrative* has come to be seen by many as a challenging but essential text in the canon of black eighteenth-century literature.

Note on the Text

The text of the work presented here is based on the first edition of *A Narrative of the Life and Adventures of Venture, A Native of Africa: But resident above sixty years in the United States of America*, printed by Charles Holt in New London in 1798. Spelling and punctuation have been modernized in accordance with the practices of this anthology.

⌘ ⌘ ⌘

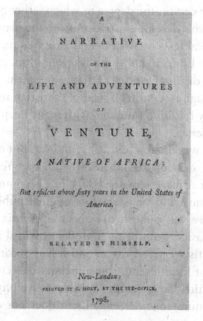

A

NARRATIVE

OF THE

LIFE AND ADVENTURES

OF

VENTURE,

A NATIVE OF AFRICA:

But resident above sixty years in the United States of America.

RELATED BY HIMSELF.

New-London:
PRINTED BY C. HOLT, AT THE BEE-OFFICE.
1798.

A Narrative of the Life and Adventures of Venture, A Native of Africa: But resident above sixty years in the United States of America

PREFACE

The following account of the life of Venture, is a relation of simple facts, in which nothing is added in substance to what he related himself. Many other interesting and curious passages of his life might have been inserted; but on account of the bulk to which they must necessarily have swelled this narrative, they were omitted. If any should suspect the truth of what is here related, they are referred to people now living who are acquainted with most of the facts mentioned in the narrative.

The reader is here presented with an account, not of a renowned politician or warrior, but of an untutored African slave, brought into this Christian country at eight years of age, wholly destitute of all education but what he received in common with other domesticated animals, enjoying no advantages that could lead him to suppose himself superior to the beasts, his fellow servants. And if he[1] shall derive no other advantage from perusing this narrative, he may experience those sensations of shame and indignation, that will prove him to be not wholly destitute of every noble and generous feeling.

The subject of the following pages, had he received only a common education, might have been a man of high respectability and usefulness; and had his education been suited to his genius, he might have been an ornament and an honor to human nature. It may perhaps, not be unpleasing to see the efforts of a great mind wholly uncultivated, enfeebled and depressed by slavery, and struggling under every disadvantage. The reader may here see a Franklin and a Washington, in a state of nature, or rather in a state of slavery.[2] Destitute as he is of all education, and broken by hardships and infirmities of age, he still exhibits striking traces of native ingenuity and good sense.

This narrative exhibits a pattern of honesty, prudence and industry, to people of his own colour; and perhaps some white people would not find themselves degraded by imitating such an example.

---

1 *he* I.e., the reader.
2 *see a … slavery* I.e., see American founders Benjamin Franklin and George Washington as they might have been had they been born into slavery.

The following account is published in compliance with the earnest desire of the subject of it, and likewise a number of respectable persons who are acquainted with him.

A NARRATIVE OF THE LIFE, ETC.

CHAPTER I
CONTAINING AN ACCOUNT OF HIS LIFE, FROM HIS BIRTH TO THE TIME OF HIS LEAVING HIS NATIVE COUNTRY.

I was born at Dukandarra, in Guinea,[1] about the year 1729. My father's name was Saungm Furro, Prince of the Tribe of Dukandarra. My father had three wives. Polygamy was not uncommon in that country, especially among the rich, as every man was allowed to keep as many wives as he could maintain. By his first wife he had three children. The eldest of them was myself, named by my father, Broteer. The other two were named Cundazo and Soozaduka. My father had two children by his second wife, and one by his third. I descended from a very large, tall and stout[2] race of beings, much larger than the generality of people in other parts of the globe, being commonly considerable above six feet in height, and every way well proportioned.

The first thing worthy of notice which I remember was, a contention between my father and mother, on account of my father's marrying his third wife without the consent of his first and eldest, which was contrary to the custom generally observed among my countrymen. In consequence of this rupture, my mother left her husband and country, and travelled away with her three children to the eastward. I was then five years old. She took not the least sustenance along with her, to support either herself or children. I was able to travel by her side; the other two of her offspring she carried one on her back, and the other being a sucking child,[3] in her arms. When we became hungry, my mother used to set us down on the ground, and gather some of the fruits which grew spontaneously in that climate. These served us for food on the way. At night we all lay down together in the most secure place we could find, and reposed ourselves until morning. Though there were many noxious[4] animals there; yet so kind was our Almighty protector, that none of them were ever permitted to hurt or molest us. Thus we went on our journey until the second day after our departure from Dukandarra, when we came to the entrance of a great desert. During our travel in that we were often affrighted

1 *Guinea* In the 1700s this term referred to a large portion of West Africa.
2 *stout* Powerfully built.
3 *sucking child* I.e., a breastfeeding infant.
4 *noxious* Dangerous.

with the doleful howlings and yellings of wolves, lions, and other animals. After five days' travel we came to the end of this desert, and immediately entered into a beautiful and extensive interval country. Here my mother was pleased to stop and seek a refuge for me. She left me at the house of a very rich farmer. I was then, as I should judge, not less than one hundred and forty miles from my native place, separated from all my relations and acquaintance. At this place my mother took her farewell of me, and set out for her own country. My new guardian, as I shall call the man with whom I was left, put me into the business of tending sheep, immediately after I was left with him. The flock which I kept with the assistance of a boy, consisted of about forty. We drove them every morning between two and three miles to pasture, into the wide and delightful plains. When night drew on, we drove them home and secured them in the cote.[1] In this round I continued during my stay there. One incident which befell me when I was driving my flock from pasture, was so dreadful to me in that age, and is to this time so fresh in my memory, that I cannot help noticing[2] it in this place. Two large dogs sallied out of a certain house and set upon me. One of them took me by the arm, and the other by the thigh, and before their master could come and relieve me, they lacerated my flesh to such a degree that the scars are very visible to the present day. My master was immediately sent for. He came and carried me home, as I was unable to go[3] myself on account of my wounds. Nothing remarkable happened afterwards until my father sent for me to return home.

Before I dismiss[4] this country, I must just inform my reader what I remember concerning this place. A large river runs through this country in a westerly course. The land for a great way on each side is flat and level, hedged in by a considerable rise of the country at a great distance from it. It scarce ever rains there, yet the land is fertile; great dews fall in the night, which refresh the soil. About the latter end of June or first of July, the river begins to rise, and gradually increases until it has inundated the country for a great distance, to the height of seven or eight feet. This brings on a slime which enriches the land surprisingly. When the river has subsided, the natives begin to sow and plant, and the vegetation is exceeding rapid. Near this rich river my guardian's land lay. He possessed, I cannot exactly tell how much, yet this I am certain of respecting it, that he owned an immense tract. He possessed likewise a great many cattle and goats. During my stay with him I was kindly used, and with as much tenderness, for what I saw, as [though I was] his only son, although I was an entire stranger to him, remote from friends and relations. The principal

---

1 *cote* Shelter for animals.
2 *noticing* I.e., making note of; mentioning.
3 *go* Walk.
4 *dismiss* Stop writing about.

occupations of the inhabitants there were the cultivation of the soil and the care of their flocks. They were a people pretty similar in every respect to that of mine, except in their persons, which were not so tall and stout. They appeared to be very kind and friendly. I will now return to my departure from that place.

My father sent a man and horse after me. After settling with my guardian for keeping me, he took me away and went for home. It was then about one year since my mother brought me here. Nothing remarkable occurred to us on our journey until we arrived safe home.

I found then that the difference[1] between my parents had been made up previous to their sending for me. On my return, I was received both by my father and mother with great joy and affection, and was once more restored to my paternal dwelling in peace and happiness. I was then about six years old.

Not more than six weeks had passed after my return, before a message was brought by an inhabitant of the place where I lived the preceding year to my father, that that place had been invaded by a numerous army, from a nation not far distant, furnished with musical instruments, and all kinds of arms[2] then in use; that they were instigated by some white nation who equipped and sent them to subdue and possess the country; that his nation[3] had made no preparation for war, having been for a long time in profound peace, that they could not defend themselves against such a formidable train of invaders, and must therefore necessarily evacuate their lands to the fierce enemy, and fly to the protection of some chief; and that if he[4] would permit them they should come under his rule and protection when they had to retreat from their own possessions. He was a kind and merciful prince, and therefore consented to these proposals.

He had scarcely returned to his nation with the message, before the whole of his people were obliged to retreat from their country, and come to my father's dominions.

He gave them every privilege and all the protection his government could afford. But they had not been there longer than four days before news came to them that the invaders had laid waste their country, and were coming speedily to destroy them in my father's territories. This affrighted them, and therefore they immediately pushed off to the southward, into the unknown countries there, and were never more heard of.

Two days after their retreat, the report turned out to be but too true. A detachment from the enemy came to my father and informed him, that the

---

1 *difference* Dispute.
2 *arms* Weapons.
3 *his nation* I.e., the nation among whom Smith had lived in the previous year.
4 *he* I.e., Smith's father.

whole army was encamped not far out of his dominions, and would invade the territory and deprive his people of their liberties and rights, if he did not comply with the following terms. These were to pay them a large sum of money, three hundred fat cattle, and a great number of goats, sheep, asses, etc.

My father told the messenger he would comply rather than [accept] that his subjects should be deprived of their rights and privileges, which he was not then in circumstances to defend from so sudden an invasion. Upon turning out those articles, the enemy pledged their faith and honor that they would not attack him. On these he relied and therefore thought it unnecessary to be on his guard against the enemy. But their pledges of faith and honor proved no better than those of other unprincipled hostile nations; for, a few days after[wards], a certain relation of the king came and informed him that the enemy who sent terms of accommodation to him and received tribute to their satisfaction, yet meditated an attack upon his subjects by surprise, and that probably they would commence their attack in less than one day; and concluded with advising him, as he was not prepared for war, to order a speedy retreat of his family and subjects. He complied with this advice.

The same night which was fixed upon to retreat, my father and his family set off about break of day. The king and his two younger wives went in one company, and my mother and her children in another. We left our dwellings in succession, and my father's company went on first. We directed our course for a large shrub plain, some distance off, where we intended to conceal ourselves from the approaching enemy, until we could refresh and rest ourselves a little. But we presently found that our retreat was not secure. For having struck up a little fire for the purpose of cooking victuals,[1] the enemy, who happened to be encamped a little distance off, had sent out a scouting party who discovered us by the smoke of the fire, just as we were extinguishing it, and about to eat. As soon as we had finished eating, my father discovered the party, and immediately began to discharge arrows at them. This was what I first saw, and it alarmed both me and the women, who being unable to make any resistance, immediately betook ourselves to the tall thick reeds not far off, and left the old king to fight alone. For some time I beheld him from the reeds defending himself with great courage and firmness, till at last he was obliged to surrender himself into their hands.

They then came to us in the reeds, and the very first salute I had from them was a violent blow on the head with the fore part of a gun, and at the same time a grasp round the neck. I then had a rope put about my neck, as had all the women in the thicket with me, and were immediately led to my father,

1 *victuals* Food.

who was likewise pinioned[1] and haltered for leading. In this condition we were all led to the camp. The women and myself being pretty submissive, had tolerable treatment from the enemy, while my father was closely interrogated respecting his money, which they knew he must have. But as he gave them no account of it, he was instantly cut and pounded on his body with great inhumanity, [so] that he might be induced by the torture he suffered to make the discovery.[2] All this availed not in the least to make him give up his money, but he despised[3] all the tortures which they inflicted, until the continued exercise and increase of torment, obliged him to sink and expire. He thus died without informing his enemies of the place where his money lay. I saw him while he was thus tortured to death. The shocking scene is to this day fresh in my mind, and I have often been overcome while thinking on it. He was a man of remarkable stature. I should judge as much as six feet and six or seven inches high, two feet across his shoulders, and every way well proportioned. He was a man of remarkable strength and resolution, affable, kind and gentle, ruling with equity and moderation.

The army of the enemy was large, I should suppose consisting of about six thousand men. Their leader was called Baukurre. After destroying the old prince, they decamped and immediately marched towards the sea, lying to the west, taking with them myself and the women prisoners. In the march a scouting party was detached from the main army. To the leader of this party I was made waiter, having to carry his gun, etc. As we were a-scouting we came across a herd of fat cattle, consisting of about thirty in number. These we set upon, and immediately wrested from their keepers, and afterwards converted them into food for the army. The enemy had remarkable success in destroying the country wherever they went. For as far as they had penetrated, they laid the habitations waste and captured the people. The distance they had now brought me was about four hundred miles. All the march I had very hard tasks imposed on me, which I [was told I] must perform on pain of punishment. I was obliged to carry on my head a large flat stone used for grinding our corn, weighing, as I should suppose, as much as 25 pounds; besides victuals, mat and cooking utensils. Though I was pretty large and stout of my age, yet these burdens were very grievous to me, being only about six years and an half old.

We were then come to a place called Malagasco. When we entered the place we could not see the least appearance of either houses or inhabitants, but upon stricter search found, that instead of houses above ground they had dens in the sides of hillocks, contiguous to ponds and streams of water. In these we

---

1 *pinioned* Bound by the arms.
2 *make the discovery* Reveal to them (where the money was).
3 *despised* Defied; was dismissive of.

perceived they had all hid themselves, as I suppose they usually did upon such occasions. In order to compel them to surrender, the enemy contrived to smoke them out with faggots.[1] These they put to the entrance of the caves and set them on fire. While they were engaged in this business, to their great surprise some of them were desperately wounded with arrows which fell from above on them. This mystery they soon found out. They perceived that the enemy[2] discharged these arrows through holes on the top of the dens directly into the air. Their weight brought them back, point downwards, on their enemies'[3] heads, whilst they were smoking the inhabitants out. The points of their arrows were poisoned, but their enemy had an antidote for it, which they instantly applied to the wounded part. The smoke at last obliged the people to give themselves up. They came out of their caves, first spatting[4] the palms of their hands together, and immediately after extended their arms, crossed at their wrists, ready to be bound and pinioned. I should judge that the dens above mentioned were extended about eight feet horizontally into the earth, six feet in height and as many wide. They were arched overhead and lined with earth, which was of the clay kind, and made the surface of their walls firm and smooth.

The invaders then pinioned the prisoners of all ages and sexes indiscriminately, took their flocks and all their effects, and moved on their way towards the sea. On the march the prisoners were treated with clemency, on account of their being submissive and humble. Having come to the next tribe, the enemy laid siege and immediately took men, women, children, flocks, and all their valuable effects. They then went on to the next district, which was contiguous to the sea, called in Africa, Anamaboo.[5] The enemy's provisions were then almost spent, as well as their strength. The inhabitants knowing what conduct they had pursued, and what were their present intentions, improved the favorable opportunity, attacked them, and took enemy, prisoners, flocks and all their effects. I was then taken a second time. All of us were then put into the castle,[6] and kept for market. On a certain time I and other prisoners were put on board a canoe, under our master, and rowed away to a vessel belonging to Rhode Island, commanded by Capt. Collingwood, and the mate Thomas Mumford. While we were going to the vessel, our master told us all

---

1   *faggots*   Bundles of kindling.

2   *the enemy*   I.e., the people hiding in the caves.

3   *their enemies*   I.e., the invading slavers.

4   *spatting*   Clapping.

5   *Anamaboo*   Town on the coast of present-day Ghana, an important center of the transatlantic slave trade on the Gold Coast.

6   *the castle*   One of the many coastal slave-trading fortresses controlled by the British; scholars are unsure in which particular castle Smith was held captive.

to appear to the best possible advantage for sale. I was bought on board by one Robertson[1] Mumford, steward of said vessel, for four gallons of rum, and a piece of calico, and called VENTURE, on account of his having purchased me with his own private venture. Thus I came by my name. All the slaves that were bought for that vessel's cargo were two hundred and sixty.

CHAPTER 2
CONTAINING AN ACCOUNT OF HIS LIFE, FROM THE TIME OF HIS LEAVING AFRICA, TO THAT OF HIS BECOMING FREE.

After all the business was ended on the coast of Africa, the ship sailed from thence to Barbados. After an ordinary passage, except great mortality by the smallpox, which broke out on board, we arrived at the island of Barbados: but when we reached it, there were found out of the two hundred and sixty that [had] sailed from Africa, not more than two hundred alive. These were all sold, except myself and three more, to the planters there.

The vessel then sailed for Rhode Island, and arrived there after a comfortable passage. Here my master sent me to live with one of his sisters, until he could carry me to Fisher's Island, the place of his residence. I had then completed my eighth year. After staying with his sister some time I was taken to my master's place to live.

When we arrived at Narraganset, my master went ashore in order to return a part of the way by land, and gave me the charge of the keys of his trunks on board the vessel, and charged me not to deliver them up to anybody, not even to his father, without his orders. To his directions I promised faithfully to conform. When I arrived with my master's articles at his house, my master's father asked me for his son's keys, as he wanted to see what his trunks contained. I told him that my master [had] intrusted me with the care of them until he should return, and that I had given him my word to be faithful to the trust, and could not therefore give him or any other person the keys without my master's directions. He insisted that I should deliver to him the keys, threatening to punish me if I did not. But I let him know that he should not have them let him say what he would. He then laid aside trying to get them. But notwithstanding he appeared to give up trying to obtain them from me, yet I mistrusted that he would take some time when I was off my guard, either in the daytime or at night to get them. Therefore I slung them round my neck, and in the daytime concealed them in my bosom, and at night I always lay with them under me, that no person might take them from me without being

---

1   *Robertson*   An error on the part of either Smith or his amanuensis; Mumford's given name was Robinson.

apprized of it. Thus I kept the keys from everybody until my master came home. When he returned he asked where Venture was. As I was then within hearing, I came, and said, here sir, at your service. He asked me for his keys, and I immediately took them off my neck and reached them out to him. He took them, stroked my hair, and commended me, saying in presence of his father that his young Venture was so faithful that he never would have been able to have taken the keys from him but by violence; that he should not fear to trust him with his whole fortune, for that he[1] had been in his native place so habituated to keeping his word that he would sacrifice even his life to maintain it.

The first of the time of living at my master's own place, I was pretty much employed in the house at carding wool[2] and other household business. In this situation I continued for some years, after which my master put me to work out of doors. After many proofs of my faithfulness and honesty, my master began to put great confidence in me. My behavior to him had as yet been submissive and obedient. I then began to have hard tasks imposed on me. Some of these were to pound four bushels of ears of corn every night in a barrel for the poultry, or be rigorously punished. At other seasons of the year I had to card wool until a very late hour. These tasks I had to perform when I was about nine years old.

Some time after I had another difficulty and oppression which was greater than any I had ever experienced since I came into this country. This was to serve two masters.[3] James Mumford, my master's son, when his father had gone from home in the morning, and given me a stint to perform that day, would order me to do *this* and *that* business different from what my master directed me. One day in particular, the authority which my master's son had set up had like to have produced melancholy effects. For my master having set me off my business to perform that day and then left me to perform it, his son came up to me in the course of the day, big with authority, and commanded me very arrogantly to quit my present business and go directly about what he should order me. I replied to him that my master had given me so much to perform that day, and that I must therefore faithfully complete it in that time. He then broke out into a great rage, snatched a pitchfork and went to lay[4] me over the head therewith; but I as soon got another and defended myself with it, or otherwise he might have murdered me in his outrage. He immediately called some people who were within hearing at work for him, and ordered them to

---

1   *he*   I.e., Venture.
2   *carding wool*   Cleaning and detangling raw wool in preparation for spinning.
3   *to serve two masters*   See Matthew 6.24: "No man can serve two masters: for either he will hate the one, and love the other; or else he will hold to the one, and despise the other."
4   *lay*   Strike.

take his hair rope and come and bind me with it. They all tried to bind me but in vain, though there were three assistants in number. My upstart master then desisted, put his pocket handkerchief before his eyes and went home with a design to tell his mother of the struggle with young Venture. He told her that their young Venture had become so stubborn that he could not control him, and asked her what he should do with him. In the meantime I recovered my temper, voluntarily caused myself to be bound by the same men who [had] tried in vain before, and [was] carried before my young master, that he might do what he pleased with me. He took me to a gallows made for the purpose of hanging cattle on, and suspended me on it. Afterwards he ordered one of his hands to go to the peach orchard and cut him three dozen of whips to punish me with. These were brought to him, and that was all that was done with them, as I was released and went to work after hanging on the gallows about an hour.

After I had lived with my master thirteen years, being then about twenty-two years old, I married Meg, a slave of his who was about my age. My master owned a certain Irishman,[1] named Heddy, who about that time formed a plan of secretly leaving his master. After he had long had this plan in meditation he suggested it to me. At first I cast a deaf ear to it, and rebuked Heddy for harboring in his mind such a rash undertaking. But after he had persuaded and much enchanted me with the prospect of gaining my freedom by such a method, I at length agreed to accompany him. Heddy next inveigled two of his fellow servants to accompany us. The place to which we designed[2] to go was the Mississippi. Our next business was to lay in a sufficient store of provisions for our voyage. We privately collected out of our master's store six great old cheeses, two firkins[3] of butter, and one whole batch of new bread. When we had gathered all our own clothes and some more, we took them all about midnight, and went to the water side. We stole our master's boat, embarked, and then directed our course for the Mississippi River.

We mutually confederated not to betray or desert one another on pain of death. We first steered our course for Montauk Point, the east end of Long Island. After our arrival there we landed, and Heddy and I made an incursion into the island after fresh water, while our two comrades were left at a little distance from the boat, employed at cooking. When Heddy and I had sought some time for water, he returned to our companions, and I continued on looking for my object. When Heddy had performed his business with

---

1 *owned a certain Irishman* I.e., held him as an indentured servant. Indentured servants would be held by their masters for a predetermined number of years, usually seven or ten. Though indentured servants—especially those from Ireland—might in some cases have been treated very poorly by their masters, they were not considered chattel in the way enslaved persons were.
2 *designed* Planned.
3 *firkins* Small casks.

our companions who were engaged in cooking, he went directly to the boat, stole all the clothes in it, and then travelled away for East Hampton, as I was informed. I returned to my fellows not long after. They informed me that our clothes were stolen, but could not determine who was the thief, yet they suspected Heddy as he was missing. After reproving my two comrades for not taking care of our things which were in the boat, I advertised Heddy and sent two men in search of him. They pursued and overtook him at Southampton and returned him to the boat. I then thought it might afford some chance for my freedom, or at least a palliation for my running away, to return Heddy immediately to his master, and inform him that I was induced to go away by Heddy's address. Accordingly I set off with him and the rest of my companions for our master's, and arrived there without any difficulty. I informed my master that Heddy was the ringleader of our revolt, and that he had used us ill. He immediately put Heddy into custody, and myself and companions were well received and went to work as usual.

Not a long time passed after that, before Heddy was sent by my master to New London gaol. At the close of that year I was sold to a Thomas Stanton, and had to be separated from my wife and one daughter, who was about one month old. He resided at Stonington Point. To this place I brought with me from my late master's, two johannes,[1] three old Spanish dollars, and two thousand of coppers, besides five pounds of my wife's money. This money I got by cleaning gentlemen's shoes and drawing[2] boots, by catching muskrats and minks, raising potatoes and carrots, etc. and by fishing in the night, and at odd spells.

All this money, amounting to near twenty-one pounds York currency,[3] my master's brother, Robert Stanton, hired of me, for which he gave me his note.[4] About one year and a half after that time, my master purchased my wife and her child for seven hundred pounds old tenor.[5] One time my master sent me two miles after a barrel of molasses, and ordered me to carry it on my shoulders. I made out to carry it all the way to my master's house. When I lived with Captain George Mumford, only to try my strength, I took up on my knees a tierce of salt containing seven bushels, and carried it two or three rods.[6] Of this fact there are several eye witnesses now living.

---

1   *johannes*   Portuguese gold coins, worth approximately 36 shillings.
2   *drawing*   Mending.
3   *York currency*   I.e., paper money printed in the colony of New York.
4   *hired of ... his note*   I.e., Stanton borrowed the twenty-one pounds from Smith, giving him a promissory note stating he would return the money.
5   *old tenor*   Paper money issued in Massachusetts or Rhode Island before 1741, after which it was replaced by a new currency.
6   *tierce ... seven bushels*   Cask of salt weighing approximately 450 pounds;   *rods*   Units of measure equalling about five and a half yards.

Towards the close of the time that I resided with this master, I had a falling out with my mistress. This happened one time when my master was gone to Long Island a gunning. At first the quarrel began between my wife and her mistress. I was then at work in the barn, and hearing a racket in the house, induced me to run there and see what had broken out. When I entered the house, I found my mistress in a violent passion with my wife, for what she informed me was a mere trifle; such a small affair that I forbear to put my mistress to the shame of having it known. I earnestly requested my wife to beg pardon of her mistress for the sake of peace, even if she had given no just occasion for offence. But whilst I was thus saying, my mistress turned the blows which she was repeating on my wife to me. She took down her horse-whip, and while she was glutting her fury with it, I reached out my great black hand, raised it up and received the blows of the whip on it which were designed for my head. Then I immediately committed the whip to the devouring fire.

When my master returned from the island, his wife told him of the affair, but for the present he seemed to take no notice of it, and mentioned not a word about it to me. Some days after his return, in the morning as I was putting on a log in the fireplace, not suspecting harm from anyone, I received a most violent stroke on the crown of my head with a club two feet long and as large round as a chair-post. This blow very badly wounded my head, and the scar of it remains to this day. The first blow made me have my wits about me you may suppose, for as soon as he went to renew it, I snatched the club out of his hands and dragged him out of the door. He then sent for his brother to come and assist him, but I presently left my master, took the club he wounded me with, carried it to a neighboring Justice of the Peace, and complained of my master. He finally advised me to return to my master, and live contented with him till he abused me again, and then complain. I consented to do accordingly. But before I set out for my master's, up he come and his brother Robert after me. The Justice improved[1] this convenient opportunity to caution my master. He asked him for what he treated his slave thus hastily and unjustly, and told him what would be the consequence if he continued the same treatment towards me.[2] After the Justice had ended his discourse with my master, he and his brother set out with me for home, one before and the

---

1 *improved* I.e., made use of.
2 *carried it ... towards me* In appealing to the law for protection from his enslaver, Smith may have been inspired by the recent story of Sharper, an enslaved ten-year-old boy who had approached a justice of the peace in New London on 9 September 1753, having suffered astonishing physical abuse at the hands of his enslaver, James Rogers. The case was brought to court in 1755, with the jury ultimately siding with Sharper and two others who had been cruelly abused by Rogers; the three enslaved plaintiffs were not freed, but were rather sent to live in new households. The story was widely publicized in local newspapers at the time.

other behind me. When they had come to a bye place,[1] they both dismounted their respective horses, and fell to beating me with great violence. I became enraged at this and immediately turned them both under me, laid one of them across the other, and stamped both with my feet what I would.

This occasioned my master's brother to advise him to put me off. A short time after this I was taken by a constable and two men. They carried me to a blacksmith's shop and had me handcuffed. When I returned home my mistress enquired much of her waiters,[2] whether Venture was handcuffed. When she was informed that I was, she appeared to be very contented and was much transported with the news. In the midst of this content and joy, I presented myself before my mistress, showed her my handcuffs, and gave her thanks for my gold rings. For this my master commanded a negro of his to fetch him a large ox chain. This my master locked on my legs with two padlocks. I continued to wear the chain peaceably for two or three days, when my master asked me with contemptuous hard names whether I had not better be freed from my chains and go to work. I answered him, No. Well then, said he, I will send you to the West Indies[3] or banish you, for I am resolved not to keep you. I answered him I crossed the waters to come here, and I am willing to cross them to return.

For a day or two after this not anyone said much to me, until one Hempsted Miner, of Stonington, asked me if I would live with him. I answered him that I would. He then requested me to make myself discontented and to appear as unreconciled to my master as I could before that he bargained with him for me; and that in return he would give me a good chance to gain my freedom when I came to live with him. I did as he requested me. Not long after Hempsted Miner purchased me of my master for fifty-six pounds lawful. He took the chain and padlocks from off me immediately after.

It may here be remembered that I related a few pages back that I hired out a sum of money to Mr. Robert Stanton, and took his note for it. In the fray between my master Stanton and myself, he broke open my chest containing his brother's note to me, and destroyed it. Immediately after my present master bought me, he determined to sell me at Hartford. As soon as I became apprized of it, I bethought myself that I would secure a certain sum of money which lay by me, safer than to hire it out to a Stanton. Accordingly I buried it in the earth, a little distance from Thomas Stanton's, in the road over which he passed daily. A short time after my master carried me to Hartford, and first proposed to sell me to one William Hooker of that place. Hooker asked

---

1   bye place   Hidden or unfrequented area.
2   enquired ... waiters   I.e., kept asking those attending her.
3   send you ... West Indies   A severe threat, given the exceptionally harsh conditions of slavery on the sugar plantations of the West Indies.

whether I would go to the German Flats[1] with him. I answered, No. He said I should, if not by fair means I should by foul. If you will go by no other measures, I will tie you down in my sleigh. I replied to him, that if he carried me in that manner, no person would purchase me, for it would be thought that he had a murderer for sale. After this he tried no more, and said he would not have me as a gift.

My master next offered me to Daniel Edwards, Esq. of Hartford, for sale. But not purchasing me, my master pawned me to him for ten pounds, and returned to Stonington. After some trial of my honesty, Mr. Edwards placed considerable trust and confidence in me. He put me to serve as his cup-bearer and waiter. When there was company at his house, he would send me into his cellar and other parts of his house to fetch wine and other articles occasionally for them. When I had been with him some time, he asked me why my master wished to part with such an honest negro, and why he did not keep me himself. I replied that I could not give him the reason, unless it was to convert me into cash, and speculate with me as with other commodities. I hope that he can never justly say it was on account of my ill conduct that he did not keep me himself. Mr. Edwards told me that he should be very willing to keep me himself, and that he would never let me go from him to live, if it was not unreasonable and inconvenient for me to be parted from my wife and children; therefore he would furnish me with a horse to return to Stonington, if I had a mind for it. As Miner did not appear to redeem me I went, and called at my old master Stanton's first to see my wife, who was then owned by him. As my old master appeared much ruffled at my being there, I left my wife before I had spent any considerable time with her, and went to Colonel O. Smith's. Miner had not as yet wholly settled with Stanton for me, and had before my return from Hartford given Col. Smith a bill of sale of me. These men once met to determine which of them should hold me, and upon my expressing a desire to be owned by Col. Smith, and upon my master's settling the remainder of the money which was due to Stanton for me, it was agreed that I should live with Col. Smith. This was the third time of my being sold, and I was then thirty-one years old. As I never had an opportunity of redeeming myself whilst I was owned by Miner, though he promised to give me a chance, I was then very ambitious of obtaining it. I asked my master one time if he would consent to have me purchase my freedom. He replied that he would. I was then very happy, knowing that I was at that time able to pay part of the purchase money, by means of the money which I some time since buried. This I took out of the earth and tendered to my master, having previously engaged a free negro man to take his security for it, as I was the property

---

1   *German Flats*   Town in New York.

of my master, and therefore could not safely take his obligation myself. What was wanting[1] in redeeming myself, my master agreed to wait on me for, until I could procure it for him. I still continued to work for Col. Smith. There was continually some interest accruing on my master's note to my friend the free negro man above named, which I received, and with some besides which I got by fishing, I laid out in land adjoining my old master Stanton's. By cultivating this land with the greatest diligence and economy, at times when my master did not require my labor,[2] in two years I laid up ten pounds. This my friend tendered my master for myself, and received his note for it.

Being encouraged by the success which I had met in redeeming myself, I again solicited my master for a further chance of completing it. The chance for which I solicited him was that of going out to work the ensuing winter. He agreed to this on condition that I would give him one quarter of my earnings. On these terms I worked the following winter, and earned four pounds sixteen shillings, one quarter of which went to my master for the privilege, and the rest was paid him on my own account. This, added to the other payments, made up forty-four pounds, eight shillings, which I had paid on my own account. I was then about thirty-five years old.

The next summer I again desired he would give me a chance of going out to work. But he refused and answered that he must have my labor this summer, as he did not have it the past winter. I replied that I considered it as hard that I could not have a chance to work out when the season became advantageous, and that I must only be permitted to hire myself out in the poorest season of the year. He asked me after this what I would give him for the privilege per month. I replied that I would leave it wholly with his own generosity to determine what I should return him a month. Well then, said he, if so two pounds a month. I answered him that if that was the least he would take I would be contented.

Accordingly I hired myself out at Fisher's Island, and earned twenty pounds, thirteen pounds six shillings of which my master drew for the privilege, and the remainder I paid him for my freedom. This made fifty-one pounds two shillings which I paid him. In October following I went and wrought[3] six months at Long Island. In that six month's time I cut and corded four hundred cords[4] of wood, besides threshing out seventy-five bushels of grain, and

---

1   *wanting*   Lacking.
2   *labor*   This word is spelled in this fashion six times in the original 1798 publication, and spelled *labour* three times. The policy of this anthology is to retain British spellings in early American works wherever they are consistently used. In cases such as this one, however, where it is not entirely clear if either spelling was preferred, the inconsistency has been retained.
3   *wrought*   Worked.
4   *cords*   Large piles of firewood, measuring about eight by four by four feet.

received of my wages down only twenty pounds, which left remaining a larger sum. Whilst I was out that time, I took up on my wages only one pair of shoes. At night I lay on the hearth, with one coverlet over and another under me. I returned to my master and gave him what I received of my six months labor. This left only thirteen pounds eighteen shillings to make up the full sum for my redemption. My master liberated me, saying that I might pay what was behind if I could ever make it convenient, otherwise it would be well. The amount of the money which I had paid my master towards redeeming my time was seventy-one pounds two shillings. The reason of my master for asking such an unreasonable price was, he said, to secure himself in case I should ever come to want. Being thirty-six years old, I left Col. Smith once for all. I had already been sold three different times, made considerable money with seemingly nothing to derive it from, been cheated out of a large sum of money, lost much by misfortunes, and paid an enormous sum for my freedom.

CHAPTER 3
CONTAINING AN ACCOUNT OF HIS LIFE, FROM THE TIME OF HIS PURCHASING HIS FREEDOM TO THE PRESENT DAY.

My wife and children were yet in bondage to Mr. Thomas Stanton. About this time I lost a chest containing, besides clothing, about thirty-eight pounds in paper money. It was burnt by accident. A short time after I sold all my possessions at Stonington, consisting of a pretty piece of land and one dwelling house thereon, and went to reside at Long Island. For the first four years of my residence there, I spent my time in working for various people on that and at the neighboring islands. In the space of six months I cut and corded upwards of four hundred cords of wood. Many other singular and wonderful labors I performed in cutting wood there, which would not be inferior to those just recited, but for brevity sake I must omit them. In the aforementioned four years, what wood I cut at Long Island amounted to several thousand cords, and the money which I earned thereby amounted to two hundred and seven pounds ten shillings. This money I laid up carefully by me. Perhaps some may enquire what maintained me all the time I was laying up money. I would inform them that I bought nothing which I did not absolutely want.[1] All fine clothes I despised in comparison with my interest, and never kept but just what clothes were comfortable for common days, and perhaps I would have a garment or two which I did not have on at all times, but as for superfluous finery I never thought it to be compared with a decent homespun dress,[2] a

---

1 *want* Need.
2 *decent homespun dress* Decent homemade clothing.

good supply of money and prudence. Expensive gatherings of my mates I commonly shunned, and all kinds of luxuries I was perfectly a stranger to; and during the time I was employed in cutting the aforementioned quantity of wood, I never was at the expense of six-pence worth of spirits.[1] Being after this labour forty years of age, I worked at various places, and in particular on Ram Island, where I purchased Solomon and Cuff, two sons of mine, for two hundred dollars each.

It will here be remembered how much money I earned by cutting wood in four years. Besides this I had considerable money, amounting in all to near three hundred pounds. When I had purchased my two sons, I had then left more than one hundred pounds. After this I purchased a negro man, for no other reason than to oblige him, and gave for him sixty pounds. But in a short time after he run away from me, and I thereby lost all that I gave for him, except twenty pounds which he paid me previous to his absconding.[2] The rest of my money I laid out in land, in addition to a farm which I owned before, and a dwelling house thereon. Forty-four years had then completed their revolution since my entrance into this existence of servitude and misfortune. Solomon, my eldest son, being then in his seventeenth year, and all my hope and dependence for help, I hired him out to one Charles Church of Rhode Island for one year, on consideration of his giving him twelve pounds and an opportunity of acquiring some learning. In the course of the year, Church fitted out a vessel for a whaling voyage, and being in want of hands to man her, he induced my son to go, with the promise of giving him on his return a pair of silver buckles, besides his wages. As soon as I heard of his going to sea, I immediately set out to go and prevent it if possible. But on my arrival at Church's, to my great grief, I could only see the vessel my son was in almost out of sight going to sea. My son died of the scurvy in this voyage, and Church has never yet paid me the least of his wages. In my son, besides the loss of his life, I lost equal to seventy-five pounds.

My other son being but a youth, still lived with me. About this time I chartered a sloop of about thirty tons burden,[3] and hired men to assist me in navigating her. I employed her mostly in the wood trade to Rhode Island, and made clear of all expenses above one hundred dollars with her in better than one year. I had then become something forehanded,[4] and being in my forty-fourth year, I purchased my wife Meg, and thereby prevented having another child to buy, as she was then pregnant. I gave forty pounds for her.

---

1   *spirits* I.e., hard alcohol.

2   *I purchased ... absconding* It seems that the man was purchased with the intention that he pay Smith back in full before properly claiming his freedom.

3   *burden* Carrying capacity of a ship.

4   *forehanded* Financially stable; having money set aside for the future.

During my residence at Long Island, I raised one year with another, ten cartloads of watermelons, and lost a great many every year besides by the thievishness of the sailors. What I made by the watermelons I sold there, amounted to nearly five hundred dollars. Various other methods I pursued in order to enable me to redeem my family. In the night time I fished with set-nets and pots for eels and lobsters, and shortly after went [on] a whaling voyage in the service of Col. Smith. After being out seven months, the vessel returned, laden with four hundred barrels of oil.[1] About this time, I become possessed of another dwelling-house, and my temporal affairs were in a pretty prosperous condition. This and my industry was what alone saved me from being expelled [from] that part of the island in which I resided, as an act was passed by the select-men of the place, that all negroes residing there should be expelled.

Next after my wife, I purchased a negro man for four hundred dollars. But he having an inclination to return to his old master, I therefore let him go. Shortly after I purchased another negro man for twenty-five pounds, whom I parted with shortly after.

Being about forty-six years old, I bought my oldest child Hannah of[2] Ray Mumford, for forty-four pounds, and she still resided with him. I had already redeemed from slavery myself, my wife and three children, besides three negro men.

About the forty-seventh year of my life, I disposed of all my property at Long Island, and came from thence into East Haddam. I hired myself out at first to Timothy Chapman for five weeks, the earnings of which time I put up carefully by me. After this I wrought for Abel Bingham about six weeks. I then put my money together and purchased of said Bingham ten acres of land, lying at Haddam Neck,[3] where I now reside. On this land I labored with great diligence for two years, and shortly after purchased six acres more of land contiguous to my other. One year from that time I purchased seventy acres more of the same man, and paid for it mostly with the produce of my other land. Soon after I bought this last lot of land, I set up a comfortable dwelling house on my farm, and built it from the produce thereof. Shortly after I had much trouble and expense with my daughter Hannah, whose name has before been mentioned in this account. She was married soon after I redeemed her, to one Isaac, a free negro, and shortly after her marriage fell sick of a mortal disease; her husband, a dissolute and abandoned[4] wretch, paid but little attention to her in her illness. I therefore thought it best to

---

1 *oil* Whale oil (at the time the most widely used fuel for lamps).
2 *of* From.
3 *Haddam Neck* In Connecticut.
4 *abandoned* Given to abandoning himself to uncontrolled impulses; unrestrained.

bring her to my house and nurse her there. I procured her all the aid mortals could afford, but notwithstanding this she fell a prey to her disease, after a lingering and painful endurance of it.

The physician's bills for attending her during her illness amounted to forty pounds. Having reached my fifty-fourth year, I hired two negro men, one named William Jacklin, and the other Mingo. Mingo lived with me one year, and having received his wages, run in debt to me eight dollars, for which he gave me his note. Presently after he tried to run away from me without troubling himself to pay up his note. I procured a warrant, took him, and requested him to go to Justice Throop's of his own accord, but he refusing, I took him on my shoulders, and carried him there, distant about two miles. The justice, asking me if I had my prisoner's note with me, and replying that I had not, he told me that I must return with him and get it. Accordingly I carried Mingo back on my shoulders, but before we arrived at my dwelling, he complained of being hurt, and asked me if this was not a hard way of treating our fellow creatures. I answered him that it would be hard thus to treat our honest fellow creatures. He then told me that if I would let him off my shoulders, he had a pair of silver shoe-buckles, one shirt and a pocket handkerchief, which he would turn out to me. I agreed, and let him return home with me on foot; but the very following night, he slipped from me, stole my horse and has never paid me even his note. The other negro man, Jacklin, being a comb-maker by trade, he requested me to set him up, and promised to reward me well with his labor. Accordingly I bought him a set of tools for making combs, and procured him stock. He worked at my house about one year, and then run away from me with all his combs, and owed me for all his board.

Since my residence at Haddam Neck, I have owned of boats, canoes and sail vessels, not less than twenty. These I mostly employed in the fishing and trafficking[1] business, and in these occupations I have been cheated out of considerable money by people whom I traded with taking advantage of my ignorance of numbers.

About twelve years ago, I hired a whale-boat and four black men, and proceeded to Long Island after a load of round clams. Having arrived there, I first purchased of James Webb, son of Orange Webb, six hundred and sixty clams, and afterwards, with the help of my men, finished loading my boat. The same evening, however, this Webb stole my boat, and went in her to Connecticut River, and sold her cargo for his own benefit. I thereupon pursued him, and at length, after an additional expense of nine crowns, recovered the boat; but for the proceeds of her cargo I never could obtain any compensation.

---

1 *trafficking* Transport.

Four years after, I met with another loss, far superior to this in value, and I think by no less wicked means. Being going to New London with a grand-child, I took passage in an Indian's boat, and went there with him. On our return, the Indian took on board two hogsheads[1] of molasses, one of which belonged to Capt. Elisha Hart, of Saybrook, to be delivered on his wharf. When we arrived there, and while I was gone, at the request of the Indian, to inform Captain Hart of his arrival, and receive the freight for him, one hogshead of the molasses had been lost overboard by the people in attempting to land it on the wharf. Although I was absent at the time, and had no concern whatever in the business, as was known to a number of respectable witnesses, I was nevertheless prosecuted by this conscientious gentleman (the Indian not being able to pay for it) and obliged to pay upwards of ten pounds lawful money, with all the costs of court. I applied to several gentlemen for counsel in this affair, and they advised me, as my adversary was rich, and threatened to carry the matter from court to court till it would cost me more than the first damages would be to pay the sum and submit to the injury; which I accord-ing did, and he has often since insultingly taunted me with my unmerited misfortune. Such a proceeding as this, committed on a defenceless stranger, almost worn out in the hard service of the world, without any foundation in reason or justice, whatever it may be called in a Christian land, would in my native country have been branded as a crime equal to highway robbery. But Captain Hart was a *white gentleman*, and I a *poor African; therefore it was all right, and good enough for the black dog.*

I am now sixty-nine years old. Though once straight and tall, measuring without shoes six feet one inch and an half, and every way well proportioned, I am now bowed down with age and hardship. My strength, which was once equal if not superior to any man whom I have ever seen, is now enfeebled so that life is a burden, and it is with fatigue that I can walk a couple of miles, stooping over my staff. Other griefs are still behind, on account of which some aged people, at least, will pity me. My eyesight has gradually failed, till I am almost blind, and whenever I go abroad[2] one of my grandchildren must direct my way; besides for many years I have been much pained and troubled with an ulcer on one of my legs. But amidst all my griefs and pains, I have many con-solations; Meg, the wife of my youth, whom I married for love, and bought with my money, is still alive. My freedom is a privilege which nothing else can equal. Notwithstanding all the losses I have suffered by fire, by the injustice of knaves, by the cruelty and oppression of false hearted friends, and the perfidy of my own countrymen whom I have assisted and redeemed from bondage, I

---

1   *hogsheads*   Large casks.
2   *abroad*   Outside the home.

am now possessed of more than one hundred acres of land, and three habitable dwelling houses. It gives me joy to think that I have and that I *deserve* so good a character, especially for *truth* and *integrity*. While I am now looking to the grave as my home, my joy for this world would be full—IF my children, Cuff for whom I paid two hundred dollars when a boy, and Solomon[1] who was born soon after I purchased his mother—If Cuff and Solomon—O! that they had walked in the way of their father. But a father's lips are closed in silence and in grief!—Vanity[2] of vanities, all is vanity!

F I N I S.

CERTIFICATE

STONINGTON, *November* 3, 1798

THESE certify, that VENTURE, a free negro man, aged about 69 years, and was, as we have ever understood, a native of Africa, and formerly a slave to Mr. James Mumford, of Fisher's Island, in the state of New York; who sold him to Mr. Thomas Stanton, 2d, of Stonington, in the state of Connecticut, and said Stanton sold said VENTURE to Col. Oliver Smith, of the aforesaid place. That said VENTURE hath sustained the character of a faithful servant, and that of a temperate, honest and industrious man, and being ever intent on obtaining his freedom, he was indulged by his masters after the ordinary labour on the days of his servitude, to improve the nights in fishing and other employments to his own emolument, in which time he procured so much money as to purchase his freedom from his late master Col. Smith; after which he took upon himself the name of VENTURE SMITH, and has, since his freedom, purchased a negro woman, called Meg, to whom he was previously married, and also his

---

1   *Solomon*   Smith had two sons named Solomon; the younger, born in 1774, was named after the elder Solomon who had died the year before. While some scholars have interpreted this lament as an implicit criticism of the elder Solomon's pursuit of riches—including the promised "silver buckles"—at sea, a note in the 1896 edition of the text suggests that it is the younger Solomon who is being referred to here. That note reads: "The closing words ... were omitted in the later editions. It is probable that both [sons] improved later, especially so in the case of Solomon, who is well spoken of by elderly men now living, as having maintained a good character." A second note further reads: "Venture in the closing words of his autobiography disparages his sons Cuff and Solomon. The compiler, on inquiry among the elderly people who remembered them well, fails to find sufficient warrant for the language of criticism. Evidently, if any youthful foibles early appeared, they were soon overcome."

2   *Vanity*   In this context, the quality of being without substance or significance—as various forms of Christianity teach is true of all worldly things. See Ecclesiastes 1.2–4: "Vanity of vanities, saith the Preacher, vanity of vanities; all is vanity. What profit hath a man of all his labour which he taketh under the sun? One generation passeth away, and another generation cometh: but the earth abideth for ever."

children who were slaves, and said VENTURE has since removed himself and family to the town of East-Haddam, in this state, where he hath purchased lands on which he hath built a house, and there taken up his abode.

NATHANIEL MINOR, Esq.
ELIJAH PALMER, Esq.
Capt. AMOS PALMER
ACORS SHEFFIELD
EDWARD SMITH[1]

—1798

---

1   *EDWARD SMITH* Son of Colonel Oliver Smith.

Olaudah Equiano or Gustavus Vassa
c. 1745 – 1797

Olaudah Equiano's *The Interesting Narrative of the Life of Olaudah Equiano* was one of the first slave narratives written in English, and is now universally acknowledged to be among the most significant and influential of all eighteenth-century texts. His narrative was a document of central importance for the abolitionist movement, showing readers the horrors of slavery while also demonstrating the eloquence of a native-born African who had been educated in the Western tradition, and displaying to the devout that black people were as capable of spiritual enlightenment as were white people.

Until the beginning of this century Equiano's account of his early years was generally taken entirely at face value: it was accepted that he had been born in what is now southern Nigeria, into the Igbo nation; that he had been kidnaped at the age of eleven and enslaved for some time in Africa; and that he was eventually brought across the Atlantic in slavery. In a 1999 article and then in his 2005 biography of Equiano, historian Vincent Carretta challenged this account, citing two documents suggesting that Equiano had been born not in Africa, but in Carolina. The issue remains disputed and may never be entirely resolved. It is significant, however, that neither Carretta nor other scholars have challenged the authenticity of the information Equiano provides about life in Africa, the passage across the Atlantic, and so on; if Equiano himself was indeed born into American slavery, he would have obtained such information directly from enslaved Africans he knew. At issue, then, is not the fundamental reality of the account Equiano provides, but only whether the early part of his narrative represents a first-hand account or an act of creative imagination based on first-hand research.

Equiano's account of his life following his purchase in Virginia by the British naval captain Michael Henry Pascal is not in dispute. While enslaved by Pascal (who renamed him "Gustavus Vassa") Equiano began his career as a mariner. For the next ten or eleven years, Equiano traveled widely around the Mediterranean, Europe, and the Americas with a series of enslavers; he was engaged in several battles during the Seven Years' War (1756–63), including the 1758 siege of Louisbourg in what is now Nova Scotia. He was sold in May of 1763 for £40 to Robert King, a Philadelphia Quaker who owned property on the Caribbean island of Monserrat and had various shipping interests. After working for King for approximately three years, Equiano was by 1766 able to purchase his freedom.

After securing his freedom, Equiano settled in England. (While slavery was still permitted in England's overseas colonies, it had no legal standing in

England itself, where there was a relatively large population of free black people.) From time to time he earned his living there—working for some time as a hair-dresser, for example—but for many years he kept returning to the sea to earn a living, working on vessels traveling not only to American ports such as Savannah and Charleston but also to Turkey, to the Caribbean, and to South America. In 1773 he served on a scientific expedition to the Arctic, and in 1775–76 he was hired to assist in the setting up of a plantation colony in Central America, where his duties included acting as an overseer of enslaved workers.

Equiano had been taught to read and write while still enslaved and in the 1780s he began to use these skills to draw attention to the plight of enslaved people and to petition for the abolition of slavery. He played a key role in helping to bring to the attention of the public the 1781 case of the slave ship *Zong*, from which 132 enslaved people had been thrown overboard; he was a founder (together with Ottobah Cugoano and others) of the Sons of Africa, which became an influential abolitionist group; he worked closely over many years with prominent white abolitionists (including Granville Sharpe, Thomas Clarkson, and William Wilberforce); his narrative made a deep impression on John Wesley, the Methodist leader (Equiano himself became a Methodist, as he recounts in his narrative); and it made an impression too on the hundreds of influential Britons whose support Equiano enlisted when he published his *Interesting Narrative* in 1789. By that time Equiano was himself a leader of the campaign against the slave trade, and he was as tireless—and as effective—in promoting the book after it had been published as he had been in soliciting support beforehand.

When in 1792 he married Susannah Cullen, a woman he had met while promoting his book in Cambridge, the occasion was considered worthy of notice in the provincial press as well as in London. The *Derby Mercury* was among the newspapers reporting on the event:

> On the 9th instant was married at Soham, in Cambridgeshire, Gustavus Vassa, the African, well known in England as the champion and advocate for procuring a suppression of the slave trade, to Miss Cullen, daughter of Mr. Cullen, of Ely. A vast number of people were assembled on the occasion.

The change in Equiano's circumstances occasioned only a brief pause in Equiano's efforts on behalf of the abolitionist cause: "when I have given her eight or ten days comfort," he wrote a friend, "I mean directly to go to Scot-land and sell my fifth editions."

The *Interesting Narrative* went through several more English editions in Equi-ano's lifetime, and he appears to have become quite well-to-do in his later years, both from the proceeds of book sales and from other ventures (including as a money-lender to some of his influential London contacts). He and Susannah had two children—both daughters. He died in London of unknown causes, on the 31st of March 1797.

The reception history of the *Interesting Narrative* in America differs strikingly from that in Britain. When the book was first published in London in 1789, it was prefaced by a letter addressed jointly to the British Houses of Parliament and accompanied by a list of 311 subscribers, including not only prominent names associated with the British abolitionist movement but also many names from the highest ranks of British society (among them the Prince of Wales, the Duke of York, and the Bishop of London). The book was widely reviewed in Britain, and widely read; several other editions followed, typically including the names of additional influential subscribers, together with fresh testimonials. Reviewers' discussions of the book typically focused on those aspects of the *Interesting Narrative* to which Equiano had drawn attention in his letter to Parliament, and treated the book as a whole as "an instrument" that aimed to bring change to Equiano's "suffering countrymen" who had been enslaved: "may the God of heaven inspire benevolence on that important day when the question of Abolition is to be discussed," Equiano implored the members of the House of Lords and House of Commons.

The circumstances were quite different when the book was published in the United States in 1791. The book was published by a New York printer largely known for publishing religious books. It included a list of just 113 subscribers, none of them particularly prominent in society and none of them especially notable as abolitionists. Indeed (as the research of Akiyo Ito has revealed), the American subscribers were very largely of the artisan class—"bakers, grocers, cartmen, cabinetmakers, carpenters, tailors, watchmakers, blacksmiths" and so on, many of whom owned enslaved people. Ito persuasively suggests that these early American readers may have valued Equiano's narrative less as an antislavery tract than as a travel and adventure narrative. Interestingly, even when Equiano's *Interesting Narrative* was re-issued in America (some thirty years after its initial edition had received so little attention), this aspect of the book seems to have been emphasized; a bookseller's 1837 description that was published more than once in William Lloyd Garrison's antislavery newspaper *The Liberator* mentions that Equiano had "lived as a slave," but places more emphasis on the book's "great variety of wonderful scenes, which give his narrative an interest scarcely surpassed by Robinson Crusoe."

It is perhaps unsurprising that, as an abolitionist text, the *Interesting Narrative* exerted far less influence in America than in Britain. For one thing, Equiano himself declared a strong connection to "old England," and little if any to America; for another, relatively little of the time that Equiano had spent enslaved had been in any part of what later became the United States. The text nevertheless has a good deal to say about slavery in the continental American colonies; the various encounters that Equiano reports (in Chapters 6, 7, and 8) having experienced in Savannah alone provide a searing indictment of the institution as it existed in the Thirteen Colonies.

Interest in Equiano's narrative—along with interest in slave narratives generally—dropped off in the late nineteenth and early twentieth centuries, and it was not until the latter part of the twentieth century that the *Interesting Narrative* began to be again widely read and widely studied. By the early twenty-first century, however, it had become one of the most widely taught texts in the canons of British and American literature—and in the newly formed canon of transatlantic literature. For the most part it has been studied fruitfully as an abolitionist text; an awareness of the book's early American reception history is a reminder that the *Interesting Narrative* can also be appreciated from numerous other angles as well. It is among other things a lively adventure narrative, a Christian conversion narrative, a remarkable tour of the transatlantic economic world—and a richly layered portrait of a man of extraordinary and sometimes contradictory character. Curious about all manner of things, blessed with seemingly boundless entrepreneurial energy, and blessed as well with keen descriptive and storytelling powers, Equiano reveals himself to be a highly talented self-fashioner. He is by turns boastful and self-deprecating, deeply religious and highly worldly. An impassioned and effective opponent of slavery, he was also an apologist for the slave trade within Africa, and a man who allowed himself to be employed for a time as an overseer of enslaved people. "My life and fortune have been extremely chequered, and my adventures various," Equiano declares near the end of the *Interesting Life*. His narrative has often been read, in the words of Joanna Brooks, as "a collective autobiography for millions who survived the slave trade," and unquestionably the text has much to tell us of that collective experience. But—as its earliest American readers appear to have recognized—it has much to tell us too of one of the most extraordinary individuals of his time.

Note on the Text

The texts of the various editions of the *Interesting Narrative* do not vary greatly; the changes Equiano made for the later British editions very largely involved the addition of testimonials and quotations from favorable reviews of the book. The American edition carried a different title page and subscriber list, but the text itself closely followed that of the first two London editions. The first edition, published in 1789, has here been used as a base text. Some paragraph breaks have been added, and spelling and punctuation have been modernized in accordance with the practices of this anthology.

⌘ ⌘ ⌘

from *The Interesting Narrative of the Life of Olaudah Equiano, or Gustavus Vassa, The African. Written by Himself*

CHAPTER I

The author's account of his country, and their manners and customs—Administration of justice—Embrenche—Marriage ceremony, and public entertainments—Mode of living—Dress—Manufactures—Buildings—Commerce—Agriculture—War and religion—Superstition of the natives—Funeral ceremonies of the priests or magicians —Curious mode of discovering poison—Some hints concerning the origin of the author's countrymen, with the opinions of different writers on that subject.

I believe it is difficult for those who publish their own memoirs to escape the imputation of vanity; nor is this the only disadvantage under which they labour: it is also their misfortune that what is uncommon is rarely, if ever, believed, and what is obvious we are apt to turn from with disgust, and to charge the writer with impertinence. People generally think those memoirs only worthy to be read or remembered which abound in great or striking events, those, in short, which in a high degree excite either admiration or pity: all others they consign to contempt and oblivion. It is therefore, I confess, not a little hazardous in a private and obscure individual, and a stranger too, thus to solicit the indulgent attention of the public; especially when I own[1] I offer here the history of neither a saint, a hero, nor a tyrant. I believe there are few events in my life which have not happened to many: it is true the

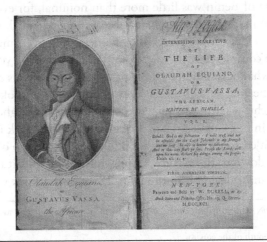

---

1 *own* Admit.

incidents of it are numerous; and, did I consider myself an European, I might say my sufferings were great: but when I compare my lot with that of most of my countrymen, I regard myself as a particular favourite of Heaven, and acknowledge the mercies of Providence in every occurrence of my life. If then the following narrative does not appear sufficiently interesting to engage general attention, let my motive be some excuse for its publication. I am not so foolishly vain as to expect from it either immortality or literary reputation. If it affords any satisfaction to my numerous friends, at whose request it has been written, or in the smallest degree promotes the interests of humanity, the ends for which it was undertaken will be fully attained, and every wish of my heart gratified. Let it therefore be remembered that, in wishing to avoid censure, I do not aspire to praise.

That part of Africa, known by the name of Guinea, to which the trade for slaves is carried on, extends along the coast above 3400 miles, from the Senegal to Angola, and includes a variety of kingdoms. Of these the most considerable is the kingdom of Benin,[1] both as to extent and wealth, the richness and cultivation of the soil, the power of its king, and the number and warlike disposition of the inhabitants. It is situated nearly under the line,[2] and extends along the coast about 170 miles, but runs back into the interior part of Africa to a distance hitherto I believe unexplored by any traveller; and seems only terminated at length by the empire of Abyssinia, near 1500 miles from its beginning. This kingdom is divided into many provinces or districts: in one of the most remote and fertile of which, called Eboe, I was born, in the year 1745, in a charming fruitful vale named Essaka. The distance of this province from the capital of Benin and the sea coast must be very considerable; for I had never heard of white men or Europeans, nor of the sea. And our subjection to the king of Benin was little more than nominal, for every transaction of the government, as far as my slender observation extended, was conducted by the chiefs or elders of the place. The manners and government of a people who have little commerce with other countries are generally very simple, and the history of what passes in one family or village may serve as a specimen of a nation. My father was one of those elders or chiefs I have spoken of, and was styled Embrenche; a term, as I remember, importing the highest distinction, and signifying in our language a *mark* of grandeur. This mark is conferred on the person entitled to it by cutting the skin across at the top of the forehead, and drawing it down to the eyebrows; and while it is in this situation applying a warm hand, and rubbing it until it shrinks up into a thick weal[3] across the

---

1   *kingdom of Benin* This kingdom extended over part of present-day Nigeria as well as present-day Benin.
2   *under the line* South of the equator.
3   *weal* Mark; welt.

lower part of the forehead. Most of the judges and senators were thus marked; my father had long borne it. I had seen it conferred on one of my brothers, and I was also *destined* to receive it by my parents. Those Embrenche, or chief men, decided disputes and punished crimes, for which purpose they always assembled together. The proceedings were generally short, and in most cases the law of retaliation prevailed. I remember a man was brought before my father and the other judges for kidnapping a boy; and, although he was the son of a chief or senator, he was condemned to make recompense by a man or woman slave. Adultery, however, was sometimes punished with slavery or death, a punishment which I believe is inflicted on it throughout most of the nations of Africa, so sacred among them is the honour of the marriage bed, and so jealous are they of the fidelity of their wives. Of this I recollect an instance: a woman was convicted before the judges of adultery, and delivered over, as the custom was, to her husband to be punished. Accordingly he determined to put her to death; but it being found, just before her execution, that she had an infant at her breast; and no woman being prevailed on to perform the part of a nurse, she was spared on account of the child. The men, however, do not preserve the same constancy to their wives which they expect from them; for they indulge in a plurality, though seldom in more than two. Their mode of marriage is thus: both parties are usually betrothed when young by their parents (though I have known the males to betroth themselves). On this occasion a feast is prepared, and the bride and bridegroom stand up in the midst of all their friends, who are assembled for the purpose, while he declares she is thenceforth to be looked upon as his wife, and that no other person is to pay any addresses to her. This is also immediately proclaimed in the vicinity, on which the bride retires from the assembly. Some time after she is brought home to her husband, and then another feast is made, to which the relations of both parties are invited. Her parents then deliver her to the bridegroom, accompanied with a number of blessings, and at the same time they tie round her waist a cotton string of the thickness of a goose-quill, which none but married women are permitted to wear: she is now considered as completely his wife; and at this time the dowry is given to the new married pair, which generally consists of portions of land, slaves, and cattle, household goods, and implements of husbandry. These are offered by the friends of both parties; besides which the parents of the bridegroom present gifts to those of the bride, whose property she is looked upon before marriage; but after it she is esteemed the sole property of her husband. The ceremony being now ended, the festival begins, which is celebrated with bonfires, and loud acclamations of joy, accompanied with music and dancing.

We are almost a nation of dancers, musicians, and poets. Thus every great event, such as a triumphant return from battle or other cause of public rejoicing, is celebrated in public dances, which are accompanied with songs and music suited to the occasion. The assembly is separated into four divisions which dance either apart or in succession, and each with a character peculiar to itself. The first division contains the married men, who in their dances frequently exhibit feats of arms, and the representation of a battle. To these succeed the married women, who dance in the second division. The young men occupy the third; and the maidens the fourth. Each represents some interesting scene of real life, such as a great achievement, domestic employment, a pathetic[1] story, or some rural sport; and as the subject is generally founded on some recent event, it is therefore ever new. This gives our dances a spirit and variety which I have scarcely seen elsewhere.[2] We have many musical instruments, particularly drums of different kinds, a piece of music which resembles a guitar, and another much like a stickado.[3] These last are chiefly used by betrothed virgins, who play on them on all grand festivals.

As our manners are simple, our luxuries are few. The dress of both sexes is nearly the same. It generally consists of a long piece of calico, or muslin, wrapped loosely round the body, somewhat in the form of a highland plaid. This is usually dyed blue, which is our favourite colour. It is extracted from a berry, and is brighter and richer than any I have seen in Europe. Besides this, our women of distinction wear golden ornaments; which they dispose with some profusion on their arms and legs. When our women are not employed with the men in tillage, their usual occupation is spinning and weaving cotton, which they afterwards dye and make it into garments. They also manufacture earthen vessels, of which we have many kinds. Among the rest tobacco pipes, made after the same fashion, and used in the same manner, as those in Turkey.[4]

Our manner of living is entirely plain; for as yet the natives are unacquainted with those refinements in cookery which debauch the taste: bullocks, goats, and poultry supply the greatest part of their food. These constitute likewise the principal wealth of the country, and the chief articles of its commerce. The flesh is usually stewed in a pan; to make it savoury we sometimes use also pepper and other spices, and we have salt made of wood ashes. Our vegetables are mostly plantains, eadas, yams, beans, and Indian corn.[5] The head of the family usually eats alone; his wives and slaves have also their separate tables. Before we taste food we always wash our hands: indeed our cleanliness on all occasions is extreme; but on this it is an indispensable ceremony. After

---

1   *pathetic* Conveying a sense of pathos; emotionally affecting.

2   [Equiano's note] When I was in Smyrna I have frequently seen the Greeks dance after this manner.

3   *stickado* Musical instrument similar to a xylophone.

4   [Equiano's note] The bowl is earthen, curiously figured, to which a long reed is fixed as a tube. This tube is sometimes so long as to be borne by one, and frequently out of grandeur by two boys.

5   *Indian corn* Maize; corn.

washing, libation is made by pouring out a small portion of the drink in a certain place, for the spirits of departed relations, which the natives suppose to preside over their conduct and guard them from evil. They are totally unacquainted with strong or spirituous liquours, and their principal beverage is palm wine. This is gotten from a tree of that name by tapping it at the top and fastening a large gourd to it; and sometimes one tree will yield three or four gallons in a night. When just drawn it is of a most delicious sweetness; but in a few days it acquires a tartish and more spirituous flavour, though I never saw any one intoxicated by it. The same tree also produces nuts and oil. Our principal luxury is in perfumes; one sort of these is an odoriferous wood of delicious fragrance; the other a kind of earth, a small portion of which thrown into the fire diffuses a most powerful odour.[1] We beat this wood into powder, and mix it with palm oil; with which both men and women perfume themselves.

In our buildings we study convenience rather than ornament. Each master of a family has a large square piece of ground, surrounded with a moat or fence, or enclosed with a wall made of red earth tempered, which, when dry, is as hard as brick. Within this are his houses to accommodate his family and slaves, which, if numerous, frequently present the appearance of a village. In the middle stands the principal building, appropriated to the sole use of the master and consisting of two apartments, in one of which he sits in the day with his family; the other is left apart for the reception of his friends. He has besides these a distinct apartment in which he sleeps, together with his male children. On each side are the apartments of his wives, who have also their separate day and night houses. The habitations of the slaves and their families are distributed throughout the rest of the enclosure. These houses never exceed one story in height; they are always built of wood, or stakes driven into the ground, crossed with wattles and neatly plastered within and without. The roof is thatched with reeds. Our dayhouses are left open at the sides; but those in which we sleep are always covered and plastered in the inside with a composition mixed with cow-dung, to keep off the different insects which annoy us during the night. The walls and floors also of these are generally covered with mats. Our beds consist of a platform, raised three or four feet from the ground, on which are laid skins and different parts of a spongy tree called plantain. Our covering is calico or muslin, the same as our dress. The usual seats are a few logs of wood, but we have benches, which are generally perfumed, to accommodate strangers. These compose the greater part of our

---

1   [Equiano's note]   When I was in Smyrna I saw the same kind of earth, and brought some of it with me to England; it resembles musk in strength, but is more delicious in scent, and is not unlike the smell of a rose.

household furniture. Houses so constructed and furnished require but little skill to erect them. Every man is a sufficient architect for the purpose. The whole neighbourhood afford their unanimous assistance in building them and in return receive, and expect, no other recompense than a feast.

As we live in a country where nature is prodigal of her favours, our wants are few and easily supplied; of course, we have few manufactures. They consist for the most part of calicoes, earthen ware, ornaments, and instruments of war and husbandry. But these make no part of our commerce, the principal articles of which, as I have observed, are provisions. In such a state money is of little use; however, we have some small pieces of coin, if I may call them such. They are made something like an anchor, but I do not remember either their value or denomination. We have also markets, at which I have been frequently with my mother. These are sometimes visited by stout mahogany-coloured men from the south west of us: we call them Oye-Eboe, which term signifies "red men living at a distance." They generally bring us firearms, gunpowder, hats, beads, and dried fish. The last we esteemed a great rarity, as our waters were only brooks and springs. These articles they barter with us for odoriferous woods and earth, and our salt of wood ashes. They always carry slaves through our land; but the strictest account is exacted of their manner of procuring them before they are suffered to pass. Sometimes indeed we sold slaves to them, but they were only prisoners of war, or such among us as had been convicted of kidnapping, or adultery, and some other crimes which we esteemed heinous. This practice of kidnapping induces me to think that, notwithstanding all our strictness, their principal business among us was to trepan[1] our people. I remember too they carried great sacks along with them, which not long after I had an opportunity of fatally seeing applied to that infamous purpose.

Our land is uncommonly rich and fruitful, and produces all kinds of veg-etables in great abundance. We have plenty of Indian corn, and vast quantities of cotton and tobacco. Our pineapples grow without culture; they are about the size of the largest sugar-loaf,[2] and finely flavoured. We have also spices of different kinds, particularly pepper, and a variety of delicious fruits which I have never seen in Europe, together with gums of various kinds, and honey in abundance. All our industry is exerted to improve those blessings of nature. Agriculture is our chief employment, and everyone, even the children and women, are engaged in it. Thus we are all habituated to labour from our earli-est years. Everyone contributes something to the common stock, and as we are unacquainted with idleness, we have no beggars. The benefits of such a

---

1 *trepan* Trick or coerce into slavery.
2 *sugar-loaf* Variety of pineapple popular in England at the time.

mode of living are obvious. The West India planters prefer the slaves of Benin or Eboe to those of any other part of Guinea, for their hardiness, intelligence, integrity, and zeal. Those benefits are felt by us in the general healthiness of the people, and in their vigour and activity; I might have added too in their comeliness.[1] Deformity is indeed unknown amongst us—I mean that of shape. Numbers of the natives of Eboe now in London might be brought in support of this assertion: for, in regard to complexion, ideas of beauty are wholly relative. I remember while in Africa to have seen three negro children who were tawny, and another quite white, who were universally regarded by myself and the natives in general, as far as related to their complexions, as deformed. Our women too were in my eyes at least uncommonly graceful, alert, and modest to a degree of bashfulness; nor do I remember to have ever heard of an instance of incontinence[2] amongst them before marriage. They are also remarkably cheerful. Indeed cheerfulness and affability are two of the leading characteristics of our nation.

Our tillage is exercised in a large plain or common some hours' walk from our dwellings, and all the neighbours resort thither in a body. They use no beasts of husbandry, and their only instruments are hoes, axes, shovels, and beaks, or pointed iron to dig with. Sometimes we are visited by locusts, which come in large clouds, so as to darken the air, and destroy our harvest. This however happens rarely, but when it does, a famine is produced by it. I remember an instance or two wherein this happened. This common is often the theatre of war; and therefore when our people go out to till their land, they not only go in a body, but generally take their arms with them for fear of a surprise; and when they apprehend an invasion they guard the avenue to their dwellings by driving sticks into the ground, which are so sharp at one end as to pierce the foot, and are generally dipped in poison. From what I can recollect of these battles, they appear to have been irruptions[3] of one little state or district on the other, to obtain prisoners or booty. Perhaps they were incited to this by those traders who brought the European goods I mentioned amongst us. Such a mode of obtaining slaves in Africa is common, and I believe more are procured this way, and by kidnapping, than any other.[4] When a trader wants slaves, he applies to a chief for them, and tempts him with his wares. It is not extraordinary if on this occasion he yields to the temptation with as little firmness and accepts the price of his fellow creatures' liberty with as little reluctance as the enlightened merchant. Accordingly he falls on his neighbours, and a desperate battle ensues. If he prevails and

---

1   *comeliness*   Pleasing appearance; beauty of form.
2   *incontinence*   Unchastity.
3   *irruptions*   Invasions.
4   [Equiano's note]   See Benezet's "Account of Africa" throughout.

takes prisoners, he gratifies his avarice by selling them; but, if his party be vanquished, and he falls into the hands of the enemy, he is put to death: for, as he has been known to foment[1] their quarrels, it is thought dangerous to let him survive, and no ransom can save him, though all other prisoners may be redeemed. We have firearms, bows and arrows, broad two-edged swords and javelins; we have shields also which cover a man from head to foot. All are taught the use of these weapons; even our women are warriors, and march boldly out to fight along with the men. Our whole district is a kind of militia: on a certain signal given, such as the firing of a gun at night, they all rise in arms and rush upon their enemy. It is perhaps something remarkable that when our people march to the field a red flag or banner is borne before them. I was once a witness to a battle in our common. We had been all at work in it one day as usual when our people were suddenly attacked. I climbed a tree at some distance, from which I beheld the fight. There were many women as well as men on both sides; among others my mother was there, and armed with a broad sword. After fighting for a considerable time with great fury, and after many had been killed, our people obtained the victory and took their enemy's chief prisoner. He was carried off in great triumph, and, though he offered a large ransom for his life, he was put to death. A virgin of note among our enemies had been slain in the battle, and her arm was exposed in our market-place, where our trophies were always exhibited. The spoils were divided according to the merit of the warriors. Those prisoners which were not sold or redeemed we kept as slaves: but how different was their condition from that of the slaves in the West Indies! With us they do no more work than other members of the community, even their masters; their food, clothing, and lodging were nearly the same as theirs (except that they were not permitted to eat with those who were free-born), and there was scarce any other difference between them than a superior degree of importance which the head of a family possesses in our state, and that authority which, as such, he exercises over every part of his household. Some of these slaves have even slaves under them as their own property and for their own use.

As to religion, the natives believe that there is one Creator of all things,[2] and that he lives in the sun and is girded round with a belt; that he may never eat or drink; but, according to some, he smokes a pipe, which is our own favourite luxury. They believe he governs events, especially our deaths or captivity; but, as for the doctrine of eternity, I do not remember to have ever heard of it: some however believe in the transmigration of souls in a

---

1 *foment* Stir up.

2 *believe ... things* For an interesting comparison, see the discussion of West African religion in Gronniosaw's *Narrative* (included elsewhere in this anthology).

certain degree. Those spirits which are not transmigrated, such as our dear friends or relations, they believe always attend them and guard them from the bad spirits or their foes. For this reason they always before eating, as I have observed, put some small portion of the meat, and pour some of their drink, on the ground for them; and they often make oblations of the blood of beasts or fowls at their graves. I was very fond of my mother, and almost constantly with her. When she went to make these oblations at her mother's tomb, which was a kind of small solitary thatched house, I sometimes attended her. There she made her libations and spent most of the night in cries and lamentations. I have been often extremely terrified on these occasions. The loneliness of the place, the darkness of the night, and the ceremony of libation, naturally awful and gloomy, were heightened by my mother's lamentations; and these, concurring with the cries of doleful birds by which these places were frequented, gave an inexpressible terror to the scene.

We compute the year from the day on which the sun crosses the line, and on its setting that evening there is a general shout throughout the land—at least, I can speak from my own knowledge, throughout our vicinity. The people at the same time make a great noise with rattles, not unlike the basket rattles used by children here, though much larger, and hold up their hands to heaven for a blessing. It is then the greatest offerings are made, and those children whom our wise men foretell will be fortunate are then presented to different people. I remember many used to come to see me, and I was carried about to others for that purpose. They have many offerings, particularly at full moons, generally two at harvest before the fruits are taken out of the ground; and when any young animals are killed, sometimes they offer up part of them as a sacrifice. These offerings, when made by one of the heads of a family, serve for the whole. I remember we often had them at my father's and my uncle's, and their families have been present. Some of our offerings are eaten with bitter herbs. We had a saying among us to any one of a cross temper, that "if they were to be eaten, they should be eaten with bitter herbs."

We practised circumcision like the Jews, and made offerings and feasts on that occasion in the same manner as they did. Like them also, our children were named from some event, some circumstance or fancied foreboding, at the time of their birth. I was named *Olaudah*, which, in our language, signifies "vicissitude" or "fortunate," also, one favoured, and having a loud voice and well spoken. I remember we never polluted the name of the object of our adoration; on the contrary, it was always mentioned with the greatest reverence; and we were totally unacquainted with swearing, and all those terms of abuse and reproach which find their way so readily and copiously into the languages of more civilized people. The only expressions of that kind I remember were "May you rot," or "May you swell," or "May a beast take you."

I have before remarked that the natives of this part of Africa are extremely cleanly. This necessary habit of decency was with us a part of religion, and therefore we had many purifications and washings; indeed almost as many and used on the same occasions, if my recollection does not fail me, as the Jews. Those that touched the dead at any time were obliged to wash and purify themselves before they could enter a dwelling-house. Every woman too, at certain times, was forbidden to come into a dwelling-house, or touch any person or any thing we ate. I was so fond of my mother I could not keep from her or avoid touching her at some of those periods, in consequence of which I was obliged to be kept out with her, in a little house made for that purpose, till offering was made, and then we were purified.

Though we had no places of public worship, we had priests and magicians, or wise men. I do not remember whether they had different offices, or whether they were united in the same persons, but they were held in great reverence by the people. They calculated our time and foretold events, as their name imported, for we called them Ah-affoe-way-cah, which signifies "calculators" or "yearly men," our year being called Ah-affoe. They wore their beards, and when they died they were succeeded by their sons. Most of their implements and things of value were interred along with them. Pipes and tobacco were also put into the grave with the corpse, which was always perfumed and ornamented, and animals were offered in sacrifice to them. None accompanied their funerals but those of the same profession or tribe. These buried them after sunset, and always returned from the grave by a different way from that which they went.

These magicians were also our doctors or physicians. They practised bleeding by cupping, and were very successful in healing wounds and expelling poisons. They had likewise some extraordinary method of discovering jealousy, theft, and poisoning; the success of which no doubt they derived from their unbounded influence over the credulity and superstition of the people. I do not remember what those methods were, except that as to poisoning: I recollect an instance or two, which I hope it will not be deemed impertinent here to insert, as it may serve as a kind of specimen of the rest, and is still used by the negroes in the West Indies. A virgin had been poisoned, but it was not known by whom. The doctors ordered the corpse to be taken up by some persons and carried to the grave. As soon as the bearers had raised it on their shoulders, they seemed seized with some sudden impulse, and ran to and fro unable to stop themselves. At last, after having passed through a number of thorns and prickly bushes unhurt, the corpse fell from them close to a house, and defaced it in the fall; and, the owner being taken up, he immediately confessed the poisoning.[1]

The natives are extremely cautious about poison. When they buy any eatable the seller kisses it all round before the buyer, to show him it is not poisoned; and the same is done when any meat or drink is presented, particularly to a stranger. We have serpents of different kinds, some of which are esteemed ominous when they appear in our houses, and these we never molest. I remember two of those ominous snakes, each of which was as thick as the calf of a man's leg, and in colour resembling a dolphin in the water, crept at different times into my mother's night-house, where I always lay with her, and coiled themselves into folds, and each time they crowed like a cock. I was desired by some of our wise men to touch these, that I might be interested in the good omens, which I did, for they were quite harmless and would tamely suffer themselves to be handled; and then they were put into a large open earthen pan and set on one side of the highway. Some of our snakes, however, were poisonous: one of them crossed the road one day when I was standing on it, and passed between my feet without offering to touch me, to the great surprise of many who saw it; and these incidents were accounted by the wise men, and therefore by my mother and the rest of the people, as remarkable omens in my favour.

Such is the imperfect sketch my memory has furnished me with of the manners and customs of a people among whom I first drew my breath. And here I cannot forbear suggesting what has long struck me very forcibly, namely, the strong analogy which even by this sketch, imperfect as it is, appears to prevail in the manners and customs of my countrymen and those of the Jews before they reached the Land of Promise, and particularly the patriarchs while they were yet in that pastoral state which is described in Genesis—an analogy which alone would induce me to think that the one people had sprung from the other. Indeed this is the opinion of Dr. Gill,[2] who, in his commentary on

---

1   [Equiano's note]   An instance of this kind happened at Montserrat in the West Indies in the year 1763. I then belonged to the *Charming Sally*, Capt. Doran. The chief mate, Mr. Mansfield, and some of the crew, being one day on shore, were present at the burying of a poisoned negro girl. Though they had often heard of the circumstance of the running in such cases, and had even seen it, they imagined it to be a trick of the corpse-bearers. The mate therefore desired two of the sailors to take up the coffin and carry it to the grave. The sailors, who were all of the same opinion, readily obeyed; but they had scarcely raised it to their shoulders before they began to run furiously about, quite unable to direct themselves, till at last, without intention, they came to the hut of him who had poisoned the girl. The coffin then immediately fell from their shoulders against the hut, and damaged part of the wall. The owner of the hut was taken into custody on this, and confessed the poisoning. I give this story as it was related by the mate and crew on their return to the ship. The credit which is due to it I leave with the reader.

2   *Dr. Gill*   John Gill (1697–1771), the Baptist author of *An Exposition of the Old Testament, in which Are Recorded the Original of Mankind, of the Several Nations of the World, and of the Jewish Nation in Particular. ...* (1788).

Genesis, very ably deduces the pedigree of the Africans from Afer and Afra, the descendants of Abraham by Keturah, his wife and concubine (for both these titles are applied to her). It is also conformable to the sentiments of Dr. John Clarke, formerly Dean of Sarum, in his *Truth of the Christian Religion*:[1] both these authors concur in ascribing to us this original. The reasonings of these gentlemen are still further confirmed by the scripture chronology; and if any further corroboration were required, this resemblance in so many respects is a strong evidence in support of the opinion. Like the Israelites in their primitive state, our government was conducted by our chiefs or judges, our wise men and elders; and the head of a family with us enjoyed a similar authority over his household with that which is ascribed to Abraham and the other patriarchs. The law of retaliation obtained almost universally with us as with them; and even their religion appeared to have shed upon us a ray of its glory, though broken and spent in its passage, or eclipsed by the cloud with which time, tradition, and ignorance might have enveloped it; for we had our circumcision (a rule I believe peculiar to that people); we had also our sacrifices and burnt-offerings, our washings and purifications, on the same occasions as they had.

As to the difference of colour between the Eboan Africans and the modern Jews, I shall not presume to account for it. It is a subject which has engaged the pens of men of both genius and learning, and is far above my strength. The most able and Reverend Mr. T. Clarkson, however, in his much admired *Essay on the Slavery and Commerce of the Human Species*, has ascertained the cause in a manner that at once solves every objection on that account and, on my mind at least, has produced the fullest conviction. I shall therefore refer to that performance for the theory, contenting myself with extracting a fact as related by Dr. Mitchel.[2] "The Spaniards, who have inhabited America, under the torrid zone, for any time, are become as dark coloured as our native Indians of Virginia; of which *I myself have been a witness*." There is also another instance of a Portuguese settlement at Mitomba, a river in Sierra Leona, where the inhabitants are bred from a mixture of the first Portuguese discoverers with the natives, and are now become, in their complexion, and in the wooly quality of their hair, perfect negroes, retaining however a smattering of the Portuguese language.

These instances, and a great many more which might be adduced, while they show how the complexions of the same persons vary in different climates, it is hoped may tend also to remove the prejudice that some conceive against

---

1   *Dr. John ... Religion* John Clarke (1682–1757) published a translation of a seventeenth-century religious work by Hugo Grotius, *The Truth of the Christian Religion* (1627), in 1743.
2   [Equiano's note]   Philos. Trans. No. 476, Sect. 4, cited by Mr. Clarkson, p. 205.

the natives of Africa on account of their colour. Surely the minds of the Span-iards did not change with their complexions! Are there not causes enough to which the apparent inferiority of an African may be ascribed, without limiting the goodness of God, and supposing he forbore to stamp understanding on certainly his own image, because "carved in ebony"?[1] Might it not naturally be ascribed to their situation?

When they come among Europeans, they are ignorant of their language, religion, manners, and customs. Are any pains taken to teach them these? Are they treated as men? Does not slavery itself depress the mind, and extinguish all its fire and every noble sentiment? But, above all, what advantages do not a refined people possess over those who are rude and uncultivated. Let the polished and haughty European recollect that his ancestors were once, like the Africans, uncivilized, and even barbarous. Did Nature make *them* inferior to their sons? And should *they too* have been made slaves? Every rational mind answers, No. Let such reflections as these melt the pride of their superiority into sympathy for the wants and miseries of their sable brethren, and compel them to acknowledge that understanding is not confined to feature or colour. If, when they look round the world, they feel exultation, let it be tempered with benevolence to others, and gratitude to God, "who hath made of one blood all nations of men for to dwell on all the face of the earth;[2] and whose wisdom is not our wisdom, neither are our ways his ways."

CHAPTER 2

The author's birth and parentage—His being kidnapped with his sister—Their separation—Surprise at meeting again—Are finally separated—Account of the different places and incidents the author met with till his arrival on the coast—The effect the sight of a slave ship had on him—He sails for the West Indies—Horrors of a slave ship—Arrives at Barbados, where the cargo is sold and dispersed.

I hope the reader will not think I have trespassed on his patience in introduc-ing myself to him with some account of the manners and customs of my country. They had been implanted in me with great care, and made an impres-sion on my mind which time could not erase, and which all the adversity and variety of fortune I have since experienced served only to rivet and record; for, whether the love of one's country be real or imaginary, or a lesson of reason, or an instinct of nature, I still look back with pleasure on the first scenes of my life, though that pleasure has been for the most part mingled with sorrow.

---

1   *carved in ebony*   Cf. Thomas Fuller's *The Holy State and the Profane State*, 2.20 (1642): "But our captain counts the Image of God nevertheless his image, cut in ebony as if done in ivory."
2   [Equiano's note]   Acts, c. 17 v. 26.

I have already acquainted the reader with the time and place of my birth. My father, besides many slaves, had a numerous family, of which seven lived to grow up, including myself and a sister, who was the only daughter. As I was the youngest of the sons, I became, of course, the greatest favourite with my mother, and was always with her; and she used to take particular pains to form my mind. I was trained up from my earliest years in the art of war; my daily exercise was shooting and throwing javelins, and my mother adorned me with emblems after the manner of our greatest warriors. In this way I grew up till I was turned the age of eleven, when an end was put to my happiness in the following manner. Generally, when the grown people in the neighbourhood were gone far in the fields to labour, the children assembled together in some of the neighbours' premises to play; and commonly some of us used to get up a tree to look out for any assailant or kidnapper that might come upon us; for they sometimes took those opportunities of our parents' absence to attack and carry off as many as they could seize. One day, as I was watching at the top of a tree in our yard, I saw one of those people come into the yard of our next neighbour but one, to kidnap, there being many stout[1] young people in it. Immediately on this I gave the alarm of the rogue, and he was surrounded by the stoutest of them, who entangled him with cords, so that he could not escape till some of the grown people came and secured him. But alas! ere long it was my fate to be thus attacked, and to be carried off, when none of the grown people were nigh. One day, when all our people were gone out to their works as usual, and only I and my dear sister were left to mind the house, two men and a woman got over our walls and in a moment seized us both, and, without giving us time to cry out or make resistance, they stopped our mouths and ran off with us into the nearest wood. Here they tied our hands and continued to carry us as far as they could, till night came on, when we reached a small house where the robbers halted for refreshment and spent the night. We were then unbound, but were unable to take any food; and, being quite overpowered by fatigue and grief, our only relief was some sleep, which allayed our misfortune for a short time.

The next morning we left the house and continued travelling all the day. For a long time we had kept the woods, but at last we came into a road, which I believed I knew. I had now some hopes of being delivered, for we had advanced but a little way before I discovered some people at a distance, on which I began to cry out for their assistance. But my cries had no other effect than to make them tie me faster and stop my mouth, and then they put me into a large sack. They also stopped my sister's mouth and tied her hands, and in this manner we proceeded till we were out of the sight of these people.

---

1   *stout*   Sturdily built; strong.

When we went to rest the following night they offered us some victuals, but we refused it, and the only comfort we had was in being in one another's arms all that night, and bathing each other with our tears. But alas! we were soon deprived of even the small comfort of weeping together. The next day proved a day of greater sorrow than I had yet experienced, for my sister and I were then separated while we lay clasped in each other's arms. It was in vain that we besought them not to part us; she was torn from me and immediately carried away, while I was left in a state of distraction not to be described. I cried and grieved continually, and for several days I did not eat anything but what they forced into my mouth.

At length, after many days travelling, during which I had often changed masters, I got into the hands of a chieftain in a very pleasant country. This man had two wives and some children, and they all used[1] me extremely well, and did all they could to comfort me—particularly the first wife, who was something like my mother. Although I was a great many days' journey from my father's house, yet these people spoke exactly the same language with us. This first master of mine, as I may call him, was a smith,[2] and my principal employment was working his bellows, which were the same kind as I had seen in my vicinity. They were in some respects not unlike the stoves here in gentlemen's kitchens, and were covered over with leather; and in the middle of that leather a stick was fixed, and a person stood up and worked it in the same manner as is done to pump water out of a cask with a hand pump. I believe it was gold he worked, for it was of a lovely bright yellow colour, and was worn by the women on their wrists and ankles.

I was there I suppose about a month, and they at last used to trust me some little distance from the house. This liberty I used in embracing every opportunity to inquire the way to my own home; and I also sometimes, for the same purpose, went with the maidens in the cool of the evenings to bring pitchers of water from the springs for the use of the house. I had also remarked where the sun rose in the morning and set in the evening as I had travelled along, and I had observed that my father's house was towards the rising of the sun. I therefore determined to seize the first opportunity of making my escape, and to shape my course for that quarter; for I was quite oppressed and weighed down by grief after my mother and friends; and my love of liberty, ever great, was strengthened by the mortifying circumstance of not daring to eat with the free-born children, although I was mostly their companion.

While I was projecting my escape, one day an unlucky event happened which quite disconcerted my plan and put an end to my hopes. I used to be

---

1   *used*   Treated.
2   *smith*   One who works with metals.

sometimes employed in assisting an elderly woman slave to cook and take care of the poultry, and one morning while I was feeding some chickens, I happened to toss a small pebble at one of them, which hit it on the middle and directly killed it. The old slave, having soon after missed the chicken, inquired after it; and on my relating the accident (for I told her the truth, because my mother would never suffer me to tell a lie), she flew into a violent passion, threatened that I should suffer for it, and, my master being out, she immediately went and told her mistress what I had done. This alarmed me very much, and I expected an instant flogging, which to me was uncommonly dreadful, for I had seldom been beaten at home. I therefore resolved to fly, and accordingly I ran into a thicket that was hard by and hid myself in the bushes. Soon afterwards my mistress and the slave returned, and, not seeing me, they searched all the house; but, not finding me, and I not making answer when they called to me, they thought I had run away, and the whole neighbourhood was raised in the pursuit of me. In that part of the country (as in ours) the houses and villages were skirted with woods, or shrubberies, and the bushes were so thick that a man could readily conceal himself in them so as to elude the strictest search. The neighbours continued the whole day looking for me, and several times many of them came within a few yards of the place where I lay hid. I then gave myself up for lost entirely and expected every moment, when I heard a rustling among the trees, to be found out and punished by my master. But they never discovered me, though they were often so near that I even heard their conjectures as they were looking about for me; and I now learned from them that any attempt to return home would be hopeless. Most of them supposed I had fled towards home, but the distance was so great, and the way so intricate, that they thought I could never reach it, and that I should be lost in the woods. When I heard this I was seized with a violent panic and abandoned myself to despair. Night too began to approach, and aggravated all my fears. I had before entertained hopes of getting home, and I had determined when it should be dark to make the attempt; but I was now convinced it was fruitless, and I began to consider that, if possibly I could escape all other animals, I could not those of the human kind, and that, not knowing the way, I must perish in the woods. Thus was I like the hunted deer:

> Ev'ry leaf and ev'ry whisp'ring breath
> Conveyed a foe, and ev'ry foe a death.[1]

---

1   *Ev'ry ... death*   See lines 287–88 of John Denham's "Cooper's Hill": "Now every leaf, and every moving breath / Presents a foe, and every foe a death."

I heard frequent ruftlings among the leaves; and, being pretty fure they were snakes, I expected every inftant to be ftung by them. This increafed my anguifh, and the horror of my fituation became now quite infupportable. I at length quitted the thicket, very faint and hungry, for I had not eaten or drank any thing all the day; and crept to my mafter's kitchen, from whence I fet out at firft, and which was an open shed, and laid myfelf down in the afhes with an anxious wifh for death to relieve me from all my pains. I was fcarcely awake in the morning when the old woman flave, who was the firft up, came to light the fire, and faw me in the fire place. She was very much furprifed to fee me, and could scarcely believe her own eyes. She now promifed to intercede for me, and went for her mafter, who foon after came, and, having flightly reprimanded me, ordered me to be taken care of, and not ill treated.

Soon after this my master's only daughter, and child by his first wife, sickened and died, which affected him so much that for some time he was almost frantic, and really would have killed himself, had he not been watched and prevented. However, in a small time afterwards he recovered, and I was again sold. I was now carried to the left of the sun's rising, through many different countries and a number of large woods. The people I was sold to used to carry me very often, when I was tired, either on their shoulders or on their backs. I saw many convenient, well built sheds along the roads, at proper distances to accommodate the merchants and travellers, who lay in those buildings along with their wives, who often accompany them; and they always go well armed.

From the time I left my own nation, I always found somebody that understood me, till I came to the sea coast. The languages of different nations did not totally differ,[1] nor were they so copious as those of the Europeans, particularly the English. They were therefore easily learned, and while I was journeying thus through Africa I acquired two or three different tongues. In this manner I had been travelling for a considerable time when one evening, to my great surprise, whom should I see brought to the house where I was but my dear sister! As soon as she saw me she gave a loud shriek and ran into my arms. I was quite overpowered: neither of us could speak, but for a considerable time clung to each other in mutual embraces, unable to do anything but weep. Our meeting affected all who saw us; and indeed I must acknowledge, in honour of those sable[2] destroyers of human rights, that I never met with any ill treatment, or saw any offered to their slaves, except tying them when necessary, to keep them from running away. When these people knew we were brother and sister they indulged us together, and the man to whom I

---

1   *languages ... differ*   The Igbo languages and other languages in the Niger-Congo language family share many features not only with each other but also with many Bantu languages.
2   *sable*   Dark skinned.

supposed we belonged lay with us, he in the middle, while she and I held one another by the hands across his breast all night; and thus for a while we forgot our misfortunes in the joy of being together. But even this small comfort was soon to have an end, for scarcely had the fatal morning appeared when she was again torn from me forever! I was now more miserable, if possible, than before. The small relief which her presence gave me from pain was gone, and the wretchedness of my situation was redoubled by my anxiety after her fate and my apprehensions lest her sufferings should be greater than mine, when I could not be with her to alleviate them. Yes, thou dear partner of all my childish sports! thou sharer of my joys and sorrows! happy should I have ever esteemed myself to encounter every misery for you, and to procure your freedom by the sacrifice of my own. Though you were early forced from my arms, your image has been always riveted in my heart, from which neither time nor fortune have been able to remove it; so that, while the thoughts of your sufferings have damped my prosperity, they have mingled with adversity and increased its bitterness. To that Heaven which protects the weak from the strong, I commit the care of your innocence and virtues, if they have not already received their full reward, and if your youth and delicacy have not long since fallen victims to the violence of the African trader, the pestilential stench of a Guinea ship,[1] the seasoning in the European colonies, or the lash and lust of a brutal and unrelenting overseer.

I did not long remain after my sister. I was again sold and carried through a number of places, till, after travelling a considerable time, I came to a town called Tinmah, in the most beautiful country I had yet seen in Africa. It was extremely rich, and there were many rivulets which flowed through it and supplied a large pond in the centre of the town, where the people washed. Here I first saw and tasted cocoa-nuts, which I thought superior to any nuts I had ever tasted before; and the trees, which were loaded, were also interspersed amongst the houses, which had commodious shades adjoining and were in the same manner as ours, the insides being neatly plastered and whitewashed. Here I also saw and tasted for the first time sugar cane. Their money consisted of little white shells the size of the fingernail. I was sold here for one hundred and seventy-two of them by a merchant who lived, and brought me, there. I had been about two or three days at his house when a wealthy widow, a neighbour of his, came there one evening and brought with her an only son, a young gentleman about my own age and size. Here they saw me; and, having taken a fancy to me, I was bought of the merchant and went home with them. Her house and premises were situated close to one of those rivulets I have mentioned, and were the finest I ever saw in Africa: they were very

---

1 *Guinea ship* Slave ship from Guinea.

extensive, and she had a number of slaves to attend her. The next day I was washed and perfumed, and when mealtime came I was led into the presence of my mistress, and ate and drank before her with her son. This filled me with astonishment, and I could scarce help expressing my surprise that the young gentleman should suffer[1] me, who was bound, to eat with him, who was free; and not only so, but that he would not at any time either eat or drink till I had taken first, because I was the eldest (which was agreeable to our custom). Indeed, everything here, and all their treatment of me, made me forget that I was a slave. The language of these people resembled ours so nearly that we understood each other perfectly. They had also the very same customs as we. There were likewise slaves daily to attend us, while my young master and I with other boys sported with our darts and bows and arrows, as I had been used to do at home. In this resemblance to my former happy state I passed about two months; and I now began to think I was to be adopted into the family, and was beginning to be reconciled to my situation and to forget by degrees my misfortunes, when all at once the delusion vanished; for, without the least previous knowledge, one morning early, while my dear master and companion was still asleep, I was wakened out of my reverie to fresh sorrow, and hurried away even amongst the uncircumcised.[2]

Thus at the very moment I dreamed of the greatest happiness I found myself most miserable, and it seemed as if fortune wished to give me this taste of joy only to render the reverse more poignant. The change I now experienced was as painful as it was sudden and unexpected. It was a change indeed from a state of bliss to a scene which is inexpressible by me, as it discovered[3] to me an element I had never before beheld, and till then had no idea of, and wherein such instances of hardship and cruelty continually occurred, as I can never reflect on but with horror.

All the nations and people I had hitherto passed through resembled our own in their manners, customs, and language, but I came at length to a country, the inhabitants of which differed from us in all those particulars. I was very much struck with this difference, especially when I came among a people who did not circumcise, and ate without washing their hands. They cooked also in iron pots, and had European cutlasses and cross bows, which were unknown to us, and fought with their fists amongst themselves. Their women were not so modest as ours, for they ate and drank and slept with their men. But, above all, I was amazed to see no sacrifices or offerings among them. In some of those places the people ornamented themselves with scars, and likewise filed

---

1 *suffer* Permit.
2 *uncircumcised* I.e., heathens, foreigners.
3 *discovered* Revealed.

their teeth very sharp. They wanted sometimes to ornament me in the same manner, but I would not suffer them, hoping that I might sometime be among a people who did not thus disfigure themselves, as I thought they did. At last I came to the banks of a large river which was covered with canoes, in which the people appeared to live with their household utensils and provisions of all kinds. I was beyond measure astonished at this, as I had never before seen any water larger than a pond or a rivulet, and my surprise was mingled with no small fear when I was put into one of these canoes and we began to paddle and move along the river. We continued going on thus till night; and when we came to land and made fires on the banks, each family by themselves, some dragged their canoes on shore, others stayed and cooked in theirs and laid in them all night. Those on the land had mats, of which they made tents, some in the shape of little houses. In these we slept, and after the morning meal we embarked again and proceeded as before. I was often very much astonished to see some of the women, as well as the men, jump into the water, dive to the bottom, come up again, and swim about.

Thus I continued to travel, sometimes by land, sometimes by water, through different countries and various nations, till, at the end of six or seven months after I had been kidnapped, I arrived at the seacoast. It would be tedious and uninteresting to relate all the incidents which befell me during this journey, and which I have not yet forgotten; of the various hands I passed through, and the manners and customs of all the different people among whom I lived. I shall therefore only observe that in all the places where I was the soil was exceedingly rich; the pumpkins, eadas,[1] plantains, yams, etc., etc., were in great abundance, and of incredible size. There were also vast quantities of different gums, though not used for any purpose, and everywhere a great deal of tobacco. The cotton even grew quite wild, and there was plenty of redwood. I saw no mechanics[2] whatever in all the way, except such as I have mentioned. The chief employment in all these countries was agriculture, and both the males and females, as with us, were brought up to it, and trained in the arts of war.

The first object which saluted my eyes when I arrived on the coast was the sea, and a slave ship, which was then riding at anchor and waiting for its cargo. These filled me with astonishment, which was soon converted into terror when I was carried on board. I was immediately handled and tossed up, to see if I were sound, by some of the crew; and I was now persuaded that I had gotten into a world of bad spirits, and that they were going to kill me. Their complexions, too, differing so much from ours, their long hair,

---

1   *eadas*   Eddoes (a variety of tropical vegetable).
2   *mechanics*   Artisans.

and the language they spoke (which was very different from any I had ever heard) united to confirm me in this belief. Indeed, such were the horrors of my views and fears at the moment that, if ten thousand worlds had been my own, I would have freely parted with them all to have exchanged my condition with that of the meanest[1] slave in my own country. When I looked round the ship, too, and saw a large furnace of copper boiling, and a multitude of black people of every description chained together, every one of their countenances expressing dejection and sorrow, I no longer doubted of my fate; and, quite overpowered with horror and anguish, I fell motionless on the deck and fainted. When I recovered a little I found some black people about me who I believed were some of those who brought me on board and had been receiving their pay; they talked to me in order to cheer me, but all in vain. I asked them if we were not to be eaten by those white men with horrible looks, red faces, and loose hair. They told me I was not, and one of the crew brought me a small portion of spirituous liquor in a wine glass; but, being afraid of him, I would not take it out of his hand. One of the blacks therefore took it from him and gave it to me, and I took a little down my palate, which, instead of reviving me as they thought it would, threw me into the greatest consternation at the strange feeling it produced, having never tasted any such liquor before.

Soon after this the blacks who brought me on board went off, and left me abandoned to despair. I now saw myself deprived of all chance of returning to my native country, or even the least glimpse of hope of gaining the shore, which I now considered as friendly; and I even wished for my former slavery in preference to my present situation, which was filled with horrors of every kind, still heightened by my ignorance of what I was to undergo. I was not long suffered to indulge my grief; I was soon put down under the decks, and there I received such a salutation in my nostrils as I had never experienced in my life; so that, with the loathsomeness of the stench and crying together, I became so sick and low that I was not able to eat, nor had I the least desire to taste anything. I now wished for the last friend, death, to relieve me; but soon, to my grief, two of the white men offered me eatables; and, on my refusing to eat, one of them held me fast by the hands and laid me across, I think, the windlass,[2] and tied my feet while the other flogged me severely. I had never experienced anything of this kind before; and although, not being used to the water, I naturally feared that element the first time I saw it, yet nevertheless, could I have got over the nettings, I would have jumped over the side. But I could not, and besides, the crew used to watch us very closely who were not

---

1   *meanest*   Most lowly; worst treated.
2   *windlass*   On board ship, a mechanical contrivance used for winding ropes or chains.

chained down to the decks, lest we should leap into the water, and I have seen some of these poor African prisoners most severely cut for attempting to do so, and hourly whipped for not eating. This indeed was often the case with myself.

In a little time after, amongst the poor chained men I found some of my own nation, which in a small degree gave ease to my mind. I inquired of these what was to be done with us; they gave me to understand we were to be carried to these white people's country to work for them. I then was a little revived and thought, if it were no worse than working, my situation was not so desperate. But still I feared I should be put to death; the white people looked and acted, as I thought, in so savage a manner—for I had never seen among any people such instances of brutal cruelty, and this not only shown towards us blacks, but also to some of the whites themselves. One white man in particular I saw, when we were permitted to be on deck, flogged so unmercifully with a large rope near the foremast that he died in consequence of it, and they tossed him over the side as they would have done a brute.[1] This made me fear these people the more, and I expected nothing less than to be treated in the same manner. I could not help expressing my fears and apprehensions to some of my countrymen. I asked them if these people had no country, but lived in this hollow place (the ship). They told me they did not, but came from a distant one. "Then," said I, "how comes it in all our country we never heard of them?" They told me because they lived so very far off. I then asked, where were their women? had they any like themselves? I was told they had. "And why," said I, "do we not see them?" They answered, because they were left behind. I asked how the vessel could go. They told me they could not tell, but that there were cloths put upon the masts by the help of the ropes I saw, and then the vessel went on; and the white men had some spell or magic they put in the water when they liked in order to stop the vessel. I was exceedingly amazed at this account, and really thought they were spirits. I therefore wished much to be from amongst them,[2] for I expected they would sacrifice me. But my wishes were vain, for we were so quartered that it was impossible for any of us to make our escape.

While we stayed on the coast I was mostly on deck, and one day, to my great astonishment, I saw one of these vessels coming in with the sails up. As soon as the whites saw it, they gave a great shout, at which we were amazed; and the more so as the vessel appeared larger by approaching nearer. At last she came to an anchor in my sight, and when the anchor was let go I and my countrymen who saw it were lost in astonishment to observe the vessel

---

1 *brute* Non-human animal.
2 *from amongst them* Away from them.

stop, and were now convinced it was done by magic. Soon after this the other ship got her boats out, and they came on board of us, and the people of both ships seemed very glad to see each other. Several of the strangers also shook hands with us black people and made motions with their hands, signifying, I suppose, we were to go to their country; but we did not understand them.

At last, when the ship we were in had got in all her cargo, they made ready with many fearful noises, and we were all put under deck, so that we could not see how they managed the vessel. But this disappointment was the least of my sorrow. The stench of the hold while we were on the coast was so intolerably loathsome that it was dangerous to remain there for any time, and some of us had been permitted to stay on the deck for the fresh air, but now that the whole ship's cargo were confined together, it became absolutely pestilential. The closeness of the place and the heat of the climate, added to the number in the ship, which was so crowded that each had scarcely room to turn himself, almost suffocated us. This produced copious perspirations, so that the air soon became unfit for respiration from a variety of loathsome smells, and brought on a sickness among the slaves, of which many died, thus falling victims to the improvident avarice, as I may call it, of their purchasers. This wretched situation was again aggravated by the galling[1] of the chains, now become insupportable, and the filth of the necessary tubs,[2] into which the children often fell, and were almost suffocated. The shrieks of the women and the groans of the dying rendered the whole a scene of horror almost inconceivable. Happily perhaps for myself, I was soon reduced so low here that it was thought necessary to keep me almost always on deck; and from my extreme youth I was not put in fetters. In this situation I expected every hour to share the fate of my companions, some of whom were almost daily brought upon deck at the point of death, which I began to hope would soon put an end to my miseries. Often did I think many of the inhabitants of the deep much more happy than myself. I envied them the freedom they enjoyed, and as often wished I could change my condition for theirs. Every circumstance I met with served only to render my state more painful and heighten my apprehensions and my opinion of the cruelty of the whites.

One day they had taken a number of fishes; and when they had killed and satisfied themselves with as many as they thought fit, to our astonishment who were on the deck, rather than give any of them to us to eat as we expected, they tossed the remaining fish into the sea again, although we begged and prayed for some as well as we could, but in vain; and some of my countrymen, being pressed by hunger, took an opportunity, when they thought no one saw them,

---

1   *galling* Chafing.
2   *necessary tubs* Containers for human excrement.

of trying to get a little privately; but they were discovered, and the attempt procured them some very severe floggings.

One day, when we had a smooth sea and moderate wind, two of my wearied countrymen who were chained together (I was near them at the time), preferring death to such a life of misery, somehow made through the nettings and jumped into the sea. Immediately another quite dejected fellow, who, on account of his illness, was suffered to be out of irons, also followed their example; and I believe many more would very soon have done the same if they had not been prevented by the ship's crew, who were instantly alarmed. Those of us that were the most active were in a moment put down under the deck, and there was such a noise and confusion amongst the people of the ship as I never heard before, to stop her and get the boat out to go after the slaves. However, two of the wretches were drowned; but they got the other, and afterwards flogged him unmercifully for thus attempting to prefer death to slavery.

In this manner we continued to undergo more hardships than I can now relate, hardships which are inseparable from this accursed trade. Many a time we were near suffocation from the want of fresh air, which we were often without for whole days together. This, and the stench of the necessary tubs, carried off many.

During our passage I first saw flying fishes, which surprised me very much: they used frequently to fly across the ship, and many of them fell on the deck. I also now first saw the use of the quadrant;[1] I had often with astonishment seen the mariners make observations with it, and I could not think what it meant. They at last took notice of my surprise, and one of them, willing to increase it, as well as to gratify my curiosity, made me one day look through it. The clouds appeared to me to be land, which disappeared as they passed along. This heightened my wonder, and I was now more persuaded than ever that I was in another world, and that everything about me was magic.

At last we came in sight of the island of Barbados, at which the whites on board gave a great shout and made many signs of joy to us. We did not know what to think of this, but as the vessel drew nearer we plainly saw the harbour and other ships of different kinds and sizes, and we soon anchored amongst them off Bridgetown. Many merchants and planters now came on board, though it was in the evening. They put us in separate parcels[2] and examined us attentively. They also made us jump, and pointed to the land, signifying we were to go there. We thought by this we should be eaten by these ugly men, as they appeared to us; and, when soon after we were all put down under the

---

1 *quadrant* Instrument used for taking altitudes.
2 *parcels* Groups.

deck again, there was much dread and trembling among us, and nothing but bitter cries to be heard all the night from these apprehensions, insomuch that at last the white people got some old slaves from the land to pacify us. They told us we were not to be eaten, but to work, and were soon to go on land, where we should see many of our country people. This report eased us much; and sure enough, soon after we were landed, there came to us Africans of all languages.

We were conducted immediately to the merchant's yard, where we were all pent up together like so many sheep in a fold, without regard to sex or age. As every object was new to me, everything I saw filled me with surprise. What struck me first was that the houses were built with stories, and in every other respect different from those in Africa. But I was still more astonished on seeing people on horseback. I did not know what this could mean, and indeed I thought these people were full of nothing but magical arts. While I was in this astonishment, one of my fellow prisoners spoke to a countryman of his about the horses, who said they were the same kind they had in their country. I understood them, though they were from a distant part of Africa, and I thought it odd I had not seen any horses there; but afterwards, when I came to converse with different Africans, I found they had many horses amongst them, and much larger than those I then saw.

We were not many days in the merchant's custody before we were sold after their usual manner, which is this: on a signal given (as the beat of a drum), the buyers rush at once into the yard where the slaves are confined, and make choice of that parcel they like best. The noise and clamour with which this is attended, and the eagerness visible in the countenances of the buyers, serve not a little to increase the apprehensions of the terrified Africans, who may well be supposed to consider them as the ministers of that destruction to which they think themselves devoted. In this manner, without scruple, are relations and friends separated, most of them never to see each other again. I remember in the vessel in which I was brought over, in the men's apartment there were several brothers who, in the sale, were sold in different lots; and it was very moving on this occasion to see and hear their cries at parting. O ye nominal Christians![1] Might not an African ask you, "Learned you this from your God, who says unto you, 'Do unto all men as you would men should do unto you'? Is it not enough that we are torn from our country and friends to toil for your luxury and lust of gain?[2] Must every tender feeling be likewise sacrificed to your avarice? Are the dearest friends and relations, now rendered more dear by their separation from their kindred, still to be parted from each

---

1   *nominal Christians*   So-called Christians.
2   *lust of gain*   Desire for riches.

other, and thus prevented from cheering the gloom of slavery with the small comfort of being together and mingling their sufferings and sorrows? Why are parents to lose their children, brothers their sisters, or husbands their wives?" Surely this is a new refinement in cruelty, which, while it has no advantage to atone for it, thus aggravates distress and adds fresh horrors even to the wretchedness of slavery.

from CHAPTER 3

The author is carried to Virginia—His distress—Surprise at seeing a picture and a watch—Is bought by Captain Pascal, and sets out for England—His terror during the voyage—Arrives in England—His wonder at a fall of snow—Is sent to Guernsey, and in some time goes on board a ship of war with his master—Some account of the expedition against Louisbourgh under the command of Admiral Boscawen, in 1758.

I now totally lost the small remains of comfort I had enjoyed in conversing with my countrymen; the women too, who used to wash and take care of me, were all gone different ways, and I never saw one of them afterwards.

I stayed in this island for a few days; I believe it could not be above a fortnight; when I and some few more slaves, that were not saleable amongst the rest, from very much fretting, were shipped off in a sloop for North America. On the passage we were better treated than when we were coming from Africa, and we had plenty of rice and fat pork. We were landed up a river a good way from the sea, about Virginia county, where we saw few or none of our native Africans, and not one soul who could talk to me. I was a few weeks weeding grass, and gathering stones in a plantation; and at last all my companions were distributed different ways, and only myself was left. I was now exceedingly miserable, and thought myself worse off than any of the rest of my companions; for they could talk to each other, but I had no person to speak to that I could understand. In this state I was constantly grieving and pining,[1] and wishing for death rather than anything else.

While I was in this plantation the gentleman, to whom I suppose the estate belonged, being unwell, I was one day sent for to his dwelling house to fan him; when I came into the room where he was I was very much affrighted at some things I saw, and the more so as I had seen a black woman slave as I came through the house, who was cooking the dinner, and the poor creature was cruelly loaded with various kinds of iron machines; she had one particularly on her head, which locked her mouth so fast that she could scarcely speak; and could not eat nor drink. I was much astonished and shocked at this contrivance, which I afterward learned was called the iron muzzle. Soon after I had a

---

1 *pining* Becoming exhausted with mental suffering.

fan put into my hand, to fan the gentleman while he slept; and so I did indeed with great fear. While he was fast asleep, I indulged myself a great deal in looking about the room, which to me appeared very fine and curious. The first object that engaged my attention was a watch which hung on the chimney, and was going. I was quite surprised at the noise it made and was afraid it would tell the gentleman anything I might do amiss: and when I immediately after observed a picture hanging in the room, which appeared constantly to look at me, I was still more affrighted, having never seen such things as these before. At one time I thought it was something relative to magic; and not seeing it move I thought it might be some way the whites had to keep their great men when they died, and offer them libation as we used to do to our friendly spirits. In this state of anxiety I remained till my master awoke, when I was dismissed out of the room, to my no small satisfaction and relief; for I thought that these people were all made up of wonders. In this place I was called Jacob; but on board the *African Snow* I was called Michael.

I had been some time in this miserable, forlorn, and much dejected state, without having anyone to talk to, which made my life a burden, when the kind and unknown hand of the Creator (who in very deed leads the blind in a way they know not) now began to appear, to my comfort; for one day the captain of a merchant ship, called the *Industrious Bee*, came on some business to my master's house. This gentleman, whose name was Michael Henry Pascal, was a lieutenant in the royal navy, but now commanded this trading ship, which was somewhere in the confines of the county many miles off. While he was at my master's house it happened that he saw me, and liked me so well that he made a purchase of me. I think I have often heard him say he gave thirty or forty pounds sterling for me; but I do not now remember which. However, he meant me for a present to some of his friends in England: and I was sent accordingly from the house of my then master, one Mr. Campbell, to the place where the ship lay; I was conducted on horseback by an elderly black man (a mode of travelling which appeared very odd to me). When I arrived I was carried on board a fine large ship, loaded with tobacco, etc. and just ready to sail for England. I now thought my condition much mended; I had sails to lie on, and plenty of good vitals[1] to eat; and everybody on board used me very kindly, quite contrary to what I had seen of any white people before; I therefore began to think that they were not all of the same disposition. A few days after I was on board we sailed for England.

I was still at a loss to conjecture my destiny. By this time, however, I could smatter a little imperfect English; and I wanted to know as well as I could where we were going. Some of the people of the ship used to tell me they were

---

1   *vitals* Nutritious foods.

going to carry me back to my own country, and this made me very happy. I was quite rejoiced at the sound of going back; and thought if I should get home what wonders I should have to tell. But I was reserved for another fate, and was soon undeceived when we came within sight of the English coast. While I was on board this ship, my captain and master named me Gustavus Vassa.[1] I at that time began to understand him a little, and refused to be called so, and told him as well as I could that I would be called Jacob; but he said I should not, and still called me Gustavus; and when I refused to answer to my new name, which at first I did, it gained me many a cuff; so at length I submitted, and was obliged to bear the present name, by which I have been known ever since.

The ship had a very long passage; and on that account we had very short allowance of provisions. Towards the last we had only one pound and a half of bread per week, and about the same quantity of meat, and one quart of water a day. We spoke with only one vessel the whole time we were at sea, and but once we caught a few fishes. In our extremities the captain and people told me in jest they would kill and eat me; but I thought them in earnest, and was depressed beyond measure, expecting every moment to be my last. While I was in this situation one evening they caught with a good deal of trouble, a large shark, and got it on board. This gladdened my poor heart exceedingly, as I thought it would serve the people to eat instead of their eating me; but very soon, to my astonishment, they cut off a small part of the tail, and tossed the rest over the side. This renewed my consternation; and I did not know what to think of these white people, though I very much feared they would kill and eat me.

There was on board the ship a young lad who had never been at sea before, about four or five years older than myself: his name was Richard Baker. He was a native of America, had received an excellent education, and was of a most amiable temper. Soon after I went on board he shewed me a great deal of partiality and attention, and in return I grew extremely fond of him. We at length became inseparable; and, for the space of two years, he was of very great use to me, and was my constant companion and instructor. Although this dear youth had many slaves of his own, yet he and I have gone through many sufferings together on shipboard; and we have many nights lain in each other's bosoms when we were in great distress. Thus such a friendship was cemented between us as we cherished till his death, which, to my very great sorrow, happened in the year 1759, when he was up the Archipelago, on board

---

1   *Gustavus Vassa*   The sixteenth-century Swedish monarch Gustav Vasa was widely regarded as a hero to his people; a 1739 play by Henry Brooke, *Gustavus Vasa, the Deliverer of His Country*, helped to make Vasa well-known in the English-speaking world.

his majesty's ship the *Preston*: an event which I have never ceased to regret, as I lost at once a kind interpreter, an agreeable companion, and a faithful friend; who, at the age of fifteen, discovered a mind superior to prejudice; and who was not ashamed to notice, to associate with, and to be the friend and instructor of one who was ignorant, a stranger, of a different complexion, and a slave! My master had lodged in his mother's house in America: he respected him very much, and made him always eat with him in the cabin. He used often to tell him jocularly that he would kill me to eat. Sometimes he would say to me the black people were not good to eat, and would ask me if we did not eat people in my country. I said, No: then he said he would kill Dick (as he always called him) first, and afterwards me. Though this hearing relieved my mind a little as to myself, I was alarmed for Dick and whenever he was called I used to be very much afraid he was to be killed; and I would peep and watch to see if they were going to kill him: nor was I free from this consternation till we made the land.

One night we lost a man overboard; and the cries and noise were so great and confused in stopping the ship, that I, who did not know what was the matter, began, as usual, to be very much afraid, and to think they were going to make an offering with me, and perform some magic; which I still believed they dealt in. As the waves were very high, I thought the ruler of the seas was angry, and I expected to be offered up to appease him. This filled my mind with agony, and I could not any more that night close my eyes again to rest. However, when daylight appeared I was a little eased in my mind; but still every time I was called, I used to think it was to be killed.

Sometime after this we saw some very large fish, which I afterwards found were called grampusses.[1] They looked to me extremely terrible, and made their appearance just at dusk and were so near as to blow the water on the ship's deck. I believed them to be the rulers of the sea; and, as the white people did not make any offerings at anytime, I thought they were angry with them: and, at last, what confirmed my belief was, the wind just then died away, and a calm ensued, and in consequence of it the ship stopped going. I supposed that the fish had performed this, and I hid myself in the fore part of the ship, through fear of being offered up to appease them, every minute peeping and quaking: but my good friend Dick came shortly towards me, and I took an opportunity to ask him, as well as I could, what these fish were. Not being able to talk much English, I could but just make him understand my question; and not at all, when I asked him if any offerings were to be made to them: however, he told me these fish would swallow anybody; which sufficiently alarmed me. Here he was called away by the captain, who was leaning over the quarter-deck

---

1   *grampusses*   The name "grampus" is applied to several species of whale and dolphin.

railing and looking at the fish; and most of the people were busied in getting a barrel of pitch to light, for them to play with. The captain now called me to him, having learned some of my apprehensions from Dick; and having diverted himself and others for some time with my fears, which appeared ludicrous enough in my crying and trembling, he dismissed me. The barrel of pitch was now lighted and put over the side into the water: by this time it was just dark, and the fish went after it; and, to my great joy, I saw them no more.

However, all my alarms began to subside when we got sight of land; and at last the ship arrived at Falmouth, after a passage of thirteen weeks. Every heart on board seemed gladdened on our reaching the shore, and none more than mine. The captain immediately went on shore, and sent on board some fresh provisions, which we wanted very much: we made good use of them, and our famine was soon turned into feasting, almost without ending. It was about the beginning of the spring 1757 when I arrived in England; and I was nearly twelve years of age at that time. I was very much struck with the buildings and the pavement of the streets in Falmouth; and, indeed, any object I saw filled me with new surprise. One morning when I got upon deck, I saw it covered all over with the snow that fell overnight: as I had never seen anything of the kind before, I thought it was salt; so I immediately ran down to the mate and desired him, as well as I could, to come and see how somebody in the night had thrown salt all over the deck. He, knowing what it was, desired me to bring some of it down to him: accordingly, I took up a handful of it, which I found very cold indeed; and when I brought it to him he desired me to taste it. I did so, and I was surprised beyond measure. I then asked him what it was; he told me it was snow: but I could not in anywise understand him. He asked me if we had no such thing in my country; and I told him, No. I then asked him the use of it, and who made it; he told me a great man in the heavens, called God: but here again I was to all intents and purposes at a loss to understand him; and the more so when a little after I saw the air filled with it, in a heavy shower, which fell down on the same day. After this I went to church; and having never been at such a place before, I was again amazed at seeing and hearing the service. I asked all I could about it; and they gave me to understand it was worshipping God, who made us and all things. I was still at a great loss, and soon got into an endless field of inquiries, as well as I was able to speak and ask about things. However, my little friend Dick used to be my best interpreter; for I could make free with him, and he always instructed me with pleasure: and from what I could understand by him of this God, and in seeing these white people did not sell one another, as we did, I was much pleased; and in this I thought they were much happier than we Africans. I was astonished at the wisdom of the white people in all things I saw; but was amazed at their not sacrificing, or making any offerings, and eating with unwashed hands, and touching the dead. I likewise could not help remarking the particular slenderness of their women, which I did not at first like; and I thought they were not so modest and shamefaced as the African women.

I had often seen my master and Dick employed in reading; and I had a great curiosity to talk to the books, as I thought they did; and so to learn how all things had a beginning: for that purpose I have often taken up a book, and have talked to it, and then put my ears to it, when alone, in hopes it would answer me; and I have been very much concerned when I found it remained silent.[1]

My master lodged at the house of a gentleman in Falmouth, who had a fine little daughter about six or seven years of age, and she grew prodigiously fond of me; insomuch that we used to eat together, and had servants to wait on us. I was so much caressed by this family that it often reminded me of the treatment I had received from my little noble African master. After I had been here a few days, I was sent on board of the ship; but the child cried so much after me that nothing could pacify her till I was sent for again. It is ludicrous enough, that I began to fear I should be betrothed to this young lady; and when my master asked me if I would stay there with her behind him, as he was going away with the ship, which had taken in the tobacco again, I cried immediately, and said I would not leave her. At last, by stealth, one night I was sent on board the ship again; and in a little time we sailed for Guernsey, where she was in part owned by a merchant, one Nicholas Doberry. As I was now amongst a people who had not their faces scarred, like some of the African nations where I had been, I was very glad I did not let them ornament me in that manner when I was with them. When we arrived at Guernsey, my master placed me to board and lodge with one of his mates, who had a wife and family there; and some months afterwards he went to England, and left me in care of this mate, together with my friend Dick: This mate had a little daughter, aged about five or six years, with whom I used to be much delighted. I had often observed that when her

---

1   *I had often ... remained silent*   A similar episode is recounted in James Albert Ukawsaw Gronniosaw's 1772 *A Narrative of the Most Remarkable Particulars in the Life of James Albert Ukawsaw Gronniosaw, an African Prince, as Related by Himself* (included elsewhere in this anthology). Before he learned to read, Gronniosaw reports that he believed that books could talk:

> I was never so surprised in my whole life as when I saw the book talk to my master, for I thought it did, as I observed him to look upon it and move his lips. I wished it would do so to me. As soon as my master had done reading, I followed him to the place where he put the book, being mightily delighted with it, and when nobody saw me, I opened it and put my ear down close upon it in great hope that it would say something to me, but was very sorry and greatly disappointed when I found it would not speak.

As Henry Louis Gates Jr. has noted, the "trope of the talking book" appears in at least five slave narratives between 1770 and 1815 (those of Gronniosaw, Equiano, John Marant [1785], Ottobah Cuguano [1787], and John Jea [1811]).

mother washed her face it looked very rosy; but when she washed mine it did not look so: I therefore tried oftentimes myself if I could not by washing make my face of the same colour as my little playmate (Mary), but it was all in vain; and I now began to be mortified at the difference in our complexions. This woman behaved to me with great kindness and attention; and taught me every thing in the same manner as she did her own child, and indeed in every respect treated me as such. I remained here till the summer of the year 1757; when my master, being appointed first lieutenant of his majesty's ship the *Roebuck*, sent for Dick and me, and his old mate: on this we all left Guernsey, and set out for England in a sloop bound for London. As we were coming up towards the Nore, where the *Roebuck* lay, a man-of-war's boat came alongside to press our people; on which each man ran to hide himself. I was very much frightened at this, though I did not know what it meant, or what to think or do. However, I went and hid myself also under a hencoop. Immediately afterwards the press-gang[1] came on board with their swords drawn, and searched all about, pulled the people out by force, and put them into the boat. At last I was found out also: the man that found me held me up by the heels while they all made their sport of me, I roaring and crying out all the time most lustily: but at last the mate, who was my conductor, seeing this, came to my assistance, and did all he could to pacify me; but all to very little purpose, till I had seen the boat go off. Soon afterwards we came to the Nore, where the *Roebuck* lay; and, to our great joy, my master came on board to us, and brought us to the ship. When I went on board this large ship, I was amazed indeed to see the quantity of men and the guns. However, my surprise began to diminish as my knowledge increased; and I ceased to feel those apprehensions and alarms which had taken such strong possession of me when I first came among the Europeans, and for some time after. I began now to pass to an opposite extreme; I was so far from being afraid of anything new which I saw, that, after I had been some time in this ship, I even began to long for a battle. ...

The *Royal George* was the largest ship I had ever seen; so that when I came on board of her I was surprised at the number of people, men, women, and children of every denomination; and the largeness of the guns, many of them also of brass, which I had never seen before. Here were also shops or stalls of every kind of goods, and people crying their different commodities about the ship as in a town. To me it appeared a little world, into which I was again cast without a friend, for I had no longer my dear companion Dick.

We did not stay long here. My master was not many weeks on board before he got an appointment to be sixth lieutenant of the *Namur*, which was then

---

1   *press-gang*   Group formed to "impress" men into the service of the navy—force them to serve against their will.

at Spithead, fitting up for Vice-admiral Boscawen, who was going with a large fleet on an expedition against Louisbourgh. The crew of the *Royal George* were turned over to her, and the flag of that gallant admiral was hoisted on board, the blue at the maintop gallant mast head. There was a very great fleet of men of war of every description assembled together for this expedition, and I was in hopes soon to have an opportunity of being gratified with a sea-fight. All things being now in readiness, this mighty fleet (for there was also Admiral Cornish's fleet in company, destined for the East Indies) at last weighed anchor, and sailed. The two fleets continued in company for several days, and then parted; Admiral Cornish, in the *Lennox*, having first saluted our admiral in the *Namur*, which he returned. We then steered for America; but, by contrary winds, we were driven to Teneriffe, where I was struck with its noted peak. Its prodigious height, and its form, resembling a sugar-loaf, filled me with wonder. We remained in sight of this island some days, and then proceeded for America, which we soon made, and got into a very commodious harbour called St. George, in Halifax, where we had fish in great plenty, and all other fresh provisions. We were here joined by different men of war and transport ships with soldiers; after which, our fleet being increased to a prodigious number of ships of all kinds, we sailed for Cape Breton in Nova Scotia.

We had the good and gallant General Wolfe[1] on board our ship, whose affability made him highly esteemed and beloved by all the men. He often honoured me, as well as other boys, with marks of his notice; and saved me once a flogging for fighting with a young gentleman. We arrived at Cape Breton in the summer of 1758: and here the soldiers were to be landed, in order to make an attack upon Louisbourgh. My master had some part in superintending the landing; and here I was in a small measure gratified in seeing an encounter between our men and the enemy. The French were posted on the shore to receive us, and disputed our landing for a long time; but at last they were driven from their trenches, and a complete landing was effected. Our troops pursued them as far as the town of Louisbourgh. In this action many were killed on both sides. One thing remarkable I saw this day: A lieutenant of the *Princess Amelia*, who, as well as my master, superintended the landing, was giving the word of command, and while his mouth was open a musket ball went through it, and passed out at his cheek. I had that day in my hand the scalp of an Indian king, who was killed in the engagement: the scalp had been taken off by an Highlander. I saw this king's ornaments too, which were very curious, and made of feathers.

---

1 *General Wolfe* James Wolfe (1727–59), later to become famous for leading the British forces at the Battle of the Plains of Abraham in Quebec, where he died.

Our land forces laid siege to the town of Louisbourgh, while the French men-of-war were blocked up in the harbour by the fleet, the batteries at the same time playing upon them from the land. This they did with such effect, that one day I saw some of the ships set on fire by the shells from the batteries, and I believe two or three of them were quite burnt. At another time, about fifty boats belonging to the English men-of-war, commanded by Captain George Balfour of the *Aetna* fire-ship, and another junior captain, Laforey, attacked and boarded the only two remaining French men-of-war in the harbour. They also set fire to a seventy-gun ship, but a sixty-four called the *Bienfaisant*, they brought off. During my stay here I had often an opportunity of being near Captain Balfour, who was pleased to notice me, and liked me so much that he often asked my master to let him have me, but he would not part with me; and no consideration could have induced me to leave him. At last Louisbourgh was taken, and the English men-of-war came into the harbour before it, to my very great joy; for I had now more liberty of indulging myself, and I went often on shore. When the ships were in the harbour we had the most beautiful procession on the water I ever saw. All the admirals and captains of the men-of-war, full dressed, and in their barges, well ornamented with pendants, came alongside of the *Namur*. The vice-admiral then went on shore in his barge, followed by the other officers in order of seniority, to take possession, as I suppose, of the town and fort. Some time after this the French governor and his lady, and other persons of note, came on board our ship to dine. On this occasion our ships were dressed with colours of all kinds, from the top gallant mast head to the deck; and this, with the firing of guns, formed a most grand and magnificent spectacle.

As soon as everything here was settled Admiral Boscawen sailed with part of the fleet for England, leaving some ships behind with Rear-admirals Sir Charles Hardy and Durrell. It was now winter; and one evening, during our passage home, about dusk when we were in the channel, or near soundings, and were beginning to look for land, we descried seven sail[s] of large men-of-war, which stood off shore several people on board of our ship said, as the two fleets were (in forty minutes from the first fight) within hail of each other, that they were English men-of-war; and some of our people even began to name some of the ships. By this time both fleets began to mingle, and our admiral ordered his flag to be hoisted. At that instant the other fleet, which were French, hoisted their ensigns, and gave us a broadside as they passed by. Nothing could create greater surprise and confusion among us than this: the wind was high, the sea rough, and we had our lower and middle deck guns housed in, so that not a single gun on board was ready to be fired at any of the French ships. However, the *Royal William* and the *Somerset* being our sternmost ships, became a little prepared, and each gave the French ships a broadside as they passed by. I afterwards heard this was a French Squadron, commanded by Mons. Conflans. ...

from CHAPTER 4

The author is baptized—Narrowly escapes drowning—Goes on an expedition to the Mediterranean—Incidents he met with there—Is witness to an engagement between some English and French ships—A particular account of the celebrated engagement between Admiral Boscawen and Mons. Le Clue, off Cape Logas, in August 1759—Dreadful explosion of a French ship—The author sails for England— His master appointed to the command of a fire-ship—Meets a negro boy, from whom he experiences much benevolence—Prepares for an expedition against Belle-Isle—A remarkable story of a disaster which befell his ship—Arrives at Belle-Isle— Operations of the landing.

It was now between two and three years since I first came to England, a great part of which I had spent at sea; so that I became inured to that service,[1] and began to consider myself as happily situated; for my master treated me always extremely well; and my attachment and gratitude to him were very great. From the various scenes I had beheld on ship-board, I soon grew a stranger to terror of every kind, and was, in that respect at least, almost an Englishman. I have often reflected with surprise that I never felt half the alarm at any of the numerous dangers I have been in, that I was filled with at the first sight of the Europeans, and at every act of theirs, even the most trifling, when I first came among them, and for some time afterwards. That fear, however, which was the effect of my ignorance, wore away as I began to know them. I could now speak English tolerably well, and I perfectly understood everything that was said. I now not only felt myself quite easy with these new countrymen, but relished their society and manners. I no longer looked upon them as spirits, but as men superior to us; and therefore I had the stronger desire to resemble them; to imbibe their spirit, and imitate their manners; I therefore embraced every occasion of improvement; and every new thing that I observed I treasured up in my memory. I had long wished to be able to read and write; and for this purpose I took every opportunity to gain instruction, but had made as yet very little progress. However, when I went to London with my master, I had soon an opportunity of improving myself, which I gladly embraced. Shortly after my arrival, he sent me to wait upon the Miss Guerins,[2] who had treated me with much kindness when I was there before; and they sent me to school.

While I was attending these ladies their servants told me I could not go to Heaven unless I was baptized. This made me very uneasy; for I had now some

---

1   *became inured to that service*   Grew accustomed to life at sea.
2   *the Miss Guerins*   Elizabeth Martha Guerin and Mary Guerin, cousins of Michael Henry Pascal.

faint idea of a future state: accordingly I communicated my anxiety to the eldest Miss Guerin, with whom I was become a favourite, and pressed her to have me baptized; when to my great joy she told me I should. She had formerly asked my master to let me be baptized, but he had refused; however she now insisted on it; and he being under some obligation to her brother complied with her request; so I was baptized in St. Margaret's Church, Westminster, in February 1759, by my present name. The clergyman, at the same time, gave me a book, called *A Guide to the Indians*,[1] written by the Bishop of Sodor and Man. On this occasion Miss Guerin did me the honour to stand as godmother, and afterwards gave me a treat. I used to attend these ladies about the town, in which service I was extremely happy; as I had thus many opportunities of seeing London, which I desired of all things. I was sometimes, however, with my master at his rendezvous house, which was at the foot of Westminster Bridge. Here I used to enjoy myself in playing about the bridge stairs, and often in the watermen's wherries,[2] with other boys. On one of these occasions there was another boy with me in a wherry, and we went out into the current of the river: while we were there two more stout boys came to us in another wherry, and, abusing us for taking the boat, desired me to get into the other wherry-boat. Accordingly I went to get out of the wherry I was in; but just as I had got one of my feet into the other boat the boys shoved it off, so that I fell into the Thames; and, not being able to swim, I should unavoidably have been drowned, but for the assistance of some watermen who providentially came to my relief.

The *Namur* being again got ready for sea, my master, with his gang,[3] was ordered on board; and, to my no small grief I was obliged to leave my schoolmaster, whom I liked very much, and always attended[4] while I stayed in London, to repair on board with my master. Nor did I leave my kind patronesses, the Miss Guerins, without uneasiness and regret. They often used to teach me to read, and took great pains to instruct me in the principles of religion and the knowledge of God. I therefore parted from those amiable ladies with reluctance; after receiving from them many friendly cautions how to conduct myself, and some valuable presents.

When I came to Spithead, I found we were destined for the Mediterranean, with a large fleet, which was now ready to put to sea. We only waited for the arrival of the admiral, who soon came on board; and about the beginning of the spring, 1759, having weighed anchor and got under way, sailed for the

---

1 *A Guide to the Indians* Bishop Thomas Wilson's *An Essay Towards an Instruction for the Indians* was published in London in 1740; this is likely the book Equiano is thinking of.
2 *watermen's wherries* Small boats belonging to those offering ferry services on the river.
3 *gang* Crew.
4 *attended* Called on; was friendly towards.

Mediterranean; and in eleven days from the Land's End, we got to Gibraltar. While we were here I used to be often on shore, and got various fruits in great plenty, and very cheap.

I had frequently told several people, in my excursions on shore, the story of my being kidnapped with my sister, and of our being separated, as I have related before; and I had as often expressed my anxiety for her fate, and my sorrow at having never met her again. One day, when I was on shore, and mentioning these circumstances to some persons, one of them told me he knew where my sister was, and, if I would accompany him, he would bring me to her. Improbable as this story was I believed it immediately, and agreed to go with him, while my heart leaped for joy: and, indeed, he conducted me to a black young woman, who was so like my sister that at first sight I really thought it was her: but I was quickly undeceived; and, on talking to her, I found her to be of another nation.

While we lay here the *Preston* came in from the Levant. As soon as she arrived, my master told me I should now see my old companion, Dick, who had gone in her when she sailed for Turkey. I was much rejoiced at this news, and expected every minute to embrace him; and when the captain came on board of our ship, which he did immediately after, I ran to inquire after my friend; but, with inexpressible sorrow, I learned from the boat's crew that the dear youth was dead! and that they had brought his chest, and all his other things, to my master. These he afterwards gave to me, and I regarded them as a memorial of my friend, whom I loved, and grieved for as a brother.

While we were at Gibraltar, I saw a soldier hanging by his heels, at one of the moles:[1] I thought this a strange sight, as I had seen a man hanged in London by his neck. At another time I saw the master of a frigate towed to shore on a grating, by several of the men-of-war boats, and discharged the fleet, which I understood was a mark of disgrace for cowardice. On board the same ship there was also a sailor hung up at the yard-arm. ...

After the taking of this island [Belle-Isle] our ships, with some others commanded by Commodore Stanhope in the *Swiftsure*, went to Basse-road, where we blocked up a French fleet. Our ships were there from June till February following; and in that time I saw a great many scenes of war, and stratagems on both sides to destroy each other's fleet. Sometimes we would attack the French with some ships of the line; at other times with boats; and frequently we made prizes.[2] Once or twice the French attacked us by throwing shells with their bomb-vessels: and one day as a French vessel was throwing shells at our ships she broke from her springs, behind the isle of I de Re: the tide being

---

1   *moles*   Stone structures forming breakwaters or piers.
2   *made prizes*   Captured enemy ships with valuable cargo aboard.

complicated, she came within a gun shot of the *Nassau* but the *Nassau* could not bring a gun to bear upon her, and thereby the Frenchman got off. We were twice attacked by their fire-floats, which they chained together, and then let them float down with the tide; but each time we sent boats with graplings, and towed them safe out of the fleet.

We had different commanders while we were at this place, Commodores Stanhope, Dennis, Lord Howe, etc. From hence, before the Spanish war began, our ship and the *Wasp* sloop were sent to St. Sebastian in Spain, by Commodore Stanhope; and Commodore Dennis afterwards sent our ship as a cartel to Bayonne in France, after which we went in February in 1762 to Belle-Isle, and there stayed till the summer, when we left it, and returned to Portsmouth.

After our ship was fitted out again for service, in September she went to Guernsey, where I was very glad to see my old hostess, who was now a widow, and my former little charming companion, her daughter. I spent some time here very happily with them, till October, when we had orders to repair to Portsmouth. We parted from each other with a great deal of affection; and I promised to return soon, and see them again, not knowing what all-powerful fate had determined for me. Our ship having arrived at Portsmouth, we went into the harbour, and remained there till the latter end of November, when we heard great talk about a peace;[1] and, to our very great joy, in the beginning of December we had orders to go up to London with our ship to be paid off. We received this news with loud huzzas, and every other demonstration of gladness; and nothing but mirth was to be seen throughout every part of the ship. I too was not without my share of the general joy on this occasion. I thought now of nothing but being freed, and working for myself and thereby getting money to enable me to get a good education; for I always had a great desire to be able at least to read and write; and while I was on ship-board I had endeavoured to improve myself in both. While I was in the *Aetna* particularly, the captain's clerk taught me to write, and gave me a smattering of arithmetic as far as the rule of three.[2] There was also one Daniel Queen, about forty years of age, a man very well educated, who messed with me on board this ship, and he likewise dressed and attended the captain.

Fortunately, this man soon became very much attached to me, and took very great pains to instruct me in many things. He taught me to shave and dress hair a little, and also to read in the Bible, explaining many passages to me, which I did not comprehend. I was wonderfully surprised to see the laws

---

1   *a peace* The Seven Years' War ended in February of 1763 with the signing of the Treaty of Paris.
2   *the rule of three* Method for discovering a fourth number in a series involving proportions, once the first three are known.

and rules of my country written almost exactly here; a circumstance which I believe tended to impress our manners and customs more deeply on my memory. I used to tell him of this resemblance; and many a time we have sat up the whole night together at this employment. In short, he was like a father to me; and some even used to call me after his name; they also styled me the black Christian. Indeed, I almost loved him with the affection of a son. Many things I have denied myself that he might have them; and when I used to play at marbles or any other game, and won a few halfpence, or got any little money, which I sometimes did, for shaving anyone, I used to buy him a little sugar or tobacco, as far as my stock of money would go. He used to say, that he and I never should part; and that when our ship was paid off, as I was as free as himself or any other man on board, he would instruct me in his business, by which I might gain a good livelihood. This gave me new life and spirits and my heart burned within me, while I thought the time long till I obtained my freedom. For though my master had not promised it to me, yet, besides the assurances I had received that he had no right to detain me, he always treated me with the greatest kindness, and reposed in me an unbounded confidence; he even paid attention to my morals; and would never suffer me to deceive him, or tell lies, of which he used to tell me the consequences; and that if I did so God would not love me; so that, from all this tenderness, I had never once supposed, in all my dreams of freedom, that he would think of detaining me any longer than I wished.

In pursuance of our orders, we sailed from Portsmouth for the Thames, and arrived at Deptford the 10th of December, where we cast anchor just as it was high water. The ship was up about half an hour, when my master ordered the barge to be manned; and all in an instant, without having before given me the least reason to suspect anything of the matter, he forced me into the barge; saying, I was going to leave him, but he would take care I should not. I was so struck with the unexpectedness of this proceeding, that for some time I did not make a reply, only I made an offer to go for my books and chest of clothes, but he swore I should not move out of his sight; and if I did, he would cut my throat, at the same time taking his hanger.[1] I began, however, to collect myself and, plucking up courage, I told him I was free, and he could not by law serve[2] me so. But this only enraged him the more; and he continued to swear, and said he would soon let me know whether he would or not, and at that instant sprung himself into the barge from the ship, to the astonishment and sorrow of all on board. The tide, rather unluckily for me, had just turned downward, so that we quickly fell down the river along with it, till we came among some

---

1   *hanger* Short, curved sword.
2   *serve* Treat.

outward-bound West Indiamen; for he was resolved to put me on board the first vessel he could get to receive me. The boat's crew, who pulled against their will, became quite faint different times, and would have gone ashore; but he would not let them. Some of them strove them to cheer me, and told me he could not sell me, and that they would stand by me, which revived me a little; and I still entertained hopes; for as they pulled along he asked some vessels to receive me, but they could not. But, just as we had got a little below Gravesend, we came alongside of a ship which was going away the next tide for the West Indies; her name was the *Charming Sally*, Captain James Doran; and my master went on board and agreed with him for me; and in a little time I was sent for into the cabin.

When I came there, Captain Doran asked me if I knew him; I answered that I did not; "Then," said he, "you are now my slave." I told him my master could not sell me to him, nor to anyone else. "Why," said he, "did not your master buy you?" I confessed he did. "But I have served him," said I, "many years, and he has taken all my wages and prize-money,[1] for I only got one sixpence during the war; besides this I have been baptized; and by the laws of the land no man has a right to sell me." And I added, that I had heard a lawyer and others at different times tell my master so. They both then said that those people who told me so were not my friends; but I replied, it was very extraordinary that other people did not know the law as well as they. Upon this Captain Doran said I talked too much English; and if I did not behave myself well, and be quiet, he had a method on board to make me. I was too well convinced of his power over me to doubt what he said; and, my former sufferings in the slave ship presenting themselves to my mind, the recollection of them made me shudder. However, before I retired I told them that as I could not get any right among men here I hoped I should hereafter in Heaven; and I immediately left the cabin, filled with resentment and sorrow. The only coat I had with me my master took away with him, and said if my prize-money had been £10,000 he had a right to it all, and would have taken it. I had about nine guineas, which, during my long sea-faring life, I had scraped together from trifling perquisites and little ventures; and I hid it that instant, lest my master should take that from me likewise, still hoping that by some means or other I should make my escape to the shore; and indeed some of my old shipmates told me not to despair, for they would get me back again; and that, as soon as they could get their pay, they would immediately come to Portsmouth to me, where this ship was going. But, alas! all my hopes were baffled, and the hour of my deliverance was yet far off. My master, having soon concluded his bargain with the captain, came out of the cabin, and he and his people got into the boat and

---

1   *prize-money*   Share of the valuables seized when capturing other vessels.

put off; I followed them with aching eyes as long as I could, and when they were out of sight I threw myself on the deck, while my heart was ready to burst with sorrow and anguish.

CHAPTER 5

The author's reflections on his situation—Is deceived by a promise of being delivered —His despair at sailing for the West Indies—Arrives at Montserrat, where he is sold to Mr. King—Various interesting instances of oppression, cruelty, and extortion, which the author saw practiced upon the slaves in the West Indies during his captivity from the year 1763 to 1766—Address on it to the planters.

Thus, at the moment I expected all my toils to end, was I plunged, as I supposed, in a new slavery; in comparison to which all my service hitherto had been "perfect freedom"; and whose horrors, always present to my mind, now rushed on it with tenfold aggravation. I wept very bitterly for some time: and began to think that I must have done something to displease the Lord, that he thus punished me so severely. This filled me with painful reflections on my past conduct; I recollected that on the morning of our arrival at Deptford[1] I had rashly sworn that as soon as we reached London I would spend the day in rambling and sport. My conscience smote me for this unguarded expression: I felt that the Lord was able to disappoint me in all things, and immediately considered my present situation as a judgment of Heaven on account of my presumption in swearing: I therefore, with contrition of heart, acknowledged my transgression to God, and poured out my soul before him with unfeigned repentance, and with earnest supplications I besought him not to abandon me in my distress, nor cast me from his mercy for ever. In a little time my grief, spent with its own violence, began to subside; and after the first confusion of my thoughts was over I reflected with more calmness on my present condition: I considered that trials and disappointments are sometimes for our good, and I thought God might perhaps have permitted this in order to teach me wisdom and resignation; for he had hitherto shadowed me with the wings of his mercy, and by his invisible but powerful hand brought me the way I knew not. These reflections gave me a little comfort, and I rose at last from the deck with dejection and sorrow in my countenance, yet mixed with some faint hope that the *Lord would appear* for my deliverance.

Soon afterwards, as my new master was going ashore, he called me to him, and told me to behave myself well, and do the business of the ship the same as any of the rest of the boys, and that I should fare the better for it; but I made

---

1 *Deptford* Southeast London area on the River Thames's south bank. Equiano arrived at Deptford on 10 December 1762.

him no answer. I was then asked if I could swim, and I said, No. However I was made to go under the deck, and was well watched. The next tide the ship got under way, and soon after arrived at the Mother Bank, Portsmouth; where she waited a few days for some of the West India convoy. While I was here I tried every means I could devise amongst the people of the ship to get me a boat from the shore, as there was none suffered to come alongside of the ship; and their own, whenever it was used, was hoisted in again immediately. A sailor on board took a guinea from me on pretence of getting me a boat; and promised me, time after time, that it was hourly to come off. When he had the watch upon deck I watched also; and looked long enough, but all in vain; I could never see either the boat or my guinea again. And what I thought was still the worst of all, the fellow gave information, as I afterwards found, all the while to the mates, of my intention to go off, if I could in any way do it; but, rogue like, he never told them he had got a guinea from me to procure my escape. However, after we had sailed, and his trick was made known to the ship's crew, I had some satisfaction in seeing him detested and despised by them all for his behaviour to me. I was still in hopes that my old shipmates would not forget their promise to come for me to Portsmouth: and, indeed, at last, but not till the day before we sailed, some of them did come there, and sent me off some oranges, and other tokens of their regard. They also sent me word they would come off to me themselves the next day or the day after; and a lady also, who lived in Gosport,[1] wrote to me that she would come and take me out of the ship at the same time. This lady had been once very intimate with my former master: I used to sell and take care of a great deal of property for her, in different ships; and in return she always showed great friendship for me, and used to tell my master that she would take me away to live with her: but, unfortunately for me, a disagreement soon afterwards took place between them; and she was succeeded in my master's good graces by another lady, who appeared sole mistress of the *Aetna*, and mostly lodged on board. I was not so great a favourite with this lady as with the former; she had conceived a pique against me on some occasion when she was on board, and she did not fail to instigate my master to treat me in the manner he did.[2]

---

1   *Gosport*   Major naval and military center primarily associated with the defense and supply of Portsmouth Harbor.

2   [Equiano's note]   Thus was I sacrificed to the envy and resentment of this woman for knowing that the lady whom she had succeeded in my master's good graces designed to take me into her service; which, had I once got on shore, she would not have been able to prevent. She felt her pride alarmed at the superiority of her rival in being attended by a black servant: it was not less to prevent this than to be revenged on me, that she caused the captain to treat me thus cruelly.

However the next morning, the 30th of December, the wind being brisk and easterly, the *Œolus* frigate,[1] which was to escort the convoy, made a signal for sailing. All the ships then got up their anchors; and, before any of my friends had an opportunity to come off to my relief, to my inexpressible anguish our ship had got under way. What tumultuous emotions agitated my soul when the convoy got under sail, and I a prisoner on board, now without hope! I kept my swimming eyes upon the land in a state of unutterable grief; not knowing what to do, and despairing how to help myself. While my mind was in this situation the fleet sailed on, and in one day's time I lost sight of the wished-for land. In the first expressions of my grief I reproached my fate, and wished I had never been born. I was ready to curse the tide that bore us, the gale that wafted my prison, and even the ship that conducted us; and I called on death to relieve me from the horrors I felt and dreaded, that I might be in that place

> Where slaves are free, and men oppress no more.
> Fool that I was, inur'd so long to pain,
> To trust to hope, or dream of joy again.
>
>   *   *   *   *   *   *
>
> Now dragg'd once more beyond the western main,
> To groan beneath some dastard planter's chain;
> Where my poor countrymen in bondage wait
> The long enfranchisement of ling'ring fate:
> Hard ling'ring fate! while, ere the dawn of day,
> Rous'd by the lash they go their cheerless way;
> And as their souls with shame and anguish burn,
> Salute with groans unwelcome morn's return,
> And, chiding ev'ry hour the slow-pac'd sun,
> Pursue their toils till all his race is run.
> No eye to mark their suff'rings with a tear;
> No friend to comfort, and no hope to cheer:
> Then, like the dull unpity'd brutes, repair
> To stalls as wretched, and as coarse a fare:
> Thank heaven one day of mis'ry was o'er,
> Then sink to sleep, and wish to wake no more.[2]

---

1 *Œolus frigate*   Because Britain had not yet officially ended its war with Spain and France, convoys bound for the West Indies were escorted by navy ships. When the *Charming Sally* set sail on 30 December 1762, it was escorted by the *H.M.S. Œolus*. The presence of the navy ship effectively put an end to Equiano's hopes of escape.

2 [Equiano's note]   "The Dying Negro," a poem originally published in 1773. Perhaps it may not be deemed impertinent here to add, that this elegant and pathetic little poem was occasioned, as appears by the advertisement prefixed to it, by the following incident. "A black, who, a few days before had ran away from his master, and got himself christened, with intent to marry a white woman his fellow-servant, being taken and sent on board a ship in the Thames, took an opportunity of shooting himself through the head."

The turbulence of my emotions, however, naturally gave way to calmer thoughts, and I soon perceived what fate had decreed no mortal on earth could prevent. The convoy sailed on without any accident, with a pleasant gale and smooth sea, for six weeks, till February, when one morning the *Œolus* ran down a brig, one of the convoy, and she instantly went down and was engulfed in the dark recesses of the ocean. The convoy was immediately thrown into great confusion till it was day-light; and the *Œolus* was illumined with lights to prevent any farther mischief. On the 13th of February 1763, from the mast-head, we descried our destined island Montserrat; and soon after I beheld those

> Regions of sorrow, doleful shades, where peace
> And rest can rarely dwell. Hope never comes
> That comes to all, but torture without end
> Still urges.[1]

At the sight of this land of bondage,[2] a fresh horror ran through all my frame, and chilled me to the heart. My former slavery now rose in dreadful review to my mind, and displayed nothing but misery, stripes, and chains; and, in the first paroxysm of my grief, I called upon God's thunder, and his avenging power, to direct the stroke of death to me, rather than permit me to become a slave, and be sold from lord to lord.

In this state of my mind our ship came to an anchor, and soon after discharged her cargo. I now knew what it was to work hard; I was made to help to unload and load the ship. And, to comfort me in my distress in that time, two of the sailors robbed me of all my money, and ran away from the ship. I had been so long used to an European climate that at first I felt the scorching West India sun very painful, while the dashing surf would toss the boat and the people in it frequently above high water mark. Sometimes our limbs were broken with this, or even attended with instant death, and I was day by day mangled and torn.

About the middle of May, when the ship was got ready to sail for England, I all the time believing that Fate's blackest clouds were gathering over my head, and expecting their bursting would mix me with the dead, Captain Doran sent for me ashore one morning, and I was told by the messenger that my fate was then determined. With trembling steps and fluttering heart I came to the

---

1 *Regions of sorrow … Still urges* Cf. John Milton, *Paradise Lost* (1.65–68). This verse offers the poem's first view of hell, but Equiano somewhat mitigates the bleaker meaning of Milton's lines, changing "rest can never dwell" to "rest can rarely dwell."

2 *land of bondage* Phrase often used in reference to Egypt as the site of the Israelites' captivity and slavery in the Hebrew Bible (the Old Testament).

captain, and found with him one Mr. Robert King, a Quaker,[1] and the first merchant in the place. The captain then told me my former master had sent me there to be sold; but that he had desired him to get me the best master he could, as he told him I was a very deserving boy, which Captain Doran said he found to be true; and if he were to stay in the West Indies he would be glad to keep me himself; but he could not venture to take me to London, for he was very sure that when I came there I would leave him. I at that instant burst out a crying, and begged much of him to take me to England with him, but all to no purpose. He told me he had got me the very best master in the whole island, with whom I should be as happy as if I were in England, and for that reason he chose to let him have me, though he could sell me to his own brother-in-law for a great deal more money than what he got from this gentleman. Mr. King, my new master, then made a reply, and said the reason he had bought me was on account of my good character; and, as he had not the least doubt of my good behaviour, I should be very well off with him. He also told me he did not live in the West Indies, but at Philadelphia, where he was going soon; and, as I understood something of the rules of arithmetic, when we got there he would put me to school, and fit me for a clerk. This conversation relieved my mind a little, and I left those gentlemen considerably more at ease in myself than when I came to them; and I was very grateful to Captain Doran, and even to my old master, for the character they had given me; a character which I afterward found of infinite service to me. I went on board again, and took leave of all my shipmates; and the next day the ship sailed. When she weighed anchor I went to the waterside and looked at her with a very wishful and aching heart, and followed her with my eyes and tears until she was totally out of sight. I was so bowed down with grief that I could not hold up my head for many months; and if my new master had not been kind to me I believe I should have died under it at last. And indeed I soon found that he fully deserved the good character which Captain Doran had given me of him; for he possessed a most amiable disposition and temper, and was very charitable and humane. If any of his slaves behaved amiss he did not beat or use them ill, but parted with them. This made them afraid of disobliging him; and as he treated his slaves better than any other man on the island, so he was better and more faithfully served by them in return. By this kind treatment I did at last endeavour to compose myself; and with fortitude, though moneyless, determined to face whatever fate had decreed for me. Mr. King soon asked me what I could do; and at the same time said he did not mean to

---

1   *Quaker*   The Quakers (formally known as the Society of Friends) are a Protestant sect that was and is committed to pacifism, equality of the sexes, and social reform. They typically sought to avoid worldly vanities, adhering to customs of plain dress, and using an old-fashioned diction (employing the pronouns *thee* and *thou* for example).

treat me as a common slave. I told him I knew something of seamanship, and could shave and dress hair pretty well; and I could refine wines, which I had learned on shipboard, where I had often done it; and that I could write, and understood arithmetic tolerably well as far as the rule of three. He then asked me if I knew anything of gauging;[1] and, on my answering that I did not, he said one of his clerks should teach me to gauge.

Mr. King dealt in all manner of merchandise, and kept from one to six clerks. He loaded many vessels in a year; particularly to Philadelphia, where he was born, and was connected with a great mercantile house in that city. He had besides many vessels and droggers,[2] of different sizes, which used to go about the island; and others to collect rum, sugar, and other goods. I understood pulling and managing those boats very well; and this hard work, which was the first that he set me to, in the sugar seasons used to be my constant employment. I have rowed the boat, and slaved at the oars, from one hour to sixteen in the twenty-four; during which I had fifteen pence sterling per day to live on, though sometimes only ten pence. However this was considerably more than was allowed to other slaves that used to work with me, and belonged to other gentlemen on the island: those poor souls had never more than nine pence per day, and seldom more than six pence, from their masters or owners, though they earned them three or four pisterines:[3] for it is a common practice in the West Indies for men to purchase slaves though they have not plantations themselves, in order to let them out to planters and merchants at so much a piece by the day, and they give what allowance they choose out of this produce of their daily work to their slaves for subsistence; this allowance is often very scanty. My master often gave the owners of these slaves two and a half of these pieces per day, and found the poor fellows in victuals[4] himself, because he thought the owners did not feed them well enough according to the work they did. The slaves used to like this very well; and, as they knew my master to be a man of feeling, they were always glad to work for him in preference to any other gentleman: some of whom, after they had been paid for these poor people's labours, would not give them their allowance out of it. Many times have I even seen these unfortunate wretches beaten for asking for their pay; and often severely flogged by their owners if they did not bring them their daily or weekly money exactly to the time; though the poor creatures were obliged to wait on the gentlemen they had worked for sometimes for more than half the day before they could get their pay; and this generally on Sundays, when they wanted the time for themselves. In particular, I knew a

---

1   *gauging*   Calculating the holding capacity or contents of a ship or other container.
2   *droggers*   Slow, awkward coasting vessels used in the West Indies.
3   [Equiano's note]   These pisterines are of the value of a shilling [twelve pence].
4   *found ... victuals*   I.e., gave them food.

countryman of mine who once did not bring the weekly money directly that it was earned; and though he brought it the same day to his master, yet he was staked to the ground for this pretended negligence, and was just going to receive a hundred lashes, but for a gentleman who begged him off fifty. This poor man was very industrious; and, by his frugality, had saved so much money by working on shipboard, that he had got a white man to buy him a boat, unknown to his master. Some time after he had this little estate the governor wanted a boat to bring his sugar from different parts of the island; and, knowing this to be a negro-man's boat, he seized upon it for himself, and would not pay the owner a farthing. The man on this went to his master, and complained to him of this act of the governor; but the only satisfaction he received was to be damned very heartily by his master, who asked him how dared any of his negroes to have a boat. If the justly-merited ruin of the governor's fortune could be any gratification to the poor man he had thus robbed, he was not without consolation. Extortion and rapine are poor providers; and some time after this the governor died in the King's Bench[1] in England, as I was told, in great poverty. The last war favoured this poor negro man, and he found some means to escape from his Christian master: he came to England; where I saw him afterwards several times. Such treatment as this often drives these miserable wretches to despair, and they run away from their masters at the hazard of their lives. Many of them, in this place, unable to get their pay when they have earned it, and fearing to be flogged, as usual, if they return home without it, run away where they can for shelter, and a reward is often offered to bring them in dead or alive. My master used sometimes, in these cases, to agree with their owners,[2] and to settle with them himself; and thereby he saved many of them a flogging.

Once, for a few days, I was let out to fit a vessel, and I had no victuals allowed me by either party; at last I told my master of this treatment, and he took me away from it. In many of the estates, on the different islands where I used to be sent for rum or sugar, they would not deliver it to me, or any other negro; he was therefore obliged to send a white man along with me to those places; and then he used to pay him six to ten pisterines a day. From being thus employed, during the time I served Mr. King, in going about the different estates on the island, I had all the opportunity I could wish for to see the dreadful usage of the poor men; usage that reconciled me to my situation, and made me bless God for the hands into which I had fallen.

I had the good fortune to please my master in every department in which he employed me; and there was scarcely any part of his business, or household

---

1   *King's Bench*   King's Bench Prison, where debtors were often held.
2   *to agree ... owners*   I.e., to make matters harmonious between enslaved people and their enslavers.

affairs, in which I was not occasionally engaged. I often supplied the place of a clerk,[1] in receiving and delivering cargoes to the ships, in tending stores, and delivering goods: and, besides this, I used to shave and dress my master when convenient, and take care of his horse; and when it was necessary, which was very often, I worked likewise on board of different vessels of his. By these means I became very useful to my master; and saved him, as he used to acknowledge, above a hundred pounds a year. Nor did he scruple to say I was of more advantage to him than any of his clerks; though their usual wages in the West Indies are from sixty to a hundred pounds current[2] a year.

I have sometimes heard it asserted that a negro cannot earn his master the first cost;[3] but nothing can be further from the truth. I suppose nine tenths of the mechanics throughout the West Indies are negro slaves; and I well know the coopers[4] among them earn two dollars a day; the carpenters the same, and oftentimes more; as also the masons, smiths, and fishermen, &c. and I have known many slaves whose masters would not take a thousand pounds current for them. But surely this assertion refutes itself; for, if it be true, why do the planters and merchants pay such a price for slaves? And, above all, why do those who make this assertion exclaim the most loudly against the abolition of the slave trade? So much are men blinded, and to such inconsistent arguments are they driven by mistaken interest! I grant, indeed, that slaves are sometimes, by half-feeding, half-clothing, over-working and stripes,[5] reduced so low, that they are turned out as unfit for service, and left to perish in the woods, or expire on a dunghill.

My master was several times offered by different gentlemen one hundred guineas for me; but he always told them he would not sell me, to my great joy: and I used to double my diligence and care for fear of getting into the hands of those men who did not allow a valuable slave the common support of life. Many of them even used to find fault with my master for feeding his slaves so well as he did; although I often went hungry, and an Englishman might think my fare very indifferent; but he used to tell them he always would do it, because the slaves thereby looked better and did more work.

While I was thus employed by my master I was often witness to cruelties of every kind, which were exercised on my unhappy fellow slaves. I used frequently to have different cargoes of new negroes in my care for sale; and it was almost a constant practice with our clerks, and other whites, to commit violent depredations on the chastity of the female slaves; and these I was,

---

1   *supplied the place of a clerk*   Filled the position of clerk.
2   *current*   Currency.
3   *first cost*   Price paid for an enslaved person.
4   *coopers*   Makers of wooden casks, barrels, and other vessels for storing goods.
5   *stripes*   Lashes of the whip.

though with reluctance, obliged to submit to at all times, being unable to help them. When we have had some of these slaves on board my master's vessels to carry them to other islands, or to America, I have known our mates to commit these acts most shamefully, to the disgrace, not of Christians only, but of men. I have even known them gratify their brutal passion with females not ten years old; and these abominations some of them practised to such scandalous excess, that one of our captains discharged the mate and others on that account. And yet in Montserrat I have seen a negro-man staked to the ground, and cut most shockingly,[1] and then his ears cut off bit by bit, because he had been connected with a white woman who was a common prostitute: as if it were no crime in the whites to rob an innocent African girl of her virtue; but most heinous in a black man only to gratify a passion of nature, where the temptation was offered by one of a different colour, though the most abandoned woman of her species.[2]

Another negro man was half-hanged, and then burnt, for attempting to poison a cruel overseer. Thus by repeated cruelties are the wretched first urged to despair, and then murdered, because they still retain so much of human nature about them as to wish to put an end to their misery, and retaliate on their tyrants! These overseers are indeed for the most part persons of the worst character of any denomination of men in the West Indies. Unfortunately, many humane gentlemen, by not residing on their estates, are obliged to leave the management of them in the hands of these human butchers, who cut and mangle the slaves in a shocking manner on the most trifling occasions, and altogether treat them in every respect like brutes. They pay no regard to the situation of pregnant women, nor the least attention to the lodging of the field negroes. Their huts, which ought to be well covered, and the place dry where they take their little repose, are often open sheds, built in damp places; so that, when the poor creatures return tired from the toil of the field, they contract many disorders, from being exposed to the damp air in this uncomfortable state, while they are heated, and their pores are open. This neglect certainly conspires with many others to cause a decrease in the births as well as in the lives of the grown negroes. I can quote many instances of gentlemen who reside on their estates in the West Indies, and then the scene is quite changed;

---

1 *cut most shockingly* The likely punishment implied here is castration.

2 The following paragraph was added here by Equiano in some later editions: "One Mr. D[rummond] told me that he had sold 41,000 negroes, and that he once cut off a negro-man's leg for running away. I asked him if the man had died in the operation, how he, as a Christian, could answer for the horrid act before God? and he told me, answering was a thing of another world, but what he thought and did were policy. I told him that the Christian doctrine taught us to do unto others as we would that others should do unto us. He then said that his scheme had the desired effect—it cured that man and some others of running away."

the negroes are treated with lenity and proper care, by which their lives are prolonged, and their masters are profited. To the honour of humanity, I knew several gentlemen who managed their estates in this manner; and they found that benevolence was their true interest. And, among many I could mention in several of the islands, I knew one in Montserrat[1] whose slaves looked remarkably well, and never needed any fresh supplies of negroes; and there are many other estates, especially in Barbados, which, from such judicious treatment, need no fresh stock of negroes at any time. I have the honour of knowing a most worthy and humane gentleman, who is a native of Barbados, and has estates there.[2] This gentleman has written a treatise on the usage of his own slaves. He allows them two hours for refreshment at mid-day; and many other indulgencies and comforts, particularly in their lying; and, besides this, he raises more provisions on his estate than they can destroy; so that by these attentions he saves the lives of his negroes, and keeps them healthy, and as happy as the condition of slavery can admit. I myself, as shall appear in the sequel,[3] managed an estate, where, by those attentions, the negroes were uncommonly cheerful and healthy, and did more work by half than by the common mode of treatment they usually do. For want,[4] therefore, of such care and attention to the poor negroes, and otherwise oppressed as they are, it is no wonder that the decrease should require 20,000 new negroes annually to fill up the vacant places of the dead.

Even in Barbados, notwithstanding those humane exceptions which I have mentioned, and others I am acquainted with, which justly make it quoted as a place where slaves meet with the best treatment, and need fewest recruits of any in the West Indies, yet this island requires 1000 negroes annually to keep up the original stock, which is only 80,000. So that the whole term of a negro's life may be said to be there but sixteen years![5] And yet the climate here is in every respect the same as that from which they are taken, except in being more wholesome. Do the British colonies decrease in this manner? And yet what a prodigious difference is there between an English and West India climate?

While I was in Montserrat I knew a negro man, named Emanuel Sankey, who endeavoured to escape from his miserable bondage, by concealing himself on board of a London ship: but fate did not favour the poor oppressed man; for, being discovered when the vessel was under sail, he was delivered up again

---

1   [Equiano's note]   Mr. Dubury, and many others, Montserrat.

2   [Equiano's note]   Sir Philip Bibbes, Baronet, Barbados.

3   *in the sequel* Hereafter. The first three editions of *The Interesting Narrative* were published in two volumes, with Chapters 1–6 included in the first volume and Chapters 7–12 in the second. See Chapter 11 for Equiano's account of his time spent as an overseer.

4   *want* Lack.

5   [Equiano's note]   Benezet's "Account of Guinea," p. 16.

to his master. This *Christian master* immediately pinned the wretch down to the ground at each wrist and ankle, and then took some sticks of sealing wax, and lighted them, and dropped it all over his back. There was another master who was noted for cruelty; and I believe he had not a slave but what had been cut, and had pieces fairly taken out of the flesh: and, after they had been punished thus, he used to make them get into a long wooden box or case he had for that purpose, in which he shut them up during pleasure.[1] It was just about the height and breadth of a man; and the poor wretches had no room, when in the case, to move.

It was very common in several of the islands, particularly in St. Kitt's, for the slaves to be branded with the initial letters of their master's name; and a load of heavy iron hooks hung about their necks. Indeed on the most trifling occasions they were loaded with chains; and often instruments of torture were added. The iron muzzle, thumb-screws, &c. are so well known, as not to need a description, and were sometimes applied for the slightest faults. I have seen a negro beaten till some of his bones were broken, for even letting a pot boil over.[2] Is it surprising that usage like this should drive the poor creatures to despair and make them seek a refuge in death from those evils which render their lives intolerable—while,

> With shudd'ring horror pale, and eyes aghast,
> They view their lamentable lot, and find
> No rest![3]

This they frequently do. A negro man on board a vessel of my master, while I belonged to her, having been put in irons for some trifling misdemeanor, and kept in that state for some days, being weary of life, took an opportunity of jumping overboard into the sea; however, he was picked up without being drowned. Another, whose life was also a burden to him, resolved to starve himself to death, and refused to eat any victuals; this procured him a severe flogging: and he also, on the first occasion which offered, jumped overboard at Charles Town,[4] but was saved.

---

1   *during pleasure*   At discretion.
2   The following lines appear in some later editions: "It is not uncommon after a flogging, to make slaves go on their knees, and thank their owners, and pray, or rather say, God bless them. I have often asked many of the men slaves (who used to go several miles to their wives, and late in the night, after having been wearied with a hard day's labour) why they went so far for wives, and why they did not take them of their own master's negro women, and particularly those who lived together as household slaves? Their answers have ever been—'Because when the master or mistress choose to punish the women, they make the husbands flog their own wives, and that they could not bear to do.'"
3   *With shudd'ring ... No rest!*   Cf. John Milton, *Paradise Lost* (2.616–18).
4   *Charles Town*   Charleston, South Carolina.

Nor is there any greater regard shown to the little property than there is to the persons and lives of the negroes. I have already related an instance or two of particular oppression out of many which I have witnessed; but the following is frequent in all the islands. The wretched field-slaves, after toiling all the day for an unfeeling owner, who gives them but little victuals, steal sometimes a few moments from rest or refreshment to gather some small portion of grass, according as their time will admit. This they commonly tie up in a parcel; either a bit's worth (six pence) or half a bit's worth; and bring it to town, or to the market to sell. Nothing is more common than for the white people on this occasion to take the grass from them without paying for it; and not only so, but too often also, to my knowledge, our clerks, and many others, at the same time have committed acts of violence on the poor, wretched, and helpless females, whom I have seen for hours stand crying to no purpose, and get no redress or pay of any kind. Is not this one common and crying sin enough to bring down God's judgments on the islands? He tells us the oppressor and the oppressed are both in his hands; and if these are not the poor, the broken-hearted, the blind, the captive, the bruised, which our Saviour speaks of, who are they? One of these depredators once, in St. Eustatia,[1] came on board of our vessel, and bought some fowls and pigs of me; and a whole day after his departure with the things he returned again and wanted his money back: I refused to give it; and, not seeing my captain on board, he began the common pranks with me; and swore he would even break open my chest and take my money. I therefore expected, as my captain was absent, that he would be as good as his word: and he was just proceeding to strike me, when fortunately a British seaman on board, whose heart had not been debauched by a West India climate, interposed and prevented him. But had the cruel man struck me, I certainly should have defended myself at the hazard of my life; for what is life to a man thus oppressed! He went away, however, swearing; and threatened that whenever he caught me on shore he would shoot me, and pay for me afterwards.

The small account in which the life of a negro is held in the West Indies is so universally known, that it might seem impertinent to quote the following extract, if some people had not been hardy enough of late to assert that negroes are on the same footing in that respect as Europeans. By the 329th Act, page 125, of the Assembly of Barbados, it is enacted "That if any negro, or other slave, under punishment by his master, or his order, for running away, or any other crime or misdemeanor towards his said master, unfortunately shall suffer in life or member, no person whatsoever shall be liable to a fine; but if any man

---

1 *St. Eustatia* Officially known as Saint Eustatius, one of the islands that constitute the Netherlands Antilles in the northern West Indies.

shall out of *wantonness, or only of bloody mindedness, or cruel intention, willfully kill a negro, or other slave, of his own, he shall pay into the public treasury fifteen pounds sterling.*" And it is the same in most, if not all, of the West India islands. Is not this one of the many acts of the islands which call loudly for redress? And do not the assembly which enacted it deserve the appellation of savages and brutes rather than of Christians and men? It is an act at once unmerciful, unjust, and unwise; which for cruelty would disgrace an assembly of those who are called barbarians; and for its injustice and *insanity* would shock the morality and common sense of a Samaide or a Hottentot.[1]

Shocking as this and many more acts of the bloody West India code at first view appear, how is the iniquity of it heightened when we consider to whom it may be extended! Mr. James Tobin, a zealous labourer in the vineyard of slavery, gives an account[2] of a French planter of his acquaintance, in the Island of Martinico, who showed him many mulattoes working in the fields like beasts of burden; and he told Mr. Tobin these were all the produce of his own loins! And I myself have known similar instances. Pray, reader, are these sons and daughters of the French planter less his children by being begotten on a black woman? And what must be the virtue of those legislators, and the feelings of those fathers, who estimate the lives of their sons, however begotten, at no more than fifteen pounds; though they should be murdered, as the act says, *out of wantonness and bloody-mindedness*? But is not the slave trade entirely a war with the heart of man? And surely that which is begun by breaking down the barriers of virtue involves in its continuance destruction to every principle, and buries all sentiments in ruin!

I have often seen slaves, particularly those who were meagre, in different islands, put into scales and weighed; and then sold from three-pence to six-pence, or nine-pence a pound. My master, however, whose humanity was shocked at this mode, used to sell such by the lump. And at or after a sale, even those negroes born in the islands, it is not uncommon to see negroes taken from their wives, wives taken from their husbands, and children from their parents, and sent off to other islands, and wherever else their merciless lords chose; and probably never more during life to see each other! Oftentimes my heart has bled at these partings; when the friends of the departed have been

---

1   *Samaide*   According to Oliver Goldsmith's *History of the Earth, and Animated Nature* (1774), "the Samoeid Tartars" are, along with "the Laplanders, the Esquimaux Indians, … the inhabitants of Nova Zembla, the Borandians, the Greenlanders, and the natives of Kamtschatka," the first distinct race of people, originating in the polar regions;   *Hottentot*   The native inhabitants of southwestern Africa. It is perhaps notable that Equiano chooses as his examples people who are considered to be neither black nor white.

2   *Mr. James … an account*   The account can be found in a footnote in Tobin's *Cursory Remarks upon the Reverend Mr. Ramsay's Essays* (1785). Ramsay's *Essay on the Treatment and Conversion of African Slaves in the Sugar Colonies* (1784) twice mentions Equiano.

at the water side, and, with sighs and tears, have kept their eyes fixed on the vessel till it went out of sight.

A poor Creole negro I knew well, who, after having been often thus transported from island to island, at last resided in Montserrat. This man used to tell me many melancholy tales of himself. Generally, after he had done working for his master, he used to employ his few leisure moments to go a fishing. When he had caught any fish, his master would frequently take them from him without paying him; and at other times some other white people would serve him in the same manner. One day he said to me, very movingly, "Sometimes when a white man take away my fish, I go to my master, and he get me my right; and when my master by strength take away my fishes, what me must do? I can't go to anybody to be righted"; then, said the poor man, looking up above, "I must look up to God Mighty in the top for right." This artless tale moved me much, and I could not help feeling the just cause Moses had in redressing his brother against the Egyptian.[1] I exhorted the man to look up still to the God on the top, since there was no redress below. Though I little thought then that I myself should more than once experience such imposition, and need the same exhortation hereafter, in my own transactions in the islands; and that even this poor man and I should some time after suffer together in the same manner, as shall be related hereafter.

Nor was such usage as this confined to particular places or individuals; for, in all the different islands in which I have been (and I have visited no less than fifteen) the treatment of the slaves was nearly the same; so nearly indeed, that the history of an island, or even a plantation, with a few such exceptions as I mentioned, might serve for a history of the whole. Such a tendency has the slave-trade to debauch men's minds, and harden them to every feeling of humanity! For I will not suppose that the dealers in slaves are born worse than other men—No; it is the fatality of this mistaken avarice, that it corrupts the milk of human kindness and turns it into gall. And, had the pursuits of those men been different, they might have been as generous, as tender-hearted and just, as they are unfeeling, rapacious and cruel. Surely this traffic cannot be good, which spreads like a pestilence, and taints what it touches! Which violates that first natural right of mankind, equality and independency, and gives one man a dominion over his fellows which God could never intend! For it raises the owner to a state as far above man as it depresses the slave below it; and, with all the presumption of human pride, sets a distinction between them, immeasurable in extent, and endless in duration! Yet how mistaken is

---

1 *Moses … Egyptian* Cf. Exodus 7.1–25. After Aaron's appeal to the Pharaoh to let the Israelites leave Egypt is denied, Moses is promised that God will visit judgment on Egypt and deliver the Israelites from captivity.

the avarice even of the planters. Are slaves more useful by being thus humbled to the condition of brutes, than they would be if suffered to enjoy the privileges of men? The freedom which diffuses health and prosperity throughout Britain answers you—No. When you make men slaves, you deprive them of half their virtue, you set them in your own conduct an example of fraud, rapine, and cruelty, and compel them to live with you in a state of war; and yet you complain that they are not honest or faithful! You stupefy them with stripes, and think it necessary to keep them in a state of ignorance; and yet you assert that they are incapable of learning; that their minds are such a barren soil or moor, that culture would be lost on them; and that they come from a climate, where nature, though prodigal of her bounties in a degree unknown to yourselves, has left man alone scant and unfinished, and incapable of enjoying the treasures she has poured out for him!—An assertion at once impious and absurd.[1] Why do you use those instruments of torture? Are they fit to be applied by one rational being to another? And are ye not struck with shame and mortification, to see the partakers of your nature reduced so low? But, above all, are there no dangers attending this mode of treatment? Are you not hourly in dread of an insurrection? Nor would it be surprising: for when

> ... No peace is given
> To us enslav'd, but custody severe;
> And stripes and arbitrary punishment
> Inflicted—What peace can we return?
> But to our power, hostility and hate;
> Untam'd reluctance, and revenge, though slow,
> Yet ever plotting how the conqueror least
> May reap his conquest, and may least rejoice
> In doing what we most in suffering feel.[2]

But by changing your conduct, and treating your slaves as men, every cause of fear would be banished. They would be faithful, honest, intelligent and vigorous; and peace, prosperity, and happiness, would attend you.

from CHAPTER 6

Some account of Brimstone-Hill in Montserrat—Favourable change in the author's situation—He commences merchant with three pence—His various success in dealing

---

1 *An assertion ... absurd* For the eighth and ninth editions, Equiano added the following note: "See the Observations on a Guinea Voyage, in a series of letters to the Rev. T. Clarkson, by James Field, Stanfield, in 1788, p. 21, 22.—'The subjects of the king of Benin, at Gatoe, where I was, had their markets regular and well-stocked; they teemed with luxuries unknown to the Europeans.'"
2 *No peace ... feel* Cf. John Milton, *Paradise Lost* (2.332–40).

in the different islands, and America, and the impositions he meets with in his transactions with Europeans—A curious imposition on human nature—Danger of the surfs in the West Indies—Remarkable instance of kidnapping a free mulatto—The author is nearly murdered by Doctor Perkins in Savannah.

In the preceding chapter I have set before the reader a few of those many instances of oppression, extortion, and cruelty, which I have been a witness to in the West Indies: but, were I to enumerate them all, the catalogue would be tedious and disgusting. The punishments of the slaves on every trifling occasion are so frequent, and so well known, together with the different instruments with which they are tortured, that it cannot any longer afford novelty to recite them; and they are too shocking to yield delight either to the writer or the reader. I shall therefore hereafter only mention such as incidentally befell myself in the course of my adventures. …

Some time in the year 1763 kind Providence seemed to appear rather more favourable to me. One of my master's vessels, a Bermudas sloop, about sixty tons, was commanded by one Captain Thomas Farmer, an Englishman, a very alert and active man, who gained my master a great deal of money by his good management in carrying passengers from one island to another; but very often his sailors used to get drunk and run away from the vessel, which hindered him in his business very much. This man had taken a liking to me; and many different times begged of my master to let me go a trip with him as a sailor; but he would tell him he could not spare me, though the vessel sometimes could not go for want of hands, for sailors were generally very scarce in the island. However, at last, from necessity or force, my master was prevailed on, though very reluctantly, to let me go with this captain; but he gave great charge to him to take care that I did not run away, for if I did he would make him pay for me. This being the case, the captain had for some time a sharp eye upon me whenever the vessel anchored; and as soon as she returned I was sent for on shore again. Thus was I slaving as it were for life, sometimes at one thing, and sometimes at another; so that the captain and I were nearly the most useful men in my master's employment. I also became so useful to the captain on shipboard, that many times, when he used to ask for me to go with him, though it should be but for twenty-four hours, to some of the islands near us, my master would answer he could not spare me, at which the captain would swear, and would not go the trip; and tell my master I was better to him on board than any three white men he had; for they used to behave ill in many respects, particularly in getting drunk; and then they frequently got the boat stove,[1] so as to hinder the vessel from coming back as soon as she

---

1 *got the boat stove* Stove the boat in; made a hole in the boat.

might have done. This my master knew very well; and at last, by the captain's constant entreaties, after I had been several times with him, one day, to my great joy, my master told me the captain would not let him rest, and asked me whether I would go aboard as a sailor, or stay on shore and mind the stores, for he could not bear any longer to be plagued in this manner. I was very happy at this proposal, for I immediately thought I might in time stand some chance by being on board to get a little money, or possibly make my escape if I should be used ill: I also expected to get better food, and in greater abundance; for I had felt much hunger oftentimes, though my master treated his slaves, as I have observed, uncommonly well. I therefore, without hesitation, answered him, that I would go and be a sailor if he pleased. Accordingly, I was ordered on board directly. Nevertheless, between the vessel and the shore, when she was in port, I had little or no rest, as my master always wished to have me along with him. Indeed, he was a very pleasant gentleman, and but for my expectations on shipboard I should not have thought of leaving him. But the captain liked me also very much, and I was entirely his right-hand man. I did all I could to deserve his favour, and in return I received better treatment from him than any other I believe ever met with in the West Indies in my situation.

After I had been sailing for some time with this captain, at length I endeavoured to try my luck and commence merchant. I had but a very small capital to begin with; for one single half bit, which is equal to three pence in England,[1] made up my whole stock. However I trusted to the Lord to be with me; and at one of our trips to St. Eustatia, a Dutch island, I bought a glass tumbler with my half bit, and when I came to Montserrat I sold it for a bit, or sixpence. Luckily we made several successive trips to St. Eustatia (which was a general mart for the West Indies, about twenty leagues from Montserrat); and in our next, finding my tumbler so profitable, with this one bit I bought two tumblers more; and when I came back I sold them for two bits, equal to a shilling sterling. When we went again, I bought with these two bits four more of these glasses, which I sold for four bits on our return to Montserrat; and in our next voyage to St. Eustatia I bought two glasses with one bit, and with the other three I bought a jug of Geneva,[2] nearly about three pints in measure. When we came to Montserrat I sold the gin for eight bits, and the tumblers for two, so that my capital now amounted in all to a dollar, well husbanded[3] and acquired in the space of a month or six weeks, when I blessed the Lord that I was so rich. As we sailed to different islands, I laid this money out in various

---

1   *single half bit ... England* A half bit was a unit of Spanish currency; three English pence would be the equivalent of perhaps a couple of American dollars today in purchasing power.
2   *Geneva* Geneva gin (in the late eighteenth century a very inexpensive and widely available type of liquor).
3   *well husbanded* Carefully managed.

things occasionally, and it used to turn out to very good account, especially when we went to Guadaloupe, Grenada, and the rest of the French islands.

Thus was I going all about the islands upwards of four years, and ever trading as I went, during which I experienced many instances of ill usage, and have seen many injuries done to other negroes in our dealings with Europeans: and, amidst our recreations, when we have been dancing and merry-making, they, without cause, have molested and insulted us. Indeed, I was more than once obliged to look up to God on high, as I had advised the poor fisherman some time before. And I had not been long trading for myself in the manner I have related above, when I experienced the like trial in company with him as follows: This man being used to the water, was upon an emergency put on board of us by his master to work as another hand, on a voyage to Santa Cruz; and at our sailing he had brought his little all for a venture, which consisted of six bits' worth of limes and oranges in a bag; I had also my whole stock, which was about twelve bits' worth of the same kind of goods, separate in two bags; for we had heard these fruits sold well in that island. When we came there, in some little convenient time he and I went ashore with our fruits to sell them; but we had scarcely landed when we were met by two white men, who presently took our three bags from us. We could not at first guess what they meant to do; and for some time we thought they were jesting with us; but they too soon let us know otherwise, for they took our ventures immediately to a house hard by, and adjoining the fort, while we followed all the way begging of them to give us our fruits, but in vain. They not only refused to return them, but swore at us, and threatened if we did not immediately depart they would flog us well. We told them these three bags were all we were worth in the world, and that we brought them with us to sell when we came from Montserrat, and shewed them the vessel. But this was rather against us, as they now saw we were strangers as well as slaves. They still therefore swore, and desired us to be gone, and even took sticks to beat us; while we, seeing they meant what they said, went off in the greatest confusion and despair. Thus, in the very minute of gaining more by three times than I ever did by any venture in my life before, was I deprived of every farthing I was worth. An insupportable misfortune! But how to help ourselves we knew not.

In our consternation we went to the commanding officer of the fort and told him how we had been served[1] by some of his people; but we obtained not the least redress: he answered our complaints only by a volley of imprecations against us, and immediately took a horse-whip, in order to chastise us, so that we were obliged to turn out much faster than we came in. I now, in the agony of distress and indignation, wished that the ire of God in his forked lightning might transfix these cruel oppressors among the dead.

---

1 *served* Treated.

Still however we persevered; went back again to the house, and begged and besought them again and again for our fruits, till at last some other people that were in the house asked if we would be contented if they kept one bag and gave us the other two. We, seeing no remedy whatever, consented to this; and they, observing one bag to have both kinds of fruit in it, which belonged to my companion, kept that; and the other two, which were mine, they gave us back. As soon as I got them, I ran as fast as I could, and got the first negro man I could to help me off; my companion, however, stayed a little longer to plead; he told them the bag they had was his, and likewise all that he was worth in the world; but this was of no avail, and he was obliged to return without it. The poor old man, wringing his hands, cried bitterly for his loss; and, indeed, he then did look up to God on high, which so moved me with pity for him, that I gave him nearly one third of my fruits. We then proceeded to the markets to sell them; and Providence was more favourable to us than we could have expected, for we sold our fruits uncommonly well; I got for mine about thirty-seven bits. Such a surprising reverse of fortune in so short a space of time seemed like a dream to me, and proved no small encouragement for me to trust the Lord in any situation. My captain afterwards frequently used to take my part, and get me my right, when I have been plundered or used ill by these tender Christian depredators; among whom I have shuddered to observe the unceasing blasphemous execrations which are wantonly thrown out by persons of all ages and conditions, not only without occasion, but even as if they were indulgences and pleasure.

At one of our trips to St. Kitt's I had eleven bits of my own; and my friendly captain lent me five bits more, with which I bought a Bible. I was very glad to get this book, which I scarcely could meet with anywhere. I think there was none sold in Montserrat; and, much to my grief, from being forced out of the *Aetna* in the manner I have related, my Bible, and the *Guide to the Indians*, the two books I loved above all others, were left behind.

While I was in this place, St. Kitt's, a very curious imposition on human nature took place. A white man wanted to marry in the church a free black woman that had land and slaves in Montserrat: but the clergyman told him it was against the law of the place to marry a white and a black in the church. The man then asked to be married on the water, to which the parson consented, and the two lovers went in one boat, and the parson and clerk in another, and thus the ceremony was performed. After this the loving pair came on board our vessel, and my captain treated them extremely well, and brought them safe to Montserrat.

The reader cannot but judge of the irksomeness of this situation to a mind like mine, in being daily exposed to new hardships and impositions, after having seen many better days, and having been as it were in a state of freedom and plenty; added to which, every part of the world I had hitherto been in seemed to me a paradise in comparison of the West Indies. My mind was therefore hourly replete with inventions and thoughts of being freed, and, if possible, by honest and honourable means; for I always remembered the old adage; and I trust it has ever been my ruling principle, that honesty is the best policy; and likewise that other golden precept—to do unto all men as I would they should do unto me. However, as I was from early years a predestinarian,[1] I thought whatever fate had determined must ever come to pass; and therefore, if ever it were my lot to be freed nothing could prevent me, although I should at present see no means or hope to obtain my freedom; on the other hand, if it were my fate not to be freed, I never should be so, and all my endeavours for that purpose would be fruitless.

In the midst of these thoughts, I therefore looked up with prayers anxiously to God for my liberty; and at the same time I used every honest means, and endeavoured all that was possible on my part to obtain it. In process of time I became master of a few pounds, and in a fair way of[2] making more, which my friendly captain knew very well; this occasioned him sometimes to take liberties with me: but whenever he treated me waspishly I used plainly to tell him my mind, and that I would die before I would be imposed on as other negroes were, and that to me life had lost its relish when liberty was gone. This I said although I foresaw my then well-being or future hopes of freedom (humanly speaking) depended on this man. However, as he could not bear the thoughts of my not sailing with him, he always became mild on my threats. I therefore continued with him; and, from my great attention to his orders and his business, I gained him credit, and through his kindness to me I at last procured my liberty. While I thus went on, filled with the thoughts of freedom, and resisting oppression as well as I was able, my life hung daily in suspense, particularly in the surfs I have formerly mentioned, as I could not swim. These are extremely violent throughout the West Indies, and I was ever exposed to their howling rage and devouring fury in all the islands. I have seen them strike and toss a boat right up an end, and maim several on board. Once in the Grenada islands, when I and about eight others were pulling a large boat with two puncheons[3] of water in it, a surf struck us, and drove the boat and all in it about half a stone's throw, among some trees, and above the high-water mark. We were obliged to get all the assistance we could from the nearest estate to mend the boat, and launch it into the water again. At Montserrat one night, in

---

1 *predestinarian* One who believes that all that occurs is predestined by God. (The question of to what degree human events are predestined was the subject of heated dispute at the time within the Methodist church, which Equiano joined in 1774.)
2 *in a fair way of* On the way to.
3 *puncheons* Barrels.

pressing hard to get off the shore on board, the punt[1] was overset with us four times; the first time I was very near being drowned; however the jacket I had on kept me up above water a little space of time, while I called on a man near me who was a good swimmer, and told him I could not swim; he then made haste to me, and, just as I was sinking, he caught hold of me, and brought me to sounding,[2] and then he went and brought the punt also. As soon as we had turned the water out of her, lest we should be used ill for being absent, we attempted again three times more, and as often the horrid surfs served us as at first; but at last, the fifth time we attempted, we gained our point, at the imminent hazard of our lives.

One day also, at Old Road in Montserrat, our captain, and three men besides myself, were going in a large canoe in quest of rum and sugar, when a single surf tossed the canoe an amazing distance from the water, and some of us even a stone's throw from each other: most of us were very much bruised; so that I and many more often said, and really thought, that there was not such another place under the heavens as this. I longed therefore much to leave it, and daily wished to see my master's promise performed of going to Philadelphia. While we lay in this place a very cruel thing happened on board of our sloop which filled me with horror; though I found afterwards such practices were frequent. There was a very clever and decent free young mulatto-man who sailed a long time with us: he had a free woman for his wife, by whom he had a child; and she was then living on shore, and all very happy. Our captain and mate, and other people on board, and several elsewhere, even the natives of Bermudas, all knew this young man from a child that he was always free, and no one had ever claimed him as their property: however, as might too often overcomes right in these parts, it happened that a Bermudas captain, whose vessel lay there for a few days in the road, came on board of us, and seeing the mulatto-man, whose name was Joseph Clipson, he told him he was not free, and that he had orders from his master to bring him to Bermudas. The poor man could not believe the captain to be in earnest; but he was very soon undeceived, his men laying violent hands on him: and although he shewed a certificate of his being born free in St. Kitt's, and most people on board knew that he served his time to boat building,[3] and always passed for a free man, yet he was taken forcibly out of our vessel. He then asked to be carried ashore before the secretary or magistrates, and these infernal invaders of human rights promised him he should; but, instead of that, they carried him on board of the other vessel: and the next day, without giving the poor

---

1 *punt* Small boat.
2 *to sounding* To where one could find sound footing underwater.
3 *served his time to boat building* Was apprenticed as a boat builder.

man any hearing on shore, or suffering him even to see his wife or child, he was carried away, and probably doomed never more in this world to see them again.

Nor was this the only instance of this kind of barbarity I was a witness to. I have since often seen in Jamaica and other islands free men, whom I have known in America, thus villainously trepanned and held in bondage. I have heard of two similar practices even in Philadelphia—and, were it not for the benevolence of the Quakers in that city, many of the sable race, who now breathe the air of liberty, would, I believe, be groaning indeed under some planter's chains. These things opened my mind to a new scene of horror to which I had been before a stranger. Hitherto I had thought only slavery dreadful; but the state of a free negro appeared to me now equally so at least, and in some respects even worse, for they live in constant alarm for their liberty; and even this is but nominal, for they are universally insulted and plundered without the possibility of redress; for such is the equity of the West Indian laws, that no free negro's evidence will be admitted in their courts of justice. In this situation, is it surprising that slaves, when mildly treated, should prefer even the misery of slavery to such a mockery of freedom? I was now completely disgusted with the West Indies, and thought I never should be entirely free until I had left them. ...

About the latter end of the year 1764 my master bought a larger sloop, called the *Providence*, about seventy or eighty tons, of which my captain had the command. I went with him into this vessel, and we took a load of new slaves for Georgia and Charles Town. My master now left me entirely to the captain, though he still wished for me to be with him; but I, who always much wished to lose sight of the West Indies, was not a little rejoiced at the thoughts of seeing any other country. Therefore, relying on the goodness of my captain, I got ready all the little venture I could; and, when the vessel was ready, we sailed, to my great joy. When we got to our destined places, Georgia and Charles Town, I expected I should have an opportunity of selling my little property to advantage: but here, particularly in Charles Town, I met with buyers, white men, who imposed on me as in other places. Notwithstanding, I was resolved to have fortitude; thinking no lot or trial is too hard when kind Heaven is the rewarder.

We soon got loaded again, and returned to Montserrat; and there, amongst the rest of the islands, I sold my goods well; and in this manner I continued trading during the year 1764; meeting with various scenes of imposition, as usual.

After this, my master fitted out his vessel for Philadelphia, in the year 1765; and during the time we were loading her, and getting ready for the voyage, I worked with redoubled alacrity, from the hope of getting money enough by these voyages to buy my freedom in time, if it should please God; and also to see the town of Philadelphia, which I had heard a great deal about for some years past; besides which, I had always longed to prove my master's promise the first day I came to him. In the midst of these elevated ideas, and while I was about getting my little merchandize in readiness, one Sunday my master sent for me to his house. When I came there, I found him and the captain together; and, on my going in, I was struck with astonishment at his telling me he heard that I meant to run away from him when I got to Philadelphia: "And therefore," said he, "I must sell you again: you cost me a great deal of money, no less than forty pounds sterling; and it will not do to lose so much. You are a valuable fellow," continued he; "and I can get any day for you one hundred guineas, from many gentlemen in this island." And then he told me of Captain Doran's brother-in-law, a severe master, who ever wanted to buy me to make me his overseer. My captain also said he could get much more than a hundred guineas for me in Carolina. This I knew to be a fact; for the gentleman that wanted to buy me came off several times on board of us, and spoke to me to live with him, and said he would use me well.

When I asked what work he would put me to he said, as I was a sailor, he would make me a captain of one of his rice vessels. But I refused: and fearing, at the same time, by a sudden turn I saw in the captain's temper, he might mean to sell me, I told the gentleman I would not live with him on any condition, and that I certainly would run away with his vessel: but he said he did not fear that, as he would catch me again; and then he told me how cruelly he would serve me if I should do so. My captain, however, gave him to understand that I knew something of navigation, so he thought better of it; and, to my great joy, he went away. I now told my master I did not say I would run away in Philadelphia; neither did I mean it, as he did not use me ill, nor yet the captain: for if they did I certainly would have made some attempts before now; but as I thought that if it were God's will I ever should be freed it would be so, and, on the contrary, if it was not his will it would not happen; so I hoped, if ever I were freed, whilst I was used well, it should be by honest means; but, as I could not help myself, he must do as he pleased; I could only hope and trust to the God of Heaven; and at that instant my mind was big with inventions and full of schemes to escape. I then appealed to the captain whether he ever saw any sign of my making the least attempt to run away; and asked him if I did not always come on board according to the time for which he gave me liberty; and, more particularly, when all our men left us at Gaurdeloupe and went on board of the French fleet, and advised me to go with them, whether I might not, and that he could not have got me again. To my no small surprise, and very great joy, the captain confirmed every syllable that I had said: and even more; for he said he had tried different times to see if I would make any attempt of this kind, both at St. Eustatia and in America, and he never found that I made the smallest; but, on the contrary, I always came on board according to his orders; and he did really believe, if I ever meant to run away, that, as I could never have had a better opportunity, I would have done it the night the mate and all the people left our vessel at Gaurdeloupe.

The captain then informed my master, who had been thus imposed on by our mate, though I did not know who was my enemy, the reason the mate had for imposing this lie upon him; which was, because I had acquainted the captain of the provisions the mate had given away or taken out of the vessel. This speech of the captain was like life to the dead to me, and instantly my soul glorified God; and still more so on hearing my master immediately say that I was a sensible fellow, and he never did intend to use me as a common slave; and that but for the entreaties of the captain, and his character of me, he would not have let me go from the stores about as I had done; that also, in so doing, he thought by carrying one little thing or other to different places to sell I might make money. That he also intended to encourage me in this by crediting me with half a puncheon of rum and half a hogshead of sugar at a time; so that, from being careful, I might have money enough, in some time, to purchase my freedom; and, when that was the case, I might depend upon it he would let me have it for forty pounds sterling money, which was only the same price he gave for me. This sound gladdened my poor heart beyond measure; though indeed it was no more than the very idea I had formed in my mind of my master long before, and I immediately made him this reply: "Sir, I always had that very thought of you, indeed I had, and that made me so diligent in serving you." He then gave me a large piece of silver coin, such as I never had seen or had before, and told me to get ready for the voyage, and he would credit me with a tierce[1] of sugar, and another of rum; he also said that he had two amiable sisters in Philadelphia, from whom I might get some necessary things. Upon this my noble captain desired me to go aboard; and, knowing the African metal,[2] he charged me not to say anything of this matter to anybody; and he promised that the lying mate should not go with him any more. This was a change indeed; in the same hour to feel the most exquisite pain, and in the turn of a moment the fullest joy. It caused in me such sensations as I was only able to express in my looks; my heart was so overpowered with gratitude that I could have kissed both of their feet. When I left the room I immediately went, or rather flew, to the vessel, which being loaded, my master, as good as his word, trusted me with a tierce of rum, and another of sugar, when we sailed, and arrived safe at the elegant town of Philadelphia.

---

1 *a tierce* One third of a barrel.
2 *metal* Character.

I soon sold my goods here pretty well; and in this charming place I found everything plentiful and cheap.

While I was in this place a very extraordinary occurrence befell me. I had been told one evening of a wise woman, a Mrs. Davis, who revealed secrets, foretold events, etc. I put little faith in this story at first, as I could not conceive that any mortal could foresee the future disposals[1] of Providence, nor did I believe in any other revelation than that of the Holy Scriptures; however, I was greatly astonished at seeing this woman in a dream that night, though a person I never before beheld in my life; this made such an impression on me that I could not get the idea the next day out of my mind, and I then became as anxious to see her as I was before indifferent; accordingly in the evening, after we left off working, I inquired where she lived, and being directed to her, to my inexpressible surprise, beheld the very woman in the very same dress she appeared to me to wear in the vision. She immediately told me I had dreamed of her the preceding night; related to me many things that had happened with a correctness that astonished me; and finally told me I should not be long a slave: this was the more agreeable news, as I believed it the more readily from her having so faithfully related the past incidents of my life. She said I should be twice in very great danger of my life within eighteen months, which, if I escaped, I should afterwards go on well; so, giving me her blessing, we parted. After staying here some time till our vessel was loaded, and I had bought in my little traffic, we sailed from this agreeable spot for Montserrat, once more to encounter the raging surfs.

We arrived safe at Montserrat, where we discharged our cargo; and soon after that we took slaves on board for St. Eustatia, and from thence to Georgia. I had always exerted myself and did double work, in order to make our voyages as short as possible; and from thus overworking myself while we were at Georgia I caught a fever and ague. I was very ill for eleven days and near dying; eternity was now exceedingly impressed on my mind, and I feared very much that awful event. I prayed the Lord therefore to spare me; and I made a promise in my mind to God, that I would be good if ever I should recover. At length, from having an eminent doctor to attend me, I was restored again to health; and soon after we got the vessel loaded, and set off for Montserrat. During the passage, as I was perfectly restored, and had much business of the vessel to mind, all my endeavours to keep up my integrity, and perform my promise to God, began to fail; and, in spite of all I could do, as we drew nearer and nearer to the islands, my resolutions more and more declined, as if the very air of that country or climate seemed fatal to piety. When we were safe arrived at Montserrat, and I had got ashore, I forgot my former resolutions.

---

1 *disposals* Arrangements.

Alas! How prone is the heart to leave that God it wishes to love! and how strongly do the things of this world strike the senses and captivate the soul!

After our vessel was discharged, we soon got her ready, and took in, as usual, some of the poor oppressed natives of Africa, and other negroes; we then set off again for Georgia and Charles Town. We arrived at Georgia, and, having landed part of our cargo, proceeded to Charles Town with the remainder. While we were there, I saw the town illuminated; the guns were fired, and bonfires and other demonstrations of joy shown, on account of the repeal of the Stamp Act.[1]

Here I disposed of some goods on my own account; the white men buying them with smooth promises and fair words, giving me however but very indifferent payment. ...

We soon came to Georgia, where we were to complete our lading; and here worse fate than ever attended me: for one Sunday night, as I was with some negroes in their master's yard in the town of Savannah, it happened that their master, one Doctor Perkins, who was a very severe and cruel man, came in drunk; and, not liking to see any strange negroes in his yard, he and a ruffian of a white man he had in his service beset me in an instant, and both of them struck me with the first weapons they could get hold of. I cried out as long as I could for help and mercy; but, though I gave a good account of myself, and he knew my captain, who lodged hard by him, it was to no purpose. They beat and mangled me in a shameful manner, leaving me near dead. I lost so much blood from the wounds I received that I lay quite motionless, and was so benumbed that I could not feel anything for many hours. Early in the morning they took me away to the jail. As I did not return to the ship all night, my captain, not knowing where I was, and being uneasy that I did not then make my appearance, he made inquiry after me; and, having found where I was, immediately came to me. As soon as the good man saw me so cut and mangled, he could not forbear weeping; he soon got me out of jail to his lodgings, and immediately sent for the best doctors in the place, who at first declared it as their opinion that I could not recover. My captain on this went to all the lawyers in the town for their advice, but they told him they could do nothing for me as I was a negro. He then went to Doctor Perkins, the hero who had vanquished me, and menaced him, swearing he would be revenged of him, and challenged him to fight. But cowardice is ever the companion of cruelty—and the Doctor refused.

---

1 *Stamp Act* The 1765 Stamp Act (requiring that various printed papers be produced on stamped paper of English manufacture) was a form of tax imposed on the American colonies by the Parliament of Great Britain. The Stamp Act inspired outrage in the colonies, and was repealed the following year.

However, by the skilfulness of one Doctor Brady of that place, I began at last to mend; but, although I was so sore and bad with the wounds I had all over me that I could not rest in any posture, yet I was in more pain on account of the captain's uneasiness about me than I otherwise should have been. The worthy man nursed and watched me all the hours of the night; and I was, through his attention and that of the doctor, able to get out of bed in about sixteen or eighteen days. All this time I was very much wanted on board, as I used frequently to go up and down the river for rafts, and other parts of our cargo, and stow them when the mate was sick or absent.

In about four weeks I was able to go on duty; and in a fortnight after, having got in all our lading, our vessel set sail for Montserrat; and in less than three weeks we arrived there safe towards the end of the year. This ended my adventures in 1764 [1765]; for I did not leave Montserrat again till the beginning of the following year.

END OF THE FIRST VOLUME

CHAPTER 7

The author's disgust at the West Indies—Forms schemes to obtain his freedom—Ludicrous disappointment he and his Captain meet with in Georgia—At last, by several successful voyages, he acquires a sum of money sufficient to purchase it—Applies to his master, who accepts it, and grants his manumission, to his great joy—He afterwards enters as a freeman on board one of Mr. King's ships, and sails for Georgia—Impositions on free negroes as usual—His venture of turkeys—Sails for Montserrat, and on his passage his friend, the Captain, falls ill and dies.

Every day now brought me nearer my freedom, and I was impatient till we proceeded again to sea, that I might have an opportunity of getting a sum large enough to purchase it. I was not long ungratified; for, in the beginning of the year 1766, my master bought another sloop, named the *Nancy*, the largest I had ever seen. She was partly laden, and was to proceed to Philadelphia; our Captain had his choice of three, and I was well pleased he chose this, which was the largest; for, from his having a large vessel, I had more room, and could carry a larger quantity of goods with me. Accordingly, when we had delivered our old vessel, the *Prudence*, and completed the lading of the *Nancy*, having made near three hundred per cent, by four barrels of pork I brought from Charles Town, I laid in as large a cargo as I could, trusting to God's providence to prosper my undertaking.

With these views I sailed for Philadelphia. On our passage, when we drew near the land, I was for the first time surprised at the sight of some whales, having never seen any such large sea monsters before; and as we sailed by the land one morning I saw a puppy whale close by the vessel; it was about the length of a wherry boat, and it followed us all the day till we got within the Capes.[1] We arrived safe and in good time at Philadelphia, and I sold my goods there chiefly to the Quakers. They always appeared to be a very honest discreet sort of people, and never attempted to impose on me;[2] I therefore liked them, and ever after chose to deal with them in preference to any others.

One Sunday morning while I was here, as I was going to church, I chanced to pass a meeting-house.[3] The doors being open, and the house full of people, it excited my curiosity to go in. When I entered the house, to my great surprise, I saw a very tall woman standing in the midst of them, speaking in an audible voice something which I could not understand. Having never seen anything of this kind before, I stood and stared about me for some time, wondering at this odd scene. As soon as it was over I took an opportunity to make inquiry about the place and people, when I was informed they were called Quakers. I particularly asked what that woman I saw in the midst of them had said, but none of them were pleased to satisfy me; so I quitted them, and soon after, as I was returning, I came to a church crowded with people; the church-yard was full likewise, and a number of people were even mounted on ladders, looking in at the windows. I thought this a strange sight, as I had never seen churches, either in England or the West Indies, crowded in this manner before. I therefore made bold to ask some people the meaning of all this, and they told me the Rev. Mr. George Whitfield[4] was preaching. I had often heard of this gentleman, and had wished to see and hear him; but I had never before had an opportunity. I now therefore resolved to gratify myself with the sight, and I pressed in amidst the multitude. When I got into the church, I saw this pious man exhorting the people with the greatest fervour and earnestness, and sweating as much as I ever did while in slavery on Montserrat beach. I was very much struck and impressed with this; I thought it strange I had never seen divines exert themselves in this manner before, and I was no longer at a loss to account for the thin congregations they preached to.

When we had discharged our cargo here, and were loaded again, we left this fruitful land once more, and set sail for Montserrat. My traffic had hitherto succeeded so well with me, that I thought, by selling my goods when we

---

1   *got within the Capes*   Delaware Bay (which leads to the Delaware River and the city of Philadelphia) is entered as one passes between Cape May to the north and Cape Henlopen to the south.

2   *impose on me*   Treat me unfairly or dishonestly.

3   *meeting-house*   In early America churches were often referred to as meeting houses.

4   *Rev. Mr. George Whitfield*   Whitfield (also spelled Whitefield) (1714–70) was originally an Anglican minister; renowned for his charismatic preaching, he became one of the founders of Methodism and one of the leaders of the Great Awakening of the 1730s and 1740s.

arrived at Montserrat, I should have enough to purchase my freedom. But, as soon as our vessel arrived there, my master came on board, and gave orders for us to go to St. Eustatia, and discharge our cargo there, and from thence proceed for Georgia. I was much disappointed at this; but thinking, as usual, it was of no use to encounter with the decrees of fate, I submitted without repining, and we went to St. Eustatia. After we had discharged our cargo there we took in a live cargo, as we call a cargo of slaves. Here I sold my goods tolerably well; but, not being able to lay out all my money in this small island to as much advantage as in many other places, I laid out only part, and the remainder I brought away with me net.[1] We sailed from hence for Georgia, and I was glad when we got there, though I had not much reason to like the place from my last adventure in Savannah; but I longed to get back to Montserrat and procure my freedom, which I expected to be able to purchase when I returned.

As soon as we arrived here I waited on my careful doctor, Mr. Brady, to whom I made the most grateful acknowledgments in my power for his former kindness and attention during my illness. While we were here an odd circumstance happened to the Captain and me, which disappointed us both a good deal. A silversmith, whom we had brought to this place some voyages before, agreed with the Captain to return with us to the West Indies, and promised at the same time to give the Captain a great deal of money, having pretended to take a liking to him, and being, as we thought, very rich. But while we stayed to load our vessel this man was taken ill in a house where he worked, and in a week's time became very bad. The worse he grew the more he used to speak of giving the Captain what he had promised him, so that he expected something considerable from the death of this man, who had no wife or child, and he attended him day and night. I used also to go with the Captain, at his own desire, to attend him. Especially when we saw there was no appearance of his recovery, and, in order to recompense me for my trouble, the Captain promised me ten pounds, when he should get the man's property. I thought this would be of great service to me, although I had nearly money enough to purchase my freedom, if I should get safe this voyage to Montserrat. In this expectation I laid out above eight pounds of my money for a suit of superfine clothes to dance with at my freedom, which I hoped was then at hand. We still continued to attend this man, and were with him even on the last day he lived, till very late at night, when we went on board. After we were got to bed, about one or two o'clock in the morning, the Captain was sent for, and informed the man was dead. On this he came to my bed, and, waking me, informed me of it, and desired me to get up and procure a light, and immediately go to him. I

---

1   net   Without having made any additional payments.

told him I was very sleepy, and wished he would take somebody else with him; or else, as the man was dead, and could want no farther attendance, to let all things remain as they were till the next morning. "No, no," said he, "we will have the money tonight, I cannot wait till tomorrow; so let us go." Accordingly I got up and struck a light, and away we both went and saw the man as dead as we could wish. The Captain said he would give him a grand burial, in gratitude for the promised treasure; and desired that all the things belonging to the deceased might be brought forth. Among others, there was a nest of trunks of which he had kept the keys whilst the man was ill, and when they were produced we opened them with no small eagerness and expectation; and as there were a great number within one another, with much impatience we took them one out of the other. At last, when we came to the smallest, and had opened it, we saw it was full of papers, which we supposed to be notes, at the sight of which our hearts leapt for joy; and that instant the Captain, clapping his hands, cried out, "Thank God, here it is." But when we took up the trunk, and began to examine the supposed treasure and long-looked-for bounty (alas! alas! how uncertain and deceitful are all human affairs!), what had we found? While we thought we were embracing a substance we grasped an empty nothing. The whole amount that was in the nest of trunks was only one dollar and a half; and all that the man possessed would not pay for his coffin. Our sudden and exquisite joy was now succeeded by a sudden and exquisite pain, and my Captain and I exhibited, for some time, most ridiculous figures—pictures of chagrin and disappointment! We went away greatly mortified, and left the deceased to do as well as he could for himself, as we had taken so good care of him when alive for nothing.

We set sail once more for Montserrat, and arrived there safe; but much out of humour with our friend the silversmith. When we had unladen the vessel, and I had sold my venture, finding myself master of about forty-seven pounds, I consulted my true friend, the Captain, how I should proceed in offering my master the money for my freedom. He told me to come on a certain morning, when he and my master would be at breakfast together. Accordingly, on that morning I went, and met the Captain there, as he had appointed. When I went in, I made my obeisance to my master, and with my money in my hand, and many fears in my heart, I prayed him to be as good as his offer to me, when he was pleased to promise me my freedom as soon as I could purchase it. This speech seemed to confound him; he began to recoil: and my heart that instant sunk within me. "What," said he, "give you your freedom? Why, where did you get the money? Have you got forty pounds sterling?" "Yes, sir," I answered. "How did you get it?" replied he. I told him, very honestly. The Captain then said he knew I got the money very honestly and with much industry, and that I was particularly careful. On which my master replied, I got money much faster than he did; and said he would not have made me the promise he did if he had thought I should have got money so soon. "Come, come," said my worthy Captain, clapping my master on the back, "Come, Robert, (which was his name) I think you must let him have his freedom; you have laid your money out very well; you have received good interest for it all this time, and here is now the principal at last. I know Gustavus has earned you more than an hundred a-year, and he will still save you money, as he will not leave you—Come, Robert, take the money." My master then said he would not be worse than his promise; and, taking the money, told me to go to the Secretary at the Register Office, and get my manumission[1] drawn up.

These words of my master were like a voice from heaven to me: in an instant all my trepidation was turned into unutterable bliss; and I most reverently bowed myself with gratitude, unable to express my feelings, but by the overflowing of my eyes, while my true and worthy friend, the Captain, congratulated us both with a peculiar degree of heartfelt pleasure.

As soon as the first transports of my joy were over, and that I had expressed my thanks to these my worthy friends in the best manner I was able, I rose with a heart full of affection and reverence, and left the room, in order to obey my master's joyful mandate of going to the Register Office. As I was leaving the house I called to mind the words of the Psalmist, in the 126th Psalm, and like him, "I glorified God in my heart, in whom I trusted."[2] These words had been impressed on my mind from the very day I was forced from Deptford to the present hour, and I now saw them, as I thought, fulfilled and verified. My imagination was all rapture as I flew to the Register Office, and, in this respect, like the apostle Peter,[3] (whose deliverance from prison was so sudden and extraordinary, that he thought he was in a vision) I could scarcely believe I was awake. Heavens! who could do justice to my feelings at this moment! Not conquering heroes themselves, in the midst of a triumph—Not the tender mother who has just regained her long-lost infant, and presses it to her heart—Not the weary hungry mariner, at the sight of the desired friendly port—Not the lover, when he once more embraces his beloved mistress, after she had been ravished from his arms!—All within my breast was tumult, wildness, and delirium! My feet scarcely touched the ground, for they were winged with joy, and, like Elijah, as he rose to heaven,[4] they "were with lightning sped as I went on." Every one I met I told of my happiness, and blazed about the virtue of my amiable master and captain.

---

1   *manumission*   Release from enslavement.
2   *the Psalmist ... trusted*   The words quoted by Equiano do not appear in this psalm; it is not entirely clear what passage he may have had in mind—possibly Psalm 28.
3   [Equiano's note]   Acts, Ch. 12, verse 9.
4   *rose to heaven*   See 2 Kings 2.1–18.

When I got to the office and acquainted the Register with my errand he congratulated me on the occasion, and told me he would draw up my manumission for half price, which was a guinea. I thanked him for his kindness; and, having received it and paid him, I hastened to my master to get him to sign it, that I might be fully released. Accordingly, he signed the manumission that day, so that, before night, I who had been a slave in the morning, trembling at the will of another, was become my own master, and completely free. I thought this was the happiest day I had ever experienced; and my joy was still heightened by the blessings and prayers of the sable race, particularly the aged, to whom my heart had ever been attached with reverence.

As the form of my manumission has something peculiar in it, and expresses the absolute power and dominion one man claims over his fellow, I shall beg leave to present it before my readers at full length:

> *Montserrat*—To all men unto whom these presents shall come:[1] I Robert King, of the parish of St. Anthony in the said island, merchant, send greeting: Know ye, that I, the aforesaid Robert King, for and in consideration of the sum of seventy pounds current money of the said island, to me in hand paid, and to the intent that a negro man-slave, named Gustavus Vassa, shall and may become free, have manumitted, emancipated, enfranchised, and set free, and by these presents do manumit, emancipate, enfranchise, and set free, the aforesaid negro man-slave, named Gustavus Vassa, for ever, hereby giving, granting, and releasing unto him, the said Gustavus Vassa, all right, title, dominion, sovereignty, and property, which, as lord and master over the aforesaid Gustavus Vassa, I had, or now I have, or by any means whatsoever I may or can hereafter possibly have over him the aforesaid negro, for ever. In witness whereof I the abovesaid Robert King have unto these presents set my hand and seal, this tenth day of July, in the year of our Lord one thousand seven hundred and sixty-six.
>
> ROBERT KING
>
> Signed, sealed, and delivered in the presence of Terrylegay, Montserrat. Registered the within manumission at full length, this eleventh day of July, 1766, in liber[2]
>
> D. TERRYLEGAY, Register.

In short, the fair as well as black people immediately styled me by a new appellation, to me the most desirable in the world, which was Freeman, and at the

---

1 *these presents shall come* The present words shall be shown.
2 *liber* Latin: book.

dances I gave,[1] my Georgia superfine blue clothes made no indifferent appearance, as I thought. Some of the sable females, who formerly stood aloof, now began to relax and appear less coy; but my heart was still fixed on London, where I hoped to be ere long. So that my worthy captain and his owner, my late master, finding that the bent of my mind was towards London, said to me, "We hope you won't leave us, but that you will still be with the vessels." Here gratitude bowed me down; and none but the generous mind can judge of my feelings, struggling between inclination and duty. However, notwithstanding my wish to be in London, I obediently answered my benefactors that I would go in the vessel, and not leave them; and from that day I was entered on board as an able-bodied sailor, at thirty-six shillings per month, besides what perquisites I could make. My intention was to make a voyage or two, entirely to please these my honoured patrons; but I determined that the year following, if it pleased God, I would see Old England once more, and surprise my old master, Capt. Pascal, who was hourly in my mind; for I still loved him, notwithstanding his usage of me, and I pleased myself with thinking of what he would say when he saw what the Lord had done for me in so short a time, instead of being, as he might perhaps suppose, under the cruel yoke of some planter.

With these kind of reveries, I used often to entertain myself, and shorten the time till my return; and now, being as in my original free African state, I embarked on board the *Nancy*, after having got all things ready for our voyage. In this state of serenity, we sailed for St. Eustatia; and, having smooth seas and calm weather, we soon arrived there: after taking our cargo on board, we proceeded to Savannah in Georgia, in August, 1766. While we were there, as usual, I used to go for the cargo up the rivers in boats; and on this business I have been frequently beset by alligators, which were very numerous on that coast, and I have shot many of them when they have been near getting into our boats; which we have with great difficulty sometimes prevented, and have been very much frightened at them. I have seen a young one sold in Georgia alive for six pence. During our stay at this place, one evening a slave belonging to Mr. Read, a merchant of Savannah, came near our vessel, and began to use me very ill. I entreated him, with all the patience I was master of, to desist, as I knew there was little or no law for a free negro here; but the fellow, instead of taking my advice, persevered in his insults, and even struck me. At this I lost all temper, and I fell on him and beat him soundly.

The next morning his master came to our vessel as we lay alongside the wharf, and desired me to come ashore that he might have me flogged all round the town, for beating his negro slave. I told him he had insulted me, and had

---

1 *gave* Attended.

given the provocation, by first striking me. I had told my captain also the whole affair that morning, and wished him to have gone along with me to Mr. Read, to prevent bad consequences; but he said that it did not signify, and if Mr. Read said any thing he would make matters up, and had desired me to go to work, which I accordingly did. The Captain being on board when Mr. Read came, he told him I was a free man; and when Mr. Read applied to him to deliver me up, he said he knew nothing of the matter. I was astonished and frightened at this, and thought I had better keep where I was than go ashore and be flogged round the town, without judge or jury. I therefore refused to stir; and Mr. Read went away, swearing he would bring all the constables in the town, for he would have me out of the vessel. When he was gone, I thought his threat might prove too true to my sorrow; and I was confirmed in this belief, as well by the many instances I had seen of the treatment of free negroes, as from a fact that had happened within my own knowledge here a short time before. There was a free black man, a carpenter, that I knew, who, for asking a gentleman that he worked for for the money he had earned, was put into jail; and afterwards this oppressed man was sent from Georgia, with false accusations, of an intention to set the gentleman's house on fire, and run away with his slaves. I was therefore much embarrassed, and very apprehensive of a flogging at least. I dreaded, of all things, the thoughts of being striped, as I never in my life had the marks of any violence of that kind.

At that instant a rage seized my soul, and for a little I determined to resist the first man that should offer to lay violent hands on me, or basely use me without a trial; for I would sooner die like a free man, than suffer myself to be scourged by the hands of ruffians, and my blood drawn like a slave. The captain and others, more cautious, advised me to make haste and conceal myself; for they said Mr. Read was a very spiteful man, and he would soon come on board with constables and take me. At first I refused this counsel, being determined to stand my ground; but at length, by the prevailing entreaties of the captain and Mr. Dixon, with whom he lodged, I went to Mr. Dixon's house, which was a little out of town, at a place called Yea-ma-chra.[1] I was but just gone when Mr. Read, with the constables, came for me, and searched the vessel; but, not finding me there, he swore he would have me dead or alive.

I was secreted about five days; however, the good character which my captain always gave me as well as some other gentlemen who also knew me, procured me some friends. At last some of them told my captain that he did not use me well, in suffering me[2] thus to be imposed upon, and said they would see me redressed, and get me on board some other vessel. My captain,

---

1   Yea-ma-chra   Indigenous name for the area near Savannah, Georgia.
2   suffering me   Allowing me.

on this, immediately went to Mr. Read, and told him that ever since I eloped from the vessel his work had been neglected, and he could not go on with her loading, himself and mate not being well; and, as I had managed things on board for them, my absence must retard his voyage, and consequently hurt the owner; he therefore begged of him to forgive me, as he said he never had any complaint of me before, for the many years that I had been with him. After repeated entreaties, Mr. Read said I might go to hell, and that he would not meddle with me; on which my captain came immediately to me at his lodging, and, telling me how pleasantly matters had gone on, he desired me to go on board. Some of my other friends then asked him if he had got the constable's warrant from them; the captain said, No. On this I was desired by them to stay in the house; and they said they would get me on board of some other vessel before the evening. When the captain heard this, he became almost distracted. He went immediately for the warrant, and, after using every exertion in his power, he at last got it from my hunters; but I had all the expenses to pay. After I had thanked all my friends for their attention, I went on board again to my work, of which I had always plenty.

We were in haste to complete our lading, and were to carry twenty head of cattle with us to the West Indies, where they are a very profitable article. In order to encourage me in working, and to make up for the time I had lost, my captain promised me the privilege of carrying two bullocks[1] of my own with me; and this made me work with redoubled ardour. As soon as I had got the vessel loaded, in doing which I was obliged to perform the duty of the mate as well as my own work, and that the bullocks were near coming on board, I asked the captain leave to bring my two, according to his promise; but, to my great surprise, he told me there was no room for them. I then asked him to permit me to take one; but he said he could not. I was a good deal mortified at this usage, and told him I had no notion that he intended thus to impose on me; nor could I think well of any man that was so much worse than his word. On this we had some disagreement, and I gave him to understand that I intended to leave the vessel. At this he appeared to be very much dejected; and our mate, who had been very sickly, and whose duty had long devolved upon me, advised him to persuade me to stay: in consequence of which he spoke very kindly to me, making many fair promises, telling me that, as the mate was so sickly, he could not do without me, and that, as the safety of the vessel and cargo depended greatly upon me, he therefore hoped that I would not be offended at what had passed between us, and swore he would make up all matters when we arrived in the West Indies. So I consented to slave on as before.

---

1   *bullocks*   Young bulls.

Soon after this, as the bullocks were coming on board, one of them ran at the captain, and butted him so furiously in the breast that he never recovered of the blow. In order to make me some amends for his treatment about the bullocks, the captain now pressed me very much to take some turkeys, and other fowls, with me, and gave me liberty to take as many as I could find room for; but I told him he knew very well I had never carried any turkeys before, as I always thought they were such tender birds that they were not fit to cross the seas. However, he continued to press me to buy them for once; and, what was very surprising to me, the more I was against it, the more he urged my taking them, insomuch that he insured me from all losses that might happen by them, and I was prevailed on to take them; but I thought this very strange, as he had never acted so with me before. This, and not being able to dispose of my paper-money in any other way, induced me at length to take four dozen. The turkeys, however, I was so dissatisfied about that I determined to make no more voyages to this quarter, nor with this captain; and was very apprehensive that my free voyage would be the worst I had ever made.

We set sail for Montserrat. The captain and mate had been both complaining of sickness when we sailed, and as we proceeded on our voyage they grew worse. This was about November, and we had not been long at sea before we began to meet with strong northerly gales and rough seas; and in about seven or eight days all the bullocks were near being drowned, and four or five of them died. Our vessel, which had not been tight[1] at first, was much less so now; and, though we were but nine in the whole, including five sailors and myself, yet we were obliged to attend to the pumps every half or three quarters of an hour. The captain and mate came on deck as often as they were able, which was now but seldom; for they declined so fast, that they were not well enough to make observations above four or five times the whole voyage. The whole care of the vessel rested, therefore, upon me, and I was obliged to direct her by my former experience, not being able to work a traverse.[2] The captain was now very sorry he had not taught me navigation, and protested, if ever he should get well again, he would not fail to do so; but in about seventeen days his illness increased so much, that he was obliged to keep [to] his bed, continuing sensible, however, till the last, constantly having the owner's interest at heart; for this just and benevolent man ever appeared much concerned about the welfare of what he was entrusted with. When this dear friend found the symptoms of death approaching, he called me by my name; and, when I came to him, he asked (with almost his last breath) if he had ever done me any harm? "God forbid I should think so," I replied. "I should then be the most

---

1 *tight* Watertight.
2 *work a traverse* Calculate a series of different courses to be followed by a sailing ship.

ungrateful of wretches to the best of benefactors." While I was thus expressing my affection and sorrow by his bedside, he expired without saying another word; and the day following we committed his body to the deep.

Every man on board loved this man, and regretted his death; but I was exceedingly affected at it, and I found that I did not know, till he was gone, the strength of my regard for him. Indeed, I had every reason in the world to be attached to him; for, besides that he was in general mild, affable, generous, faithful, benevolent, and just, he was to me a friend and a father; and, had it pleased Providence that he had died but five months before, I verily believe I should not have obtained my freedom when I did; and it is not improbable that I might not have been able to get it at any rate afterwards.

The captain being dead, the mate came on the deck, and made such observations as he was able, but to no purpose. In the course of a few days more, the few bullocks that remained were found dead; but the turkeys I had, though on the deck and exposed to so much wet and bad weather, did well, and I afterwards gained near three hundred per cent on the sale of them; so that in the event it proved a happy circumstance for me that I had not bought the bullocks I intended, for they must have perished with the rest; and I could not help looking on this otherwise trifling circumstance as a particular providence of God, and I was thankful accordingly.

The care of the vessel took up all my time, and engaged my attention entirely. As we were now out of the variable winds, I thought I should not be much puzzled to hit upon the islands. I was persuaded I steered right for Antigua, which I wished to reach, as the nearest to us; and in the course of nine or ten days we made this island, to our great joy; and the next day after we came safe to Montserrat. Many were surprised when they heard of my conducting the sloop into the port, and I now obtained a new appellation, and was called Captain. This elated me not a little, and it was quite flattering to my vanity to be thus styled by as high a title as any free man in this place possessed. When the death of the captain became known, he was much regretted by all who knew him; for he was a man universally respected. At the same time the sable captain lost no fame;[1] for the success I had met with increased the affection of my friends in no small measure.

from CHAPTER 8

The author, to oblige Mr. King, once more embarks for Georgia in one of his vessels— A new captain is appointed—They sail, and steer a new course—Three remarkable dreams—The vessel is shipwrecked on the Bahama bank, but the crew are preserved,

---

1 *the sable captain lost no fame* The dark-skinned captain (i.e., Equiano himself) emerged with an enhanced reputation.

principally by means of the author—He sets out from the island with the captain, in a small boat, in quest of a ship—Their distress—Meet with a wrecker—Sail for Providence—Are overtaken again by a terrible storm, and are all near perishing —Arrive at New Providence—The author, after some time, sails from thence to Georgia—Meets with another storm, and is obliged to put back and refit—Arrives at Georgia—Meets new impositions—Two white men attempt to kidnap him— Officiates as a parson at a funeral ceremony—Bids adieu to Georgia, and sails for Martinico.

... We stayed in New Providence[1] about seventeen or eighteen days; during which time I met with many friends, who gave me encouragement to stay there with them: but I declined it; though, had not my heart been fixed on England, I should have stayed, as I liked the place extremely, and there were some free black people here who were very happy, and we passed our time pleasantly together, with the melodious sound of the catguts,[2] under the lime and lemon trees. At length Captain Phillips hired a sloop to carry him and some of the slaves that he could not sell to Georgia; and I agreed to go with him in this vessel, meaning now to take my farewell of that place. When the vessel was ready, we all embarked; and I took my leave of New Providence, not without regret. We sailed about four o'clock in the morning, with a fair wind, for Georgia; and about eleven o'clock the same morning a short and sudden gale sprung up and blew away most of our sails; and, as we were still amongst the keys, in a very few minutes it dashed the sloop against the rocks. Luckily for us the water was deep; and the sea was not so angry but that, after having for some time laboured hard, and being many in number, we were saved through God's mercy; and, by using our greatest exertions, we got the vessel off. The next day we returned to Providence, where we soon got her again refitted. Some of the people swore that we had spells set upon us by somebody in Montserrat; and others that we had witches and wizards amongst the poor helpless slaves; and that we never should arrive safe at Georgia. But these things did not deter me; I said, "Let us again face the winds and seas, and swear not, but trust to God, and he will deliver us." We therefore once more set sail; and, with hard labour, in seven days' time arrived safe at Georgia.

After our arrival we went up to the town of Savannah; and the same evening I went to a friend's house to lodge, whose name was Mosa, a black man. We were very happy at meeting each other; and after supper we had a light till it was between nine and ten o'clock at night. About that time the watch or patrol came by; and, discerning a light in the house, they knocked at the door: we opened it; and they came in and sat down, and drank some punch with us:

---

1 *New Providence* The largest of the Bahama Islands.
2 *the melodious sound of the catguts* Catgut was commonly used to make strings for stringed instruments (such as fiddles).

they also begged some limes of me, as they understood I had some, which I readily gave them. A little after this they told me I must go to the watch-house with them: this surprised me a good deal, after our kindness to them; and I asked them, why so? They said that all negroes who had light in their houses after nine o'clock were to be taken into custody, and either pay some dollars or be flogged. Some of those people knew that I was a free man; but, as the man of the house was not free, and had his master to protect him, they did not take the same liberty with him they did with me. I told them that I was a free man, and just arrived from Providence; that we were not making any noise, and that I was not a stranger in that place, but was very well known there: "Besides," said I, "what will you do with me?"—"That you shall see," replied they, "but you must go to the watch-house with us." Now whether they meant to get money from me or not I was at a loss to know; but I thought immediately of the oranges and limes at Santa Cruz: and seeing that nothing would pacify them I went with them to the watch-house, where I remained during the night. Early the next morning these imposing ruffians flogged a negro man and woman that they had in the watch-house, and then they told me that I must be flogged too. I asked why? and if there was no law for free men? And told them if there was I would have it put in force against them. But this only exasperated them the more; and instantly they swore they would serve[1] me as Doctor Perkins had done; and they were going to lay violent hands on me; when one of them, more humane than the rest, said that as I was a free man they could not justify stripping me by law. I then immediately sent for Doctor Brady, who was known to be an honest and worthy man; and on his coming to my assistance they let me go.

This was not the only disagreeable incident I met with while I was in this place; for, one day, while I was a little way out of the town of Savannah, I was beset by two white men, who meant to play their usual tricks with me in the way of kidnapping. As soon as these men accosted me, one of them said to the other, "This is the very fellow we are looking for that you lost": and the other swore immediately that I was the identical person. On this they made up to me, and were about to handle me; but I told them to be still and keep off; for I had seen those kind of tricks played upon other free blacks, and they must not think to serve me so. At this they paused a little, and one said to the other—it will not do; and the other answered that I talked too good English. I replied, I believed I did; and I had also with me a revengeful stick equal to the occasion; and my mind was likewise good. Happily however it was not used; and, after we had talked together a little in this manner, the rogues left me. I stayed in Savannah some time, anxiously trying to get to Montserrat once more to see

---

1   serve   Treat.

Mr. King, my old master, and then to take a final farewell of the American quarter of the globe. At last I met with a sloop called the *Speedwell*, Captain John Bunton, which belonged to Grenada, and was bound to Martinico, a French island, with a cargo of rice, and I shipped myself on board of her. Before I left Georgia a black woman, who had a child lying dead, being very tenacious of the church burial service,[1] and not able to get any white person to perform it, applied to me for that purpose. I told her I was no parson; and besides, that the service over the dead did not affect the soul. This, however, did not satisfy her; she still urged me very hard: I therefore complied with her earnest entreaties, and at last consented to act the parson for the first time in my life. As she was much respected, there was a great company both of white and black people at the grave. I then accordingly assumed my new vocation, and performed the funeral ceremony to the satisfaction of all present; after which I bade adieu to Georgia, and sailed for Martinico.

from CHAPTER 9

The author arrives at Martinico—Meets with new difficulties—Gets to Montserrat, where he takes leave of his old master, and sails for England—Meets Capt. Pascal—Learns the French horn—Hires himself with Doctor Irving, where he learns to freshen sea water—Leaves the doctor, and goes a voyage to Turkey and Portugal; and afterwards goes a voyage to Grenada, and another to Jamaica—Returns to the Doctor, and they embark together on a voyage to the North Pole, with the Hon. Capt. Phipps—Some account of that voyage, and the dangers the author was in—He returns to England.

I thus took a final leave of Georgia; for the treatment I had received in it disgusted me very much against the place; and when I left it and sailed for Martinico I determined never more to revisit it. My new captain conducted his vessel safer than my former one; and, after an agreeable voyage, we got safe to our intended port. While I was on this island I went about a good deal, and found it very pleasant: in particular I admired the town of St. Pierre, which is the principal one in the island, and built more like an European town than any I had seen in the West Indies. In general also, slaves were better treated, had more holidays, and looked better than those in the English islands. After we had done our business here, I wanted my discharge, which was necessary; for it was then the month of May, and I wished much to be at Montserrat to bid farewell to Mr. King, and all my other friends there, in time to sail for Old England in the July fleet. ...

---

1   *very tenacious of the church burial service*   Determined to have a church burial service for her child.

We ... set sail, and the next day, the 23d, I arrived at the wished-for place, after an absence of six months, in which I had more than once experienced the delivering hand of Providence, when all human means of escaping destruction seemed hopeless. I saw my friends with a gladness of heart which was increased by my absence and the dangers I had escaped, and I was received with great friendship by them all, but particularly by Mr. King, to whom I related the fate of his sloop, the *Nancy*, and the causes of her being wrecked. I now learned with extreme sorrow, that his house was washed away during my absence, by the bursting of a pond at the top of a mountain that was opposite the town of Plymouth. It swept [a] great part of the town away, and Mr. King lost a great deal of property from the inundation, and nearly his life. When I told him I intended to go to London that season, and that I had come to visit him before my departure, the good man expressed a great deal of affection for me, and sorrow that I should leave him, and warmly advised me to stay there; insisting, as I was much respected by all the gentlemen in the place, that I might do very well, and in a short time have land and slaves of my own. I thanked him for this instance of his friendship; but, as I wished very much to be in London, I declined remaining any longer there, and begged he would excuse me. I then requested he would be kind enough to give me a certificate of my behaviour while in his service, which he very readily complied with, and gave me the following:

Montserrat, January 26, 1767.
The bearer hereof, Gustavus Vassa, was my slave for upwards of three years, during which he has always behaved himself well, and discharged his duty with honesty and assiduity.

Robert King
To all whom this may concern

Having obtained this, I parted from my kind master, after many sincere professions of gratitude and regard, and prepared for my departure for London. I immediately agreed to go with one Capt. John Hamer, for seven guineas, the passage to London, on board a ship called the *Andromache*; and on the 24th and 25th I had free dances, as they are called, with some of my countrymen, previous to my setting off; after which I took leave of all my friends, and on the 26th I embarked for London, exceedingly glad to see myself once more on board of a ship; and still more so, in steering the course I had long wished for. With a light heart I bade Montserrat farewell, and never had my feet on it since; and with it I bade adieu to the sound of the cruel whip, and all other dreadful instruments of torture; adieu to the offensive sight of the violated chastity of the sable females, which has too often accosted my eyes; adieu to oppressions (although to me less severe than most of my countrymen); and adieu to the angry howling, dashing surfs. I wished for a grateful and thankful heart to praise the Lord God on high for all his mercies!

We had a most prosperous voyage, and, at the end of seven weeks, arrived at Cherry-Garden stairs.[1] Thus were my longing eyes once more gratified with a sight of London, after having been absent from it above four years. I immediately received my wages, and I never had earned seven guineas so quick in my life before; I had thirty-seven guineas in all, when I got cleared of the ship. I now entered upon a scene, quite new to me, but full of hope.

In this situation my first thoughts were to look out for some of my former friends, and amongst the first of those were the Miss Guerins. As soon, therefore, as I had regaled myself I went in quest of those kind ladies, whom I was very impatient to see; and with some difficulty and perseverance, I found them at May's-hill, Greenwich. They were most agreeably surprised to see me, and I quite overjoyed at meeting with them. I told them my history, at which they expressed great wonder, and freely acknowledged it did their cousin, Capt. Pascal, no honour. He then visited there frequently; and I met him four or five days after in Greenwich Park. When he saw me he appeared a good deal surprised, and asked me how I came back? I answered, "In a ship." To which he replied dryly, "I suppose you did not walk back to London on the water." As I saw, by his manner, that he did not seem to be sorry for his behaviour to me, and that I had not much reason to expect any favour from him, I told him that he had used me very ill, after I had been such a faithful servant to him for so many years; on which, without saying any more, he turned about and went away. A few days after this I met Capt. Pascal at Miss Guerin's house, and asked him for my prize-money. He said there was none due to me; for, if my prize-money had been £10,000, he had a right to it all. I told him I was informed otherwise; on which he bade me defiance; and, in a bantering tone, desired me to commence a lawsuit against him for it: "There are lawyers enough," said he, "that will take the cause in hand, and you had better try it." I told him then that I would try it, which enraged him very much; however, out of regard to the ladies, I remained still, and never made any farther demand of my right.

Sometime afterwards these friendly ladies asked me what I meant to do with myself, and how they could assist me. I thanked them, and said, if they pleased, I would be their servant; but if not, as I had thirty-seven guineas, which would support me for some time, I would be much obliged to them to recommend me to some person who would teach me a business whereby I

---

1   *Cherry-Garden stairs* Landing area on the Thames, in London's east end.

might earn my living. They answered me very politely, that they were sorry it did not suit them to take me as their servant, and asked me what business I should like to learn? I said, hair-dressing. They then promised to assist me in this; and soon after they recommended me to a gentleman whom I had known before, one Capt. O'Hara, who treated me with much kindness, and procured me a master, a hair-dresser, in Coventry-court, Haymarket, with whom he placed me. I was with this man from September till the February following.

In that time we had a neighbour in the same court who taught the French horn. He used to blow it so well that I was charmed with it, and agreed with him to teach me to blow it. Accordingly he took me in hand, and began to instruct me, and I soon learned all the three parts. I took great delight in blowing on this instrument, the evenings being long; and besides that, I was fond of it. I did not like to be idle, and it filled up my vacant hours innocently.

At this time also I agreed with the Rev. Mr. Gregory, who lived in the same court, where he kept an academy and an evening-school, to improve me in arithmetic. This he did as far as barter and alligation; so that all the time I was there I was entirely employed. In February 1768 I hired myself to Dr. Charles Irving, in Pall Mall, so celebrated for his successful experiments in making sea water fresh; and here I had plenty of hair-dressing to improve my hand. This gentleman was an excellent master; he was exceedingly kind and good tempered; and allowed me in the evenings to attend my schools, which I esteemed a great blessing; therefore I thanked God and him for it, and used all my diligence to improve the opportunity.

This diligence and attention recommended me to the notice and care of my three preceptors, who on their parts bestowed a great deal of pains in my instruction, and besides were all very kind to me. My wages, however, which were by two thirds less than I ever had in my life (for I had only £12 per annum) I soon found would not be sufficient to defray this extraordinary expense of masters, and my own necessary expenses; my old thirty-seven guineas had by this time worn all away to one. I thought it best, therefore, to try the sea again in quest of more money, as I had been bred to it, and had hitherto found the profession of it successful. I had also a very great desire to see Turkey, and I now determined to gratify it. Accordingly, in the month of May, 1768, I told the doctor my wish to go to sea again, to which he made no opposition; and we parted on friendly terms.

The same day I went into the city in quest of a master. I was extremely fortunate in my inquiry; for I soon heard of a gentleman who had a ship going to Italy and Turkey, and he wanted a man who could dress hair well. I was overjoyed at this, and went immediately on board of his ship, as I had been directed, which I found to be fitted up with great taste, and I already foreboded no small pleasure in sailing in her. Not finding the gentleman on board, I was directed to his lodgings, where I met with him the next day, and gave him a specimen of my dressing. He liked it so well that he hired me immediately, so that I was perfectly happy; for the ship, master, and voyage, were entirely to my mind. The ship was called the *Delawar*, and my master's name was John Jolly, a neat smart good-humoured man, just such a one as I wished to serve. We sailed from England in July following, and our voyage was extremely pleasant. We went to Villa Franca, Nice, and Leghorn;[1] and in all these places I was charmed with the richness and beauty of the countries, and struck with the elegant buildings with which they abound. We had always in them plenty of extraordinary good wines and rich fruits, which I was very fond of; and I had frequent occasions of gratifying both my taste and curiosity; for my captain always lodged on shore in those places, which afforded me opportunities to see the country around. I also learned navigation of the mate, which I was very fond of. When we left Italy we had delightful sailing among the Archipelago islands, and from thence to Smyrna in Turkey. This is a very ancient city; the houses are built of stone, and most of them have graves adjoining to them; so that they sometimes present the appearance of church-yards. Provisions are very plentiful in this city, and good wine less than a penny a pint. The grapes, pomegranates, and many other fruits, were also the richest and largest I ever tasted. The natives are well looking and strong made, and treated me always with great civility. In general, I believe they are fond of black people; and several of them gave me pressing invitations to stay amongst them, although they keep the franks, or Christians,[2] separate, and do not suffer them to dwell immediately amongst them. I was astonished in not seeing women in any of their shops, and very rarely any in the streets; and whenever I did they were covered with a veil from head to foot, so that I could not see their faces, except when any of them out of curiosity uncovered them to look at me, which they sometimes did. I was surprised to see how the Greeks are, in some measure, kept under by the Turks,[3] as the negroes are in the West Indies by the white people. The less refined Greeks, as I have already hinted, dance here in the same manner as we do in my nation. On the whole, during our stay here, which was about five months, I liked the place and the Turks extremely well. I could not help observing one very remarkable circumstance there: the tails of the sheep are flat, and so very large, that I have known the tail even of a lamb to weigh from eleven to thirteen pounds. The

---

1 *Leghorn* Livorno (a seaport in northwest Italy).

2 *franks, or Christians* "Frank," originally a term for members of the ancient tribes that inhabited what is now France, came in medieval times to be widely used in the Middle East as a term for Western European Christians; this usage persisted into the eighteenth century and beyond.

3 *the Greeks … the Turks* Greece was under the control of the Turkish Ottoman Empire from late medieval times until Greek independence was declared in 1832.

fat of them is very white and rich, and is excellent in puddings, for which it is much used. Our ship being at length richly loaded with silk, and other articles, we sailed for England.

In May 1769, soon after our return from Turkey, our ship made a delightful voyage to Oporto in Portugal, where we arrived at the time of the carnival.[1] On our arrival, there were sent on board to us thirty-six articles to observe, with very heavy penalties if we should break any of them; and none of us even dared to go on board any other vessel or on shore till the Inquisition had sent on board and searched for every thing illegal, especially bibles.[2] Such as were produced, and certain other things, were sent on shore till the ships were going away; and any person in whose custody a bible was found concealed was to be imprisoned and flogged, and sent into slavery for ten years. I saw here many very magnificent sights, particularly the garden of Eden, where many of the clergy and laity went in procession in their several orders with the Host,[3] and sung Te Deum.[4] I had a great curiosity to go into some of their churches, but could not gain admittance without using the necessary sprinkling of holy water at my entrance. From curiosity, and a wish to be holy, I therefore complied with this ceremony, but its virtues were lost on me, for I found myself nothing the better for it. This place abounds with plenty of all kinds of provisions. The town is well built and pretty, and commands a fine prospect. Our ship having taken in a load of wine, and other commodities, we sailed for London, and arrived in July following. Our next voyage was to the Mediterranean. The ship was again got ready, and we sailed in September for Genoa. This is one of the finest cities I ever saw; some of the edifices were of beautiful marble, and made a most noble appearance; and many had very curious fountains before them. The churches were rich and magnificent, and curiously adorned both in the inside and out. But all this grandeur was in my eyes disgraced by the galley slaves,[5] whose condition both there and in other parts of Italy is truly piteous and wretched. After we had stayed there some weeks, during which we bought many different things which we wanted, and got them very cheap, we sailed to Naples, a charming city, and remarkably clean. The bay is the most beautiful I ever saw; the moles for shipping are

---

1   *the carnival*   Probably the festival of São João (St. John), a major celebration held in Porto in June.

2   *Inquisition ... bibles*   From the thirteenth until the early nineteenth centuries the Roman Catholic church operated a set of institutions known collectively as the "Holy Inquisition," the purpose of which was to combat heresy. Roman Catholic practice did not encourage private study of the Bible by individuals; preferred practice was for the clergy to interpret the Bible to the laity. (Protestant denominations, in contrast, encouraged individuals to read and study the Bible on their own.)

3   *the Host*   Communion wafers.

4   *Te Deum*   Latin: To God. The *Te Deum* prayer is recited or sung during Catholic services.

5   *galley slaves*   Galleys were ships propelled either by sail or by oars—with the rowing done by enslaved people (generally, war captives).

excellent. I thought it extraordinary to see grand operas acted here on Sunday nights, and even attended by their majesties. I too, like these great ones, went to those sights, and vainly served God in the day while I thus served mammon effectually at night. While we remained here there happened an eruption of Mount Vesuvius, of which I had a perfect view. It was extremely awful; and we were so near that the ashes from it used to be thick on our deck.

After we had transacted our business at Naples we sailed with a fair wind once more for Smyrna, where we arrived in December. A seraskier[1] or officer took a liking to me here, and wanted me to stay, and offered me two wives; however I refused the temptation. The merchants here travel in caravans or large companies. I have seen many caravans from India, with some hundreds of camels, laden with different goods. The people of these caravans are quite brown. Among other articles, they brought with them a great quantity of locusts,[2] which are a kind of pulse, sweet and pleasant to the palate, and in shape resembling French beans, but longer. Each kind of goods is sold in a street by itself, and I always found the Turks very honest in their dealings. They let no Christians into their mosques or churches, for which I was very sorry; as I was always fond of going to see the different modes of worship of the people wherever I went. The plague broke out while we were in Smyrna, and we stopped taking goods into the ship till it was over. She was then richly laden, and we sailed in about March 1770 for England. One day in our passage we met with an accident which was near burning the ship. A black cook, in melting some fat, overset the pan into the fire under the deck, which imme-diately began to blaze, and the flame went up very high under the foretop. With the fright the poor cook became almost white, and altogether speechless. Happily however we got the fire out without doing much mischief. After vari-ous delays in this passage, which was tedious, we arrived in Standgate Creek[3] in July; and, at the latter end of the year, some new event occurred, so that my noble captain, the ship, and I all separated.

In April 1771 I shipped myself as a steward with Capt. Wm. Robertson of the ship *Grenada Planter*, once more to try my fortune in the West Indies; and we sailed from London for Madeira, Barbados, and the Grenades. ...

[At the end of the voyage] we arrived in England, and I got clear of this ship. But, being still of a roving disposition, and desirous of seeing as many different parts of the world as I could, I shipped myself soon after, in the same year, as steward on board of a fine large ship, called the *Jamaica*, Captain David Watt; and we sailed from England in December 1771 for Nevis and Jamaica. I found

---

1   *seraskier*   High-ranking military official.
2   *locusts*   I.e., legumes from the carob tree, also known in English as the locust tree, which grows in the Mediterranean region and the Middle East.
3   *Standgate Creek*   Harbor located near the mouth of the Thames in southeast England.

Jamaica to be a very fine large island, well peopled, and the most considerable of the West India islands. There was a vast number of negroes here, whom I found as usual exceedingly imposed upon by the white people, and the slaves punished as in the other islands. There are negroes whose business it is to flog slaves; they go about to different people for employment, and the usual pay is from one to four bits. I saw many cruel punishments inflicted on the slaves in the short time I stayed here. In particular I was present when a poor fellow was tied up and kept hanging by the wrists at some distance from the ground, and then some half hundred weights were fixed to his ankles, in which posture he was flogged most unmercifully. There were also, as I heard, two different masters noted for cruelty on the island, who had staked up two negroes naked, and in two hours the vermin stung them to death. I heard a gentleman I well knew tell my captain that he passed sentence on a negro man to be burnt alive for attempting to poison an overseer. I pass over numerous other instances, in order to relieve the reader by a milder scene of roguery. Before I had been long on the island, one Mr. Smith at Port Morant bought goods of me to the amount of twenty-five pounds sterling; but when I demanded payment from him, he was going each time to beat me, and threatened that he would put me in jail. One time he would say I was going to set his house on fire, at another he would swear I was going to run away with his slaves. I was astonished at this usage from a person who was in the situation of a gentleman, but I had no alternative; I was therefore obliged to submit. When I came to Kingston, I was surprised to see the number of Africans who were assembled together on Sundays; particularly at a large commodious place, called Spring Path. Here each different nation of Africa meet and dance after the manner of their own country. They still retain most of their native customs: they bury their dead, and put victuals, pipes and tobacco, and other things, in the grave with the corpse, in the same manner as in Africa. Our ship having got her loading we sailed for London, where we arrived in the August following. On my return to London, I waited on my old and good master, Dr. Irving, who made me an offer of his service again. Being now tired of the sea I gladly accepted it. I was very happy in living with this gentleman once more; during which time we were daily employed in reducing old Neptune's dominions by purifying the briny element and making it fresh. Thus I went on till May 1773, when I was roused by the sound of fame, to seek new adventures, and to find, towards the North Pole, what our Creator never intended we should, a passage to India. An expedition was now fitting out to explore a north-east passage, conducted by the Honourable John Constantine Phipps, since Lord Mulgrave, in his Majesty's sloop of war, the *Race Horse*. My master being anxious for the reputation of this adventure, we therefore prepared everything for our voyage, and I attended him on board the *Race Horse*, the 24th day of May

1773. We proceeded to Sheerness, where we were joined by his Majesty's sloop the *Carcass*, commanded by Captain Lutwidge. On the 4th of June we sailed towards our destined place, the pole; and on the 15th of the same month we were off Shetland. ...

The weather now became extremely cold; and as we sailed between north and east, which was our course, we saw many very high and curious mountains of ice; and also a great number of very large whales, which used to come close to our ship, and blow the water up to a very great height in the air. One morning we had vast quantities of sea-horses about the ship, which neighed exactly like any other horses. We fired some harpoon guns amongst them, in order to take some, but we could not get any. The 30th, the captain of a Greenland ship came on board, and told us of three ships that were lost in the ice; however, we still held on our course till July the 11th, when we were stopped by one compact impenetrable body of ice. We ran along it from east to west above ten degrees; and on the 27th we got as far north as 80, 37; and in 19 or 20 degrees east longitude from London. On the 29th and 30th of July we saw one continued plain of smooth unbroken ice, bounded only by the horizon; and we fastened to a piece of ice that was eight yards eleven inches thick. We had generally sunshine, and constant daylight; which gave cheerfulness and novelty to the whole of this striking, grand, and uncommon scene; and, to heighten it still more, the reflection of the sun from the ice gave the clouds a most beautiful appearance. We killed many different animals at this time, and among the rest nine bears. Though they had nothing in their paunches but water yet they were all very fat. We used to decoy them to the ship sometimes by burning feathers or skins. I thought them coarse eating, but some of the ship's company relished them very much. ...

Our deplorable condition, which kept up the constant apprehension of our perishing in the ice, brought me gradually to think of eternity in such a manner as I never had done before. I had the fears of death hourly upon me, and shuddered at the thoughts of meeting the grim king of terrors in the natural state I then was in, and was exceedingly doubtful of a happy eternity if I should die in it. I had no hopes of my life being prolonged for any time; for we saw that our existence could not be long on the ice after leaving the ships, which were now out of sight, and some miles from the boats. Our appearance now became truly lamentable; pale dejection seized every countenance; many, who had been before blasphemers, in this our distress began to call on the good God of heaven for his help; and in the time of our utter need he heard us, and against hope or human probability delivered us!

It was the eleventh day of the ships being thus fastened, and the fourth of our drawing the boats in this manner, that the wind changed to the E.N.E. The weather immediately became mild, and the ice broke towards the sea, which was to the S.W. of us. Many of us on this got on board again, and with all our might we hove the ships into every open water we could find, and made all the sail on them in our power; and now, having a prospect of success, we made signals for the boats and the remainder of the people. This seemed to us like a reprieve from death; and happy was the man who could first get on board of any ship, or the first boat he could meet. We then proceeded in this manner till we got into the open water again, which we accomplished in about thirty hours, to our infinite joy and gladness of heart. As soon as we were out of danger we came to anchor and refitted; and on the 19th of August we sailed from this uninhabited extremity of the world, where the inhospitable climate affords neither food nor shelter, and not a tree or shrub of any kind grows amongst its barren rocks; but all is one desolate and expanded waste of ice, which even the constant beams of the sun for six months in the year cannot penetrate or dissolve.

The sun now being on the decline, the days shortened as we sailed to the southward; and, on the 28th, in latitude 73, it was dark by ten o'clock at night. September the 10th, in latitude 58–59, we met a very severe gale of wind and high seas, and shipped a great deal of water in the space of ten hours. This made us work exceedingly hard at all our pumps a whole day; and one sea, which struck the ship with more force than anything I ever met with of the kind before, laid her under water for some time, so that we thought she would have gone down. Two boats were washed from the booms, and the long-boat from the chucks: all other moveable things on the deck were also washed away, among which were many curious things of different kinds which we had brought from Greenland; and we were obliged, in order to lighten the ship, to toss some of our guns overboard. We saw a ship, at the same time, in very great distress, and her masts were gone; but we were unable to assist her. We now lost sight of the *Carcass* till the 26th, when we saw land about Orfordness,[1] off which place she joined us. From thence we sailed for London, and on the 30th came up to Deptford. And thus ended our Arctic voyage, to the no small joy of all on board, after having been absent four months; in which time, at the imminent hazard of our lives, we explored nearly as far towards the Pole as 81 degrees north, and 20 degrees east longitude; being much farther, by all accounts, than any navigator had ever ventured before; in which we fully proved the impracticability of finding a passage that way to India.

---

1   *Orfordness*   Near Ipswich, on the east coast of England.

from Chapter 10

The author leaves Doctor Irving and engages on board a Turkey ship—Account of a black man's being kidnapped on board and sent to the West Indies, and the author's fruitless endeavours to procure his freedom—Some account of the manner of the author's conversion to the faith of Jesus Christ.

Our voyage to the North Pole being ended, I returned to London with Doctor Irving, with whom I continued for some time, during which I began seriously to reflect on the dangers I had escaped, particularly those of my last voyage, which made a lasting impression on my mind, and, by the grace of God, proved afterwards a mercy to me; it caused me to reflect deeply on my eternal state, and to seek the Lord with full purpose of heart ere it was too late. I rejoiced greatly; and heartily thanked the Lord for directing me to London, where I was determined to work out my own salvation, and in so doing procure a title to heaven, being the result of a mind blended by ignorance and sin.

In process of time I left my master, Doctor Irving, the purifier of waters, and lodged in Coventry Court, Haymarket, where I was continually oppressed and much concerned about the salvation of my soul, and was determined (in my own strength) to be a first-rate Christian. I used every means for this purpose; and, not being able to find any person amongst my acquaintance that agreed with me in point of religion, or, in scripture language, "that would shew me any good"; I was much dejected, and knew not where to seek relief; however, I first frequented the neighbouring churches, St. James's, and others, two or three times a day, for many weeks: still I came away dissatisfied; something was wanting that I could not obtain, and I really found more heartfelt relief in reading my bible at home than in attending the church; and, being resolved to be saved, I pursued other methods still. First I went among the Quakers, where the word of God was neither read or preached, so that I remained as much in the dark as ever. I then searched into the Roman Catholic principles, but was not in the least satisfied. At length I had recourse to the Jews, which availed me nothing, for the fear of eternity daily harassed my mind, and I knew not where to seek shelter from the wrath to come. However, this was my conclusion, at all events—to read the four evangelists, and whatever sect or party I found adhering thereto such I would join. Thus I went on heavily without any guide to direct me the way that leadeth to eternal life. I asked different people questions about the manner of going to heaven, and was told different ways. Here I was much staggered, and could not find any at that time more righteous than myself, or indeed so much inclined to devotion. I thought we should not all be saved (this is agreeable to the holy scriptures), nor would all be damned. I found none among the circle of my acquaintance that kept wholly the ten commandments.

So righteous was I in my own eyes, that I was convinced I excelled many of them in that point, by keeping eight out of ten; and finding those who in general termed themselves Christians not so honest or so good in their morals as the Turks, I really thought the Turks were in a safer way of salvation than my neighbours: so that between hopes and fears I went on, and the chief comforts I enjoyed were in the musical French horn, which I then practised, and also dressing of hair. Such was my situation some months, experiencing the dishonesty of many people here. I determined at last to set out for Turkey, and there to end my days. It was now early in the spring 1774. I sought for a master, and found a captain John Hughes, commander of a ship called *Anglicania*, fitting out in the River Thames, and bound to Smyrna in Turkey. I shipped myself with him as a steward; at the same time, I recommended to him a very clever black man, John Annis, as a cook. This man was on board the ship near two months doing his duty: he had formerly lived many years with Mr. William Kirkpatrick, a gentleman of the island of St. Kitts, from whom he parted by consent, though he afterwards tried many schemes to inveigle the poor man. He had applied to many captains who traded to St. Kitts to trepan him; and when all their attempts and schemes of kidnapping proved abortive, Mr. Kirkpatrick came to our ship at Union Stairs[1] on Easter Monday, April the fourth, with two wherry boats and six men, having learned that the man was on board; and tied, and forcibly took him away from the ship, in the presence of the crew and the chief mate, who had detained him after he had notice to come away. I believe that this was a combined piece of business: but, at any rate, it certainly reflected great disgrace on the mate and captain also, who, although they had desired the oppressed man to stay on board, yet he did not in the least assist to recover him, or pay me a farthing of his wages, which was about five pounds. I proved the only friend he had, who attempted to regain him his liberty if possible, having known the want of liberty myself. I sent as soon as I could to Gravesend, and got knowledge of the ship in which he was; but unluckily she had sailed the first tide after he was put on board.

My intention was then immediately to apprehend Mr. Kirkpatrick, who was about setting off for Scotland; and, having obtained a habeas corpus for him, and got a tipstaff to go with me to St. Paul's church-yard, where he lived, he, suspecting something of this kind, set a watch to look out. My being known to them occasioned me to use the following deception: I whitened my face, that they might not know me, and this had its desired effect. He did not go out of his house that night, and next morning I contrived a well plotted stratagem

---

1 *Union Stairs* Landing area in the docks district of East London.

notwithstanding he had a gentleman in his house to personate him. My direction to the tipstaff, who got admittance into the house, was to conduct him to a judge, according to the writ. When he came there, his plea was, that he had not the body in custody, on which he was admitted to bail. I proceeded immediately to that philanthropist, Granville Sharp,[1] Esq. who received me with the utmost kindness, and gave me every instruction that was needful on the occasion. I left him in full hope that I should gain the unhappy man his liberty, with the warmest sense of gratitude towards Mr. Sharp for his kindness; but, alas! my attorney proved unfaithful; he took my money, lost me many months employ, and did not do the least good in the cause: and when the poor man arrived at St. Kitts, he was, according to custom, staked to the ground with four pins through a cord, two on his wrists, and two on his ankles, was cut and flogged most unmercifully, and afterwards loaded cruelly with irons about his neck. I had two very moving letters from him, while he was in this situation; and also was told of it by some very respectable families now in London, who saw him in St. Kitts, in the same state in which he remained till kind death released him out of the hands of his tyrants.

During this disagreeable business I was under strong convictions of sin, and thought that my state was worse than any man's; my mind was unaccountably disturbed; I often wished for death, though at the same time convinced I was altogether unprepared for that awful summons. Suffering much by villains in the late cause, and being much concerned about the state of my soul, these things (but particularly the latter) brought me very low; so that I became a burden to myself, and viewed all things around me as emptiness and vanity, which could give no satisfaction to a troubled conscience. I was again determined to go to Turkey, and resolved, at that time, never more to return to England. I engaged as steward on board a Turkeyman (the *Wester Hall*, Capt. Linna); but was prevented by means of my late captain, Mr. Hughes, and others. All this appeared to be against me, and the only comfort I then experienced was, in reading the holy scriptures, where I saw that "there is no new thing under the sun," Eccles. 1.9; and what was appointed for me I must submit to. Thus I continued to travel in much heaviness, and frequently murmured against the Almighty, particularly in his providential dealings; and, awful to think! I began to blaspheme, and wished often to be anything but a human being. In these severe conflicts the Lord answered me by awful "visions of the night, when deep sleep falleth upon men, in slumberings upon the bed," Job xxxiii. 15. He was pleased, in much mercy, to give me to see, and in some measure to understand, the great and awful scene of the judgment-day, that "no unclean

---

1 *Granville Sharp* Sharp (1735–1813) was one of the leading British figures in the campaign to abolish the slave trade.

person, no unholy thing, can enter into the kingdom of God," Eph. v. 5. I would then, if it had been possible, have changed my nature with the meanest worm on the earth; and was ready to say to the mountains and rocks "fall on me," Rev. vi. 16; but all in vain. I then requested the divine Creator that he would grant me a small space of time to repent of my follies and vile iniquities, which I felt were grievous. The Lord, in his manifold mercies, was pleased to grant my request, and being yet in a state of time, the sense of God's mercies was so great on my mind when I awoke, that my strength entirely failed me for many minutes, and I was exceedingly weak. This was the first spiritual mercy I ever was sensible of, and being on praying ground, as soon as I recovered a little strength, and got out of bed and dressed myself, I invoked Heaven from my inmost soul, and fervently begged that God would never again permit me to blaspheme his most holy name. The Lord, who is long-suffering, and full of compassion to such poor rebels as we are, condescended to hear and answer. I felt that I was altogether unholy, and saw clearly what a bad use I had made of the faculties I was endowed with; they were given me to glorify God with; I thought, therefore, I had better want them here, and enter into life eternal, than abuse them and be cast into hell fire. I prayed to be directed, if there were any holier than those with whom I was acquainted, that the Lord would point them out to me. I appealed to the Searcher of hearts, whether I did not wish to love him more, and serve him better. Notwithstanding all this, the reader may easily discern, if he is a believer, that I was still in nature's darkness. At length I hated the house in which I lodged, because God's most holy name was blasphemed in it; then I saw the word of God verified, viz. "Before they call, I will answer; and while they are yet speaking, I will hear."[1]

I had a great desire to read the bible the whole day at home; but not having a convenient place for retirement, I left the house in the day, rather than stay amongst the wicked ones; and that day as I was walking, it pleased God to direct me to a house where there was an old sea-faring man, who experienced much of the love of God shed abroad in his heart. He began to discourse with me; and, as I desired to love the Lord, his conversation rejoiced me greatly; and indeed I had never heard before the love of Christ to believers set forth in such a manner, and in so clear a point of view. ...

When the wished-for hour came I went, and happily the old man was there, who kindly seated me, as he belonged to the place. I was much astonished to see the place filled with people, and no signs of eating and drinking. There were many ministers in the company. At last they began by giving out hymns, and between the singing the minister engaged in prayer; in short, I knew not what to make of this sight, having never seen anything of the kind

---

1 *Before ... hear* See Isaiah 65.24.

in my life before now. Some of the guests began to speak their experience, agreeable to what I read in the Scriptures; much was said by every speaker of the providence of God, and his unspeakable mercies, to each of them. This I knew in a great measure, and could most heartily join them. But when they spoke of a future state, they seemed to be altogether certain of their calling and election of God; and that no one could ever separate them from the love of Christ, or pluck them out of his hands. This filled me with utter consternation, intermingled with admiration. I was so amazed as not to know what to think of the company; my heart was attracted and my affections were enlarged. I wished to be as happy as them, and was persuaded in my mind that they were different from the world "that lieth in wickedness," 1 John v. 19. Their language and singing, &c. did well harmonize; I was entirely overcome, and wished to live and die thus. Lastly, some persons in the place produced some neat baskets full of buns, which they distributed about; and each person communicated with his neighbour, and sipped water out of different mugs, which they handed about to all who were present. This kind of Christian fellowship I had never seen, nor ever thought of seeing on earth; it fully reminded me of what I had read in the holy scriptures, of the primitive Christians, who loved each other and broke bread. In partaking of it, even from house to house, this entertainment (which lasted about four hours) ended in singing and prayer. It was the first soul feast I ever was present at. This last twenty-four hours produced me things, spiritual and temporal, sleeping and waking, judgment and mercy, that I could not but admire the goodness of God, in directing the blind, blasphemous sinner in the path that he knew not of, even among the just; and instead of judgment he has shewed mercy, and will hear and answer the prayers and supplications of every returning prodigal:

> O! to grace how great a debtor
> Daily I'm constrained to be![1]

After this I was resolved to win Heaven if possible; and if I perished I thought it should be at the feet of Jesus, in praying to him for salvation. After having been an eye-witness to some of the happiness which attended those who feared God, I knew not how, with any propriety, to return to my lodgings, where the name of God was continually profaned, at which I felt the greatest horror. I paused in my mind for some time, not knowing what to do; whether to hire a bed elsewhere, or go home again. At last, fearing an evil report might arise, I went home, with a farewell to card-playing and vain jesting, &c. I saw that time was very short, eternity long, and very near, and I

---

1   *O ... to be*   The lines are from a Methodist hymn, "Come, Thou Font of Every Blessing."

viewed those persons alone blessed who were found ready at midnight call, or when the Judge of all, both quick and dead, cometh.

The next day I took courage, and went to Holborn, to see my new and worthy acquaintance, the old man, Mr. C——; he, with his wife, a gracious woman, were at work at silk weaving; they seemed mutually happy, and both quite glad to see me, and I more so to see them. I sat down, and we conversed much about soul matters, &c. Their discourse was amazingly delightful, edifying, and pleasant. I knew not at last how to leave this agreeable pair, till time summoned me away. As I was going they lent me a little book, entitled *The Conversion of an Indian*.[1] It was in questions and answers. The poor man came over the sea to London, to inquire after the Christians' God, who, (through rich mercy) he found, and had not his journey in vain. The above book was of great use to me, and at that time was a means of strengthening my faith; however, in parting, they both invited me to call on them when I pleased. This delighted me, and I took care to make all the improvement from it I could; and so far I thanked God for such company and desires. I prayed that the many evils I felt within might be done away, and that I might be weaned from my former carnal acquaintances. This was quickly heard and answered, and I was soon connected with those whom the scripture calls the excellent of the earth. I heard the gospel preached, and the thoughts of my heart and actions were laid open by the preachers, and the way of salvation by Christ alone was evidently set forth. Thus I went on happily for near two months; and I once heard, during this period, a reverend gentleman speak of a man who had departed this life in full assurance of his going to glory. I was much astonished at the assertion; and did very deliberately inquire how he could get at this knowledge. I was answered fully, agreeable to what I read in the oracles of truth; and was told also, that if I did not experience the new birth, and the pardon of my sins, through the blood of Christ, before I died, I could not enter the kingdom of heaven. I knew not what to think of this report, as I thought I kept eight commandments out of ten; then my worthy interpreter told me I did not do it, nor could I; and he added, that no man ever did or could keep the commandments, without offending in one point. I thought this sounded very strange, and puzzled me much for many weeks; for I thought it a hard saying. I then asked my friend, Mr. L——d, who was a clerk in a chapel, why the commandments of God were given, if we could not be saved by them? To which he replied, "The law is a schoolmaster to bring us to Christ," who alone could and did keep the commandments. ...

---

1   *The Conversion of an Indian*   The full title is *The Conversion of an Indian, in a Letter to a Friend*; the book was written by Laurence Harlow and published in London in 1774.

from CHAPTER II

The author embarks on board a ship bound for Cadiz [in March 1775]—Is near being shipwrecked—Goes to Malaga—Remarkable fine cathedral there—The author disputes with a popish priest—Picking up eleven miserable men at sea in returning to England—Engages again with Doctor Irving to accompany him to Jamaica and the Musquito Shore—Meets with an Indian prince on board—The author attempts to instruct him in the truths of the Gospel—Frustrated by the bad example of some in the ship—They arrive on the Musquito Shore with some slaves they purchased at Jamaica, and begin to cultivate a plantation—Some account of the manners and customs of the Musquito Indians—Successful device of the author's to quell a riot among them—Curious entertainment given by them to Doctor Irving and the author, who leaves the shore and goes for Jamaica—Is barbarously treated by a man with whom he engaged for his passage—Escapes and goes to the Musquito admiral, who treats him kindly—He gets another vessel and goes on board—Instances of bad treatment—Meets Doctor Irving—Gets to Jamaica—Is cheated by his captain—Leaves the Doctor and goes for England.

… When we had dispatched our business at Cadiz, we went to Gibraltar, and from thence to Malaga, a very pleasant and rich city, where there is one of the finest cathedrals I had ever seen. It had been above fifty years in building, as I heard, though it was not then quite finished; great part of the inside, however, was completed and highly decorated with the richest marble columns and many superb paintings; it was lighted occasionally by an amazing number of wax tapers of different sizes, some of which were as thick as a man's thigh; these, however, were only used on some of their grand festivals.

I was very much shocked at the custom of bull-baiting, and other diversions which prevailed here on Sunday evenings, to the great scandal of Christianity and morals. I used to express my abhorrence of it to a priest whom I met with. I had frequent contests about religion with the reverend father, in which he took great pains to make a proselyte of me to his church; and I no less to convert him to mine. On these occasions I used to produce my Bible, and shew him in what points his church erred. He then said he had been in England, and that every person there read the Bible, which was very wrong; but I answered him that Christ desired us to search the Scriptures. In his zeal for my conversion, he solicited me to go to one of the universities in Spain, and declared that I should have my education free; and told me, if I got myself made a priest, I might in time become even pope; and that Pope Benedict was a black man.[1] As I was ever desirous of learning, I paused for some time upon this temptation; and thought by being crafty I might catch some with

---

1   *Pope Benedict … black man*   Benedict XIV (1675–1758; pope from 1740 to 1758) was in fact white; Equiano's informant may well have confused Pope Benedict XIV with St. Benedict the Moor (1526–89).

guile; but I began to think that it would be only hypocrisy in me to embrace his offer, as I could not in conscience conform to the opinions of his church. I was therefore enabled to regard the word of God, which says, "Come out from amongst them," and refused Father Vincent's offer. So we parted without conviction on either side. ...

On the fifth of January [1776] we made Antigua and Montserrat, and ran along the rest of the islands: and on the fourteenth we arrived at Jamaica. One Sunday while we were there I took the Musquito Prince George to church, where he saw the sacrament administered. When we came out we saw all kinds of people, almost from the church door for the space of half a mile down to the waterside, buying and selling all kinds of commodities: and these acts afforded me great matter of exhortation to this youth, who was much astonished. Our vessel being ready to sail for the Musquito shore, I went with the Doctor on board a Guinea-man, to purchase some slaves to carry with us, and cultivate a plantation; and I chose them all my own countrymen. On the twelfth of February we sailed from Jamaica, and on the eighteenth arrived at the Musquito shore, at a place called Dupeupy. All our Indian guests now, after I had admonished them and a few cases of liquor given them by the Doctor, took an affectionate leave of us, and went ashore, where they were met by the Musquito king, and we never saw one of them afterwards. We then sailed to the southward of the shore, to a place called Cape Gracias a Dios, where there was a large lagoon or lake, which received the emptying of two or three very fine large rivers, and abounded much in fish and land tortoise.

Some of the native Indians came on board of us here; and we used them well, and told them we were come to dwell amongst them, which they seemed pleased at. So the Doctor and I, with some others, went with them ashore; and they took us to different places to view the land, in order to choose a place to make a plantation of. We fixed on a spot near a river's bank, in a rich soil; and, having got our necessaries out of the sloop, we began to clear away the woods, and plant different kinds of vegetables, which had a quick growth. While we were employed in this manner, our vessel went northward to Black River to trade. While she was there, a Spanish guarda costa met with and took her. This proved very hurtful, and a great embarrassment to us. However, we went on with the culture of the land. We used to make fires every night all around us, to keep off wild beasts, which, as soon as it was dark, set up a most hideous roaring. Our habitation being far up in the woods, we frequently saw different kinds of animals; but none of them ever hurt us, except poisonous snakes, the bite of which the Doctor used to cure by giving to the patient, as soon as possible, about half a tumbler of strong rum, with a good deal of Cayenne pepper in it. In this manner he cured two natives and one of his own slaves. The Indians were exceedingly fond of the Doctor, and they had good reason for it; for I believe they never had such an useful man amongst them. They came from all quarters to our dwelling; and some woolwow, or flat-headed Indians, who lived fifty or sixty miles above our river, and this side of the South Sea, brought us a good deal of silver in exchange for our goods.

The principal articles we could get from our neighbouring Indians, were turtle oil, and shells, little silk grass, and some provisions; but they would not work at anything for us, except fishing; and a few times they assisted to cut some trees down, in order to build us houses; which they did exactly like the Africans, by the joint labour of men, women, and children. I do not recollect any of them to have had more than two wives. These always accompanied their husbands when they came to our dwelling; and then they generally carried whatever they brought to us, and always squatted down behind their husbands. Whenever we gave them anything to eat, the men and their wives ate it separate. I never saw the least sign of incontinence[1] amongst them. The women are ornamented with beads, and fond of painting themselves; the men also paint, even to excess, both their faces and shirts: their favourite colour is red. The women generally cultivate the ground, and the men are all fishermen and canoe makers. Upon the whole, I never met any nation that were so simple in their manners as these people, or had so little ornament in their houses. Neither had they, as I ever could learn, one word expressive of an oath. The worst word I ever heard amongst them when they were quarreling, was one that they had got from the English, which was, "you rascal." I never saw any mode of worship among them; but in this they were not worse than their European brethren or neighbours: for I am sorry to say that there was not one white person in our dwelling, nor anywhere else that I saw in different places I was at on the shore, that was better or more pious than those unenlightened Indians; but they either worked or slept on Sundays: and, to my sorrow, working was too much Sunday's employment with ourselves; so much so, that in some length of time we really did not know one day from another. This mode of living laid the foundation of my decamping at last.

The natives are well made and warlike; and they particularly boast of having never been conquered by the Spaniards. They are great drinkers of strong liquors when they can get them. We used to distil rum from pine apples, which were very plentiful here; and then we could not get them away from our place. Yet they seemed to be singular, in point of honesty, above any other nation I was ever amongst. The country being hot, we lived under an open shed, where we had all kinds of goods, without a door or a lock to any one article; yet we slept in safety, and never lost anything, or were disturbed. This surprised us a good deal; and the Doctor, myself, and others, used to say, if we

---

1   *incontinence* Lack of control, especially with regard to sexual propriety.

were to lie in that manner in Europe we should have our throats cut the first night. The Indian governor goes once in a certain time all about the province or district, and has a number of men with him as attendants and assistants. He settles all the differences among the people, like the judge here, and is treated with very great respect. He took care to give us timely notice before he came to our habitation, by sending his stick as a token, for rum, sugar, and gunpowder, which we did not refuse sending; and at the same time we made the utmost preparation to receive his honour and his train. When he came with his tribe, and all our neighbouring chieftains, we expected to find him a grave reverend judge, solid and sagacious; but instead of that, before he and his gang came in sight, we heard them very clamorous; and they even had plundered some of our good neighbouring Indians, having intoxicated themselves with our liquor. When they arrived we did not know what to make of our new guests, and would gladly have dispensed with the honour of their company. However, having no alternative, we feasted them plentifully all the day till the evening; when the governor, getting quite drunk, grew very unruly, and struck one of our most friendly chiefs, who was our nearest neighbour, and also took his gold-laced hat from him. At this a great commotion taken place; and the Doctor interfered to make peace, as we could all understand one another, but to no purpose; and at last they became so outrageous that the Doctor, fearing he might get into trouble, left the house, and made the best of his way to the nearest wood, leaving me to do as well as I could among them. I was so enraged with the Governor, that I could have wished to have seen him tied fast to a tree and flogged for his behaviour; but I had not people enough to cope with his party. I therefore thought of a stratagem to appease the riot. Recollecting a passage I had read in the life of Columbus, when he was amongst the Indians in Mexico or Peru, where, on some occasion, he frightened them, by telling them of certain events in the heavens,[1] I had recourse to the same expedient; and it succeeded beyond my most sanguine expectations. When I had formed my determination, I went in the midst of them; and, taking hold of the Governor, I pointed up to the heavens. I menaced him and the rest: I told them God lived there, and that he was angry with them, and they must not quarrel so; that they were all brothers, and if they did not leave off, and go away quietly, I would take the book (pointing to the Bible), read, and tell God to make them dead. This was something like magic. The clamour immediately ceased, and I gave them some rum and a few other things; after which they

---

1   *a passage I had read … the heavens*   On 29 February 1504, Columbus deceived a group of Indigenous people on the island of Jamaica, drawing on his knowledge of an impending lunar eclipse to foretell the moon's disappearance as a sign from the "Great Spirit who dwells in heaven." When the moon disappeared just as Columbus had said it would, the frightened Jamaicans agreed to provide him with continued help.

went away peaceably; and the Governor afterwards gave our neighbour, who was called Captain Plasmyah, his hat again. When the Doctor returned, he was exceedingly glad at my success in thus getting rid of our troublesome guests. …

The rainy season came on here about the latter end of May, which continued till August very heavily; so that the rivers were overflowed, and our provisions then in the ground were washed away. I thought this was in some measure a judgment upon us for working on Sundays, and it hurt my mind very much. I often wished to leave this place and sail for Europe; for our mode of procedure and living in this heathenish form was very irksome to me. The word of God saith, "What does it avail a man if he gain the whole world, and lose his own soul?"[1] This was much and heavily impressed on my mind; and, though I did not know how to speak to the Doctor for my discharge, it was disagreeable for me to stay any longer. But about the middle of June I took courage enough to ask him for it. He was very unwilling at first to grant my request; but I gave him so many reasons for it, that at last he consented to my going, and gave me the following certificate of my behaviour:

> The bearer, Gustavus Vassa, has served me several years with strict honesty, sobriety, and fidelity. I can, therefore, with justice recommend him for these qualifications; and indeed in every respect I consider him as an excellent servant. I do hereby certify that he always behaved well, and that he is perfectly trust-worthy.
>
> Charles Irving
>
> Musquito Shore, June 15, 1776.

Though I was much attached to the doctor, I was happy when he consented. I got everything ready for my departure, and hired some Indians, with a large canoe, to carry me off. All my poor countrymen, the slaves, when they heard of my leaving them, were very sorry, as I had always treated them with care and affection, and did everything I could to comfort the poor creatures, and render their condition easy.

Having taken leave of my old friends and companions, on the 18th of June, accompanied by the doctor, I left that spot of the world, and went southward above twenty miles along the river. There I found a sloop, the captain of which told me he was going to Jamaica. Having agreed for my passage with him and one of the owners, who was also on board, named Hughes, the doctor and I parted, not without shedding tears on both sides. …

---

1   *What does … own soul?*   See Mark 8.36; Matthew 16.26.

from CHAPTER 12

Different transactions of the author's life till the present time—His application to the late Bishop of London to be appointed a missionary to Africa—Some account of his share in the conduct of the late expedition to Sierra Leone[1]—Petition to the Queen—Conclusion.

Such were the various scenes which I was a witness to, and the fortune I experienced until the year 1777. Since that period my life has been more uniform, and the incidents of it fewer, than in any other equal number of years preceding; I therefore hasten to the conclusion of a narrative, which I fear the reader may think already sufficiently tedious.

I had suffered so many impositions in my commercial transactions in different parts of the world, that I became heartily disgusted with the sea-faring life, and I was determined not to return to it, at least for some time. I therefore once more engaged in service shortly after my return, and continued for the most part in this situation until 1784. ...

In October 1785 I was accompanied by some of the Africans, and presented this address of thanks to the gentlemen called Friends or Quakers, in Gracechurch-Court Lombard-Street:

Gentlemen,

By reading your book, entitled *A Caution to Great Britain and Her Colonies*, concerning the calamitous state of the enslaved negroes: We the poor, oppressed, needy, and much-degraded negroes, desire to approach you with this address of thanks, with our inmost love and warmest acknowledgment; and with the deepest sense of your benevolence, unwearied labour, and kind interposition, towards breaking the yoke of slavery, and to administer a little comfort and ease to thousands and tens of thousands of very grievously afflicted, and too heavy burdened negroes.

Gentlemen, could you, by perseverance, at last be enabled, under God, to lighten in any degree the heavy burden of the afflicted, no doubt it would, in some measure, be the possible means, under God, of saving the souls of many of the oppressors; and, if so, sure we are that the God, whose eyes are ever upon all his creatures, and always rewards every true act of virtue, and regards the prayers of the oppressed, will give to you and yours those blessings which it is not in our power to express or conceive, but which we, as a part of those captived, oppressed, and afflicted people, most earnestly wish and pray for.

---

1 *the late expedition to Sierra Leone* The project had involved a ship sailing to Sierra Leone in West Africa, in order to transport black people from Britain for resettlement.

These gentlemen received us very kindly, with a promise to exert themselves on behalf of the oppressed Africans, and we parted.

While in town I chanced once to be invited to a Quaker's wedding. The simple and yet expressive mode used at their solemnizations is worthy of note. The following is the true form of it:

After the company have met they have seasonable exhortations by several of the members; the bride and bridegroom stand up, and, taking each other by the hand in a solemn manner, the man audibly declares to this purpose:

> Friends, in the fear of the Lord, and in the presence of this assembly, whom I desire to be my witnesses, I take this my friend, M.N. to be my wife; promising, through divine assistance, to be unto her a loving and faithful husband till death separate us.

and the woman makes the like declaration. Then the two first sign their names to the record, and as many more witnesses as have a mind. I had the honour to subscribe mine to a register in Gracechurch-Court, Lombard-Street.

We returned to London in August; and our ship not going immediately to sea, I shipped as a steward in an American ship called the *Harmony*, Captain John Willet, and left London in March 1786, bound to Philadelphia. Eleven days after sailing we carried our foremast away. We had a nine weeks passage, which caused our trip not to succeed well, the market for our goods proving bad; and, to make it worse, my commander began to play me the like tricks as others too often practise on free negroes in the West Indies. But I thank God I found many friends here, who in some measure prevented him. On my return to London in August I was very agreeably surprised to find that the benevolence of government had adopted the plan of some philanthropic individuals to send the Africans from hence to their native quarter; and that some vessels were then engaged to carry them to Sierra Leone; an act which redounded to the honour of all concerned in its promotion, and filled me with prayers and much rejoicing. There was then in the city a select committee of gentlemen for the black poor, to some of whom I had the honour of being known; and, as soon as they heard of my arrival they sent for me to the committee. When I came there they informed me of the intention of government; and as they seemed to think me qualified to superintend part of the undertaking, they asked me to go with the black poor to Africa. I pointed out to them many objections to my going; and particularly I expressed some difficulties on the account of the slave dealers, as I would certainly oppose their traffic in the human species by every means in my power. However these objections were over-ruled by the gentlemen of the committee, who prevailed on me to go, and recommended me to the honourable Commissioners of his

Majesty's Navy as a proper person to act as commissary for government in the intended expedition; and they accordingly appointed me in November 1786 to that office, and gave me sufficient power to act for the government in the capacity of commissary, having received my warrant and the following order:

By the principal officers and commissioners of his Majesty's navy

Whereas you were directed, by our warrant of the 4th of last month, to receive into your charge from Mr. Irving the surplus provisions remaining of what was provided for the voyage, as well as the provisions for the support of the black poor, after the landing at Sierra Leone, with the clothing, tools, and all other articles provided at government's expense; and as the provisions were laid in at the rate of two months for the voyage, and for four months after the landing, but the number embarked being so much less than was expected, whereby there may be a considerable surplus of provisions, clothing, &c. These are, in addition to former orders, to direct and require you to appropriate or dispose of such surplus to the best advantage you can for the benefit of government, keeping and rendering to us a faithful account of what you do herein. And for your guidance in preventing any white persons going, who are not intended to have the indulgences of being carried thither, we send you herewith a list of those recommended by the Committee for the black poor as proper persons to be permitted to embark, and acquaint you that you are not to suffer any others to go who do not produce a certificate from the committee for the black poor, of their having their permission for it. For which this shall be your warrant. Dated at the Navy Office, January 16, 1787.

J. Hinslow
Geo. Marsh
W. Palmer
To Mr. Gustavus Vassa,
    Commissary of Provisions and Stores for the Black Poor going to Sierra Leone

I proceeded immediately to the execution of my duty on board the vessels destined for the voyage, where I continued till the March following.

During my continuance in the employment of government, I was struck with the flagrant abuses committed by the agent, and endeavoured to remedy them, but without effect. One instance, among many which I could produce, may serve as a specimen. Government had ordered to be provided all necessaries (slops, as they are called, included) for 750 persons; however, not being able to muster more than 426, I was ordered to send the superfluous slops, &c. to the king's stores at Portsmouth; but, when I demanded them for that purpose from the agent, it appeared they had never been bought, though paid for by government. But that was not all, government were not the only objects of peculation; these poor people suffered infinitely more; their accommodations were most wretched; many of them wanted beds, and many more clothing and other necessaries. For the truth of this, and much more, I do not seek credit from my own assertion. I appeal to the testimony of Capt. Thompson, of the *Nautilus*, who convoyed us, to whom I applied in February 1787 for a remedy, when I had remonstrated to the agent in vain, and even brought him to be a witness of the injustice and oppression I complained of. I appeal also to a letter written by these wretched people, so early as the beginning of the preceding January, and published in the Morning Herald of the 4th of that month, signed by twenty of their chiefs.

I could not silently suffer government to be thus cheated, and my country-men plundered and oppressed, and even left destitute of the necessaries for almost their existence. I therefore informed the Commissioners of the Navy of the agent's proceeding; but my dismission was soon after procured, by means of a gentleman in the city, whom the agent, conscious of his peculation, had deceived by letter, and whom, moreover, empowered the same agent to receive on board, at the government expense, a number of persons as passengers, contrary to the orders I received. By this I suffered a considerable loss in my property: however, the commissioners were satisfied with my conduct, and wrote to Capt. Thompson, expressing their approbation of it.

Thus provided, they proceeded on their voyage; and at last, worn out by treatment, perhaps not the most mild, and wasted by sickness, brought on by want of medicine, cloaths, bedding, &c. they reached Sierra Leone just at the commencement of the rains. At that season of the year it is impossible to cultivate the lands; their provisions therefore were exhausted before they could derive any benefit from agriculture; and it is not surprising that many, especially the lascars,[1] whose constitutions are very tender, and who had been cooped up in ships from October to June, and accommodated in the manner I have mentioned, should be so wasted by their confinement as not long to survive it.

Thus ended my part of the long-talked-of expedition to Sierra Leone; an expedition which, however unfortunate in the event, was humane and politic in its design, nor was its failure owing to government: everything was done on their part; but there was evidently sufficient mismanagement attending the conduct and execution of it to defeat its success.

I should not have been so ample in my account of this transaction, had not the share I bore in it been made the subject of partial animadversion, and even

---

1 *lascars* Sailors from the East Indies.

my dismission from my employment thought worthy of being made by some a matter of public triumph.[1] The motives which might influence any person to descend to a petty contest with an obscure African, and to seek gratification by his depression, perhaps it is not proper here to inquire into or relate, even if its detection were necessary to my vindication; but I thank Heaven it is not. I wish to stand by my own integrity, and not to shelter myself under the impropriety of another; and I trust the behaviour of the Commissioners of the Navy to me entitle me to make this assertion; for after I had been dismissed, March 24, I drew up a memorial thus:

To the Right Honourable the Lords Commissioners of his Majesty's Treasury:
The Memorial and Petition of Gustavus Vassa, a Black Man, late[2] Commissary to the Black Poor going to Africa.

HUMBLY SHEWETH

That your Lordships' memorialist was, by the Honourable the Commissioners of his Majesty's Navy, on the 4th of December last, appointed to the above employment by warrant from that board;

That he accordingly proceeded to the execution of his duty on board of the *Vernon*, being one of the ships appointed to proceed to Africa with the above poor;

That your memorialist, to his great grief and astonishment, received a letter of dismission from the Honourable Commissioners of the Navy, by your Lordships' orders;

That, conscious of having acted with the most perfect fidelity and the greatest assiduity in discharging the trust reposed in him, he is altogether at a loss to conceive the reasons of your Lordships' having altered the favourable opinion you were pleased to conceive of him, sensible that your Lordships would not proceed to so severe a measure without some apparent good cause; he therefore has every reason to believe that his conduct has been grossly misrepresented to your Lordships; and he is the more confirmed in his opinion, because, by opposing measures of others concerned in the same expedition, which tended to defeat your Lordships' humane intentions, and to put the government to a very considerable additional expense, he created a number of enemies, whose misrepresentations, he has too much reason

---

1   [Equiano's note]   See the *Public Advertiser*, July 14, 1787. [That issue of the newspaper carried a letter from Equiano, providing a defense of his actions.]
2   *late* Recent.

to believe, laid the foundation of his dismission. Unsupported by friends, and unaided by the advantages of a liberal education, he can only hope for redress from the justice of his cause, in addition to the mortification of having been removed from his employment, and the advantage which he reasonably might have expected to have derived therefrom. He has had the misfortune to have sunk a considerable part of his little property in fitting himself out, and in other expenses arising out of his situation, an account of which he here annexes. Your memorialist will not trouble your Lordships with a vindication of any part of his conduct, because he knows not of what crimes he is accused; he, however, earnestly entreats that you will be pleased to direct an inquiry into his behaviour during the time he acted in the public service; and, if it be found that his dismission arose from false representations, he is confident that in your Lordships' justice he shall find redress.

Your petitioner therefore humbly prays that your Lordships will take his case into consideration, and that you will be pleased to order payment of the above referred-to account, amounting to 32£. 4s. and also the wages intended, which is most humbly submitted.

London, May 12, 1787.

The above petition was delivered into the hands of their Lordships, who were kind enough, in the space of some few months afterwards, without hearing, to order me £50 sterling—that is, £18 wages for the time (upwards of four months) I acted a faithful part in their service. Certainly the sum is more than a free negro would have had in the western colonies!!![1] ...

As the inhuman traffic of slavery is to be taken into the consideration of the British legislature, I doubt not, if a system of commerce was established in Africa, the demand for manufactures would most rapidly augment, as the native inhabitants will insensibly adopt the British fashions, manners, customs, &c. In proportion to the civilization, so will be the consumption of British manufactures.

The wear and tear of a continent, nearly twice as large as Europe, and rich in vegetable and mineral productions, is much easier conceived than calculated.

A case in point—It cost the Aborigines of Britain little or nothing in clothing, &c. The difference between their forefathers and the present generation, in point of consumption, is literally infinite. The supposition is most obvious. It will be equally immense in Africa—The same cause, viz. civilization, will ever have the same effect.

---

1   *the western colonies*   In later editions Equiano added the following at this point: "From that point to the present time my life has passed in an even tenor, and a great part of my study and attention has been to assist in the cause of my much injured countrymen."

It is trading upon safe grounds. A commercial intercourse with Africa opens an inexhaustible source of wealth to the manufacturing interests of Great Britain, and to all which the slave trade is an objection.

If I am not misinformed, the manufacturing interest is equal, if not superior, to the landed interest, as to the value, for reasons which will soon appear. The abolition of slavery, so diabolical, will give a most rapid extension of manufactures, which is totally and diametrically opposite to what some interested people assert.

The manufacturers of this country must and will, in the nature and reason of things, have a full and constant employ by supplying the African markets.

Population, the bowels and surface of Africa, abound in valuable and useful returns; the hidden treasures of centuries will be brought to light and into circulation. Industry, enterprise, and mining, will have their full scope, proportionably as they civilize. In a word, it lays open an endless field of commerce to the British manufactures and merchant adventurer. The manufacturing interest and the general interests are synonymous. The abolition of slavery would be in reality a universal good.

Tortures, murder, and every other imaginable barbarity and iniquity, are practised upon the poor slaves with impunity. I hope the slave trade will be abolished. I pray it may be an event at hand. The great body of manufacturers, uniting in the cause, will considerably facilitate and expedite it; and, as I have already stated, it is most substantially their interest and advantage, and as such the nation's at large, (except those persons concerned in the manufacturing neck-yokes, collars, chains, hand-cuffs, leg-bolts, drags, thumb-screws, iron muzzles, and coffins; cats, scourges, and other instruments of torture used in the slave trade). In a short time one sentiment alone will prevail, from motives of interest as well as justice and humanity. Europe contains one hundred and twenty millions of inhabitants. Query—How many millions doth Africa contain? Supposing the Africans, collectively and individually, to expend £5 a head in raiment and furniture yearly when civilized, &c. an immensity beyond the reach of imagination!

This I conceive to be a theory founded upon facts, and therefore an infallible one. If the blacks were permitted to remain in their own country, they would double themselves every fifteen years. In proportion to such increase will be the demand for manufactures. Cotton and indigo grow spontaneously in most parts of Africa; a consideration this of no small consequence to the manufacturing towns of Great Britain. It opens a most immense, glorious, and happy prospect—the clothing, &c. of a continent ten thousand miles in circumference, and immensely rich in productions of every denomination in return for manufactures.

I have only therefore to request the reader's indulgence and conclude. I am far from the vanity of thinking there is any merit in this narrative: I hope censure will be suspended, when it is considered that it was written by one who was as unwilling as unable to adorn the plainness of truth by the colouring of imagination. My life and fortune have been extremely chequered, and my adventures various. Even those I have related are considerably abridged. If any incident in this little work should appear uninteresting and trifling to most readers, I can only say, as my excuse for mentioning it, that almost every event of my life made an impression on my mind and influenced my conduct. I early accustomed myself to look for the hand of God in the minutest occurrence, and to learn from it a lesson of morality and religion; and in this light every circumstance I have related was to me of importance. After all, what makes any event important, unless by its observation we become better and wiser, and learn "to do justly, to love mercy, and to walk humbly before God?"[1] To those who are possessed of this spirit, there is scarcely any book or incident so trifling that does not afford some profit, while to others the experience of ages seems of no use; and even to pour out to them the treasures of wisdom is throwing the jewels of instruction away.

The End
—1789

---

1   *to do ... before God*   See Micah 6.8.

In Context

Equiano's Narrative as a Philadelphia Abolitionist Pamphlet

The first illustrated edition of any part of Equiano's *Interesting Narrative* seems to have been a 36-page pamphlet largely made up of excerpts from Equiano's work. The pamphlet was issued in 1829 in Philadelphia by Samuel Wood, a Quaker printer who had been publishing abolitionist broadsides and pamphlets since the early years of the century. As illustrations, Wood included several woodcuts (several of which had appeared in his earlier publications and were now re-purposed); he also appended to the Equiano material "the following *Remarks upon the Slave Trade*," which Wood had originally published in 1807 as a reprint of "a pamphlet lately published by a society at Plymouth, in Great Britain, from which the Philadelphia Society for Promoting the Abolition of Slavery have taken the following extracts, and have added a copy of the plate, which accompanied it." The plate (shown right) bears a close resemblance to Thomas Clarkson's 1787 diagram of the hold of the slave ship *Brooks*, which had been widely reprinted and was credited with helping significantly to spur abolitionist sentiment.

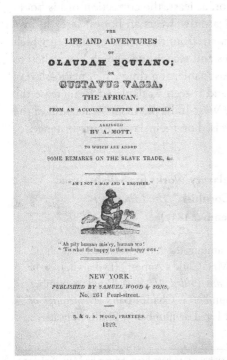 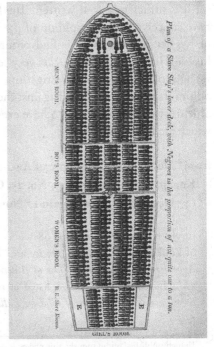

Title page and illustration, *The Life and Adventures of Olaudah Equiano* (1829).

Reactions to Olaudah Equiano's Work

from *The Analytic Review* (May 1789)[1]

The life of an African, written by himself, is certainly a curiosity, as it has been a favourite philosophic whim to degrade the numerous nations, on whom the sun-beams more directly dart, below the common level of humanity, and hastily to conclude that nature, by making them inferior to the rest of the human race, designed to stamp them with a mark of slavery. … If these volumes do not exhibit extraordinary intellectual powers, sufficient to wipe off the stigma, yet the activity and ingenuity, which conspicuously appear in the character of Gustavus, place him on a par with the general mass of men, who fill the subordinate stations in a more civilized society than that which he was thrown into at his birth.

from *The Monthly Review* (June 1789)

We entertain no doubt of the general authenticity of this very intelligent African's story; though it is not improbable that some English writer has assisted him in the compilement, or, at least, the correction of his book; for it is sufficiently well-written. The Narrative wears an honest face; and we have conceived a good opinion of the man, from the artless manner in which he has detailed the variety of adventures and vicissitudes which have fallen to his lot. His publication appears very seasonable, at a time when negro-slavery is the subject of public investigation; and it seems calculated to increase the odium that has been excited against the West-India planters, on account of the cruelties that some are said to have exercised on their slaves, many instances of which are here detailed.

from "Descriptive Catalogue of Anti-Slavery Works for Sale by Isaac Knaap, at the Depository, No. 25, Cornhill," *The Liberator* (27 October 1837 and again 17 November 1837)

In all, Knapp's list includes 68 works; among the more notable listed ahead of Equiano's *Interesting Narrative* are "Mrs. Child's Appeal" (Lydia Child's *An Appeal in Favor of That Class of Americans Called Africans*), listed at number 2; Archy Moore's *The Slave*, listed at number 4; Charles Ball's *A Narrative of the Life and Adventures of Charles Ball*, listed at number 5; Phillis Wheatley's

---

1 Though published anonymously, this review is now known to have been written by Mary Wollstonecraft.

Memoir and Poems, listed at number 18; Whittier's *Poems*, listed at number 20; and a collection of Lemuel Haynes's writings, listed at number 30.

36.   GUSTAVUS VASSA.   294 pp. 12 mo. Cloth 62 1-2-
The life of Olaudah Equiano, or Gustavus Vassa, the African, written by himself. With two lithographic Prints.

This is the life of a native African, of powerful intellect, who was 'stolen out of his own land,' lived as a slave in Pennsylvania, went several voyages to the West Indies, and to several ports in Europe, narrowly escaped death several times, and passed through a great variety of wonderful scenes, which give his narrative an interest scarcely surpassed by Robinson Crusoe.

Mary Prince
1788 – after 1833

"I will say the truth to the English people," declared the abolitionist Mary Prince, whose autobiography detailing her life in the West Indies is the earliest extant slave narrative by a woman. Published at a crucial moment in the campaign to end slavery in British possessions, *The History of Mary Prince* represents an important contribution to the abolitionist movement, as well as a work of historical and literary interest in its own right.

Mary Prince was born into bondage in the British colony of Bermuda, where for the first twelve years of her life she was, relatively speaking, spared the cruelty that dominated her adult years. Both her parents were also enslaved, the property of Charles Myners. After Myners died, Mary and her mother were sold to a Captain Williams, whose daughter Betsey treated her with racist condescension, but with relative compassion. Williams sold Prince to another family to raise money for his marriage, and in 1806 she was sent to work in the salt ponds of Turks Island: "This work was perfectly new to me. I was given a half barrel and shovel, and had to stand up to my knees in the water, from four o'clock in the morning till nine, when we were given some Indian corn boiled in water, which we were obliged to swallow as fast as we could for fear the rain should come on and melt the salt." In addition to these intolerable working conditions, Prince also endured physical and probably sexual abuse from her master.

In 1818, Prince was sold for three hundred dollars to John Wood, a plantation owner in Antigua, who beat, overworked, and otherwise abused her. By this time Prince had developed a serious skin problem, and while working for the Woods she became essentially crippled by severe rheumatism; her mistreatment would also eventually lead to damaged eyesight. Prince began attending meetings held at the Moravian Church, where various women taught her to read: "After we had done spelling, we tried to read in the Bible. After reading was over, the missionary gave out a hymn for us to sing." Prince was married in this church to Daniel Jones, a formerly enslaved man who had purchased his own freedom. Wood horsewhipped Prince when he discovered the marriage. In 1828 Wood took Prince to London as his servant. Abolitionist sympathizers helped her escape (which they were able to do because slavery was illegal in England), and she found employment as a domestic servant of Thomas Pringle, a Methodist and secretary of the Society for the Abolition of Slavery.

Pringle encouraged Prince to tell the story of her life and, in 1831, he arranged for the publication of her book, *The History of Mary Prince, a West-Indian*

Slave, Related by Herself. In his "Preface" to the work, Pringle wrote: "The idea of writing Mary Prince's history was first suggested by herself. She wished it to be done, she said, that good people in England might hear from a slave what a slave had felt and suffered." Mary Prince told her story to Susanna Strickland (later Moodie), who recorded it in writing. It seems improbable that Strickland—who would later come to be regarded as one of Canada's most accomplished writers in the nineteenth century—would not at a minimum have edited the dictated narrative for grammar and syntax, and some have suggested that Pringle may have had some hand in shaping the manuscript so as to better serve abolitionist ends. (His insistence that the rhetorical flourish at the end of Prince's first paragraph is "given verbatim as uttered by Mary Prince" has struck more than one reader as rather forced.) But most scholars have stopped short of suggesting that material was fabricated by Pringle and Strickland, or that this is not in essence Prince's own narrative. Strickland herself attested that she had "been writing Mr. Pringle's black Mary's life from her own dictation and for her benefit adhering to her own simple story and language without deviating to the paths of flourish or romance."

The book was a great success, and gave rise to considerable controversy. *Blackwood's Magazine* and *The Glasgow Courier* claimed it was fraudulent and propagandistic. A number of libel suits resulted, with Wood suing Pringle and Pringle counter-suing. Wood claimed that the book had "endeavored to injure the character of my family by the most vile and infamous falsehoods." Wood lost the case, and the libel scandal served only to make Prince's work more widely known. It reached a third edition in the same year it was published, and it has since that time retained its place as one of the most moving, detailed, and comprehensive narratives of the life of an enslaved person.

Slavery was legally abolished in almost all British colonies in 1833. Little is known of Prince's life after the publication of her *History*, and we do not know when, where, or how she died.

Note on the Text

The text reproduced below is based on that printed in the 1831 first edition of *The History of Mary Prince*. Spelling and punctuation have been modernized in accordance with the practices of this anthology.

⌘ ⌘ ⌘

The History of Mary Prince, A West Indian Slave, Related by Herself

PREFACE [BY THOMAS PRINGLE][1]

The idea of writing Mary Prince's history was first suggested by herself. She wished it to be done, she said, that good people in England might hear from a slave what a slave had felt and suffered; and a letter of her late master's, which will be found in the Supplement, induced me to accede to her wish without farther delay. The more immediate object of the publication will afterwards appear.

The narrative was taken down from Mary's own lips by a lady who happened to be at the time residing in my family as a visitor. It was written out fully, with all the narrator's repetitions and prolixities,[2] and afterwards pruned into its present shape; retaining, as far as was practicable, Mary's exact expressions and peculiar phraseology. No fact of importance has been omitted, and not a single circumstance or sentiment has been added. It is essentially her own, without any material alteration farther than was requisite to exclude redundances and gross grammatical errors, so as to render it clearly intelligible.

After it had been thus written out, I went over the whole, carefully examining her on every fact and circumstance detailed; and in all that relates to her residence in Antigua I had the advantage of being assisted in this scrutiny by Mr. Joseph Phillips, who was a resident in that colony during the same period, and had known her there.

The names of all the persons mentioned by the narrator have been printed in full, except those of Capt. I— and his wife, and that of Mr. D—, to whom conduct of peculiar atrocity is ascribed. These three individuals are now gone to answer at a far more awful tribunal than that of public opinion, for the deeds of which their former bondwoman accuses them; and to hold them up more openly to human reprobation could no longer affect themselves, while it might deeply lacerate the feelings of their surviving and perhaps innocent relatives, without any commensurate public advantage.

Without detaining the reader with remarks on other points which will be adverted to more conveniently in the Supplement, I shall here merely notice

---

1 THOMAS PRINGLE Poet and abolitionist Thomas Pringle (1789–1834) was born in Scotland and lived in South Africa between 1820 and 1826, where he published a newspaper and a magazine. In 1826 he returned to England, where he devoted himself to the antislavery movement as secretary to the Society for the Abolition of Slavery.
2 *prolixities* Instances of wordiness.

farther, that the Anti-Slavery Society have no concern whatever with this publication, nor are they in any degree responsible for the statements it contains. I have published the tract, not as their Secretary, but in my private capacity; and any profits that may arise from the sale will be exclusively appropriated to the benefit of Mary Prince herself.

THOMAS PRINGLE

7, Solly Terrace, Claremont Square,
January 25, 1831

P.S. Since writing the above, I have been furnished by my friend Mr. George Stephen, with the interesting narrative of Asa-Asa,[1] a captured African, now under his protection; and have printed it as a suitable appendix to this little history.

T.P.

The History of Mary Prince

I was born at Brackish-Pond, in Bermuda, on a farm belonging to Mr. Charles Myners. My mother was a household slave; and my father, whose name was Prince, was a sawyer[2] belonging to Mr. Trimmingham, a shipbuilder at Crow-Lane. When I was an infant, old Mr. Myners died, and there was a division of the slaves and other property among the family. I was bought along with my mother by old Captain Darrel, and given to his grandchild, little Miss Betsey Williams. Captain Williams, Mr. Darrel's son-in-law, was master of a vessel which traded to several places in America and the West Indies, and he was seldom at home long together.

Mrs. Williams was a kind-hearted good woman, and she treated all her slaves well. She had only one daughter, Miss Betsey, for whom I was purchased, and who was about my own age. I was made quite a pet of by Miss Betsey, and loved her very much. She used to lead me about by the hand, and call me her little nigger.[3] This was the happiest period of my life; for I was too young to understand rightly my condition as a slave, and too thoughtless and full of spirits to look forward to the days of toil and sorrow.

---

1   *the interesting narrative of Asa-Asa*   This narrative does not appear in the present anthology.
2   *sawyer*   Worker whose job it is to saw timber.
3   *nigger*   By the early nineteenth century, this word (today widely acknowledged to be an utterly unacceptable expression of racism) had firmly established itself in the vernacular of white people in both the British empire and the United States as an emphatically pejorative alternative to the then-more neutral term "negro."

My mother was a household slave in the same family. I was under her own care, and my little brothers and sisters were my play-fellows and companions. My mother had us several fine children after she came to Mrs. Williams, three girls and two boys. The tasks given out to us children were light, and we used to play together with Miss Betsey, with as much freedom almost as if she had been our sister.

My master, however, was a very harsh, selfish man; and we always dreaded his return from sea. His wife was herself much afraid of him; and, during his stay at home, seldom dared to show her usual kindness to the slaves. He often left her, in the most distressed circumstances, to reside in other female society, at some place in the West Indies of which I have forgot the name. My poor mistress bore his ill-treatment with great patience, and all her slaves loved and pitied her. I was truly attached to her, and, next to my own mother, loved her better than any creature in the world. My obedience to her commands was cheerfully given: it sprung solely from the affection I felt for her, and not from fear of the power which the white people's law had given her over me.

I had scarcely reached my twelfth year when my mistress became too poor to keep so many of us at home; and she hired me out to Mrs. Pruden, a lady who lived about five miles off, in the adjoining parish, in a large house near the sea. I cried bitterly at parting with my dear mistress and Miss Betsey, and when I kissed my mother and brothers and sisters, I thought my young heart would break, it pained me so. But there was no help; I was forced to go. Good Mrs. Williams comforted me by saying that I should still be near the home I was about to quit, and might come over and see her and my kindred whenever I could obtain leave of absence from Mrs. Pruden. A few hours after this I was taken to a strange house, and found myself among strange people. This separation seemed a sore trial to me then; but oh! 'twas light, light to the trials I have since endured!—'twas nothing—nothing to be mentioned with them; but I was a child then, and it was according to my strength.

I knew that Mrs. Williams could no longer maintain me; that she was fain to part with me for my food and clothing; and I tried to submit myself to the change. My new mistress was a passionate woman; but yet she did not treat me very unkindly. I do not remember her striking me but once, and that was for going to see Mrs. Williams when I heard she was sick, and staying longer than she had given me leave to do. All my employment at this time was nursing a sweet baby, little Master Daniel; and I grew so fond of my nursling that it was my greatest delight to walk out with him by the sea-shore, accompanied by his brother and sister, Miss Fanny and Master James. Dear Miss Fanny! She was a sweet, kind young lady, and so fond of me that she wished me to learn all that she knew herself; and her method of teaching me was as follows: Directly she had said her lessons to her grandmamma, she used to come running to me, and make me repeat them one by one after her; and in a few months I was able not only to say my letters but to spell many small words. But this happy state was not to last long. Those days were too pleasant to last. My heart always softens when I think of them.

At this time Mrs. Williams died. I was told suddenly of her death, and my grief was so great that, forgetting I had the baby in my arms, I ran away directly to my poor mistress's house; but reached it only in time to see the corpse carried out. Oh, that was a day of sorrow—a heavy day! All the slaves cried. My mother cried and lamented her sore; and I (foolish creature!) vainly entreated them to bring my dear mistress back to life. I knew nothing rightly about death then, and it seemed a hard thing to bear. When I thought about my mistress I felt as if the world was all gone wrong; and for many days and weeks I could think of nothing else. I returned to Mrs. Pruden's; but my sorrow was too great to be comforted, for my own dear mistress was always in my mind. Whether in the house or abroad, my thoughts were always talking to me about her.

I stayed at Mrs. Pruden's about three months after this; I was then sent back to Mr. Williams to be sold. Oh, that was a sad sad time! I recollect the day well. Mrs. Pruden came to me and said, "Mary, you will have to go home directly; your master is going to be married, and he means to sell you and two of your sisters to raise money for the wedding." Hearing this I burst out a crying—though I was then far from being sensible of the full weight of my misfortune, or of the misery that waited for me. Besides, I did not like to leave Mrs. Pruden, and the dear baby, who had grown very fond of me. For some time I could scarcely believe that Mrs. Pruden was in earnest, till I received orders for my immediate return. Dear Miss Fanny! how she cried at parting with me, whilst I kissed and hugged the baby, thinking I should never see him again. I left Mrs. Pruden's, and walked home with a heart full of sorrow. The idea of being sold away from my mother and Miss Betsey was so frightful, that I dared not trust myself to think about it. We had been bought of Mrs. Myners, as I have mentioned, by Miss Betsey's grandfather, and given to her, so that we were by right *her* property, and I never thought we should be separated or sold away from her.

When I reached the house, I went in directly to Miss Betsey. I found her in great distress; and she cried out as soon as she saw me, "Oh, Mary! my father is going to sell you all to raise money to marry that wicked woman. You are *my* slaves, and he has no right to sell you; but it is all to please her." She then told me that my mother was living with her father's sister at a house close by, and I went there to see her. It was a sorrowful meeting; and we lamented with a great and sore crying our unfortunate situation. "Here comes one of my poor piccaninnies!"[1] she said, the moment I came in, "one of the poor slave-brood who are to be sold tomorrow."

Oh dear! I cannot bear to think of that day—it is too much. It recalls the great grief that filled my heart, and the woeful thoughts that passed to and fro through my mind, whilst listening to the pitiful words of my poor mother, weeping for the loss of her children. I wish I could find words to tell you all I then felt and suffered. The great God above alone knows the thoughts of the poor slave's heart, and the bitter pains which follow such separations as these. All that we love taken away from us—oh, it is sad, sad! and sore to be borne! I got no sleep that night for thinking of the morrow; and dear Miss Betsey was scarcely less distressed. She could not bear to part with her old playmates and she cried sore and would not be pacified.

The black morning at length came; it came too soon for my poor mother and us. Whilst she was putting on us the new osnaburgs[2] in which we were to be sold, she said, in a sorrowful voice, (I shall never forget it!) "See, I am *shrouding* my poor children; what a task for a mother!" She then called Miss Betsey to take leave of us. "I am going to carry my little chickens to market," (these were her very words) "take your last look of them; may be you will see them no more." "Oh, my poor slaves! my own slaves!" said dear Miss Betsey, "you belong to me; and it grieves my heart to part with you." Miss Betsey kissed us all, and, when she left us, my mother called the rest of the slaves to bid us good bye. One of them, a woman named Moll, came with her infant in her arms. "Ay!" said my mother, seeing her turn away and look at her child with the tears in her eyes, "your turn will come next." The slaves could say nothing to comfort us; they could only weep and lament with us. When I left my dear little brothers and the house in which I had been brought up, I thought my heart would burst.

Our mother, weeping as she went, called me away with the children Hannah and Dinah, and we took the road that led to Hamble Town, which we reached about four o'clock in the afternoon. We followed my mother to the market-place, where she placed us in a row against a large house, with our backs to the wall and our arms folded across our breasts. I, as the eldest, stood first, Hannah next to me, then Dinah; and our mother stood beside, crying over us. My heart throbbed with grief and terror so violently, that I pressed my hands quite tightly across my breast, but I could not keep it still, and it continued to leap as though it would burst out of my body. But who cared for that? Did one of the many bystanders, who were looking at us so carelessly, think of the pain that wrung the hearts of the negro woman and her young ones? No, no! They

---

1 *piccaninnies* Derogatory term for black children.
2 *osnaburgs* Clothes made of osnaburg, a coarse linen.

were not all bad, I dare say, but slavery hardens white people's hearts towards the blacks; and many of them were not slow to make their remarks upon us aloud, without regard to our grief—though their light words fell like cayenne on the fresh wounds of our hearts. Oh those white people have small hearts who can only feel for themselves.

At length the vendue[1] master, who was to offer us for sale like sheep or cattle, arrived, and asked my mother which was the eldest. She said nothing, but pointed to me. He took me by the hand, and led me out into the middle of the street, and, turning me slowly round, exposed me to the view of those who attended the vendue. I was soon surrounded by strange men, who examined and handled me in the same manner that a butcher would a calf or a lamb he was about to purchase, and who talked about my shape and size in like words—as if I could no more understand their meaning than the dumb beasts. I was then put up for sale. The bidding commenced at a few pounds, and gradually rose to fifty-seven, when I was knocked down to the highest bidder; and the people who stood by said that I had fetched a great sum for so young a slave.

I then saw my sisters led forth, and sold to different owners; so that we had not the sad satisfaction of being partners in bondage. When the sale was over, my mother hugged and kissed us, and mourned over us, begging of us to keep up a good heart, and do our duty to our new masters. It was a sad parting; one went one way, one another, and our poor mammy went home with nothing.

My new master was a Captain I—, who lived at Spanish Point. After parting with my mother and sisters, I followed him to his store, and he gave me into the charge of his son, a lad about my own age, Master Benjy, who took me to my new home. I did not know where I was going, or what my new master would do with me. My heart was quite broken with grief, and my thoughts went back continually to those from whom I had been so suddenly parted. "Oh, my mother! my mother!" I kept saying to myself, "Oh, my mammy and my sisters and my brothers, shall I never see you again!"

Oh, the trials! the trials! they make the salt water come into my eyes when I think of the days in which I was afflicted—the times that are gone; when I mourned and grieved with a young heart for those whom I loved. It was night when I reached my new home. The house was large, and built at the bottom of a very high hill; but I could not see much of it that night. I saw too much of it afterwards. The stones and the timber were the best things in it; they were not so hard as the hearts of the owners.

Before I entered the house, two slave women, hired from another owner, who were at work in the yard, spoke to me, and asked who I belonged to? I

---

1 *vendue* Sale.

replied, "I am come to live here." "Poor child, poor child!" they both said; "you must keep a good heart, if you are to live here." When I went in, I stood up crying in a corner. Mrs. I— came and took off my hat, a little black silk hat Miss Pruden made for me, and said in a rough voice, "You are not come here to stand up in corners and cry, you are come here to work." She then put a child into my arms, and, tired as I was, I was forced instantly to take up my old occupation of a nurse. I could not bear to look at my mistress, her countenance was so stern. She was a stout tall woman with a very dark complexion, and her brows were always drawn together into a frown. I thought of the words of the two slave women when I saw Mrs. I—, and heard the harsh sound of her voice.

The person I took the most notice of that night was a French Black called Hetty, whom my master took in privateering from another vessel, and made his slave. She was the most active woman I ever saw, and she was tasked to her utmost. A few minutes after my arrival she came in from milking the cows, and put the sweet-potatoes on for supper. She then fetched home the sheep, and penned them in the fold; drove home the cattle, and staked them about the pond side; fed and rubbed down my master's horse, and gave the hog and the fed cow their suppers; prepared the beds, and undressed the children, and laid them to sleep. I liked to look at her and watch all her doings, for hers was the only friendly face I had as yet seen, and I felt glad that she was there. She gave me my supper of potatoes and milk, and a blanket to sleep upon, which she spread for me in the passage before the door of Mrs. I—'s chamber.

I got a sad fright, that night. I was just going to sleep, when I heard a noise in my mistress's room; and she presently called out to inquire if some work was finished that she had ordered Hetty to do. "No, Ma'am, not yet," was Hetty's answer from below. On hearing this, my master started up from his bed, and just as he was, in his shirt, ran down stairs with a long cow-skin in his hand. I heard immediately after, the cracking of the thong, and the house rang to the shrieks of poor Hetty, who kept crying out, "Oh, Massa! Massa! me dead. Massa! have mercy upon me—don't kill me outright." This was a sad beginning for me. I sat up upon my blanket, trembling with terror, like a frightened hound, and thinking that my turn would come next. At length the house became still, and I forgot for a little while all my sorrows by falling fast asleep.

The next morning my mistress set about instructing me in my tasks. She taught me to do all sorts of household work; to wash and bake, pick cotton and wool, and wash floors, and cook. And she taught me (how can I ever forget it!) more things than these; she caused me to know the exact difference between the smart of the rope, the cart-whip, and the cow-skin, when applied to my naked body by her own cruel hand. And there was scarcely any punishment more dreadful than the blows I received on my face and head from her hard heavy fist. She was a fearful woman, and a savage mistress to her slaves.

There were two little slave boys in the house, on whom she vented her bad temper in a special manner. One of these children was a mulatto, called Cyrus, who had been bought while an infant in his mother's arms; the other, Jack, was an African from the coast of Guinea, whom a sailor had given or sold to my master. Seldom a day passed without these boys receiving the most severe treatment, and often for no fault at all. Both my master and mistress seemed to think that they had a right to ill-use them at their pleasure; and very often accompanied their commands with blows, whether the children were behaving well or ill. I have seen their flesh ragged and raw with licks. Lick—lick—they were never secure one moment from a blow, and their lives were passed in continual fear. My mistress was not contented with using the whip, but often pinched their cheeks and arms in the most cruel manner. My pity for these poor boys was soon transferred to myself; for I was licked, and flogged, and pinched by her pitiless fingers in the neck and arms, exactly as they were. To strip me naked—to hang me up by the wrists and lay my flesh open with the cow-skin, was an ordinary punishment for even a slight offence. My mistress often robbed me too of the hours that belong to sleep. She used to sit up very late, frequently even until morning; and I had then to stand at a bench and wash during the greater part of the night, or pick wool and cotton and often I have dropped down overcome by sleep and fatigue, till roused from a state of stupor by the whip, and forced to start up to my tasks.

Poor Hetty, my fellow slave, was very kind to me, and I used to call her my Aunt; but she led a most miserable life, and her death was hastened (at least the slaves all believed and said so) by the dreadful chastisement she received from my master during her pregnancy. It happened as follows. One of the cows had dragged the rope away from the stake to which Hetty had fastened it, and got loose. My master flew into a terrible passion, and ordered the poor creature to be stripped quite naked, notwithstanding her pregnancy, and to be tied up to a tree in the yard. He then flogged her as hard as he could lick, both with the whip and cow-skin, till she was all over streaming with blood. He rested, and then beat her again and again. Her shrieks were terrible. The consequence was that poor Hetty was brought to bed before her time, and was delivered after severe labour of a dead child. She appeared to recover after her confinement, so far that she was repeatedly flogged by both master and mistress afterwards; but her former strength never returned to her. Ere long her body and limbs swelled to a great size; and she lay on a mat in the kitchen, till the water burst out of her body and she died. All the slaves said that death was a good thing for poor Hetty; but I cried very much for her death. The manner of it filled me with horror. I could not bear to think about it; yet it was always present to my mind for many a day.

After Hetty died all her labours fell upon me, in addition to my own. I had now to milk eleven cows every morning before sunrise, sitting among the damp weeds; to take care of the cattle as well as the children; and to do the work of the house. There was no end to my toils—no end to my blows. I lay down at night and rose up in the morning in fear and sorrow; and often wished that like poor Hetty I could escape from this cruel bondage and be at rest in the grave. But the hand of that God whom then I knew not, was stretched over me; and I was mercifully preserved for better things. It was then, however, my heavy lot to weep, weep, weep, and that for years; to pass from one misery to another, and from one cruel master to a worse. But I must go on with the thread of my story. One day a heavy squall of wind and rain came on suddenly, and my mistress sent me round the corner of the house to empty a large earthen jar. The jar was already cracked with an old deep crack that divided it in the middle, and in turning it upside down to empty it, it parted in my hand. I could not help the accident, but I was dreadfully frightened, looking forward to a severe punishment. I ran crying to my mistress, "O mistress, the jar has come in two." "You have broken it, have you?" she replied; "come directly here to me." I came trembling: she stripped and flogged me long and severely with the cow-skin; as long as she had strength to use the lash, for she did not give over till she was quite tired. When my master came home at night, she told him of my fault; and oh, frightful! how he fell a swearing. After abusing me with every ill name he could think of, (too, too bad to speak in England) and giving me several heavy blows with his hand, he said, "I shall come home tomorrow morning at twelve, on purpose to give you a round hundred." He kept his word—Oh sad for me! I cannot easily forget it. He tied me up upon a ladder, and gave me a hundred lashes with his own hand, and master Benjy stood by to count them for him. When he had licked me for some time he sat down to take breath; then after resting, he beat me again and again, until he was quite wearied, and so hot (for the weather was very sultry), that he sank back in his chair, almost like to faint. While my mistress went to bring him drink, there was a dreadful earthquake. Part of the roof fell down, and everything in the house went—clatter, clatter, clatter. Oh I thought the end of all things near at hand; and I was so sore with the flogging, that I scarcely cared whether I lived or died. The earth was groaning and shaking; everything tumbling about; and my mistress and the slaves were shrieking and crying out, "The earthquake! the earthquake!" It was an awful day for us all.

During the confusion I crawled away on my hands and knees, and laid myself down under the steps of the piazza, in front of the house. I was in a dreadful state—my body all blood and bruises, and I could not help moaning piteously. The other slaves, when they saw me, shook their heads and said, "Poor child! poor child"—I lay there till the morning, careless of what might happen, for life was very weak in me, and I wished more than ever to die. But when we are very young, death always seems a great way off, and it would not come that night to me. The next morning I was forced by my master to rise and go about my usual work, though my body and limbs were so stiff and sore, that I could not move without the greatest pain. Nevertheless, even after all this severe punishment, I never heard the last of that jar; my mistress was always throwing it in my face.

Some little time after this, one of the cows got loose from the stake, and eat one of the sweet-potato slips. I was milking when my master found it out. He came to me, and without any more ado, stooped down, and taking off his heavy boot, he struck me such a severe blow in the small of my back, that I shrieked with agony, and thought I was killed; and I feel a weakness in that part to this day. The cow was frightened by his violence, and kicked down the pail and spilt the milk all about. My master knew that this accident was his own fault, but he was so enraged that he seemed glad of an excuse to go on with his ill usage. I cannot remember how many licks he gave me then, but he beat me till I was unable to stand, and till he himself was weary.

After this I ran away and went to my mother, who was living with Mr. Richard Darrel. My poor mother was both grieved and glad to see me; grieved because I had been so ill used, and glad because she had not seen me for a long, long while. She dared not receive me into the house, but she hid me up in a hole in the rocks near, and brought me food at night, after everybody was asleep. My father, who lived at Crow-Lane, over the salt-water channel, at last heard of my being hid up in the cavern, and he came and took me back to my master. Oh I was loath, loath to go back; but as there was no remedy, I was obliged to submit.

When we got home, my poor father said to Capt. I—, "Sir, I am sorry that my child should be forced to run away from her owner; but the treatment she has received is enough to break her heart. The sight of her wounds has nearly broke mine. I entreat you, for the love of God, to forgive her for running away, and that you will be a kind master to her in future." Capt. I— said I was used as well as I deserved, and that I ought to be punished for running away. I then took courage and said that I could stand the floggings no longer; that I was weary of my life, and therefore I had run away to my mother; but mothers could only weep and mourn over their children, they could not save them from cruel masters—from the whip, the rope, and the cow-skin. He told me to hold my tongue and go about my work, or he would find a way to settle me. He did not, however, flog me that day.

For five years after this I remained in his house, and almost daily received the same harsh treatment. At length he put me on board a sloop, and to my great joy sent me away to Turk's Island.[1] I was not permitted to see my mother or father, or poor sisters and brothers, to say good bye, though going away to a strange land, and might never see them again. Oh the Buckra[2] people who keep slaves think that black people are like cattle, without natural affection. But my heart tells me it is far otherwise.

We were nearly four weeks on the voyage, which was unusually long. Sometimes we had a light breeze, sometimes a great calm, and the ship made no way; so that our provisions and water ran very low, and we were put upon short allowance. I should almost have been starved had it not been for the kindness of a black man called Anthony, and his wife, who had brought their own victuals, and shared them with me.

When we went ashore at the Grand Quay, the captain sent me to the house of my new master, Mr. D——, to whom Captain I—— had sold me. Grand Quay is a small town upon a sandbank; the houses low and built of wood. Such was my new master's. The first person I saw, on my arrival, was Mr. D——, a stout sulky looking man, who carried me through the hall to show me to his wife and children. Next day I was put up by the vendue master to know how much I was worth, and I was valued at one hundred pounds currency.

My new master was one of the owners or holders of the salt ponds, and he received a certain sum for every slave that worked upon his premises, whether they were young or old. This sum was allowed him out of the profits arising from the salt works. I was immediately sent to work in the salt water with the rest of the slaves. This work was perfectly new to me. I was given a half barrel and a shovel, and had to stand up to my knees in the water, from four o'clock in the morning till nine, when we were given some Indian corn boiled in water, which we were obliged to swallow as fast as we could for fear the rain should come on and melt the salt. We were then called again to our tasks, and worked through the heat of the day; the sun flaming upon our heads like fire, and raising salt blisters in those parts which were not completely covered. Our feet and legs, from standing in the salt water for so many hours, soon became full of dreadful boils, which eat down in some cases to the very bone, afflicting the sufferers with great torment. We came home at twelve; ate our corn soup, called *blawly*, as fast as we could, and went back to our employment till dark at night. We then shovelled up the salt in large heaps, and went down to the sea, where we washed the pickle from our limbs, and cleaned the barrows and shovels from the salt. When we returned to the house, our master gave us

---

1 *sloop* Small ship; *Turk's Island* The southernmost and easternmost island of the Bahamas.
2 *Buckra* White.

each our allowance of raw Indian corn, which we pounded in a mortar and boiled in water for our suppers. We slept in a long shed, divided into narrow slips, like the stalls used for cattle. Boards fixed upon stakes driven into the ground, without mat or covering, were our only beds. On Sundays, after we had washed the salt bags, and done other work required of us, we went into the bush and cut the long soft grass, of which we made trusses for our legs and feet to rest upon, for they were so full of the salt boils that we could get no rest lying upon the bare boards.

Though we worked from morning till night, there was no satisfying Mr. D—. I hoped, when I left Capt. I—, that I should have been better off, but I found it was but going from one butcher to another. There was this difference between them: my former master used to beat me while raging and foaming with passion; Mr. D— was usually quite calm. He would stand by and give orders for a slave to be cruelly whipped, and assist in the punishment, without moving a muscle of his face; walking about and taking snuff with the greatest composure. Nothing could touch his hard heart—neither sighs, nor tears, nor prayers, nor streaming blood; he was deaf to our cries, and careless of our sufferings. Mr. D— has often stripped me naked, hung me up by the wrists, and beat me with the cow-skin, with his own hand, till my body was raw with gashes. Yet there was nothing very remarkable in this; for it might serve as a sample of the common usage of the slaves on that horrible island.

Owing to the boils in my feet, I was unable to wheel the barrow fast through the sand, which got into the sores, and made me stumble at every step; and my master, having no pity for my sufferings from this cause, rendered them far more intolerable, by chastising me for not being able to move so fast as he wished me. Another of our employments was to row a little way off from the shore in a boat, and dive for large stones to build a wall round our master's house. This was very hard work; and the great waves breaking over us continually, made us often so giddy that we lost our footing, and were in danger of being drowned.

Ah, poor me!—my tasks were never ended. Sick or well, it was work—work—work!—After the diving season was over, we were sent to the South Creek, with large bills, to cut up mangoes to burn lime with. Whilst one party of slaves were thus employed, another were sent to the other side of the island to break up coral out of the sea.

When we were ill, let our complaint be what it might, the only medicine given to us was a great bowl of hot salt water, with salt mixed with it, which made us very sick. If we could not keep up with the rest of the gang of slaves, we were put in the stocks,[1] and severely flogged the next morning. Yet, not the less, our master expected, after we had thus been kept from our rest, and our

---

1   *stocks*   Device for confining the ankles and sometimes the wrists.

limbs rendered stiff and sore with ill usage, that we should still go through the ordinary tasks of the day all the same.——Sometimes we had to work all night, measuring salt to load a vessel; or turning a machine to draw water out of the sea for the salt-making. Then we had no sleep—no rest—but were forced to work as fast as we could, and go on again all next day the same as usual. Work—work—work—Oh that Turk's Island was a horrible place! The people in England, I am sure, have never found out what is carried on there. Cruel, horrible place!

Mr. D— had a slave called old Daniel, whom he used to treat in the most cruel manner. Poor Daniel was lame in the hip, and could not keep up with the rest of the slaves; and our master would order him to be stripped and laid down on the ground, and have him beaten with a rod of rough briar till his skin was quite red and raw. He would then call for a bucket of salt, and fling upon the raw flesh till the man writhed on the ground like a worm, and screamed aloud with agony. This poor man's wounds were never healed, and I have often seen them full of maggots, which increased his torments to an intolerable degree. He was an object of pity and terror to the whole gang of slaves, and in his wretched case we saw, each of us, our own lot, if we should live to be as old.

Oh the horrors of slavery! How the thought of it pains my heart! But the truth ought to be told of it; and what my eyes have seen I think it is my duty to relate; for few people in England know what slavery is. I have been a slave—I have felt what a slave feels, and I know what a slave knows; and I would have all the good people in England to know it too, that they may break our chains, and set us free.

Mr. D— had another slave called Ben. He being very hungry, stole a little rice one night after he came in from work, and cooked it for his supper. But his master soon discovered the theft; locked him up all night; and kept him without food till one o'clock the next day. He then hung Ben up by his hands, and beat him from time to time till the slaves came in at night. We found the poor creature hung up when we came home; with a pool of blood beneath him, and our master still licking him, but this was not the worst. My master's son was in the habit of stealing the rice and rum. Ben had seen him do this, and thought he might do the same, and when master found out that Ben had stolen the rice and swore to punish him, he tried to excuse himself by saying that Master Dickey did the same thing every night. The lad denied it to his father, and was so angry with Ben for informing against him, that out of revenge he ran and got a bayonet, and whilst the poor wretch was suspended by his hands and writhing under his wounds, he run it quite through his foot. I was not by when he did it, but I saw the wound when I came home, and heard Ben tell the manner in which it was done.

I must say something more about this cruel son of a cruel father. He had no heart—no fear of God; he had been brought up by a bad father in a bad path, and he delighted to follow in the same steps. There was a little old woman among the slaves called Sarah, who was nearly past work; and, Master Dickey being the overseer of the slaves just then, this poor creature, who was subject to several bodily infirmities, and was not quite right in her head, did not wheel the barrow fast enough to please him. He threw her down on the ground, and after beating her severely, he took her up in his arms and flung her among the prickly-pear[1] bushes, which are all covered over with sharp venomous prickles. By this her naked flesh was so grievously wounded, that her body swelled and festered all over, and she died in a few days after. In telling my own sorrows, I cannot pass by those of my fellow-slaves—for when I think of my own griefs, I remember theirs.

I think it was about ten years I had worked in the salt ponds at Turk's Island, when my master left off business, and retired to a house he had in Bermuda, leaving his son to succeed him in the island. He took me with him to wait upon his daughters; and I was joyful, for I was sick, sick of Turk's Island, and my heart yearned to see my native place again, my mother, and my kindred.

I had seen my poor mother during the time I was a slave in Turk's Island. One Sunday morning I was on the beach with some of the slaves, and we saw a sloop come in loaded with slaves to work in the salt water. We got a boat and went aboard. When I came upon the deck I asked the black people, "Is there any one here for me?" "Yes," they said, "your mother." I thought they said this in jest—I could scarcely believe them for joy; but when I saw my poor mammy my joy was turned to sorrow, for she had gone from her senses. "Mammy," I said, "is this you!" She did not know me. "Mammy," I said, "what's the matter?" She began to talk foolishly and said that she had been under the vessel's bottom. They had been overtaken by a violent storm at sea. My poor mother had never been on the sea before, and she was so ill, that she lost her senses, and it was long before she came quite to herself again. She had a sweet child with her—a little sister I had never seen, about four years of age, called Rebecca. I took her on shore with me, for I felt I should love her directly; and I kept her with me a week. Poor little thing! hers has been a sad life, and continues so to this day. My mother worked for some years on the island, but was taken back to Bermuda some time before my master carried me again thither.

After I left Turk's Island, I was told by some negroes that came over from it, that the poor slaves had built up a place with boughs and leaves, where they might meet for prayers, but the white people pulled it down twice, and would

---

1 *prickly-pear* Type of cactus.

not allow them even a shed for prayers. A flood came down soon after and washed away many houses, filled the place with sand, and overflowed the ponds: and I do think that this was for their wickedness; for the Buckra men there were very wicked. I saw and heard much that was very very bad at that place.

I was several years the slave of Mr. D— after I returned to my native place. Here I worked in the grounds. My work was planting and hoeing sweet-potatoes, Indian corn, plaintains, bananas, cabbages, pumpkins, onions, &c. I did all the household work, and attended upon a horse and cow besides, going also upon all errands. I had to curry the horse—to clean and feed him—and sometimes to ride him a little. I had more than enough to do—but still it was not so very bad as Turk's Island.

My old master often got drunk, and then he would get in a fury with his daughter, and beat her till she was not fit to be seen. I remember on one occasion, I had gone to fetch water, and when I was coming up the hill I heard a great screaming; I ran as fast as I could to the house, put down the water, and went into the chamber, where I found my master beating Miss D— dreadfully. I strove with all my strength to get her away from him; for she was all black and blue with bruises. He had beat her with his fist, and almost killed her. The people gave me credit for getting her away. He turned round and began to lick me. Then I said, "Sir, this is not Turk's Island." I can't repeat his answer, the words were too wicked—too bad to say. He wanted to treat me the same in Bermuda as he had done in Turk's Island.

He had an ugly fashion of stripping himself quite naked and ordering me then to wash him in a tub of water. This was worse to me than all the licks. Sometimes when he called me to wash him I would not come, my eyes were so full of shame. He would then come to beat me. One time I had plates and knives in my hand, and I dropped both plates and knives, and some of the plates were broken. He struck me so severely for this, that at last I defended myself, for I thought it was high time to do so. I then told him I would not live longer with him, for he was a very indecent man—very spiteful, and too indecent; with no shame for his servants, no shame for his own flesh. So I went away to a neighbouring house and sat down and cried till the next morning, when I went home again, not knowing what else to do.

After that I was hired to work at Cedar Hills, and every Saturday night I paid the money to my master. I had plenty of work to do there—plenty of washing; but yet I made myself pretty comfortable. I earned two dollars and a quarter a week, which is twenty pence a day.

During the time I worked there, I heard that Mr. John Wood was going to Antigua. I felt a great wish to go there, and I went to Mr. D—, and asked him to let me go in Mr. Wood's service. Mr. Wood did not then want to purchase me; it was my own fault that I came under him, I was so anxious to go. It was ordained to be, I suppose; God led me there. The truth is, I did not wish to be any longer the slave of my indecent master.

Mr. Wood took me with him to Antigua, to the town of St. John's, where he lived. This was about fifteen years ago. He did not then know whether I was to be sold; but Mrs. Wood found that I could work, and she wanted to buy me. Her husband then wrote to my master to inquire whether I was to be sold? Mr. D— wrote in reply, "that I should not be sold to any one that would treat me ill." It was strange he should say this, when he had treated me so ill himself. So I was purchased by Mr. Wood for 300 dollars (or £100 Bermuda currency).

My work there was to attend the chambers and nurse the child, and to go down to the pond and wash clothes. But I soon fell ill of the rheumatism, and grew so very lame that I was forced to walk with a stick. I got the Saint Anthony's fire,[1] also, in my left leg, and became quite a cripple. No one cared much to come near me, and I was ill a long long time; for several months I could not lift the limb. I had to lie in a little old out-house, that was swarming with bugs and other vermin, which tormented me greatly; but I had no other place to lie in. I got the rheumatism by catching cold at the pond side, from washing in the fresh water; in the salt water I never got cold. The person who lived in next yard (a Mrs. Greene) could not bear to hear my cries and groans. She was kind, and used to send an old slave woman to help me, who sometimes brought me a little soup. When the doctor found I was so ill, he said I must be put into a bath of hot water. The old slave got the bark of some bush that was good for pains, which she boiled in the hot water, and every night she came and put me into the bath, and did what she could for me; I don't know what I should have done, or what would have become of me, had it not been for her. My mistress, it is true, did send me a little food; but no one from our family came near me but the cook, who used to shove my food in at the door, and say, "Molly, Molly, there's your dinner." My mistress did not care to take any trouble about me; and if the Lord had not put it into the hearts of the neighbours to be kind to me, I must, I really think, have lain and died.

It was a long time before I got well enough to work in the house. Mrs. Wood, in the meanwhile, hired a mulatto woman to nurse the child; but she was such a fine lady she wanted to be mistress over me. I thought it very hard for a coloured woman to have rule over me because I was a slave and she was free. Her name was Martha Wilcox; she was a saucy woman, very saucy; and she went and complained of me, without cause, to my mistress, and made her angry with me. Mrs. Wood told me that if I did not mind what I was about, she would get my master to strip me and give me fifty lashes: "You have been

---

1   *Saint Anthony's fire*   Erysipelas or ergotism, diseases that cause intense redness, swelling of the skin, and severe pain.

used to the whip," she said, "and you shall have it here." This was the first time she threatened to have me flogged; and she gave me the threatening so strong of what she would have done to me, that I thought I should have fallen down at her feet, I was so vexed and hurt by her words. The mulatto woman was rejoiced to have power to keep me down. She was constantly making mischief; there was no living for the slaves—no peace after she came.

I was also sent by Mrs. Wood to be put in the Cage one night, and was next morning flogged, by the magistrate's order, at her desire; and this all for a quarrel I had about a pig with another slave woman. I was flogged on my naked back on this occasion; although I was in no fault after all; for old Justice Dyett, when we came before him, said that I was in the right, and ordered the pig to be given to me. This was about two or three years after I came to Antigua.

When we moved from the middle of the town to the Point, I used to be in the house and do all the work and mind the children, though still very ill with the rheumatism. Every week I had to wash two large bundles of clothes, as much as a boy could help me to lift; but I could give no satisfaction. My mistress was always abusing and fretting after me. It is not possible to tell all her ill language. One day she followed me foot after foot scolding and rating me. I bore in silence a great deal of ill words: at last my heart was quite full, and I told her that she ought not to use me so; that when I was ill I might have lain and died for what she cared; and no one would then come near me to nurse me, because they were afraid of my mistress. This was a great affront. She called her husband and told him what I had said. He flew into a passion: but did not beat me then; he only abused and swore at me; and then gave me a note and bade me go and look for an owner. Not that he meant to sell me; but he did this to please his wife and to frighten me. I went to Adam White, a cooper,[1] a free black who had money, and asked him to buy me. He went directly to Mr. Wood, but was informed that I was not to be sold. The next day my master whipped me.

Another time (about five years ago) my mistress got vexed with me because I fell sick and I could not keep on with my work. She complained to her husband, and he sent me off again to look for an owner. I went to a Mr. Burchell, showed him the note, and asked him to buy me for my own benefit; for I had saved about 100 dollars, and hoped with a little help, to purchase my freedom. He accordingly went to my master: "Mr. Wood," he said, "Molly has brought me a note that she wants an owner. If you intend to sell her, I may as well buy her as another." My master put him off and said that he did not mean to sell me. I was very sorry at this, for I had no comfort with Mrs. Wood, and I wished greatly to get my freedom.

---

1   *cooper*   Barrel- and tub-maker.

The way in which I made my money was this. When my master and mistress went from home, as they sometimes did, and left me to take care of the house and premises, I had a good deal of time to myself and made the most of it. I took in washing, and sold coffee and yams and other provisions to the captains of ships. I did not sit still idling during the absence of my owners; for I wanted, by all honest means, to earn money to buy my freedom. Sometimes I bought a hog cheap on board ship, and sold it for double the money on shore; and I also earned a good deal by selling coffee. By this means I by degrees acquired a little cash. A gentleman also lent me some to help to buy my freedom—but when I could not get free he got it back again. His name was Captain Abbot.

My master and mistress went on one occasion into the country, to Date Hill, for a change of air, and carried me with them to take charge of the children, and to do the work of the house. While I was in the country, I saw how the field negroes are worked in Antigua. They are worked very hard and fed but scantily. They are called out to work before daybreak, and come home after dark; and then each has to heave his bundle of grass for the cattle in the pen. Then, on Sunday morning, each slave has to go out and gather a large bundle of grass; and, when they bring it home, they have all to sit at the manager's door and wait till he comes out: often have they to wait there till past eleven o'clock without any breakfast. After that, those that have yams or potatoes, or fire-wood to sell, hasten to market to buy a dog's[1] worth of salt fish, or pork, which is a great treat for them. Some of them buy a little pickle out of the shad barrels, which they call sauce, to season their yams and Indian corn. It is very wrong, I know, to work on Sunday or go to market; but will not God call the Buckra men to answer for this on the great day of judgment—since they will give the slaves no other day?

While we were at Date Hill Christmas came; and the slave woman who had the care of the place (which then belonged to Mr. Roberts the marshal), asked me to go with her to her husband's house, to a Methodist meeting for prayer, at a plantation called Winthorps. I went; and they were the first prayers I ever understood. One woman prayed; and then they all sung a hymn; then there was another prayer and another hymn; and then they all spoke by turns of their own griefs as sinners. The husband of the woman I went with was a black driver. His name was Henry. He confessed that he had treated the slaves very cruelly; but said that he was compelled to obey the orders of his master. He prayed them all to forgive him, and he prayed that God would forgive him. He said it was a horrid thing for a ranger to have sometimes to beat his own wife or sister; but he must do so if ordered by his master.

---

1   *dog*   Coin of low value.

I felt sorry for my sins also. I cried the whole night, but I was too much ashamed to speak. I prayed God to forgive me. This meeting had a great impression on my mind, and led my spirit to the Moravian church; so that when I got back to town, I went and prayed to have my name put down in the Missionaries' book; and I followed the church earnestly every opportunity. I did not then tell my mistress about it; for I knew that she would not give me leave to go. But I felt I *must* go. Whenever I carried the children their lunch at school, I ran round and went to hear the teachers.

The Moravian ladies (Mrs. Richter, Mrs. Olufsen, and Mrs. Sauter) taught me to read in the class; and I got on very fast. In this class there were all sorts of people, old and young, grey headed folks and children; but most of them were free people. After we had done spelling, we tried to read in the Bible. After the reading was over, the missionary gave out a hymn for us to sing. I dearly loved to go to the church, it was so solemn. I never knew rightly that I had much sin till I went there. When I found out that I was a great sinner, I was very sorely grieved, and very much frightened. I used to pray God to pardon my sins for Christ's sake, and forgive me for everything I had done amiss; and when I went home to my work, I always thought about what I had heard from the missionaries, and wished to be good that I might go to heaven. After a while I was admitted a candidate for the holy Communion. I had been baptized long before this, in August 1817, by the Rev. Mr. Curtin, of the English Church, after I had been taught to repeat the Creed and the Lord's Prayer. I wished at that time to attend a Sunday School taught by Mr. Curtin, but he would not receive me without a written note from my master, granting his permission. I did not ask my owner's permission, from the belief that it would be refused; so that I got no farther instruction at that time from the English Church.

Some time after I began to attend the Moravian Church, I met with Daniel James, afterwards my dear husband. He was a carpenter and cooper to his trade; an honest, hard-working, decent black man, and a widower. He had purchased his freedom of his mistress, old Mrs. Baker, with money he had earned whilst a slave. When he asked me to marry him, I took time to consider the matter over with myself, and would not say yes till he went to church with me and joined the Moravians. He was very industrious after he bought his freedom; and he had hired a comfortable house, and had convenient things about him. We were joined in marriage, about Christmas 1826, in the Moravian Chapel at Spring Gardens, by the Rev. Mr. Olufsen. We could not be married in the English Church. English marriage is not allowed to slaves; and no free man can marry a slave woman.

When Mr. Wood heard of my marriage, he flew into a great rage, and sent for Daniel, who was helping to build a house for his old mistress. Mr. Wood asked him who gave him a right to marry a slave of his? My husband said, "Sir,

I am a free man, and thought I had a right to choose a wife; but if I had known Molly was not allowed to have a husband, I should not have asked her to marry me." Mrs. Wood was more vexed about my marriage than her husband. She could not forgive me for getting married, but stirred up Mr. Wood to flog me dreadfully with his horsewhip. I thought it very hard to be whipped at my time of life for getting a husband—I told her so. She said that she would not have nigger men about the yards and premises, or allow a nigger man's clothes to be washed in the same tub where hers were washed. She was fearful, I think, that I should lose her time, in order to wash and do things for my husband: but I had then no time to wash for myself; I was obliged to put out my own clothes, though I was always at the wash-tub.

I had not much happiness in my marriage, owing to my being a slave. It made my husband sad to see me so ill-treated. Mrs. Wood was always abusing me about him. She did not lick me herself, but she got her husband to do it for her, whilst she fretted the flesh off my bones. Yet for all this she would not sell me. She sold five slaves whilst I was with her; but though she was always finding fault with me, she would not part with me. However, Mr. Wood afterwards allowed Daniel to have a place to live in our yard, which we were very thankful for.

After this, I fell ill again with the rheumatism, and was sick a long time; but whether sick or well, I had my work to do. About this time I asked my master and mistress to let me buy my own freedom. With the help of Mr. Burchell, I could have found the means to pay Mr. Wood; for it was agreed that I should afterwards serve Mr. Burchell a while, for the cash he was to advance for me. I was earnest in the request to my owners; but their hearts were hard—too hard to consent. Mrs. Wood was very angry—she grew quite outrageous—she called me a black devil, and asked me who had put freedom into my head. "To be free is very sweet," I said: but she took good care to keep me a slave. I saw her change colour, and I left the room.

About this time my master and mistress were going to England to put their son in school, and bring their daughters home; and they took me with them to take care of the child. I was willing to come to England: I thought that by going there I should probably get cured of my rheumatism, and should return with my master and mistress, quite well, to my husband. My husband was willing for me to come away, for he had heard that my master would free me, and I also hoped this might prove true; but it was all a false report.

The steward of the ship was very kind to me. He and my husband were in the same class in the Moravian Church. I was thankful that he was so friendly, for my mistress was not kind to me on the passage; and she told me, when she was angry, that she did not intend to treat me any better in England than in the West Indies—that I need not expect it. And she was as good as her word.

When we drew near to England, the rheumatism seized all my limbs worse than ever, and my body was dreadfully swelled. When we landed at the Tower, I showed my flesh to my mistress, but she took no great notice of it. We were obliged to stop at the tavern till my master got a house; and a day or two after, my mistress sent me down into the wash-house to learn to wash in the English way. In the West Indies we wash with cold water—in England with hot. I told my mistress I was afraid that putting my hands first into the hot water and then into the cold, would increase the pain in my limbs. The doctor had told my mistress long before I came from the West Indies, that I was a sickly body and the washing did not agree with me. But Mrs. Wood would not release me from the tub, so I was forced to do as I could. I grew worse, and could not stand to wash. I was then forced to sit down with the tub before me, and often through pain and weakness was reduced to kneel or to sit down on the floor, to finish my task. When I complained to my mistress of this, she only got into a passion as usual, and said washing in hot water could not hurt any one; that I was lazy and insolent, and wanted to be free of my work; but that she would make me do it. I thought her very hard on me, and my heart rose up within me. However I kept still at that time, and went down again to wash the child's things; but the English washerwomen who were at work there, when they saw that I was so ill, had pity upon me and washed them for me.

After that, when we came up to live in Leigh Street, Mrs. Wood sorted out five bags of clothes which we had used at sea, and also such as had been worn since we came on shore, for me and the cook to wash. Elizabeth the cook told her, that she did not think that I was able to stand to the tub, and that she had better hire a woman. I also said myself, that I had come over to nurse the child, and that I was sorry I had come from Antigua, since mistress would work me so hard, without compassion for my rheumatism. Mr. and Mrs. Wood, when they heard this, rose up in a passion against me. They opened the door and bade me get out. But I was a stranger, and did not know one door in the street from another, and was unwilling to go away. They made a dreadful uproar, and from that day they constantly kept cursing and abusing me. I was obliged to wash, though I was very ill. Mrs. Wood, indeed once hired a washerwoman, but she was not well treated, and would come no more.

My master quarrelled with me another time, about one of our great wash-ings, his wife having stirred him up to do so. He said he would compel me to do the whole of the washing given out to me, or if I again refused, he would take a short course with me: he would either send me down to the brig in the river, to carry me back to Antigua, or he would turn me at once out of doors, and let me provide for myself. I said I would willingly go back, if he would let me purchase my own freedom. But this enraged him more than all the rest: he cursed and swore at me dreadfully, and said he would never sell my freedom—if I wished to be free, I was free in England, and I might go and try what freedom would do for me, and be d——d. My heart was very sore with this treatment, but I had to go on. I continued to do my work, and did all I could to give satisfaction, but all would not do.

Shortly after, the cook left them, and then matters went on ten times worse. I always washed the child's clothes without being commanded to do it, and anything else that was wanted in the family; though still I was very sick—very sick indeed. When the great washing came round, which was every two months, my mistress got together again a great many heavy things, such as bed-ticks, bed-coverlets, &c. for me to wash. I told her I was too ill to wash such heavy things that day. She said, she supposed I thought myself a free woman, but I was not; and if I did not do it directly I should be instantly turned out of doors. I stood a long time before I could answer, for I did not know well what to do. I knew that I was free in England, but I did not know where to go, or how to get my living; and therefore, I did not like to leave the house. But Mr. Wood said he would send for a constable to thrust me out; and at last I took courage and resolved that I would not be longer thus treated, but would go and trust to Providence. This was the fourth time they had threatened to turn me out, and, go where I might, I was determined now to take them at their word; though I thought it very hard, after I had lived with them for thirteen years, and worked for them like a horse, to be driven out in this way, like a beggar. My only fault was being sick, and therefore unable to please my mistress, who thought she never could get work enough out of her slaves; and I told them so: but they only abused me and drove me out. This took place from two to three months, I think, after we came to England.

When I came away, I went to the man (one Mash) who used to black the shoes of the family, and asked his wife to get somebody to go with me to Hatton Garden to the Moravian Missionaries: these were the only persons I knew in England. The woman sent a young girl with me to the mission house, and I saw there a gentleman called Mr. Moore. I told him my whole story, and how my owners had treated me, and asked him to take in my trunk with what few clothes I had. The missionaries were very kind to me—they were sorry for my destitute situation, and gave me leave to bring my things to be placed under their care. They were very good people, and they told me to come to the church.

When I went back to Mr. Wood's to get my trunk, I saw a lady, Mrs. Pell, who was on a visit to my mistress. When Mr. and Mrs. Wood heard me come in, they set this lady to stop me, finding that they had gone too far with me. Mrs. Pell came out to me, and said, "Are you really going to leave, Molly? Don't leave, but come into the country with me." I believe she said this because she thought Mrs. Wood would easily get me back again. I replied to her, "Ma'am, this is the fourth time my master and mistress have driven me out, or threatened to drive me—and I will give them no more occasion to bid me go. I was not willing to leave them, for I am a stranger in this country, but now I must go—I can stay no longer to be used." Mrs. Pell then went up stairs to my mistress, and told that I would go, and that she could not stop me. Mrs. Wood was very much hurt and frightened when she found I was determined to go out that day. She said, "If she goes the people will rob her, and then turn her adrift." She did not say this to me, but she spoke it loud enough for me to hear; that it might induce me not to go, I suppose. Mr. Wood also asked me where I was going to. I told him where I had been, and that I should never have gone away had I not been driven out by my owners. He had given me a written paper some time before, which said that I had come with them to England by my own desire; and that was true. It said also that I left them of my own free will, because I was a free woman in England; and that I was idle and would not do my work which was not true. I gave this paper afterwards to a gentleman who inquired into my case.

I went into the kitchen and got my clothes out. The nurse and the servant girl were there, and I said to the man who was going to take out my trunk, "Stop, before you take up this trunk, and hear what I have to say before these people. I am going out of this house, as I was ordered; but I have done no wrong at all to my owners, neither here nor in the West Indies. I always worked very hard to please them, both by night and day; but there was no giving satisfaction, for my mistress could never be satisfied with reasonable service. I told my mistress I was sick, and yet she has ordered me out of doors. This is the fourth time; and now I am going out."

And so I came out, and went and carried my trunk to the Moravians. I then returned back to Mash the shoeblack's house, and begged his wife to take me in. I had a little West Indian money in my trunk; and they got it changed for me. This helped to support me for a little while. The man's wife was very kind to me. I was very sick, and she boiled nourishing things up for me. She also sent for a doctor to see me, and sent me medicine, which did me good, though I was ill for a long time with the rheumatic pains. I lived a good many months with these poor people, and they nursed me, and did all that lay in their power to serve me. The man was well acquainted with my situation, as he used to go to and fro to Mr. Wood's house to clean shoes and knives; and he and his wife were sorry for me.

About this time, a woman of the name of Hill told me of the Anti-Slavery Society, and went with me to their office, to inquire if they could do anything to get me my freedom, and send me back to the West Indies. The gentlemen of the Society took me to a lawyer, who examined very strictly into my case; but told me that the laws of England could do nothing to make me free in

Antigua. However they did all they could for me: they gave me a little money from time to time to keep me from want; and some of them went to Mr. Wood to try to persuade him to let me return a free woman to my husband; but though they offered him, as I have heard, a large sum for my freedom, he was sulky and obstinate, and would not consent to let me go free.

This was the first winter I spent in England, and I suffered much from the severe cold, and from the rheumatic pains, which still at times torment me. However, Providence was very good to me, and I got many friends—especially some Quaker ladies, who hearing of my case, came and sought me out, and gave me good warm clothing and money. Thus I had great cause to bless God in my affliction.

When I got better I was anxious to get some work to do, as I was unwilling to eat the bread of idleness. Mrs. Mash, who was a laundress, recommended me to a lady for a charwoman. She paid me very handsomely for what work I did, and I divided the money with Mrs. Mash; for though very poor, they gave me food when my own money was done, and never suffered me to want.

In the spring, I got into service with a lady, who saw me at the house where I sometimes worked as a charwoman. This lady's name was Mrs. Forsyth. She had been in the West Indies, and was accustomed to Blacks, and liked them. I was with her six months, and went with her to Margate. She treated me well, and gave me a good character when she left London.

After Mrs. Forsyth went away, I was again out of place, and went to lodgings, for which I paid two shillings a week, and found coals and candle. After eleven weeks, the money I had saved in service was all gone, and I was forced to go back to the Anti-Slavery office to ask a supply, till I could get another situation. I did not like to go back—I did not like to be idle. I would rather work for my living than get it for nothing. They were very good to give me a supply, but I felt shame at being obliged to apply for relief whilst I had strength to work.

At last I went into the service of Mr. and Mrs. Pringle, where I have been ever since, and am as comfortable as I can be while separated from my dear husband, and away from my own country and all old friends and connections. My dear mistress teaches me daily to read the word of God, and takes great pains to make me understand it. I enjoy the great privilege of being enabled to attend church three times on the Sunday; and I have met with many kind friends since I have been here, both clergymen and others. The Rev. Mr. Young, who lives in the next house, has shown me much kindness, and taken much pains to instruct me, particularly while my master and mistress were absent in Scotland. Nor must I forget, among my friends, the Rev. Mr. Mortimer, the good clergyman of the parish, under whose ministry I have now sat for upwards of twelve months. I trust in God I have profited by what I have heard from him. He never keeps back the truth, and I think he has been the means of opening my eyes and ears much better to understand the word of God. Mr. Mortimer tells me that he cannot open the eyes of my heart, but that I must pray to God to change my heart, and make me to know the truth, and the truth will make me free.

I still live in the hope that God will find a way to give me my liberty, and give me back to my husband. I endeavour to keep down my fretting, and to leave all to Him, for he knows what is good for me better than I know myself. Yet, I must confess, I find it a hard and heavy task to do so.

I am often much vexed, and I feel great sorrow when I hear some people in this country say, that the slaves do not need better usage, and do not want to be free. They believe the foreign people, who deceive them, and say slaves are happy. I say, Not so. How can slaves be happy when they have the halter round their neck and the whip upon their back? and are disgraced and thought no more of than beasts? and are separated from their mothers, and husbands, and children, and sisters, just as cattle are sold and separated? Is it happiness for a driver in the field to take down his wife or sister or child, and strip them, and whip them in such a disgraceful manner?—women that have had children exposed in the open field to shame! There is no modesty or decency shown by the owner to his slaves; men, women, and children are exposed alike. Since I have been here I have often wondered how English people can go out into the West Indies and act in such a beastly manner. But when they go to the West Indies, they forget God and all feeling of shame, I think, since they can see and do such things. They tie up slaves like hogs—moor them up like cattle, and they lick them, so as hogs, or cattle, or horses never were flogged—and yet they come home and say, and make some good people believe, that slaves don't want to get out of slavery. But they put a cloak about the truth. It is not so. All slaves want to be free—to be free is very sweet. I will say the truth to English people who may read this history that my good friend, Miss S——, is now writing down for me. I have been a slave myself—I know what slaves feel—I can tell by myself what other slaves feel, and by what they have told me. The man that says slaves be quite happy in slavery—that they don't want to be free—that man is either ignorant or a lying person. I never heard a slave say so. I never heard a Buckra man say so, till I heard tell of it in England. Such people ought to be ashamed of themselves. They can't do without slaves they say. What's the reason they can't do without slaves as well as in England? No slaves here—no whips—no stocks—no punishment, except for wicked people. They hire servants in England; and if they don't like them, they send them away: they can't lick them. Let them work ever so hard in England, they are far better off than slaves. If they get a bad master, they give warning and go hire to another. They have their liberty. That's just what *we* want. We don't mind hard work, if we had proper treatment, and proper wages like English servants, and proper time given in the week to keep us from breaking the Sabbath. But they won't give it; they will have work—work—work, night and day, sick or well, till we are quite done up; and we must not speak up nor look amiss, however much we be abused. And then when we are quite done up, who cares for us, more than for a lame horse? This is slavery. I tell it to let English people know the truth; and I hope they will never leave off to pray God, and call loud to the great King of England, till all the poor blacks be given free, and slavery done up for evermore.

—1831

In Context

Mary Prince and Slavery

Mary Prince's Petition Presented to Parliament (24 June 1829)

A Petition of Mary Prince or James, commonly called Molly Wood, was presented, and read; setting forth, That the Petitioner was born a Slave in the colony of Bermuda, and is now about forty years of age; That the Petitioner was sold some years ago for the sum of 300 dollars to Mr. John Wood, by whom the Petitioner was carried to Antigua, where she has since, until lately resided as a domestic slave on his establishment; that in December 1826, the Petitioner who is connected with the Moravian Congregation, was married in a Moravian Chapel at Spring Gardens, in the parish of Saint John's, by the Moravian minister, Mr. Ellesen, to a free Black of the name of Daniel James, who is a carpenter at Saint John's, in Antigua, and also a member of the same congregation; that the Petitioner and the said Daniel James have lived together ever since as man and wife; that about ten months ago the Petitioner arrived in London, with her master and mistress, in the capacity of nurse to their child; that the Petitioner's master has offered to send her back in his brig to the West Indies, to work in the yard; that the Petitioner expressed her desire to return to the West Indies, but not as a slave, and has entreated her master to sell her, her freedom on account of her services as a nurse to his child, but he has refused, and still does refuse; further stating the particulars of her case; and praying the House to take the same into their consideration, and to grant such relief as to them may, under the circumstances, appear right. Ordered, That the said Petition do lie upon the Table.

from Thomas Pringle, Supplement to *The History of Mary Prince* (1831)

It was through the auspices of Thomas Pringle that Mary Prince's narrative came to be published, and that Prince found employment in London. Pringle contributed a substantial supplement to the *History* when it was first published; excerpts are reproduced below.

By the Original Editor, Thomas Pringle

Leaving Mary's narrative, for the present, without comment to the reader's reflections, I proceed to state some circumstances connected with her case which have fallen more particularly under my own notice, and which I consider it incumbent now to lay fully before the public.

About the latter end of November, 1828, this poor woman found her way to the office of the Anti-Slavery Society in Aldermanbury, by the aid of a person who had become acquainted with her situation, and had advised her to apply there for advice and assistance. After some preliminary examination into the accuracy of the circumstances related by her, I went along with her to Mr. George Stephen, solicitor, and requested him to investigate and draw up a statement of her case, and have it submitted to counsel, in order to ascertain whether or not, under the circumstances, her freedom could be legally established on her return to Antigua. On this occasion, in Mr. Stephen's presence and mine, she expressed, in very strong terms, her anxiety to return thither if she could go as a free person, and, at the same time, her extreme apprehensions of the fate that would probably await her if she returned as a slave. Her words were, "I would rather go into my grave than go back a slave to Antigua, though I wish to go back to my husband very much—very much—very much! I am much afraid my owners would separate me from my husband, and use me very hard, or perhaps sell me for a field negro—and slavery is too too bad. I would rather go into my grave!"

The paper which Mr. Wood had given her before she left his house, was placed by her in Mr. Stephen's hands. It was expressed in the following terms:

> I have already told Molly, and now give it her in writing, in order that there may be no misunderstanding on her part, that as I brought her from Antigua at her own request and entreaty, and that she is consequently now free, she is of course at liberty to take her baggage and go where she pleases. And, in consequence of her late conduct, she must do one of two things—either quit the house, or return to Antigua by the earliest opportunity, as she does not evince a disposition to make herself useful. As she is a stranger in London, I do not wish to turn her out, or would do so, as two female servants are sufficient for my establishment. If after this she does remain, it will be only during her good behaviour; but on no consideration will I allow her wages or any other remuneration for her services.
>
> JOHN A. WOOD
> London, 18 August 1828

This paper, though not devoid of inconsistencies, which will be apparent to any attentive reader, is craftily expressed; and was well devised to serve the purpose which the writer had obviously in view, namely, to frustrate any appeal which the friendless black woman might make to the sympathy of strangers, and thus prevent her from obtaining an asylum, if she left his house, from any respectable family. As she had no one to refer to for a character in this country except himself, he doubtless calculated securely on her being speedily driven back, as soon as the slender fund she had in her possession was expended, to throw herself unconditionally upon his tender mercies; and his disappointment in this expectation appears to have exasperated his feelings of resentment towards the poor woman, to a degree which few persons alive to the claims of common justice, not to speak of Christianity or common humanity, could easily have anticipated. Such, at least, seems the only intelligible inference that can be drawn from his subsequent conduct.

The case having been submitted, by desire of the Anti-Slavery Committee, to the consideration of Dr. Lushington and Mr. Sergeant Stephen, it was found that there existed no legal means of compelling Mary's master to grant her manumission; and that if she returned to Antigua, she would inevitably fall again under his power, or that of his attorneys, as a slave. It was, however, resolved to try what could be effected for her by amicable negotiation; and with this view Mr. Ravenscroft, a solicitor (Mr. Stephen's relative), called upon Mr. Wood, in order to ascertain whether he would consent to Mary's manumission on any reasonable terms, and to refer, if required, the amount of compensation for her value to arbitration. Mr. Ravenscroft with some difficulty obtained one or two interviews, but found Mr. Wood so full of animosity against the woman, and so firmly bent against any arrangement having her freedom for its object, that the negotiation was soon broken off as hopeless. The angry slave-owner declared "that he would not move a finger about her in this country, or grant her manumission on any terms whatever; and that if she went back to the West Indies, she must take the consequences."

This unreasonable conduct of Mr. Wood, induced the Anti-Slavery Committee, after several other abortive attempts to effect a compromise, to think of bringing the case under the notice of Parliament. The heads of Mary's statement were accordingly engrossed in a Petition, which Dr. Lushington offered to present, and to give notice at the same time of his intention to bring in a Bill to provide for the entire emancipation of all slaves brought to England with the owner's consent. But before this step was taken, Dr. Lushington again had recourse to negotiation with the master; and, partly through the friendly intervention of Mr. Manning, partly by personal conference, used every persuasion in his power to induce Mr. Wood to relent and let the bondwoman go free. Seeing the matter thus seriously taken up, Mr. Wood became at length alarmed—not relishing, it appears, the idea of having the case publicly discussed in the House of Commons; and to avert this result he submitted to temporize—assumed a demeanour of unwonted civility, and even hinted to Mr. Manning (as I was given to understand) that if he was not driven to utter hostility by the threatened exposure, he would probably meet our wishes "in his own time and way." Having gained time by these manoeuvres, he adroitly endeavoured to cool the ardour of Mary's new friends, in her cause, by representing her as an abandoned and worthless woman, ungrateful towards him, and undeserving of sympathy from others; allegations which he supported by the ready affirmation of some of his West India friends, and by one or two plausible letters procured from Antigua. By these and like artifices he appears completely to have imposed on Mr. Manning, the respectable West India merchant whom Dr. Lushington had asked to negotiate with him; and he prevailed so far as to induce Dr. Lushington himself (actuated by the benevolent view of thereby best serving Mary's cause), to abstain from any remarks upon his conduct when the petition was at last presented in Parliament. In this way he dextrously contrived to neutralize all our efforts, until the close of the Session of 1829; soon after which he embarked with his family for the West Indies.

Every exertion for Mary's relief having thus failed; and being fully convinced from a twelvemonth's observation of her conduct, that she was really a well-disposed and respectable woman; I engaged her, in December 1829, as a domestic servant in my own family. In this capacity she has remained ever since; and I am thus enabled to speak of her conduct and character with a degree of confidence I could not have otherwise done. ...

I may here add a few words respecting the earlier portion of Mary Prince's narrative. The facts there stated must necessarily rest entirely—since we have no collateral evidence—upon their intrinsic claims to probability, and upon the reliance the reader may feel disposed, after perusing the foregoing pages, to place on her veracity. To my judgment, the internal evidence of the truth of her narrative appears remarkably strong. The circumstances are related in a tone of natural sincerity, and are accompanied in almost every case with characteristic and minute details, which must, I conceive, carry with them full conviction to every candid mind that this negro woman has actually seen, felt, and suffered all that she so impressively describes; and that the picture she has given of West Indian slavery is not less true than it is revolting.

But there may be some persons into whose hands this tract may fall, so imperfectly acquainted with the real character of Negro Slavery, as to be shocked into partial, if not absolute incredulity, by the acts of inhuman oppression and brutality related of Capt. I— and his wife, and of Mr. D—, the salt manufacturer of Turk's Island. Here, at least, such persons may be disposed to think, there surely must be *some* exaggeration; the facts are too shocking to be credible. The facts are indeed shocking, but unhappily not the less credible on that account. Slavery is a curse to the oppressor scarcely less than to the oppressed: its natural tendency is to brutalize both.

from *The Narrative of Ashton Warner*

The History of Mary Prince was published in January of 1831. The following month Susanna Strickland recorded the narrative of the life of another slave, Ashton Warner, which was published March 1st. No doubt inevitably, there is some similarity in the descriptions of horrific abuse in the two narratives, but there is also a good deal to suggest that Strickland was not being disingenuous in her assertion that she was quite faithful in recording these narratives as they were related to her; certainly there are noticeable differences between the narrative style of Warner and that of Prince. (Strickland's note inviting readers to "see and converse with themselves" if they doubt that someone of Warner's background would be able to express himself so well is particularly interesting in this connection.)

Advertisement

In consequence of the unexpected decease of Ashton Warner, while this little volume was in the press, the profits that may arise from its sale will no longer be required, as was originally designed, for his personal benefit. But, in compliance with a wish expressed by the poor negro on his death-bed, it is now proposed to appropriate the proceeds to the benefit of his aged mother, and the enfranchisement (should the amount prove so considerable) of his enslaved wife and child. And I have the satisfaction of being authorized to add, for the information of benevolent individuals disposed to contribute liberally towards the objects now intimated—whether by the purchase of copies of this volume, or by pecuniary donations—that the little charitable fund thus contemplated, will be placed under the immediate management of George Stephen, Esq., Solicitor, 17, King's Arms Yard, Coleman Street, and Thomas Pringle, Esq., Secretary of the Anti-Slavery Society, 18, Aldermanbury, who have kindly undertaken to superintend its proper application.

S. STRICKLAND.

from Introduction

In writing Ashton's narrative, I have adhered strictly to the simple facts, adopting, wherever it could conveniently be done, his own language, which, for a person in his condition, is remarkably expressive and appropriate. Had I been inclined to give a recital of revolting cruelty, I should have chosen another case; and for such, unhappily, I had not far to seek. But those who wish to read such mournful narratives of human depravity will find enough for their information (far too many for the honour of human nature!) recorded in the publications of the Anti-Slavery Society.

The profits arising from the sale of this tract will be appropriated to the benefit of Ashton, who has been for the last three months in England, endeavouring to establish his claims to freedom; and who is at present suffering under severe illness, without any adequate means of subsistence.

With a view to render this Sketch of Colonial Slavery more complete, and to enable the reader to compare the details given by Ashton with those recorded by intelligent and conscientious eye-witnesses from England, I have subjoined, as an Appendix, the very important testimonies on this subject of three highly respectable clergymen of the established Church, and of an excellent Wesleyan Missionary[1]—testimonies as yet but partially known to the public, and which comprise a mass of information equally recent and interesting.

Should this little tract assist, however feebly, in the diffusion of correct information in regard to the general condition and the feelings of the slaves, and thus tend to promote the great and good cause of justice and mercy, the writer's object will be fully accomplished. Like the widow's mite cast into the sacred treasury,[2] those who love the truth will not deem it unworthy because its value is but humble.

London, 19 February 1831
S.S.

NEGRO SLAVERY
DESCRIBED
BY A NEGRO:
BEING
THE NARRATIVE OF ASHTON WARNER,
A NATIVE OF ST. VINCENT'S.
With an Appendix,
CONTAINING THE
TESTIMONY OF FOUR CHRISTIAN MINISTERS,
RECENTLY RETURNED FROM THE COLONIES,
ON THE SYSTEM OF SLAVERY AS IT NOW EXISTS.
BY
S. STRICKLAND.

"And tears and toil have been my lot
Since I the white man's thrall became;
And sorer griefs I wish forgot—

---

1   *I have subjoined ... Missionary*   These testimonies are not included in this anthology.
2   *widow's ... treasury*   See Luke 21.1–4.

Harsh blows and burning shame!
Oh, Englishman! thou ne'er canst know
The injured bondman's bitter woe
When round his heart, like scorpions, cling
Black thoughts that madden while they sting!"

LONDON:
SAMUEL MAUNDER, NEWGATE STREET.
1831.

I was born in the Island of St. Vincent's, and baptized by the name of Ashton Warner, in the parish church, by the Rev. Mr. Gildon. My father and mother, at the time of my birth, were slaves on Cane Grove estate, in Bucumar Valley, then the property of Mr. Ottley. I was an infant at the breast when Mr. Ottley died; and shortly after the estate was put to sale, that the property might be divided among his family. Before Cane Grove was sold, my aunt, Daphne Crosbie, took the opportunity of buying my mother and me of Mr. Ottley's trustees. My aunt had been a slave, but a favoured one. She had money left her by a coloured gentleman of the name of Crosbie, with whom she lived, and whose name she took. After his death she went to reside at Kingston. Finding it a good thing to be free, aunt Daphne wished to make all her friends free also, particularly the slaves on the estate where she was born, and with whom she had shared, in her early days, all the sorrows of negro servitude. She had a large heart, and felt great kindness for her own people; but her means were not equal to her good wishes. She bought her old parents of Mr. Jackson, Mr. Ottley's executor; and, as it was her earnest desire to make us all happy, she would have bought my uncle John Baptiste (my mother's brother) too; but Mr. Wilson, the gentleman who purchased the estate, would not sell him. His reason for refusing my aunt never knew, for my uncle was an old man then, and nearly past work. Mr. Wilson sent him away to the Island of St. Lucia, and it was some years before aunt Daphne heard any tidings of him. At last some persons, coming from St. Lucia to St. Vincent's, told her that he lay very sick on Mr. Grant's estate. My aunt was glad to find that he was still living, and she went herself to make him free. She had never crossed the water, or been on the great sea, but she overcame her fears, and hired a small boat, and went directly to St. Lucia. She found my poor uncle in a very miserable state, and in this condition she bought him of his master, and brought him back to St. Vincent's. He was ill a long, long time; it was many long weary months before he could even take up a broom to sweep the house. He was very grateful to aunt Daphne for all that she had done for him; and so were we all. She was a very good, kind woman, and a Christian, though a black woman; and we (her relations) all loved her very, very much. We had no one else to love—she was all the world to us.

Whilst I lived with my aunt at Kingston I was very happy. I had no heavy tasks to do; and she was as careful over me as if she had been my own mother, and used to keep me with her in the house, that I might not be playing about in the streets with bad companions. My mother made sausages and *souse*,[1] and I used to help her to carry them to gentlemen's houses for sale. This was light labour to her, for she had been a field slave, kept at hard work, and driven to it by the whip. I am sure our best days were spent with my dear aunt; nor did she make us alone happy; all the money she could save went to purchase the freedom of slaves who had formerly been her companions in bondage at Cane Grove, or to make their condition better. There was not a person upon the island who did not speak well of Daphne Crosbie; black or white it was all the same. She bore a good character until the day she died.

I lived with my aunt till I was ten years old, when I was claimed as a slave belonging to the Cane Grove estate, by Mr. Wilson. This was a hard and unjust claim; but Mr. Wilson said, that though my mother was sold I was not—that the best slaves had been sold off the estate—that I was *his* property, and he would claim me wherever I was to be found. Now, he was wrong in all this, and I can prove to you, in two short minutes, that I did not belong to him. When my aunt manumitted my mother and me, Mr. Wilson had not-yet bought the estate; and in the Island of St. Vincent's it has always been a customary rule that the young child at the breast is sold as one with its mother, and does not become separate property till it is five or six years old; so that Mr. Wilson's claim was very unjust and oppressive.[2]

When my aunt found Mr. Wilson bent on taking me away by force, she went to Mr. Jackson, the gentleman from whom she had purchased my mother, and told him the state of the case, and he gave her a written paper to take to the Chief Justice of the island, to prove that I belonged to Daphne Crosbie, should Mr. Wilson continue to claim me. My aunt went to the Governor and showed him this paper, and also the manumission paper she had received from Mr. Jackson. The Governor, after looking at it, said that Mr. Wilson had no legal right to claim me upon the estate, and he promised my aunt that he would write to him to that effect. But we never knew whether he did or not, for we never got an answer from him. It is of no use trusting to what the white people in the West Indies say; they always forget their promises to slaves. Before this happened, my aunt had bound me apprentice to a cooper, to learn

---

1   [Strickland's note] Slices of pig's head, salted and prepared in a particular manner, and sold in the markets by the slaves.

2   [Strickland's note] This is poor Ashton's own statement. Whether the Colonial *Slave Law* will support his claim for freedom on this ground, is a question which remains to be determined.—S.S.

his trade. I was bound for seven years, and had signed the indenture myself, as a free black, by making a cross for my name.

My master's name was Pierre Wynn. He was a kind good master, and I never ceased to lament the cause which parted me from him. I had been with him between two and three months, and was busy one morning at work in the cooper's yard, helping the journeyman to truss a molasses-cask, when Mr. Wilson's manager, Mr. Donald, with two coloured men, and a white named Newman, came into the yard. This man, Newman, had informed Mr. Wilson where I was, and he sent his people to take me away by force. When the manager came into the yard, he said, "Which is Ashton?" I answered, quite innocently, not suspecting any mischief, "I am Ashton." Directly I said so the manager caught hold of me by the back of my neck. I did not know why he held me. I did not know what to think—I could not get my breath to speak—I was dreadfully frightened, and trembled all over. The other men got hold of me, and held me fast. They then led me away to Mr. Dalzell, Mr. Wilson's attorney, and shut me up in his office till Mr. Wilson came. Mr. Dalzell was afraid that I would try to make my escape, and to make sure of me one man kept watch at the window and another at the door. When Mr. Wilson came in he did not know me, and asked who I was. One of the men told him that I was Ashton. He said, "Very well; keep him here till I am ready to send him down to the estate." He then came up to the place where I was standing, and examined me from head to foot; then turned to Mr. Dalzell, and began talking to him about me. I was too young, and too much frightened at being stolen away, to remember much of their discourse; but I am very sure that I shall never forget that day.

Before Mr. Wilson left the office, my mother and Daphne Crosbie came to hear what was to be done with me, and why I had been taken away. But all they said was of no use; they could do no good where there was no justice to be had. Mr. Wilson insisted that I was a slave, and *his* slave, and he would have it so, in spite of my mother's tears and my aunt's entreaties. My poor mother was greatly distressed, and cried very bitterly. She entreated Mr. Wilson, if he thought he had a just claim for me, to put me in gaol till the question as to my freedom could be fairly settled; but he refused to do this, and when she continued her entreaties he grew angry, and ordered her not to stop in the yard, but to go away directly. And she and aunt Crosbie, on finding that nothing could be done for me there, were obliged to leave me in his hands.

The manager then put me into a boat, and took me down to the estate. It was rather late in the afternoon when we got there. I had nothing given me to do that day. It was Saturday, and I was not set to work till the Monday morning. I was very sad, and wished very much to run away. I could not bear the thought of being a slave, and I was very restless and unhappy.

On the Monday morning, John, the head cooper, took me down to the sugar works to help him; but I had no heart to work—I did nothing but think how I might run away. I was not knowing enough, however, to make my escape; and, after consulting with myself a long time, I found it would be the best plan to make myself as patient as I could. But still I was always thinking of my mother and aunt, and of Pierre Wynn, and the home I had been taken from. The estate of Cane Grove was in the middle of a deep valley, near the sea shore. Mr. Wilson's house stood upon the brow of the hill, and overlooked the whole sugar plantation. He had about three hundred slaves, and was considered one of the severest masters in the whole island.

As I have spoken of the condition of the field negroes as being so much worse than that of the mechanics among whom I was ranked on the estate, I shall here endeavour to describe the manner in which the field gang were worked on Cane Grove estate. They were obliged to be in the field before five o'clock in the morning; and, as the negro houses were at the distance of from three to four miles from the cane pieces, they were generally obliged to rise as early as four o'clock, to be at their work in time. The driver is first in the field, and calls the slaves together by cracking the whip or blowing the conch shell. Before five o'clock the overseer calls over the roll; and if any of the slaves are so unfortunate as to be too late, even by a few minutes, which, owing to the distance, is often the case, the driver flogs them as they come in, with the cart-whip, or with a scourge of tamarind rods. When flogged with the whip, they are stripped and held down upon the ground, and exposed in the most shameful manner.

In the cultivation of the canes the slaves work in a row. Each person has a hoe, and the women are expected to do as much as the men. This work is so hard that any slave, newly put to it, in the course of a month becomes so weak that often he is totally unfit for labour. If he falls back behind the rest, the driver keeps forcing him up with the whip.

They work from five o'clock to nine, when they are allowed to sit down for half an hour in the field, and take such food as they have been able to prepare over night. But many have no food ready, and so fast till mid-day.

They go to work again directly after half an hour's respite, and labour till twelve o'clock, when they leave off for dinner. They are allowed two hours of mid-day intermission, out of crop time, and an hour and a half in crop time.

During this interval every slave must pick a bundle of grass to bring home for the cattle at night. The grass grows in tufts, often scattered over a great space of ground, and, when the season is dry, it is very scarce and withered, so that the slaves collect it slowly and with difficulty, and are often employed most of the time allowed them for mid-day rest, in seeking for it. I have frequently known them occupied the whole two hours in collecting it.

They work again in gang from two till seven o'clock. It is then dark. When they return home the overseer calls over the roll, and demands of every man and woman their bundles of grass. He weighs with his hand each bundle as it is given in, and, if it be too light, the person who presents it is either instantly laid down and flogged severely with the cart-whip, or is put into the stocks for the whole night. If the slaves bring home no grass, they are not only put into the stocks all night, but are more severely flogged the next morning. This grass-picking is a very sore grievance to the field slaves.

When they are manuring the ground, the slaves are forced to carry the wet manure in open baskets upon their heads. This is most unpleasant as well as severe work. It is a usual occupation for wet weather, and the moisture from the manure drips constantly down upon the faces, and over the body and clothes of the slaves. They are forced to run with their loads as fast as they can; and, if they flag, the driver is instantly at their heels with the cart-whip.

The crop-time usually commences in January and lasts till June, and, if the season is wet, till July. During this season every slave must bring in a bundle of cane-tops for the cattle, instead of a bundle of grass. They then go immediately to the sugar works, where they have to take up the *mogass* which was spread out at nine o'clock in the morning to dry for fuel to boil the sugar. This mogass is the stalks of the cane after the juice has been squeezed out by the mill. The slaves are employed till ten at night in gathering in the mogass, that it may not be wetted with the dew and rendered unfit for immediate use. The overseer then calls over the roll, and issues orders for a certain spell of them to be up and at the works at one o'clock in the morning. After this the slaves have to prepare their suppers; for, if they have no very aged parents or friends belonging to them, they must do this themselves, which occupies them another hour. Every creature that is capable of work must take a part in the labours of the crop; and no person remains at home but those who are totally unfit for work. Slaves who are too old and weak to go to the field have to make up bundles of mogass, cut grass for the stock, &c.

During this season all the mechanics on the estate are employed to pot the sugar; carpenters, coopers, masons, and rum-distillers, even the pasture-boys who tend the cattle, are called in to assist. To the little people are given small tubs to carry the sugar into the curing house; and the grown-up slaves have shovels to fill the tubs for them. When employed in potting the sugar, we did not leave off to get our breakfast till ten or eleven o'clock, and I have known it mid-day before we have tasted food.

The whole gang of field slaves are divided into spells, and every man and woman able to work has not only to endure during crop-time the severe daily labour, but to work half the night also, or three whole nights in the week. The work is very severe, and great numbers of the slaves, during this period, sink under it, and become ill; but if they complain, their complaints are not readily believed, or are considered only a pretence to escape from labour. If they are so very ill that their inability to work can be no longer doubted, they are at length sent to the sick house.

The sick-house is just like a pen to keep pigs in; if you wish to keep yourself clean and decent, you cannot. It is one of the greatest punishments to the slaves to be sent there. When we were hard pressed, and had much sugar to pot, the manager would often send to the sick-house for the people who were sick, or lame with sores, to help us. If they refused to come, and said that they were unable to work, they were taken down and severely flogged, by the manager's order, with the cart-whip. There is nothing in slavery harder to bear than this. When you are ill and cannot work, your pains are made light of, and your complaints neither listened to, nor believed. I have seen people who were so sick that they could scarcely stand, dragged out of the sick-house, and tied up to a tree, and flogged in a shocking manner; then driven with the whip to the work. I have seen slaves in this state crawl away, and lie down among the wet trash to get a little ease, though they knew that it would most likely cause their death.

The quantity of food allowed the slaves is from two pounds and a half to three pounds of salt-fish per week, for each grown person. They could easily eat this in two days, but they must make it last till they receive a fresh allowance from the overseer. The rest of their food they raise upon their provision grounds. The owner gives to each slave from thirty to forty feet square of ground; not the best ground, but such as has been over-cropped, and is no longer productive for canes. This is taken from them the next year, when, by manuring and planting with yams and other things, it has been brought round, and recovered strength for the cultivation of sugar. The slaves are likewise permitted to cultivate waste pieces of ground, and the headlands of fields, that are unfit for planting. They work this ground every Sunday. It is generally given to them in March or April, and it is taken away in December or January. Besides the Sunday, they get part of twenty-six Saturdays, out of crop-time, to cultivate their grounds. What I mean by saying they get only *part* of these Saturdays is this—that they are employed in their master's work, such as carrying out trash, &c., from five to ten o'clock in the forenoon; and in the evening they must bring each his bundle of grass to deliver as usual at the calling of the lists; so that about seven hours, even of the day which is called their own, is occupied with their owner's work. They are obliged to work on these days at the provision grounds, if they wish ever so much for a holiday. If they are absent when the overseer inspects the grounds, they are flogged, or put in the stocks. The grounds produce plantains, yams, potatoes, pumpkins, calabashes, &c. On the Sunday, at every town, a market is held, in which the slaves are allowed to sell the produce of their grounds. Those that can save a little money, buy a pig and fatten it, that, in case of any death happening among their friends, they may sell the pig to provide a few necessaries for the funeral. They bury the dead during the night, being allowed no time during the day for their funerals.

In building their houses, they are allowed as much board as will form a window and a door. They go to the woods and cut wild canes, to form the walls and roof. The huts are thatched with cane-trash or tops.

For clothing, the owner gives to each slave in the year six yards of blue stuff, called bamboo, and six yards of brown. The young people and children are given a less allowance, in proportion to their size and age; the young children getting only a small stripe to tie round the waist. For bed-clothing, they give them only a blanket once in four or five years; and they are obliged to wear this till it falls in pieces. If the slaves require other clothes, they must buy them out of their own little savings. Many of the field negroes are very badly off for clothing. A good many are always to be seen with only a rag of cloth round their loins in all weathers.

People so hardly, so harshly, treated, and so destitute of every comfort, cannot be supposed to work with a willing mind. They have no home which they can well call their own. They are worked beyond their strength, and live in perpetual fear of the whip. They are insulted, tormented, and indecently exposed and degraded; yet English people wonder that they are not contented. Some have even said that they are happy! Let such people place themselves for a few minutes under the same yoke, and see if they could bear it. Such bondage is ruin both to the soul and body of the slave; and I hope every good Englishman will daily pray to God, that the yoke of slavery may soon be broken from off the necks of my unfortunate countrymen for ever.[1]

What made me feel more deeply for the sad condition of the field slaves was the circumstance of my having taken a wife from among them, after I had resided several years on Cane Grove estate. When I was about twenty-one years of age, finding my condition lonely, because I had no friends to manage for me, as the other slaves had, I wished to marry, and have a home of my own, and a kind partner to do for me. Among the field slaves there was a very respectable young woman, called Sally, for whom I had long felt a great deal of regard. At last I asked her to be my wife; and we stood up in her father's house, before her mother, and her uncle, and her sisters, and, holding each other by the hand, pledged our troth as husband and wife, and promised before God

---

1   [Strickland's note]   Such is the impressive language in which Ashton speaks of slavery. The above are his own expressions; for, though an uneducated, he is a very intelligent negro, and speaks remarkably good English. Any reader, who wishes it, may see and converse with himself, by making application through the publisher.—S.S.

to be good and kind to each other, and to love and help each other, as long as we lived.

And so we married. And though it was not as white folks marry, before the parson, yet I considered her as much my wife, and I loved her as well, as though we had been married in the church; and she was as careful, and managed as well for me, as if she had been my mother. I could not bear to see her work in the field. It is, as I have already said, a very sad and hard condition of slavery; and the more my wife suffered, the more I wished to be free, and to make her so. When she was with child, she was flogged for not coming out early enough to work, and afterwards, when far advanced in pregnancy, she was put into the stocks by the manager, because she said she was unable to go to the field. My heart was almost broken to see her so treated, but I could do nothing to help her; and it would have made matters worse if I had attempted to speak up for her. She was twice punished in this cruel manner, though the overseer must have known that she was in no condition to work. After our child was born, she was again repeatedly flogged for not coming sooner to the field, though she had stopped merely to attend and suckle the baby. But they had no feeling for the mother or for her child, they cared only for the work. It is a dreadful thing to be a field negro; and it is scarcely less dreadful, if one's heart is not quite hardened, to have a wife, or a husband, or a child, in that condition. On this account I was often grieved that I had taken poor Sally to be my wife; for it caused her more suffering as a mother, while her cruel treatment wrung my heart, without my being able to move a finger, or utter a word, in her behalf.

—1831

David George

c. 1742 – 1810

David George's *An Account of the Life of Mr. David George* is a remarkable early slave narrative and conversion narrative, as well as an essential document in the history of the black Atlantic. In this dictated autobiography, George—whose varied experiences took him throughout the South, northward to what would later be Canada, and across the Atlantic to England and West Africa—demonstrates both the lengths to which black Americans before and after the Revolutionary War might go to pursue freedom, and the often-tenuous nature of the freedom they were able to secure.

David George was born into slavery in Virginia in the mid-eighteenth century, the son of John and Judith, Africans who had been kidnapped and brought to America as part of the transatlantic slave trade. His narrative recounts the vicious cruelty of the family's enslaver, which drove George to run away as a young man. George's escape did not lead to outright freedom, but he found numerous white and Indigenous communities willing to provide him with temporary shelter from his pursuant enslavers, including a Muskogg (Creek) tribe among whom he was also enslaved but was treated with kindness. Eventually, George was purchased by another, less cruel white enslaver named Gaulfin, whose extensive property spanned portions of South Carolina and Georgia; he would live here for several more years, marrying an enslaved woman named Phillis and having a number of children.

Although by the 1770s the period of religious revivalism known to historians as the First Great Awakening had subsided throughout most of colonial America, revival movements persisted in more rural areas in the South, and George soon found himself swept up in one of these waves. Stimulated by a conversation with a fellow black man who warned George that if he continued to live without religion he would "never see the face of God in glory," George underwent a profound conversion experience; before long, he was baptized and had begun to preach in the surrounding community. Around 1774, George and a small number of fellow believers formed the Silver Bluff Baptist Church, thought to be among the first black churches in America. George found he had immense skill as a preacher; under his ministry, the church at Silver Bluff more than tripled in size in just a few years. During this period, George taught himself to read—despite stringent Southern laws that sought to prevent literacy among enslaved people.

Like many black Americans, George's life was radically transformed by the advent of the American Revolutionary War, particularly as British troops began to gain ground in the South in the late 1770s. Gaulfin, a supporter of the Revolution, fled his property following the British capture of Savannah in 1778. He thus left George, his wife and children, and dozens of others able to cross the British lines, where enslaved people willing to support the Loyalist cause were promised freedom in accordance with the terms of Dunmore's Proclamation. George and his family spent the next few years living primarily in Savannah, joining a majority-black population whose collective labors became essential to the continuation of the British occupation; George made a living as a butcher, while his wife Phillis worked as a laundress for a British general.

At war's end, as the defeated British troops rushed to evacuate the South, George and a small number of other Black Loyalists were offered free transport to the British colony of Nova Scotia. George's time in Nova Scotia was marked both by highly successful evangelical efforts—he prompted conversions among and performed baptisms upon numerous white and black settlers—and by repeated outbreaks of highly racialized violence. Around 1784, Shelburne, Nova Scotia, was the site of numerous racially motivated riots instigated by white settlers; George was himself the target of several attacks. By the early 1790s, word of the black settlers' negative experiences in Nova Scotia—including the re-institution of a system that was in many cases tantamount to slavery—had reached a number of government officials in Britain. In response, the British government sent John Clarkson, an abolitionist and agent for the newly established Sierra Leone Company, to Nova Scotia with yet another offer of relocation: the company would pay for the passage for several hundred black people to resettle in the British colony at Freetown. George accepted, along with over a thousand other black recruits; in 1792 they began the brutal seven weeks' voyage to Sierra Leone.

Shortly after the move to Freetown, George took to sea yet again, this time to undertake a tour of England and meet with various Baptist leaders. It was here that he dictated his dramatic life story to the white ministers John Rippon and Samuel Pearce, who printed it (along with several white-authored testimonials to George's character and power as a preacher) in the *Baptist Annual Register* in 1793. He then returned to Sierra Leone, where he spent the rest of his life working as a religious and civic leader, bearing witness to the tumultuous beginnings of the colony. George died in Freetown in 1810. His *An Account of the Life of Mr. David George, from Sierra Leone in Africa* remains among the most important extant documents testifying to the lives and experiences of the group known today as the Black Loyalists.

Note on the Text

The text reproduced below is based on that first printed in *The Baptist Annual Register* (1793) as *An Account of the Life of Mr. David George, from Sierra Leone in Africa; Given by Himself in a Conversation with Brother Rippon of London, and Brother Pearce of Birmingham.* Spelling and punctuation have been modernized in accordance with the practices of this anthology.

⌘ ⌘ ⌘

An Account of the Life of Mr. David George, from Sierra Leone in Africa

I was born in Essex County, Virginia, about 50 or 60 miles from Williamsburg, on Nottaway River, of parents who were brought from Africa, but who had not the fear of God before their eyes. The first work I did was fetching water, and carding of cotton;[1] afterwards I was sent into the field to work about the Indian corn and tobacco, till I was about 19 years old. My father's name was John, and my mother's Judith. I had four brothers, and four sisters, who, with myself, were all born in slavery: our master's name was Chapel—a very bad man to the Negroes. My older sister was called Patty; I have seen her several times so whipped that her back has been all corruption, as though it would rot. My brother Dick ran away, but they caught him, and brought him home; and as they were going to tie him up, he broke away again, and they hunted him with horses and dogs, till they took him; then they hung him up to a cherry-tree in the yard, by his two hands, quite naked, except his breeches, with his feet about half a yard from the ground. They tied his legs close together, and put a pole between them, at one end of which one of the owner's sons sat, to keep him down, and another son at the other. After he had received 500 lashes, or more, they washed his back with salt water, and whipped it in, as well as rubbed it in with a rag; and then directly set him to work in pulling off the suckers[2] of tobacco. I also have been whipped many a time on my naked skin, and sometimes till the blood has run down over my waistband; but the greatest grief I then had was to see them whip my mother, and to hear her, on her knees, begging for mercy. She was master's cook, and if they only thought she might do anything better than she did, instead of speaking to her as to a servant, they would strip her directly, and cut away.[3] I believe she was on her death-bed when I got off, but I have never heard since. Master's rough and cruel usage was the reason of my running away. Before this time I used to drink, but did not steal; did not fear hell; was without knowledge; though I went sometimes to Nottaway, the English church,[4] about eight or nine miles off. I left the plantation about midnight, walked all night, got into Brunswick County, then over Roanoak River, and soon met with some White travelling

---

1 *carding of cotton* Cleaning and detangling raw cotton fibers in preparation for spinning.
2 *suckers* Undesired new leaf shoots; the continuous "suckering" of plants to maintain uniform growth is an essential part of tobacco cultivation.
3 *directly* Immediately; *cut away* I.e., punish with whips.
4 *English church* I.e., an Anglican church.

people, who helped me on to Pedee River.[1] When I had been at work there two or three weeks, a hue and cry found me out, and the master said to me, there are 30 guineas offered for you, but I will have no hand in it: I would advise you to make your way towards Savannah River.[2] I hearkened to him, but was several weeks going. I worked there, I suppose, as long as two years, with John Green, a white man, before they came after me again. Then I ran away up among the Creek Indians. As I travelled from Savannah River, I came to Okemulgee River,[3] near which the Indians observed my track. They can tell the Black people's track from their own, because they are hollow in the midst of their feet, and the Black's feet are flatter than theirs. They followed my track down to the river, where I was making a long raft to cross over with. One of these Indians was a king, called Blue Salt;[4] he could talk a little broken English. He took and carried me about 17 or 18 miles into the woods to his camp, where they had bear meat, deer meat, turkeys, and wild potatoes. I was his prize, and lived with him from the Christmas month till April, when he went into his town, Augusta, in the Creek nation. I made fences, dug the ground, planted corn, and worked hard; but the people were kind to me. S.C., my master's son, came there for me, from Virginia, I suppose 800 miles, and paid king Blue Salt for me in rum, linen, and a gun; but before he could take me out of the Creek nation, I escaped and went to the Nautchee[5] Indians, and got to live with their king, Jack, who employed me a few weeks. S.C. was waiting this while in hopes to have me. Mr. Gaulfin, who lived on Savannah River, at Silver Bluff, and who was afterwards my master, traded in these parts among the Indians in deer skins. He had a manager here, whose name was John Miller. Mr. Miller knew king Jack, and agreed with him and S.C. as to the price Mr. Gaulfin was to pay for me. So I came away from king Jack, who gave me into the hands of John Miller. Now I mended deer skins, and kept their horses together, that they might not wander too far and be lost. I used also once a year to go down with the horses, carrying deer skins, to Mr. Gaulfin's, at Silver Bluff. The distance, I think, was 400 miles, over five or six rivers, which we crossed in leather boats. After three years, when I came down, I told Mr. Gaulfin, that I wished to live with him at Silver Bluff. He told me I should: so he took me to wait upon him,[6] and was very kind to me. I was with

---

1 *Pedee River* I.e., Pee Dee River, which flows through both Carolinas.
2 *Savannah River* River that forms part of the border between South Carolina and Georgia.
3 *Okemulgee River* Alternative spelling of Ocmulgee, river that flows through central Georgia.
4 *king* Term often erroneously applied by English-language writers to Indigenous political leaders; among the Muskogee (Creek), the most important political leader is known as a "mico"; *Blue Salt* Although the exact identity of this leader is unknown, it is possible that the name George provides references the Salt Clan of the Muskogee.
5 *Nautchee* I.e., Natchez.
6 *to wait upon him* I.e., to work as a house servant.

him about four years, I think, before I was married.[1] Here I lived a bad life, and had no serious thoughts about my soul; but after my wife was delivered of our first child, a man of my own color, named Cyrus, who came from Charlestown,[2] South Carolina, to Silver Bluff, told me one day in the woods, that if I lived so, I should never see the face of God in glory. (Whether he himself was a converted man or not, I do not know.) This was the first thing that disturbed me, and gave me much concern. I thought then that I must be saved by prayer. I used to say the Lord's prayer,[3] that it might make me better, but I feared that I grew worse; and I continued worse and worse, as long as I thought I would do something to make me better;[4] till at last it seemed as if there was no possibility of relief, and that I must go to hell. I saw myself a mass of sin. I could not read, and had no scriptures. I did not think of Adam and Eve's sin,[5] but *I* was sin. I felt my *own* plague; and I was so overcome that I could not wait upon my master. I told him *I was ill*. I felt myself at the disposal of Sovereign mercy. At last in prayer to God I began to think that he would deliver me, but I did not know how. Soon after I saw that I could not be saved by my own doings, but that it must be by God's mercy—that my sins had crucified Christ; and now the Lord took away my distress. I was sure that the Lord took it away, because I had such pleasure and joy in my soul, that no man could give me. Soon after I heard brother George Liele preach, who, as you both[6] know, is at Kingston in Jamaica. I knew him ever since he was a boy. I am older than he; I am about fifty. His sermon was very suitable, on "Come unto me all ye that labour, and are heavy laden, and I will give you rest."[7] When it was ended, I went to him and told him I was so: That I was weary and heavy laden, and that the grace of God had given me rest. Indeed his whole discourse seemed for me. Afterwards brother Palmer, who was pastor at some distance from Silver Bluff, came and preached to a large congregation at a mill of Mr. Gaulfin's. He was a very powerful preacher; and as he was returning home Lord's-day[8] evening, I went with him two or three miles, and told him how it was with me. About this time more of my fellow-creatures began to

---

1   *married*   George's wife's name was Phillis.

2   *Charlestown*   Today spelled Charleston.

3   *the Lord's prayer*   Commonly recited Christian prayer; see Matthew 6.9–13 and Luke 11.2–4.

4   *as long as … better*   I.e., as long as I held to the belief that my individual actions could improve the state of my soul. Among many Protestant denominations, a central tenet is a belief in salvation through faith in God and his teachings, and not through one's good works on earth.

5   *Adam and Eve's sin*   The eating of the forbidden fruit in the Garden of Eden; many Christians hold this to be the first sin, and believe that all humans born thereafter have inherited Adam and Eve's original sin.

6   *you both*   John Rippon and Samuel Pearce, the Baptist ministers to whom George narrated his autobiography.

7   *Come unto … you rest*   See Matthew 11.28.

8   *Lord's-day*   Sunday.

seek the Lord. Afterwards Brother Palmer came again and wished us to beg Master to let him preach to us; and he had leave, and came frequently. There were eight of us now who had found the great blessing and mercy from the Lord, and my wife was one of them, and my brother Jesse Gaulfin that you mention in the history of us poor slaves,[1] was another. Brother Palmer appointed a Saturday evening to hear what the Lord had done for us,[2] and the next day he baptized us in the mill stream. Some time afterwards, when Brother George Liele came again, and preached in a corn field, I had a great desire to pray with the people myself, but I was ashamed, and went to a swamp and poured out my heart before the Lord. I then came back to Brother George Liele, and told him my case. He said, "In the intervals of service you should engage in prayer with the friends." At another time, when he was preaching, I felt the same desire, and after he had done, I began in prayer—it gave me great relief, and I went home with a desire for nothing else but to talk to the brothers and sisters about the Lord. Brother Palmer formed us into a church, and gave us the Lord's supper[3] at Silver Bluff. Then I began to exhort in the church, and learned to sing hymns. The first I learned out of book was a hymn by that great writing man, Watts,[4] which begins with "Thus saith the wisdom of the Lord." Afterwards the church advised with Brother Palmer about my speaking to them, and keeping them together; I refused, and felt I was unfit for all that, but Brother Palmer said this word to me, "Take care that you don't offend the Lord." Then I thought that he knew best, and I agreed that I would do as well as I could. So I was appointed to the office of an Elder and received instruction from Brother Palmer how to conduct myself. I proceeded in this way till the American war[5] was coming on, when the Ministers were not allowed to come amongst us lest they should furnish us with too much knowledge.[6] The Black people all around attended with us, and as Brother Palmer must not come, I had the whole management, and used to preach among them myself. Then I

---

1   *my brother Jesse Gaulfin*   George here assigns his brother the surname of their mutual enslaver, Mr. Gaulfin, as was common practice at the time;   *the history of us poor slaves*   George refers to George Liele's *Account of Several Baptist Churches, Consisting Chiefly of Negro Slaves* (1793), which appears in the same volume of the *Baptist Annual Register* that George's autobiography was published in.

2   *to hear ... for us*   Spoken accounts of one's spiritual conversion are an essential element of worship in many revivalist denominations, and a prerequisite of baptism in churches that perform only believer's baptism, such as the Baptist Church.

3   *gave us the Lord's supper*   I.e., conducted the rite of Holy Communion, which involves consuming bread and wine that have been consecrated and are therefore meant to symbolize the body and blood of Jesus.

4   *that great ... Watts*   Celebrated English hymn writer Isaac Watts (1674–1748).

5   *the American war*   I.e., the Revolutionary War.

6   *lest they ... too much knowledge*   Many white Americans felt that enslaved people should have minimal knowledge of the war and its causes, lest the rhetoric around freedom incite discontent and rebellion among them.

got a spelling book and began to read. As Master was a great man, he kept a White school-master to teach the White children to read. I used to go to the little children to teach me a, b, c. They would give me a lesson, which I tried to learn, and then I would go to them again, and ask them if I was right? The reading so ran in my mind, that I think I learned in my sleep as really as when I was awake; and I can now read the Bible, so that what I have in my heart, I can see again in the Scriptures. I continued preaching at Silver Bluff, till the church, constituted with eight, increased to thirty or more, and till the British came to the city Savannah and took it.[1] My Master was an anti-loyalist;[2] and being afraid, he now retired from home and left the slaves behind. My wife and I, and the two children we then had, and fifty or more of my Master's people, went to Ebenezer, about twenty miles from Savannah, where the King's forces were. The General[3] sent us over the big Ogeechee River to Savages' Plantation, where the White people, who were Loyalists, reported that I was planning to carry the Black people back to their slavery;[4] and I was thrown into prison, and laid there about a month, when Colonel Brown, belonging to the British, took me out. I stayed some time in Savannah, and at Yamacraw a little distance from it, preaching with brother George Liele. He and I worked together also a month or two: he used to plow, and I to weed Indian-corn. I and my family went into Savannah, at the beginning of the siege.[5] A ball[6] came through the roof of the stable where we lived, and much shattered it, which made us remove to Yamacraw, where we sheltered ourselves under the floor of a house on the ground. Not long after the siege was raised, I caught the small pox, in the fall of the year, and thought I should have died, nor could I do any more than just walk in the spring. My wife used to wash[7] for General Clinton,[8] and out of the little she got maintained us. I was then about a mile from Savannah, when the Americans were coming towards it a second time. I wished my wife to escape, and to take care of herself and of the children, and let me die there. She went: I had about two quarts Indian corn, which I boiled; I ate a little, and a dog came in and devoured the rest; but it pleased God some

---

1   *till the British ... took it*   Reference to the 29 December 1778 capture of Savannah, which remained a Loyalist stronghold until 1782.
2   *anti-loyalist*   I.e., a Patriot, or supporter of the Revolution.
3   *The General*   British general Augustine Prévost (1723–86).
4   *that I ... their slavery*   I.e., that I was planning to betray the British and lead the black people back across rebel lines, where they would be returned to slavery. Under the terms of the war measure known as Dunmore's Proclamation (1775), the British had offered freedom to any enslaved people who would flee their rebel enslavers and support the Loyalist cause.
5   *the siege*   Unsuccessful 1779 attempt by the Continental Army to recapture Savannah.
6   *ball*   I.e., cannonball.
7   *wash*   I.e., do the laundry.
8   *General Clinton*   Henry Clinton, who served as British Commander-in-Chief in North America between 1778 and 1782.

people who came along the road gave me a little rice: I grew better, and as the troops did not come so near as was expected, I went into Savannah, where I met my family, and tarried there about two years, in a hut belonging to Lawyer Gibbons, where I kept a butcher's stall. My wife had a brother, who was half an Indian by his mother's side, and half a Negro. He sent us a steer, which I sold, and had now in all 13 dollars, and about three guineas[1] besides, with which I designed to pay our passage, and set off for Charlestown;[2] but the British light horse[3] came in, and took it all away. However as it was a good time for the sale of meat, I borrowed money from some of the Black people to buy hogs, and soon re-paid them, and agreed for a passage to Charlestown, where Major P.[4] the British commander, was very kind to me. When the English were going to evacuate Charlestown, they advised me to go to Halifax, in Nova Scotia, and gave the few Black people, and it may be as many as 500 White people, their passage for nothing. We were 22 days on the passage, and used[5] very ill on board. When we came off Halifax, I got leave to go ashore. On showing my papers to General Patterson, he sent orders, by a sergeant, for my wife and children to follow me. This was before Christmas, and we stayed there till June; but as no way was open for me to preach to my own color, I got leave to go to Shelburn (150 miles, or more, I suppose, by sea), in the suit of General Patterson, leaving my wife and children for a while behind. Numbers of my own color were here, but I found the White people were against me. I began to sing the first night, in the woods, at a camp, for there were no houses then built; they were just clearing and preparing to erect a town. The Black people came far and near, it was so new to them: I kept on so every night in the week, and appointed a meeting for the first Lord's-day, in a valley between two hills, close by the river; and a great number of White and Black people came, and I was so overjoyed with having an opportunity once more of preaching the word of God, that after I had given out the hymn, I could not speak for tears. In the afternoon we met again, in the same place, and I had great

---

1 *13 dollars ... guineas* The dollars referred to here are Spanish dollars, which were widely used in America prior to the introduction of the U.S. dollar in 1792; the guinea was a British coin valued at twenty-one shillings, or one pound and one shilling. Currency was extremely heterogeneous in pre-revolutionary America (and various forms of currency besides U.S. dollars continued to be in circulation well into the nineteenth century).

2 *Charlestown* Charleston was a British stronghold from May 1780 until its evacuation in December 1782.

3 *light horse* Cavalry; troop of mounted soldiers that would engage in reconnaissance, skirmishes, and other engagements requiring speed. Though George's meaning here is not clear, one possible interpretation is that he spent all his money preparing for the journey to Charleston, but that a battle in which the British Light Horse took part subsequently made it impossible to go there.

4 *Major P.* Major-general James Paterson, who served as military commander of British-held Charleston.

5 *used* Treated.

liberty from the Lord. We had a meeting now every evening, and those poor creatures who had never heard the gospel before, listened to me very attentively: but the White people, the justices, and all, were in an uproar, and said that I might go out into the woods, for I should not stay there. I ought to except one White man, who knew me at Savannah, and who said I should have his lot to live upon as long as I would, and build a house if I pleased. I then cut down poles, stripped bark, and made a smart hut, and the people came flocking to the preaching every evening for a month, as though they had come for their supper. Then Governor Parr[1] came from Halifax, brought my wife and children, gave me six months provisions for my family, and a quarter an acre of land to cultivate for our subsistence. It was a spot where there was plenty of water, and which I had secretly wished for, as I knew it would be convenient for baptizing at any time. The weather being severe, and the ground covered with snow, we raised a platform of poles for the hearers to stand upon, but there was nothing over their heads. Continuing to attend, they desired to have a meeting house[2] built. We had then a day of hearing what the Lord had done, and I and my wife heard their experiences,[3] and I received four of my own color; brother Sampson, brother John, sister Offee, and sister Dinah; these all wear well,[4] at Sierra Leone, except brother Sampson, an excellent man, who died on his voyage to that place. The first time I baptized here was a little before Christmas, in the creek which ran through my lot. I preached to a great number of people on the occasion, who behaved very well. I now formed the church with us six, and administered the Lord's supper in the meeting-house before it was finished. They went on with the building, and we appointed a time every other week to hear experiences. A few months after I baptized nine more, and the congregation very much increased. The worldly[5] Blacks, as well as the members of the church, assisted in cutting timber in the woods, and in getting shingles; and we used to give a few coppers to buy nails. We were increasing all the winter, and baptized almost every month, and administered the Lord's supper first of all once in two months; but the frame of the meeting [house] was not all up, nor had we covered it with shingles till about the middle of the summer, and then it had no pulpit, seats, nor flooring. About this time, Mr. William Taylor and his wife, two Baptists, who came from London to Shelburn, heard of me. She came to my house when I was so poor that I had no money to buy any potatoes for feed, and was so good as to give my children somewhat, and me money enough to

---

1   *Governor Parr*   John Parr, who served as governor of Nova Scotia from 1783 to 1791.
2   *meeting house*   Churches were commonly referred to as meeting houses during this period.
3   *heard their experiences*   I.e., listened to their accounts of conversion before baptizing them.
4   *wear well*   I.e., are doing well.
5   *worldly*   In this context, not associated with the church; unbaptized.

buy a bushel of potatoes; which one produced thirty-five bushels. The church was now grown to about fifty members. At this time a White person, William Holmes, who, with Deborah his wife, had been converted by reading the scriptures, and lived at Jones's Harbour, about twenty miles down the river, came up for me, and would have me go with him in his schooner to his house. I went with him, first to his own house, and then to a town they called Liverpool,[1] inhabited by White people. Many have been baptized there by Mr. Chippenham, of Annapolis, in Nova Scotia. Mr. Jesse Dexter preached to them, but was not their pastor. It is a mixed communion church.[2] I preached there; the Christians were all alive,[3] and we had a little heaven together. We then returned to brother Holmes's, and he and his wife came up with me to Shelburn, and gave their experiences to the church on Thursday, and were baptized on Lord's-day. Their relations who lived in the town were very angry, raised a mob, and endeavoured to hinder their being baptized. Mrs. Holmes's sister especially laid hold of her hair to keep her from going down into the water; but the justices commanded peace, and said that she should be baptized as she herself desired it. Then they were all quiet. Soon after this the persecution increased, and became so great, that it did not seem possible to preach, and I thought I must leave Shelburn. Several of the Black people had houses upon my lot; but forty or fifty disbanded soldiers were employed, who came with the tackle of ships, and turned my dwelling house, and every one of their houses, quite over; and the meeting house they would have burned down, had not the ring-leader of the mob himself prevented it. But I continued preaching in it till they came one night, and stood before the pulpit, and swore how they would treat me if I preached again. But I stayed and preached, and the next day they came and beat me with sticks, and drove me into a swamp. I returned in the evening, and took my wife and children over the river to Birch Town, where some Black people were settled, and there seemed a greater prospect of doing good than at Shelburn. I preached at Birch Town from the fall till about the middle of December, and was frequently hearing experiences, and baptized about twenty there. Those who desired to hear the word of God, invited me from house to house, and so I preached. A little before Christmas, as my own color persecuted me there, I set off with my family, to return to Shelburn; and coming down the river the boat was frozen, but we took whip-saws[4] and cut away the ice till we came to Shelburn. In my absence the meeting house was occupied by a sort of tavern-keeper, who said, "The old Negro wanted to make a heaven of this place, but I'll make a hell of it." Then I preached in it as

---

1   *Liverpool*   Town in southwestern Nova Scotia.
2   *mixed communion church*   I.e., a church made up of followers of various Christian denominations.
3   *alive*   Full of Christian spirit.
4   *whip-saws*   Saws with long, narrow blades.

before, and as my house was pulled down, lived in it also. The people began to attend again, and in the summer there was a considerable revival of religion. Now I went down about twenty miles to a place called Ragged Island, among some White people, who desired to hear the word. One White sister was converted there while I was preaching concerning the disciples, who left all and followed Christ. She came up afterwards, gave her experience to our church, and was baptized, and two Black sisters with her. Then her other sister gave in her experience; and joined us without baptism, to which she would have submitted, had not her family cruelly hindered her; but she was the only one in our society who was not baptized.

By this time, the Christians at St. John's,[1] about 200 miles from Shelburn, over the Bay of Fundy, in New Brunswick, had heard of me, and wished me to visit them. Part of the first Saturday I was there was spent in hearing the experiences of the Black people; four were approved, some of whom had been converted in Virginia: a fortnight after, I baptized them in the river, on the Lord's-day. Numerous spectators, White and Black, were present, who behaved very well. But on Monday many of the inhabitants made a disturbance, declaring that nobody should preach there again without a licence from the Governor. He lived at Frederick town,[2] about an hundred miles from thence up St. John's River. I went off in the packet[3] to him. Colonel Allen, who knew me in Charlestown, lived but a few miles from the Governor, and introduced me to him, upon which his secretary gave me a licence.[4] I returned then to St. John's, and preached again, and left brother Peter Richards to exhort among them. He afterwards died on the passage, just going into Sierra Leone, and we buried him there. When I got back to Shelburn, I sent brother Sampson Colbert, one of my Elders, to St. John's, to stay there. He was a loving brother, and the Lord had endowed him with great gifts. When the experiences of nine or ten had been related there, they sent for me to come and baptize them. I went by water to Halifax, and walked from thence to Haughton about 80 miles from Annapolis, not far from New Brunswick. There is a large church at Haughton, I think the largest in Nova Scotia. They are all Baptists; Mr. Scott is their minister. We spent one Sabbath together, and all day long was a day to be remembered. When I was landing at St. John's, some of the people who

---

1 *St. John's* Now Saint John, New Brunswick.
2 *Frederick town* Now Fredericton, New Brunswick.
3 *packet* Type of ship that travels on a regular schedule between two locations to convey goods and passengers.
4 [Rippon's note] Secretary's Office, Frederick-town, 17th July, 1792.

   I do hereby certify, that David George, a free Negro man, has permission from his Excellency the Lieutenant Governor, to instruct the Black people in the knowledge, and exhort them to the practice of the Christian religion.

Jon. Odell, Secretary.

intended to be baptized were so full of joy that they ran out from waiting at table on their masters, with the knives and forks in their hands, to meet me at the water side. This second time of my being at St. John's I stayed preaching about a fortnight, and baptized ten people. Our going down into the water seemed to be a pleasing sight to the whole town, White people and Black. I had now to go to Frederick Town again, from whence I obtained the licence before; for one of our brethren had been there, and heard the experiences of three of the people, and they sent to me, intreating that I would not return until I had been and baptized them. Two brethren took me to Frederick Town in a boat. I baptized on the Lord's-day, about 12 o'clock: a great number of people attended. The Governor said he was sorry he could not come down to see it; but he had a great deal of company that day, which also hindered one of his servants from being baptized. I came back to St. John's, and home to Shelburn. Then I was sent for to Preston, and left brother Hector Peters, one of my Elders, with them. In returning to Shelburn, with about 30 passengers, we were blown off into the sea, and lost our course. I had no blanket to cover me, and got frost-bitten in both my legs up to my knees, and was so ill when I came towards land, that I could not walk. The church met me at the river side, and carried me home. Afterwards, when I could walk a little, I wanted to speak of the Lord's goodness, and the brethren made a wooden sledge, and drew me to Meeting. In the spring of the year I could walk again, but have never been strong since.

The next fall, Agent (afterwards Governor) Clarkson came to Halifax, about settling the new colony at Sierra Leone.[1] The White people in Nova Scotia were very unwilling that we should go, though they had been very cruel to us, and treated many of us as bad as though we had been slaves.[2] They attempted to persuade us that if we went away we should be made slaves again. The brethren and sisters all round at St. John's, Halifax, and other places, Mr. Wesley's people[3] and all, consulted what was best to do, and sent in their names to me, to give to Mr. Clarkson, and I was to tell him that they were willing to go. I carried him their names, and he appointed to meet us at Birch Town the next day. We gathered together there, in the meeting house of brother Moses, a blind man, one of Mr. Wesley's preachers. Then the Governor read the proclamation, which contained what was offered, in case we had a mind willingly to go, and the greatest part of us were pleased and agreed to go. We appointed a day over at Shelburn, when the names were to

---

1 *Agent ... Sierra Leone* British Lieutenant John Clarkson (1764–1828) was a leading abolitionist and a leader of the Sierra Leone Company, which sought to resettle Black Loyalists from Nova Scotia in the newly established British colony of Sierra Leone. Clarkson was later appointed governor of the colony.

2 [Rippon's note] This Governor Clarkson also has confirmed to the Editor.

3 *Mr. Wesley's people* I.e., the Methodists; John Wesley (1703–91) was a founder of Methodism.

be given to the Governor. Almost all the Baptists went, except a few of the sisters whose husbands were inclined to go back to New York; and sister Lizze, a Quebec Indian, and brother Lewis, her husband, who was an half Indian, both of whom were converted under my ministry, and had been baptized by me. There are a few scattered Baptists yet at Shelburn, St. John's, Jones's Harbour, and Ragged Island, beside the congregations at the other places I mentioned before. The meeting house lot, and all our land at Shelburn, it may be half an acre, was sold to merchant Black for about 7£.

We departed and called at Liverpool, a place I mentioned before. I preached a farewell sermon there; I longed to do it. Before I left the town, Major Collins, who with his wife used to hear me at this place, was very kind to me, and gave me some salted herrings, which were very acceptable all the way to Sierra Leone. We sailed from Liverpool to Halifax, where we tarried three or four weeks, and I preached from house to house, and [delivered] my farewell sermon in Mr. Marchington's Methodist Meeting-house. There is also a Mr. William Black, at Halifax, a smart preacher, one of Mr. Wesley's, who baptizes those Christians who desire it by immersion.[1]

Our passage from Halifax to Sierra Leone was seven weeks, in which we had very stormy weather. Several persons died on the voyage, of a catching fever, among whom were three of my Elders, Sampson Colwell, a loving man, Peter Richards, and John Williams.

There was great joy to see the land. The high mountain, at some distance from Free-town,[2] where we now live, appeared like a cloud to us. I preached the first Lord's day, it was a blessed time, under a sail, and so I did for several weeks after. We then erected a hovel for a meeting house, which is made of posts put into the ground, and poles over our heads, which are covered with grass. While I was preaching under the sails, sisters Patty Webb and Lucy Lawrence were converted, and they, with old sister Peggy, brother Bill Taylor, and brother Sampson Haywood, three who were awakened before they came this voyage, have since been baptized in the river.

On the voyage from Halifax to Sierra Leone, I asked the Governor if I might not hereafter go to England? and some time after we arrived there, I told him I wished to see the Baptist brethren who live in his country. He was a very kind man to me and to everybody; he is very free and good natured, and used to come to hear me preach, and would sometimes sit down at our private meetings; and he liked that I should call my last child by his name. And I sent

---

1 *one of ... by immersion* Although baptism by sprinkling or pouring water over the believer's head is more typical in Methodist churches, many offer baptism by full immersion upon the believer's request.

2 *Free-town* First continuous settlement by colonists sponsored by the Sierra Leone Company, and today the capital of Sierra Leone.

to[1] Mr. Henry Thornton,[2] O what a blessed man is that! he is brother, father, everything. He ordered me five guineas, and I had leave to come over. When I came away from Sierra Leone, I preached a farewell sermon to the church, and encouraged them to look to the Lord, and submit to one another, and regard what is said to them by my three Elders, brethren Hector Peters, and John Colbert, who are two exhorters, and brother John Ramsey.

—1793

---

1   *sent to*   I.e., sent word; sent a letter.
2   *Mr. Henry Thornton*   One of the directors of the Sierra Leone Company (1760–1815).

Solomon Northup
1807/08 – c. 1870?

Solomon Northup's *Twelve Years a Slave* is today acknowledged to be among the most unusual—and most powerful—slave narratives of the nineteenth century. Born a free man in upstate New York, in his early thirties Northup was kidnapped and sold into Louisiana, where he endured over a decade of plantation slavery before, in 1853, he managed to secure his freedom. Published mere months after the rescue, Northup's narrative not only gave a vivid picture of slavery's horrors in the South; it also laid bare the fragility of freedom for African Americans in the North.

Northup was born in northeastern New York in 1807 or 1808,[1] less than a decade after the passage of the state's Gradual Abolition Act, and only a few years after his father, Mintus Northup, had been freed (through the will of his late enslaver). Northup married in 1829, and he and his wife, Anne, were soon supporting a growing family. Both Northup and Anne regularly worked at hotels and restaurants during the busy tourist season; Northup worked periodically as a farmer, carpenter, and general laborer, and was also a highly skilled violinist, supplementing the family's income through performances.

It was as a violinist that Northup was "hired" in 1841 by two men identifying themselves as Merrill Brown and Abram Hamilton; they convinced Northup to join their traveling circus on a tour to New York City and ultimately to Washington, D.C. Though the men were friendly and appeared by all accounts to have Northup's best interests at heart, the trip ended in disaster. On the seventh of April 1841, Northup grew suddenly and severely ill; upon waking, he found himself locked in a slave pen, his free papers gone, Brown and Hamilton nowhere to be seen.

Northup had been kidnapped and sold into slavery, evidently through the collusion of the two white men. Without formal written evidence or the testimony of white people to prove his free status, Northup was effectively powerless. Following a brutal episode in which he was beaten for asserting that he was free, Northup found himself part of a large group of captives bound for New Orleans—a number of whom, he discovered, had also been unlawfully kidnapped. While en route to Louisiana Northup made two attempts at escape. Both fell through, and before long he was up for sale in the nation's slave-trading capital.

---

1   In his narrative Northup states that he was born in July 1808, but in later court testimony he claimed to have turned 47 in July 1854, meaning he would have been born in 1807. Most modern accounts of his life give more weight to this later testimony and give his year of birth as 1807, but there is no proof either way; some have suggested it to be more likely that a person would remember their year of birth correctly but sometimes get their age wrong than it would be for them to be mistaken in the other direction.

In New Orleans, Northup was purchased by cotton planter and minister William Ford; over the coming months Northup gained Ford's favor through his industrious work ethic and creative improvements to the estate's operation. Northup's initial experience of slavery under Ford was far less severe than that endured by many others enslaved in the Deep South. But it was not long before a change in Ford's financial situation resulted in Northup's being sold to the much more brutal John Tibaut (spelled "Tibeats" in the narrative). After numerous clashes with Tibaut—including narrowly escaping a lynching—Northup was sold again to cotton planter Edwin Epps, a violent and unpredictable man sarcastically described by Northup as "a shrewd calculator … [who] knew how to manage his own animals, drunk or sober." It was under Epps that Northup was to be enslaved for the next decade.

Northup's chance for escape came in June 1852 when he met Samuel Bass, a Canadian carpenter who earned Northup's trust through his kindness and apparent antislavery sympathies. With Bass's help, Northup was able to send three letters to New York; one of these eventually reached Henry B. Northup, a lawyer and the nephew of Mintus Northup's former enslaver, who had known Solomon throughout his youth. Though the rescue was several months in coming, in January 1853 Henry Northup arrived at Epps's plantation armed with proof of Northup's free status. The return to New York was not without incident. In Washington, Northup and his lawyer tried to press charges against James Burch, Northup's first purchaser; the charges were dropped in part because the court would not accept testimony from a black person. But on the twenty-first of January, Northup was finally reunited with his family.

Northup's rescue made national headlines. He soon began appearing on the abolitionist lecture circuit, and his case was widely discussed in the abolitionist press (some abolitionists petitioned Congress to provide financial compensation for Northup's time in unlawful servitude, but these petitions were never given serious consideration by those in power).

Within half a year of his rescue, Northup had produced a memoir, *Twelve Years a Slave*. Published in July 1853, the book was an almost instant bestseller; by 1856 it had sold over 30,000 copies, making it one of the most successful slave narratives of the nineteenth century. Northup had authored it in collaboration with white writer David Wilson, generally described as Northup's amanuensis; the degree of Northup's direct involvement in writing the text is unclear, though Wilson's preface claims that Northup "carefully perused the manuscript, dictating an alteration wherever the most trivial inaccuracy … appeared." Wilson was not known as an abolitionist, but had a minor reputation as the author of a handful of fairly sensational histories and biographies. This literary experience probably contributed to the success of *Twelve Years*, as did its illustrations (by prominent magazine illustrator Frederick M. Coffin).

The book's popularity was such that it was adapted for the stage in 1854 as *The Free Slave*—a play that Northup helped produce and in which he performed the starring role. He also continued to go on abolitionist lecture tours over the coming years. But by 1857 his career had begun to flag; the stage adaptations were drawing smaller and smaller audiences, and Northup was viciously attacked by a hostile crowd while attempting to deliver an antislavery lecture in what is now Ontario. This period was also marked by the failure of the legal proceedings against Northup's kidnappers (now revealed to be Alexander Merrill and Joseph Russell), which had begun late in 1853 when a reader of *Twelve Years* recognized Northup's descriptions of "Brown" and "Hamilton." Though the evidence against Merrill and Russell was strong, the proceedings stagnated and ultimately charges were dropped, likely for a variety of political reasons as well as due to persistent rumors that Northup had in fact colluded with his kidnappers in a botched attempt to defraud James Burch. Northup's near disappearance from public view after 1857 led to unsubstantiated rumors that he had been kidnapped again or murdered; in fact, there is scattered evidence to indicate that he was alive until at least the mid-1860s, possibly involved with the Underground Railroad. The general consensus is that Northup died in the early 1870s.

Twelve Years a Slave was widely praised upon its first publication, with reviewers citing its emotional weight, its "thrilling" plot, and its honesty (indeed, some reviewers felt that the narrative would be more convincing as abolitionist literature "because, instead of indiscriminate accusations, [Northup] gives you the good and evil of slavery just as he found it"). Several new editions were published over the next few decades. By the twentieth century the narrative tended to be referenced primarily for its contribution to the historical record; only infrequently was it studied as literature. For some critics, *Twelve Years* belonged to the same category as the other white-authored slave narratives that they judged to be historically interesting but factually unreliable, overly conventional in style and structure, and inauthentic as autobiography. Today, scholars give far more credence to Northup as an author and as an eyewitness to slavery, pointing out that almost all the events described in *Twelve Years* have since been authenticated, and noting as well the significant ways in which the work differs—in its perspective, its style, and Northup's narrative voice—from the conventional slave narrative.

Note on the Text

The excerpts included below are based on the first 1853 edition of *Twelve Years a Slave. Narrative of Solomon Northup, a citizen of New-York, kidnapped in Washington City in 1841, and rescued in 1853, from a cotton plantation near the Red River, in Louisiana.* Spelling and punctuation have been modernized in accordance with the practices of this anthology.

⌘⌘⌘

from *Twelve Years a Slave*

from CHAPTER I

Having been born a freeman, and for more than thirty years enjoyed the blessings of liberty in a free state—and having at the end of that time been kidnapped and sold into slavery, where I remained, until happily rescued in the month of January, 1853, after a bondage of twelve years—it has been suggested that an account of my life and fortunes would not be uninteresting to the public.

Since my return to liberty, I have not failed to perceive the increasing interest throughout the Northern states, in regard to the subject of slavery. Works of fiction, professing to portray its features in their more pleasing as well as more repugnant aspects, have been circulated to an extent unprecedented, and, as I understand, have created a fruitful topic of comment and discussion.

I can speak of slavery only so far as it came under my own observation—only so far as I have known and experienced it in my own person. My object[1] is to give a candid and truthful statement of facts: to repeat the story of my life without exaggeration, leaving it for others to determine whether even the pages of fiction present a picture of more cruel wrong or a severer bondage.

As far back as I have been able to ascertain, my ancestors on the paternal side were slaves in Rhode Island. They belonged to a family by the name of Northup, one of whom, removing to the state of New-York, settled at Hoosick, in Rensselaer County. He brought with him Mintus Northup, my father. On the death of this gentleman, which must have occurred some fifty years ago, my father became free, having been emancipated by a direction in his will.

Henry B. Northup, Esq., of Sandy Hill, a distinguished counselor at law, and the man to whom, under Providence, I am indebted for my present liberty, and my return to the society of my wife and children, is a relative of the family in which my forefathers were thus held to service, and from which they took the name I bear. To this fact may be attributed the persevering interest he has taken in my behalf.

Sometime after my father's liberation, he removed to the town of Minerva, Essex County, N.Y., where I was born, in the month of July, 1808.[2] How long he remained in the latter place I have not the means of definitely ascertaining. From thence he removed to Granville, Washington County, near a place

---

1   *object*   Goal.
2   *born ... 1808*   In later court testimony, Northup claimed to have turned forty-seven on 10 July 1854, which would make his year of birth 1807.

known as Slyborough, where, for some years, he labored on the farm of Clark Northup, also a relative of his old master; from thence he removed to the Alden farm, at Moss Street, a short distance north of the village of Sandy Hill; and from thence to the farm now owned by Russel Pratt, situated on the road leading from Fort Edward to Argyle, where he continued to reside until his death, which took place on the 22d day of November, 1829. He left a widow and two children—myself, and Joseph, an elder brother. The latter is still living in the county of Oswego, near the city of that name; my mother died during the period of my captivity.

SOLOMON IN HIS PLANTATION SUIT.

Solomon Northup

Illustration of Solomon Northup, used as the frontispiece for the first edition of *Twelve Years a Slave*. The seven illustrations in the book (four of which are included in this selection) were drawn by popular magazine illustrator Frederick M. Coffin and engraved by Nathaniel Orr.

Though born a slave, and laboring under the disadvantages to which my unfortunate race is subjected, my father was a man respected for his industry and integrity, as many now living, who well remember him, are ready to testify. His whole life was passed in the peaceful pursuits of agriculture, never seeking employment in those more menial positions, which seem to be especially allotted to the children of Africa. Besides giving us an education surpassing that ordinarily bestowed upon children in our condition, he acquired, by his diligence and economy, a sufficient property qualification to entitle him to the right of suffrage.[1] He was accustomed to speak to us of his early life; and although at all times cherishing the warmest emotions of kindness, and even of affection towards the family, in whose house he had been a bondsman, he nevertheless comprehended the system of slavery, and dwelt with sorrow on the degradation of his race. He endeavored to imbue our minds with sentiments of morality, and to teach us to place our trust and confidence in Him who regards the humblest as well

---

1   *a sufficient property ... suffrage*   Like those of many other states, New York's original constitution granted suffrage to all adult male residents who owned a certain amount of property, without any explicit race-based restrictions. The constitution was revised, however, in 1821, granting near-universal suffrage to white male residents while limiting suffrage among African Americans to those who owned property of at least $250 in value—effectively disenfranchising a large portion of New York's free black population.

as the highest of his creatures. How often since that time has the recollection of his paternal counsels occurred to me, while lying in a slave hut in the distant and sickly regions of Louisiana, smarting with the undeserved wounds which an inhuman master had inflicted, and longing only for the grave which had covered him, to shield me also from the lash of the oppressor. In the churchyard at Sandy Hill, an humble stone marks the spot where he reposes, after having worthily performed the duties appertaining to the lowly sphere wherein God had appointed him to walk.

Up to this period I had been principally engaged with my father in the labors of the farm. The leisure hours allowed me were generally either employed over my books, or playing on the violin—an amusement which was the ruling passion of my youth. It has also been the source of consolation since, affording pleasure to the simple beings with whom my lot was cast, and beguiling my own thoughts, for many hours, from the painful contemplation of my fate.

On Christmas day, 1829, I was married to Anne Hampton, a colored girl then living in the vicinity of our residence. The ceremony was performed at Fort Edward, by Timothy Eddy, Esq., a magistrate of that town, and still a prominent citizen of the place. She had resided a long time at Sandy Hill, with Mr. Baird, proprietor of the Eagle Tavern, and also in the family of Rev. Alexander Proudfit, of Salem. This gentleman for many years had presided over the Presbyterian society at the latter place, and was widely distinguished for his learning and piety. Anne still holds in grateful remembrance the exceeding kindness and the excellent counsels of that good man. She is not able to determine the exact line of her descent, but the blood of three races mingles in her veins. It is difficult to tell whether the red, white, or black predominates. The union of them all, however, in her origin, has given her a singular but pleasing expression, such as is rarely to be seen. Though somewhat resembling, yet she cannot properly be styled a quadroon,[1] a class to which, I have omitted to mention, my mother belonged.

I had just now passed the period of my minority, having reached the age of twenty-one years in the month of July previous. Deprived of the advice and assistance of my father, with a wife dependent upon me for support, I resolved to enter upon a life of industry; and notwithstanding the obstacle of color, and the consciousness of my lowly state, indulged in pleasant dreams of a good time coming, when the possession of some humble habitation, with a few surrounding acres, should reward my labors, and bring me the means of happiness and comfort.

---

1 *quadroon* Term commonly used in the nineteenth century to classify a person of mixed racial background—specifically, someone with one black and three white grandparents.

From the time of my marriage to this day the love I have borne my wife has been sincere and unabated; and only those who have felt the glowing tenderness a father cherishes for his offspring, can appreciate my affection for the beloved children which have since been born to us. This much I deem appropriate and necessary to say, in order that those who read these pages, may comprehend the poignancy of those sufferings I have been doomed to bear. ...

While living at the United States Hotel,[1] I frequently met with slaves, who had accompanied their masters from the South. They were always well dressed and well provided for, leading apparently an easy life, with but few of its ordinary troubles to perplex them. Many times they entered into conversation with me on the subject of slavery. Almost uniformly I found they cherished a secret desire for liberty. Some of them expressed the most ardent anxiety to escape, and consulted me on the best method of effecting it. The fear of punishment, however, which they knew was certain to attend their re-capture and return, in all cases proved sufficient to deter them from the experiment. Having all my life breathed the free air of the North, and conscious that I possessed the same feelings and affections that find a place in the white man's breast; conscious, moreover, of an intelligence equal to that of some men, at least, with a fairer skin, I was too ignorant, perhaps too independent, to conceive how anyone could be content to live in the abject condition of a slave. I could not comprehend the justice of that law, or that religion, which upholds or recognizes the principle of slavery; and never once, I am proud to say, did I fail to counsel anyone who came to me, to watch his opportunity, and strike for freedom. ...

At this time we were the parents of three children—Elizabeth, Margaret, and Alonzo. Elizabeth, the eldest, was in her tenth year; Margaret was two years younger, and little Alonzo had just passed his fifth birthday. They filled our house with gladness. Their young voices were music in our ears. Many an airy castle did their mother and myself build for the little innocents. When not at labor I was always walking with them, clad in their best attire, through the streets and groves of Saratoga. Their presence was my delight; and I clasped them to my bosom with as warm and tender love as if their clouded skins had been as white as snow.

Thus far the history of my life presents nothing whatever unusual—nothing but the common hopes, and loves, and labors of an obscure colored man, making his humble progress in the world. But now I had reached a turning point in my existence—reached the threshold of unutterable wrong, and sorrow, and despair. Now had I approached within the shadow of the cloud,

---

1   *United States Hotel*   Establishment in Saratoga Springs, New York, at which both Northup and his wife had been working during the winter season since about 1836.

into the thick darkness whereof I was soon to disappear, thenceforward to be hidden from the eyes of all my kindred, and shut out from the sweet light of liberty, for many a weary year.

from CHAPTER 2

One morning, towards the latter part of the month of March, 1841, having at that time no particular business to engage my attention, I was walking about the village of Saratoga Springs, thinking to myself where I might obtain some present employment, until the busy season should arrive. Anne, as was her usual custom, had gone over to Sandy Hill, a distance of some twenty miles, to take charge of the culinary department at Sherrill's Coffee House, during the session of the court. Elizabeth, I think, had accompanied her. Margaret and Alonzo were with their aunt at Saratoga.

On the corner of Congress Street and Broadway, near the tavern then—and for aught I know to the contrary, still—kept by Mr. Moon, I was met by two gentlemen of respectable appearance, both of whom were entirely unknown to me. I have the impression that they were introduced to me by some one of my acquaintances, but who, I have in vain endeavored to recall, with the remark that I was an expert player on the violin.

At any rate, they immediately entered into conversation on that subject, making numerous inquiries touching my proficiency in that respect. My responses being to all appearances satisfactory, they proposed to engage my services for a short period, stating, at the same time, I was just such a person as their business required. Their names, as they afterwards gave them to me, were Merrill Brown and Abram Hamilton, though whether these were their true appellations, I have strong reasons to doubt. The former was a man apparently forty years of age, somewhat short and thick-set, with a countenance indicating shrewdness and intelligence. He wore a black frock coat and black hat, and said he resided either at Rochester or at Syracuse. The latter was a young man of fair complexion and light eyes, and, I should judge, had not passed the age of twenty-five. He was tall and slender, dressed in a snuff-colored coat, with glossy hat, and vest of elegant pattern. His whole apparel was in the extreme of fashion. His appearance was somewhat effeminate, but prepossessing, and there was about him an easy air, that showed he had mingled with the world. They were connected, as they informed me, with a circus company, then in the city of Washington; that they were on their way thither to rejoin it, having left it for a short time to make an excursion northward, for the purpose of seeing the country, and were paying their expenses by an occasional exhibition. They also remarked that they had found much difficulty in procuring music for their entertainments, and that if I would accompany them as far as New-York, they would give me one dollar for each day's services, and three dollars in addition for every night I played at their performances, besides sufficient to pay the expenses of my return from New-York to Saratoga.

I at once accepted the tempting offer, both for the reward it promised, and from a desire to visit the metropolis. They were anxious to leave immediately. Thinking my absence would be brief, I did not deem it necessary to write to Anne whither I had gone; in fact supposing that my return, perhaps, would be as soon as hers. So taking a change of linen and my violin, I was ready to depart. The carriage was brought round—a covered one, drawn by a pair of noble bays, altogether forming an elegant establishment. Their baggage, consisting of three large trunks, was fastened on the rack, and mounting to the driver's seat, while they took their places in the rear, I drove away from Saratoga on the road to Albany, elated with my new position, and happy as I had ever been, on any day in all my life. ...

Brown and Hamilton ... began to importune me to continue with them to Washington. They alleged that immediately on their arrival, now that the summer season was approaching, the circus would set out for the north. They promised me a situation and high wages if I would accompany them. Largely did they expatiate on the advantages that would result to me, and such were the flattering representations they made, that I finally concluded to accept the offer.

The next morning they suggested that, inasmuch as we were about entering a slave state, it would be well, before leaving New-York, to procure free papers. The idea struck me as a prudent one, though I think it would scarcely have occurred to me, had they not proposed it. We proceeded at once to what I understood to be the Custom House. They made oath to certain facts showing I was a free man. ... Some further formalities were gone through with before it was completed, when, paying the officer two dollars, I placed the papers in my pocket, and started with my two friends to our hotel. I thought at the time, I must confess, that the papers were scarcely worth the cost of obtaining them—the apprehension of danger to my personal safety never having suggested itself to me in the remotest manner. ...

[The group arrives in Washington on 6 April 1841, the evening before the funeral procession of the recently deceased William Henry Harrison.]

After supper they called me to their apartments, and paid me forty-three dollars, a sum greater than my wages amounted to, which act of generosity was in consequence, they said, of their not having exhibited as often as they had given me to anticipate, during our trip from Saratoga. They moreover informed me that it had been the intention of the circus company to leave Washington the next morning, but that on account of the funeral, they had concluded to remain another day. They were then, as they had been from the time of our first meeting, extremely kind. No opportunity was omitted of addressing me in the language of approbation; while, on the other hand, I was certainly much prepossessed in their favor. I gave them my confidence without reserve, and would freely have trusted them to almost any extent. Their constant conversation and manner towards me—their foresight in suggesting the idea of free papers, and a hundred other little acts, unnecessary to be repeated—all indicated that they were friends indeed, sincerely solicitous for my welfare. I know not but they were. I know not but they were innocent of the great wickedness of which I now believe them guilty. Whether they were accessory to my misfortunes— subtle and inhuman monsters in the shape of men—designedly luring me away from home and family, and liberty, for the sake of gold—those who read these pages will have the same means of determining as myself. If they were innocent, my sudden disappearance must have been unaccountable indeed; but revolving in my mind all the attending circumstances, I never yet could indulge, towards them, so charitable a supposition.

After receiving the money from them, of which they appeared to have an abundance, they advised me not to go into the streets that night, inasmuch as I was unacquainted with the customs of the city. Promising to remember their advice, I left them together, and soon after was shown by a colored servant to a sleeping room in the back part of the hotel, on the ground floor. I laid down to rest, thinking of home and wife, and children, and the long distance that stretched between us, until I fell asleep. But no good angel of pity came to my bedside, bidding me to fly[1]—no voice of mercy forewarned me in my dreams of the trials that were just at hand.

The next day there was a great pageant in Washington. The roar of cannon and the tolling of bells filled the air, while many houses were shrouded with crape,[2] and the streets were black with people. As the day advanced, the procession made its appearance, coming slowly through the Avenue, carriage after carriage, in long succession, while thousands upon thousands followed on foot—all moving to the sound of melancholy music. They were bearing the dead body of Harrison to the grave.

From early in the morning, I was constantly in the company of Hamilton and Brown. They were the only persons I knew in Washington. We stood together as the funeral pomp passed by. I remember distinctly how the window glass would break and rattle to the ground, after each report[3] of the cannon

---

1 *fly* Flee.
2 *crape* Fabric typically dyed black and associated with mourning.
3 *each report* The sound of each shot.

they were firing in the burial ground. We went to the Capitol, and walked a long time about the grounds. In the afternoon, they strolled towards the President's House,[1] all the time keeping me near to them, and pointing out various places of interest. As yet, I had seen nothing of the circus. In fact, I had thought of it but little, if at all, amidst the excitement of the day.

My friends, several times during the afternoon, entered drinking saloons, and called for liquor. They were by no means in the habit, however, so far as I knew them, of indulging to excess. On these occasions, after serving themselves, they would pour out a glass and hand it to me. I did not become intoxicated, as may be inferred from what subsequently occurred. Towards evening, and soon after partaking of one of these potations, I began to experience most unpleasant sensations. I felt extremely ill. My head commenced aching—a dull, heavy pain, inexpressibly disagreeable. At the supper table, I was without appetite; the sight and flavor of food was nauseous. About dark the same servant conducted me to the room I had occupied the previous night. Brown and Hamilton advised me to retire, commiserating me kindly, and expressing hopes that I would be better in the morning. Divesting myself of coat and boots merely, I threw myself upon the bed. It was impossible to sleep. The pain in my head continued to increase, until it became almost unbearable. In a short time I became thirsty. My lips were parched. I could think of nothing but water—of lakes and flowing rivers, of brooks where I had stooped to drink, and of the dripping bucket, rising with its cool and overflowing nectar, from the bottom of the well. Towards midnight, as near as I could judge, I arose, unable longer to bear such intensity of thirst. I was a stranger in the house, and knew nothing of its apartments. There was no one up, as I could observe. Groping about at random, I knew not where, I found the way at last to a kitchen in the basement. Two or three colored servants were moving through it, one of whom, a woman, gave me two glasses of water. It afforded momentary relief, but by the time I had reached my room again, the same burning desire of drink, the same tormenting thirst, had again returned. It was even more torturing than before, as was also the wild pain in my head, if such a thing could be. I was in sore distress—in most excruciating agony! I seemed to stand on the brink of madness! The memory of that night of horrible suffering will follow me to the grave.

In the course of an hour or more after my return from the kitchen, I was conscious of someone entering my room. There seemed to be several—a mingling of various voices—but how many, or who they were, I cannot tell. Whether Brown and Hamilton were among them, is a mere matter of conjecture. I only

---

1 *the President's House* While the use of the name "White House" has been recorded at least as early as 1811, it did not become the standard name for the presidential residence until the early 1900s.

remember, with any degree of distinctness, that I was told it was necessary to go to a physician and procure medicine, and that pulling on my boots, without coat or hat, I followed them through a long passageway, or alley, into the open street. It ran out at right angles from Pennsylvania Avenue. On the opposite side there was a light burning in a window. My impression is there were then three persons with me, but it is altogether indefinite and vague, and like the memory of a painful dream. Going towards the light, which I imagined proceeded from a physician's office, and which seemed to recede as I advanced, is the last glimmering recollection I can now recall. From that moment I was insensible. How long I remained in that condition—whether only that night, or many days and nights—I do not know; but when consciousness returned, I found myself alone, in utter darkness, and in chains.

The pain in my head had subsided in a measure, but I was very faint and weak. I was sitting upon a low bench, made of rough boards, and without coat or hat. I was handcuffed. Around my ankles also were a pair of heavy fetters. One end of a chain was fastened to a large ring in the floor, the other to the fetters on my ankles. I tried in vain to stand upon my feet. Waking from such a painful trance, it was some time before I could collect my thoughts. Where was I? What was the meaning of these chains? Where were Brown and Hamilton? What had I done to deserve imprisonment in such a dungeon? I could not comprehend. There was a blank of some indefinite period, preceding my awakening in that lonely place, the events of which the utmost stretch of memory was unable to recall. I listened intently for some sign or sound of life, but nothing broke the oppressive silence, save the clinking of my chains, whenever I chanced to move. I spoke aloud, but the sound of my voice startled me. I felt of my pockets, so far as the fetters would allow—far enough, indeed, to ascertain that I had not only been robbed of liberty, but that my money and free papers were also gone! Then did the idea begin to break upon my mind, at first dim and confused, that I had been kidnapped. But that I thought was incredible. There must have been some misapprehension—some unfortunate mistake. It could not be that a free citizen of New-York, who had wronged no man, nor violated any law, should be dealt with thus inhumanly. The more I contemplated my situation, however, the more I became confirmed in my suspicions. It was a desolate thought, indeed. I felt there was no trust or mercy in unfeeling man; and commending myself to the God of the oppressed, bowed my head upon my fettered hands, and wept most bitterly.

from CHAPTER 3

Some three hours elapsed, during which time I remained seated on the low bench, absorbed in painful meditations. At length I heard the crowing of a cock, and soon a distant rumbling sound, as of carriages hurrying through the streets, came to my ears, and I knew that it was day. No ray of light, however, penetrated my prison. Finally, I heard footsteps immediately overhead, as of someone walking to and fro. It occurred to me then that I must be in an underground apartment, and the damp, mouldy odors of the place confirmed the supposition. The noise above continued for at least an hour, when, at last, I heard footsteps approaching from without: A key rattled in the lock—a strong door swung back upon its hinges, admitting a flood of light, and two men entered and stood before me. One of them was a large, powerful man, forty years of age, perhaps, with dark, chestnut-colored hair, slightly interspersed with gray. His face was full, his complexion flush, his features grossly coarse, expressive of nothing but cruelty and cunning. He was about five feet ten inches high, of full habit, and, without prejudice, I must be allowed to say, was a man whose whole appearance was sinister and repugnant. His name was James H. Burch, as I learned afterwards—a well-known slave-dealer in Washington; and then, or lately, connected in business, as a partner, with Theophilus Freeman, of New-Orleans. The person who accompanied him was a simple lackey, named Ebenezer Radburn, who acted merely in the capacity of turnkey. Both of these men still live in Washington, or did, at the time of my return through that city from slavery in January last.

The light admitted through the open door enabled me to observe the room in which I was confined. It was about twelve feet square—the walls of solid masonry. The floor was of heavy plank. There was one small window, crossed with great iron bars, with an outside shutter, securely fastened.

An iron-bound door led into an adjoining cell, or vault, wholly destitute of windows, or any means of admitting light. The furniture of the room in which I was, consisted of the wooden bench on which I sat, an old-fashioned, dirty box stove, and besides these, in either cell, there was neither bed, nor blanket, nor any other thing whatever. The door, through which Burch and Radburn entered, led through a small passage, up a flight of steps into a yard, surrounded by a brick wall ten or twelve feet high, immediately in rear of a building of the same width as itself. The yard extended rearward from the house about thirty feet. In one part of the wall there was a strongly ironed door, opening into a narrow, covered passage, leading along one side of the house into the street. The doom of the colored man, upon whom the door leading out of that narrow passage closed, was sealed. The top of the wall supported one end of a roof, which ascended inwards, forming a kind of open shed. Underneath the roof there was a crazy loft all round, where slaves, if so disposed, might sleep at night, or in inclement weather seek shelter from the storm. It was like a farmer's barnyard in most respects, save it was so constructed that the outside world could never see the human cattle that were herded there.

The building to which the yard was attached was two stories high, fronting on one of the public streets of Washington. Its outside presented only the appearance of a quiet private residence. A stranger looking at it would never have dreamed of its execrable uses. Strange as it may seem, within plain sight of this same house, looking down from its commanding height upon it, was the Capitol. The voices of patriotic representatives boasting of freedom and equality, and the rattling of the poor slave's chains, almost commingled. A slave pen within the very shadow of the Capitol!

Such is a correct description as it was in 1841, of Williams' slave pen in Washington, in one of the cellars of which I found myself so unaccountably confined.

"Well, my boy, how do you feel now?" said Burch, as he entered through the open door. I replied that I was sick, and inquired the cause of my imprisonment. He answered that I was his slave—that he had bought me, and that he was about to send me to New-Orleans. I asserted, aloud and boldly, that I was a free man—a resident of Saratoga, where I had a wife and children, who were also free, and that my name was Northup. I complained bitterly of the strange treatment I had received, and threatened, upon my liberation, to have satisfaction for the wrong. He denied that I was free, and with an emphatic oath, declared that I came from Georgia. Again and again I asserted I was no man's slave, and insisted upon his taking off my chains at once. He endeavored to hush me, as if he feared my voice would be overheard. But I would not be silent, and denounced the authors of my imprisonment, whoever they might be, as unmitigated villains. Finding he could not quiet me, he flew into a towering passion. With blasphemous oaths, he called me a black liar, a runaway from Georgia, and every other profane and vulgar epithet that the most indecent fancy could conceive.

During this time Radburn was standing silently by. His business was to oversee this human, or rather inhuman,

SCENE IN THE SLAVE PEN AT WASHINGTON.

stable, receiving slaves, feeding and whipping them, at the rate of two shillings a head per day. Turning to him, Burch ordered the paddle and cat-o'-ninetails to be brought in. He disappeared, and in a few moments returned with these instruments of torture. The paddle, as it is termed in slave-beating parlance, or at least the one with which I first became acquainted, and of which I now speak, was a piece of hard-wood board, eighteen or twenty inches long, moulded to the shape of an old-fashioned pudding stick, or ordinary oar. The flattened portion, which was about the size in circumference of two open hands, was bored with a small auger in numerous places. The cat was a large rope of many strands—the strands unraveled, and a knot tied at the extremity of each.

As soon as these formidable whips appeared, I was seized by both of them, and roughly divested of my clothing. My feet, as has been stated, were fastened to the floor. Drawing me over the bench, face downwards, Radburn placed his heavy foot upon the fetters, between my wrists, holding them painfully to the floor. With the paddle, Burch commenced beating me. Blow after blow was inflicted upon my naked body. When his unrelenting arm grew tired, he stopped and asked if I still insisted I was a free man. I did insist upon it, and then the blows were renewed, faster and more energetically, if possible, than before. When again tired, he would repeat the same question, and receiving the same answer, continue his cruel labor. All this time, the incarnate devil was uttering most fiendish oaths. At length the paddle broke, leaving the useless handle in his hand. Still I would not yield. All his brutal blows could not force from my lips the foul lie that I was a slave. Casting madly on the floor the handle of the broken paddle, he seized the rope. This was far more painful than the other. I struggled with all my power, but it was in vain. I prayed for mercy, but my prayer was only answered with imprecations and with stripes. I thought I must die beneath the lashes of the accursed brute. Even now the flesh crawls upon my bones, as I recall the scene. I was all on fire. My sufferings I can compare to nothing else than the burning agonies of hell!

At last I became silent to his repeated questions. I would make no reply. In fact, I was becoming almost unable to speak. Still he plied the lash without stint upon my poor body, until it seemed that the lacerated flesh was stripped from my bones at every stroke. A man with a particle of mercy in his soul would not have beaten even a dog so cruelly. At length Radburn said that it was useless to whip me any more—that I would be sore enough. Thereupon, Burch desisted, saying, with an admonitory shake of his fist in my face, and hissing the words through his firm-set teeth, that if ever I dared to utter again that I was entitled to my freedom, that I had been kidnapped, or anything whatever of the kind, the castigation I had just received was nothing in comparison with what would follow. He swore that he would either conquer or kill me. With these consolatory words, the fetters were taken from my wrists, my feet still remaining fastened to the ring; the shutter of the little barred window, which had been opened, was again closed, and going out, locking the great door behind them, I was left in darkness as before.

In an hour, perhaps two, my heart leaped to my throat, as the key rattled in the door again. I, who had been so lonely, and who had longed so ardently to see someone, I cared not who, now shuddered at the thought of man's approach. A human face was fearful to me, especially a white one. Radburn entered, bringing with him, on a tin plate, a piece of shriveled fried pork, a slice of bread and a cup of water. He asked me how I felt, and remarked that I had received a pretty severe flogging. He remonstrated with me against the propriety of asserting my freedom. In rather a patronizing and confidential manner, he gave it to me as his advice, that the less I said on that subject the better it would be for me. The man evidently endeavored to appear kind—whether touched at the sight of my sad condition, or with the view of silencing, on my part, any further expression of my rights, it is not necessary now to conjecture. He unlocked the fetters from my ankles, opened the shutters of the little window, and departed, leaving me again alone.

By this time I had become stiff and sore; my body was covered with blisters, and it was with great pain and difficulty that I could move. From the window I could observe nothing but the roof resting on the adjacent wall. At night I laid down upon the damp, hard floor, without any pillow or covering whatever. Punctually, twice a day, Radburn came in, with his pork, and bread, and water. I had but little appetite, though I was tormented with continual thirst. My wounds would not permit me to remain but a few minutes in any one position; so, sitting, or standing, or moving slowly round, I passed the days and nights. I was heartsick and discouraged. Thoughts of my family, of my wife and children, continually occupied my mind. When sleep overpowered me I dreamed of them—dreamed I was again in Saratoga—that I could see their faces, and hear their voices calling me. Awakening from the pleasant phantasms of sleep to the bitter realities around me, I could but groan and weep. Still my spirit was not broken. I indulged the anticipation of escape, and that speedily. It was impossible, I reasoned, that men could be so unjust as to detain me as a slave, when the truth of my case was known. Burch, ascertaining I was no runaway from Georgia, would certainly let me go. Though suspicions of Brown and Hamilton were not unfrequent, I could not reconcile myself to the idea that they were instrumental to my imprisonment. Surely they would seek me out—they would deliver me from thralldom. Alas! I had not then learned the measure of "man's inhumanity to man," nor to what limitless extent of wickedness he will go for the love of gain.

[Northup ultimately finds himself part of a large group of enslaved people—some of whom, he discovers, have also been illegally kidnapped. The captives are then shipped downriver to New Orleans, where Northup is purchased along with a woman named Eliza—who has just been forcibly separated from her young daughter—and a man named Harry.]

from Chapter 7

On leaving the New-Orleans slave pen, Harry and I followed our new master through the streets, while Eliza, crying and turning back, was forced along by Freeman and his minions, until we found ourselves on board the steamboat *Rodolph*, then lying at the levee. In the course of half an hour we were moving briskly up the Mississippi, bound for some point on Red River.[1] There were quite a number of slaves on board beside ourselves, just purchased in the New-Orleans market. I remember a Mr. Kelsow, who was said to be a well-known and extensive planter, had in charge a gang of women.

Our master's name was William Ford. He resided then in the "Great Pine Woods," in the parish of Avoyelles,[2] situated on the right bank of Red River, in the heart of Louisiana. He is now a Baptist preacher. Throughout the whole parish of Avoyelles, and especially along both shores of Bayou Boeuf, where he is more intimately known, he is accounted by his fellow-citizens as a worthy minister of God. In many northern minds, perhaps, the idea of a man holding his brother man in servitude, and the traffic in human flesh, may seem altogether incompatible with their conceptions of a moral or religious life. From descriptions of such men as Burch and Freeman, and others hereinafter mentioned, they are led to despise and execrate the whole class of slaveholders, indiscriminately. But I was sometime his slave, and had an opportunity of learning well his character and disposition, and it is but simple justice to him when I say, in my opinion, there never was a more kind, noble, candid, Christian man than William Ford. The influences and associations that had always surrounded him, blinded him to the inherent wrong at the bottom of the system of slavery. He never doubted the moral right of one man holding another in subjection. Looking through the same medium with his fathers before him, he saw things in the same light. Brought up under other circumstances and other influences, his notions would undoubtedly have been different. Nevertheless, he was a model master, walking uprightly, according to the light of his understanding, and fortunate was the slave who came to his possession. Were all men such as he, slavery would be deprived of more than half its bitterness.

---

1   *Red River*   River that flows through central Louisiana.
2   *parish of Avoyelles*   In east-central Louisiana, approximately 140 miles northwest of New Orleans.

We were two days and three nights on board the steamboat *Rodolph*, during which time nothing of particular interest occurred. I was now known as Platt, the name given me by Burch, and by which I was designated through the whole period of my servitude. Eliza was sold by the name of "Dradey." She was so distinguished in the conveyance to Ford, now on record in the recorder's office in New-Orleans.

On our passage I was constantly reflecting on my situation, and consulting with myself on the best course to pursue in order to effect my ultimate escape. Sometimes, not only then, but afterwards, I was almost on the point of disclosing fully to Ford the facts of my history. I am inclined now to the opinion it would have resulted in my benefit. This course was often considered, but through fear of its miscarriage, never put into execution, until eventually my transfer and his pecuniary embarrassments[1] rendered it evidently unsafe. Afterwards, under other masters, unlike William Ford, I knew well enough the slightest knowledge of my real character would consign me at once to the remoter depths of slavery. I was too costly a chattel to be lost, and was well aware that I would be taken farther on, into some by-place, over the Texan border, perhaps, and sold; that I would be disposed of as the thief disposes of his stolen horse, if my right to freedom was even whispered. So I resolved to lock the secret closely in my heart—never to utter one word or syllable as to who or what I was—trusting in Providence and my own shrewdness for deliverance. ....

We usually spent our Sabbaths at the opening,[2] on which days our master would gather all his slaves about him, and read and expound the Scriptures. He sought to inculcate in our minds feelings of kindness towards each other, of dependence upon God—setting forth the rewards promised unto those who lead an upright and prayerful life. Seated in the doorway of his house, surrounded by his man-servants and his maid-servants, who looked earnestly into the good man's face, he spoke of the loving kindness of the Creator, and of the life that is to come. Often did the voice of prayer ascend from his lips to heaven, the only sound that broke the solitude of the place.

In the course of the summer Sam became deeply convicted, his mind dwelling intensely on the subject of religion. His mistress gave him a Bible, which he carried with him to his work. Whatever leisure time was allowed him, he spent in perusing it, though it was only with great difficulty that he could master any part of it. I often read to him, a favor which he well repaid me by many expressions of gratitude. Sam's piety was frequently observed by white men who came to the mill, and the remark it most generally provoked was

---

1 *pecuniary embarrassments* Financial difficulties.
2 *the opening* I.e., the open area in which the main house was situated.

that a man like Ford, who allowed his slaves to have Bibles, was "not fit to own a nigger."[1]

He, however, lost nothing by his kindness. It is a fact I have more than once observed, that those who treated their slaves most leniently, were rewarded by the greatest amount of labor. I know it from my own experience. It was a source of pleasure to surprise Master Ford with a greater day's work than was required, while, under subsequent masters, there was no prompter to extra effort but the overseer's lash. ...

At this time one John M. Tibeats, a carpenter, came to the opening to do some work on master's house. I was directed to quit the looms[2] and assist him. For two weeks I was in his company, planning and matching boards for ceiling, a plastered room being a rare thing in the parish of Avoyelles.

John M. Tibeats was the opposite of Ford in all respects. He was a small, crabbed, quick-tempered, spiteful man. He had no fixed residence that I ever heard of, but passed from one plantation to another, wherever he could find employment. He was without standing in the community, not esteemed by white men, nor even respected by slaves. He was ignorant, withal, and of a revengeful disposition. He left the parish long before I did, and I know not whether he is at present alive or dead. Certain it is, it was a most unlucky day for me that brought us together. During my residence with Master Ford I had seen only the bright side of slavery. His was no heavy hand crushing us to the earth. *He* pointed upwards, and with benign and cheering words addressed us as his fellow-mortals, accountable, like himself, to the Maker of us all. I think of him with affection, and had my family been with me, could have borne his gentle servitude, without murmuring, all my days. But clouds were gathering in the horizon—forerunners of a pitiless storm that was soon to break over me. I was doomed to endure such bitter trials as the poor slave only knows, and to lead no more the comparatively happy life which I had led in the "Great Pine Woods."

[Ford's financial circumstances take a turn, leading him to sell Northup to John Tibeats, a carpenter regularly employed by Ford. Northup and Tibeats go to Ford's plantation at Bayou Boeuf, where Tibeats is working on a number of construction projects.]

---

1   *nigger*   By the nineteenth century, this word had acquired the extremely derogatory connotations it holds today; nevertheless, it was regularly used in print.

2   *looms*   Northup has been constructing looms for a weaving house to be used by Ford's wife.

from Chapter 8

As the day began to open, Tibeats came out of the house to where I was, hard at work. He seemed to be that morning even more morose and disagreeable than usual. He was my master, entitled by law to my flesh and blood, and to exercise over me such tyrannical control as his mean nature prompted; but there was no law that could prevent my looking upon him with intense contempt. I despised both his disposition and his intellect. I had just come round to the keg for a further supply of nails, as he reached the weaving-house.

"I thought I told you to commence putting on weather-boards this morning," he remarked.

"Yes, master, and I am about it," I replied.

"Where?" he demanded.

"On the other side," was my answer.

He walked round to the other side, examined my work for a while, muttering to himself in a fault-finding tone.

"Didn't I tell you last night to get a keg of nails of Chapin?"[1] he broke forth again.

"Yes, master, and so I did; and overseer said he would get another size for you, if you wanted them, when he came back from the field."

Tibeats walked to the keg, looked a moment at the contents, then kicked it violently. Coming towards me in a great passion, he exclaimed,

"G—d d—n you! I thought you *knowed* something."

I made answer: "I tried to do as you told me, master. I didn't mean anything wrong. Overseer said—" But he interrupted me with such a flood of curses that I was unable to finish the sentence. At length he ran towards the house, and going to the piazza, took down one of the overseer's whips. The whip had a short wooden stock, braided over with leather, and was loaded at the butt. The lash was three feet long, or thereabouts, and made of raw-hide strands.

At first I was somewhat frightened, and my impulse was to run. There was no one about except Rachel, the cook, and Chapin's wife, and neither of them were to be seen. The rest were in the field. I knew he intended to whip me, and it was the first time any one had attempted it since my arrival at Avoyelles. I felt, moreover, that I had been faithful—that I was guilty of no wrong whatever, and deserved commendation rather than punishment. My fear changed to anger, and before he reached me I had made up my mind fully not to be whipped, let the result be life or death.

Winding the lash around his hand, and taking hold of the small end of the stock, he walked up to me, and with a malignant look, ordered me to strip.

---

1   *Chapin*   Ford's overseer at Bayou Boeuf, described by Northup as a relatively kind man.

"Master Tibeats," said I, looking him boldly in the face, "I will *not*." I was about to say something further in justification, but with concentrated vengeance, he sprang upon me, seizing me by the throat with one hand, raising the whip with the other, in the act of striking. Before the blow descended, however, I had caught him by the collar of the coat, and drawn him closely to me. Reaching down, I seized him by the ankle, and pushing him back with the other hand, he fell over on the ground. Putting one arm around his leg, and holding it to my breast, so that his head and shoulders only touched the ground, I placed my foot upon his neck. He was completely in my power. My blood was up. It seemed to course through my veins like fire. In the frenzy of my madness I snatched the whip from his hand. He struggled with all his power; swore that I should not live to see another day; and that he would tear out my heart. But his struggles and his threats were alike in vain. I cannot tell how many times I struck him. Blow after blow fell fast and heavy upon his wriggling form. At length he screamed—cried murder—and at last the blasphemous tyrant called on God for mercy. But he who had never shown mercy did not receive it. The stiff stock of the whip warped round his cringing body until my right arm ached.

Until this time I had been too busy to look about me. Desisting for a moment, I saw Mrs. Chapin looking from the window, and Rachel standing in the kitchen door. Their attitudes expressed the utmost excitement and alarm. His screams had been heard in the field. Chapin was coming as fast as he could ride. I struck him a blow or two more, then pushed him from me with such a well-directed kick that he went rolling over on the ground.

[Tibeats returns with a group of accomplices and attempts to hang Northup in revenge for the fight, but Chapin and Ford ultimately step in to prevent the lynching. After several more weeks under Tibeats, he is sold without warning to a planter named Edwin Epps, a cruel man who keeps those he enslaves in terrible living conditions. At this point, it has been two years since Northup's abduction. Over time, Northup earns Epps's confidence as a laborer and is raised to the position of "slave driver," forcing upon him authority over the others enslaved on the plantation—including the task of doling out punishments.]

from CHAPTER 13

Patsey was slim and straight. She stood erect as the human form is capable of standing. There was an air of loftiness in her movement, that neither labor, nor weariness, nor punishment could destroy. Truly, Patsey was a splendid animal, and were it not that bondage had enshrouded her intellect in utter and everlasting darkness, would have been chief among ten thousand of her people. She could leap the highest fences, and a fleet hound it was indeed that could outstrip her in a race. No horse could fling her from his back. She was a skillful teamster.[1] She turned as true a furrow as the best, and at splitting rails there were none who could excel her. When the order to halt was heard at night, she would have her mules at the crib, unharnessed, fed and curried, before uncle Abram had found his hat. Not, however, for all or any of these, was she chiefly famous. Such lightning-like motion was in her fingers as no other fingers ever possessed, and therefore it was, that in cotton picking time, Patsey was queen of the field.

She had a genial and pleasant temper, and was faithful and obedient. Naturally, she was a joyous creature, a laughing, light-hearted girl, rejoicing in the mere sense of existence. Yet Patsey wept oftener, and suffered more, than any of her companions. She had been literally excoriated. Her back bore the scars of a thousand stripes; not because she was backward in her work, nor because she was of an unmindful and rebellious spirit, but because it had fallen to her lot to be the slave of a licentious master and a jealous mistress. She shrank before the lustful eye of the one, and was in danger even of her life at the hands of the other, and between the two, she was indeed accursed. In the great house, for days together, there were high and angry words, poutings and estrangement, whereof she was the innocent cause. Nothing delighted the mistress so much as to see her suffer, and more than once, when Epps had refused to sell her, has she tempted me with bribes to put her secretly to death, and bury her body in some lonely place in the margin of the swamp. Gladly would Patsey have appeased this unforgiving spirit, if it had been in her power, but not like Joseph, dared she escape from Master Epps, leaving her garment in his hand.[2] Patsey walked under a cloud. If she uttered a word in opposition to her master's will, the lash was resorted to at once, to bring her to subjection; if she was not watchful when about her cabin, or when walking in the yard, a billet of wood, or a broken bottle perhaps, hurled from her mistress' hand, would smite her unexpectedly in the face. The enslaved victim of lust and hate, Patsey had no comfort of her life. ...

from CHAPTER 14

To be rid of Patsey—to place her beyond sight or reach, by sale, or death, or in any other manner—of late years, seemed to be the ruling thought and passion of my mistress. Patsey had been a favorite when a child, even in the great house. She had been petted and admired for her uncommon sprightliness and

---

1   *teamster*   One who drives a team of animals.

2   *not like Joseph ... hand*   See Genesis 39.1–12; Joseph, who is enslaved by Potiphar, manages to evade the lustful pursuit of Potiphar's wife by running away when she grabs him, leaving only his coat in her hands.

pleasant disposition. She had been fed many a time, so Uncle Abram said, even on biscuit and milk, when the madam, in her younger days, was wont to[1] call her to the piazza, and fondle her as she would a playful kitten. But a sad change had come over the spirit of the woman. Now, only black and angry fiends ministered in the temple of her heart, until she could look on Patsey but with concentrated venom.

Mistress Epps was not naturally such an evil woman, after all. She was possessed of the devil, jealousy, it is true, but aside from that, there was much in her character to admire. Her father, Mr. Roberts, resided in Cheneyville, an influential and honorable man, and as much respected throughout the parish as any other citizen. She had been well educated at some institution this side the Mississippi; was beautiful, accomplished, and usually good-humored. She was kind to all of us but Patsey—frequently, in the absence of her husband, sending out to us some little dainty from her own table. In other situations—in a different society from that which exists on the shores of Bayou Boeuf—she would have been pronounced an elegant and fascinating woman. An ill wind it was that blew her into the arms of Epps. ...

from CHAPTER 18

... On a Sabbath day in hoeing time, not long ago, we were on the bayou bank, washing our clothes, as was our usual custom. Presently Patsey was missing. Epps called aloud, but there was no answer. No one had observed her leaving the yard, and it was a wonder with us whither she had gone. In the course of a couple of hours she was seen approaching from the direction of Shaw's. This man, as has been intimated, was a notorious profligate, and withal not on the most friendly terms with Epps. Harriet, his black wife, knowing Patsey's troubles, was kind to her, in consequence of which the latter was in the habit of going over to see her every opportunity. Her visits were prompted by friendship merely, but the suspicion gradually entered the brain of Epps, that another and a baser passion led her thither—that it was not Harriet she desired to meet, but rather the unblushing libertine, his neighbor. Patsey found her master in a fearful rage on her return. His violence so alarmed her that at first she attempted to evade direct answers to his questions, which only served to increase his suspicions. She finally, however, drew herself up proudly, and in a spirit of indignation boldly denied his charges.

"Missus don't give me soap to wash with, as she does the rest," said Patsey, "and you know why. I went over to Harriet's to get a piece," and saying this, she drew it forth from a pocket in her dress and exhibited it to him. "That's

---

1 *wont to* In the habit of.

what I went to Shaw's for, Massa Epps," continued she; "the Lord knows that was all."

"You lie, you black wench!" shouted Epps.

"I *don't* lie, massa. If you kill me, I'll stick to that."

"Oh! I'll fetch you down. I'll learn you to go to Shaw's. I'll take the starch out of ye," he muttered fiercely through his shut teeth.

Then turning to me, he ordered four stakes to be driven into the ground, pointing with the toe of his boot to the places where he wanted them. When the stakes were driven down, he ordered her to be stripped of every article of dress. Ropes were then brought,

THE STAKING OUT AND FLOGGING OF THE GIRL PATSEY.

and the naked girl was laid upon her face, her wrists and feet each tied firmly to a stake. Stepping to the piazza, he took down a heavy whip, and placing it in my hands, commanded me to lash her. Unpleasant as it was, I was compelled to obey him. Nowhere that day, on the face of the whole earth, I venture to say, was there such a demoniac exhibition witnessed as then ensued.

Mistress Epps stood on the piazza among her children, gazing on the scene with an air of heartless satisfaction. The slaves were huddled together at a little distance, their countenances indicating the sorrow of their hearts. Poor Patsey prayed piteously for mercy, but her prayers were vain. Epps ground his teeth, and stamped upon the ground, screaming at me, like a mad fiend, to strike *harder*.

"Strike harder, or *your* turn will come next, you scoundrel," he yelled.

"Oh, mercy, massa!—oh! have mercy, *do*. Oh, God! pity me," Patsey exclaimed continually, struggling fruitlessly, and the flesh quivering at every stroke.

When I had struck her as many as thirty times, I stopped, and turned round toward Epps, hoping he was satisfied; but with bitter oaths and threats, he ordered me to continue. I inflicted ten or fifteen blows more. By this time her back was covered with long welts, intersecting each other like net work. Epps was yet furious and savage as ever, demanding if she would like to go to Shaw's again, and swearing he would flog her until she wished she was in h—l. Throwing down the whip, I declared I could punish her no more. He ordered me to go on, threatening me with a severer flogging than she had received, in case of refusal. My heart revolted at the inhuman scene, and risking the consequences, I absolutely refused to raise the whip. He then seized it himself, and applied it with ten-fold greater force than I had. The painful cries and shrieks of the tortured Patsey, mingling with the loud and angry curses of Epps, loaded the air. She was terribly lacerated—I may say, without exaggeration, literally flayed. The lash was wet with blood, which flowed down her sides and dropped upon the ground. At length she ceased struggling. Her head sank listlessly on the ground. Her screams and supplications gradually decreased and died away into a low moan. She no longer writhed and shrank beneath the lash when it bit out small pieces of her flesh. I thought that she was dying!

It was the Sabbath of the Lord. The fields smiled in the warm sunlight—the birds chirped merrily amidst the foliage of the trees—peace and happiness seemed to reign everywhere, save in the bosoms of Epps and his panting victim and the silent witnesses around him. The tempestuous emotions that were raging there were little in harmony with the calm and quiet beauty of the day. I could look on Epps only with unutterable loathing and abhorrence, and thought within myself—"Thou devil, sooner or later, somewhere in the course of eternal justice, thou shalt answer for this sin!"

Finally, he ceased whipping from mere exhaustion, and ordered Phebe to bring a bucket of salt and water. After washing her thoroughly with this, I was told to take her to her cabin. Untying the ropes, I raised her in my arms. She was unable to stand, and as her head rested on my shoulder, she repeated many times, in a faint voice scarcely perceptible, "Oh, Platt—oh, Platt!" but nothing further. Her dress was replaced, but it clung to her back, and was soon stiff with blood. We laid her on some boards in the hut, where she remained a long time, with eyes closed and groaning in agony. At night Phebe applied melted tallow to her wounds, and so far as we were able, all endeavored to assist and console her. Day after day she lay in her cabin upon her face, the sores preventing her resting in any other position.

A blessed thing it would have been for her—days and weeks and months of misery it would have saved her—had she never lifted up her head in life again. Indeed, from that time forward she was not what she had been. The burden of a deep melancholy weighed heavily on her spirits. She no longer moved with that buoyant and elastic step—there was not that mirthful sparkle in her eyes that formerly distinguished her. The bounding vigor—the sprightly, laughter-loving spirit of her youth, were gone. She fell into a mournful and desponding mood, and oftentimes would start up in her sleep, and with raised hands, plead for mercy. She became more silent than she was, toiling all day in our midst, not uttering a word. A care-worn, pitiful expression settled on her face, and it was her humor now to weep, rather than rejoice. If ever there was a broken heart—one crushed and blighted by the rude grasp of suffering and misfortune—it was Patsey's.

She had been reared no better than her master's beast—looked upon merely as a valuable and handsome animal—and consequently possessed but a limited amount of knowledge. And yet a faint light cast its rays over her intellect, so that it was not wholly dark. She had a dim perception of God and of eternity, and a still more dim perception of a Saviour who had died even for such as her. She entertained but confused notions of a future life—not comprehending the distinction between the corporeal and spiritual existence. Happiness, in her mind, was exemption from stripes—from labor—from the cruelty of masters and overseers. Her idea of the joy of heaven was simply *rest*, and is fully expressed in these lines of a melancholy bard:

> I ask no paradise on high,
> With cares on earth oppressed,
> The only heaven for which I sigh,
> Is rest, eternal rest.[1]

It is a mistaken opinion that prevails in some quarters that the slave does not understand the term—does not comprehend the idea—of freedom. Even on Bayou Boeuf, where I conceive slavery exists in its most abject and cruel form—where it exhibits features altogether unknown in more northern states—the most ignorant of them generally know full well its meaning. They understand the privileges and exemptions that belong to it—that it would bestow upon them the fruits of their own labors, and that it would secure to them the enjoyment of domestic happiness. They do not fail to observe the difference between their own condition and the meanest white man's, and to realize the injustice of the laws which place it in his power not only to appropriate the profits of their industry, but to subject them to unmerited and unprovoked punishment, without remedy, or the right to resist, or to remonstrate.

Patsey's life, especially after her whipping, was one long dream of liberty. Far away, to her fancy an immeasurable distance, she knew there was a land of freedom. A thousand times she had heard that somewhere in the distant North there were no slaves—no masters. In her imagination it was an enchanted region, the Paradise of the earth. To dwell where the black man may work

---

1   *I ask ... eternal rest*   Reference to a stanza (slightly altered by Northup) from John Malcolm's poem "Byron's Prayer," published in the *Edinburgh Literary Journal* in 1831 and in the *American Masonic Register* in 1841.

for himself—live in his own cabin—till his own soil, was a blissful dream of Patsey's—a dream, alas! the fulfillment of which she can never realize.

The effect of these exhibitions of brutality on the household of the slave-holder is apparent. Epps' oldest son is an intelligent lad of ten or twelve years of age. It is pitiable, sometimes, to see him chastising, for instance, the venerable Uncle Abram. He will call the old man to account, and if in his childish judgment it is necessary, sentence him to a certain number of lashes, which he proceeds to inflict with much gravity and deliberation. Mounted on his pony, he often rides into the field with his whip, playing the overseer, greatly to his father's delight. Without discrimination, at such times, he applies the rawhide, urging the slaves forward with shouts, and occasional expressions of profanity, while the old man laughs, and commends him as a thorough-going boy.

"The child is father to the man,"[1] and with such training, whatever may be his natural disposition, it cannot well be otherwise than that, on arriving at maturity, the sufferings and miseries of the slave will be looked upon with entire indifference. The influence of the iniquitous system necessarily fosters an unfeeling and cruel spirit, even in the bosoms of those who, among their equals, are regarded as humane and generous.

Young Master Epps possessed some noble qualities, yet no process of reasoning could lead him to comprehend that in the eye of the Almighty there is no distinction of color. He looked upon the black man simply as an animal, differing in no respect from any other animal, save in the gift of speech and the possession of somewhat higher instincts, and, therefore, the more valuable. To work like his father's mules—to be whipped and kicked and scourged through life—to address the white man with hat in hand, and eyes bent servilely on the earth, in his mind, was the natural and proper destiny of the slave. Brought up with such ideas—in the notion that we stand without the pale[2] of humanity—no wonder the oppressors of my people are a pitiless and unrelenting race.

[Northup is tasked with the construction of a new house for Epps. During this project he encounters white carpenter Samuel Bass, an eccentric character who is well-liked by most other white people in the community despite his many unorthodox views (including a strong dislike of slavery).]

from CHAPTER 19

... [Bass] remained at Epps' through the summer, visiting Marksville generally once a fortnight. The more I saw of him, the more I became convinced he was a man in whom I could confide. Nevertheless, my previous ill-fortune had

---

1 *The child ... man* From "My Heart Leaps Up" (1802), by the British poet William Wordsworth.
2 *without the pale* Outside the realm.

taught me to be extremely cautious. It was not my place to speak to a white man except when spoken to, but I omitted no opportunity of throwing myself in his way, and endeavored constantly in every possible manner to attract his attention. In the early part of August he and myself were at work alone in the house, the other carpenters having left, and Epps being absent in the field. Now was the time, if ever, to broach the subject, and I resolved to do it, and submit to whatever consequences might ensue. We were busily at work in the afternoon, when I stopped suddenly and said—

"Master Bass, I want to ask you what part of the country you came from?"

"Why, Platt, what put that into your head?" he answered. "You wouldn't know if I should tell you." After a moment or two he added—"I was born in Canada; now guess where that is."

"Oh, I know where Canada is," said I, "I have been there myself."

"Yes, I expect you are well acquainted all through that country," he remarked, laughing incredulously.

"As sure as I live, Master Bass," I replied, "I have been there. I have been in Montreal and Kingston, and Queenston, and a great many places in Canada, and I have been in York State, too—in Buffalo, and Rochester, and Albany, and can tell you the names of the villages on the Erie canal and the Champlain canal."

Bass turned round and gazed at me a long time without uttering a syllable.

"How came you here?" he inquired, at length.

"Master Bass," I answered, "if justice had been done, I never would have been here."

"Well, how's this?" said he. "Who are you? You have been in Canada sure enough; I know all the places you mention. How did you happen to get here? Come, tell me all about it."

"I have no friends here," was my reply, "that I can put confidence in. I am afraid to tell you, though I don't believe you would tell Master Epps if I should."

He assured me earnestly he would keep every word I might speak to him a profound secret, and his curiosity was evidently strongly excited. It was a long story, I informed him, and would take some time to relate it. Master Epps would be back soon, but if he would see me that night after all were asleep, I would repeat it to him. He consented readily to the arrangement, and directed me to come into the building where we were then at work, and I would find him there. About midnight, when all was still and quiet, I crept cautiously from my cabin, and silently entering the unfinished building, found him awaiting me.

After further assurances on his part that I should not be betrayed, I began a relation of the history of my life and misfortunes. He was deeply interested, asking numerous questions in reference to localities and events. Having ended my story I besought him to write to some of my friends at the North, acquainting them with my situation, and begging them to forward free papers, or take such steps as they might consider proper to secure my release. He promised to do so, but dwelt upon the danger of such an act in case of detection, and now impressed upon me the great necessity of strict silence and secrecy. Before we parted our plan of operation was arranged.

We agreed to meet the next night at a specified place among the high weeds on the bank of the bayou, some distance from master's dwelling. There he was to write down on paper the names and address of several persons, old friends in the North, to whom he would direct letters during his next visit to Marksville. It was not deemed prudent to meet in the new house, inasmuch as the light it would be necessary to use might possibly be discovered. In the course of the day I managed to obtain a few matches and a piece of candle, unperceived, from the kitchen, during a temporary absence of Aunt Phebe. Bass had pencil and paper in his tool chest.

At the appointed hour we met on the bayou bank, and creeping among the high weeds, I lighted the candle, while he drew forth pencil and paper and prepared for business. I gave him the names of William Perry, Cephas Parker and Judge Marvin, all of Saratoga Springs, Saratoga county, New-York. I had been employed by the latter in the United States Hotel, and had transacted business with the former to a considerable extent, and trusted that at least one of them would be still living at that place. He carefully wrote the names, and then remarked, thoughtfully—

"It is so many years since you left Saratoga, all these men may be dead, or may have removed. You say you obtained papers at the custom house in New-York. Probably there is a record of them there, and I think it would be well to write and ascertain."

I agreed with him, and again repeated the circumstances related heretofore, connected with my visit to the custom house with Brown and Hamilton. We lingered on the bank of the bayou an hour or more, conversing upon the subject which now engrossed our thoughts. I could no longer doubt his fidelity, and freely spoke to him of the many sorrows I had borne in silence, and so long. I spoke of my wife and children, mentioning their names and ages, and dwelling upon the unspeakable happiness it would be to clasp them to my heart once more before I died. I caught him by the hand, and with tears and passionate entreaties implored him to befriend me—to restore me to my kindred and to liberty—promising I would weary Heaven the remainder of my life with prayers that it would bless and prosper him. In the enjoyment of freedom—surrounded by the associations of youth, and restored to the bosom of my family—that promise is not yet forgotten, nor shall it ever be so long as I have strength to raise my imploring eyes on high.

Oh, blessings on his kindly voice and on his silver hair,
And blessings on his whole life long, until he meet me there.[1]

He overwhelmed me with assurances of friendship and faithfulness, saying he had never before taken so deep an interest in the fate of anyone. He spoke of himself in a somewhat mournful tone, as a lonely man, a wanderer about the world—that he was growing old, and must soon reach the end of his earthly journey, and lie down to his final rest without kith or kin to mourn for him, or to remember him—that his life was of little value to himself, and henceforth should be devoted to the accomplishment of my liberty, and to an unceasing warfare against the accursed shame of slavery.

After this time we seldom spoke to, or recognized each other. He was, moreover, less free in his conversation with Epps on the subject of slavery. The remotest suspicion that there was any unusual intimacy—any secret understanding between us—never once entered the mind of Epps, or any other person, white or black, on the plantation.

I am often asked, with an air of incredulity, how I succeeded so many years in keeping from my daily and constant companions the knowledge of my true name and history. The terrible lesson Burch taught me, impressed indelibly upon my mind the danger and uselessness of asserting I was a freeman. There was no possibility of any slave being able to assist me, while, on the other hand, there *was* a possibility of his exposing me. When it is recollected the whole current of my thoughts, for twelve years, turned to the contemplation of escape, it will not be wondered at, that I was always cautious and on my guard. It would have been an act of folly to have proclaimed my *right* to freedom; it would only have subjected me to severer scrutiny—probably have consigned me to some more distant and inaccessible region than even Bayou Boeuf. Edwin Epps was a person utterly regardless of a black man's rights or wrongs—utterly destitute of any natural sense of justice, as I well knew. It was important, therefore, not only as regarded my hope of deliverance, but also as regarded the few personal privileges I was permitted to enjoy, to keep from him the history of my life.

The Saturday night subsequent to our interview at the water's edge, Bass went home to Marksville. The next day, being Sunday, he employed himself in his own room writing letters. One he directed to the Collector of Customs at New-York, another to Judge Marvin, and another to Messrs. Parker and Perry

---

1   *Oh, blessings ... me there*   See Alfred, Lord Tennyson's poem "The May Queen" (1842).

jointly. The latter was the one which led to my recovery. He subscribed my true name, but in the postscript intimated I was not the writer. The letter itself shows that he considered himself engaged in a dangerous undertaking—no less than running "the risk of his life, if detected." I did not see the letter before it was mailed, but have since obtained a copy, which is here inserted:

Bayou Boeuf, August 15, 1852

Mr. WILLIAM PERRY or Mr. CEPHAS PARKER:

Gentlemen—It having been a long time since I have seen or heard from you, and not knowing that you are living, it is with uncertainty that I write to you, but the necessity of the case must be my excuse.

Having been born free, just across the river from you, I am certain you must know me, and I am here now a slave. I wish you to obtain free papers for me, and forward them to me at Marksville, Louisiana, Parish of Avoyelles, and oblige

Yours, SOLOMON NORTHUP.

The way I came to be a slave, I was taken sick in Washington City, and was insensible for some time. When I recovered my reason, I was robbed of my free-papers, and in irons on my way to this state, and have never been able to get anyone to write for me until now; and he that is writing for me runs the risk of his life if detected.

The allusion to myself in the work recently issued, entitled "A Key to Uncle Tom's Cabin,"[1] contains the first part of this letter, omitting the postscript. Neither are the full names of the gentlemen to whom it is directed correctly stated, there being a slight discrepancy, probably a typographical error. To the postscript more than to the body of the communication am I indebted for my liberation, as will presently be seen.

When Bass returned from Marksville he informed me of what he had done. We continued our midnight consultations, never speaking to each other through the day, excepting as it was necessary about the work. As nearly as he was able to ascertain, it would require two weeks for the letter to reach Saratoga in due course of mail, and the same length of time for an answer to return. Within six weeks, at the farthest, we concluded, an answer would arrive, if it arrived at all. A great many suggestions were now made, and a great deal of conversation took place between us, as to the most safe and proper course

---

1   *A Key … Tom's Cabin*   Book compiled by Harriet Beecher Stowe in 1853 as a follow-up to her bestselling abolitionist novel, *Uncle Tom's Cabin* (1852); it contains non-fiction accounts of slavery from a wide variety of sources, including newspapers and excerpts from slave narratives such as Northup's. It was intended to counter the arguments of those who claimed that the cruelties depicted in her novel had been exaggerated.

to pursue on receipt of the free papers. They would stand between him and harm, in case we were overtaken and arrested leaving the country altogether. It would be no infringement of law, however much it might provoke individual hostility, to assist a freeman to regain his freedom.

At the end of four weeks he was again at Marksville, but no answer had arrived. I was sorely disappointed, but still reconciled myself with the reflection that sufficient length of time had not yet elapsed—that there might have been delays—and that I could not reasonably expect one so soon. Six, seven, eight, and ten weeks passed by, however, and nothing came. I was in a fever of suspense whenever Bass visited Marksville, and could scarcely close my eyes until his return. Finally my master's house was finished, and the time came when Bass must leave me. The night before his departure I was wholly given up to despair. I had clung to him as a drowning man clings to the floating spar, knowing if it slips from his grasp he must forever sink beneath the waves. The all-glorious hope, upon which I had laid such eager hold, was crumbling to ashes in my hands. I felt as if sinking down, down, amidst the bitter waters of slavery, from the unfathomable depths of which I should never rise again.

The generous heart of my friend and benefactor was touched with pity at the sight of my distress. He endeavored to cheer me up, promising to return the day before Christmas, and if no intelligence was received in the meantime, some further step would be undertaken to effect our design. He exhorted me to keep up my spirits—to rely upon his continued efforts in my behalf, assuring me, in most earnest and impressive language, that my liberation should, from thenceforth, be the chief object of his thoughts.

In his absence the time passed slowly indeed. I looked forward to Christmas with intense anxiety and impatience. I had about given up the expectation of receiving any answer to the letters. They might have miscarried, or might have been misdirected. Perhaps those at Saratoga, to whom they had been addressed, were all dead; perhaps, engaged in their pursuits, they did not consider the fate of an obscure, unhappy black man of sufficient importance to be noticed. My whole reliance was in Bass. The faith I had in him was continually re-assuring me, and enabled me to stand up against the tide of disappointment that had overwhelmed me.

So wholly was I absorbed in reflecting upon my situation and prospects, that the hands with whom I labored in the field often observed it. Patsey would ask me if I was sick, and Uncle Abram, and Bob, and Wiley frequently expressed a curiosity to know what I could be thinking about so steadily. But I evaded their inquiries with some light remark, and kept my thoughts locked closely in my breast.

[Chapter 21 opens with an account of the arrival of the letter in New York, where it is received by Parker and Perry, who in turn forward it to Northup's wife, Anne. She ultimately delivers the letter to Henry B. Northup, the white lawyer described in the narrative's opening pages, who takes the information before a legislative council in Washington; he then receives a commission to head South to search for Northup. Having arrived in Marksville, he enlists the assistance of Judge John Waddill.]

from CHAPTER 21

I am indebted to Mr. Henry B. Northup and others for many of the particulars contained in this chapter. ...

"I can scarcely comprehend the nice[1] distinctions and shades of political parties in your State," observed Mr. Waddill. "I read of soft-shells and hard-shells, hunkers and barnburners, woolly-heads and silver-grays,[2] and am unable to understand the precise difference between them. Pray, what is it?"

Mr. Northup, re-filling his pipe, entered into quite an elaborate narrative of the origin of the various sections of parties, and concluded by saying there was another party in New-York, known as free-soilers or abolitionists. "You have seen none of those in this part of the country, I presume?" Mr. Northup remarked.

"Never, but one," answered Waddill, laughingly. "We have one here in Marksville, an eccentric creature, who preaches abolitionism as vehemently as any fanatic at the North. He is a generous, inoffensive man, but always maintaining the wrong side of an argument. It affords us a deal of amusement. He is an excellent mechanic, and almost indispensable in this community. He is a carpenter. His name is Bass."

Some further good-natured conversation was had at the expense of Bass' peculiarities, when Waddill all at once fell into a reflective mood, and asked for the mysterious letter again.

"Let me see—l-e-t m-e s-e-e!" he repeated, thoughtfully to himself, running his eyes over the letter once more. "'Bayou Boeuf, August 15.' August 15—post-marked here. 'He that is writing for me—' Where did Bass work last summer?" he inquired, turning suddenly to his brother. His brother was unable to inform him, but rising, left the office, and soon returned with the intelligence that "Bass worked last summer somewhere on Bayou Boeuf."

"He is the man," bringing down his hand emphatically on the table, "who can tell us all about Solomon Northup," exclaimed Waddill.

---

1 *nice* Precise, fussy.
2 *soft-shells ... silver-grays* Nicknames for a variety of mid-nineteenth-century Northern political factions.

Bass was immediately searched for, but could not be found. After some inquiry, it was ascertained he was at the landing on Red River. Procuring a conveyance, young Waddill and Northup were not long in traversing the few miles to the latter place. On their arrival, Bass was found, just on the point of leaving, to be absent a fortnight or more. After an introduction, Northup begged the privilege of speaking to him privately a moment. They walked together towards the river, when the following conversation ensued:

"Mr. Bass," said Northup, "allow me to ask you if you were on Bayou Boeuf last August?"

"Yes, sir, I was there in August," was the reply.

"Did you write a letter for a colored man at that place to some gentleman in Saratoga Springs?"

"Excuse me, sir, if I say that is none of your business," answered Bass, stopping and looking his interrogator searchingly in the face.

"Perhaps I am rather hasty, Mr. Bass; I beg your pardon; but I have come from the State of New-York to accomplish the purpose the writer of a letter dated the 15th of August, post-marked at Marksville, had in view. Circumstances have led me to think that you are perhaps the man who wrote it. I am in search of Solomon Northup. If you know him, I beg you to inform me frankly where he is, and I assure you the source of any information you may give me shall not be divulged, if you desire it not to be."

A long time Bass looked his new acquaintance steadily in the eyes, without opening his lips. He seemed to be doubting in his own mind if there was not an attempt to practice some deception upon him. Finally he said, deliberately—

"I have done nothing to be ashamed of. I am the man who wrote the letter. If you have come to rescue Solomon Northup, I am glad to see you."

"When did you last see him, and where is he?" Northup inquired.

"I last saw him Christmas, a week ago today. He is the slave of Edwin Epps, a planter on Bayou Boeuf, near Holmesville. He is not known as Solomon Northup; he is called Platt."

The secret was out—the mystery was unraveled. Through the thick, black cloud, amid whose dark and dismal shadows I had walked twelve years, broke the star that was to light me back to liberty. All mistrust and hesitation were soon thrown aside, and the two men conversed long and freely upon the subject uppermost in their thoughts. Bass expressed the interest he had taken in my behalf—his intention of going north in the spring, and declaring that he had resolved to accomplish my emancipation, if it were in his power. He described the commencement and progress of his acquaintance with me, and listened with eager curiosity to the account given him of my family, and the history of my early life. Before separating, he drew a map of the bayou on a strip of paper with a piece of red chalk, showing the locality of Epps' plantation, and the road leading most directly to it. ...

... [T]hey came in sight of the plantation, and discovered us at work. Alighting from the carriage, and directing the driver to proceed to the great house, with instructions not to mention to anyone the object of their errand until they met again, Northup and the sheriff turned from the highway, and came towards us across the cotton field. We observed them, on looking up at the carriage—one several rods[1] in advance of the other. It was a singular and unusual thing to see white men approaching us in that manner, and especially at that early hour in the morning, and Uncle Abram and Patsey made some remarks, expressive of their astonishment. Walking up to Bob, the sheriff inquired:

"Where's the boy they call Platt?"

"Thar he is, massa," answered Bob, pointing to me, and twitching off his hat.

I wondered to myself what business he could possibly have with me, and turning round, gazed at him until he had approached within a step. During my long residence on the bayou, I had become familiar with the face of every planter within many miles; but this man was an utter stranger—certainly I had never seen him before.

"Your name is Platt, is it?" he asked.

"Yes, master," I responded.

Pointing towards Northup, standing a few rods distant, he demanded—"Do you know that man?"

I looked in the direction indicated, and as my eyes rested on his countenance, a world of images thronged my brain; a multitude of well-known faces—Anne's, and the dear children's, and my old dead father's; all the scenes and associations of childhood and youth; all the friends of other and happier days, appeared and disappeared, flitting and floating like dissolving shadows before the vision of my imagination, until at last the perfect memory of the man recurred to me, and throwing up my hands towards Heaven, I exclaimed, in a voice louder than I could utter in a less exciting moment—

"*Henry B. Northup*! Thank God—thank God!"

In an instant I comprehended the nature of his business, and felt that the hour of my deliverance was at hand. I started towards him, but the sheriff stepped before me.

"Stop a moment," said he; "have you any other name than Platt?"

"Solomon Northup is my name, master," I replied.

"Have you a family?" he inquired.

---

1   *rods*   Units of measurement, each equal to approximately five and a half yards.

"I *had* a wife and three children."

"What were your children's names?"

"Elizabeth, Margaret and Alonzo."

"And your wife's name before her marriage?"

"Anne Hampton."

"Who married you?"

"Timothy Eddy, of Fort Edward."

"Where does that gentleman live?" again pointing to Northup, who remained standing in the same place where I had first recognized him.

"He lives in Sandy Hill, Washington county, New-York," was the reply.

He was proceeding to ask further questions, but I pushed past him, unable longer to restrain myself. I seized my old acquaintance by both hands. I could not speak. I could not refrain from tears.

"Sol," he said at length, "I'm glad to see you."

I essayed to make some answer, but emotion choked all utterance, and I was silent. The slaves, utterly confounded, stood gazing upon the scene, their open mouths and rolling eyes indicating the utmost wonder and astonishment. For ten years I had dwelt among them, in the field and in the cabin, borne the same hardships, partaken the same fare, mingled my griefs with theirs, participated in the same scanty joys; nevertheless, not until this hour, the last I was to remain among them, had the remotest suspicion of my true name, or the slightest knowledge of my real history, been entertained by any one of them.

Not a word was spoken for several minutes, during which time I clung fast to Northup, looking up into his face, fearful I should awake and find it all a dream.

"Throw down that sack," Northup added, finally; "your cotton-picking days are over. Come with us to the man you live with." ...

I walked out into the yard, and was entering the kitchen door, when something struck me in the back. Aunt Phebe, emerging from the back door of the great house with a pan of potatoes, had thrown one of them with unnecessary violence, thereby giving me to understand that she wished to speak to me a moment confidentially. Running up to me, she whispered in my ear with great earnestness,

"Lor a' mity, Platt! what d'ye think? Dem two men come after ye. Heard 'em tell massa you free—got wife and tree children back thar whar you come from. Goin' wid 'em? Fool if ye don't—wish I could go," and Aunt Phebe ran on in this manner at a rapid rate.

Presently Mistress Epps made her appearance in the kitchen. She said many things to me, and wondered why I had not told her who I was. She expressed her regret, complimenting me by saying she had rather lose any other servant on the plantation. Had Patsey that day stood in my place, the measure of my mistress' joy would have overflowed. Now there was no one left who could mend a chair or a piece of furniture—no one who was of any use about the house—no one who could play for her on the violin—and Mistress Epps was actually affected to tears.

Epps had called to Bob to bring up his saddle horse. The other slaves, also, overcoming their fear of the penalty, had left their work and come to the yard. They were standing behind the cabins, out of sight of Epps. They beckoned me to come to them, and with all the eagerness of curiosity, excited to the highest pitch, conversed with and questioned me. If I could repeat the exact words they uttered, with the same emphasis—if I could paint their several attitudes, and the expression of their countenances—it would be indeed an interesting picture. In their estimation, I had suddenly arisen to an immeasurable height—had become a being of immense importance.

The legal papers having been served, and arrangements made with Epps to meet them the next day at Marksville, Northup and the sheriff entered the carriage to return to the latter place. As I was about mounting to the driver's seat, the sheriff said I ought to bid Mr. and Mrs. Epps goodbye. I ran back to the piazza where they were standing, and taking off my hat, said,

"Goodbye, missis."

"Goodbye, Platt," said Mrs. Epps, kindly.

"Goodbye, master."

"Ah! you d—d nigger," muttered Epps, in a surly, malicious tone of voice, "you needn't feel so cussed tickled—you ain't gone yet—I'll see about this business at Marksville tomorrow."

I was only a "*nigger*" and knew my place, but felt as strongly as if I had been a white man, that it would have been an inward comfort, had I dared to have given him a parting kick. On my way back to the carriage, Patsey ran from behind a cabin and threw her arms about my neck.

"Oh! Platt," she cried, tears streaming down her face, "you're goin' to be free—you're goin' way off yonder where we'll neber see ye any more. You've saved me a good many whippins, Platt; I'm glad you're goin' to be free—but oh! de Lord, de Lord! what'll become of me?"

I disengaged myself from her, and entered the carriage. The driver cracked his whip and away we rolled. I looked back and saw Patsey, with drooping head, half reclining on the ground; Mrs. Epps was on the piazza; Uncle Abram, and Bob, and Wiley, and Aunt Phebe stood by the gate, gazing after me. I waved my hand, but the carriage turned a bend of the bayou, hiding them from my eyes forever.

We stopped a moment at Carey's sugar house, where a great number of slaves were at work, such an establishment being a curiosity to a Northern man. Epps dashed by us on horseback at full speed—on the way, as we learned next day, to the "Pine Woods," to see William Ford, who had brought me into the country.

Tuesday, the fourth of January, Epps and his counsel, the Hon. H. Taylor, Northup, Waddill, the Judge and sheriff of Avoyelles, and myself, met in a room in the village of Marksville. Mr. Northup stated the facts in regard to me, and presented his commission, and the affidavits accompanying it. The sheriff described the scene in the cotton field. I was also interrogated at great length. Finally, Mr. Taylor assured his client that he was satisfied, and that litigation would not only be expensive, but utterly useless. In accordance with his advice, a paper was drawn up and signed by the proper parties, wherein Epps acknowledged he was satisfied of my right to freedom, and formally surrendered me to the authorities of New-York. It was also stipulated that it be entered of record in the recorder's office of Avoyelles.

Mr. Northup and myself immediately hastened to the landing, and taking passage on the first steamer that arrived, were soon floating down Red River, up which, with such desponding thoughts, I had been borne twelve years before.

—1853

SCENE IN THE COTTON FIELD, SOLOMON DELIVERED UP

In Context

Roaring River

The sheet music reproduced here was included at the end of *Twelve Years a Slave*, just before the book's appendices. The song is first referenced in Chapter 15, where its lyrics are given as an example of the sorts of songs that Northup heard sung by the enslaved during their Christmas celebrations—"the only respite from constant labor the slave has through the whole year." It is impossible to know for certain who composed the sheet music or decided to include it in the book, though given Northup's musical proficiency, it is likely (according to scholar Lara Langer Cohen) that he had some involvement. It is also impossible to tell how closely the lyrics provided actually resemble those Northup would have encountered on the plantation. Similar lyrics had appeared in various publications since at least 1843, often presented as minstrel songs —and versions of the lyrics continued to appear in various publications in the later decades of the nineteenth century.

ROARING RIVER.

A REFRAIN OF THE RED RIVER PLANTATION.

"Harper's creek and roarin' ribber,
Thar, my dear, we'll live forebber;
Den we'll go to de Ingin nation,
All I want in dis creation,
Is pretty little wife and big plantation.

CHORUS.
Up dat oak and down dat ribber,
Two overseers and one little nigger."

Solomon Northup in the Popular Press

from *The Morning Express*, Buffalo, New York (26 January 1853) [reprinted from *The New York Times*]

The Kidnapping Case.

Narrative of the Seizure and Recovery of Solomon Northrup—Interesting Disclosures.

From the New York Times.

We have obtained from Washington the subjoined statement of the circumstances attending the seizure and recovery of the negro man Solomon Northrup, whose case has excited so high a degree of interest. The material facts in the history of the transaction have already been given, but this narrative will be found more complete and authentic record than has yet appeared:

Solomon Northrup, the subject of the following narrative, is a free colored citizen of the United States; was born in Essex County, New York, about the year 1808; became early a resident of Washington County, and married there in 1829. His father and mother resided in the County of Washington about fifty years, till their decease and were both free. With his wife and children he resided at Saratoga Springs, in the winter of 1841, and while there was employed by two gentlemen to drive a team South, at the rate of a dollar a day. In fulfilment of his employment he proceeded to New York. and having taken out free papers, to show that he was a citizen, he went on to Washington City, where he arrived the second day of April, the same year, and put up at Gadby's Hotel. Soon after he arrived, he felt unwell and went to bed.

While suffering with severe pain, some persons came in, and, seeing the condition he was in, proposed to give him some medicine, and did so.— That is the last thing of which he had any recollection until he found himself chained to the floor of Williams' slave pen in this City, and handcuffed. In the course of a few hours, James H Burch, a slave dealer, came in, and the colored man asked him to take the irons off from him, and wanted to know why they were put on. Burch told him it was none of his business. The colored man said he was free and told where he was born Burch called in a man by the name of Ebenezer Rodbury, and they two stripped the man and laid him across a bench, Rodbury holding him down by his wrists. Burch whipped him with a cat-o'-nine tails, giving him a hundred lashes, and he swore he would kill him if he ever stated to any one that he was a free man. From that time forward the man saw he did not communicate th

.These statements regarding the condition of Solomon while with Eppes, and the punishment and brutal treatment of the colored girls, are taken from Solomon himself. It has been stated that the nearest plantation was distant from that of Eppes a half mile, and of course there could be no interference on the part of neighbors in any punishment however cruel or however well disposed to interfere they might be.

By the laws of Louisiana no man can be punished for having sold Solomon into slavery wrongfully, because more than two years had elapsed since he was sold; and no recovery can be had for his services, because he was bought without the knowledge that he was a free citizen.

[Over two newspaper columns, the account provides the full story of Northup's enslavement in summary form, before concluding with the following observations concerning Louisiana law.]

from *The Buffalo Courier*, **Buffalo, New York (11 January 1854)**

Solomon Northrup, the Slave,

WILL LECTURE and tell his narrative, at AMERICAN HALL., on THURSDAY EVENING, the 12th inst.   jan11-2t*

PIANOS TO RENT.

A FEW EXCELLENT ONES if applied for soon at
         SAGE & SONS', Music Store,
jan11   209 M in street.

To Rent.

A DESIRABLE Two Story Brick Dwelling House, No. 23 Carolina street. Possession given immediately. Enquire on the premises.   jan10-2t*   H. McCROSSAN.

from *The Daily Delta*, New Orleans (19 July 1854)

[This short article was printed in many newspapers; it appeared in *The Brooklyn Daily Eagle* on 12 July, for example, and in the *Buffalo Courier* on 15 July.]

The examination of Alexander Merrill and Joseph Russell, on the charge of kidnapping Solomon Northrup, and selling him into slavery, was progressing at Balston Spa, New York, on the 11th. Northrup positively swears to their being the persons, and told how he was hired at Saratoga Springs in 1841, to go to the South with them to join a circus company; that he was treated at Washington by them with drugged liquor, &c. The witness was in court who drank with Northrup and the kidnappers at Washington on the night before he was put in the slave pen. It is expected that this witness will come forward and testify to having heard Merrill tell of selling Northrup. The accused were discovered from the description and incidents given in Northrup's book.

from *The Daily Picayune*, New Orleans (27 May 1857)

Unsubstantiated claims such as that made by "T.A." in the letter below, which attempted to call into question the character of any black person who made allegations against white people, were printed frequently in Southern newspapers of the era.

[Special correspondence of the Picayune.]
Washington, Miss., May 20, 1857

... D uring my cruise in that bayou region, I first met with that precious production, entitled "Solomon Northup, or twelve years a slave." The copy I saw had evidently done good service; having been loaned from hand to hand, to those who wished to read it, so as to avoid buying more copies. A good idea with such a book. The scene is laid in that region—on Bayou Rouge. I found that much of Solomon or Platt's account of himself was true; that he was no doubt a native of New York and free. But, it is also clear, that Solomon was one of those cute Yankee niggers[1] who permit themselves to be sold occasionally, pocketing half the proceeds, and then claiming and proving their freedom, under the plea of having been kidnapped. Solomon was not so wise as his name would indicate,[2] and allowed himself to be thus sold once too often. He is spoken of on the bayou as a very decent and generally well behaved negro. And, as in "Uncle Tom's Cabin," just enough of truth has been worked up, to give the abundance of lies a *vraisemblance*,[3] it is evident that some most unprincipled scoundrel, possessed of considerable ability as a cross-examiner and writer, has led the negro on, and has worked up his simple tale in the most plausible manner, without the slightest reference to actual truth. For instance, he speaks of a girl Patsy, as having been most cruelly punished at the instigation of her mistress—cut most fearfully. Master Solomon's own gallantries lead the poor girl repeatedly into trouble, it seems. But I had the assurance of the resident physician, whose statement no one would pretend to doubt, that six or twelve months before Solomon's removal, and long after the time that he pretends these severe punishments were given, he had occasion to cup this girl, and found her back without a scar. What a consummate and unprincipled scoundrel must be he who could work up such a book as that, introducing as he has the names of respectable and excellent families.

But again I must close.

Yours, etc.,

T.A.

---

1   *cute* Acute; clever;   *niggers* By the nineteenth century, this term had acquired the unequivocally derogatory connotations it carries today; nevertheless, it continued to be used freely in many contexts by white writers.

2   *Solomon ... would indicate* Reference to King Solomon, the biblical King of Israel known for his profound wisdom.

3   *vraisemblance* Semblance of truth.

Sojourner Truth
c. 1797 – 1883

Abolitionist and women's rights activist Sojourner Truth was among the most celebrated and compelling orators of nineteenth-century America. Born into slavery near the turn of the century, Truth spent the first seventeen years of her free life working as a domestic servant in New York City before undergoing the spiritual transformation that, in 1843, compelled her to begin a career as an itinerant evangelist. Truth soon became a national celebrity, renowned both for her moving religious exhortations and for her uniquely powerful campaigning for racial and gender equality. Throughout her career, Truth thought and spoke about the intersections of race, class, and gender in a way that few of her fellow activists fully appreciated. Truth never learned to read or write herself; her ideas have come down to us primarily through the accounts of her contemporaries—a fact that has for decades challenged scholars seeking an "authentic" account of this exceptionally charismatic figure.

Isabella (Truth's birth name) was born to parents Elizabeth and James Baumfree or Bomefree around 1797 in Ulster County, two years before the passage of New York State's Gradual Abolition Act, and three decades before that act would take effect for all enslaved people in the state. Speaking Low Dutch as her first language, Isabella learned English when she was sold to an English-speaker, John Neely, around the age of nine. She lived under five different enslavers over the course of her enslaved life, enduring forced separation from her family as well as numerous instances of severe abuse. Forbidden from marrying her first love, Robert, because he belonged to another owner, Isabella was instead arranged to be married to Thomas, with whom she had five children.

Isabella's final enslaver was John Dumont, under whom some scholars speculate she experienced sexual abuse, and with whom she lived for sixteen years until the autumn of 1826. When Dumont broke a promise he had made to emancipate her that summer, Isabella emancipated herself. Leaving in the early hours of the morning, she walked twelve miles to a Quaker settlement with her youngest daughter in tow, leaving her other children with their father, who did not join her. The Quakers provided shelter for Isabella, and provided for her purchase from Dumont when he later came to demand her return. She was taken into the household of Isaac Van Wagenen, for whom she worked voluntarily—though legally still enslaved—as a domestic helper over the course of the next year. While working for Van Wagenen, Isabella discovered that her five-year-old son Peter had been illegally sold into slavery in Alabama by Dumont. When the Gradual Abolition Act came into effect and she was officially freed, Isabella sued to regain custody of her son, and, remarkably, succeeded.

In 1828 Isabella underwent a conversion experience, upon which she moved to New York City; she lived there for the next fifteen years, working as a domestic servant, preaching in various contexts including within the Methodist Church and at revivalist camp meetings, and briefly becoming involved in a controversial cult called the Kingdom of Matthias. She underwent a second religious experience in 1843; leaving behind what she now believed to be a sinful city, Isabella adopted the new name Sojourner Truth and began her travels to spread God's word.

Truth discovered a talent for oratory and religious ministry, and soon became something of a regional celebrity. As her fame increased, Truth took to posing for photographs, which she had printed in the popular form of *cartes de visite* that she then sold to collectors to fund her missionary travels. Though she did not initially demonstrate a vocal interest in either abolitionism or women's rights, the religious circles in which she moved often had a strongly antislavery bent. In the mid-1840s, Truth began living at the Northampton Association for Education and Industry, one of the era's many utopian, reform-minded communities. Here she met several prominent abolitionists—among them William Lloyd Garrison, David Ruggles, and, perhaps most significantly, the formerly enslaved orator Frederick Douglass. Douglass and Truth, though very different in their personalities, made profound impressions on one another here; it was at this point that Truth seems to have dedicated herself to the antislavery cause.

Around 1848, Garrison encouraged Truth to compose an autobiography focused on her time in slavery, in the vein of similar slave narratives by individuals such as Douglass. Having never learned to read or write, Truth dictated her life story to abolitionist Olive Gilbert, and had it published in 1850 as *The Narrative of Sojourner Truth, a Northern Slave*. It was printed cheaply, and sold in large numbers at abolitionist conferences. The *Narrative* contributed to Truth's growing abolitionist fame; she began speaking publicly on the subject that fall.

In May 1851, Truth spoke at a women's rights conference held at a church in Akron, Ohio, at which she appears to have been the only African American woman in attendance. In contemporary records of the speech, Truth affirmed the physical capabilities of women, using herself as an example; argued for their intellectual rights; and sharply repudiated the biblically derived objections to the equality of women that opponents of women's rights commonly offered. In the best-known contemporaneous report of the speech, Marius Robinson claimed that it was "impossible to transfer it to paper, or convey any adequate idea of the effect [Truth's speech] produced upon the audience." Another account of Truth's speech, however, eventually became more famous; it was produced in 1863, over a decade after the speech had been given, by Frances Dana Gage, who had presided over the Akron convention. In her version, Gage significantly expanded upon the content of Truth's speech, portraying her as speaking in a strong dialect reflective of stereotypical Southern "slave" accents. (Truth, as a native Dutch speaker from the North, would almost certainly not have spoken with such an accent.) Gage also added the famous refrain, "Ar'n't I a Woman?," which has since lent the speech its popular name. Gage's version appeared in revised editions of Truth's *Narrative* published in the 1870s and 1880s, as well as in the first volume of Elizabeth Cady Stanton's monumental *History of Woman Suffrage* (1881); it remained throughout much of the twentieth century the most widely known and reproduced.

Truth's speeches continued to garner her influence and notoriety. Her highly animated, song-filled lectures were the subject of much comment, as was her physical appearance; she stood nearly six feet tall, and is said to have bared both her arms and her breasts on stage to prove her strength and womanhood to skeptics. She was regularly discussed in abolitionist and feminist media; Harriet Beecher Stowe famously wrote of her in *The Atlantic* in 1863, describing her as "the Libyan Sibyl."

Though a pacifist at heart, Truth welcomed the Civil War as a national spiritual purge. She met (and posed for a photograph with) Abraham Lincoln during the period at which the Emancipation Proclamation was being drafted, and, after the end of the war, she provided aid and advice to newly emancipated men and women. Over the following years she agitated for healthcare, housing, and land reform for African Americans; for the desegregation of transportation; for temperance; for the abolition of capital punishment; and for universal suffrage.

Truth died in 1883, at the age of eighty-six, having by then established a vivid presence in the American public imagination. She had often aroused puzzlement in her admirers, including in Frederick Douglass, who described her as a "strange compound of wit and wisdom, of wild enthusiasm and flint-like common sense. She was a genuine specimen of the uncultured negro. She cared very little for elegance of speech or refinement of manners." Long after her death, monikers such as "the Negro Joan of Arc" remained associated with her name. Later scholarship has often pivoted on the question of authenticity, especially as it relates to her apparently intentional rejection of conventional literacy; on her highly dynamic lectures; and on her intersectional politics. Her life, career, and words continue to both challenge and fascinate.

Note on the Texts

The text of Truth's narrative is taken from the first edition of the *Narrative of Sojourner Truth, a Northern Slave, emancipated from bodily servitude by the state of New York, in 1828* (1850). Truth's famous 1851 speech is presented in two versions: the first is based on that printed in *The Anti-Slavery Bugle* on 21 June 1851, transcribed with commentary by Marius Robinson; the second is based on that published in the 1875 edition *Narrative of Sojourner Truth; A Bondswoman of Olden Time, emancipated by the New York Legislature in the early part of the present century; with a history of her Labors and Correspondence, drawn from her "Book of life,"* edited by Frances Titus with reminiscences by Frances Dana Gage. Spelling and punctuation have been lightly modernized in accordance with the practices of this anthology, but any writing that aims to reproduce (authentically or not) Truth's speech patterns remains unaltered.

⌘ ⌘ ⌘

from *The Narrative of Sojourner Truth, a Northern Slave*

Her Religious Instruction

Isabella[1] and Peter (her youngest brother) remained, with their parents, the legal property of Charles Ardinburgh till his decease, which took place when Isabella was near nine years old.

After this event, she was often surprised to find her mother in tears; and when, in her simplicity, she inquired, "Mau-mau, what makes you cry?" she would answer, "Oh, my child, I am thinking of your brothers and sisters that have been sold away from me." And she would proceed to detail many circumstances respecting them. But Isabella long since concluded that it was the impending fate of her only remaining children, which her mother but too well understood, even then, that called up those memories from the past, and made them crucify her heart afresh.

In the evening, when her mother's work was done, she would sit down under the sparkling vault of heaven, and calling her children to her, would talk to them of the only Being that could effectually aid or protect them. Her teachings were delivered in Low Dutch, her only language, and, translated into English, ran nearly as follows:

"My children, there is a God, who hears and sees you."

"A *God*, mau-mau! Where does he live?" asked the children.

"He lives in the sky," she replied; "and when you are beaten, or cruelly treated, or fall into any trouble, you must ask help of him, and he will always hear and help you." She taught them to kneel and say the Lord's Prayer. She entreated them to refrain from lying and stealing, and to strive to obey their masters.

At times, a groan would escape her, and she would break out in the language of the Psalmist—"Oh Lord, how long?[2] Oh Lord, how long?" And in reply to Isabella's question—"What ails you, mau-mau?" her only answer was, "Oh, a good deal ails me—Enough ails me." Then again, she would point them to the stars, and say, in her peculiar language, "Those are the same stars, and that is the same moon, that look down upon your brothers and sisters, and which they see as they look up to them, though they are ever so far away from us, and each other."

Thus, in her humble way, did she endeavor to show them their Heavenly Father, as the only being who could protect them in their perilous condition;

---

1   *Isabella*   Truth's birth name.

2   *Oh Lord, how long?*   See Psalm 13.1: "How long wilt thou forget me, O Lord? for ever? how long wilt thou hide thy face from me?"

at the same time, she would strengthen and brighten the chain of family affection, which she trusted extended itself sufficiently to connect the widely scattered members of her precious flock. These instructions of the mother were treasured up and held sacred by Isabella, as our future narrative will show.

THE AUCTION

At length, the never-to-be-forgotten day of the terrible auction arrived, when the "slaves, horses, and other cattle" of Charles Ardinburgh, deceased, were to be put under the hammer, and again change masters. Not only Isabella and Peter, but their mother, were now destined to the auction block, and would have been struck off with the rest to the highest bidder, but for the following circumstance: A question arose among the heirs, "Who shall be burdened with Bomefree, when we have sent away his faithful Mau-mau Bett?"[1] He was becoming weak and infirm; his limbs were painfully rheumatic and distorted—more from exposure and hardship than from old age, though he was several years older than Mau-mau Bett; he was no longer considered of value, but must soon be a burden and care to some one. After some contention on the point at issue, none being willing to be burdened with him, it was finally agreed, as most expedient for the heirs, that the price of Mau-mau Bett should be sacrificed, and she receive her freedom, on condition that she take care of and support her faithful James—faithful, not only to her as a husband, but proverbially faithful as a slave to those who would not willingly sacrifice a dollar for *his* comfort, now that he had commenced his descent into the dark vale of decrepitude and suffering. This important decision was received as joyful news indeed to our ancient couple, who were the objects of it, and who were trying to prepare their hearts for a severe struggle, and one altogether new to them, as they had never before been separated; for, though ignorant, helpless, crushed in spirit, and weighed down with hardship and cruel bereavement, they were still human, and their human hearts beat within them with as true an affection as ever caused a human heart to beat. And their anticipated separation now, in the decline of life, after the last child had been torn from them, must have been truly appalling. Another privilege was granted them—that of remaining occupants of the same dark, humid cellar I have before described: otherwise, they were to support themselves as they best could. And as her mother was still able to do considerable work, and her father a little, they got on for some time very comfortably. The strangers who rented the house were humane people, and very kind to them; they were not rich, and owned no slaves. How long this state of things continued, we are unable

---

1   *Bomefree* Truth's father, James Baumfree;   *Mau-mau Bett* Truth's mother Elizabeth.

to say, as Isabella had not then sufficiently cultivated her organ[1] of time to calculate years, or even weeks or hours. But she thinks her mother must have lived several years after the death of Master Charles. She remembers going to visit her parents some three or four times before the death of her mother, and a good deal of time seemed to her to intervene between each visit.

At length her mother's health began to decline—a fever-sore made its ravages on one of her limbs, and the palsy[2] began to shake her frame; still, she and James tottered about, picking up a little here and there, which, added to the mites[3] contributed by their kind neighbors, sufficed to sustain life, and drive famine from the door. ...

THE CAUSE OF HER LEAVING THE CITY

The first years spent by Isabella in the city, she accumulated more than enough to satisfy all her wants, and she placed all the overplus in the Savings Bank. Afterwards, while living with Mr. Pierson,[4] he prevailed on her to take it all thence, and invest it in a common fund which he was about establishing, as a fund to be drawn from by all the faithful; the faithful, of course, were the handful that should subscribe to his peculiar creed. This fund, commenced by Mr. Pierson, afterwards became part and parcel of the kingdom of which Matthias assumed to be head;[5] and at the breaking up of the kingdom, her little property was merged in the general ruin—or went to enrich those who profited by the loss of others, if any such there were. Mr. Pierson and others had so assured her that the fund would supply all her wants, at all times, and in all emergencies, and to the end of life, that she became perfectly careless on the subject—asking for no interest when she drew her money from the bank, and taking no account of the sum she placed in the fund. She recovered a few articles of the furniture from the wreck of the kingdom, and received a small sum of money from Mr. B. Folger, as the price of Mrs. Folger's attempt to convict her of murder.[6] With this to start upon, she commenced anew her labors, in the hope of yet being able to accumulate a sufficiency to make a

---

1 *organ* Mental sense.
2 *palsy* Paralysis or tremor.
3 *mites* Small donations.
4 *Mr. Pierson* Isabella's employer, businessperson Elias Pierson.
5 *the kingdom ... head* Elias Pierson had been converted by itinerant preacher Robert Matthews, also known as Matthias, in the 1830s, following which he helped fund a new religious cult called the Kingdom of Matthias. Matthias became a notorious figure both for his unorthodox—and rampantly misogynistic—theology and for the controversy that surrounded his cult's dissolution.
6 *Mr. B. Folger ... murder* The Kingdom of Matthias fell apart after Pierson died under suspicious circumstances, upon which both Matthias and Isabella were accused of his murder. Isabella successfully sued their accusers, the Folgers, for libel.

little home for herself, in her advancing age. With this stimulus before her, she toiled hard, working early and late, doing a great deal for a little money, and turning her hand to almost anything that promised good pay. Still, she did not prosper, and somehow, could not contrive to lay by a single dollar for a "rainy day."

When this had been the state of her affairs some time, she suddenly paused, and taking a retrospective view of what had passed, inquired within herself why it was that, for all her unwearied labors, she had nothing to show; why it was that others, with much less care and labor, could hoard up treasures for themselves and children? She became more and more convinced, as she reasoned, that everything she had undertaken in the city of New York had finally proved a failure; and where her hopes had been raised the highest, there she felt the failure had been the greatest, and the disappointment most severe.

After turning it in her mind for some time, she came to the conclusion that she had been taking part in a great drama, which was, in itself, but one great system of robbery and wrong. "Yes," she said, "the rich rob the poor, and the poor rob one another." True, she had not received labor from others, and stinted their pay, as she felt had been practised against her; but she had taken their work from them, which was their only means to get money, and was the same to them in the end. For instance—a gentleman where she lived would give her a dollar to hire a poor man to clear the new-fallen snow from the steps and sidewalks. She would arise early, and perform the labor herself, putting the money into her own pocket. A poor man would come along, saying she ought to have let him have the job; he was poor, and needed the pay for his family. She would harden her heart against him, and answer—"I am poor too, and I need it for mine." But, in her retrospection, she thought of all the misery she might have been adding to, in her selfish grasping, and it troubled her conscience sorely; and this insensibility to the claims of human brotherhood, and the wants of the destitute and wretched poor, she now saw, as she never had done before, to be unfeeling, selfish and wicked. These reflections and convictions gave rise to a sudden revulsion of feeling in the heart of Isabella, and she began to look upon money and property with great indifference, if not contempt—being at that time unable, probably, to discern any difference between a miserly grasping at and hoarding of money and means, and a true use of the good things of this life for one's own comfort, and the relief of such as she might be enabled to befriend and assist. One thing she was sure of—that the precepts, "Do unto others as ye would that others should do unto you," "Love your neighbor as yourself,"[1] and so forth, were maxims that had been but little thought of by herself, or practised by those about her.

---

1   *Do unto others ... as yourself*   See Luke 6.31 and Mark 12.31, respectively.

Her next decision was that she must leave the city; it was no place for her; yea, she felt called in spirit to leave it, and to travel east and lecture. She had never been further east than the city, neither had she any friends there of whom she had particular reason to expect anything; yet to her it was plain that her mission lay in the east, and that she would find friends there. She determined on leaving; but these determinations and convictions she kept close locked in her own breast, knowing that if her children and friends were aware of it, they would make such an ado about it as would render it very unpleasant, if not distressing to all parties. Having made what preparations for leaving she deemed necessary—which was, to put up a few articles of clothing in a pillow-case, all else being deemed an unnecessary incumbrance—about an hour before she left, she informed Mrs. Whiting, the woman of the house where she was stopping, that her name was no longer Isabella, but SOJOURNER, and that she was going east. And to her inquiry, "What are you going east for?" her answer was, "The Spirit calls me there, and I must go."

She left the city on the morning of the 1st of June, 1843, crossing over to Brooklyn, L.I.;[1] and taking the rising sun for her only compass and guide, she "remembered Lot's wife,"[2] and hoping to avoid her fate, she resolved not to look back till she felt sure the wicked city from which she was fleeing was left too far behind to be visible in the distance; and when she first ventured to look back, she could just discern the blue cloud of smoke that hung over it, and she thanked the Lord that she was thus far removed from what seemed to *her* a second Sodom.

She was now fairly started on her pilgrimage; her bundle in one hand, and a little basket of provisions in the other, and two York shillings[3] in her purse—her heart strong in the faith that her true work lay before her, and that the Lord was her director; and she doubted not he would provide for and protect her, and that it would be very censurable in her to burden herself with anything more than a moderate supply for her then present needs. Her mission was not merely to travel east, but to "lecture," as she designated it, "testifying of the hope that was in her"—exhorting the people to embrace Jesus, and refrain from sin, the nature and origin of which she explained to them in accordance with her own most curious and original views. Through

---

1   *L.I.*   Long Island.
2   *remembered Lot's wife*   In Genesis 19, the virtuous man Lot and his unnamed wife are permitted by God to flee the city of Sodom, which God is about to destroy because its inhabitants have been sinful; Lot and his wife are instructed not to look back upon the burning city, but Lot's wife disobeys, and as a punishment is turned into a pillar of salt. The story is referenced in the New Testament; Luke 17.32 instructs Christians to "Remember Lot's wife."
3   *York shillings*   Colonial form of currency still then in circulation in New York; one shilling was the equivalent of approximately twelve cents.

her life, and all its chequered changes, she has ever clung fast to her first permanent impressions on religious subjects.

Wherever night overtook her, there she sought for lodgings—free, if she might—if not, she paid; at a tavern, if she chanced to be at one—if not, at a private dwelling; with the rich, if they would receive her—if not, with the poor.

But she soon discovered that the largest houses were nearly always full; if not quite full, company was soon expected; and that it was much easier to find an unoccupied corner in a small house than in a large one; and if a person possessed but a miserable roof over his head, you might be sure of a welcome to part of it.

But this, she had penetration enough to see, was quite as much the effect of a want of sympathy as of benevolence; and this was also very apparent in her religious conversations with people who were strangers to her. She said, "she never could find out that the rich had any religion. If *I* had been rich and accomplished, I could; for the rich could always find religion in the rich, and *I* could find it among the poor."

At first, she attended such meetings as she heard of, in the vicinity of her travels, and spoke to the people as she found them assembled. Afterwards, she advertised meetings of her own, and held forth to large audiences, having, as she said, "a good time."

When she became weary of travelling, and wished a place to stop a while and rest herself, she said some opening for her was always near at hand; and the first time she needed rest, a man accosted her as she was walking, inquiring if she was looking for work. She told him that was not the object of her travels, but that she would willingly work a few days, if anyone wanted. He requested her to go to his family, who were sadly in want of assistance, which he had been thus far unable to supply. She went to the house where she was directed, and was received by his family, one of whom was ill, as a "Godsend"; and when she felt constrained to resume her journey, they were very sorry, and would fain have detained her longer; but as she urged the necessity of leaving, they offered her what seemed in her eyes a great deal of money as a remuneration for her labor, and an expression of their gratitude for her opportune assistance; but she would only receive a very little of it; enough, as she says, to enable her to pay tribute to Cæsar,[1] if it was demanded of her; and two or three York shillings at a time were all she allowed herself to take; and then,

---

1   *pay tribute to Cæsar*   Truth is likely referencing the biblical saying regarding taxation, "Render unto Caesar the things that are Caesar's, and unto God the things that are God's" (Matthew 22.21); the "things that are Caesar's" referred to taxes or other fees relating to secular matters. In other words, Truth will accept only as much money as she needs to pay for the demands of earthly life, which may have included road and bridge taxes as well as things such as food and shelter.

with purse replenished, and strength renewed, she would once more set out to perform her mission.

The Consequences of Refusing a Traveller a Night's Lodging

As she drew near the centre of the Island,[1] she commenced, one evening at nightfall, to solicit the favor of a night's lodging. She had repeated her request a great many, it seemed to her some twenty times, and as many times she received a negative answer. She walked on, the stars and the tiny horns of the new moon shed but a dim light on her lonely way, when she was familiarly accosted by two Indians, who took her for an acquaintance. She told them they were mistaken in the person; she was a stranger there, and asked them the direction to a tavern. They informed her it was yet a long way—some two miles or so—and inquired if she were alone. Not wishing for their protection, or knowing what might be the character of their kindness, she answered, "No, not exactly," and passed on. At the end of a weary way, she came to the tavern—rather, to a large building, which was occupied as a courthouse, tavern, and jail—and on asking for a night's lodging, was informed she could stay, if she would consent to be locked in. This to her mind was an insuperable objection. To have a key turned on her was a thing not to be thought of, at least not to be endured, and she again took up her line of march, preferring to walk beneath the open sky, to being locked up by a stranger in such a place. She had not walked far, before she heard the voice of a woman under an open shed; she ventured to accost her, and inquired if she knew where she could get in for the night. The woman answered that she did not, unless she went home with them; and turning to her "good man," asked him if the stranger could not share their home for the night, to which he cheerfully assented. Sojourner thought it evident he had been taking a drop too much, but as he was civil and good-natured, and she did not feel inclined to spend the night alone in the open air, she felt driven to the necessity of accepting their hospitality, whatever it might prove to be. The woman soon informed her that there was a ball in the place, at which they would like to drop in a while, before they went to their home.

Balls being no part of Sojourner's mission, she was not desirous of attending; but her hostess could be satisfied with nothing short of a taste of it, and she was forced to go with her, or relinquish their company at once, in which move there might be more exposure than in accompanying her. She went, and soon found herself surrounded by an assemblage of people, collected from

---

1   *the Island*   I.e., Long Island.

the very dregs of society, too ignorant and degraded to understand, much less entertain, a high or bright idea—in a dirty hovel, destitute of every comfort, and where the fumes of whiskey were abundant and powerful.

Sojourner's guide there was too much charmed with the combined entertainments of the place to be able to tear herself away, till she found her faculties for enjoyment failing her, from a too free use of liquor; and she betook herself to bed till she could recover them. Sojourner, seated in a corner, had time for many reflections, and refrained from lecturing them, in obedience to the recommendation, "Cast not your pearls,"[1] etc. When the night was far spent, the husband of the sleeping woman aroused the sleeper, and reminded her that she was not very polite to the woman she had invited to sleep at her house, and of the propriety of returning home. They once more emerged into the pure air, which to our friend Sojourner, after so long breathing the noisome air of the ballroom, was most refreshing and grateful. Just as day dawned, they reached the place they called their home. Sojourner now saw that she had lost nothing in the shape of rest by remaining so long at the ball, as their miserable cabin afforded but one bunk or pallet for sleeping; and had there been many such, she would have preferred sitting up all night to occupying one like it. They very politely offered her the bed, if she would use it; but civilly declining, she waited for morning with an eagerness of desire she never felt before on the subject, and was never more happy than when the eye of day shed its golden light once more over the earth. She was once more free, and while daylight should last, independent, and needed no invitation to pursue her journey. Let these facts teach us that every pedestrian in the world is not a vagabond, and that it is a dangerous thing to compel anyone to receive that hospitality from the vicious and abandoned which they should have received from us—as thousands can testify, who have thus been caught in the snares of the wicked.

The fourth of July, Isabella arrived at Huntingdon; from thence she went to Cold Springs, where she found the people making preparations for a mass temperance meeting. With her usual alacrity, she entered into their labors, getting up dishes *à la New York*,[2] greatly to the satisfaction of those she assisted. After remaining at Cold Springs some three weeks, she returned to Huntingdon, where she took boat for Connecticut. Landing at Bridgeport, she again resumed her travels towards the northeast, lecturing some, and working some, to get wherewith to pay tribute to Cæsar, as she called it; and in this manner

---

1   *Cast not your pearls*   See Matthew 7.6: "Give not that which is holy unto the dogs, neither cast ye your pearls before swine, lest they trample them under their feet, and turn again and rend you."

2   *getting up dishes à la New York*   Preparing meals in New York style. The expression "à la New York" is tongue-in-cheek; nineteenth-century American cuisine was typically quite unrefined, but restaurants often tried to suggest a higher level of sophistication by dressing up the dishes they served with French or other European names (*potatoes Parisienne, macaroni à la Milanese*, etc.).

she presently came to the city of New Haven, where she found many meetings, which she attended—at some of which, she was allowed to express her views freely, and without reservation. She also called meetings expressly to give herself an opportunity to be heard; and found in the city many true friends of Jesus, as she judged, with whom she held communion of spirit, having no preference for one sect more than another, but being well satisfied with all who gave her evidence of having known or loved the Saviour.

After thus delivering her testimony in this pleasant city, feeling she had not as yet found an abiding place, she went from thence to Bristol, at the request of a zealous sister who desired her to go to the latter place and hold a religious conversation with some friends of hers there. She went as requested, found the people kindly and religiously disposed, and through them she became acquainted with several very interesting persons.

A spiritually-minded brother in Bristol, becoming interested in her new views and original opinions, requested as a favor that she would go to Hartford, to see and converse with friends of his there. Standing ready to perform any service in the Lord, she went to Hartford as desired, bearing in her hand the following note from this brother:

> SISTER—I send you this living messenger, as I believe her to be one that God loves. Ethiopia is stretching forth her hands unto God.[1] You can see by this sister, that God does by his Spirit alone teach his own children things to come. Please receive her, and she will tell you some new things. Let her tell her story without interrupting her, and give close attention, and you will see she has got the lever of truth, that God helps her to pry where but few can. She cannot read or write, but the law is in her heart.
>
> Send her to brother—brother—and where she can do the most good.
> From your brother,
> H.L.B.

SOME OF HER VIEWS AND REASONINGS

As soon as Isabella saw God as an all-powerful, all-pervading spirit, she became desirous of hearing all that had been written of him, and listened to the account of the creation of the world and its first inhabitants, as contained in the first chapters of Genesis, with peculiar interest. For some time she received it all literally, though it appeared strange to her that "God worked by the day, got tired, and stopped to rest," etc. But after a little time, she began to reason

---

1 *Ethiopia ... unto God* See Psalm 68.31: "Princes shall come out of Egypt; Ethiopia shall soon stretch out her hands unto God." In the nineteenth century, this biblical line was often referenced by abolitionists, with "Ethiopia" being used as a shorthand for the African continent and African-descended people as a whole.

upon it, thus—"Why, if God works by the day, and one day's work tires him, and he is obliged to rest, either from weariness or on account of darkness, or if he waited for the 'cool of the day' to walk in the garden,'[1] because he was inconvenienced by the heat of the sun, why then it seems that God cannot do as much as *I* can; for *I* can bear the sun at noon, and work several days and nights in succession without being much tired. Or, if he rested nights because of the darkness, it is very queer that he should make the night so dark that he could not see himself. If *I* had been God, I would have made the night light enough for my own convenience, surely." But the moment she placed this idea of God by the side of the impression she had once so suddenly received of his inconceivable greatness and entire spirituality, that moment she exclaimed mentally, "No, God does not stop to rest, for he is a spirit, and cannot tire; he cannot want for light, for he hath all light in himself. And if 'God is all in all,' and 'worketh all in all,'[2] as I have heard them read, then it is impossible he should rest at all; for if he did, every other thing would stop and rest too; the waters would not flow, and the fishes could not swim; and all motion must cease. God could have no pauses in his work, and he needed no Sabbaths of rest. Man might need them, and he should take them when he needed them, whenever he required rest. As it regarded the worship of God, he was to be worshipped at all times and in all places; and one portion of time never seemed to her more holy than another."

These views, which were the results of the workings of her own mind, assisted solely by the light of her own experience and very limited knowledge, were, for a long time after their adoption, closely locked in her own breast, fearing lest their avowal might bring upon her the imputation of "infidelity"—the usual charge preferred by all religionists, against those who entertain religious views and feelings differing materially from their own. If, from their own sad experience, they are withheld from shouting the cry of "infidel," they fail not to see and to feel, ay, and to say, that the dissenters are not of the right spirit, and that their spiritual eyes have never been unsealed.

While travelling in Connecticut, she met a minister, with whom she held a long discussion on these points, as well as on various other topics, such as the origin of all things, especially the origin of evil, at the same time bearing her testimony strongly against a paid ministry. He belonged to that class, and, as a matter of course, as strongly advocated his own side of the question.

I had forgotten to mention, in its proper place, a very important fact, that when she was examining the scriptures, she wished to hear them without

---

1   *cool of … the garden*   See Genesis 3.8: "And they [Adam and Eve] heard the voice of the Lord God walking in the garden in the cool of the day."

2   *God is … in all*   See 1 Corinthians 12.6: "And there are diversities of operations, but it is the same God which worketh all in all."

comment; but if she employed adult persons to read them to her, and she asked them to read a passage over again, they invariably commenced to explain, by giving her their version of it; and in this way, they tried her feelings exceedingly. In consequence of this, she ceased to ask adult persons to read the Bible to her, and substituted children in their stead. Children, as soon as they could read distinctly, would re-read the same sentence to her, as often as she wished, and without comment—and in that way she was enabled to see what her own mind could make out of the record, and that, she said, was what she wanted, and not what others thought it to mean. She wished to compare the teachings of the Bible with the witness within her; and she came to the conclusion, that the spirit of truth spoke in those records, but that the recorders of those truths had intermingled with them ideas and suppositions of their own. This is one among the many proofs of her energy and independence of character.

When it became known to her children that Sojourner had left New York, they were filled with wonder and alarm. Where could she have gone, and why had she left? were questions no one could answer satisfactorily. Now, their imaginations painted her as a wandering maniac—and again they feared she had been left to commit suicide; and many were the tears they shed at the loss of her.

But when she reached Berlin, Conn., she wrote to them by amanuensis, informing them of her whereabouts, and waiting an answer to her letter; thus quieting their fears, and gladdening their hearts once more with assurances of her continued life and her love.

—1850

In Context

Speech at the Akron, Ohio Women's Rights Convention, 1851

On the 29th of May 1851, Sojourner Truth attended a women's rights convention held at the Old Stone Church in Akron, Ohio, where she ventured before the crowd, apparently spontaneously, and delivered what would become one of the most famous speeches of the burgeoning women's rights movement. Numerous reports of her speech were published in newspapers at the time; most notable among them was that written by Marius Robinson for the Salem *Anti-Slavery Bugle*. Nearly twelve years later, another account was published in the 23 April 1863 issue of the *New York Independent*, written by Frances Dana Gage, who had presided over the 1851 Akron event. This version differed substantially from the earlier transcription, portraying Truth as speaking with a dialect that modern scholars argue was almost certainly not representative of her actual mode of speaking. Nevertheless, Gage's version was reprinted in an 1875 edition of the *Narrative of Sojourner Truth; A Bondswoman of Olden Time*, and again in Volume 1 of Elizabeth Cady Stanton's *History of Woman Suffrage* (1881). It prevailed as the standard rendition of Truth's speech well into the twentieth century.

[*1851 VERSION*]

WOMEN'S RIGHTS CONVENTION

SOJOURNER TRUTH

One of the most unique and interesting speeches of the Convention was made by Sojourner Truth, an emancipated slave. It is impossible to transfer it to paper, or convey any adequate idea of the effect it produced upon the audience. Those only can appreciate it who saw her powerful form, her whole-souled, earnest gesture, and listened to her strong and truthful tones. She came forward to the platform and addressing the President said with great simplicity:

May I say a few words? Receiving an affirmative answer, she proceeded: I want to say a few words about this matter. I am a woman's rights. I have as much muscle as any man, and can do as much work as any man. I have plowed and reaped and husked and chopped and mowed, and can any man do more than that? I have heard much about the sexes being equal; I can carry as much as any man, and can eat as much too, if I can get it. I am as strong as any man that is now. As for intellect, all I can say is, if woman have a pint and man a quart—why can't she have her little pint full? You need not be afraid to give us our rights for fear we will take too much—for we can't take more than our pint'll hold. The poor men seem to be all in confusion, and don't know what to do. Why children, if you have woman's rights give it to her and you will feel better. You will have your own rights, and they won't be so much trouble. I can't read, but I can hear. I have heard the Bible and have learned that Eve caused man to sin. Well if woman upset the world, do give her a chance to set it right side up again. The Lady has spoken about Jesus, how he never spurned woman from him, and she was right. When Lazarus died, Mary and Martha came to him with faith and love and besought him to raise their brother. And Jesus wept—and Lazarus came forth.[1] And how came Jesus into the world? Through God who created him and woman who bore him. Man, where is your part? But the women are coming up blessed by God and a few of the men are coming up with them. But man is in a tight place, the poor slave is on him, woman is coming on him, and he is surely between a hawk and a buzzard.

[*1875 VERSION*]

The cause [of women's rights] was unpopular then. The leaders of the movement trembled on seeing a tall, gaunt black woman, in a gray dress and white turban, surmounted by an uncouth sun-bonnet, march deliberately into the church, walk with the air of a queen up the aisle, and take her seat upon the pulpit steps. A buzz of disapprobation was heard all over the house, and such words as these fell upon listening ears:

"An abolition affair!" "Woman's rights and niggers!"[2] "We told you so!" "Go it, old darkey!"

I chanced upon that occasion to wear my first laurels in public life as president of the meeting. At my request, order was restored and the business of the hour went on. The morning session was held; the evening exercises came and went. Old Sojourner, quiet and reticent as the "Libyan Statue,"[3] sat crouched against the wall on the corner of the pulpit stairs, her sun-bonnet shading her eyes, her elbows on her knees, and her chin resting upon her broad, hard palm. At intermission she was busy, selling "The Life of Sojourner Truth," a

---

1   *When Lazarus ... came forth*   In John 11, Jesus is asked by Mary and Martha of Bethany to come to the aid of their ailing brother Lazarus. Jesus arrives in Bethany four days after Lazarus' death, but because of the sisters' faith, Jesus raises Lazarus from the dead.

2   *niggers*   By the mid-nineteenth century, as the context here suggests, this word (today universally acknowledged to be an utterly unacceptable expression of racism) had firmly established itself in white American vernacular as an emphatically pejorative alternative to the then-more neutral term "negro."

3   *Libyan Statue*   Reference to an 1861 marble sculpture by William Wetmore Story.

narrative of her own strange and adventurous life. Again and again timorous and trembling ones came to me and said with earnestness, "Don't let her speak, Mrs. Gage, it will ruin us. Every newspaper in the land will have our cause mixed with abolition and niggers, and we shall be utterly denounced." My only answer was, "We shall see when the time comes."

The second day the work waxed warm. Methodist, Baptist, Episcopal, Presbyterian, and Universalist ministers came in to hear and discuss the resolutions presented. One claimed superior rights and privileges for man on the ground of superior intellect; another, because of the manhood of Christ. "If God had desired the equality of woman, he would have given some token of his will through the birth, life, and death of the Saviour." Another gave us a theological view of the sin of our first mother. There were few women in those days that dared to "speak in meeting," and the august teachers of the people were seeming to get the better of us, while the boys in the galleries and the sneerers among the pews were hugely enjoying the discomfiture, as they supposed, of the "strong minded." Some of the tender-skinned friends were on the point of losing dignity, and the atmosphere of the convention betokened a storm.

Slowly from her seat in the corner rose Sojourner Truth, who, till now, had scarcely lifted her head. "Don't let her speak!" gasped half a dozen in my ear. She moved slowly and solemnly to the front, laid her old bonnet at her feet, and turned her great, speaking eyes to me. There was a hissing sound of disapprobation above and below. I rose and announced "Sojourner Truth," and begged the audience to keep silence for a few moments. The tumult subsided at once, and every eye was fixed on this almost Amazon[1] form, which stood nearly six feet high, head erect, and eye piercing the upper air, like one in a dream. At her first word, there was a profound hush. She spoke in deep tones, which, though not loud, reached every ear in the house, and away through the throng at the doors and windows:

"Well, chilern, whar dar is so much racket dar must be something out o' kilter. I tink dat 'twixt de niggers of de Souf and de women at de Norf all a talkin' 'bout rights, de white men will be in a fix pretty soon. But what's all dis here talkin' 'bout? Dat man ober dar say dat women needs to be helped into carriages, and lifted ober ditches, and to have de best place every whar. Nobody eber help me into carriages, or ober mud puddles, or gives me any best place," and raising herself to her full height and her voice to a pitch like rolling thunder, she asked, "and ar'n't I a woman? Look at me! Look at my arm!" And she bared her right arm to the shoulder, showing her tremendous muscular power. "I have plowed, and planted, and gathered into barns, and no man could head me—and ar'n't I a woman? I could work as much and eat

---

1   *Amazon*   Legendary race of tall, strong women warriors in Greek mythology.

as much as a man (when I could get it), and bear de lash as well—and ar'n't I a woman? I have borne thirteen chilern and seen 'em mos' all sold off into slavery,[1] and when I cried out with a mother's grief, none but Jesus heard—and ar'n't I a woman? Den dey talks 'bout dis ting in de head—what dis dey call it?" "Intellect," whispered some one near. "Dat's it honey. What's dat got to do with women's rights or nigger's rights? If my cup won't hold but a pint and yourn holds a quart, would n't ye be mean[2] not to let me have my little half-measure full?" And she pointed her significant finger and sent a keen glance at the minister who had made the argument. The cheering was long and loud.

"Den dat little man in black dar, he say woman can't have as much rights as man, cause Christ want[3] a woman. Whar did your Christ come from?" Rolling thunder could not have stilled that crowd as did those deep, wonderful tones, as she stood there with outstretched arms and eye of fire. Raising her voice still louder, she repeated, "Whar did your Christ come from? From God and a woman. Man had nothing to do with him." Oh! what a rebuke she gave the little man.

Turning again to another objector, she took up the defense of mother Eve.[4] I cannot follow her through it all. It was pointed, and witty, and solemn, eliciting at almost every sentence deafening applause; and she ended by asserting that "if de fust woman God ever made was strong enough to turn the world upside down, all 'lone, dese togedder," and she glanced her eye over us, "ought to be able to turn it back and get it right side up again, and now dey is asking to do it, de men better let em." Long continued cheering. "Bleeged[5] to ye for hearin' on me, and now ole Sojourner ha'n't got nothing more to say."

Amid roars of applause, she turned to her corner, leaving more than one of us with streaming eyes and hearts beating with gratitude. She had taken us up in her strong arms and carried us safely over the slough of difficulty, turning the whole tide in our favor. I have never in my life seen anything like the magical influence that subdued the mobbish spirit of the day and turned the jibes and sneers of an excited crowd into notes of respect and admiration. Hundreds rushed up to shake hands, and congratulate the glorious old mother and bid her God speed on her mission of "testifying again concerning the wickedness of this 'ere people."

---

1 *I have ... into slavery*   In fact, as Truth relates in her *Narrative*, she had only five children, all of whom were born into slavery, and all of whom she lived with until she left Dumont's farm in 1826. (One son was sold—illegally—to a slaveholder in Alabama shortly before New York emancipated all its enslaved inhabitants, but Truth successfully sued for his return.)

2 *mean*   Selfish; small-minded.

3 *want*   Wasn't.

4 *defense of mother Eve*   I.e., an attack against Christian arguments by which Eve is considered to have introduced sin to the world through her actions in the Garden of Eden, and thereby to have rendered all women sinful.

5 *Bleeged*   Obliged.

Sojourner Truth's *Cartes de Visite*

In the 1860s, Sojourner Truth started regularly posing for photographs, which she printed in mass and sold at speeches and events to fund her activist travels. In 1864 she began having her photographs copyrighted under her own name—as opposed to that of the photographer—and adding the distinctive caption: "I sell the Shadow to Support the Substance." Many of her early portraits were printed in the form of *cartes de visite*, small (approximately the size of modern playing cards), inexpensive photo cards that in the 1860s became hugely popular as collectors' items, especially those that depicted politicians and celebrities. The *carte de visite* was among several innovations in early photography that led many at the time to praise photography as democratizing the tradition of portraiture, both by making it more accessible and affordable and by making portraits easier to reproduce and share. In the late 1870s the *cartes de visite* format was largely supplanted by that of the somewhat larger cabinet card, and Truth adapted her practice to suit. She continued posing for and selling her photographs until not long before her death.

Photographer unknown. The first known extant photograph of Truth, this 1861 portrait depicts Truth just prior to her appearance at an event in Indiana, whose state constitution included an article forbidding African Americans from traveling into the state. Some reports suggest that Truth's unusual outfit, consisting of numerous layers of heavy, padded, red-white-and-blue garments, was given her by her white colleagues as a sort of coat of soft armor against the disorderly and potentially hostile crowd. Truth was also escorted to the event by the state's Home Guard. She was arrested and released several times over the course of her Indiana speaking tour, but her abolitionist following also grew with every speech.

Photographer unknown, 1864. This photograph is among the few which clearly show Truth's right hand, which had lost part of its index finger in an accident during her time enslaved by John Dumont.

I SELL THE SHADOW TO SUPPORT THE SUBSTANCE. SOJOURNER TRUTH.

I Sell the Shadow to Support the Substance. SOJOURNER TRUTH.

Photographer unknown, 1864. Knitting exploded in popularity during the Civil War, with many women knitting garments, especially socks, to be sent to the soldiers. Several photographs depict Truth with her knitting.

Photographer unknown, 1866. The framed portrait sitting on her lap is a photograph of her grandson, James Caldwell, who had fought with the 54th Massachusetts Regiment during the Civil War.

Randall Studio, c. 1870. The backdrop in this photograph (which would have been supplied by the studio) is among the most ornate of those to be seen in Truth's portraits.

Harriet Jacobs
c. 1813 – 1897

For a hundred and twenty years, Harriet Jacobs's groundbreaking narrative, *Incidents in the Life of a Slave Girl* (1861), went largely unnoticed. When it did receive commentary, it was assumed that the narrative was not autobiography but fiction, and that its true author was the white abolitionist writer Lydia Maria Child (who in fact edited the volume). It was not until scholar Jean Fagan Yellin published a groundbreaking article on the narrative in 1981 that Jacobs's authorship was authenticated. This meant that Jacobs's gripping and eloquent narrative, one of the earliest written by an enslaved woman in the United States, did not impact American literature and history until late in the twentieth century. Since then, Jacobs's achievement as a writer and activist has been widely recognized, and her profound influence on American literature has taken firm root. Jacobs's *Incidents* is brave and revolutionary in that it openly discusses the particular evils that slavery systemically inflicted on women—sexual abuse, rape, and the knowledge that any children born would be born enslaved. As critic Henry Louis Gates Jr. wrote, "Whereas the black male slave narrators' accounts of sexual brutality remain suggestive, if gruesome, Jacobs's ... charts in vivid detail precisely how the shape of her life and the choices she makes are defined by her reduction to a sexual object, an object to be raped, bred or abused." Jacobs herself put it very simply: "Slavery is terrible for men; but it is far more terrible for women."

Jacobs was born in Edenton, North Carolina; most biographers date her birth in 1813, though her tombstone states she was born in 1815. Her mother, Delilah Horniblow, was enslaved by Margaret Horniblow, and her father, Elijah Knox, was enslaved by Andrew Knox. As a young child, Jacobs was unaware of her own enslaved condition; her father, a skilled carpenter, was allowed to keep a portion of his earnings, and the family lived in tolerable independence. Jacobs's maternal grandmother, Molly Horniblow, was a formative influence and support to the family, particularly to Jacobs. "I was so fondly shielded," she recalled, "that I never dreamed I was a piece of merchandise." Jacobs's mother died when she was six, breaking up the family circle; Margaret Horniblow, who had owned Delilah and thus owned her daughter, brought Jacobs to her home. Jacobs was treated kindly, and Horniblow taught her to read, write, and sew. When Jacobs was almost twelve years old, Horniblow died. Although Jacobs had believed that her mistress would set her free, she was instead bequeathed to Horniblow's five-year-old niece. Jacobs came under the control of the girl's father, Dr. James Norcom (who is given the pseudonym Dr. Flint in *Incidents*), a cruel man who soon began persecuting Jacobs with unwanted sexual attention.

Norcom's harassment of Jacobs was persistent, and her life in his house became more and more unbearable, both because of the sexual pressure and because of Mrs. Norcom's jealousy. Jacobs was increasingly isolated by what she perceived to be the shame of her situation: she usually went to her grandmother for advice, but she did not want to communicate the sexual nature of Norcom's persecution. In an effort to find security, Jacobs took a lover, Samuel Tredwell Sawyer, a local white attorney. With Sawyer, Jacobs would have two children, Joseph and Louisa. "I knew nothing would enrage [Norcom] so much as to know that I favored another," Jacobs wrote, "and it was something to triumph over my tyrant even in that small way." This relationship did not free her, however, from Norcom's threats, and, in the summer of 1835, Jacobs ran away and hid in a small crawlspace just below her grandmother's roof. She spent seven years in this tiny garret, watching her children grow up through a small hole she made to peer through. She managed to sew and read the Bible, but those years in hiding were plagued by isolation, by discomfort brought on by the weather—cold, heat, and rain all made her hideaway a miserable place—and by illness. In 1842, Jacobs escaped and went by boat to Pennsylvania, and from there to New York City.

While Jacobs was in hiding, Sawyer, who had been elected to Congress in 1837, had managed to purchase his and Jacobs's two children from Norcom, and he had sent the girl, Louisa, to Brooklyn to work as a servant (he did not keep his promise to free the children). Jacobs settled in New York to be close to her daughter—her son also eventually joined them—and took a job as nursemaid in the house of Mary Stace Willis, wife of the well-known poet and editor Nathaniel Parker Willis. Periodically, Norcom would try to find Jacobs, and she would have to temporarily leave New York. On one such occasion in 1845, while Jacobs was hiding in Boston, her employer, Mary Willis, died; when Nathaniel Willis subsequently decided to take a trip to England with his daughter, Jacobs accepted his offer to go with them and act as nursemaid. Jacobs experienced little racism in England, and she was impressed that the poor people in that country had access to education. In 1849, again fleeing Norcom, Jacobs went to Rochester, New York, where she worked with her brother, John Jacobs, in an antislavery reading room and bookstore. Rochester was a thriving center for abolitionist and feminist activism—Jacobs and her brother's reading room was located above the offices of Frederick Douglass's newspaper—and Jacobs began to find likeminded friends there, including Amy Post, who encouraged Jacobs to write and publish her experience.

In the meantime, Nathaniel Parker Willis remarried, and his second wife, Cornelia Grinell, employed Jacobs as a nursemaid for her new baby. In 1852, when Jacobs was again threatened with capture, Cornelia bought her for $300, ensuring her freedom. Though it deflated Jacobs to be traded like merchandise, having her freedom was a significant relief, and in 1853 she began her writing career in earnest. She wrote anonymous letters to the *New York Tribune*, including "Letter from a Fugitive Slave. Slaves Sold under Peculiar Circumstances" (21 June 1853), which touches on what would become a central theme in *Incidents*: the sexual abuse faced by enslaved women, and the struggle enslaved mothers endured to attempt to protect their children. Jacobs wrote *Incidents* while still working as a nursemaid in the Willis household; she kept her writing private, because she was not convinced that Nathaniel Willis supported abolition (though his wife certainly did). In the summer of 1857, Jacobs wrote to Amy Post that she had finished "a true and just account of my own life in Slavery," and that she hoped it "might do something for the Antislavery Cause."

Jacobs faced hurdles, however, in publishing *Incidents*, traveling to England in 1858 in an unsuccessful search for a publisher. The Boston company Phillips and Samson eventually agreed to take the book if Willis, Jacobs's employer, or Harriet Beecher Stowe would write an introduction. Jacobs didn't feel Willis would support the book, so she asked Stowe, but Stowe rejected the idea of collaborating with Jacobs. A different publisher, Thayer and Eldridge, then agreed to publish, stipulating this time an introduction by Lydia Maria Child, and, though very reluctant to do so, Jacobs asked Child if she would contribute to the project. Child agreed to not only write an introduction, but to edit the book. Though many people thought Child's involvement was extensive, Jean Fagan Yellin's research makes it clear that Child did not exceed the role she herself described in the introduction to the volume: "I have not added anything to the incidents, or changed the import of [Jacobs's] very pertinent remarks. With trifling exceptions, both the ideas and the language are her own. I pruned excrescences a little, but otherwise I had no reason for changing her lively and dramatic way of telling her own story."

When Thayer and Eldridge dissolved as a company, Jacobs secured the typeset pages of *Incidents* and determined to publish it herself; it was finally published in 1861, followed by a British edition in 1862. Jacobs used a pseudonym, Linda Brent, and she changed the names of all the characters in the book to protect their anonymity. *Incidents* was warmly received by audiences in the North and across the Atlantic, but it was not financially successful, and the Civil War soon drew much of the public's attention. After the war, Jacobs's work fell into obscurity, and only since the 1980s have readership and scholarship of it flourished; it has since become one of the most often-taught and frequently-read slave narratives.

Jacobs's writing style was influenced by the Bible, by other slave narratives— such as those by Olaudah Equiano and Frederick Douglass—and by the work of various contemporary women writers, including Lydia Maria Child, Fanny Fern, and Harriet Beecher Stowe. Like Stowe, Jacobs uses the rhetorical tools of the sentimental novel to add emotional power to her attack on slavery, and to frame some of her own experiences. In sentimental novels such as Samuel Richardson's *Pamela* (1740), for example, a servant girl is persecuted by the sexual attentions of her master, whom she continually rejects, thereby preserving her virtue. Jacobs's persistence in escaping Norcom is presented within this framework, as she bravely and successfully keeps her abuser at bay; on the other hand, the shame she feels at having an unmarried affair with Sawyer is felt as a failure to live up to the idealization of what it means to be a virtuous young woman. While Jacobs clearly judged herself against such ideals, she also forcefully questions their application to a person who is trapped in the misery of slavery: "... in looking back, calmly, on the events of my life, I feel that the slave woman ought not to be judged by the same standard as others."

Jacobs's story, focusing as it does on the bonds of women and seeking as it does an inter-racial and inter-regional political alliance, has become a crucial feminist text. *Incidents* has also taken a vital place in the history of African American literature, influencing writers such as Toni Morrison, Alice Walker, bell hooks, Ta-Nehisi Coates, and Claudia Rankine, among many others. As writers consider what it means to lead a dignified life in an America still convulsed with sexism and racism, Jacobs's narrative is a touchstone and inspiration. It has been translated into many languages and is read and taught around the world.

Jacobs dedicated her life not only to exposing the sexual violence of slavery—a secret she said was "concealed like those of the Inquisition"—but also to bettering the condition of black people across the United States. Following the publication of *Incidents*, Jacobs delivered numerous speeches in support of abolition, nursed wounded black troops during the Civil War, and assisted newly-emancipated African Americans. In 1864, she established a school for black children in Alexandria, Virginia, where her daughter Louisa was a teacher. Jacobs died in Washington, D.C. in 1897 and was buried in Cambridge, Massachusetts, in Mount Auburn Cemetery.

Note on the Text

The text presented here is based on the first 1861 edition of Jacobs's *Incidents in the Life of a Slave Girl, Written by Herself*, edited by Lydia Maria Child. Spelling and punctuation have been modernized in accordance with the practices of this anthology.

⌘ ⌘ ⌘

Incidents in the Life of a Slave Girl, Written by Herself

Northerners know nothing at all about Slavery. They think it is perpetual
bondage only. They have no conception of the depth of *degradation*
involved in
that word, SLAVERY; if they had, they would never cease
their efforts until so horrible a system was overthrown.
A WOMAN OF NORTH CAROLINA

Rise up, ye women that are at ease! Hear my voice,
ye careless daughters! Give ear unto my speech.
ISAIAH 32.9

PREFACE BY THE AUTHOR

Reader, be assured this narrative is no fiction. I am aware that some of my
adventures may seem incredible; but they are, nevertheless, strictly true.
I have not exaggerated the wrongs inflicted by Slavery; on the contrary, my
descriptions fall far short of the facts. I have concealed the names of places,
and given persons fictitious names. I had no motive for secrecy on my own
account, but I deemed it kind and considerate towards others to pursue this
course.

I wish I were more competent to the task I have undertaken. But I trust
my readers will excuse deficiencies in consideration of circumstances. I was
born and reared in Slavery; and I remained in a Slave State twenty-seven years.
Since I have been at the North, it has been necessary for me to work diligently
for my own support, and the education of my children. This has not left me
much leisure to make up for the loss of early opportunities to improve myself;
and it has compelled me to write these pages at irregular intervals, whenever I
could snatch an hour from household duties.

When I first arrived in Philadelphia, Bishop Paine[1] advised me to publish
a sketch of my life, but I told him I was altogether incompetent to such an
undertaking. Though I have improved my mind somewhat since that time,
I still remain of the same opinion; but I trust my motives will excuse what
might otherwise seem presumptuous. I have not written my experiences in
order to attract attention to myself; on the contrary, it would have been more
pleasant to me to have been silent about my own history. Neither do I care to

---

1   *Bishop Paine*   Daniel Alexander Payne was a writer, educator, and bishop in the African Methodist
    Episcopal Church. In the early 1840s, he worked on the Philadelphia Vigilance Committee, which
    provided clothing and shelter for enslaved people escaping to the North.

excite sympathy for my own sufferings. But I do earnestly desire to arouse the women of the North to a realizing sense of the condition of two millions of women at the South, still in bondage, suffering what I suffered, and most of them far worse. I want to add my testimony to that of abler pens to convince the people of the Free States what Slavery really is. Only by experience can anyone realize how deep, and dark, and foul is that pit of abominations. May the blessing of God rest on this imperfect effort in behalf of my persecuted people!

Linda Brent[1]

INTRODUCTION BY THE EDITOR

The author of the following autobiography is personally known to me, and her conversation and manners inspire me with confidence. During the last seventeen years, she has lived the greater part of the time with a distinguished family in New York, and has so deported[2] herself as to be highly esteemed by them. This fact is sufficient, without further credentials of her character. I believe those who know her will not be disposed to doubt her veracity, though some incidents in her story are more romantic[3] than fiction.

At her request, I have revised her manuscript; but such changes as I have made have been mainly for purposes of condensation and orderly arrangement. I have not added anything to the incidents, or changed the import of her very pertinent remarks. With trifling exceptions, both the ideas and the language are her own. I pruned excrescences a little, but otherwise I had no reason for changing her lively and dramatic way of telling her own story. The names of both persons and places are known to me; but for good reasons I suppress them.

It will naturally excite surprise that a woman reared in Slavery should be able to write so well. But circumstances will explain this. In the first place, nature endowed her with quick perceptions. Secondly, the mistress, with whom she lived till she was twelve years old, was a kind, considerate friend, who taught her to read and spell. Thirdly, she was placed in favorable circumstances after she came to the North; having frequent intercourse with intelligent persons, who felt a friendly interest in her welfare, and were disposed to give her opportunities for self-improvement.

I am well aware that many will accuse me of indecorum for presenting these pages to the public; for the experiences of this intelligent and much-injured

---

1   *Linda Brent*   Harriet Jacobs's pseudonym.
2   *deported*   Conducted.
3   *romantic*   Unlikely or implausible.

woman belong to a class which some call delicate subjects, and others indelicate. This peculiar phase of Slavery[1] has generally been kept veiled; but the public ought to be made acquainted with its monstrous features, and I willingly take the responsibility of presenting them with the veil withdrawn. I do this for the sake of my sisters in bondage, who are suffering wrongs so foul, that our ears are too delicate to listen to them. I do it with the hope of arousing conscientious and reflecting women at the North to a sense of their duty in the exertion of moral influence on the question of Slavery, on all possible occasions. I do it with the hope that every man who reads this narrative will swear solemnly before God that, so far as he has power to prevent it, no fugitive from Slavery shall ever be sent back to suffer in that loathsome den of corruption and cruelty.

L. Maria Child

Chapter i. Childhood

I was born a slave; but I never knew it till six years of happy childhood had passed away. My father was a carpenter, and considered so intelligent and skillful in his trade, that, when buildings out of the common line were to be erected, he was sent for from long distances, to be head workman. On condition of paying his mistress two hundred dollars a year,[2] and supporting himself, he was allowed to work at his trade, and manage his own affairs. His strongest wish was to purchase his children; but, though he several times offered his hard earnings for that purpose, he never succeeded. In complexion my parents were a light shade of brownish yellow, and were termed mulattoes.[3] They lived together in a comfortable home; and, though we were all slaves, I was so fondly shielded that I never dreamed I was a piece of merchandise, trusted to them for safe keeping, and liable to be demanded of them at any moment. I had one brother, William, who was two years younger than myself—a bright, affectionate child. I had also a great treasure in my maternal grandmother, who was a remarkable woman in many respects. She was the daughter of a planter in South Carolina, who, at his death, left her mother and his three children free, with money to go to St. Augustine,[4] where they had relatives. It was during the Revolutionary War; and they were captured on their passage, carried back, and sold to different purchasers. Such was the story

---

1 *peculiar phase of Slavery* I.e., the particular abuses, such as sexual violence, that slavery systemically encouraged and enabled.

2 *two hundred dollars a year* Equivalent to about $6,000.

3 *mulattoes* The term "mulatto," which is today considered archaic and offensive, was commonly used in the nineteenth century to classify individuals of mixed racial background—most frequently, those with one white and one black parent.

4 *St. Augustine* City on the northeast coast of Florida.

my grandmother used to tell me; but I do not remember all the particulars. She was a little girl when she was captured and sold to the keeper of a large hotel. I have often heard her tell how hard she fared during childhood. But as she grew older she evinced so much intelligence, and was so faithful, that her master and mistress could not help seeing it was for their interest to take care of such a valuable piece of property. She became an indispensable personage in the household, officiating in all capacities, from cook and wet nurse to seamstress. She was much praised for her cooking; and her nice[1] crackers became so famous in the neighborhood that many people were desirous of obtaining them. In consequence of numerous requests of this kind, she asked permission of her mistress to bake crackers at night, after all the household work was done; and she obtained leave to do it, provided she would clothe herself and her children from the profits. Upon these terms, after working hard all day for her mistress, she began her midnight bakings, assisted by her two oldest children. The business proved profitable; and each year she laid by a little, which was saved for a fund to purchase her children. Her master died, and the property was divided among his heirs. The widow had her dower in the hotel, which she continued to keep open. My grandmother remained in her service as a slave; but her children were divided among her master's children. As she had five, Benjamin, the youngest one, was sold, in order that each heir might have an equal portion of dollars and cents. There was so little difference in our ages that he seemed more like my brother than my uncle. He was a bright, handsome lad, nearly white; for he inherited the complexion my grandmother had derived from Anglo-Saxon ancestors. Though only ten years old, seven hundred and twenty dollars were paid for him. His sale was a terrible blow to my grandmother; but she was naturally hopeful, and she went to work with renewed energy, trusting in time to be able to purchase some of her children. She had laid up three hundred dollars, which her mistress one day begged as a loan, promising to pay her soon. The reader probably knows that no promise or writing given to a slave is legally binding; for, according to Southern laws, a slave, being property, can hold no property. When my grandmother lent her hard earnings to her mistress, she trusted solely to her honor. The honor of a slaveholder to a slave!

To this good grandmother I was indebted for many comforts. My brother Willie and I often received portions of the crackers, cakes, and preserves, she made to sell; and after we ceased to be children we were indebted to her for many more important services.

Such were the unusually fortunate circumstances of my early childhood. When I was six years old, my mother died; and then, for the first time, I

---

1   *nice* Tasty, delicate.

learned, by the talk around me, that I was a slave. My mother's mistress was the daughter of my grandmother's mistress. She was the foster sister of my mother; they were both nourished at my grandmother's breast. In fact, my mother had been weaned at three months old, that the babe of the mistress might obtain sufficient food. They played together as children; and, when they became women, my mother was a most faithful servant to her whiter foster sister. On her death-bed her mistress promised that her children should never suffer for anything; and during her lifetime she kept her word. They all spoke kindly of my dead mother, who had been a slave merely in name, but in nature was noble and womanly. I grieved for her, and my young mind was troubled with the thought who would now take care of me and my little brother. I was told that my home was now to be with her mistress; and I found it a happy one. No toilsome or disagreeable duties were imposed upon me. My mistress was so kind to me that I was always glad to do her bidding, and proud to labor for her as much as my young years would permit. I would sit by her side for hours, sewing diligently, with a heart as free from care as that of any free-born white child. When she thought I was tired, she would send me out to run and jump; and away I bounded, to gather berries or flowers to decorate her room. Those were happy days—too happy to last. The slave child had no thought for the morrow; but there came that blight, which too surely waits on every human being born to be a chattel.

When I was nearly twelve years old, my kind mistress sickened and died. As I saw the cheek grow paler, and the eye more glassy, how earnestly I prayed in my heart that she might live! I loved her; for she had been almost like a mother to me. My prayers were not answered. She died, and they buried her in the little churchyard, where, day after day, my tears fell upon her grave.

I was sent to spend a week with my grandmother. I was now old enough to begin to think of the future; and again and again I asked myself what they would do with me. I felt sure I should never find another mistress so kind as the one who was gone. She had promised my dying mother that her children should never suffer for anything; and when I remembered that, and recalled her many proofs of attachment to me, I could not help having some hopes that she had left me free. My friends were almost certain it would be so. They thought she would be sure to do it, on account of my mother's love and faithful service. But, alas! we all know that the memory of a faithful slave does not avail much to save her children from the auction block.

After a brief period of suspense, the will of my mistress was read, and we learned that she had bequeathed me to her sister's daughter, a child of five years old. So vanished our hopes. My mistress had taught me the precepts of God's Word: "Thou shalt love thy neighbor as thyself." "Whatsoever ye would that men should do unto you, do ye even so unto them."[1] But I was her slave, and I suppose she did not recognize me as her neighbor. I would give much to blot out from my memory that one great wrong. As a child, I loved my mistress; and, looking back on the happy days I spent with her, I try to think with less bitterness of this act of injustice. While I was with her, she taught me to read and spell; and for this privilege, which so rarely falls to the lot of a slave, I bless her memory.

She possessed but few slaves; and at her death those were all distributed among her relatives. Five of them were my grandmother's children, and had shared the same milk that nourished her mother's children. Notwithstanding my grandmother's long and faithful service to her owners, not one of her children escaped the auction block. These God-breathing machines are no more, in the sight of their masters, than the cotton they plant, or the horses they tend.

Chapter 2. The New Master and Mistress

Dr. Flint, a physician in the neighborhood, had married the sister of my mistress, and I was now the property of their little daughter. It was not without murmuring[2] that I prepared for my new home; and what added to my unhappiness, was the fact that my brother William was purchased by the same family. My father, by his nature, as well as by the habit of transacting business as a skillful mechanic, had more of the feelings of a freeman than is common among slaves. My brother was a spirited boy; and being brought up under such influences, he early detested the name of master and mistress. One day, when his father and his mistress both happened to call him at the same time, he hesitated between the two; being perplexed to know which had the strongest claim upon his obedience. He finally concluded to go to his mistress. When my father reproved him for it, he said, "You both called me, and I didn't know which I ought to go to first."

"You are *my* child," replied our father, "and when I call you, you should come immediately, if you have to pass through fire and water."[3]

---

1   *Thou shalt ... thyself* The second of Christ's commandments, see Matthew 22.39; *Whatsoever ye would ... unto them* This saying is known as the "golden rule." See Leviticus 19.18 and Matthew 7.12.

2   *not without murmuring* See Philippians 2.14–15: "Do all things without murmurings and disputings; / That ye may be blameless and harmless, the sons of God, without rebuke, in the midst of a crooked and perverse nation, among whom ye shine as lights in the world."

3   *pass through fire and water* See Isaiah 43.2: "When thou passest through the waters, I will be with thee; and through the rivers, they shall not overflow thee: when thou walkest through the fire, thou shalt not be burned; neither shall the flame kindle upon thee."

Poor Willie! He was now to learn his first lesson of obedience to a master. Grandmother tried to cheer us with hopeful words, and they found an echo in the credulous hearts of youth.

When we entered our new home we encountered cold looks, cold words, and cold treatment. We were glad when the night came. On my narrow bed I moaned and wept, I felt so desolate and alone.

I had been there nearly a year, when a dear little friend of mine was buried. I heard her mother sob, as the clods fell on the coffin of her only child, and I turned away from the grave, feeling thankful that I still had something left to love. I met my grandmother, who said, "Come with me, Linda"; and from her tone I knew that something sad had happened. She led me apart from the people, and then said, "My child, your father is dead." Dead! How could I believe it? He had died so suddenly I had not even heard that he was sick. I went home with my grandmother. My heart rebelled against God, who had taken from me mother, father, mistress, and friend. The good grandmother tried to comfort me. "Who knows the ways of God?" said she. "Perhaps they have been kindly taken from the evil days to come." Years afterwards I often thought of this. She promised to be a mother to her grandchildren, so far as she might be permitted to do so; and strengthened by her love, I returned to my master's. I thought I should be allowed to go to my father's house the next morning; but I was ordered to go for flowers, that my mistress's house might be decorated for an evening party. I spent the day gathering flowers and weaving them into festoons, while the dead body of my father was lying within a mile of me. What cared my owners for that? he was merely a piece of property. Moreover, they thought he had spoiled his children, by teaching them to feel that they were human beings. This was blasphemous doctrine for a slave to teach; presumptuous in him, and dangerous to the masters.

The next day I followed his remains to a humble grave beside that of my dear mother. There were those who knew my father's worth, and respected his memory.

My home now seemed more dreary than ever. The laugh of the little slave-children sounded harsh and cruel. It was selfish to feel so about the joy of others. My brother moved about with a very grave face. I tried to comfort him, by saying, "Take courage, Willie; brighter days will come by and by."

"You don't know anything about it, Linda," he replied. "We shall have to stay here all our days; we shall never be free."

I argued that we were growing older and stronger, and that perhaps we might, before long, be allowed to hire our own time, and then we could earn money to buy our freedom. William declared this was much easier to say than to do; moreover, he did not intend to buy his freedom. We held daily controversies upon this subject.

Little attention was paid to the slaves' meals in Dr. Flint's house. If they could catch a bit of food while it was going, well and good. I gave myself no trouble on that score, for on my various errands I passed my grandmother's house, where there was always something to spare for me. I was frequently threatened with punishment if I stopped there; and my grandmother, to avoid detaining me, often stood at the gate with something for my breakfast or dinner. I was indebted to her for all my comforts, spiritual or temporal. It was her labor that supplied my scanty wardrobe. I have a vivid recollection of the linsey-woolsey[1] dress given me every winter by Mrs. Flint. How I hated it! It was one of the badges of slavery.

While my grandmother was thus helping to support me from her hard earnings, the three hundred dollars she had lent her mistress were never repaid. When her mistress died, her son-in-law, Dr. Flint, was appointed executor. When grandmother applied to him for payment, he said the estate was insolvent, and the law prohibited payment. It did not, however, prohibit him from retaining the silver candelabra, which had been purchased with that money. I presume they will be handed down in the family, from generation to generation.

My grandmother's mistress had always promised her that, at her death, she should be free; and it was said that in her will she made good the promise. But when the estate was settled, Dr. Flint told the faithful old servant that, under existing circumstances, it was necessary she should be sold.

On the appointed day, the customary advertisement was posted up, proclaiming that there would be "a public sale of negroes, horses, &c." Dr. Flint called to tell my grandmother that he was unwilling to wound her feelings by putting her up at auction, and that he would prefer to dispose of her at private sale. My grandmother saw through his hypocrisy; she understood very well that he was ashamed of the job. She was a very spirited woman, and if he was base enough to sell her, when her mistress intended she should be free, she was determined the public should know it. She had for a long time supplied many families with crackers and preserves; consequently, "Aunt Marthy," as she was called, was generally known, and everybody who knew her respected her intelligence and good character. Her long and faithful service in the family was also well known, and the intention of her mistress to leave her free. When the day of sale came, she took her place among the chattels, and at the first call she sprang upon the auction-block. Many voices called out, "Shame! Shame! Who is going to sell *you*, Aunt Marthy? Don't stand there! That is no place for *you*." Without saying a word, she quietly awaited her fate. No one bid for her. At last, a feeble voice said, "Fifty dollars." It came from a maiden lady, seventy

---

1   *linsey-woolsey*   Coarse fabric made of the cheapest wool and linen.

years old, the sister of my grandmother's deceased mistress. She had lived forty years under the same roof with my grandmother; she knew how faithfully she had served her owners, and how cruelly she had been defrauded of her rights; and she resolved to protect her. The auctioneer waited for a higher bid; but her wishes were respected; no one bid above her. She could neither read nor write; and when the bill of sale was made out, she signed it with a cross. But what consequence was that, when she had a big heart overflowing with human kindness? She gave the old servant her freedom.

At that time, my grandmother was just fifty years old. Laborious years had passed since then; and now my brother and I were slaves to the man who had defrauded her of her money, and tried to defraud her of her freedom. One of my mother's sisters, called Aunt Nancy, was also a slave in his family. She was a kind, good aunt to me; and supplied the place of both housekeeper and waiting maid to her mistress. She was, in fact, at the beginning and end of everything.

Mrs. Flint, like many southern women, was totally deficient in energy. She had not strength to superintend her household affairs; but her nerves were so strong, that she could sit in her easy chair and see a woman whipped, till the blood trickled from every stroke of the lash. She was a member of the church; but partaking of the Lord's supper[1] did not seem to put her in a Christian frame of mind. If dinner was not served at the exact time on that particular Sunday, she would station herself in the kitchen, and wait till it was dished, and then spit in all the kettles and pans that had been used for cooking. She did this to prevent the cook and her children from eking out their meagre fare with the remains of the gravy and other scrapings. The slaves could get nothing to eat except what she chose to give them. Provisions were weighed out by the pound and ounce, three times a day. I can assure you she gave them no chance to eat wheat bread from her flour barrel. She knew how many biscuits a quart of flour would make, and exactly what size they ought to be.

Dr. Flint was an epicure.[2] The cook never sent a dinner to his table without fear and trembling; for if there happened to be a dish not to his liking, he would either order her to be whipped, or compel her to eat every mouthful of it in his presence. The poor, hungry creature might not have objected to eating it; but she did object to having her master cram it down her throat till she choked.

They had a pet dog, that was a nuisance in the house. The cook was ordered to make some Indian mush[3] for him. He refused to eat, and when his head was

---

1 *Lord's supper* I.e., sacrament of the Eucharist, in which the faithful drink wine and eat bread that are considered, symbolically, the blood and body of Christ.
2 *epicure* Person devoted to sensual pleasure.
3 *Indian mush* Porridge made of corn.

held over it, the froth flowed from his mouth into the basin. He died a few minutes after. When Dr. Flint came in, he said the mush had not been well cooked, and that was the reason the animal would not eat it. He sent for the cook, and compelled her to eat it. He thought that the woman's stomach was stronger than the dog's; but her sufferings afterwards proved that he was mistaken. This poor woman endured many cruelties from her master and mistress; sometimes she was locked up, away from her nursing baby, for a whole day and night.

When I had been in the family a few weeks, one of the plantation slaves was brought to town, by order of his master. It was near night when he arrived, and Dr. Flint ordered him to be taken to the work house, and tied up to the joist, so that his feet would just escape the ground. In that situation he was to wait till the doctor had taken his tea. I shall never forget that night. Never before, in my life, had I heard hundreds of blows fall, in succession, on a human being. His piteous groans, and his "O, pray don't, massa," rang in my ear for months afterwards. There were many conjectures as to the cause of this terrible punishment. Some said master accused him of stealing corn; others said the slave had quarrelled with his wife, in presence of the overseer, and had accused his master of being the father of her child. They were both black, and the child was very fair.

I went into the work house next morning, and saw the cowhide[1] still wet with blood, and the boards all covered with gore. The poor man lived, and continued to quarrel with his wife. A few months afterwards Dr. Flint handed them both over to a slave-trader. The guilty man put their value into his pocket, and had the satisfaction of knowing that they were out of sight and hearing. When the mother was delivered into the trader's hands, she said, "You *promised* to treat me well." To which he replied, "You have let your tongue run too far; damn you!" She had forgotten that it was a crime for a slave to tell who was the father of her child.

From others than the master persecution also comes in such cases. I once saw a young slave girl dying soon after the birth of a child nearly white. In her agony she cried out, "O Lord, come and take me!" Her mistress stood by, and mocked at her like an incarnate fiend. "You suffer, do you?" she exclaimed. "I am glad of it. You deserve it all, and more too."

The girl's mother said, "The baby is dead, thank God; and I hope my poor child will soon be in heaven, too."

"Heaven!" retorted the mistress. "There is no such place for the like of her and her bastard."

---

1 *cowhide* Heavy whip made of cow's hide.

The poor mother turned away, sobbing. Her dying daughter called her, feebly, and as she bent over her, I heard her say, "Don't grieve so, mother; God knows all about it; and HE will have mercy upon me."

Her sufferings, afterwards, became so intense, that her mistress felt unable to stay; but when she left the room, the scornful smile was still on her lips. Seven children called her mother. The poor black woman had but the one child, whose eyes she saw closing in death, while she thanked God for taking her away from the greater bitterness of life.

Chapter 3. The Slaves' New Year's Day

Dr. Flint owned a fine residence in town, several farms, and about fifty slaves, besides hiring a number by the year.

Hiring-day at the south takes place on the 1st of January. On the 2nd, the slaves are expected to go to their new masters. On a farm, they work until the corn and cotton are laid.[1] They then have two holidays.[2] Some masters give them a good dinner under the trees. This over, they work until Christmas eve. If no heavy charges are meantime brought against them, they are given four or five holidays, whichever the master or overseer may think proper. Then comes New Year's eve; and they gather together their little alls,[3] or more properly speaking, their little nothings, and wait anxiously for the dawning of day. At the appointed hour the grounds are thronged with men, women, and children, waiting, like criminals, to hear their doom pronounced. The slave is sure to know who is the most humane, or cruel master, within forty miles of him.

It is easy to find out, on that day, who clothes and feeds his slaves well; for he is surrounded by a crowd, begging, "Please, massa, hire me this year. I will work *very* hard, massa."

If a slave is unwilling to go with his new master, he is whipped, or locked up in jail, until he consents to go, and promises not to run away during the year. Should he chance to change his mind, thinking it justifiable to violate an extorted promise, woe unto him if he is caught! The whip is used till the blood flows at his feet; and his stiffened limbs are put in chains, to be dragged in the field for days and days!

If he lives until the next year, perhaps the same man will hire him again, without even giving him an opportunity of going to the hiring-ground. After those for hire are disposed of, those for sale are called up.

---

1 *laid* Harvested, stored.
2 *holidays* Days off.
3 *alls* Possessions.

O, you happy free women, contrast *your* New Year's day with that of the poor bond-woman! With you it is a pleasant season, and the light of the day is blessed. Friendly wishes meet you everywhere, and gifts are showered upon you. Even hearts that have been estranged from you soften at this season, and lips that have been silent echo back, "I wish you a happy New Year." Children bring their little offerings, and raise their rosy lips for a caress. They are your own, and no hand but that of death can take them from you.

But to the slave mother New Year's day comes laden with peculiar sorrows. She sits on her cold cabin floor, watching the children who may all be torn from her the next morning; and often does she wish that she and they might die before the day dawns. She may be an ignorant creature, degraded by the system that has brutalized her from childhood; but she has a mother's instincts, and is capable of feeling a mother's agonies.

On one of these sale days, I saw a mother lead seven children to the auction-block. She knew that *some* of them would be taken from her; but they took *all*. The children were sold to a slave-trader, and their mother was bought by a man in her own town. Before night her children were all far away. She begged the trader to tell her where he intended to take them; this he refused to do. How *could* he, when he knew he would sell them, one by one, wherever he could command the highest price? I met that mother in the street, and her wild, haggard face lives today in my mind. She wrung her hands in anguish, and exclaimed, "Gone! All gone! Why *don't* God kill me?" I had no words wherewith to comfort her. Instances of this kind are of daily, yea, of hourly occurrence.

Slaveholders have a method, peculiar to their institution, of getting rid of *old* slaves, whose lives have been worn out in their service. I knew an old woman, who for seventy years faithfully served her master. She had become almost helpless, from hard labor and disease. Her owners moved to Alabama, and the old black woman was left to be sold to anybody who would give twenty dollars for her.

CHAPTER 4. THE SLAVE WHO DARED TO FEEL LIKE A MAN

Two years had passed since I entered Dr. Flint's family, and those years had brought much of the knowledge that comes from experience, though they had afforded little opportunity for any other kinds of knowledge.

My grandmother had, as much as possible, been a mother to her orphan grandchildren. By perseverance and unwearied industry, she was now mistress of a snug little home, surrounded with the necessaries of life. She would have been happy could her children have shared them with her. There remained but three children and two grandchildren, all slaves. Most earnestly did she strive to make us feel that it was the will of God: that He had seen fit to place us under such circumstances; and though it seemed hard, we ought to pray for contentment.

It was a beautiful faith, coming from a mother who could not call her children her own. But I, and Benjamin, her youngest boy, condemned it. We reasoned that it was much more the will of God that we should be situated as she was. We longed for a home like hers. There we always found sweet balsam[1] for our troubles. She was so loving, so sympathizing! She always met us with a smile, and listened with patience to all our sorrows. She spoke so hopefully, that unconsciously the clouds gave place to sunshine. There was a grand big oven there, too, that baked bread and nice things for the town, and we knew there was always a choice bit in store for us.

But, alas! even the charms of the old oven failed to reconcile us to our hard lot. Benjamin was now a tall, handsome lad, strongly and gracefully made, and with a spirit too bold and daring for a slave. My brother William, now twelve years old, had the same aversion to the word master that he had when he was an urchin of seven years. I was his confidant. He came to me with all his troubles. I remember one instance in particular. It was on a lovely spring morning, and when I marked the sunlight dancing here and there, its beauty seemed to mock my sadness. For my master, whose restless, craving, vicious nature roved about day and night, seeking whom to devour, had just left me, with stinging, scorching words; words that scathed ear and brain like fire. O, how I despised him! I thought how glad I should be, if some day when he walked the earth, it would open and swallow him up, and disencumber the world of a plague.

When he told me that I was made for his use, made to obey his command in *every* thing; that I was nothing but a slave, whose will must and should surrender to his, never before had my puny arm felt half so strong.

So deeply was I absorbed in painful reflections afterwards, that I neither saw nor heard the entrance of anyone, till the voice of William sounded close beside me. "Linda," said he, "what makes you look so sad? I love you. O, Linda, isn't this a bad world? Everybody seems so cross and unhappy. I wish I had died when poor father did."

I told him that everybody was *not* cross, or unhappy; that those who had pleasant homes, and kind friends, and who were not afraid to love them, were happy. But we, who were slave-children, without father or mother, could not expect to be happy. We must be good; perhaps that would bring us contentment.

---

1   *balsam*   Resinous, aromatic medicine for soothing pain.

"Yes," he said, "I try to be good; but what's the use? They are all the time troubling me." Then he proceeded to relate his afternoon's difficulty with young master Nicholas. It seemed that the brother of master Nicholas had pleased himself with making up stories about William. Master Nicholas said he should be flogged, and he would do it. Whereupon he went to work; but William fought bravely, and the young master, finding he was getting the better of him, undertook to tie his hands behind him. He failed in that likewise. By dint of kicking and fisting, William came out of the skirmish none the worse for a few scratches.

He continued to discourse on his young master's *meanness*;[1] how he whipped the *little* boys, but was a perfect coward when a tussle ensued between him and white boys of his own size. On such occasions he always took to his legs. William had other charges to make against him. One was his rubbing up pennies with quicksilver,[2] and passing them off for quarters of a dollar on an old man who kept a fruit stall. William was often sent to buy fruit, and he earnestly inquired of me what he ought to do under such circumstances. I told him it was certainly wrong to deceive the old man, and that it was his duty to tell him of the impositions practised by his young master. I assured him the old man would not be slow to comprehend the whole, and there the matter would end. William thought it might with the old man, but not with *him*. He said he did not mind the smart of the whip, but he did not like the *idea* of being whipped.

While I advised him to be good and forgiving I was not unconscious of the beam in my own eye.[3] It was the very knowledge of my own shortcomings that urged me to retain, if possible, some sparks of my brother's God-given nature. I had not lived fourteen years in slavery for nothing. I had felt, seen, and heard enough, to read the characters, and question the motives, of those around me. The war of my life had begun; and though one of God's most powerless creatures, I resolved never to be conquered. Alas, for me!

If there was one pure, sunny spot for me, I believed it to be in Benjamin's heart, and in another's, whom I loved with all the ardor of a girl's first love. My owner knew of it, and sought in every way to render me miserable. He did not resort to corporal punishment, but to all the petty, tyrannical ways that human ingenuity could devise.

---

1   *meanness* Inferiority of character; lowliness.

2   *quicksilver* Mercury.

3   *beam ... own eye* See Matthew 7.3–5: "And why beholdest thou the mote that is in thy brother's eye, but considerest not the beam that is in thine own eye? Or how wilt thou say to thy brother, Let me pull out the mote out of thine eye; and, behold, a beam is in thine own eye? Thou hypocrite, first cast out the beam out of thine own eye; and then shalt thou see clearly to cast out the mote out of thy brother's eye."

I remember the first time I was punished. It was in the month of February. My grandmother had taken my old shoes, and replaced them with a new pair. I needed them; for several inches of snow had fallen, and it still continued to fall. When I walked through Mrs. Flint's room, their creaking grated harshly on her refined nerves. She called me to her, and asked what I had about me that made such a horrid noise. I told her it was my new shoes. "Take them off," said she; "and if you put them on again, I'll throw them into the fire."

I took them off, and my stockings also. She then sent me a long distance, on an errand. As I went through the snow, my bare feet tingled. That night I was very hoarse; and I went to bed thinking the next day would find me sick, perhaps dead. What was my grief on waking to find myself quite well!

I had imagined if I died, or was laid up for some time, that my mistress would feel a twinge of remorse that she had so hated "the little imp," as she styled me. It was my ignorance of that mistress that gave rise to such extravagant imaginings.

Dr. Flint occasionally had high prices offered for me; but he always said, "She don't belong to me. She is my daughter's property, and I have no right to sell her." Good, honest man! My young mistress was still a child, and I could look for no protection from her. I loved her, and she returned my affection. I once heard her father allude to her attachment to me; and his wife promptly replied that it proceeded from fear. This put unpleasant doubts into my mind. Did the child feign what she did not feel? or was her mother jealous of the mite of love she bestowed on me? I concluded it must be the latter. I said to myself, "Surely, little children are true."

One afternoon I sat at my sewing, feeling unusual depression of spirits. My mistress had been accusing me of an offence, of which I assured her I was perfectly innocent; but I saw, by the contemptuous curl of her lip, that she believed I was telling a lie.

I wondered for what wise purpose God was leading me through such thorny paths,[1] and whether still darker days were in store for me. As I sat musing thus, the door opened softly, and William came in. "Well, brother," said I, "what is the matter this time?"

"O Linda, Ben and his master have had a dreadful time!" said he.

My first thought was that Benjamin was killed. "Don't be frightened, Linda," said William; "I will tell you all about it."

It appeared that Benjamin's master had sent for him, and he did not immediately obey the summons. When he did, his master was angry, and began to whip him. He resisted. Master and slave fought, and finally the master was

---

1 *thorny paths* See Hosea 2.6: "Therefore, behold, I will hedge up thy way with thorns, and make a wall, that she shall not find her paths."

thrown. Benjamin had cause to tremble; for he had thrown to the ground his master—one of the richest men in town. I anxiously awaited the result.

That night I stole to my grandmother's house, and Benjamin also stole thither from his master's. My grandmother had gone to spend a day or two with an old friend living in the country.

"I have come," said Benjamin, "to tell you goodbye. I am going away."

I inquired where.

"To the north," he replied.

I looked at him to see whether he was in earnest. I saw it all in his firm, set mouth. I implored him not to go, but he paid no heed to my words. He said he was no longer a boy, and every day made his yoke more galling. He had raised his hand against his master, and was to be publicly whipped for the offence. I reminded him of the poverty and hardships he must encounter among strangers. I told him he might be caught and brought back; and that was terrible to think of.

He grew vexed, and asked if poverty and hardships with freedom, were not preferable to our treatment in slavery. "Linda," he continued, "we are dogs here; footballs, cattle, everything that's mean. No, I will not stay. Let them bring me back. We don't die but once."

He was right; but it was hard to give him up. "Go," said I, "and break your mother's heart."

I repented of my words ere they were out.

"Linda," said he, speaking as I had not heard him speak that evening, "how *could* you say that? Poor mother! be kind to her, Linda; and you, too, cousin Fanny."

Cousin Fanny was a friend who had lived some years with us.

Farewells were exchanged, and the bright, kind boy, endeared to us by so many acts of love, vanished from our sight.

It is not necessary to state how he made his escape. Suffice it to say, he was on his way to New York when a violent storm overtook the vessel. The captain said he must put into the nearest port. This alarmed Benjamin, who was aware that he would be advertised in every port near his own town. His embarrassment was noticed by the captain. To port they went. There the advertisement met the captain's eye. Benjamin so exactly answered its description, that the captain laid hold on him, and bound him in chains. The storm passed, and they proceeded to New York. Before reaching that port Benjamin managed to get off his chains and throw them overboard. He escaped from the vessel, but was pursued, captured, and carried back to his master.

When my grandmother returned home and found her youngest child had fled, great was her sorrow; but, with characteristic piety, she said, "God's will be done." Each morning, she inquired if any news had been heard from her boy. Yes, news *was* heard. The master was rejoicing over a letter, announcing the capture of his human chattel.

That day seems but as yesterday, so well do I remember it. I saw him led through the streets in chains, to jail. His face was ghastly pale, yet full of determination. He had begged one of the sailors to go to his mother's house and ask her not to meet him. He said the sight of her distress would take from him all self-control. She yearned to see him, and she went; but she screened herself in the crowd, that it might be as her child had said.

We were not allowed to visit him; but we had known the jailer for years, and he was a kind-hearted man. At midnight he opened the jail door for my grandmother and myself to enter, in disguise. When we entered the cell not a sound broke the stillness. "Benjamin, Benjamin!" whispered my grandmother. No answer. "Benjamin!" she again faltered. There was a jingle of chains. The moon had just risen, and cast an uncertain light through the bars of the window. We knelt down and took Benjamin's cold hands in ours. We did not speak. Sobs were heard, and Benjamin's lips were unsealed; for his mother was weeping on his neck. How vividly does memory bring back that sad night! Mother and son talked together. He had asked her pardon for the suffering he had caused her. She said she had nothing to forgive; she could not blame his desire for freedom. He told her that when he was captured, he broke away, and was about casting himself into the river, when thoughts of *her* came over him, and he desisted. She asked if he did not also think of God. I fancied I saw his face grow fierce in the moonlight. He answered, "No, I did not think of him. When a man is hunted like a wild beast he forgets there is a God, a heaven. He forgets everything in his struggle to get beyond the reach of the bloodhounds."

"Don't talk so, Benjamin," said she. "Put your trust in God. Be humble, my child, and your master will forgive you."

"Forgive me for *what*, mother? For not letting him treat me like a dog? No! I will never humble myself to him. I have worked for him for nothing all my life, and I am repaid with stripes[1] and imprisonment. Here I will stay till I die, or till he sells me."

The poor mother shuddered at his words. I think he felt it; for when he next spoke, his voice was calmer. "Don't fret about me, mother. I ain't worth it," said he. "I wish I had some of your goodness. You bear everything patiently, just as though you thought it was all right. I wish I could."

---

1 *stripes* Marks made on the body by a whip.

She told him she had not always been so; once, she was like him; but when sore troubles came upon her, and she had no arm to lean upon, she learned to call on God, and he lightened her burdens.[1] She besought him to do likewise.

We overstayed our time, and were obliged to hurry from the jail.

Benjamin had been imprisoned three weeks, when my grandmother went to intercede for him with his master. He was immovable. He said Benjamin should serve as an example to the rest of his slaves; he should be kept in jail till he was subdued, or be sold if he got but one dollar for him. However, he afterwards relented in some degree. The chains were taken off, and we were allowed to visit him.

As his food was of the coarsest kind, we carried him as often as possible a warm supper, accompanied with some little luxury for the jailer.

Three months elapsed, and there was no prospect of release or of a purchaser. One day he was heard to sing and laugh. This piece of indecorum was told to his master, and the overseer was ordered to re-chain him. He was now confined in an apartment with other prisoners, who were covered with filthy rags. Benjamin was chained near them, and was soon covered with vermin. He worked at his chains till he succeeded in getting out of them. He passed them through the bars of the window, with a request that they should be taken to his master, and he should be informed that he was covered with vermin.

This audacity was punished with heavier chains, and prohibition of our visits.

My grandmother continued to send him fresh changes of clothes. The old ones were burned up. The last night we saw him in jail his mother still begged him to send for his master, and beg his pardon. Neither persuasion nor argument could turn him from his purpose. He calmly answered, "I am waiting his time."

Those chains were mournful to hear.

Another three months passed, and Benjamin left his prison walls. We that loved him waited to bid him a long and last farewell. A slave trader had bought him. You remember, I told you what price he brought when ten years of age. Now he was more than twenty years old, and sold for three hundred dollars. The master had been blind to his own interest. Long confinement had made his face too pale, his form too thin; moreover, the trader had heard something of his character, and it did not strike him as suitable for a slave. He said he would give any price if the handsome lad was a girl. We thanked God that he was not.

---

1   *lightened her burdens*   See Jesus' words in Matthew 11.28–30: "Come unto me, all ye that labour and are heavy laden, and I will give you rest. Take my yoke upon me, and learn of me; for I am meek and lowly in heart: and ye shall find rest unto your souls. For my yoke is easy, and my burden is light."

Could you have seen that mother clinging to her child, when they fastened the irons upon his wrists; could you have heard her heart-rending groans, and seen her bloodshot eyes wander wildly from face to face, vainly pleading for mercy; could you have witnessed that scene as I saw it, you would exclaim, *Slavery is damnable!*

Benjamin, her youngest, her pet, was forever gone! She could not realize it. She had had an interview with the trader for the purpose of ascertaining if Benjamin could be purchased. She was told it was impossible, as he had given bonds not to sell him till he was out of the state. He promised that he would not sell him till he reached New Orleans.

With a strong arm and unvaried trust, my grandmother began her work of love. Benjamin must be free. If she succeeded, she knew they would still be separated; but the sacrifice was not too great. Day and night she labored. The trader's price would treble that he gave; but she was not discouraged.

She employed a lawyer to write to a gentleman, whom she knew, in New Orleans. She begged him to interest himself for Benjamin, and he willingly favored her request. When he saw Benjamin, and stated his business, he thanked him; but said he preferred to wait a while before making the trader an offer. He knew he had tried to obtain a high price for him, and had invariably failed. This encouraged him to make another effort for freedom. So one morning, long before day, Benjamin was missing. He was riding over the blue billows,[1] bound for Baltimore.

For once his white face did him a kindly service. They had no suspicion that it belonged to a slave; otherwise, the law would have been followed out to the letter, and the *thing* rendered back to slavery. The brightest skies are often overshadowed by the darkest clouds. Benjamin was taken sick, and compelled to remain in Baltimore three weeks. His strength was slow in returning; and his desire to continue his journey seemed to retard his recovery. How could he get strength without air and exercise? He resolved to venture on a short walk. A by-street was selected, where he thought himself secure of not being met by anyone that knew him; but a voice called out, "Halloo, Ben, my boy! what are you doing *here*?"

His first impulse was to run; but his legs trembled so that he could not stir. He turned to confront his antagonist, and behold, there stood his old master's next door neighbor! He thought it was all over with him now; but it proved otherwise. That man was a miracle. He possessed a goodly number of slaves, and yet was not quite deaf to that mystic clock, whose ticking is rarely heard in the slaveholder's breast.

---

1 *billows* Waves.

"Ben, you are sick," said he. "Why, you look like a ghost. I guess I gave you something of a start. Never mind, Ben, I am not going to touch you. You had a pretty tough time of it, and you may go on your way rejoicing for all me. But I would advise you to get out of this place plaguy[1] quick, for there are several gentlemen here from our town." He described the nearest and safest route to New York, and added, "I shall be glad to tell your mother I have seen you. Goodbye, Ben."

Benjamin turned away, filled with gratitude, and surprised that the town he hated contained such a gem—a gem worthy of a purer setting.

This gentleman was a Northerner by birth, and had married a southern lady. On his return, he told my grandmother that he had seen her son, and of the service he had rendered him.

Benjamin reached New York safely, and concluded to stop there until he had gained strength enough to proceed further. It happened that my grandmother's only remaining son had sailed for the same city on business for his mistress. Through God's providence, the brothers met. You may be sure it was a happy meeting. "O Phil," exclaimed Benjamin, "I am here at last." Then he told him how near he came to dying, almost in sight of free land, and how he prayed that he might live to get one breath of free air. He said life was worth something now, and it would be hard to die. In the old jail he had not valued it; once, he was tempted to destroy it; but something, he did not know what, had prevented him; perhaps it was fear. He had heard those who profess to be religious declare there was no heaven for self-murderers; and as his life had been pretty hot here, he did not desire a continuation of the same in another world. "If I die now," he exclaimed, "thank God, I shall die a freeman!"

He begged my uncle Phillip not to return south; but stay and work with him, till they earned enough to buy those at home. His brother told him it would kill their mother if he deserted her in her trouble. She had pledged her house, and with difficulty had raised money to buy him. Would he be bought?

"No, never!" he replied. "Do you suppose, Phil, when I have got so far out of their clutches, I will give them one red cent? No! And do you suppose I would turn mother out of her home in her old age? That I would let her pay all those hard-earned dollars for me, and never to see me? For you know she will stay south as long as her other children are slaves. What a good mother! Tell her to buy *you*, Phil. You have been a comfort to her, and I have been a trouble. And Linda, poor Linda; what'll become of her? Phil, you don't know what a life they lead her. She has told me something about it, and I wish old Flint was dead, or a better man. When I was in jail, he asked her if she didn't want *him* to ask my master to forgive me, and take me home again. She told

---

1   *plaguy*   I.e., awfully; very.

him, No; that I didn't want to go back. He got mad, and said we were all alike. I never despised my own master half as much as I do that man. There is many a worse slaveholder than my master; but for all that I would not be his slave."

While Benjamin was sick, he had parted with nearly all his clothes to pay necessary expenses. But he did not part with a little pin I fastened in his bosom when we parted. It was the most valuable thing I owned, and I thought none more worthy to wear it. He had it still.

His brother furnished him with clothes, and gave him what money he had.

They parted with moistened eyes; and as Benjamin turned away, he said, "Phil, I part with all my kindred." And so it proved. We never heard from him again.

Uncle Phillip came home; and the first words he uttered when he entered the house were, "Mother, Ben is free! I have seen him in New York." She stood looking at him with a bewildered air. "Mother, don't you believe it?" he said, laying his hand softly upon her shoulder. She raised her hands, and exclaimed, "God be praised! Let us thank him." She dropped on her knees, and poured forth her heart in prayer. Then Phillip must sit down and repeat to her every word Benjamin had said. He told her all; only he forbore to mention how sick and pale her darling looked. Why should he distress her when she could do him no good?

The brave old woman still toiled on, hoping to rescue some of her other children. After a while she succeeded in buying Phillip. She paid eight hundred dollars, and came home with the precious document that secured his freedom. The happy mother and son sat together by the old hearthstone that night, telling how proud they were of each other, and how they would prove to the world that they could take care of themselves, as they had long taken care of others. We all concluded by saying, "He that is *willing* to be a slave, let him be a slave."

CHAPTER 5. THE TRIALS OF GIRLHOOD

During the first years of my service in Dr. Flint's family, I was accustomed to share some indulgences with the children of my mistress. Though this seemed to me no more than right, I was grateful for it, and tried to merit the kindness by the faithful discharge of my duties. But I now entered on my fifteenth year—a sad epoch in the life of a slave girl. My master began to whisper foul words in my ear. Young as I was, I could not remain ignorant of their import. I tried to treat them with indifference or contempt. The master's age, my extreme youth, and the fear that his conduct would be reported to my grand-mother, made him bear this treatment for many months. He was a crafty man, and resorted to many means to accomplish his purposes. Sometimes he had stormy, terrific[1] ways, that made his victims tremble; sometimes he assumed a gentleness that he thought must surely subdue. Of the two, I preferred his stormy moods, although they left me trembling. He tried his utmost to corrupt the pure principles my grandmother had instilled. He peopled my young mind with unclean images, such as only a vile monster could think of. I turned from him with disgust and hatred. But he was my master. I was compelled to live under the same roof with him—where I saw a man forty years my senior daily violating the most sacred commandments of nature. He told me I was his property; that I must be subject to his will in all things. My soul revolted against the mean tyranny. But where could I turn for protection? No matter whether the slave girl be as black as ebony or as fair as her mistress. In either case, there is no shadow of law to protect her from insult, from violence, or even from death; all these are inflicted by fiends who bear the shape of men. The mistress, who ought to protect the helpless victim, has no other feelings towards her but those of jealousy and rage. The degradation, the wrongs, the vices, that grow out of slavery, are more than I can describe. They are greater than you would willingly believe. Surely, if you credited one half the truths that are told you concerning the helpless millions suffering in this cruel bondage, you at the north would not help to tighten the yoke.[2] You surely would refuse to do for the master, on your own soil, the mean and cruel work which trained bloodhounds and the lowest class of whites do for him at the south.

Everywhere the years bring to all enough of sin and sorrow; but in slavery the very dawn of life is darkened by these shadows. Even the little child, who is accustomed to wait on her mistress and her children, will learn, before she is twelve years old, why it is that her mistress hates such and such a one among the slaves. Perhaps the child's own mother is among those hated ones. She listens to violent outbreaks of jealous passion, and cannot help understanding what is the cause. She will become prematurely knowing in evil things. Soon she will learn to tremble when she hears her master's footfall. She will be compelled to realize that she is no longer a child. If God has bestowed beauty upon her, it will prove her greatest curse. That which commands admiration in the white woman only hastens the degradation of the female slave. I know that some are too much brutalized by slavery to feel the humiliation of their position; but many slaves feel it most acutely, and shrink from the memory of

---

1   terrific   I.e., terrifying.
2   north ... yoke   Reference to the hope that Northerners would actively resist the terms of the Fugitive Slave Act of 1850, under which it became illegal for anyone, whether in the North or the South, to give aid to people escaping slavery; citizens throughout the country were expected to actively participate in the apprehension and return of fugitives to the South. The Fugitive Slave Act was fiercely resisted by Northern abolitionists, but it was not repealed until 1864.

it. I cannot tell how much I suffered in the presence of these wrongs, nor how I am still pained by the retrospect. My master met me at every turn, reminding me that I belonged to him, and swearing by heaven and earth that he would compel me to submit to him. If I went out for a breath of fresh air, after a day of unwearied toil, his footsteps dogged me. If I knelt by my mother's grave, his dark shadow fell on me even there. The light heart which nature had given me became heavy with sad forebodings. The other slaves in my master's house noticed the change. Many of them pitied me; but none dared to ask the cause. They had no need to inquire. They knew too well the guilty practices under that roof; and they were aware that to speak of them was an offence that never went unpunished.

I longed for someone to confide in. I would have given the world to have laid my head on my grandmother's faithful bosom, and told her all my troubles. But Dr. Flint swore he would kill me, if I was not as silent as the grave. Then, although my grandmother was all in all to me, I feared her as well as loved her. I had been accustomed to look up to her with a respect bordering upon awe. I was very young, and felt shamefaced about telling her such impure things, especially as I knew her to be very strict on such subjects. Moreover, she was a woman of a high spirit. She was usually very quiet in her demeanor; but if her indignation was once roused, it was not very easily quelled. I had been told that she once chased a white gentleman with a loaded pistol, because he insulted one of her daughters. I dreaded the consequences of a violent outbreak; and both pride and fear kept me silent. But though I did not confide in my grandmother, and even evaded her vigilant watchfulness and inquiry, her presence in the neighborhood was some protection to me. Though she had been a slave, Dr. Flint was afraid of her. He dreaded her scorching rebukes. Moreover, she was known and patronized by many people; and he did not wish to have his villainy made public. It was lucky for me that I did not live on a distant plantation, but in a town not so large that the inhabitants were ignorant of each other's affairs. Bad as are the laws and customs in a slavehold-ing community, the doctor, as a professional man, deemed it prudent to keep up some outward show of decency.

O, what days and nights of fear and sorrow that man caused me! Reader, it is not to awaken sympathy for myself that I am telling you truthfully what I suffered in slavery. I do it to kindle a flame of compassion in your hearts for my sisters who are still in bondage, suffering as I once suffered.

I once saw two beautiful children playing together. One was a fair white child; the other was her slave, and also her sister. When I saw them embracing each other, and heard their joyous laughter, I turned sadly away from the lovely sight. I foresaw the inevitable blight that would fall on the little slave's heart. I knew how soon her laughter would be changed to sighs. The fair child grew up to be a still fairer woman. From childhood to womanhood her pathway was blooming with flowers, and overarched by a sunny sky. Scarcely one day of her life had been clouded when the sun rose on her happy bridal morning.

How had those years dealt with her slave sister, the little playmate of her childhood? She, also, was very beautiful; but the flowers and sunshine of love were not for her. She drank the cup of sin, and shame, and misery, whereof her persecuted race are compelled to drink.

In view of these things, why are ye silent, ye free men and women of the north? Why do your tongues falter in maintenance of the right? Would that I had more ability! But my heart is so full, and my pen is so weak! There are noble men and women who plead for us, striving to help those who cannot help themselves. God bless them! God give them strength and courage to go on! God bless those, everywhere, who are laboring to advance the cause of humanity!

CHAPTER 6. THE JEALOUS MISTRESS

I would ten thousand times rather that my children should be the half-starved paupers of Ireland than to be the most pampered among the slaves of America. I would rather drudge out my life on a cotton plantation, till the grave opened to give me rest, than to live with an unprincipled master and a jealous mistress. The felon's home in a penitentiary is preferable. He may repent, and turn from the error of his ways, and so find peace; but it is not so with a favorite slave. She is not allowed to have any pride of character. It is deemed a crime in her to wish to be virtuous.

Mrs. Flint possessed the key to her husband's character before I was born. She might have used this knowledge to counsel and to screen the young and the innocent among her slaves; but for them she had no sympathy. They were the objects of her constant suspicion and malevolence. She watched her husband with unceasing vigilance; but he was well practiced in means to evade it. What he could not find opportunity to say in words he manifested in signs. He invented more than were ever thought of in a deaf and dumb[1] asylum. I let them pass, as if I did not understand what he meant; and many were the curses and threats bestowed on me for my stupidity. One day he caught me teaching myself to write. He frowned, as if he was not well pleased, but I suppose he came to the conclusion that such an accomplishment might help to advance his favorite scheme. Before long, notes were often slipped into my hand. I would return them, saying, "I can't read them, sir." "Can't you?" he replied; "then I must read them to you." He always finished the reading by

---

1 *dumb* Unable to speak.

asking, "Do you understand?" Sometimes he would complain of the heat of the tea room, and order his supper to be placed on a small table in the piazza.[1] He would seat himself there with a well-satisfied smile, and tell me to stand by and brush away the flies. He would eat very slowly, pausing between the mouthfuls. These intervals were employed in describing the happiness I was so foolishly throwing away, and in threatening me with the penalty that finally awaited my stubborn disobedience. He boasted much of the forbearance he had exercised towards me, and reminded me that there was a limit to his patience. When I succeeded in avoiding opportunities for him to talk to me at home, I was ordered to come to his office, to do some errand. When there, I was obliged to stand and listen to such language as he saw fit to address to me. Sometimes I so openly expressed my contempt for him that he would become violently enraged, and I wondered why he did not strike me. Circumstanced as he was, he probably thought it was better policy to be forbearing. But the state of things grew worse and worse daily. In desperation I told him that I must and would apply to my grandmother for protection. He threatened me with death, and worse than death, if I made any complaint to her. Strange to say, I did not despair. I was naturally of a buoyant disposition, and always I had hope of somehow getting out of his clutches. Like many a poor, simple slave before me, I trusted that some threads of joy would yet be woven into my dark destiny.

I had entered my sixteenth year, and every day it became more apparent that my presence was intolerable to Mrs. Flint. Angry words frequently passed between her and her husband. He had never punished me himself, and he would not allow anybody else to punish me. In that respect, she was never satisfied; but, in her angry moods, no terms were too vile for her to bestow upon me. Yet I, whom she detested so bitterly, had far more pity for her than he had, whose duty it was to make her life happy. I never wronged her, or wished to wrong her; and one word of kindness from her would have brought me to her feet.

After repeated quarrels between the doctor and his wife, he announced his intention to take his youngest daughter, then four years old, to sleep in his apartment. It was necessary that a servant should sleep in the same room, to be on hand if the child stirred. I was selected for that office, and informed for what purpose that arrangement had been made. By managing to keep within sight of people, as much as possible during the day time, I had hitherto succeeded in eluding my master, though a razor was often held to my throat to force me to change this line of policy. At night I slept by the side of my great aunt, where I felt safe. He was too prudent to come into her room. She was an

---

1 *piazza* Veranda.

old woman, and had been in the family many years. Moreover, as a married man, and a professional man, he deemed it necessary to save appearances in some degree. But he resolved to remove the obstacle in the way of his scheme; and he thought he had planned it so that he should evade suspicion. He was well aware how much I prized my refuge by the side of my old aunt, and he determined to dispossess me of it. The first night the doctor had the little child in his room alone. The next morning, I was ordered to take my station as nurse the following night. A kind Providence interposed in my favor. During the day Mrs. Flint heard of this new arrangement, and a storm followed. I rejoiced to hear it rage.

After a while my mistress sent for me to come to her room. Her first question was, "Did you know you were to sleep in the doctor's room?"

"Yes, ma'am."

"Who told you?"

"My master."

"Will you answer truly all the questions I ask?"

"Yes, ma'am."

"Tell me, then, as you hope to be forgiven, are you innocent of what I have accused you?"

"I am."

She handed me a Bible, and said, "Lay your hand on your heart, kiss this holy book, and swear before God that you tell me the truth."

I took the oath she required, and I did it with a clear conscience.

"You have taken God's holy word to testify your innocence," said she. "If you have deceived me, beware! Now take this stool, sit down, look me directly in the face, and tell me all that has passed between your master and you."

I did as she ordered. As I went on with my account her color changed frequently, she wept, and sometimes groaned. She spoke in tones so sad, that I was touched by her grief. The tears came to my eyes; but I was soon convinced that her emotions arose from anger and wounded pride. She felt that her marriage vows were desecrated, her dignity insulted, but she had no compassion for the poor victim of her husband's perfidy. She pitied herself as a martyr; but she was incapable of feeling for the condition of shame and misery in which her unfortunate, helpless slave was placed.

Yet perhaps she had some touch of feeling for me; for when the conference was ended, she spoke kindly, and promised to protect me. I should have been much comforted by this assurance if I could have had confidence in it; but my experiences in slavery had filled me with distrust. She was not a very refined woman, and had not much control over her passions. I was an object of her jealousy, and, consequently, of her hatred; and I knew I could not expect kindness or confidence from her under the circumstances in which I was placed.

I could not blame her. Slave-holders' wives feel as other women would under similar circumstances. The fire of her temper kindled from small sparks, and now the flame became so intense that the doctor was obliged to give up his intended arrangement.

I knew I had ignited the torch, and I expected to suffer for it afterwards; but I felt too thankful to my mistress for the timely aid she rendered me to care much about that. She now took me to sleep in a room adjoining her own. There I was an object of her especial care, though not of her especial comfort, for she spent many a sleepless night to watch over me. Sometimes I woke up, and found her bending over me. At other times she whispered in my ear, as though it was her husband who was speaking to me, and listened to hear what I would answer. If she startled me, on such occasions, she would glide stealthily away; and the next morning she would tell me I had been talking in my sleep, and ask who I was talking to. At last, I began to be fearful for my life. It had been often threatened; and you can imagine, better than I can describe, what an unpleasant sensation it must produce to wake up in the dead of night and find a jealous woman bending over you. Terrible as this experience was, I had fears that it would give place to one more terrible.

My mistress grew weary of her vigils; they did not prove satisfactory. She changed her tactics. She now tried the trick of accusing my master of crime, in my presence, and gave my name as the author of the accusation. To my utter astonishment, he replied, "I don't believe it; but if she did acknowledge it, you tortured her into exposing me." Tortured into exposing him! Truly, Satan had no difficulty in distinguishing the color of his soul! I understood his object in making this false representation. It was to show me that I gained nothing by seeking the protection of my mistress; that the power was still all in his own hands. I pitied Mrs. Flint. She was a second wife, many years the junior of her husband; and the hoary-headed[1] miscreant was enough to try the patience of a wiser and better woman. She was completely foiled, and knew not how to proceed. She would gladly have had me flogged for my supposed false oath; but, as I have already stated, the doctor never allowed anyone to whip me. The old sinner was politic. The application of the lash might have led to remarks that would have exposed him in the eyes of his children and grandchildren. How often did I rejoice that I lived in a town where all the inhabitants knew each other! If I had been on a remote plantation, or lost among the multitude of a crowded city, I should not be a living woman at this day.

The secrets of slavery are concealed like those of the Inquisition. My master was, to my knowledge, the father of eleven slaves. But did the mothers dare to tell who was the father of their children? Did the other slaves dare to allude to

---

1 *hoary-headed* I.e., white-haired.

it, except in whispers among themselves? No, indeed! They knew too well the terrible consequences.

My grandmother could not avoid seeing things which excited her suspicions. She was uneasy about me, and tried various ways to buy me; but the never-changing answer was always repeated: "Linda does not belong to me. She is my daughter's property, and I have no legal right to sell her." The conscientious man! He was too scrupulous to sell me; but he had no scruples whatever about committing a much greater wrong against the helpless young girl placed under his guardianship, as his daughter's property. Sometimes my persecutor would ask me whether I would like to be sold. I told him I would rather be sold to anybody than to lead such a life as I did. On such occasions he would assume the air of a very injured individual, and reproach me for my ingratitude. "Did I not take you into the house, and make you the companion of my own children?" he would say. "Have I ever treated you like a negro? I have never allowed you to be punished, not even to please your mistress. And this is the recompense I get, you ungrateful girl!" I answered that he had reasons of his own for screening me from punishment, and that the course he pursued made my mistress hate me and persecute me. If I wept, he would say, "Poor child! Don't cry! don't cry! I will make peace for you with your mistress. Only let me arrange matters in my own way. Poor, foolish girl! you don't know what is for your own good. I would cherish you. I would make a lady of you. Now go, and think of all I have promised you."

I did think of it.

Reader, I draw no imaginary pictures of southern homes. I am telling you the plain truth. Yet when victims make their escape from this wild beast of Slavery, northerners consent to act the part of bloodhounds, and hunt the poor fugitive back into his den, "full of dead men's bones, and all uncleanness."[1] Nay, more, they are not only willing, but proud, to give their daughters in marriage to slaveholders. The poor girls have romantic notions of a sunny clime, and of the flowering vines that all the year round shade a happy home. To what disappointments are they destined! The young wife soon learns that the husband in whose hands she has placed her happiness pays no regard to his marriage vows. Children of every shade of complexion play with her own fair babies, and too well she knows that they are born unto him of his own household. Jealousy and hatred enter the flowery home, and it is ravaged of its loveliness.

---

1 *full … uncleanness* See Matthew 23.27: "Woe unto you, scribes and Pharisees, hypocrites! for ye are like unto whited sepulchers, which indeed appear beautiful outward, but are within full of dead men's bones, and of all uncleanness."

Southern women often marry a man knowing that he is the father of many little slaves. They do not trouble themselves about it. They regard such children as property, as marketable as the pigs on the plantation; and it is seldom that they do not make them aware of this by passing them into the slave-trader's hands as soon as possible, and thus getting them out of their sight. I am glad to say there are some honorable exceptions.

I have myself known two southern wives who exhorted their husbands to free those slaves towards whom they stood in a "parental relation"; and their request was granted. These husbands blushed before the superior nobleness of their wives' natures. Though they had only counselled them to do that which it was their duty to do, it commanded their respect, and rendered their conduct more exemplary. Concealment was at an end, and confidence took the place of distrust.

Though this bad institution deadens the moral sense, even in white women, to a fearful extent, it is not altogether extinct. I have heard southern ladies say of Mr. Such a one, "He not only thinks it no disgrace to be the father of those little niggers,[1] but he is not ashamed to call himself their master. I declare, such things ought not to be tolerated in any decent society!"

CHAPTER 7. THE LOVER

Why does the slave ever love? Why allow the tendrils of the heart to twine around objects which may at any moment be wrenched away by the hand of violence? When separations come by the hand of death, the pious soul can bow in resignation, and say, "Not my will, but thine be done, O Lord!" But when the ruthless hand of man strikes the blow, regardless of the misery he causes, it is hard to be submissive. I did not reason thus when I was a young girl. Youth will be youth. I loved, and I indulged the hope that the dark clouds around me would turn out a bright lining. I forgot that in the land of my birth the shadows are too dense for light to penetrate. A land

> Where laughter is not mirth; nor thought the mind;
> Nor words a language; nor e'en men mankind.
> Where cries reply to curses, shrieks to blows,
> And each is tortured in his separate hell.[2]

There was in the neighborhood a young colored carpenter; a free born man. We had been well acquainted in childhood, and frequently met together

---

1 *niggers* By the mid-nineteenth century, this word, when used by white people of black people, had acquired the extremely derogatory connotations it carries today.

2 *Where laughter ... separate hell* These lines are from Byron's "The Lament of Tasso," 4.84–87 (1817).

afterwards. We became mutually attached, and he proposed to marry me. I loved him with all the ardor of a young girl's first love. But when I reflected that I was a slave, and that the laws gave no sanction to the marriage of such, my heart sank within me. My lover wanted to buy me; but I knew that Dr. Flint was too willful and arbitrary a man to consent to that arrangement. From him, I was sure of experiencing all sorts of opposition, and I had nothing to hope from my mistress. She would have been delighted to have got rid of me, but not in that way. It would have relieved her mind of a burden if she could have seen me sold to some distant state, but if I was married near home I should be just as much in her husband's power as I had previously been—for the husband of a slave has no power to protect her. Moreover, my mistress, like many others, seemed to think that slaves had no right to any family ties of their own; that they were created merely to wait upon the family of the mistress. I once heard her abuse a young slave girl, who told her that a colored man wanted to make her his wife. "I will have you peeled and pickled, my lady," said she, "if I ever hear you mention that subject again. Do you suppose that I will have you tending my children with the children of that nigger?" The girl to whom she said this had a mulatto child, of course not acknowledged by its father. The poor black man who loved her would have been proud to acknowledge his helpless offspring.

Many and anxious were the thoughts I revolved in my mind. I was at a loss what to do. Above all things, I was desirous to spare my lover the insults that had cut so deeply into my own soul. I talked with my grandmother about it, and partly told her my fears. I did not dare to tell her the worst. She had long suspected all was not right, and if I confirmed her suspicions I knew a storm would rise that would prove the overthrow of all my hopes.

This love-dream had been my support through many trials; and I could not bear to run the risk of having it suddenly dissipated. There was a lady in the neighborhood, a particular friend of Dr. Flint's, who often visited the house. I had a great respect for her, and she had always manifested a friendly interest in me. Grandmother thought she would have great influence with the doctor. I went to this lady, and told her my story. I told her I was aware that my lover's being a free-born man would prove a great objection; but he wanted to buy me; and if Dr. Flint would consent to that arrangement, I felt sure he would be willing to pay any reasonable price. She knew that Mrs. Flint disliked me; therefore, I ventured to suggest that perhaps my mistress would approve of my being sold, as that would rid her of me. The lady listened, with kindly sympathy, and promised to do her utmost to promote my wishes. She had an interview with the doctor, and I believe she pleaded my cause earnestly; but it was all to no purpose.

How I dreaded my master now! Every minute I expected to be summoned to his presence; but the day passed, and I heard nothing from him. The next morning, a message was brought to me: "Master wants you in his study." I found the door ajar, and I stood a moment gazing at the hateful man who claimed a right to rule me, body and soul. I entered, and tried to appear calm. I did not want him to know how my heart was bleeding. He looked fixedly at me, with an expression which seemed to say, "I have half a mind to kill you on the spot." At last he broke the silence, and that was a relief to both of us.

"So you want to be married, do you?" said he, "and to a free nigger."

"Yes, sir."

"Well, I'll soon convince you whether I am your master, or the nigger fellow you honor so highly. If you *must* have a husband, you may take up with one of my slaves."

What a situation I should be in, as the wife of one of *his* slaves, even if my heart had been interested!

I replied, "Don't you suppose, sir, that a slave can have some preference about marrying? Do you suppose that all men are alike to her?"

"Do you love this nigger?" said he, abruptly.

"Yes, sir."

"How dare you tell me so!" he exclaimed, in great wrath. After a slight pause, he added, "I supposed you thought more of yourself; that you felt above the insults of such puppies."

I replied, "If he is a puppy I am a puppy, for we are both of the negro race. It is right and honorable for us to love each other. The man you call a puppy never insulted me, sir; and he would not love me if he did not believe me to be a virtuous woman."

He sprang upon me like a tiger, and gave me a stunning blow. It was the first time he had ever struck me; and fear did not enable me to control my anger. When I had recovered a little from the effects, I exclaimed, "You have struck me for answering you honestly. How I despise you!"

There was silence for some minutes. Perhaps he was deciding what should be my punishment; or, perhaps, he wanted to give me time to reflect on what I had said, and to whom I had said it. Finally, he asked, "Do you know what you have said?"

"Yes, sir; but your treatment drove me to it."

"Do you know that I have a right to do as I like with you—that I can kill you, if I please?"

"You have tried to kill me, and I wish you had; but you have no right to do as you like with me."

"Silence!" he exclaimed, in a thundering voice. "By heavens, girl, you forget yourself too far! Are you mad? If you are, I will soon bring you to your senses.

Do you think any other master would bear what I have borne from you this morning? Many masters would have killed you on the spot. How would you like to be sent to jail for your insolence?"

"I know I have been disrespectful, sir," I replied; "but you drove me to it; I couldn't help it. As for the jail, there would be more peace for me there than there is here."

"You deserve to go there," said he, "and to be under such treatment, that you would forget the meaning of the word *peace*. It would do you good. It would take some of your high notions out of you. But I am not ready to send you there yet, notwithstanding your ingratitude for all my kindness and forbearance. You have been the plague of my life. I have wanted to make you happy, and I have been repaid with the basest ingratitude; but though you have proved yourself incapable of appreciating my kindness, I will be lenient towards you, Linda. I will give you one more chance to redeem your character. If you behave yourself and do as I require, I will forgive you and treat you as I always have done; but if you disobey me, I will punish you as I would the meanest slave on my plantation. Never let me hear that fellow's name mentioned again. If I ever know of your speaking to him, I will cowhide you both; and if I catch him lurking about my premises, I will shoot him as soon as I would a dog. Do you hear what I say? I'll teach you a lesson about marriage and free niggers! Now go, and let this be the last time I have occasion to speak to you on this subject."

Reader, did you ever hate? I hope not. I never did but once; and I trust I never shall again. Somebody has called it "the atmosphere of hell";[1] and I believe it is so.

For a fortnight[2] the doctor did not speak to me. He thought to mortify me; to make me feel that I had disgraced myself by receiving the honorable addresses of a respectable colored man, in preference to the base proposals of a white man. But though his lips disdained to address me, his eyes were very loquacious. No animal ever watched its prey more narrowly than he watched me. He knew that I could write, though he had failed to make me read his letters; and he was now troubled lest I should exchange letters with another man. After a while he became weary of silence; and I was sorry for it. One morning, as he passed through the hall, to leave the house, he contrived to thrust a note into my hand. I thought I had better read it, and spare myself the vexation of having him read it to me. It expressed regret for the blow he had given me, and reminded me that I myself was wholly to blame for it. He

---

1   *Somebody ... hell*   English writer Martin Farquhar Tupper wrote that "hatred is the atmosphere of hell" in his book *Proverbial Philosophy* (1838).

2   *a fortnight*   Two weeks.

hoped I had become convinced of the injury I was doing myself by incurring his displeasure. He wrote that he had made up his mind to go to Louisiana; that he should take several slaves with him, and intended I should be one of the number. My mistress would remain where she was; therefore I should have nothing to fear from that quarter. If I merited kindness from him, he assured me that it would be lavishly bestowed. He begged me to think over the matter, and answer the following day.

The next morning I was called to carry a pair of scissors to his room. I laid them on the table with the letter beside them. He thought it was my answer, and did not call me back. I went as usual to attend my young mistress to and from school. He met me in the street, and ordered me to stop at his office on my way back. When I entered, he showed me his letter, and asked me why I had not answered it. I replied, "I am your daughter's property, and it is in your power to send me, or take me, wherever you please." He said he was very glad to find me so willing to go, and that we should start early in the autumn. He had a large practice in the town, and I rather thought he had made up the story merely to frighten me. However that might be, I was determined that I would never go to Louisiana with him.

Summer passed away, and early in the autumn Dr. Flint's eldest son was sent to Louisiana to examine the country, with a view to emigrating. That news did not disturb me. I knew very well that I should not be sent with *him*. That I had not been taken to the plantation before this time, was owing to the fact that his son was there. He was jealous of his son; and jealousy of the overseer had kept him from punishing me by sending me into the fields to work. Is it strange that I was not proud of these protectors? As for the overseer, he was a man for whom I had less respect than I had for a bloodhound.

Young Mr. Flint did not bring back a favorable report of Louisiana, and I heard no more of that scheme. Soon after this, my lover met me at the corner of the street, and I stopped to speak to him. Looking up, I saw my master watching us from his window. I hurried home, trembling with fear. I was sent for, immediately, to go to his room. He met me with a blow. "When is mistress to be married?" said he, in a sneering tone. A shower of oaths and imprecations followed. How thankful I was that my lover was a free man! that my tyrant had no power to flog him for speaking to me in the street!

Again and again I revolved in my mind how all this would end. There was no hope that the doctor would consent to sell me on any terms. He had an iron will, and was determined to keep me, and to conquer me. My lover was an intelligent and religious man. Even if he could have obtained permission to marry me while I was a slave, the marriage would give him no power to protect me from my master. It would have made him miserable to witness the insults I should have been subjected to. And then, if we had children, I knew they must "follow the condition of the mother."[1] What a terrible blight that would be on the heart of a free, intelligent father! For *his* sake, I felt that I ought not to link his fate with my own unhappy destiny. He was going to Savannah to see about a little property left him by an uncle; and hard as it was to bring my feelings to it, I earnestly entreated him not to come back. I advised him to go to the Free States, where his tongue would not be tied, and where his intelligence would be of more avail to him. He left me, still hoping the day would come when I could be bought. With me the lamp of hope had gone out. The dream of my girlhood was over. I felt lonely and desolate.

Still I was not stripped of all. I still had my good grandmother, and my affectionate brother. When he put his arms round my neck, and looked into my eyes, as if to read there the troubles I dared not tell, I felt that I still had something to love. But even that pleasant emotion was chilled by the reflection that he might be torn from me at any moment, by some sudden freak of my master. If he had known how we loved each other, I think he would have exulted in separating us. We often planned together how we could get to the north. But, as William remarked, such things are easier said than done. My movements were very closely watched, and we had no means of getting any money to defray our expenses. As for grandmother, she was strongly opposed to her children's undertaking any such project. She had not forgotten poor Benjamin's sufferings, and she was afraid that if another child tried to escape, he would have a similar or a worse fate. To me, nothing seemed more dreadful than my present life. I said to myself, "William *must* be free. He shall go to the north, and I will follow him." Many a slave sister has formed the same plans.

Chapter 8. What Slaves Are Taught to Think of the North

Slaveholders pride themselves upon being honorable men; but if you were to hear the enormous lies they tell their slaves, you would have small respect for their veracity. I have spoken plain English. Pardon me. I cannot use a milder term. When they visit the north, and return home, they tell their slaves of the runaways they have seen, and describe them to be in the most deplorable condition. A slaveholder once told me that he had seen a runaway friend of mine in New York, and that she besought him to take her back to her master, for she was literally dying of starvation; that many days she had only one cold potato to eat, and at other times could get nothing at all. He said he refused

---

1   *follow ... mother*   From 1662 onwards, slave law in Britain and America had followed the doctrine that children followed the status of their mother (i.e., any child born to an enslaved woman would be themselves enslaved). This law meant that enslavers who fathered children with enslaved women were not held in any way accountable and in fact profited from the practice, as they could then exploit or sell their own children.

to take her, because he knew her master would not thank him for bringing such a miserable wretch to his house. He ended by saying to me, "This is the punishment she brought on herself for running away from a kind master."

This whole story was false. I afterwards stayed with that friend in New York, and found her in comfortable circumstances. She had never thought of such a thing as wishing to go back to slavery. Many of the slaves believe such stories, and think it is not worthwhile to exchange slavery for such a hard kind of freedom. It is difficult to persuade such that freedom could make them useful men, and enable them to protect their wives and children. If those heathen in our Christian land had as much teaching as some Hindoos, they would think otherwise. They would know that liberty is more valuable than life. They would begin to understand their own capabilities, and exert themselves to become men and women.

But while the Free States sustain a law[1] which hurls fugitives back into slavery, how can the slaves resolve to become men? There are some who strive to protect wives and daughters from the insults of their masters; but those who have such sentiments have had advantages above the general mass of slaves. They have been partially civilized and Christianized by favorable circumstances. Some are bold enough to *utter* such sentiments to their masters. O, that there were more of them!

Some poor creatures have been so brutalized by the lash that they will sneak out of the way to give their masters free access to their wives and daughters. Do you think this proves the black man to belong to an inferior order of beings? What would *you* be, if you had been born and brought up a slave, with generations of slaves for ancestors? I admit that the black man *is* inferior. But what is it that makes him so? It is the ignorance in which white men compel him to live; it is the torturing whip that lashes manhood out of him; it is the fierce bloodhounds of the South, and the scarcely less cruel human bloodhounds of the north, who enforce the Fugitive Slave Law. *They* do the work.

Southern gentlemen indulge in the most contemptuous expressions about the Yankees, while they,[2] on their part, consent to do the vilest work for them, such as the ferocious bloodhounds and the despised negro-hunters are employed to do at home. When southerners go to the north, they are proud to do them honor;[3] but the northern man is not welcome south of Mason Dixon's line, unless he suppresses every thought and feeling at variance with

---

1 *Free States sustain a law* See note 2 on page 325 above.
2 *Yankees* In common American usage, this term referred originally to New Englanders, and later to Northerners in general—the sense in which Jacobs is using it here; *they* I.e., the Yankees.
3 *they .... honor* I.e., the Northerners are respectful of visiting Southerners.

their "peculiar institution."[1] Nor is it enough to be silent. The masters are not pleased, unless they obtain a greater degree of subservience than that; and they are generally accommodated. Do they respect the northerner for this? I trow[2] not. Even the slaves despise "a northern man with southern principles"; and that is the class they generally see. When northerners go to the south to reside, they prove very apt scholars. They soon imbibe the sentiments and disposition of their neighbors, and generally go beyond their teachers. Of the two, they are proverbially the hardest masters.

They seem to satisfy their consciences with the doctrine that God created the Africans to be slaves. What a libel upon the heavenly Father, who "made of one blood all nations of men"![3] And then who are Africans? Who can measure the amount of Anglo-Saxon blood coursing in the veins of American slaves?

I have spoken of the pains slaveholders take to give their slaves a bad opinion of the north; but, notwithstanding this, intelligent slaves are aware that they have many friends in the Free States. Even the most ignorant have some confused notions about it. They knew that I could read; and I was often asked if I had seen anything in the newspapers about white folks over in the big north, who were trying to get their freedom for them. Some believe that the abolitionists have already made them free, and that it is established by law, but that their masters prevent the law from going into effect. One woman begged me to get a newspaper and read it over. She said her husband told her that the black people had sent word to the queen of 'Merica that they were all slaves; that she didn't believe it, and went to Washington city to see the president about it. They quarrelled; she drew her sword upon him, and swore that he should help her to make them all free.

That poor, ignorant woman thought that America was governed by a Queen, to whom the President was subordinate. I wish the President was subordinate to Queen Justice.

CHAPTER 9. SKETCHES OF NEIGHBORING SLAVEHOLDERS

There was a planter in the country, not far from us, whom I will call Mr. Litch. He was an ill-bred, uneducated man, but very wealthy. He had six hundred slaves, many of whom he did not know by sight. His extensive plantation was managed by well-paid overseers. There was a jail and a whipping post on his grounds; and whatever cruelties were perpetrated there, they passed without

---

1   *Mason Dixon's line*   Line separating parts of Pennsylvania and Delaware from parts of Maryland and Virginia; the phrase was used as shorthand for the boundary between the Northern free states and the Southern slave states; *peculiar institution*   I.e., slavery.
2   *trow*   Believe.
3   *made ... men*   See Acts 17.26.

comment. He was so effectually screened by his great wealth that he was called to no account for his crimes, not even for murder.

Various were the punishments resorted to. A favorite one was to tie a rope round a man's body, and suspend him from the ground. A fire was kindled over him, from which was suspended a piece of fat pork. As this cooked, the scalding drops of fat continually fell on the bare flesh. On his own plantation, he required very strict obedience to the eighth commandment.[1] But depredations on the neighbors were allowable, provided the culprit managed to evade detection or suspicion. If a neighbor brought a charge of theft against any of his slaves, he was browbeaten by the master, who assured him that his slaves had enough of everything at home, and had no inducement to steal. No sooner was the neighbor's back turned, than the accused was sought out, and whipped for his lack of discretion. If a slave stole from him even a pound of meat or a peck[2] of corn, if detection followed, he was put in chains and imprisoned, and so kept till his form was attenuated by hunger and suffering.

A freshet[3] once bore his wine cellar and meat house miles away from the plantation. Some slaves followed, and secured bits of meat and bottles of wine. Two were detected; a ham and some liquor being found in their huts. They were summoned by their master. No words were used, but a club felled them to the ground. A rough box was their coffin, and their interment was a dog's burial. Nothing was said.

Murder was so common on his plantation that he feared to be alone after nightfall. He might have believed in ghosts.

His brother, if not equal in wealth, was at least equal in cruelty. His bloodhounds were well trained. Their pen was spacious, and a terror to the slaves. They were let loose on a runaway, and, if they tracked him, they literally tore the flesh from his bones. When this slaveholder died, his shrieks and groans were so frightful that they appalled his own friends. His last words were, "I am going to hell; bury my money with me."

After death his eyes remained open. To press the lids down, silver dollars were laid on them. These were buried with him. From this circumstance, a rumor went abroad that his coffin was filled with money. Three times his grave was opened, and his coffin taken out. The last time, his body was found on the ground, and a flock of buzzards were pecking at it. He was again interred, and a sentinel set over his grave. The perpetrators were never discovered.

Cruelty is contagious in uncivilized communities. Mr. Conant, a neighbor of Mr. Litch, returned from town one evening in a partial state of intoxication.

---

1   *eighth commandment*   I.e., thou shalt not steal (see Exodus 20.15)
2   *peck*   Unit of measurement equivalent to about eight quarts.
3   *freshet*   Flooding river.

His body servant[1] gave him some offence. He was divested of his clothes, except his shirt, whipped, and tied to a large tree in front of the house. It was a stormy night in winter. The wind blew bitterly cold, and the boughs of the old tree crackled under falling sleet. A member of the family, fearing he would freeze to death, begged that he might be taken down; but the master would not relent. He remained there three hours; and, when he was cut down, he was more dead than alive. Another slave, who stole a pig from this master, to appease his hunger, was terribly flogged. In desperation, he tried to run away. But at the end of two miles, he was so faint with loss of blood, he thought he was dying. He had a wife, and he longed to see her once more. Too sick to walk, he crept back that long distance on his hands and knees. When he reached his master's, it was night. He had not strength to rise and open the gate. He moaned, and tried to call for help. I had a friend living in the same family. At last his cry reached her. She went out and found the prostrate man at the gate. She ran back to the house for assistance, and two men returned with her. They carried him in, and laid him on the floor. The back of his shirt was one clot of blood. By means of lard, my friend loosened it from the raw flesh. She bandaged him, gave him cool drink, and left him to rest. The master said he deserved a hundred more lashes. When his own labor was stolen from him, he had stolen food to appease his hunger. This was his crime.

Another neighbor was a Mrs. Wade. At no hour of the day was there cessation of the lash on her premises. Her labors began with the dawn, and did not cease till long after nightfall. The barn was her particular place of torture. There she lashed the slaves with the might of a man. An old slave of hers once said to me, "It is hell in missis's house. 'Pears I can never get out. Day and night I prays to die."

The mistress died before the old woman, and, when dying, entreated her husband not to permit any one of her slaves to look on her after death. A slave who had nursed her children, and had still a child in her care, watched her chance, and stole with it in her arms to the room where lay her dead mistress. She gazed a while on her, then raised her hand and dealt two blows on her face, saying, as she did so, "The devil is got you *now!*" She forgot that the child was looking on. She had just begun to talk; and she said to her father, "I did see ma, and mammy did strike ma, so," striking her own face with her little hand. The master was startled. He could not imagine how the nurse could obtain access to the room where the corpse lay; for he kept the door locked. He questioned her. She confessed that what the child had said was true, and told how she had procured the key. She was sold to Georgia.

In my childhood I knew a valuable slave, named Charity, and loved her, as all children did. Her young mistress married, and took her to Louisiana. Her

---

1 *body servant* Enslaved person who tended on Mr. Conant personally (as a valet).

little boy, James, was sold to a good sort of master. He became involved in debt, and James was sold again to a wealthy slaveholder, noted for his cruelty. With this man he grew up to manhood, receiving the treatment of a dog. After a severe whipping, to save himself from further infliction of the lash, with which he was threatened, he took to the woods. He was in a most miserable condition—cut by the cowskin,[1] half naked, half starved, and without the means of procuring a crust of bread.

Some weeks after his escape, he was captured, tied, and carried back to his master's plantation. This man considered punishment in his jail, on bread and water, after receiving hundreds of lashes, too mild for the poor slave's offence. Therefore he decided, after the overseer should have whipped him to his satisfaction, to have him placed between the screws of the cotton gin,[2] to stay as long as he had been in the woods. This wretched creature was cut with the whip from his head to his foot, then washed with strong brine, to prevent the flesh from mortifying, and make it heal sooner than it otherwise would. He was then put into the cotton gin, which was screwed down, only allowing him room to turn on his side when he could not lie on his back. Every morning a slave was sent with a piece of bread and bowl of water, which were placed within reach of the poor fellow. The slave was charged, under penalty of severe punishment, not to speak to him.

Four days passed, and the slave continued to carry the bread and water. On the second morning, he found the bread gone, but the water untouched. When he had been in the press four days and five nights, the slave informed his master that the water had not been used for four mornings, and that a horrible stench came from the gin house. The overseer was sent to examine into it. When the press was unscrewed, the dead body was found partly eaten by rats and vermin. Perhaps the rats that devoured his bread had gnawed him before life was extinct. Poor Charity! Grandmother and I often asked each other how her affectionate heart would bear the news, if she should ever hear of the murder of her son. We had known her husband, and knew that James was like him in manliness and intelligence. These were the qualities that made it so hard for him to be a plantation slave. They put him into a rough box, and buried him with less feeling than would have been manifested for an old house dog. Nobody asked any questions. He was a slave; and the feeling was that the master had a right to do what he pleased with his own property. And what did *he* care for the value of a slave? He had hundreds of them. When they had finished their daily toil, they must hurry to eat their little morsels, and be ready to extinguish their pine knots[3] before nine o'clock, when the overseer went his

---

1   cowskin   I.e., whip.
2   cotton gin   Machine used to separate the cotton wool from the seeds.
3   pine knots   Rounded, dense pieces of pine burned as torches to provide light.

patrol rounds. He entered every cabin, to see that men and their wives had gone to bed together, lest the men, from over-fatigue, should fall asleep in the chimney corner, and remain there till the morning horn called them to their daily task. Women are considered of no value, unless they continually increase their owner's stock.[1] They are put on a par with animals. This same master shot a woman through the head, who had run away and been brought back to him. No one called him to account for it. If a slave resisted being whipped, the bloodhounds were unpacked, and set upon him, to tear his flesh from his bones. The master who did these things was highly educated, and styled a perfect gentleman. He also boasted the name and standing of a Christian, though Satan never had a truer follower.

I could tell of more slaveholders as cruel as those I have described. They are not exceptions to the general rule. I do not say there are no humane slave-holders. Such characters do exist, notwithstanding the hardening influences around them. But they are "like angels' visits—few and far between."[2]

I knew a young lady who was one of these rare specimens. She was an orphan, and inherited as slaves a woman and her six children. Their father was a free man. They had a comfortable home of their own, parents and children living together. The mother and eldest daughter served their mistress during the day, and at night returned to their dwelling, which was on the premises. The young lady was very pious, and there was some reality in her religion. She taught her slaves to lead pure lives, and wished them to enjoy the fruit of their own industry. *Her* religion was not a garb put on for Sunday, and laid aside till Sunday returned again. The eldest daughter of the slave mother was promised in marriage to a free man; and the day before the wedding this good mistress emancipated her, in order that her marriage might have the sanction of *law*.[3]

Report said that this young lady cherished an unrequited affection for a man who had resolved to marry for wealth. In the course of time a rich uncle of hers died. He left six thousand dollars to his two sons by a colored woman, and the remainder of his property to this orphan niece. The metal soon attracted the magnet. The lady and her weighty purse became his. She offered to manumit her slaves—telling them that her marriage might make unexpected changes in their destiny, and she wished to insure their happiness. They refused to take their freedom, saying that she had always been their best friend, and they could not be so happy anywhere as with her. I was not surprised. I had often seen them in their comfortable home, and thought that

---

1   *increase ... stock*   I.e., have children that would be born into slavery.

2   *like angels' ... far between*   See Thomas Campbell's poem "The Pleasures of Hope" (1799), lines 223–24: "What though my winged hours of bliss have been, / Like angel visits, few and far between."

3   *marriage ... law*   Marriages between enslaved people were not legally recognized in slave states, so in order for this marriage to be legally valid, both parties would need to be free.

the whole town did not contain a happier family. They had never felt slavery; and, when it was too late, they were convinced of its reality.

When the new master claimed this family as his property, the father became furious, and went to his mistress for protection. "I can do nothing for you now, Harry," said she. "I no longer have the power I had a week ago. I have succeeded in obtaining the freedom of your wife; but I cannot obtain it for your children." The unhappy father swore that nobody should take his children from him. He concealed them in the woods for some days; but they were discovered and taken. The father was put in jail, and the two oldest boys sold to Georgia. One little girl, too young to be of service to her master, was left with the wretched mother. The other three were carried to their master's plantation. The eldest soon became a mother; and, when the slaveholder's wife looked at the babe, she wept bitterly. She knew that her own husband had violated the purity she had so carefully inculcated. She had a second child by her master, and then he sold her and his offspring to his brother. She bore two children to the brother, and was sold again. The next sister went crazy. The life she was compelled to lead drove her mad. The third one became the mother of five daughters. Before the birth of the fourth the pious mistress died. To the last, she rendered every kindness to the slaves that her unfortunate circumstances permitted. She passed away peacefully, glad to close her eyes on a life which had been made so wretched by the man she loved.

This man squandered the fortune he had received, and sought to retrieve his affairs by a second marriage; but, having retired after a night of drunken debauch, he was found dead in the morning. He was called a good master; for he fed and clothed his slaves better than most masters, and the lash was not heard on his plantation so frequently as on many others. Had it not been for slavery, he would have been a better man, and his wife a happier woman.

No pen can give an adequate description of the all-pervading corruption produced by slavery. The slave girl is reared in an atmosphere of licentiousness and fear. The lash and the foul talk of her master and his sons are her teachers. When she is fourteen or fifteen, her owner, or his sons, or the overseer, or perhaps all of them, begin to bribe her with presents. If these fail to accomplish their purpose, she is whipped or starved into submission to their will. She may have had religious principles inculcated by some pious mother or grandmother, or some good mistress; she may have a lover, whose good opinion and peace of mind are dear to her heart; or the profligate men who have power over her may be exceedingly odious to her. But resistance is hopeless.

> The poor worm
> Shall prove her contest vain. Life's little day
> Shall pass, and she is gone![1]

---

1 *The poor worm ... she is gone* These lines are drawn from William Mason's dramatic poem *Elfrida* (1752).

The slaveholder's sons are, of course, vitiated, even while boys, by the unclean influences everywhere around them. Nor do the master's daughters always escape. Severe retributions sometimes come upon him for the wrongs he does to the daughters of the slaves. The white daughters early hear their parents quarrelling about some female slave. Their curiosity is excited, and they soon learn the cause. They are attended by the young slave girls whom their father has corrupted; and they hear such talk as should never meet youthful ears, or any other ears. They know that the women slaves are subject to their father's authority in all things; and in some cases they exercise the same authority over the men slaves. I have myself seen the master of such a household whose head was bowed down in shame; for it was known in the neighborhood that his daughter had selected one of the meanest slaves on his plantation to be the father of his first grandchild. She did not make her advances to her equals, nor even to her father's more intelligent servants. She selected the most brutalized, over whom her authority could be exercised with less fear of exposure. Her father, half frantic with rage, sought to revenge himself on the offending black man; but his daughter, foreseeing the storm that would arise, had given him free papers, and sent him out of the state.

In such cases the infant is smothered, or sent where it is never seen by any who know its history. But if the white parent is the *father*, instead of the mother, the offspring are unblushingly reared for the market. If they are girls, I have indicated plainly enough what will be their inevitable destiny.

You may believe what I say; for I write only that whereof I know. I was twenty-one years in that cage of obscene birds. I can testify, from my own experience and observation, that slavery is a curse to the whites as well as to the blacks. It makes the white fathers cruel and sensual; the sons violent and licentious; it contaminates the daughters, and makes the wives wretched. And as for the colored race, it needs an abler pen than mine to describe the extremity of their sufferings, the depth of their degradation.

Yet few slaveholders seem to be aware of the widespread moral ruin occasioned by this wicked system. Their talk is of blighted cotton crops—not of the blight on their children's souls

If you want to be fully convinced of the abominations of slavery, go on a southern plantation, and call yourself a negro trader. Then there will be no concealment; and you will see and hear things that will seem to you impossible among human beings with immortal souls.

Chapter 10. A Perilous Passage in the Slave Girl's Life

After my lover went away, Dr. Flint contrived a new plan. He seemed to have an idea that my fear of my mistress was his greatest obstacle. In the blandest tones, he told me that he was going to build a small house for me, in a secluded place, four miles away from the town. I shuddered; but I was constrained to listen, while he talked of his intention to give me a home of my own, and to make a lady of me. Hitherto, I had escaped my dreaded fate, by being in the midst of people. My grandmother had already had high words with my master about me. She had told him pretty plainly what she thought of his character, and there was considerable gossip in the neighborhood about our affairs, to which the open-mouthed jealousy of Mrs. Flint contributed not a little. When my master said he was going to build a house for me, and that he could do it with little trouble and expense, I was in hopes something would happen to frustrate his scheme; but I soon heard that the house was actually begun. I vowed before my Maker that I would never enter it. I had rather toil on the plantation from dawn till dark; I had rather live and die in jail, than drag on, from day to day, through such a living death. I was determined that the master, whom I so hated and loathed, who had blighted the prospects of my youth, and made my life a desert, should not, after my long struggle with him, succeed at last in trampling his victim under his feet. I would do anything, everything, for the sake of defeating him. What *could* I do? I thought and thought, till I became desperate, and made a plunge into the abyss.

And now, reader, I come to a period in my unhappy life, which I would gladly forget if I could. The remembrance fills me with sorrow and shame. It pains me to tell you of it; but I have promised to tell you the truth, and I will do it honestly, let it cost me what it may. I will not try to screen myself behind the plea of compulsion from a master; for it was not so. Neither can I plead ignorance or thoughtlessness. For years, my master had done his utmost to pollute my mind with foul images, and to destroy the pure principles inculcated by my grandmother, and the good mistress of my childhood. The influences of slavery had had the same effect on me that they had on other young girls; they had made me prematurely knowing, concerning the evil ways of the world. I know what I did, and I did it with deliberate calculation.

But, O, ye happy women, whose purity has been sheltered from childhood, who have been free to choose the objects of your affection, whose homes are protected by law, do not judge the poor desolate slave girl too severely! If slavery had been abolished, I, also, could have married the man of my choice; I could have had a home shielded by the laws; and I should have been spared the painful task of confessing what I am now about to relate; but all my prospects had been blighted by slavery. I wanted to keep myself pure; and, under the most adverse circumstances, I tried hard to preserve my self-respect; but I was struggling alone in the powerful grasp of the demon Slavery; and the monster proved too strong for me. I felt as if I was forsaken by God and man; as if all my efforts must be frustrated; and I became reckless in my despair.

I have told you that Dr. Flint's persecutions and his wife's jealousy had given rise to some gossip in the neighborhood. Among others, it chanced that a white unmarried gentleman had obtained some knowledge of the circumstances in which I was placed. He knew my grandmother, and often spoke to me in the street. He became interested for me, and asked questions about my master, which I answered in part. He expressed a great deal of sympathy, and a wish to aid me. He constantly sought opportunities to see me, and wrote to me frequently. I was a poor slave girl, only fifteen years old.

So much attention from a superior person was, of course, flattering; for human nature is the same in all. I also felt grateful for his sympathy, and encouraged by his kind words. It seemed to me a great thing to have such a friend. By degrees, a more tender feeling crept into my heart. He was an educated and eloquent gentleman; too eloquent, alas, for the poor slave girl who trusted in him. Of course I saw whither all this was tending. I knew the impassable gulf between us; but to be an object of interest to a man who is not married, and who is not her master, is agreeable to the pride and feelings of a slave, if her miserable situation has left her any pride or sentiment. It seems less degrading to give one's self, than to submit to compulsion. There is something akin to freedom in having a lover who has no control over you, except that which he gains by kindness and attachment. A master may treat you as rudely as he pleases, and you dare not speak; moreover, the wrong does not seem so great with an unmarried man, as with one who has a wife to be made unhappy. There may be sophistry in all this; but the condition of a slave confuses all principles of morality, and, in fact, renders the practice of them impossible.

When I found that my master had actually begun to build the lonely cottage, other feelings mixed with those I have described. Revenge, and calculations of interest, were added to flattered vanity and sincere gratitude for kindness. I knew nothing would enrage Dr. Flint so much as to know that I favored another; and it was something to triumph over my tyrant even in that small way. I thought he would revenge himself by selling me, and I was sure my friend, Mr. Sands, would buy me. He was a man of more generosity and feeling than my master, and I thought my freedom could be easily obtained from him. The crisis of my fate now came so near that I was desperate. I shuddered to think of being the mother of children that should be owned by my old tyrant. I knew that as soon as a new fancy took him, his victims were sold far off to get rid of them; especially if they had children. I had seen several women sold, with his babies at the breast. He never allowed his offspring by slaves to remain long in sight of himself and his wife. Of a man who was not my master I could ask to have my children well supported; and in this case, I felt confident I should obtain the boon. I also felt quite sure that they would be made free. With all these thoughts revolving in my mind, and seeing no other way of escaping the doom I so much dreaded, I made a headlong plunge. Pity me, and pardon me, O virtuous reader! You never knew what it is to be a slave; to be entirely unprotected by law or custom; to have the laws reduce you to the condition of a chattel, entirely subject to the will of another. You never exhausted your ingenuity in avoiding the snares, and eluding the power of a hated tyrant; you never shuddered at the sound of his footsteps, and trembled within hearing of his voice. I know I did wrong. No one can feel it more sensibly than I do. The painful and humiliating memory will haunt me to my dying day. Still, in looking back, calmly, on the events of my life, I feel that the slave woman ought not to be judged by the same standard as others.

The months passed on. I had many unhappy hours. I secretly mourned over the sorrow I was bringing on my grandmother, who had so tried to shield me from harm. I knew that I was the greatest comfort of her old age, and that it was a source of pride to her that I had not degraded myself, like most of the slaves. I wanted to confess to her that I was no longer worthy of her love; but I could not utter the dreaded words.

As for Dr. Flint, I had a feeling of satisfaction and triumph in the thought of telling *him*. From time to time he told me of his intended arrangements, and I was silent. At last, he came and told me the cottage was completed, and ordered me to go to it. I told him I would never enter it. He said, "I have heard enough of such talk as that. You shall go, if you are carried by force; and you shall remain there." I replied, "I will never go there. In a few months I shall be a mother."

He stood and looked at me in dumb amazement, and left the house without a word. I thought I should be happy in my triumph over him. But now that the truth was out, and my relatives would hear of it, I felt wretched. Humble as were their circumstances, they had pride in my good character. Now, how could I look them in the face? My self-respect was gone! I had resolved that I would be virtuous, though I was a slave. I had said, "Let the storm beat! I will brave it till I die." And now, how humiliated I felt!

I went to my grandmother. My lips moved to make confession, but the words stuck in my throat. I sat down in the shade of a tree at her door and began to sew. I think she saw something unusual was the matter with me. The mother of slaves is very watchful. She knows there is no security for her children. After they have entered their teens she lives in daily expectation of trouble. This leads to many questions. If the girl is of a sensitive nature, timidity keeps her from answering truthfully, and this well-meant course has a tendency to drive her from maternal counsels. Presently, in came my mistress, like a mad woman, and accused me concerning her husband. My grandmother, whose suspicions had been previously awakened, believed what she said. She exclaimed, "O Linda! has it come to this? I had rather see you dead than to see you as you now are. You are a disgrace to your dead mother." She tore from my fingers my mother's wedding ring and her silver thimble. "Go away!" she exclaimed, "and never come to my house, again." Her reproaches fell so hot and heavy, that they left me no chance to answer. Bitter tears, such as the eyes never shed but once, were my only answer. I rose from my seat, but fell back again, sobbing. She did not speak to me; but the tears were running down her furrowed cheeks, and they scorched me like fire. She had always been so kind to me! So kind! How I longed to throw myself at her feet, and tell her all the truth! But she had ordered me to go, and never to come there again. After a few minutes, I mustered strength, and started to obey her. With what feelings did I now close that little gate, which I used to open with such an eager hand in my childhood! It closed upon me with a sound I never heard before.

Where could I go? I was afraid to return to my master's. I walked on recklessly, not caring where I went, or what would become of me. When I had gone four or five miles, fatigue compelled me to stop. I sat down on the stump of an old tree. The stars were shining through the boughs above me. How they mocked me, with their bright, calm light! The hours passed by, and as I sat there alone a chilliness and deadly sickness came over me. I sank on the ground. My mind was full of horrid thoughts. I prayed to die; but the prayer was not answered. At last, with great effort I roused myself, and walked some distance further, to the house of a woman who had been a friend of my mother. When I told her why I was there, she spoke soothingly to me; but I could not be comforted. I thought I could bear my shame if I could only be reconciled to my grandmother. I longed to open my heart to her. I thought if she could know the real state of the case, and all I had been bearing for years, she would perhaps judge me less harshly. My friend advised me to send for her. I did so; but days of agonizing suspense passed before she came. Had she utterly forsaken me? No. She came at last. I knelt before her, and told her the things that had poisoned my life; how long I had been persecuted; that I saw no way of escape; and in an hour of extremity I had become desperate. She listened in silence. I told her I would bear anything and do anything, if in time I had hopes of obtaining her forgiveness. I begged of her to pity me, for my dead mother's sake. And she did pity me. She did not say, "I forgive you"; but she looked at me lovingly, with her eyes full of tears. She laid her old hand gently on my head, and murmured, "Poor child! Poor child!"

CHAPTER II. THE NEW TIE TO LIFE

I returned to my good grandmother's house. She had an interview with Mr. Sands. When she asked him why he could not have left her one ewe lamb—whether there were not plenty of slaves who did not care about character—he made no answer; but he spoke kind and encouraging words. He promised to care for my child, and to buy me, be the conditions what they might.

I had not seen Dr. Flint for five days. I had never seen him since I made the avowal to him. He talked of the disgrace I had brought on myself; how I had sinned against my master, and mortified my old grandmother. He intimated that if I had accepted his proposals, he, as a physician, could have saved me from exposure. He even condescended to pity me. Could he have offered wormwood[1] more bitter? He, whose persecutions had been the cause of my sin!

"Linda," said he, "though you have been criminal towards me, I feel for you, and I can pardon you if you obey my wishes. Tell me whether the fellow you wanted to marry is the father of your child. If you deceive me, you shall feel the fires of hell."

I did not feel as proud as I had done. My strongest weapon with him was gone. I was lowered in my own estimation, and had resolved to bear his abuse in silence. But when he spoke contemptuously of the lover who had always treated me honorably; when I remembered that but for him I might have been a virtuous, free, and happy wife, I lost my patience. "I have sinned against God and myself," I replied; "but not against you."

He clinched his teeth, and muttered, "Curse you!" He came towards me, with ill-suppressed rage, and exclaimed, "You obstinate girl! I could grind your bones to powder! You have thrown yourself away on some worthless rascal. You are weak-minded, and have been easily persuaded by those who don't care a straw for you. The future will settle accounts between us. You are blinded now; but hereafter you will be convinced that your master was your best friend. My lenity towards you is a proof of it. I might have punished you in many ways. I might have had you whipped till you fell dead under the lash. But I wanted you to live; I would have bettered your condition. Others cannot do it. You are my slave. Your mistress, disgusted by your conduct, forbids you to return to the house; therefore I leave you here for the present; but I shall see you often. I will call tomorrow."

He came with frowning brows, that showed a dissatisfied state of mind. After asking about my health, he inquired whether my board was paid, and who visited me. He then went on to say that he had neglected his duty; that

---

1 *wormwood* Bitter-tasting herb.

as a physician there were certain things that he ought to have explained to me. Then followed talk such as would have made the most shameless blush. He ordered me to stand up before him. I obeyed. "I command you," said he, "to tell me whether the father of your child is white or black." I hesitated. "Answer me this instant!" he exclaimed. I did answer. He sprang upon me like a wolf, and grabbed my arm as if he would have broken it. "Do you love him?" said he, in a hissing tone.

"I am thankful that I do not despise him," I replied.

He raised his hand to strike me; but it fell again. I don't know what arrested the blow. He sat down, with lips tightly compressed. At last he spoke. "I came here," said he, "to make you a friendly proposition; but your ingratitude chafes me beyond endurance. You turn aside all my good intentions towards you. I don't know what it is that keeps me from killing you." Again he rose, as if he had a mind to strike me.

But he resumed. "On one condition I will forgive your insolence and crime. You must henceforth have no communication of any kind with the father of your child. You must not ask anything from him, or receive anything from him. I will take care of you and your child. You had better promise this at once, and not wait till you are deserted by him. This is the last act of mercy I shall show towards you."

I said something about being unwilling to have my child supported by a man who had cursed it and me also. He rejoined, that a woman who had sunk to my level had no right to expect anything else. He asked, for the last time, would I accept his kindness? I answered that I would not.

"Very well," said he; "then take the consequences of your wayward course. Never look to me for help. You are my slave, and shall always be my slave. I will never sell you, that you may depend upon."

Hope died away in my heart as he closed the door after him. I had calculated that in his rage he would sell me to a slave-trader; and I knew the father of my child was on the watch to buy me.

About this time my uncle Phillip was expected to return from a voyage. The day before his departure I had officiated as bridesmaid to a young friend. My heart was then ill at ease, but my smiling countenance did not betray it. Only a year had passed; but what fearful changes it had wrought! My heart had grown gray in misery. Lives that flash in sunshine, and lives that are born in tears, receive their hue from circumstances. None of us know what a year may bring forth.

I felt no joy when they told me my uncle had come. He wanted to see me, though he knew what had happened. I shrank from him at first; but at last consented that he should come to my room. He received me as he always had done. O, how my heart smote me when I felt his tears on my burning cheeks!

The words of my grandmother came to my mind—"Perhaps your mother and father are taken from the evil days to come." My disappointed heart could now praise God that it was so. But why, thought I, did my relatives ever cherish hopes for me? What was there to save me from the usual fate of slave girls? Many more beautiful and more intelligent than I had experienced a similar fate, or a far worse one. How could they hope that I should escape?

My uncle's stay was short, and I was not sorry for it. I was too ill in mind and body to enjoy my friends as I had done. For some weeks I was unable to leave my bed. I could not have any doctor but my master, and I would not have him sent for. At last, alarmed by my increasing illness, they sent for him. I was very weak and nervous; and as soon as he entered the room, I began to scream. They told him my state was very critical. He had no wish to hasten me out of the world, and he withdrew.

When my babe was born, they said it was premature. It weighed only four pounds; but God let it live. I heard the doctor say I could not survive till morning. I had often prayed for death; but now I did not want to die, unless my child could die too. Many weeks passed before I was able to leave my bed. I was a mere wreck of my former self. For a year there was scarcely a day when I was free from chills and fever. My babe also was sickly. His little limbs were often racked with pain. Dr. Flint continued his visits, to look after my health; and he did not fail to remind me that my child was an addition to his stock of slaves.

I felt too feeble to dispute with him, and listened to his remarks in silence. His visits were less frequent; but his busy spirit could not remain quiet. He employed my brother in his office, and he was made the medium of frequent notes and messages to me. William was a bright lad, and of much use to the doctor. He had learned to put up medicines, to leech, cup, and bleed.[1] He had taught himself to read and spell. I was proud of my brother; and the old doctor suspected as much. One day, when I had not seen him for several weeks, I heard his steps approaching the door. I dreaded the encounter, and hid myself. He inquired for me, of course; but I was nowhere to be found. He went to his office, and despatched William with a note. The color mounted to my brother's face when he gave it to me; and he said, "Don't you hate me, Linda, for bringing you these things?" I told him I could not blame him; he was a slave, and obliged to obey his master's will. The note ordered me to come to his office. I went. He demanded to know where I was when he called. I told him I was at home. He flew into a passion, and said

---

1 *put up medicines* Prepare medicines; *leech* Use leeches for blood-letting, a process that doctors for thousands of years thought aided in curing many different conditions; *cup* Use of a heated cup in blood-letting that acted as a vacuum to extract more blood; *bleed* Conduct the process of blood-letting, either by leech or by lancet.

he knew better. Then he launched out upon his usual themes—my crimes against him, and my ingratitude for his forbearance. The laws were laid down to me anew, and I was dismissed. I felt humiliated that my brother should stand by, and listen to such language as would be addressed only to a slave. Poor boy! He was powerless to defend me; but I saw the tears, which he vainly strove to keep back. This manifestation of feeling irritated the doctor. William could do nothing to please him. One morning he did not arrive at the office so early as usual; and that circumstance afforded his master an opportunity to vent his spleen. He was put in jail. The next day my brother sent a trader to the doctor, with a request to be sold. His master was greatly incensed at what he called his insolence. He said he had put him there to reflect upon his bad conduct, and he certainly was not giving any evidence of repentance. For two days he harassed himself to find somebody to do his office work; but everything went wrong without William. He was released, and ordered to take his old stand,[1] with many threats, if he was not careful about his future behavior.

As the months passed on, my boy improved in health. When he was a year old, they called him beautiful. The little vine was taking deep root in my existence, though its clinging fondness excited a mixture of love and pain. When I was most sorely oppressed I found a solace in his smiles. I loved to watch his infant slumbers; but always there was a dark cloud over my enjoyment. I could never forget that he was a slave. Sometimes I wished that he might die in infancy. God tried me. My darling became very ill. The bright eyes grew dull, and the little feet and hands were so icy cold that I thought death had already touched them. I had prayed for his death, but never so earnestly as I now prayed for his life; and my prayer was heard. Alas, what mockery it is for a slave mother to try to pray back her dying child to life! Death is better than slavery. It was a sad thought that I had no name to give my child. His father caressed him and treated him kindly, whenever he had a chance to see him. He was not unwilling that he should bear his name; but he had no legal claim to it; and if I had bestowed it upon him, my master would have regarded it as a new crime, a new piece of insolence, and would, perhaps, revenge it on the boy. O, the serpent of Slavery has many and poisonous fangs!

1 *stand* Position.

CHAPTER 12. FEAR OF INSURRECTION

Not far from this time Nat Turner's insurrection[1] broke out; and the news threw our town into great commotion. Strange that they should be alarmed when their slaves were so "contented and happy"! But so it was.

It was always the custom to have a muster[2] every year. On that occasion every white man shouldered his musket. The citizens[3] and the so-called country gentlemen wore military uniforms. The poor whites took their places in the ranks in every-day dress, some without shoes, some without hats. This grand occasion had already passed; and when the slaves were told there was to be another muster, they were surprised and rejoiced. Poor creatures! They thought it was going to be a holiday. I was informed of the true state of affairs, and imparted it to the few I could trust. Most gladly would I have proclaimed it to every slave; but I dared not. All could not be relied on. Mighty is the power of the torturing lash.

By sunrise, people were pouring in from every quarter within twenty miles of the town. I knew the houses were to be searched; and I expected it would be done by country bullies and the poor whites. I knew nothing annoyed them so much as to see colored people living in comfort and respectability; so I made arrangements for them with especial care. I arranged everything in my grandmother's house as neatly as possible. I put white quilts on the beds, and decorated some of the rooms with flowers. When all was arranged, I sat down at the window to watch. Far as my eye could reach, it rested on a motley crowd of soldiers. Drums and fifes were discoursing[4] martial music. The men were divided into companies of sixteen, each headed by a captain. Orders were given, and the wild scouts rushed in every direction, wherever a colored face was to be found.

It was a grand opportunity for the low whites, who had no negroes of their own to scourge. They exulted in such a chance to exercise a little brief authority, and show their subserviency to the slaveholders; not reflecting that the power which trampled on the colored people also kept themselves in poverty, ignorance, and moral degradation. Those who never witnessed such scenes

---

1 *Nat Turner's insurrection*   In 1831, the enslaved preacher Nat Turner led an antislavery rebellion in Virginia; at least fifty-one white people were killed, and the rebellion was suppressed after four days of fighting, after which over a hundred black people were killed in retaliation. The revolt was widely depicted as a massacre in Southern media, and the events led to new restrictions on education for black people as well as to rules preventing enslaved people from meeting without a white person present.

2 *muster*   Gathering or roll-call for a militia unit, in order to count the number of persons available for potential military service.

3 *citizens*   Likely a reference to those who were entitled to vote—men in the community who paid taxes or owned property.

4 *fifes*   Small flutes that are played along with drums in military music; *discoursing*   Pouring forth.

can hardly believe what I know was inflicted at this time on innocent men, women, and children, against whom there was not the slightest ground for suspicion. Colored people and slaves who lived in remote parts of the town suffered in an especial manner. In some cases the searchers scattered powder and shot among their clothes, and then sent other parties to find them, and bring them forward as proof that they were plotting insurrection. Everywhere men, women, and children were whipped till the blood stood in puddles at their feet. Some received five hundred lashes; others were tied hands and feet, and tortured with a bucking paddle,[1] which blisters the skin terribly. The dwellings of the colored people, unless they happened to be protected by some influential white person, who was nigh at hand, were robbed of clothing and everything else the marauders thought worth carrying away. All day long these unfeeling wretches went round, like a troop of demons, terrifying and tormenting the helpless. At night, they formed themselves into patrol bands, and went wherever they chose among the colored people, acting out their brutal will. Many women hid themselves in woods and swamps, to keep out of their way. If any of the husbands or fathers told of these outrages, they were tied up to the public whipping post, and cruelly scourged for telling lies about white men. The consternation was universal. No two people that had the slightest tinge of color in their faces dared to be seen talking together.

I entertained no positive fears about our household, because we were in the midst of white families who would protect us. We were ready to receive the soldiers whenever they came. It was not long before we heard the tramp of feet and the sound of voices. The door was rudely pushed open; and in they tumbled, like a pack of hungry wolves. They snatched at everything within their reach. Every box, trunk, closet, and corner underwent a thorough examination. A box in one of the drawers containing some silver change was eagerly pounced upon. When I stepped forward to take it from them, one of the soldiers turned and said angrily, "What d'ye foller us fur? D'ye s'pose white folks is come to steal?"

I replied, "You have come to search; but you have searched that box, and I will take it, if you please."

At that moment I saw a white gentleman who was friendly to us; and I called to him, and asked him to have the goodness to come in and stay till the search was over. He readily complied. His entrance into the house brought in the captain of the company, whose business it was to guard the outside of the house, and see that none of the inmates left it. This officer was Mr. Litch, the wealthy slaveholder whom I mentioned, in the account of neighboring

---

1   *bucking paddle*   Wooden paddle—also called a "spanking paddle"—with holes in it, designed to create blisters when repeatedly used to hit someone.

planters, as being notorious for his cruelty. He felt above soiling his hands with the search. He merely gave orders; and, if a bit of writing was discovered, it was carried to him by his ignorant followers, who were unable to read.

My grandmother had a large trunk of bedding and table cloths. When that was opened, there was a great shout of surprise; and one exclaimed, "Where'd the damned niggers git all dis sheet an' table clarf?"

My grandmother, emboldened by the presence of our white protector, said, "You may be sure we didn't pilfer 'em from *your* houses."

"Look here, mammy," said a grim-looking fellow without any coat, "you seem to feel mighty gran' 'cause you got all them 'ere fixens. White folks ough-ter have 'em all."

His remarks were interrupted by a chorus of voices shouting, "We's got 'em! We's got 'em! Dis 'ere yaller gal's[1] got letters!"

There was a general rush for the supposed letter, which, upon examination, proved to be some verses written to me by a friend. In packing away my things, I had overlooked them. When their captain informed them of their contents, they seemed much disappointed. He inquired of me who wrote them. I told him it was one of my friends. "Can you read them?" he asked. When I told him I could, he swore, and raved, and tore the paper into bits. "Bring me all your letters!" said he, in a commanding tone. I told him I had none. "Don't be afraid," he continued, in an insinuating way. "Bring them all to me. Nobody shall do you any harm." Seeing I did not move to obey him, his pleasant tone changed to oaths and threats. "Who writes to you? half free niggers?" inquired he. I replied, "O, no; most of my letters are from white people. Some request me to burn them after they are read, and some I destroy without reading."

An exclamation of surprise from some of the company put a stop to our conversation. Some silver spoons which ornamented an old-fashioned buffet had just been discovered. My grandmother was in the habit of preserving fruit for many ladies in the town, and of preparing suppers for parties; con-sequently she had many jars of preserves. The closet that contained these was next invaded, and the contents tasted. One of them, who was helping himself freely, tapped his neighbor on the shoulder, and said, "Wal done! Don't wonder de niggers want to kill all de white folks, when dey live on 'sarves" [meaning preserves]. I stretched out my hand to take the jar, saying, "You were not sent here to search for sweetmeats."

"And what *were* we sent for?" said the captain, bristling up to me. I evaded the question.

The search of the house was completed, and nothing found to condemn us. They next proceeded to the garden, and knocked about every bush and vine

---

1 *yaller gal* I.e., mulatto girl.

with no better success. The captain called his men together, and, after a short consultation, the order to march was given. As they passed out of the gate, the captain turned back, and pronounced a malediction on the house. He said it ought to be burned to the ground, and each of its inmates receive thirty-nine lashes. We came out of this affair very fortunately; not losing anything except some wearing apparel.

Towards evening the turbulence increased. The soldiers, stimulated by drink, committed still greater cruelties. Shrieks and shouts continually rent the air. Not daring to go to the door, I peeped under the window curtain. I saw a mob dragging along a number of colored people, each white man, with his musket upraised, threatening instant death if they did not stop their shrieks. Among the prisoners was a respectable old colored minister. They had found a few parcels of shot in his house, which his wife had for years used to balance her scales. For this they were going to shoot him on Court House Green. What a spectacle was that for a civilized country! A rabble, staggering under intoxication, assuming to be the administrators of justice!

The better class of the community exerted their influence to save the innocent, persecuted people; and in several instances they succeeded, by keeping them shut up in jail till the excitement abated. At last the white citizens found that their own property was not safe from the lawless rabble they had summoned to protect them. They rallied[1] the drunken swarm, drove them back into the country, and set a guard over the town.

The next day, the town patrols were commissioned to search colored people that lived out of the city; and the most shocking outrages were committed with perfect impunity. Every day for a fortnight, if I looked out, I saw horsemen with some poor panting negro tied to their saddles, and compelled by the lash to keep up with their speed, till they arrived at the jail yard. Those who had been whipped too unmercifully to walk were washed with brine, tossed into a cart, and carried to jail. One black man, who had not fortitude to endure scourging, promised to give information about the conspiracy. But it turned out that he knew nothing at all. He had not even heard the name of Nat Turner. The poor fellow had, however, made up a story, which augmented his own sufferings and those of the colored people.

The day patrol continued for some weeks, and at sundown a night guard was substituted. Nothing at all was proved against the colored people, bond or free. The wrath of the slaveholders was somewhat appeased by the capture of Nat Turner. The imprisoned were released. The slaves were sent to their masters, and the free were permitted to return to their ravaged homes. Visiting was strictly forbidden on the plantations. The slaves begged the privilege of again

---

1   *rallied*   Brought back together.

meeting at their little church in the woods, with their burying ground around it. It was built by the colored people, and they had no higher happiness than to meet there and sing hymns together, and pour out their hearts in spontaneous prayer. Their request was denied, and the church was demolished. They were permitted to attend the white churches, a certain portion of the galleries being appropriated to their use. There, when everybody else had partaken of the communion, and the benediction had been pronounced, the minister said, "Come down, now, my colored friends." They obeyed the summons, and partook of the bread and wine, in commemoration of the meek and lowly Jesus, who said, "God is your Father, and all ye are brethren."

CHAPTER 13. THE CHURCH AND SLAVERY

After the alarm caused by Nat Turner's insurrection had subsided, the slaveholders came to the conclusion that it would be well to give the slaves enough of religious instruction to keep them from murdering their masters. The Episcopal clergyman offered to hold a separate service on Sundays for their benefit. His colored members were very few, and also very respectable—a fact which I presume had some weight with him. The difficulty was to decide on a suitable place for them to worship. The Methodist and Baptist churches admitted them in the afternoon, but their carpets and cushions were not so costly as those at the Episcopal church. It was at last decided that they should meet at the house of a free colored man, who was a member.

I was invited to attend, because I could read. Sunday evening came, and, trusting to the cover of night, I ventured out. I rarely ventured out by daylight, for I always went with fear, expecting at every turn to encounter Dr. Flint, who was sure to turn me back, or order me to his office to inquire where I got my bonnet, or some other article of dress. When the Rev. Mr. Pike came, there were some twenty persons present. The reverend gentleman knelt in prayer, then seated himself, and requested all present, who could read, to open their books, while he gave out the portions he wished them to repeat or respond to.

His text was, "Servants, be obedient to them that are your masters according to the flesh, with fear and trembling, in singleness of your heart, as unto Christ."[1]

---

1   *Servants ... Christ* Ephesians 6.5, one of the passages in the Bible that was commonly cited in support of slavery. The full passage (some of which is referenced in the passage that follows) reads thus: "Servants, be obedient to them that are your masters according to the flesh, with fear and trembling, in singleness of your heart, as unto Christ; Not with eyeservice, as menpleasers; but as the servants of Christ, doing the will of God from the heart; With good will doing service, as to the Lord, and not to men: Knowing that whatsoever good thing any man doeth, the same shall he receive of the Lord, whether he be bond or free. And, ye masters, do the same things unto them, forbearing threatening: knowing that your Master also is in heaven; neither is there respect of persons with him" (6.5–9).

Pious Mr. Pike brushed up his hair till it stood upright, and, in deep, solemn tones, began: "Hearken, ye servants! Give strict heed unto my words. You are rebellious sinners. Your hearts are filled with all manner of evil. 'Tis the devil who tempts you. God is angry with you, and will surely punish you, if you don't forsake your wicked ways. You that live in town are eye-servants behind your master's back. Instead of serving your masters faithfully, which is pleasing in the sight of your heavenly Master, you are idle, and shirk your work. God sees you. You tell lies. God hears you. Instead of being engaged in worshipping him, you are hidden away somewhere, feasting on your master's substance; tossing coffee-grounds with some wicked fortuneteller,[1] or cutting cards with another old hag. Your masters may not find you out, but God sees you, and will punish you. O, the depravity of your hearts! When your master's work is done, are you quietly together, thinking of the goodness of God to such sinful creatures? No; you are quarrelling, and tying up little bags of roots to bury under the door-steps to poison each other with. God sees you. You men steal away to every grog shop to sell your master's corn, that you may buy rum to drink. God sees you. You sneak into the back streets, or among the bushes, to pitch coppers.[2] Although your masters may not find you out, God sees you; and he will punish you. You must forsake your sinful ways, and be faithful servants. Obey your old master and your young master—your old mistress and your young mistress. If you disobey your earthly master, you offend your heavenly Master. You must obey God's commandments. When you go from here, don't stop at the corners of the streets to talk, but go directly home, and let your master and mistress see that you have come."

The benediction was pronounced. We went home, highly amused at brother Pike's gospel teaching, and we determined to hear him again. I went the next Sabbath evening, and heard pretty much a repetition of the last discourse. At the close of the meeting, Mr. Pike informed us that he found it very inconvenient to meet at the friend's house, and he should be glad to see us, every Sunday evening, at his own kitchen.

I went home with the feeling that I had heard the Reverend Mr. Pike for the last time. Some of his members repaired to his house, and found that the kitchen sported two tallow candles;[3] the first time, I am sure, since its present occupant owned it, for the servants never had anything but pine knots. It was

---

1   *tossing ... fortuneteller*   I.e., studying the patterns made by coffee grounds at the bottom of a cup in order to tell a person's fortune (much in the way that some fortune-tellers read tea leaves). Fortune telling was seen by many white Christians as a sinful practice.

2   *pitch coppers*   Also known as "pitching pennies," this is a game in which players throw pennies toward a wall, and the penny that lands closest to the wall wins.

3   *tallow candles*   Cheap candles made of animal fat. Tallow candles tend to smoke and produce wavering light.

so long before the reverend gentleman descended from his comfortable parlor that the slaves left, and went to enjoy a Methodist shout.[1] They never seem so happy as when shouting and singing at religious meetings. Many of them are sincere, and nearer to the gate of heaven than sanctimonious Mr. Pike, and other long-faced Christians, who see wounded Samaritans, and pass by on the other side.[2]

The slaves generally compose their own songs and hymns, and they do not trouble their heads much about the measure. They often sing the following verses:

> Old Satan is one busy ole man;
> He rolls dem blocks all in my way;
> But Jesus is my bosom friend;
> He rolls dem blocks away.
>
> If I had died when I was young,
> Den how my stam'ring tongue would have sung;
> But I am ole, and now I stand
> A narrow chance for to tread dat heavenly land.

I well remember one occasion when I attended a Methodist class meeting.[3] I went with a burdened spirit, and happened to sit next a poor, bereaved mother, whose heart was still heavier than mine. The class leader was the town constable—a man who bought and sold slaves, who whipped his brethren and sisters of the church at the public whipping post, in jail or out of jail. He was ready to perform that Christian office anywhere for fifty cents. This white-faced, black-hearted brother came near us, and said to the stricken woman, "Sister, can't you tell us how the Lord deals with your soul? Do you love him as you did formerly?"

She rose to her feet, and said, in piteous tones, "My Lord and Master, help me! My load is more than I can bear. God has hid himself from me, and I am left in darkness and misery." Then, striking her breast, she continued, "I can't tell you what is in here! They've got all my children. Last week they took the last one. God only knows where they've sold her. They let me have her sixteen

---

1   *Methodist shout*   Part of a Methodist prayer meeting in which a ring of people move or dance in a circle, clapping hands, singing, and praying. Enslaved people would sometimes gather in the woods at night for shouts.

2   *wounded ... side*   See the Parable of the Good Samaritan, Luke 10.25–37, particularly Luke 10.31: "And by chance there came down a certain priest that way: and when he saw him [the wounded man], he passed by on the other side."

3   *class meeting*   Gathering of a subdivision of a Methodist congregation.

years, and then—O! O! Pray for her brothers and sisters! I've got nothing to live for now. God make my time short!"

She sat down, quivering in every limb. I saw that constable class leader become crimson in the face with suppressed laughter, while he held up his handkerchief, that those who were weeping for the poor woman's calamity might not see his merriment. Then, with assumed gravity, he said to the bereaved mother, "Sister, pray to the Lord that every dispensation of his divine will may be sanctified to the good of your poor needy soul!"

The congregation struck up a hymn, and sung as though they were as free as the birds that warbled round us—

> Ole Satan thought he had a mighty aim;
> He missed my soul, and caught my sins.
> Cry Amen, cry Amen, cry Amen to God!
>
> He took my sins upon his back;
> Went muttering and grumbling down to hell.
> Cry Amen, cry Amen, cry Amen to God!
>
> Ole Satan's church is here below.
> Up to God's free church I hope to go.
> Cry Amen, cry Amen, cry Amen to God!

Precious are such moments to the poor slaves. If you were to hear them at such times, you might think they were happy. But can that hour of singing and shouting sustain them through the dreary week, toiling without wages, under constant dread of the lash?

The Episcopal clergyman, who, ever since my earliest recollection, had been a sort of god among the slaveholders, concluded, as his family was large, that he must go where money was more abundant. A very different clergyman took his place. The change was very agreeable to the colored people, who said, "God has sent us a good man this time." They loved him, and their children followed him for a smile or a kind word. Even the slaveholders felt his influence. He brought to the rectory five slaves. His wife taught them to read and write, and to be useful to her and themselves. As soon as he was settled, he turned his attention to the needy slaves around him. He urged upon his parishioners the duty of having a meeting expressly for them every Sunday, with a sermon adapted to their comprehension. After much argument and importunity, it was finally agreed that they might occupy the gallery of the church on Sunday evenings. Many colored people, hitherto unaccustomed to attend church, now gladly went to hear the gospel preached. The sermons were simple, and they understood them. Moreover, it was the first time they had ever been addressed as human beings. It was not long before his white parishioners began to be dissatisfied. He was accused of preaching better sermons to the negroes than he did to them. He honestly confessed that he bestowed more pains upon those sermons than upon any others; for the slaves were reared in such ignorance that it was a difficult task to adapt himself to their comprehension. Dissensions arose in the parish. Some wanted he should preach to them in the evening, and to the slaves in the afternoon. In the midst of these disputings his wife died, after a very short illness. Her slaves gathered round her dying bed in great sorrow. She said, "I have tried to do you good and promote your happiness; and if I have failed, it has not been for want[1] of interest in your welfare. Do not weep for me; but prepare for the new duties that lie before you. I leave you all free. May we meet in a better world." Her liberated slaves were sent away, with funds to establish them comfortably. The colored people will long bless the memory of that truly Christian woman. Soon after her death her husband preached his farewell sermon, and many tears were shed at his departure.

Several years after, he passed through our town and preached to his former congregation. In his afternoon sermon he addressed the colored people. "My friends," said he, "it affords me great happiness to have an opportunity of speaking to you again. For two years I have been striving to do something for the colored people of my own parish; but nothing is yet accomplished. I have not even preached a sermon to them. Try to live according to the word of God, my friends. Your skin is darker than mine; but God judges men by their hearts, not by the color of their skins." This was strange doctrine from a southern pulpit. It was very offensive to slaveholders. They said he and his wife had made fools of their slaves, and that he preached like a fool to the negroes.

I knew an old black man, whose piety and childlike trust in God were beautiful to witness. At fifty-three years old he joined the Baptist church. He had a most earnest desire to learn to read. He thought he should know how to serve God better if he could only read the Bible. He came to me, and begged me to teach him. He said he could not pay me, for he had no money, but he would bring me nice fruit when the season for it came. I asked him if he didn't know it was contrary to law; and that slaves were whipped and imprisoned for teaching each other to read. This brought the tears into his eyes. "Don't be troubled uncle Fred," said I. "I have no thoughts of refusing to teach you. I only told you of the law, that you might know the danger, and be on your guard." He thought he could plan to come three times a week without its being suspected. I selected a quiet nook, where no intruder was likely to penetrate, and there I taught him his A, B, C. Considering his age, his progress was astonishing.

---

1 *want* Lack.

As soon as he could spell in two syllables he wanted to spell out words in the Bible. The happy smile that illuminated his face put joy into my heart. After spelling out a few words, he paused, and said, "Honey, it 'pears when I can read dis good book I shall be nearer to God. White man is got all de sense. He can larn easy. It ain't easy for ole black man like me. I only wants to read dis book, dat I may know how to live, den I hab no fear 'bout dying."

I tried to encourage him by speaking of the rapid progress he had made. "Hab patience, child," he replied. "I larns slow."

I had no need of patience. His gratitude, and the happiness I imparted, were more than a recompense for all my trouble.

At the end of six months he had read through the New Testament, and could find any text in it. One day, when he had recited unusually well, I said, "Uncle Fred, how do you manage to get your lessons so well?"

"Lord bress you, chile," he replied. "You nebber gibs me a lesson dat I don't pray to God to help me to understan' what I spells and what I reads. And he does help me, chile. Bress his holy name!"

There are thousands, who, like good uncle Fred, are thirsting for the water of life; but the law forbids it, and the churches withhold it. They send the Bible to heathen abroad, and neglect the heathen at home. I am glad that missionaries go out to the dark corners of the earth; but I ask them not to overlook the dark corners at home. Talk to American slaveholders as you talk to savages in Africa. Tell *them* it is wrong to traffic in men. Tell them it is sinful to sell their own children, and atrocious to violate their own daughters. Tell them that all men are brethren, and that man has no right to shut out the light of knowledge from his brother. Tell them they are answerable to God for sealing up the Fountain of Life from souls that are thirsting for it.

There are men who would gladly undertake such missionary work as this; but, alas! their number is small. They are hated by the south, and would be driven from its soil, or dragged to prison to die, as others have been before them. The field is ripe for the harvest, and awaits the reapers. Perhaps the great grandchildren of uncle Fred may have freely imparted to them the divine treasures, which he sought by stealth, at the risk of the prison and the scourge.

Are doctors of divinity blind, or are they hypocrites? I suppose some are the one, and some the other; but I think if they felt the interest in the poor and the lowly, that they ought to feel, they would not be so *easily* blinded. A clergyman who goes to the south, for the first time, has usually some feeling, however vague, that slavery is wrong. The slaveholder suspects this, and plays his game accordingly. He makes himself as agreeable as possible; talks on theology, and other kindred topics. The reverend gentleman is asked to invoke a blessing on a table loaded with luxuries. After dinner he walks round the premises, and sees the beautiful groves and flowering vines, and the comfortable huts of favored household slaves. The southerner invites him to talk with these slaves. He asks them if they want to be free, and they say, "O, no, massa." This is sufficient to satisfy him. He comes home to publish a "South-Side View of Slavery,"[1] and to complain of the exaggerations of abolitionists. He assures people that he has been to the south, and seen slavery for himself; that it is a beautiful "patriarchal institution"; that the slaves don't want their freedom; that they have hallelujah meetings, and other religious privileges.

What does *he* know of the half-starved wretches toiling from dawn till dark on the plantations? of mothers shrieking for their children, torn from their arms by slave traders? of young girls dragged down into moral filth? of pools of blood around the whipping post? of hounds trained to tear human flesh? of men screwed into cotton gins to die? The slaveholder showed him none of these things, and the slaves dared not tell of them if he had asked them.

There is a great difference between Christianity and religion at the south. If a man goes to the communion table, and pays money into the treasury of the church, no matter if it be the price of blood, he is called religious. If a pastor has offspring by a woman not his wife, the church dismiss him, if she is a white woman; but if she is colored, it does not hinder his continuing to be their good shepherd.

When I was told that Dr. Flint had joined the Episcopal church, I was much surprised. I supposed that religion had a purifying effect on the character of men; but the worst persecutions I endured from him were after he was a communicant. The conversation of the doctor, the day after he had been confirmed, certainly gave me no indication that he had "renounced the devil and all his works."[2] In answer to some of his usual talk, I reminded him that he had just joined the church. "Yes, Linda," said he. "It was proper for me to do so. I am getting [on] in years, and my position in society requires it, and it puts an end to all the damned slang.[3] You would do well to join the church, too, Linda."

"There are sinners enough in it already," rejoined I. "If I could be allowed to live like a Christian, I should be glad."

---

1 *South-Side View of Slavery* Book by Nehemiah Adams, published in 1854. Adams, the pastor at Essex Street Congregational Church in Boston, began his career as a minister with antislavery views; after a visit to the South, he wrote this book, which chronicled what he called "the correction" of his opinions, and is a defense of slavery.

2 *renounced... works* This phrase is quoted from the profession adults make when they are baptized into the Anglican (or Episcopal) Church. The Book of Common Prayer reads thus: "[Officiant:] Dost thou renounce the devil and all his works, the vain pomp and glory of the world, with all covetous desires of the same, and the sinful desires of the flesh, so that thou wilt not follow, nor be led by them? Answer. I renounce them all; and, by God's help, will endeavour not to follow, nor be led by them."

3 *slang* Low, crass language or gossip.

"You can do what I require; and if you are faithful to me, you will be as virtuous as my wife," he replied.

I answered that the Bible didn't say so.

His voice became hoarse with rage. "How dare you preach to me about your infernal Bible!" he exclaimed. "What right have you, who are my negro, to talk to me about what you would like, and what you wouldn't like? I am your master, and you shall obey me."

No wonder the slaves sing—

> Ole Satan's church is here below;
> Up to God's free church I hope to go.

CHAPTER 14. ANOTHER LINK TO LIFE

I had not returned to my master's house since the birth of my child. The old man raved to have me thus removed from his immediate power; but his wife vowed, by all that was good and great, she would kill me if I came back; and he did not doubt her word. Sometimes he would stay away for a season. Then he would come and renew the old threadbare discourse about his forbearance and my ingratitude. He labored, most unnecessarily, to convince me that I had lowered myself. The venomous old reprobate had no need of descanting on that theme. I felt humiliated enough. My unconscious babe was the ever-present witness of my shame. I listened with silent contempt when he talked about my having forfeited *his* good opinion; but I shed bitter tears that I was no longer worthy of being respected by the good and pure. Alas! slavery still held me in its poisonous grasp. There was no chance for me to be respectable. There was no prospect of being able to lead a better life.

Sometimes, when my master found that I still refused to accept what he called his kind offers, he would threaten to sell my child. "Perhaps that will humble you," said he.

Humble *me*! Was I not already in the dust? But his threat lacerated my heart. I knew the law gave him power to fulfil it; for slaveholders have been cunning enough to enact that "the child shall follow the condition of the *mother*," not of the *father*; thus taking care that licentiousness shall not interfere with avarice. This reflection made me clasp my innocent babe all the more firmly to my heart. Horrid visions passed through my mind when I thought of his liability to fall into the slave trader's hands. I wept over him, and said, "O my child! perhaps they will leave you in some cold cabin to die, and then throw you into a hole, as if you were a dog."

When Dr. Flint learned that I was again to be a mother, he was exasperated beyond measure. He rushed from the house, and returned with a pair of shears. I had a fine head of hair; and he often railed about my pride of arranging it nicely. He cut every hair close to my head, storming and swearing all the time. I replied to some of his abuse, and he struck me. Some months before, he had pitched me down stairs in a fit of passion; and the injury I received was so serious that I was unable to turn myself in bed for many days. He then said, "Linda, I swear by God I will never raise my hand against you again"; but I knew that he would forget his promise.

After he discovered my situation, he was like a restless spirit from the pit. He came every day; and I was subjected to such insults as no pen can describe. I would not describe them if I could; they were too low, too revolting. I tried to keep them from my grandmother's knowledge as much as I could. I knew she had enough to sadden her life, without having my troubles to bear. When she saw the doctor treat me with violence, and heard him utter oaths terrible enough to palsy a man's tongue, she could not always hold her peace. It was natural and motherlike that she should try to defend me; but it only made matters worse.

When they told me my new-born babe was a girl, my heart was heavier than it had ever been before. Slavery is terrible for men; but it is far more terrible for women. Superadded to the burden common to all, *they* have wrongs, and sufferings, and mortifications peculiarly their own.

Dr. Flint had sworn that he would make me suffer, to my last day, for this new crime against *him*, as he called it; and as long as he had me in his power he kept his word. On the fourth day after the birth of my babe, he entered my room suddenly, and commanded me to rise and bring my baby to him. The nurse who took care of me had gone out of the room to prepare some nourishment, and I was alone. There was no alternative. I rose, took up my babe, and crossed the room to where he sat. "Now stand there," said he, "till I tell you to go back!" My child bore a strong resemblance to her father, and to the deceased Mrs. Sands, her grandmother. He noticed this; and while I stood before him, trembling with weakness, he heaped upon me and my little one every vile epithet he could think of. Even the grandmother in her grave did not escape his curses. In the midst of his vituperations[1] I fainted at his feet. This recalled him to his senses. He took the baby from my arms, laid it on the bed, dashed cold water on my face, took me up, and shook me violently, to restore my consciousness before any one entered the room. Just then my grandmother came in, and he hurried out of the house. I suffered in consequence of this treatment; but I begged my friends to let me die, rather than send for the doctor. There was nothing I dreaded so much as his presence. My life was spared; and I was glad for the sake of my little ones. Had it not been

---

1 *vituperations* Abusive rantings.

for these ties to life, I should have been glad to be released by death, though I had lived only nineteen years.

Always it gave me a pang that my children had no lawful claim to a name. Their father offered his; but, if I had wished to accept the offer, I dared not while my master lived. Moreover, I knew it would not be accepted at their baptism. A Christian name they were at least entitled to; and we resolved to call my boy for our dear good Benjamin, who had gone far away from us.

My grandmother belonged to the church; and she was very desirous of having the children christened. I knew Dr. Flint would forbid it, and I did not venture to attempt it. But chance favored me. He was called to visit a patient out of town, and was obliged to be absent during Sunday. "Now is the time," said my grandmother; "we will take the children to church, and have them christened."

When I entered the church, recollections of my mother came over me, and I felt subdued in spirit. There she had presented me for baptism, without any reason to feel ashamed. She had been married, and had such legal rights as slavery allows to a slave. The vows had at least been sacred to *her*, and she had never violated them. I was glad she was not alive, to know under what different circumstances her grandchildren were presented for baptism. Why had my lot been so different from my mother's? *Her* master had died when she was a child; and she remained with her mistress till she married. She was never in the power of any master; and thus she escaped one class of the evils that generally fall upon slaves.

When my baby was about to be christened, the former mistress of my father stepped up to me, and proposed to give it her Christian name. To this I added the surname of my father, who had himself no legal right to it; for my grandfather on the paternal side was a white gentleman. What tangled skeins are the genealogies of slavery! I loved my father; but it mortified me to be obliged to bestow his name on my children.

When we left the church, my father's old mistress invited me to go home with her. She clasped a gold chain round my baby's neck. I thanked her for this kindness; but I did not like the emblem. I wanted no chain to be fastened on my daughter, not even if its links were of gold. How earnestly I prayed that she might never feel the weight of slavery's chain, whose iron entereth into the soul!

My children grew finely; and Dr. Flint would often say to me, with an exulting smile, "These brats will bring me a handsome sum of money one of these days."

I thought to myself that, God being my helper, they should never pass into his hands. It seemed to me I would rather see them killed than have them given up to his power. The money for the freedom of myself and my children could be obtained; but I derived no advantage from that circumstance. Dr. Flint loved money, but he loved power more. After much discussion, my friends resolved on making another trial. There was a slaveholder about to leave for Texas, and he was commissioned to buy me. He was to begin with nine hundred dollars, and go up to twelve. My master refused his offers. "Sir," said he, "she don't belong to me. She is my daughter's property, and I have no right to sell her. I mistrust that you come from her paramour. If so, you may tell him that he cannot buy her for any money; neither can he buy her children."

The doctor came to see me the next day, and my heart beat quicker as he entered. I never had seen the old man tread with so majestic a step. He seated himself and looked at me with withering scorn. My children had learned to be afraid of him. The little one would shut her eyes and hide her face on my shoulder whenever she saw him; and Benny, who was now nearly five years old, often inquired, "What makes that bad man come here so many times? Does he want to hurt us?" I would clasp the dear boy in my arms, trusting that he would be free before he was old enough to solve the problem. And now, as the doctor sat there so grim and silent, the child left his play and came and nestled up by me. At last my tormentor spoke. "So you are left in disgust, are you?" said he. "It is no more than I expected. You remember I told you years ago that you would be treated so. So he is tired of you? Ha! ha! ha! The virtuous madam don't like to hear about it, does she? Ha! ha! ha!" There was a sting in his calling me virtuous madam. I no longer had the power of answering him as I had formerly done. He continued: "So it seems you are trying to get up another intrigue. Your new paramour came to me, and offered to buy you; but you may be assured you will not succeed. You are mine; and you shall be mine for life. There lives no human being that can take you out of slavery. I would have done it; but you rejected my kind offer."

I told him I did not wish to get up any intrigue; that I had never seen the man who offered to buy me.

"Do you tell me I lie?" exclaimed he, dragging me from my chair. "Will you say again that you never saw that man?"

I answered, "I do say so."

He clinched my arm with a volley of oaths. Ben began to scream, I told him to go to his grandmother.

"Don't you stir a step, you wretch!" said he. The child drew nearer to me, and put his arms round me, as if he wanted to protect me. This was too much for my enraged master. He caught him up and hurled him across the room. I thought he was dead, and rushed towards him to take him up.

"Not yet!" exclaimed the doctor. "Let him lie there till he comes to."

"Let me go! Let me go!" I screamed, "or I will raise the whole house." I struggled and got away; but he clinched me again. Somebody opened the door, and he released me. I picked up my insensible child, and when I turned my tormentor was gone. Anxiously I bent over the little form, so pale and still; and when the brown eyes at last opened, I don't know whether I was very happy.

All the doctor's former persecutions were renewed. He came morning, noon, and night. No jealous lover ever watched a rival more closely than he watched me and the unknown slaveholder, with whom he accused me of wishing to get up an intrigue. When my grandmother was out of the way he searched every room to find him.

In one of his visits, he happened to find a young girl, whom he had sold to a trader a few days previous. His statement was, that he sold her because she had been too familiar with the overseer. She had had a bitter life with him, and was glad to be sold. She had no mother, and no near ties. She had been torn from all her family years before. A few friends had entered into bonds for her safety,[1] if the trader would allow her to spend with them the time that intervened between her sale and the gathering up of his human stock. Such a favor was rarely granted. It saved the trader the expense of board and jail fees, and though the amount was small, it was a weighty consideration in a slave-trader's mind.

Dr. Flint always had an aversion to meeting slaves after he had sold them. He ordered Rose out of the house; but he was no longer her master, and she took no notice of him. For once the crushed Rose was the conqueror. His gray eyes flashed angrily upon her; but that was the extent of his power. "How came this girl here?" he exclaimed. "What right had you to allow it, when you knew I had sold her?"

I answered, "This is my grandmother's house, and Rose came to see her. I have no right to turn anybody out of doors, that comes here for honest purposes."

---

1   *entered ... safety*   I.e., guaranteed (by means of monetary bonds) that she would not run away or be rendered less valuable to the enslaver.

He gave me the blow that would have fallen upon Rose if she had still been his slave. My grandmother's attention had been attracted by loud voices, and she arrived in time to see a second blow dealt. She was not a woman to let such an outrage, in her own house, go unrebuked. The doctor undertook to explain that I had been insolent. Her indignant feelings rose higher and higher, and finally boiled over in words. "Get out of my house!" she exclaimed. "Go home, and take care of your wife and children, and you will have enough to do, without watching my family."

He threw the birth of my children in her face, and accused her of sanctioning the life I was leading. She told him I was living with her by compulsion of his wife; that he needn't accuse her, for he was the one to blame; he was the one who had caused all the trouble. She grew more and more excited as she went on. "I tell you what, Dr. Flint," said she, "you ain't got many more years to live, and you'd better be saying your prayers. It will take 'em all, and more too, to wash the dirt off your soul."

"Do you know whom you are talking to?" he exclaimed.

She replied, "Yes, I know very well who I am talking to."

He left the house in a great rage. I looked at my grandmother. Our eyes met. Their angry expression had passed away, but she looked sorrowful and weary—weary of incessant strife. I wondered that it did not lessen her love for me; but if it did she never showed it. She was always kind, always ready to sympathize with my troubles. There might have been peace and contentment in that lovable home if it had not been for the demon Slavery.

The winter passed undisturbed by the doctor. The beautiful spring came; and when Nature resumes her loveliness, the human soul is apt to revive also. My drooping hopes came to life again with the flowers. I was dreaming of freedom again; more for my children's sake than my own. I planned and I planned. Obstacles hit against plans. There seemed no way of overcoming them; and yet I hoped.

Back came the wily doctor. I was not at home when he called. A friend had invited me to a small party, and to gratify her I went. To my great consternation, a messenger came in haste to say that Dr. Flint was at my grandmother's, and insisted on seeing me. They did not tell him where I was, or he would have come and raised a disturbance in my friend's house. They sent me a dark wrapper;[1] I threw it on and hurried home. My speed did not save me; the doctor had gone away in anger. I dreaded the morning, but I could not delay it; it came, warm and bright. At an early hour the doctor came and asked me where I had been last night. I told him. He did not believe me, and sent to my friend's house to ascertain the facts. He came in the afternoon to assure me he

---

1   *wrapper*   Cloak or shawl.

was satisfied that I had spoken the truth. He seemed to be in a facetious mood, and I expected some jeers were coming. "I suppose you need some recreation," said he, "but I am surprised at your being there, among those negroes. It was not the place for you. Are you allowed to visit such people?"

I understood this covert fling at the white gentleman who was my friend; but I merely replied, "I went to visit my friends, and any company they keep is good enough for me."

He went on to say, "I have seen very little of you of late, but my interest in you is unchanged. When I said I would have no more mercy on you I was rash. I recall my words. Linda, you desire freedom for yourself and your children, and you can obtain it only through me. If you agree to what I am about to propose, you and they shall be free. There must be no communication of any kind between you and their father. I will procure a cottage, where you and the children can live together. Your labor shall be light, such as sewing for my family. Think what is offered you, Linda—a home and freedom! Let the past be forgotten. If I have been harsh with you at times, your willfulness drove me to it. You know I exact obedience from my own children, and I consider you as yet a child."

He paused for an answer, but I remained silent.

"Why don't you speak?" said he. "What more do you wait for?"

"Nothing, sir."

"Then you accept my offer?"

"No, sir."

His anger was ready to break loose; but he succeeded in curbing it, and replied, "You have answered without thought. But I must let you know there are two sides to my proposition; if you reject the bright side, you will be obliged to take the dark one. You must either accept my offer, or you and your children shall be sent to your young master's plantation, there to remain till your young mistress is married; and your children shall fare like the rest of the negro children. I give you a week to consider of it."

He was shrewd; but I knew he was not to be trusted. I told him I was ready to give my answer now.

"I will not receive it now," he replied. "You act too much from impulse. Remember that you and your children can be free a week from today if you choose."

On what a monstrous chance hung the destiny of my children! I knew that my master's offer was a snare, and that if I entered it escape would be impossible. As for his promise, I knew him so well that I was sure if he gave me free papers, they would be so managed as to have no legal value. The alternative was inevitable. I resolved to go to the plantation. But then I thought how completely I should be in his power, and the prospect was appalling. Even if

I should kneel before him, and implore him to spare me, for the sake of my children, I knew he would spurn me with his foot, and my weakness would be his triumph.

Before the week expired, I heard that young Mr. Flint was about to be married to a lady of his own stamp. I foresaw the position I should occupy in his establishment. I had once been sent to the plantation for punishment, and fear of the son had induced the father to recall me very soon. My mind was made up; I was resolved that I would foil my master and save my children, or I would perish in the attempt. I kept my plans to myself; I knew that friends would try to dissuade me from them, and I would not wound their feelings by rejecting their advice.

On the decisive day the doctor came, and said he hoped I had made a wise choice.

"I am ready to go to the plantation, sir," I replied.

"Have you thought how important your decision is to your children?" said he.

I told him I had.

"Very well. Go to the plantation, and my curse go with you," he replied. "Your boy shall be put to work, and he shall soon be sold; and your girl shall be raised for the purpose of selling well. Go your own ways!" He left the room with curses, not to be repeated.

As I stood rooted to the spot, my grandmother came and said, "Linda, child, what did you tell him?"

I answered that I was going to the plantation.

"Must you go?" said she. "Can't something be done to stop it?"

I told her it was useless to try; but she begged me not to give up. She said she would go to the doctor, and remind him how long and how faithfully she had served in the family, and how she had taken her own baby from her breast to nourish his wife. She would tell him I had been out of the family so long they would not miss me; that she would pay them for my time, and the money would procure a woman who had more strength for the situation than I had. I begged her not to go; but she persisted in saying, "He will listen to me, Linda." She went, and was treated as I expected. He coolly listened to what she said, but denied her request. He told her that what he did was for my good, that my feelings were entirely above my situation, and that on the plantation I would receive treatment that was suitable to my behavior.

My grandmother was much cast down. I had my secret hopes; but I must fight my battle alone. I had a woman's pride, and a mother's love for my children; and I resolved that out of the darkness of this hour a brighter dawn should rise for them. My master had power and law on his side; I had a determined will. There is might in each.

Chapter 16. Scenes at the Plantation

Early the next morning I left my grandmother's with my youngest child. My boy was ill, and I left him behind. I had many sad thoughts as the old wagon jolted on. Hitherto, I had suffered alone; now, my little one was to be treated as a slave. As we drew near the great house, I thought of the time when I was formerly sent there out of revenge. I wondered for what purpose I was now sent. I could not tell. I resolved to obey orders so far as duty required; but within myself, I determined to make my stay as short as possible. Mr. Flint was waiting to receive us, and told me to follow him upstairs to receive orders for the day. My little Ellen was left below in the kitchen. It was a change for her, who had always been so carefully tended. My young master said she might amuse herself in the yard. This was kind of him, since the child was hateful to his sight. My task was to fit up the house for the reception of the bride. In the midst of sheets, tablecloths, towels, drapery, and carpeting, my head was as busy planning, as were my fingers with the needle. At noon I was allowed to go to Ellen. She had sobbed herself to sleep. I heard Mr. Flint say to a neighbor, "I've got her down here, and I'll soon take the town notions out of her head. My father is partly to blame for her nonsense. He ought to have broke her in long ago." The remark was made within my hearing, and it would have been quite as manly to have made it to my face. He *had* said things to my face which might, or might not, have surprised his neighbor if he had known of them. He was "a chip of the old block."

I resolved to give him no cause to accuse me of being too much of a lady, so far as work was concerned. I worked day and night, with wretchedness before me. When I lay down beside my child, I felt how much easier it would be to see her die than to see her master beat her about, as I daily saw him beat other little ones. The spirit of the mothers was so crushed by the lash, that they stood by, without courage to remonstrate. How much more must I suffer, before I should be "broke in" to that degree?

I wished to appear as contented as possible. Sometimes I had an opportunity to send a few lines home; and this brought up recollections that made it difficult, for a time, to seem calm and indifferent to my lot. Notwithstanding my efforts, I saw that Mr. Flint regarded me with a suspicious eye. Ellen broke down under the trials of her new life. Separated from me, with no one to look after her, she wandered about, and in a few days cried herself sick. One day, she sat under the window where I was at work, crying that weary cry which makes a mother's heart bleed. I was obliged to steel myself to bear it. After a while it ceased. I looked out, and she was gone. As it was near noon, I ventured to go down in search of her. The great house was raised two feet above the ground. I looked under it, and saw her about midway, fast asleep. I crept under and drew her out. As I held her in my arms, I thought how well it would be for her if she never waked up; and I uttered my thought aloud. I was startled to hear someone say, "Did you speak to me?" I looked up, and saw Mr. Flint standing beside me. He said nothing further, but turned, frowning, away. That night he sent Ellen a biscuit and a cup of sweetened milk. This generosity surprised me. I learned afterwards, that in the afternoon he had killed a large snake, which crept from under the house; and I supposed that incident had prompted his unusual kindness.

The next morning the old cart was loaded with shingles for town. I put Ellen into it, and sent her to her grandmother. Mr. Flint said I ought to have asked his permission. I told him the child was sick, and required attention which I had no time to give. He let it pass; for he was aware that I had accomplished much work in a little time.

I had been three weeks on the plantation, when I planned a visit home. It must be at night, after everybody was in bed. I was six miles from town, and the road was very dreary. I was to go with a young man, who, I knew, often stole to town to see his mother. One night, when all was quiet, we started. Fear gave speed to our steps, and we were not long in performing the journey. I arrived at my grandmother's. Her bedroom was on the first floor, and the window was open, the weather being warm. I spoke to her and she awoke. She let me in and closed the window, lest some late passer-by should see me. A light was brought, and the whole household gathered round me, some smiling and some crying. I went to look at my children, and thanked God for their happy sleep. The tears fell as I leaned over them. As I moved to leave, Benny stirred. I turned back, and whispered, "Mother is here." After digging at his eyes with his little fist, they opened, and he sat up in bed, looking at me curiously. Having satisfied himself that it was I, he exclaimed, "O mother! you ain't dead, are you? They didn't cut off your head at the plantation, did they?"

My time was up too soon, and my guide was waiting for me. I laid Benny back in his bed, and dried his tears by a promise to come again soon. Rapidly we retraced our steps back to the plantation. About halfway we were met by a company of four patrols. Luckily we heard their horse's hoofs before they came in sight, and we had time to hide behind a large tree. They passed, hallooing and shouting in a manner that indicated a recent carousal.[1] How thankful we were that they had not their dogs with them! We hastened our footsteps, and when we arrived on the plantation we heard the sound of the hand-mill. The slaves were grinding their corn. We were safely in the house before the horn summoned them to their labor. I divided my little parcel of food with my

---

1 *carousal* Drinking session.

guide, knowing that he had lost the chance of grinding his corn, and must toil all day in the field.

Mr. Flint often took an inspection of the house, to see that no one was idle. The entire management of the work was trusted to me, because he knew nothing about it; and rather than hire a superintendent he contented himself with my arrangements. He had often urged upon his father the necessity of having me at the plantation to take charge of his affairs, and make clothes for the slaves; but the old man knew him too well to consent to that arrangement.

When I had been working a month at the plantation, the great aunt of Mr. Flint came to make him a visit. This was the good old lady who paid fifty dollars for my grandmother, for the purpose of making her free, when she stood on the auction block. My grandmother loved this old lady, whom we all called Miss Fanny. She often came to take tea with us. On such occasions the table was spread with a snow-white cloth, and the china cups and silver spoons were taken from the old-fashioned buffet. There were hot muffins, tea rusks,[1] and delicious sweetmeats. My grandmother kept two cows, and the fresh cream was Miss Fanny's delight. She invariably declared that it was the best in town. The old ladies had cosy times together. They would work and chat, and sometimes, while talking over old times, their spectacles would get dim with tears, and would have to be taken off and wiped. When Miss Fanny bade us goodbye, her bag was filled with grandmother's best cakes, and she was urged to come again soon.

There had been a time when Dr. Flint's wife came to take tea with us, and when her children were also sent to have a feast of "Aunt Marthy's" nice cooking. But after I became an object of her jealousy and spite, she was angry with grandmother for giving a shelter to me and my children. She would not even speak to her in the street. This wounded my grandmother's feelings, for she could not retain ill will against the woman whom she had nourished with her milk when a babe. The doctor's wife would gladly have prevented our intercourse with Miss Fanny if she could have done it, but fortunately she was not dependent on the bounty of the Flints. She had enough to be independent; and that is more than can ever be gained from charity, however lavish it may be.

Miss Fanny was endeared to me by many recollections, and I was rejoiced to see her at the plantation. The warmth of her large, loyal heart made the house seem pleasanter while she was in it. She stayed a week, and I had many talks with her. She said her principal object in coming was to see how I was treated, and whether anything could be done for me. She inquired whether she could help me in any way. I told her I believed not. She condoled with me

---

1   *rusks*   Pieces of twice-baked sweet bread.

in her own peculiar way; saying she wished that I and all my grandmother's family were at rest in our graves, for not until then should she feel any peace about us. The good old soul did not dream that I was planning to bestow peace upon her, with regard to myself and my children; not by death, but by securing our freedom.

Again and again I had traversed those dreary twelve miles, to and from the town; and all the way, I was meditating upon some means of escape for myself and my children. My friends had made every effort that ingenuity could devise to effect our purchase, but all their plans had proved abortive. Dr. Flint was suspicious, and determined not to loosen his grasp upon us. I could have made my escape alone; but it was more for my helpless children than for myself that I longed for freedom. Though the boon would have been precious to me, above all price, I would not have taken it at the expense of leaving them in slavery. Every trial I endured, every sacrifice I made for their sakes, drew them closer to my heart, and gave me fresh courage to beat back the dark waves that rolled and rolled over me in a seemingly endless night of storms.

The six weeks were nearly completed, when Mr. Flint's bride was expected to take possession of her own home. The arrangements were all completed, and Mr. Flint said I had done well. He expected to leave home on Saturday, and return with his bride the following Wednesday. After receiving various orders from him, I ventured to ask permission to spend Sunday in town. It was granted; for which favor I was thankful. It was the first I had ever asked of him, and I intended it should be the last. It needed more than one night to accomplish the project I had in view; but the whole of Sunday would give me an opportunity. I spent the Sabbath with my grandmother. A calmer, more beautiful day never came down out of heaven. To me it was a day of conflicting emotions. Perhaps it was the last day I should ever spend under that dear, old sheltered roof! Perhaps these were the last talks I should ever have with the faithful old friend of my whole life! Perhaps it was the last time I and my children should be together! Well, better so, I thought, than that they should be slaves. I knew the doom that awaited my fair baby in slavery, and I determined to save her from it, or perish in the attempt. I went to make this vow at the graves of my poor parents, in the burying-ground of the slaves. "There the wicked cease from troubling, and there the weary be at rest. There the prisoners rest together; they hear not the voice of the oppressor; the servant is free from his master."[1] I knelt by the graves of my parents, and thanked God, as I had often done before, that they had not lived to witness my trials, or to mourn over my sins. I had received my mother's blessing when she died; and in many an hour of tribulation I had seemed to hear her

1 *There the wicked ... his master* See Job 3.17–19.

voice, sometimes chiding me, sometimes whispering loving words into my wounded heart. I have shed many and bitter tears, to think that when I am gone from my children they cannot remember me with such entire satisfaction as I remembered my mother.

The graveyard was in the woods, and twilight was coming on. Nothing broke the death-like stillness except the occasional twitter of a bird. My spirit was overawed by the solemnity of the scene. For more than ten years I had frequented this spot, but never had it seemed to me so sacred as now. A black stump, at the head of my mother's grave, was all that remained of a tree my father had planted. His grave was marked by a small wooden board, bearing his name, the letters of which were nearly obliterated. I knelt down and kissed them, and poured forth a prayer to God for guidance and support in the perilous step I was about to take. As I passed the wreck of the old meeting house, where, before Nat Turner's time, the slaves had been allowed to meet for worship, I seemed to hear my father's voice come from it, bidding me not to tarry till I reached freedom or the grave. I rushed on with renovated hopes. My trust in God had been strengthened by that prayer among the graves.

My plan was to conceal myself at the house of a friend, and remain there a few weeks till the search was over. My hope was that the doctor would get discouraged, and, for fear of losing my value, and also of subsequently finding my children among the missing, he would consent to sell us; and I knew somebody would buy us. I had done all in my power to make my children comfortable during the time I expected to be separated from them. I was packing my things, when grandmother came into the room, and asked what I was doing. "I am putting my things in order," I replied. I tried to look and speak cheerfully; but her watchful eye detected something beneath the surface. She drew me towards her, and asked me to sit down. She looked earnestly at me, and said, "Linda, do you want to kill your old grandmother? Do you mean to leave your little, helpless children? I am old now, and cannot do for your babies as I once did for you."

I replied, that if I went away, perhaps their father would be able to secure their freedom.

"Ah, my child," said she, "don't trust too much to him. Stand by your own children, and suffer with them till death. Nobody respects a mother who forsakes her children; and if you leave them, you will never have a happy moment. If you go, you will make me miserable the short time I have to live. You would be taken and brought back, and your sufferings would be dreadful. Remember poor Benjamin. Do give it up, Linda. Try to bear a little longer. Things may turn out better than we expect."

My courage failed me, in view of the sorrow I should bring on that faithful, loving old heart. I promised that I would try longer, and that I would take nothing out of her house without her knowledge.

Whenever the children climbed on my knee, or laid their heads on my lap, she would say, "Poor little souls! what would you do without a mother? She don't love you as I do." And she would hug them to her own bosom, as if to reproach me for my want of affection; but she knew all the while that I loved them better than my life. I slept with her that night, and it was the last time. The memory of it haunted me for many a year.

On Monday I returned to the plantation, and busied myself with preparations for the important day. Wednesday came. It was a beautiful day, and the faces of the slaves were as bright as the sunshine. The poor creatures were merry. They were expecting little presents from the bride, and hoping for better times under her administration. I had no such hopes for them. I knew that the young wives of slaveholders often thought their authority and importance would be best established and maintained by cruelty; and what I had heard of young Mrs. Flint gave me no reason to expect that her rule over them would be less severe than that of the master and overseer. Truly, the colored race are the most cheerful and forgiving people on the face of the earth. That their masters sleep in safety is owing to their superabundance of heart; and yet they look upon their sufferings with less pity than they would bestow on those of a horse or a dog.

I stood at the door with others to receive the bridegroom and bride. She was a handsome, delicate-looking girl, and her face flushed with emotion at [the] sight of her new home. I thought it likely that visions of a happy future were rising before her. It made me sad; for I knew how soon clouds would come over her sunshine. She examined every part of the house, and told me she was delighted with the arrangements I had made. I was afraid old Mrs. Flint had tried to prejudice her against me and I did my best to please her.

All passed off smoothly for me until dinner time arrived. I did not mind the embarrassment of waiting on a dinner party, for the first time in my life, half so much as I did the meeting with Dr. Flint and his wife, who would be among the guests. It was a mystery to me why Mrs. Flint had not made her appearance at the plantation during all the time I was putting the house in order. I had not met her, face to face, for five years, and I had no wish to see her now. She was a praying woman, and, doubtless, considered my present position a special answer to her prayers. Nothing could please her better than to see me humbled and trampled upon. I was just where she would have me— in the power of a hard, unprincipled master. She did not speak to me when she took her seat at the table; but her satisfied, triumphant smile, when I handed her plate, was more eloquent than words. The old doctor was not so quiet in his demonstrations. He ordered me here and there, and spoke with peculiar emphasis when he said "your *mistress*." I was drilled like a disgraced soldier. When all was over, and the last key turned, I sought my pillow thankful that God had appointed a season of rest for the weary.

The next day my new mistress began her housekeeping. I was not exactly appointed maid of all work; but I was to do whatever I was told. Monday evening came. It was always a busy time. On that night the slaves received their weekly allowance of food. Three pounds of meat, a peck of corn, and perhaps a dozen herring were allowed to each man. Women received a pound and a half of meat, a peck of corn, and the same number of herring. Children over twelve years old had half the allowance of the women. The meat was cut and weighed by the foreman of the field hands, and piled on planks before the meat house. Then the second foreman went behind the building, and when the first foreman called out, "Who takes this piece of meat?" he answered by calling somebody's name. This method was resorted to as a means of preventing partiality in distributing the meat. The young mistress came out to see how things were done on her plantation, and she soon gave a specimen of her character. Among those in waiting for their allowance was a very old slave, who had faithfully served the Flint family through three generations. When he hobbled up to get his bit of meat, the mistress said he was too old to have any allowance; that when niggers were too old to work, they ought to be fed on grass. Poor old man! He suffered much before he found rest in the grave.

My mistress and I got along very well together. At the end of a week, old Mrs. Flint made us another visit, and was closeted a long time with her daughter-in-law. I had my suspicions what was the subject of the conference. The old doctor's wife had been informed that I could leave the plantation on one condition, and she was very desirous to keep me there. If she had trusted me, as I deserved to be trusted by her, she would have had no fears of my accepting that condition. When she entered her carriage to return home, she said to young Mrs. Flint, "Don't neglect to send for them as quick as possible." My heart was on the watch all the time, and I at once concluded that she spoke of my children. The doctor came the next day, and as I entered the room to spread the tea table, I heard him say, "Don't wait any longer. Send for them tomorrow." I saw through the plan. They thought my children's being there would fetter me to the spot, and that it was a good place to break us all in to abject submission to our lot as slaves. After the doctor left, a gentleman called, who had always manifested friendly feelings towards my grandmother and her family. Mr. Flint carried him over the plantation to show him the results of labor performed by men and women who were unpaid, miserably clothed, and half famished. The cotton crop was all they thought of. It was duly admired, and the gentleman returned with specimens to show his friends.

I was ordered to carry water to wash his hands. As I did so, he said, "Linda, how do you like your new home?" I told him I liked it as well as I expected. He replied, "They don't think you are contented, and tomorrow they are going to bring your children to be with you. I am sorry for you, Linda. I hope they will treat you kindly." I hurried from the room, unable to thank him. My suspicions were correct. My children were to be brought to the plantation to be "broke in."

To this day I feel grateful to the gentleman who gave me this timely information. It nerved me to immediate action.

Chapter 17. The Flight

Mr. Flint was hard pushed for house servants, and rather than lose me he had restrained his malice. I did my work faithfully, though not, of course, with a willing mind. They were evidently afraid I should leave them. Mr. Flint wished that I should sleep in the great house instead of the servants' quarters. His wife agreed to the proposition, but said I mustn't bring my bed into the house, because it would scatter feathers on her carpet. I knew when I went there that they would never think of such a thing as furnishing a bed of any kind for me and my little one. I therefore carried my own bed, and now I was forbidden to use it. I did as I was ordered. But now that I was certain my children were to be put in their power, in order to give them a stronger hold on me, I resolved to leave them that night. I remembered the grief this step would bring upon my dear old grandmother; and nothing less than the freedom of my children would have induced me to disregard her advice. I went about my evening work with trembling steps. Mr. Flint twice called from his chamber door to inquire why the house was not locked up. I replied that I had not done my work. "You have had time enough to do it," said he. "Take care how you answer me!"

I shut all the windows, locked all the doors, and went up to the third story, to wait till midnight. How long those hours seemed, and how fervently I prayed that God would not forsake me in this hour of utmost need! I was about to risk everything on the throw of a die; and if I failed, O what would become of me and my poor children? They would be made to suffer for my fault.

At half past twelve I stole softly downstairs. I stopped on the second floor, thinking I heard a noise. I felt my way down into the parlor, and looked out of the window. The night was so intensely dark that I could see nothing. I raised the window very softly and jumped out. Large drops of rain were falling, and the darkness bewildered me. I dropped on my knees, and breathed a short prayer to God for guidance and protection. I groped my way to the road, and rushed towards the town with almost lightning speed. I arrived at my grandmother's house, but dared not see her. She would say, "Linda, you are killing me"; and I knew that would unnerve me. I tapped softly at the window of a room, occupied by a woman, who had lived in the house several years. I knew she was a faithful friend, and could be trusted with my secret. I tapped several times before she heard me. At last she raised the window, and I whispered, "Sally, I have run away. Let me in, quick." She opened the door softly, and said in low tones, "For God's sake, don't. Your grandmother is trying to buy you and de chillern. Mr. Sands was here last week. He tole her he was going away on business, but he wanted her to go ahead about buying you and de chillern, and he would help her all he could. Don't run away, Linda. Your grandmother is all bowed down wid trouble now."

I replied, "Sally, they are going to carry my children to the plantation tomorrow; and they will never sell them to anybody so long as they have me in their power. Now, would you advise me to go back?"

"No, chile, no," answered she. "When dey finds you is gone, dey won't want de plague ob de chillern; but where is you going to hide? Dey knows ebery inch ob dis house."

I told her I had a hiding-place, and that was all it was best for her to know. I asked her to go into my room as soon as it was light, and take all my clothes out of my trunk, and pack them in hers; for I knew Mr. Flint and the constable would be there early to search my room. I feared the sight of my children would be too much for my full heart; but I could not go out into the uncertain future without one last look. I bent over the bed where lay my little Benny and baby Ellen. Poor little ones! fatherless and motherless! Memories of their father came over me. He wanted to be kind to them; but they were not all to him, as they were to my womanly heart. I knelt and prayed for the innocent little sleepers. I kissed them lightly, and turned away.

As I was about to open the street door, Sally laid her hand on my shoulder, and said, "Linda, is you gwine all alone? Let me call your uncle."

"No Sally," I replied, "I want no one to be brought into trouble on my account."

I went forth into the darkness and rain. I ran on till I came to the house of the friend who was to conceal me.

Early the next morning Mr. Flint was at my grandmother's inquiring for me. She told him she had not seen me, and supposed I was at the plantation. He watched her face narrowly, and said, "Don't you know anything about her running off?" She assured him that she did not. He went on to say, "Last night she ran off without the least provocation. We had treated her very kindly. My wife liked her. She will soon be found and brought back. Are her children with you?" When told that they were, he said, "I am very glad to hear that. If they are here, she cannot be far off. If I find out that any of my niggers have had anything to do with this damned business, I'll give 'em five hundred lashes." As he started to go to his father's, he turned round and added, persuasively, "Let her be brought back, and she shall have her children to live with her."

The tidings made the old doctor rave and storm at a furious rate. It was a busy day for them. My grandmother's house was searched from top to bottom. As my trunk was empty, they concluded I had taken my clothes with me. Before ten o'clock every vessel northward bound was thoroughly examined, and the law against harboring fugitives was read to all on board. At night a watch was set over the town. Knowing how distressed my grandmother would be, I wanted to send her a message; but it could not be done. Everyone who went in or out of her house was closely watched. The doctor said he would take my children, unless she became responsible for them; which of course she willingly did. The next day was spent in searching. Before night, the following advertisement was posted at every corner, and in every public place for miles round:

> "$300 REWARD! Ran away from the subscriber, an intelligent, bright, mulatto girl, named Linda, 21 years age. Five feet four inches high. Dark eyes, and black hair inclined to curl; but it can be made straight. Has a decayed spot on a front tooth. She can read and write, and in all probability will try to get to the Free States. All persons are forbidden, under penalty of the law, to harbor or employ said slave. $150 will be given to whoever takes her in the state, and $300 if taken out of the state and delivered to me, or lodged in jail.
> DR. FLINT."

Chapter 18. Months of Peril

The search for me was kept up with more perseverance than I had anticipated. I began to think that escape was impossible. I was in great anxiety lest I should implicate the friend who harbored me. I knew the consequences would be frightful; and much as I dreaded being caught, even that seemed better than causing an innocent person to suffer for kindness to me. A week had passed in terrible suspense, when my pursuers came into such close vicinity that I concluded they had tracked me to my hiding-place. I flew out of the house, and concealed myself in a thicket of bushes. There I remained in an agony of fear for two hours. Suddenly, a reptile of some kind seized my leg. In my fright, I struck a blow which loosened its hold, but I could not tell whether I had killed it; it was so dark, I could not see what it was; I only knew it was something cold and slimy. The pain I felt soon indicated that the bite was poisonous. I was compelled to leave my place of concealment, and I groped my way back into the house. The pain had become intense, and my friend was startled by my look of anguish. I asked her to prepare a poultice of warm ashes and vinegar, and I applied it to my leg, which was already much swollen. The application gave me some relief, but the swelling did not abate. The dread of being disabled was greater than the physical pain I endured. My friend asked an old woman, who doctored among the slaves, what was good for the bite of a snake or a lizard. She told her to steep a dozen coppers[1] in vinegar, overnight, and apply the cankered[2] vinegar to the inflamed part.[3]

I had succeeded in cautiously conveying some messages to my relatives. They were harshly threatened, and despairing of my having a chance to escape, they advised me to return to my master, ask his forgiveness, and let him make an example of me. But such counsel had no influence on me. When I started upon this hazardous undertaking, I had resolved that, come what would, there should be no turning back. "Give me liberty, or give me death,"[4] was my motto. When my friend contrived to make known to my relatives the painful situation I had been in for twenty-four hours, they said no more about my going back to my master. Something must be done, and that speedily; but where to turn for help, they knew not. God in his mercy raised up "a friend in need."[5]

Among the ladies who were acquainted with my grandmother, was one who had known her from childhood, and always been very friendly to her. She had also known my mother and her children, and felt interested for them. At this crisis of affairs she called to see my grandmother, as she not unfrequently did. She observed the sad and troubled expression of her face, and asked if she knew where Linda was, and whether she was safe. My grandmother shook her head, without answering. "Come, Aunt Martha," said the kind lady, "tell me all about it. Perhaps I can do something to help you." The husband of this lady held many slaves, and bought and sold slaves. She also held a number in her own name; but she treated them kindly, and would never allow any of them to be sold. She was unlike the majority of slaveholders' wives. My grandmother looked earnestly at her. Something in the expression of her face said "Trust

---

1   *coppers* Pennies.

2   *cankered* Corrosive.

3   [Editor's (Lydia Maria Child's) note]   The poison of a snake is a powerful acid, and is counteracted by powerful alkalies, such as potash, ammonia, &c. The Indians are accustomed to apply wet ashes, or plunge the limb into strong lye. White men, employed to lay out railroads in snaky places, often carry ammonia with them as an antidote.

4   *Give me liberty ... death* Words famously spoken by Patrick Henry at the outset of the American Revolution; the phrase became a slogan for American revolutionaries, and for revolutionary movements around the world.

5   *a friend in need* Allusion to the proverb "a friend in need is a friend indeed."

me!" and she did trust her. She listened attentively to the details of my story, and sat thinking for a while. At last she said, "Aunt Martha, I pity you both. If you think there is any chance of Linda's getting to the Free States, I will conceal her for a time. But first you must solemnly promise that my name shall never be mentioned. If such a thing should become known, it would ruin me and my family. No one in my house must know of it, except the cook. She is so faithful that I would trust my own life with her; and I know she likes Linda. It is a great risk; but I trust no harm will come of it. Get word to Linda to be ready as soon as it is dark, before the patrols are out. I will send the housemaids on errands, and Betty shall go to meet Linda." The place where we were to meet was designated and agreed upon. My grandmother was unable to thank the lady for this noble deed; overcome by her emotions, she sank on her knees and sobbed like a child.

I received a message to leave my friend's house at such an hour, and go to a certain place where a friend would be waiting for me. As a matter of prudence no names were mentioned. I had no means of conjecturing who I was to meet, or where I was going. I did not like to move thus blindfolded, but I had no choice. It would not do for me to remain where I was. I disguised myself, summoned up courage to meet the worst, and went to the appointed place. My friend Betty was there; she was the last person I expected to see. We hurried along in silence. The pain in my leg was so intense that it seemed as if I should drop; but fear gave me strength. We reached the house and entered unobserved. Her first words were: "Honey, now you is safe. Dem devils ain't coming to search *dis* house. When I get you into missis' safe place, I will bring some nice hot supper. I specs you need it after all dis skeering." Betty's vocation led her to think eating the most important thing in life. She did not realize that my heart was too full for me to care much about supper.

The mistress came to meet us, and led me upstairs to a small room over her own sleeping apartment. "You will be safe here, Linda," said she; "I keep this room to store away things that are out of use. The girls are not accustomed to be sent to it, and they will not suspect anything unless they hear some noise. I always keep it locked, and Betty shall take care of the key. But you must be very careful, for my sake as well as your own; and you must never tell my secret; for it would ruin me and my family. I will keep the girls busy in the morning, that Betty may have a chance to bring your breakfast; but it will not do for her to come to you again till night. I will come to see you sometimes. Keep up your courage. I hope this state of things will not last long." Betty came with the "nice hot supper," and the mistress hastened downstairs to keep things straight till she returned. How my heart overflowed with gratitude! Words choked in my throat; but I could have kissed the feet of my benefactress. For that deed of Christian womanhood may God forever bless her!

I went to sleep that night with the feeling that I was for the present the most fortunate slave in town. Morning came and filled my little cell with light. I thanked the heavenly Father for this safe retreat. Opposite my window was a pile of feather beds. On the top of these I could lie perfectly concealed, and command a view of the street through which Dr. Flint passed to his office. Anxious as I was, I felt a gleam of satisfaction when I saw him. Thus far I had outwitted him, and I triumphed over it. Who can blame slaves for being cunning? They are constantly compelled to resort to it. It is the only weapon of the weak and oppressed against the strength of their tyrants.

I was daily hoping to hear that my master had sold my children; for I knew who was on the watch to buy them. But Dr. Flint cared even more for revenge than he did for money. My brother William, and the good aunt who had served in his family twenty years, and my little Benny, and Ellen, who was a little over two years old, were thrust into jail, as a means of compelling my relatives to give some information about me. He swore my grandmother should never see one of them again till I was brought back. They kept these facts from me for several days. When I heard that my little ones were in a loathsome jail, my first impulse was to go to them. I was encountering dangers for the sake of freeing them, and must I be the cause of their death? The thought was agonizing. My benefactress tried to soothe me by telling me that my aunt would take good care of the children while they remained in jail. But it added to my pain to think that the good old aunt, who had always been so kind to her sister's orphan children, should be shut up in prison for no other crime than loving them. I suppose my friends feared a reckless movement on my part, knowing, as they did, that my life was bound up in my children. I received a note from my brother William. It was scarcely legible, and ran thus: "Wherever you are, dear sister, I beg of you not to come here. We are all much better off than you are. If you come, you will ruin us all. They would force you to tell where you had been, or they would kill you. Take the advice of your friends; if not for the sake of me and your children, at least for the sake of those you would ruin."

Poor William! He also must suffer for being my brother. I took his advice and kept quiet. My aunt was taken out of jail at the end of a month, because Mrs. Flint could not spare her any longer. She was tired of being her own housekeeper. It was quite too fatiguing to order her dinner and eat it too. My children remained in jail, where brother William did all he could for their comfort. Betty went to see them sometimes, and brought me tidings. She was not permitted to enter the jail; but William would hold them up to the grated window while she chatted with them. When she repeated their prattle, and told me how they wanted to see their ma, my tears would flow. Old Betty would exclaim, "Lors, chile! what's you crying 'bout? Dem young uns vil kill you dead. Don't be so chick'n hearted! If you does, you vil nebber git thro' dis world."

Good old soul! She had gone through the world childless. She had never had little ones to clasp their arms round her neck; she had never seen their soft eyes looking into hers; no sweet little voices had called her mother; she had never pressed her own infants to her heart, with the feeling that even in fetters there was something to live for. How could she realize my feelings? Betty's husband loved children dearly, and wondered why God had denied them to him. He expressed great sorrow when he came to Betty with the tidings that Ellen had been taken out of jail and carried to Dr. Flint's. She had the measles a short time before they carried her to jail, and the disease had left her eyes affected. The doctor had taken her home to attend to them. My children had always been afraid of the doctor and his wife. They had never been inside of their house. Poor little Ellen cried all day to be carried back to prison. The instincts of childhood are true. She knew she was loved in the jail. Her screams and sobs annoyed Mrs. Flint. Before night she called one of the slaves, and said, "Here, Bill, carry this brat back to the jail. I can't stand her noise. If she would be quiet I should like to keep the little minx. She would make a handy waiting maid for my daughter by and by. But if she stayed here, with her white face, I suppose I should either kill her or spoil her. I hope the doctor will sell them as far as wind and water can carry them. As for their mother, her ladyship will find out yet what she gets by running away. She hasn't so much feeling for her children as a cow has for its calf. If she had, she would have come back long ago, to get them out of jail, and save all this expense and trouble. The good-for-nothing hussy! When she is caught, she shall stay in jail, in irons, for one six months,[1] and then be sold to a sugar plantation. I shall see her broke in yet. What do you stand there for, Bill? Why don't you go off with the brat? Mind, now, that you don't let any of the niggers speak to her in the street!"

When these remarks were reported to me, I smiled at Mrs. Flint's saying that she should either kill my child or spoil her. I thought to myself there was very little danger of the latter. I have always considered it as one of God's special providences that Ellen screamed till she was carried back to jail.

That same night, Dr. Flint was called to a patient, and did not return till near morning. Passing my grandmother's, he saw a light in the house, and thought to himself, "Perhaps this has something to do with Linda." He knocked and the door was opened. "What calls you up so early?" said he. "I saw your light, and I thought I would just stop and tell you that I have found out where Linda is. I know where to put my hands on her, and I shall have her

---

1   *one six months*   I.e., one period of six months.

before twelve o'clock." When he had turned away, my grandmother and my uncle looked anxiously at each other. They did not know whether or not it was merely one of the doctor's tricks to frighten them. In their uncertainty, they thought it was best to have a message conveyed to my friend Betty. Unwilling to alarm her mistress, Betty resolved to dispose of me herself. She came to me, and told me to rise and dress quickly. We hurried downstairs, and across the yard, into the kitchen. She locked the door, and lifted up a plank in the floor. A buffalo skin and a bit of carpet were spread for me to lie on, and a quilt thrown over me. "Stay dar," said she, "till I sees if dey know 'bout you. Dey say dey vil put thar hans on you afore twelve o'clock. If dey *did* know whar you are, dey won't know *now*. Dey'll be disapinted dis time. Dat's all I got to say. If dey comes rummagin 'mong *my* tings, dey'll get one bressed sarssin[1] from dis 'ere nigger." In my shallow bed I had but just room enough to bring my hands to my face to keep the dust out of my eyes; for Betty walked over me twenty times in an hour, passing from the dresser to the fireplace. When she was alone, I could hear her pronouncing anathemas over Dr. Flint and all his tribe, every now and then saying, with a chuckling laugh, "Dis nigger's too cute[2] for 'em dis time." When the housemaids were about, she had sly ways of drawing them out, that I might hear what they would say. She would repeat stories she had heard about my being in this, or that, or the other place. To which they would answer, that I was not fool enough to be staying round there; that I was in Philadelphia or New York before this time. When all were abed and asleep, Betty raised the plank, and said, "Come out, chile; come out. Dey don't know nottin 'bout you. 'Twas only white folks' lies, to skeer de niggers."

Some days after this adventure I had a much worse fright. As I sat very still in my retreat above stairs, cheerful visions floated through my mind. I thought Dr. Flint would soon get discouraged, and would be willing to sell my children, when he lost all hopes of making them the means of my discovery. I knew who was ready to buy them. Suddenly I heard a voice that chilled my blood. The sound was too familiar to me, it had been too dreadful, for me not to recognize at once my old master. He was in the house, and I at once concluded that he had come to seize me. I looked round in terror. There was no way of escape. The voice receded. I supposed the constable was with him, and they were searching the house. In my alarm I did not forget the trouble I was bringing on my generous benefactress. It seemed as if I were born to bring sorrow on all who befriended me, and that was the bitterest drop in the bitter cup of my life. After a while I heard approaching footsteps; the key was turned in my door. I braced myself against the wall to keep from falling. I ventured to

---

1 *sarssin* I.e., sassing; scolding.
2 *cute* Acute; clever.

look up, and there stood my kind benefactress. I was too much overcome to speak, and sunk down upon the floor.

"I thought you would hear your master's voice," she said; "and knowing you would be terrified, I came to tell you there is nothing to fear. You may even indulge in a laugh at the old gentleman's expense. He is so sure you are in New York, that he came to borrow five hundred dollars to go in pursuit of you. My sister had some money to loan on interest. He has obtained it, and proposes to start for New York tonight. So, for the present, you see you are safe. The doctor will merely lighten his pocket hunting after the bird he has left behind."

Chapter 19. The Children Sold

The doctor came back from New York, of course without accomplishing his purpose. He had expended considerable money, and was rather disheartened. My brother and the children had now been in jail two months, and that also was some expense. My friends thought it was a favorable time to work on his discouraged feelings. Mr. Sands sent a speculator to offer him nine hundred dollars for my brother William, and eight hundred for the two children. These were high prices, as slaves were then selling; but the offer was rejected. If it had been merely a question of money, the doctor would have sold any boy of Benny's age for two hundred dollars; but he could not bear to give up the power of revenge. But he was hard pressed for money, and he revolved the matter in his mind. He knew that if he could keep Ellen till she was fifteen, he could sell her for a high price; but I presume he reflected that she might die, or might be stolen away. At all events, he came to the conclusion that he had better accept the slave-trader's offer. Meeting him in the street, he inquired when he would leave town. "Today, at ten o'clock," he replied. "Ah, do you go so soon?" said the doctor; "I have been reflecting upon your proposition, and I have concluded to let you have the three negroes if you will say nineteen hundred dollars." After some parley, the trader agreed to his terms. He wanted the bill of sale drawn up and signed immediately, as he had a great deal to attend to during the short time he remained in town. The doctor went to the jail and told William he would take him back into his service if he would promise to behave himself; but he replied that he would rather be sold. "And you *shall* be sold, you ungrateful rascal!" exclaimed the doctor. In less than an hour the money was paid, the papers were signed, sealed, and delivered, and my brother and children were in the hands of the trader.

It was a hurried transaction; and after it was over, the doctor's characteristic caution returned. He went back to the speculator, and said, "Sir, I have come to lay you under obligations of a thousand dollars[1] not to sell any of those negroes in this state." "You come too late," replied the trader; "our bargain is closed." He had, in fact, already sold them to Mr. Sands, but he did not mention it. The doctor required him to put irons on "that rascal, Bill," and to pass through the back streets when he took his gang out of town. The trader was privately instructed to concede to his wishes. My good old aunt went to jail to bid the children goodbye, supposing them to be the speculator's property, and that she should never see them again. As she held Benny in her lap, he said, "Aunt Nancy, I want to show you something." He led her to the door and showed her a long row of marks, saying "Uncle Will taught me to count. I have made a mark for every day I have been here, and it is sixty days. It is a long time; and the speculator is going to take me and Ellen away. He's a bad man. It's wrong for him to take grandmother's children. I want to go to my mother."

My grandmother was told that the children would be restored to her, but she was requested to act as if they were really to be sent away. Accordingly, she made up a bundle of clothes and went to the jail. When she arrived, she found William handcuffed among the gang, and the children in the trader's cart. The scene seemed too much like a reality. She was afraid there might have been some deception or mistake. She fainted, and was carried home.

When the wagon stopped at the hotel, several gentlemen came out and proposed to purchase William, but the trader refused their offers, without stating that he was already sold. And now came the trying hour for that drove of human beings, driven away like cattle, to be sold they knew not where. Husbands were torn from wives, parents from children, never to look upon each other again this side the grave. There was wringing of hands and cries of despair.

Dr. Flint had the supreme satisfaction of seeing the wagon leave town, and Mrs. Flint had the gratification of supposing that my children were going "as far as wind and water would carry them." According to the agreement, my uncle followed the wagon some miles, until they came to an old farmhouse. There the trader took the irons from William, and as he did so, he said, "You are a damned clever fellow. I should like to own you myself. Them gentlemen that wanted to buy you said you was a bright, honest chap, and I must git you a good home. I guess your old master will swear tomorrow, and call himself an old fool for selling the children. I reckon he'll never git their mammy back agin. I expect she's made tracks for the north. Goodbye, old boy. Remember, I have done you a good turn. You must thank me by coaxing all the pretty gals

---

1 *lay you ... dollars* I.e., legally obligate you, with a penalty of a thousand dollars if the obligation is breached.

to go with me next fall. That's going to be my last trip. The trading in niggers is a bad business for a fellow that's got any heart. Move on you fellows!" And the gang went on, God alone knows where.

Much as I despise and detest the class of slave-traders, whom I regard as the vilest wretches on earth, I must do this man the justice to say that he seemed to have some feeling. He took a fancy to William in the jail, and wanted to buy him. When he heard the story of my children, he was willing to aid them in getting out of Dr. Flint's power, even without charging the customary fee.

My uncle procured a wagon and carried William and the children back to town. Great was the joy in my grandmother's house! The curtains were closed, and the candles lighted. The happy grandmother cuddled the little ones to her bosom. They hugged her, and kissed her, and clapped their hands, and shouted. She knelt down and poured forth one of her heartfelt prayers of thanksgiving to God. The father was present for awhile; and though such a "parental relation" as existed between him and my children takes slight hold of the heart or consciences of slaveholders, it must be that he experienced some moments of pure joy in witnessing the happiness he had imparted.

I had no share in the rejoicings of that evening. The events of that day had not come to my knowledge. And now I will tell you something that happened to me; though you will, perhaps, think it illustrates the superstition of slaves. I sat in my usual place on the floor near the window, where I could hear much that was said in the street without being seen. The family had retired for the night, and all was still. I sat there thinking of my children, when I heard a low strain of music. A band of serenaders were under the window, playing "Home, sweet home."[1] I listened till the sounds did not seem like music, but like the moaning of children. It seemed as if my heart would burst. I rose from my sitting posture, and knelt. A streak of moonlight was on the floor before me, and in the midst of it appeared the forms of my two children. They vanished; but I had seen them distinctly. Some will call it a dream, others a vision. I know not how to account for it, but it made a strong impression on my mind, and I felt certain something had happened to my little ones.

I had not seen Betty since morning. Now I heard her softly turning the key. As soon as she entered, I clung to her, and begged her to let me know whether my children were dead, or whether they were sold; for I had seen their spirits in my room, and I was sure something had happened to them. "Lor, chile," said she, putting her arms round me, "you's got de highsterics. I'll sleep wid you tonight, 'cause you'll make a noise, and ruin missis. Something has stirred you up mightily. When you is done cryin, I'll talk wid you. De chillern is well, and mighty happy. I seed 'em myself. Does dat satisfy you? Dar, chile, be

---

1   *Home, sweet home*   Popular song written by John Howard Payne and first performed in 1823.

still! Somebody vill hear you." I tried to obey her. She lay down and was soon sound asleep; but no sleep would come to my eyelids.

At dawn, Betty was up and off to the kitchen. The hours passed on, and the vision of the night kept constantly recurring to my thought. After a while I heard the voices of two women in the entry. In one of them I recognized the housemaid. The other said to her, "Did you know Linda Brent's children was sold to the speculator yesterday. They say ole massa Flint was mighty glad to see 'em drove out of town; but they say they've come back agin. I 'spect it's all their daddy's doings. They say he's bought William too. Lor! how it will take hold of ole massa Flint! I'm going roun' to aunt Marthy's to see 'bout it."

I bit my lips till the blood came to keep from crying out. Were my children with their grandmother, or had the speculator carried them off? The suspense was dreadful. Would Betty never come, and tell me the truth about it? At last she came, and I eagerly repeated what I had overheard. Her face was one broad bright smile. "Lor, you foolish ting!" said she. "I'se gwine to tell you all 'bout it. De gals is eating thar breakfast, and missus tole me to let her tell you; but, poor creeter! t'aint right to keep you waitin', and I'se gwine to tell you. Brudder, chillern, all is bought by de daddy! I'se laugh more dan nuff, tinking 'bout ole massa Flint. Lor, how he vill swar! He's got ketched dis time, and how; but I must be getting out o' dis, or dem gals vill come and ketch me."

Betty went off laughing; and I said to myself, "Can it be true that my children are free? I have not suffered for them in vain. Thank God!"

Great surprise was expressed when it was known that my children had returned to their grandmother's. The news spread through town, and many a kind word was bestowed on the little ones.

Dr. Flint went to my grandmother's to ascertain who was the owner of my children, and she informed him. "I expected as much," said he. "I am glad to hear it. I have had news from Linda lately, and I shall soon have her. You need never expect to see her free. She shall be my slave as long as I live, and when I am dead she shall be the slave of my children. If I ever find out that you or Phillip had anything to do with her running off I'll kill him. And if I meet William in the street, and he presumes to look at me, I'll flog him within an inch of his life. Keep those brats out of my sight!"

As he turned to leave, my grandmother said something to remind him of his own doings. He looked back upon her, as if he would have been glad to strike her to the ground.

I had my season of joy and thanksgiving. It was the first time since my childhood that I had experienced any real happiness. I heard of the old doctor's threats, but they no longer had the same power to trouble me. The darkest cloud that hung over my life had rolled away. Whatever slavery might do to me, it could not shackle my children. If I fell a sacrifice, my little ones were saved. It was well for me that my simple heart believed all that had been promised for their welfare. It is always better to trust than to doubt.

CHAPTER 20. NEW PERILS

The doctor, more exasperated than ever, again tried to revenge himself on my relatives. He arrested uncle Phillip on the charge of having aided my flight. He was carried before a court, and swore truly that he knew nothing of my intention to escape, and that he had not seen me since I left my master's plantation. The doctor then demanded that he should give bail for five hundred dollars that he would have nothing to do with me. Several gentlemen offered to be security for him; but Mr. Sands told him he had better go back to jail, and he would see that he came out without giving bail.

The news of his arrest was carried to my grandmother, who conveyed it to Betty. In the kindness of her heart, she again stowed me away under the floor; and as she walked back and forth, in the performance of her culinary duties, she talked apparently to herself, but with the intention that I should hear what was going on. I hoped that my uncle's imprisonment would last but few days; still I was anxious. I thought it likely that Dr. Flint would do his utmost to taunt and insult him, and I was afraid my uncle might lose control of himself, and retort in some way that would be construed into a punishable offence; and I was well aware that in court his word would not be taken against any white man's. The search for me was renewed. Something had excited suspicions that I was in the vicinity. They searched the house I was in. I heard their steps and their voices. At night, when all were asleep, Betty came to release me from my place of confinement. The fright I had undergone, the constrained posture, and the dampness of the ground, made me ill for several days. My uncle was soon after taken out of prison; but the movements of all my relatives, and of all our friends, were very closely watched.

We all saw that I could not remain where I was much longer. I had already stayed longer than was intended, and I knew my presence must be a source of perpetual anxiety to my kind benefactress. During this time, my friends had laid many plans for my escape, but the extreme vigilance of my persecutors made it impossible to carry them into effect.

One morning I was much startled by hearing somebody trying to get into my room. Several keys were tried, but none fitted. I instantly conjectured it was one of the housemaids; and I concluded she must either have heard some noise in the room, or have noticed the entrance of Betty. When my friend came, at her usual time, I told her what had happened. "I knows who it was," said she. "'Pend upon it, 'twas dat Jenny. Dat nigger allers got de debble in her." I suggested that she might have seen or heard something that excited her curiosity.

"Tut! tut! chile!" exclaimed Betty, "she ain't seen notin', nor hearn notin'. She only 'spects something. Dat's all. She wants to fine out who hab cut and make my gownd. But she won't nebber know. Dat's sartin. I'll git missis to fix her."

I reflected a moment, and said, "Betty, I must leave here tonight."

"Do as you tink best, poor chile," she replied. "I'se mighty 'fraid dat 'ere nigger vill pop on you some time."

She reported the incident to her mistress, and received orders to keep Jenny busy in the kitchen till she could see my uncle Phillip. He told her he would send a friend for me that very evening. She told him she hoped I was going to the north, for it was very dangerous for me to remain anywhere in the vicinity. Alas, it was not an easy thing, for one in my situation, to go to the north. In order to leave the coast quite clear for me, she went into the country to spend the day with her brother, and took Jenny with her. She was afraid to come and bid me goodbye, but she left a kind message with Betty. I heard her carriage roll from the door, and I never again saw her who had so generously befriended the poor, trembling fugitive! Though she was a slaveholder, to this day my heart blesses her!

I had not the slightest idea where I was going. Betty brought me a suit of sailor's clothes—jacket, trousers, and tarpaulin hat.[1] She gave me a small bundle, saying I might need it where I was going. In cheery tones, she exclaimed, "I'se *so* glad you is gwine to free parts! Don't forget ole Betty. P'raps I'll come 'long by and by."

I tried to tell her how grateful I felt for all her kindness, but she interrupted me. "I don't want no tanks, honey. I'se glad I could help you, and I hope de good Lord vill open de path for you. I'se gwine wid you to de lower gate. Put your hands in your pockets, and walk ricketty,[2] like de sailors."

I performed to her satisfaction. At the gate I found Peter, a young colored man, waiting for me. I had known him for years. He had been an apprentice to my father, and had always borne a good character. I was not afraid to trust to him. Betty bade me a hurried goodbye, and we walked off. "Take courage, Linda," said my friend Peter. "I've got a dagger, and no man shall take you from me, unless he passes over my dead body."

It was a long time since I had taken a walk out of doors, and the fresh air revived me. It was also pleasant to hear a human voice speaking to me above a whisper. I passed several people whom I knew, but they did not recognize

---

1 *tarpaulin hat* Canvas hat waterproofed with tar.
2 *ricketty* Unsteadily.

me in my disguise. I prayed internally that, for Peter's sake, as well as my own, nothing might occur to bring out his dagger. We walked on till we came to the wharf. My aunt Nancy's husband was a seafaring man, and it had been deemed necessary to let him into our secret. He took me into his boat, rowed out to a vessel not far distant, and hoisted me on board. We three were the only occupants of the vessel. I now ventured to ask what they proposed to do with me. They said I was to remain on board till near dawn, and then they would hide me in Snaky Swamp, till my uncle Phillip had prepared a place of concealment for me. If the vessel had been bound north, it would have been of no avail to me, for it would certainly have been searched. About four o'clock, we were again seated in the boat, and rowed three miles to the swamp. My fear of snakes had been increased by the venomous bite I had received, and I dreaded to enter this hiding-place. But I was in no situation to choose, and I gratefully accepted the best that my poor, persecuted friends could do for me.

Peter landed first, and with a large knife cut a path through bamboos and briers of all descriptions. He came back, took me in his arms, and carried me to a seat made among the bamboos. Before we reached it, we were covered with hundreds of mosquitos. In an hour's time they had so poisoned my flesh that I was a pitiful sight to behold. As the light increased, I saw snake after snake crawling round us. I had been accustomed to the sight of snakes all my life, but these were larger than any I had ever seen. To this day I shudder when I remember that morning. As evening approached, the number of snakes increased so much that we were continually obliged to thrash them with sticks to keep them from crawling over us. The bamboos were so high and so thick that it was impossible to see beyond a very short distance. Just before it became dark we procured a seat nearer to the entrance of the swamp, being fearful of losing our way back to the boat. It was not long before we heard the paddle of oars, and the low whistle, which had been agreed upon as a signal. We made haste to enter the boat, and were rowed back to the vessel. I passed a wretched night; for the heat of the swamp, the mosquitos, and the constant terror of snakes, had brought on a burning fever. I had just dropped asleep, when they came and told me it was time to go back to that horrid swamp. I could scarcely summon courage to rise. But even those large, venomous snakes were less dreadful to my imagination than the white men in that community called civilized. This time Peter took a quantity of tobacco to burn, to keep off the mosquitos. It produced the desired effect on them, but gave me nausea and severe headache. At dark we returned to the vessel. I had been so sick during the day, that Peter declared I should go home that night, if the devil himself was on patrol. They told me a place of concealment had been provided for me at my grandmother's. I could not imagine how it was possible to hide me in her house, every nook and corner of which was known to the

Flint family. They told me to wait and see. We were rowed ashore, and went boldly through the streets, to my grandmother's. I wore my sailor's clothes, and had blackened my face with charcoal. I passed several people whom I knew. The father of my children came so near that I brushed against his arm; but he had no idea who it was.

"You must make the most of this walk," said my friend Peter, "for you may not have another very soon."

I thought his voice sounded sad. It was kind of him to conceal from me what a dismal hole was to be my home for a long, long time.

Chapter 21. The Loophole of Retreat

A small shed had been added to my grandmother's house years ago. Some boards were laid across the joists at the top, and between these boards and the roof was a very small garret, never occupied by anything but rats and mice. It was a pent roof, covered with nothing but shingles, according to the southern custom for such buildings. The garret was only nine feet long, and seven wide. The highest part was three feet high, and sloped down abruptly to the loose board floor. There was no admission for either light or air. My uncle Phillip, who was a carpenter, had very skillfully made a concealed trap door, which communicated with the storeroom. He had been doing this while I was waiting in the swamp. The storeroom opened upon a piazza. To this hole I was conveyed as soon as I entered the house. The air was stifling; the darkness total. A bed had been spread on the floor. I could sleep quite comfortably on one side; but the slope was so sudden that I could not turn on the other without hitting the roof. The rats and mice ran over my bed; but I was weary, and I slept such sleep as the wretched may, when a tempest has passed over them. Morning came. I knew it only by the noises I heard; for in my small den day and night were all the same. I suffered for air even more than for light. But I was not comfortless. I heard the voices of my children. There was joy and there was sadness in the sound. It made my tears flow. How I longed to speak to them! I was eager to look on their faces; but there was no hole, no crack, through which I could peep. This continued darkness was oppressive. It seemed horrible to sit or lie in a cramped position day after day, without one gleam of light. Yet I would have chosen this, rather than my lot as a slave, though white people considered it an easy one; and it was so compared with the fate of others. I was never cruelly over-worked; I was never lacerated with the whip from head to foot; I was never so beaten and bruised that I could not turn from one side to the other; I never had my heel-strings cut to prevent my running away; I was never chained to a log and forced to drag it about, while I toiled in the fields from morning till night; I was never branded with hot iron, or torn by bloodhounds. On the contrary, I had always been kindly treated, and tenderly cared for, until I came into the hands of Dr. Flint. I had never wished for freedom till then. But though my life in slavery was comparatively devoid of hardships, God pity the woman who is compelled to lead such a life!

My food was passed up to me through the trap-door my uncle had contrived; and my grandmother, my uncle Phillip, and aunt Nancy would seize such opportunities as they could, to mount up there and chat with me at the opening. But of course this was not safe in the daytime. It must all be done in darkness. It was impossible for me to move in an erect position, but I crawled about my den for exercise. One day I hit my head against something, and found it was a gimlet.[1] My uncle had left it sticking there when he made the trap-door. I was as rejoiced as Robinson Crusoe[2] could have been in finding such a treasure. It put a lucky thought into my head. I said to myself, "Now I will have some light. Now I will see my children." I did not dare to begin my work during the daytime, for fear of attracting attention. But I groped round; and having found the side next the street, where I could frequently see my children, I stuck the gimlet in and waited for evening. I bored three rows of holes, one above another; then I bored out the interstices between. I thus succeeded in making one hole about an inch long and an inch broad. I sat by it till late into the night, to enjoy the little whiff of air that floated in. In the morning I watched for my children. The first person I saw in the street was Dr. Flint. I had a shuddering, superstitious feeling that it was a bad omen. Several familiar faces passed by. At last I heard the merry laughing of children, and presently two sweet little faces were looking up at me, as though they knew I was there, and were conscious of the joy they imparted. How I longed to *tell* them I was there!

My condition was now a little improved. But for weeks I was tormented by hundreds of little red insects, fine as a needle's point, that pierced through my skin, and produced an intolerable burning. The good grandmother gave me herb teas and cooling medicines, and finally I got rid of them. The heat of my den was intense, for nothing but thin shingles protected me from the scorching summer's sun. But I had my consolations. Through my peeping-hole I could watch the children, and when they were near enough, I could hear their talk. Aunt Nancy brought me all the news she could hear at Dr. Flint's. From her I learned that the doctor had written to New York to a colored woman, who had been born and raised in our neighborhood, and had breathed his contaminating atmosphere. He offered her a reward if she could

---

1   *gimlet*   Tool used for boring holes.
2   *Robinson Crusoe*   Protagonist of Daniel Defoe's novel of the same name (1719). In the novel, Crusoe is shipwrecked on an uninhabited island and manages to build a dwelling and farm for himself with the few tools he successfully scavenges from the shipwreck.

find out anything about me. I know not what was the nature of her reply; but he soon after started for New York in haste, saying to his family that he had business of importance to transact. I peeped at him as he passed on his way to the steamboat. It was a satisfaction to have miles of land and water between us, even for a little while; and it was a still greater satisfaction to know that he believed me to be in the Free States. My little den seemed less dreary than it had done. He returned, as he did from his former journey to New York, without obtaining any satisfactory information. When he passed our house next morning, Benny was standing at the gate. He had heard them say that he had gone to find me, and he called out, "Dr. Flint, did you bring my mother home? I want to see her." The doctor stamped his foot at him in a rage, and exclaimed, "Get out of the way, you little damned rascal! If you don't, I'll cut off your head."

Benny ran terrified into the house, saying, "You can't put me in jail again. I don't belong to you now." It was well that the wind carried the words away from the doctor's ear. I told my grandmother of it, when we had our next conference at the trap-door; and begged of her not to allow the children to be impertinent to the irascible old man.

Autumn came, with a pleasant abatement of heat. My eyes had become accustomed to the dim light, and by holding my book or work in a certain position near the aperture I contrived to read and sew. That was a great relief to the tedious monotony of my life. But when winter came, the cold penetrated through the thin shingle roof, and I was dreadfully chilled. The winters there are not so long, or so severe, as in northern latitudes; but the houses are not built to shelter from cold, and my little den was peculiarly comfortless. The kind grandmother brought me bed-clothes and warm drinks. Often I was obliged to lie in bed all day to keep comfortable; but with all my precautions, my shoulders and feet were frostbitten. O, those long, gloomy days, with no object for my eye to rest upon, and no thoughts to occupy my mind, except the dreary past and the uncertain future! I was thankful when there came a day sufficiently mild for me to wrap myself up and sit at the loophole to watch the passersby. Southerners have the habit of stopping and talking in the streets, and I heard many conversations not intended to meet my ears. I heard slave-hunters planning how to catch some poor fugitive. Several times I heard allusions to Dr. Flint, myself, and the history of my children, who, perhaps, were playing near the gate. One would say, "I wouldn't move my little finger to catch her, as old Flint's property." Another would say, "I'll catch *any* nigger for the reward. A man ought to have what belongs to him, if he *is* a damned brute." The opinion was often expressed that I was in the Free States. Very rarely did anyone suggest that I might be in the vicinity. Had the least suspicion rested on my grandmother's house, it would have been burned to the ground. But it was the last place they thought of. Yet there was no place, where slavery existed, that could have afforded me so good a place of concealment.

Dr. Flint and his family repeatedly tried to coax and bribe my children to tell something they had heard said about me. One day the doctor took them into a shop, and offered them some bright little silver pieces and gay handkerchiefs if they would tell where their mother was. Ellen shrank away from him, and would not speak; but Benny spoke up, and said, "Dr. Flint, I don't know where my mother is. I guess she's in New York; and when you go there again, I wish you'd ask her to come home, for I want to see her; but if you put her in jail, or tell her you'll cut her head off, I'll tell her to go right back."

Chapter 22. Christmas Festivities

Christmas was approaching. Grandmother brought me materials, and I busied myself making some new garments and little playthings for my children. Were it not that hiring day is near at hand, and many families are fearfully looking forward to the probability of separation in a few days, Christmas might be a happy season for the poor slaves. Even slave mothers try to gladden the hearts of their little ones on that occasion. Benny and Ellen had their Christmas stockings filled. Their imprisoned mother could not have the privilege of witnessing their surprise and joy. But I had the pleasure of peeping at them as they went into the street with their new suits on. I heard Benny ask a little playmate whether Santa Claus brought him anything. "Yes," replied the boy; "but Santa Claus ain't a real man. It's the children's mothers that put things into the stockings." "No, that can't be," replied Benny, "for Santa Claus brought Ellen and me these new clothes, and my mother has been gone this long time."

How I longed to tell him that his mother made those garments, and that many a tear fell on them while she worked!

Every child rises early on Christmas morning to see the Johnkannaus. Without them, Christmas would be shorn of its greatest attraction. They consist of companies of slaves from the plantations, generally of the lower class. Two athletic men, in calico wrappers, have a net thrown over them, covered with all manner of bright-colored stripes. Cows' tails are fastened to their backs, and their heads are decorated with horns. A box, covered with sheepskin, is called the gumbo box. A dozen beat on this, while others strike triangles and jawbones, to which bands of dancers keep time. For a month previous they are composing songs, which are sung on this occasion. These companies, of a hundred each, turn out early in the morning, and are allowed to go round till twelve o'clock, begging for contributions. Not a door is left unvisited where there is the least chance of obtaining a penny or a glass of rum. They do not drink while they are out, but carry the rum home in jugs, to have a carousal. These Christmas donations frequently amount to twenty or thirty dollars. It is seldom that any white man or child refuses to give them a trifle. If he does, they regale his ears with the following song:

> Poor massa, so dey say;
> Down in de heel, so dey say;
> Got no money, so dey say;
> Not one shillin, so dey say;
> God A'mighty bress you, so dey say.

Christmas is a day of feasting, both with white and colored people. Slaves, who are lucky enough to have a few shillings, are sure to spend them for good eating; and many a turkey and pig is captured, without saying "By your leave, sir." Those who cannot obtain these, cook a 'possum, or a raccoon, from which savory dishes can be made. My grandmother raised poultry and pigs for sale; and it was her established custom to have both a turkey and a pig roasted for Christmas dinner.

On this occasion, I was warned to keep extremely quiet, because two guests had been invited. One was the town constable, and the other was a free colored man, who tried to pass himself off for white, and who was always ready to do any mean work for the sake of currying favor with white people. My grandmother had a motive for inviting them. She managed to take them all over the house. All the rooms on the lower floor were thrown open for them to pass in and out; and after dinner, they were invited upstairs to look at a fine mockingbird my uncle had just brought home. There, too, the rooms were all thrown open, that they might look in. When I heard them talking on the piazza, my heart almost stood still. I knew this colored man had spent many nights hunting for me. Everybody knew he had the blood of a slave father in his veins; but for the sake of passing himself off for white, he was ready to kiss the slaveholders' feet. How I despised him! As for the constable, he wore no false colors. The duties of his office were despicable, but he was superior to his companion, inasmuch as he did not pretend to be what he was not. Any white man, who could raise money enough to buy a slave, would have considered himself degraded by being a constable; but the office enabled its possessor to exercise authority. If he found any slave out after nine o'clock, he could whip him as much as he liked; and that was a privilege to be coveted. When the guests were ready to depart, my grandmother gave each of them some of her nice pudding, as a present for their wives. Through my peep-hole I saw them go out of the gate, and I was glad when it closed after them. So passed the first Christmas in my den.

When spring returned, and I took in the little patch of green the aperture commanded, I asked myself how many more summers and winters I must be condemned to spend thus. I longed to draw in a plentiful draught of fresh air, to stretch my cramped limbs, to have room to stand erect, to feel the earth under my feet again. My relatives were constantly on the lookout for a chance of escape; but none offered that seemed practicable, and even tolerably safe. The hot summer came again, and made the turpentine drop from the thin roof over my head.

During the long nights, I was restless for want of air, and I had no room to toss and turn. There was but one compensation; the atmosphere was so stifled that even mosquitos would not condescend to buzz in it. With all my detestation of Dr. Flint, I could hardly wish him a worse punishment, either in this world or that which is to come, than to suffer what I suffered in one single summer. Yet the laws allowed him to be out in the free air, while I, guiltless of crime, was pent up in here, as the only means of avoiding the cruelties the laws allowed him to inflict upon me! I don't know what kept life within me. Again and again, I thought I should die before long; but I saw the leaves of another autumn whirl through the air, and felt the touch of another winter. In summer the most terrible thunderstorms were acceptable, for the rain came through the roof, and I rolled up my bed that it might cool the hot boards under it. Later in the season, storms sometimes wet my clothes through and through, and that was not comfortable when the air grew chilly. Moderate storms I could keep out by filling the chinks with oakum.[1]

But uncomfortable as my situation was, I had glimpses of things out of doors, which made me thankful for my wretched hiding-place. One day I saw a slave pass our gate, muttering, "It's his own, and he can kill it if he will." My grandmother told me that woman's history. Her mistress had that day seen her baby for the first time, and in the lineaments of its fair face she saw a likeness to her husband. She turned the bondwoman and her child out of doors, and forbade her ever to return. The slave went to her master, and told him what had happened. He promised to talk with her mistress, and make it all right. The next day she and her baby were sold to a Georgia trader.

Another time I saw a woman rush wildly by, pursued by two men. She was a slave, the wet nurse of her mistress's children. For some trifling offence her mistress ordered her to be stripped and whipped. To escape the degradation

---

1   *oakum* Loose fibers from hemp ropes that have been unwound and separated, often used as a caulking material.

and the torture, she rushed to the river, jumped in, and ended her wrongs in death.

Senator Brown, of Mississippi,[1] could not be ignorant of many such facts as these, for they are of frequent occurrence in every Southern State. Yet he stood up in the Congress of the United States, and declared that slavery was "a great moral, social, and political blessing; a blessing to the master, and a blessing to the slave!"

I suffered much more during the second winter than I did during the first. My limbs were benumbed by inaction, and the cold filled them with cramp. I had a very painful sensation of coldness in my head; even my face and tongue stiffened, and I lost the power of speech. Of course it was impossible, under the circumstances, to summon any physician. My brother William came and did all he could for me. Uncle Phillip also watched tenderly over me; and poor grandmother crept up and down to inquire whether there were any signs of returning life. I was restored to consciousness by the dashing of cold water in my face, and found myself leaning against my brother's arm, while he bent over me with streaming eyes. He afterwards told me he thought I was dying, for I had been in an unconscious state sixteen hours. I next became delirious, and was in great danger of betraying myself and my friends. To prevent this, they stupefied me with drugs. I remained in bed six weeks, weary in body and sick at heart. How to get medical advice was the question. William finally went to a Thompsonian doctor,[2] and described himself as having all my pains and aches. He returned with herbs, roots, and ointment. He was especially charged to rub on the ointment by a fire; but how could a fire be made in my little den? Charcoal in a furnace was tried, but there was no outlet for the gas, and it nearly cost me my life. Afterwards coals, already kindled, were brought up in an iron pan, and placed on bricks. I was so weak, and it was so long since I had enjoyed the warmth of a fire, that those few coals actually made me weep. I think the medicines did me some good; but my recovery was very slow. Dark thoughts passed through my mind as I lay there day after day. I tried to be thankful for my little cell, dismal as it was, and even to love it, as part of the price I had paid for the redemption of my children. Sometimes I thought God was a compassionate Father, who would forgive my sins for the sake of my sufferings. At other times, it seemed to me there was no justice or mercy in the divine government. I asked why the curse of slavery was permitted to exist,

---

1   *Senator Brown, of Mississippi*   Albert Gallatin Brown (1813–80) was Democratic Senator from Mississippi from 1854 until 1861. He was a member of a group of proslavery Democrats known as Fire-Eaters; he said in a speech that he "would spread the blessings of slavery ... to the uttermost ends of the earth."

2   *Thompsonian doctor*   Person trained in "Thomsonian" medicine, a popular nineteenth-century system of medicine founded by the herbalist Samuel Thomson (1769–1843), who believed in using steam baths and herbs to rid the body of toxins and thus restore health.

and why I had been so persecuted and wronged from youth upward. These things took the shape of mystery, which is to this day not so clear to my soul as I trust it will be hereafter.

In the midst of my illness, grandmother broke down under the weight of anxiety and toil. The idea of losing her, who had always been my best friend and a mother to my children, was the sorest trial I had yet had. O, how earnestly I prayed that she might recover! How hard it seemed, that I could not tend upon her, who had so long and so tenderly watched over me!

One day the screams of a child nerved me with strength to crawl to my peeping-hole, and I saw my son covered with blood. A fierce dog, usually kept chained, had seized and bitten him. A doctor was sent for, and I heard the groans and screams of my child while the wounds were being sewed up. O, what torture to a mother's heart, to listen to this and be unable to go to him!

But childhood is like a day in spring, alternately shower and sunshine. Before night Benny was bright and lively, threatening the destruction of the dog; and great was his delight when the doctor told him the next day that the dog had bitten another boy and been shot. Benny recovered from his wounds; but it was long before he could walk.

When my grandmother's illness became known, many ladies, who were her customers, called to bring her some little comforts, and to inquire whether she had everything she wanted. Aunt Nancy one night asked permission to watch with her sick mother, and Mrs. Flint replied, "I don't see any need of your going. I can't spare you." But when she found other ladies in the neighborhood were so attentive, not wishing to be outdone in Christian charity, she also sallied forth, in magnificent condescension, and stood by the bedside of her who had loved her in her infancy, and who had been repaid by such grievous wrongs. She seemed surprised to find her so ill, and scolded uncle Phillip for not sending for Dr. Flint. She herself sent for him immediately, and he came. Secure as I was in my retreat, I should have been terrified if I had known he was so near me. He pronounced my grandmother in a very critical situation, and said if her attending physician wished it, he would visit her. Nobody wished to have him coming to the house at all hours, and we were not disposed to give him a chance to make out a long bill.

As Mrs. Flint went out, Sally told her the reason Benny was lame was, that a dog had bitten him. "I'm glad of it," she replied. "I wish he had killed him. It would be good news to send to his mother. *Her* day will come. The dogs will grab *her* yet." With these Christian words she and her husband departed, and, to my great satisfaction, returned no more.

I heard from uncle Phillip, with feelings of unspeakable joy and gratitude, that the crisis was passed and grandmother would live. I could now say from my heart, "God is merciful. He has spared me the anguish of feeling that I caused her death."

Chapter 24. The Candidate for Congress

The summer had nearly ended, when Dr. Flint made a third visit to New York, in search of me. Two candidates were running for Congress, and he returned in season to vote. The father of my children was the Whig[1] candidate. The doctor had hitherto been a staunch Whig; but now he exerted all his energies for the defeat of Mr. Sands. He invited large parties of men to dine in the shade of his trees, and supplied them with plenty of rum and brandy. If any poor fellow drowned his wits in the bowl, and, in the openness of his convivial heart, proclaimed that he did not mean to vote the Democratic ticket, he was shoved into the street without ceremony.

The doctor expended his liquor in vain. Mr. Sands was elected; an event which occasioned me some anxious thoughts. He had not emancipated my children and if he should die, they would be at the mercy of his heirs. Two little voices, that frequently met my ear, pleaded with me not to let their father depart without striving to make their freedom secure. Years had passed since I had spoken to him. I had not even seen him since the night I passed him, unrecognized in my disguise of a sailor. I supposed he would call before he left, to say something to my grandmother concerning the children, and I resolved what course to take.

The day before his departure for Washington I made arrangements, towards evening, to get from my hiding-place into the storeroom below. I found myself so stiff and clumsy that it was with great difficulty I could hitch from one resting place to another. When I reached the storeroom my ankles gave way under me, and I sank exhausted on the floor. It seemed as if I could never use my limbs again. But the purpose I had in view roused all the strength I had. I crawled on my hands and knees to the window, and, screened behind a barrel, I waited for his coming. The clock struck nine, and I knew the steamboat would leave between ten and eleven. My hopes were failing. But presently I heard his voice, saying to someone, "Wait for me a moment. I wish to see aunt Martha." When he came out, as he passed the window, I said, "Stop one moment, and let me speak for my children." He started, hesitated, and then passed on, and went out of the gate. I closed the shutter I had partially opened, and sank down behind the barrel. I had suffered much; but seldom had I experienced a

---

1 *Whig* The Whig party took shape in the 1830s in opposition to Andrew Jackson's presidency; they tended to oppose both an overly powerful executive branch and territorial expansion and drew their support mainly from the urban middle classes, in contrast to the poor farmers and working-class men who formed the Democrats' base.

leaner[1] pang than I then felt. Had my children, then, become of so little consequence to him? And had he so little feeling for their wretched mother that he would not listen a moment while she pleaded for them? Painful memories were so busy within me, that I forgot I had not hooked the shutter, till I heard someone opening it. I looked up. He had come back. "Who called me?" said he, in a low tone. "I did," I replied. "Oh, Linda," said he, "I knew your voice; but I was afraid to answer, lest my friend should hear me. Why do you come here? Is it possible you risk yourself in this house? They are mad to allow it. I shall expect to hear that you are all ruined." I did not wish to implicate him, by letting him know my place of concealment; so I merely said, "I thought you would come to bid grandmother goodbye, and so I came here to speak a few words to you about emancipating my children. Many changes may take place during the six months you are gone to Washington and it does not seem right for you to expose them to the risk of such changes. I want nothing for myself; all I ask is, that you will free my children, or authorize some friend to do it, before you go."

He promised he would do it, and also expressed a readiness to make any arrangements whereby I could be purchased.

I heard footsteps approaching, and closed the shutter hastily. I wanted to crawl back to my den, without letting the family know what I had done; for I knew they would deem it very imprudent. But he stepped back into the house to tell my grandmother that he had spoken with me at the storeroom window, and to beg of her not to allow me to remain in the house overnight. He said it was the height of madness for me to be there; that we should certainly all be ruined. Luckily, he was in too much of a hurry to wait for a reply, or the dear old woman would surely have told him all.

I tried to go back to my den, but found it more difficult to go up than I had to come down. Now that my mission was fulfilled, the little strength that had supported me through it was gone, and I sank helpless on the floor. My grandmother, alarmed at the risk I had run, came into the storeroom in the dark, and locked the door behind her. "Linda," she whispered, "where are you?"

"I am here by the window," I replied. "I *couldn't* have him go away without emancipating the children. Who knows what may happen?"

"Come, come, child," said she, "it won't do for you to stay here another minute. You've done wrong; but I can't blame you, poor thing!"

I told her I could not return without assistance, and she must call my uncle. Uncle Phillip came, and pity prevented him from scolding me. He carried me back to my dungeon, laid me tenderly on the bed, gave me some medicine, and

---

1   *leaner*   Sharper.

asked me if there was anything more he could do. Then he went away, and I was left with my own thoughts—starless as the midnight darkness around me.

My friends feared I should become a cripple for life; and I was so weary of my long imprisonment that, had it not been for the hope of serving my children, I should have been thankful to die; but, for their sakes, I was willing to bear on.

Chapter 25. Competition in Cunning

Dr. Flint had not given me up. Every now and then he would say to my grandmother that I would yet come back, and voluntarily surrender myself; and that when I did, I could be purchased by my relatives, or anyone who wished to buy me. I knew his cunning nature too well not to believe that this was a trap laid for me; and so all my friends understood it. I resolved to match my cunning against his cunning. In order to make him believe that I was in New York, I resolved to write him a letter dated from that place. I sent for my friend Peter, and asked him if he knew any trustworthy seafaring person, who would carry such a letter to New York, and put it in the post office there. He said he knew one that he would trust with his own life to the ends of the world. I reminded him that it was a hazardous thing for him to undertake. He said he knew it, but he was willing to do anything to help me. I expressed a wish for a New York paper, to ascertain the names of some of the streets. He run his hand into his pocket, and said, "Here is half a one, that was round a cap I bought of a peddler yesterday." I told him the letter would be ready the next evening. He bade me goodbye, adding, "Keep up your spirits, Linda; brighter days will come by and by."

My uncle Phillip kept watch over the gate until our brief interview was over. Early the next morning, I seated myself near the little aperture to examine the newspaper. It was a piece of the *New York Herald*; and, for once, the paper that systematically abuses the colored people, was made to render them a service.[1] Having obtained what information I wanted concerning streets and numbers, I wrote two letters, one to my grandmother, the other to Dr. Flint. I reminded him how he, a gray-headed man, had treated a helpless child, who had been placed in his power, and what years of misery he had brought upon her. To my grandmother, I expressed a wish to have my children sent to me at the north, where I could teach them to respect themselves, and set them a virtuous example; which a slave mother was not allowed to do at the south.

---

1   *New York Herald ... service* The *New York Herald* was one of the most widely circulated newspapers in mid-nineteenth-century America; its founder, James Gordon Bennett, was known for editorials that were vehemently against the abolition of slavery.

I asked her to direct her answer to a certain street in Boston, as I did not live in New York, though I went there sometimes. I dated these letters ahead, to allow for the time it would take to carry them, and sent a memorandum of the date to the messenger. When my friend came for the letters, I said, "God bless and reward you, Peter, for this disinterested kindness. Pray be careful. If you are detected, both you and I will have to suffer dreadfully. I have not a relative who would dare to do it for me." He replied, "You may trust to me, Linda. I don't forget that your father was my best friend, and I will be a friend to his children so long as God lets me live."

It was necessary to tell my grandmother what I had done, in order that she might be ready for the letter, and prepared to hear what Dr. Flint might say about my being at the north. She was sadly troubled. She felt sure mischief would come of it. I also told my plan to aunt Nancy, in order that she might report to us what was said at Dr. Flint's house. I whispered it to her through a crack, and she whispered back, "I hope it will succeed. I shan't mind being a slave all *my* life, if I can only see you and the children free."

I had directed that my letters should be put into the New York post office on the 20th of the month. On that evening of the 24th my aunt came to say that Dr. Flint and his wife had been talking in a low voice about a letter he had received, and that when he went to his office he promised to bring it when he came to tea. So I concluded I should hear my letter read the next morning. I told my grandmother Dr. Flint would be sure to come, and asked her to have him sit near a certain door, and leave it open, that I might hear what he said. The next morning I took my station within sound of that door, and remained motionless as a statue. It was not long before I heard the gate slam, and the well-known footsteps enter the house. He seated himself in the chair that was placed for him, and said, "Well, Martha, I've brought you a letter from Linda. She has sent me a letter also. I know exactly where to find her; but I don't choose to go to Boston for her. I had rather she would come back of her own accord, in a respectable manner. Her uncle Phillip is the best person to go for her. With *him*, she would feel perfectly free to act. I am willing to pay his expenses going and returning. She shall be sold to her friends. Her children are free; at least I suppose they are; and when you obtain her freedom, you'll make a happy family. I suppose, Martha, you have no objection to my reading to you the letter Linda has written to you."

He broke the seal, and I heard him read it. The old villian! He had suppressed the letter I wrote to grandmother, and prepared a substitute of his own, the purport of which was as follows:

> Dear Grandmother: I have long wanted to write to you; but the disgraceful manner in which I left you and my children made me ashamed to do it. If

you knew how much I have suffered since I ran away, you would pity and forgive me. I have purchased freedom at a dear rate. If any arrangement could be made for me to return to the south without being a slave, I would gladly come. If not, I beg of you to send my children to the north. I cannot live any longer without them. Let me know in time, and I will meet them in New York or Philadelphia, whichever place best suits my uncle's convenience. Write as soon as possible to your unhappy daughter,

LINDA

"It is very much as I expected it would be," said the old hypocrite, rising to go. "You see the foolish girl has repented of her rashness, and wants to return. We must help her to do it, Martha. Talk with Phillip about it. If he will go for her, she will trust to him, and come back. I should like an answer tomorrow. Good morning, Martha."

As he stepped out on the piazza, he stumbled over my little girl. "Ah, Ellen, is that you?" he said, in his most gracious manner. "I didn't see you. How do you do?"

"Pretty well, sir," she replied. "I heard you tell grandmother that my mother is coming home. I want to see her."

"Yes, Ellen, I am going to bring her home very soon," rejoiced he; "and you shall see her as much as you like, you little curly-headed nigger."

This was as good as a comedy to me, who had heard it all; but grandmother was frightened and distressed, because the doctor wanted my uncle to go for me.

The next evening Dr. Flint called to talk the matter over. My uncle told him that from what he had heard of Massachusetts, he judged he should be mobbed if he went there after a runaway slave.[1] "All stuff and nonsense, Phillip!" replied the doctor. "Do you suppose I want you to kick up a row in Boston? The business can all be done quietly. Linda writes that she wants to come back. You are her relative, and she would trust *you*. The case would be different if I went. She might object to coming with *me*; and the damned abolitionists, if they knew I was her master, would not believe me, if I told them she had begged to go back. They would get up a row; and I should not like to see Linda dragged through the streets like a common negro. She has been very ungrateful to me for all my kindness; but I forgive her, and want to act the part of a friend towards her. I have no wish to hold her as my slave. Her friends can buy her as soon as she arrives here."

Finding that his arguments failed to convince my uncle, the doctor "let the cat out of the bag," by saying that he had written to the mayor of Boston,

---

1 *Massachusetts ... slave* A reference to the fact that abolitionists in Boston actively attempted to protect people who had made it North to freedom from being forced back into slavery by their enslavers.

to ascertain whether there was a person of my description at the street and number from which my letter was dated. He had omitted this date in the letter he had made up to read to my grandmother. If I had dated from New York, the old man would probably have made another journey to that city. But even in that dark region, where knowledge is so carefully excluded from the slave, I had heard enough about Massachusetts to come to the conclusion that slaveholders did not consider it a comfortable place to go to in search of a runaway. That was before the Fugitive Slave Law was passed; before Massachusetts had consented to become a "nigger hunter" for the south.

My grandmother, who had become skittish by seeing her family always in danger, came to me with a very distressed countenance, and said, "What will you do if the mayor of Boston sends him word that you haven't been there? Then he will suspect the letter was a trick; and maybe he'll find out something about it, and we shall all get into trouble. O Linda, I wish you had never sent the letters."

"Don't worry yourself, grandmother," said I. "The mayor of Boston won't trouble himself to hunt niggers for Dr. Flint. The letters will do good in the end. I shall get out of this dark hole some time or other."

"I hope you will, child," replied the good, patient old friend. "You have been here a long time; almost five years; but whenever you do go, it will break your old grandmother's heart. I should be expecting every day to hear that you were brought back in irons and put in jail. God help you, poor child! Let us be thankful that some time or other we shall go 'where the wicked cease from troubling, and the weary are at rest.'" My heart responded, Amen.

The fact that Dr. Flint had written to the mayor of Boston convinced me that he believed my letter to be genuine, and of course that he had no suspicion of my being anywhere in the vicinity. It was a great object to keep up this delusion, for it made me and my friends feel less anxious, and it would be very convenient whenever there was a chance to escape. I resolved, therefore, to continue to write letters from the north from time to time.

Two or three weeks passed, and as no news came from the mayor of Boston, grandmother began to listen to my entreaty to be allowed to leave my cell, sometimes, and exercise my limbs to prevent my becoming a cripple. I was allowed to slip down into the small storeroom, early in the morning, and remain there a little while. The room was all filled up with barrels, except a small open space under my trapdoor. This faced the door, the upper part of which was of glass, and purposely left uncurtained that the curious might look in. The air of this place was close; but it was so much better than the atmosphere of my cell, that I dreaded to return. I came down as soon as it was light, and remained till eight o'clock, when people began to be about, and there was danger that someone might come on the piazza. I had tried various applications[1] to bring warmth and feeling into my limbs, but without avail. They were so numb and stiff that it was a painful effort to move; and had my enemies come upon me during the first mornings I tried to exercise them a little in the small unoccupied space of the storeroom, it would have been impossible for me to have escaped.

Chapter 26. Important Era in My Brother's Life

I missed the company and kind attentions of my brother William, who had gone to Washington with his master, Mr. Sands. We received several letters from him, written without any allusion to me, but expressed in such a manner that I knew he did not forget me. I disguised my hand,[2] and wrote to him in the same manner. It was a long session; and when it closed, William wrote to inform us that Mr. Sands was going to the north, to be gone some time, and that he was to accompany him. I knew that his master had promised to give him his freedom, but no time had been specified. Would William trust to a slave's chances? I remembered how we used to talk together, in our young days, about obtaining our freedom, and I thought it very doubtful whether he would come back to us.

Grandmother received a letter from Mr. Sands saying that William had proved a most faithful servant, and he would also say a valued friend; that no mother had ever trained a better boy. He said he had travelled through the Northern States and Canada; and though the abolitionists had tried to decoy him away, they had never succeeded. He ended by saying they should be at home shortly.

We expected letters from William, describing the novelties of his journey, but none came. In time, it was reported that Mr. Sands would return late in the autumn, accompanied by a bride. Still no letters from William. I felt almost sure I should never see him again on southern soil; but had he no word of comfort to send to his friends at home? to the poor captive in her dungeon? My thoughts wandered through the dark past, and over the uncertain future. Alone in my cell, where no eye but God's could see me, I wept bitter tears. How earnestly I prayed to him to restore me to my children, and enable me to be a useful woman and a good mother!

At last the day arrived for the return of the travellers. Grandmother had made loving preparations to welcome her absent boy back to the old hearthstone. When the dinner table was laid, William's plate occupied its old place.

---

1   *applications*   Medicated lotions or herbal preparations.
2   *hand*   I.e., handwriting.

The stagecoach[1] went by empty. My grandmother waited dinner. She thought perhaps he was necessarily detained by his master. In my prison I listened anxiously, expecting every moment to hear my dear brother's voice and step. In the course of the afternoon a lad was sent by Mr. Sands to tell grandmother that William did not return with him; that the abolitionists had decoyed him away. But he begged her not to feel troubled about it, for he felt confident she would see William in a few days. As soon as he had time to reflect he would come back, for he could never expect to be so well off at the north as he had been with him.

If you had seen the tears, and heard the sobs, you would have thought the messenger had brought tidings of death instead of freedom. Poor old grandmother felt that she should never see her darling boy again. And I was selfish. I thought more of what I had lost, than of what my brother had gained. A new anxiety began to trouble me. Mr. Sands had expended a good deal of money, and would naturally feel irritated by the loss he had incurred. I greatly feared this might injure the prospects of my children, who were now becoming valuable property. I longed to have their emancipation made certain. The more so, because their master and father was now married. I was too familiar with slavery not to know that promises made to slaves, though with kind intentions, and sincere at the time, depend upon many contingencies for their fulfillment.

Much as I wished William to be free, the step he had taken made me sad and anxious. The following Sabbath was calm and clear; so beautiful that it seemed like a Sabbath in the eternal world. My grandmother brought the children out on the piazza, that I might hear their voices. She thought it would comfort me in my despondency; and it did. They chatted merrily, as only children can. Benny said, "Grandmother, do you think uncle Will has gone for good? Won't he ever come back again? Maybe he'll find mother. If he does, won't she be glad to see him! Why don't you and uncle Phillip, and all of us, go and live where mother is? I should like it; wouldn't you, Ellen?"

"Yes, I should like it," replied Ellen; "but how could we find her? Do you know the place, grandmother? I don't remember how mother looked—do you, Benny?"

Benny was just beginning to describe me when they were interrupted by an old slave woman, a near neighbor, named Aggie. This poor creature had witnessed the sale of her children, and seen them carried off to parts unknown, without any hopes of ever hearing from them again. She saw that my grandmother had been weeping, and she said, in a sympathizing tone, "What's the matter, aunt Marthy?"

---

1   *stagecoach*   Carriage that carried passengers and packages on a scheduled journey between predetermined locations.

"O Aggie," she replied, "it seems as if I shouldn't have any of my children or grandchildren left to hand me a drink when I'm dying, and lay my old body in the ground. My boy didn't come back with Mr. Sands. He stayed at the north."

Poor old Aggie clapped her hands for joy. "Is *dat* what you's crying fur?" she exclaimed. "Git down on your knees and bress de Lord! I don't know whar my poor chillern is, and I nebber 'spect to know. You don't know whar poor Linda's gone to; but you *do* know whar her brudder is. He's in free parts; and dat's de right place. Don't murmur at de Lord's doings, but git down on your knees and tank him for his goodness."

My selfishness was rebuked by what poor Aggie said. She rejoiced over the escape of one who was merely her fellow-bondman, while his own sister was only thinking what his good fortune might cost her children. I knelt and prayed God to forgive me; and I thanked him from my heart, that one of my family was saved from the grasp of slavery.

It was not long before we received a letter from William. He wrote that Mr. Sands had always treated him kindly, and that he had tried to do his duty to him faithfully. But ever since he was a boy, he had longed to be free; and he had already gone through enough to convince him he had better not lose the chance that offered. He concluded by saying, "Don't worry about me, dear grandmother. I shall think of you always, and it will spur me on to work hard and try to do right. When I have earned money enough to give you a home, perhaps you will come to the north, and we can all live happy together."

Mr. Sands told my uncle Phillip the particulars about William's leaving him. He said, "I trusted him as if he were my own brother, and treated him as kindly. The abolitionists talked to him in several places; but I had no idea they could tempt him. However, I don't blame William. He's young and inconsiderate, and those Northern rascals decoyed him. I must confess the scamp was very bold about it. I met him coming down the steps of the Astor House[1] with his trunk on his shoulder, and I asked him where he was going. He said he was going to change his old trunk. I told him it was rather shabby, and asked if he didn't need some money. He said, No, thanked me, and went off. He did not return so soon as I expected; but I waited patiently. At last I went to see if our trunks were packed, ready for our journey. I found them locked, and a sealed note on the table informed me where I could find the keys. The fellow even tried to be religious. He wrote that he hoped God would always bless me, and reward me for my kindness; that he was not unwilling to serve me; but he wanted to be a free man; and that if I thought he did wrong, he hoped I would forgive him. I intended to give him his freedom in five years. He might have

---

1 *Astor House* Fashionable hotel in New York City.

trusted me. He has shown himself ungrateful; but I shall not go for him, or send for him. I feel confident that he will soon return to me."

I afterwards heard an account of the affair from William himself. He had not been urged away by abolitionists. He needed no information they could give him about slavery to stimulate his desire for freedom. He looked at his hands, and remembered that they were once in irons. What security had he that they would not be so again? Mr. Sands was kind to him; but he might indefinitely postpone the promise he had made to give him his freedom. He might come under pecuniary embarrassments,[1] and his property be seized by creditors; or he might die, without making any arrangements in his favor. He had too often known such accidents to happen to slaves who had kind masters, and he wisely resolved to make sure of the present opportunity to own himself. He was scrupulous about taking any money from his master on false pretences; so he sold his best clothes to pay for his passage to Boston. The slaveholders pronounced him a base, ungrateful wretch, for thus requiting his master's indulgence. What would they have done under similar circumstances?

When Dr. Flint's family heard that William had deserted Mr. Sands, they chuckled greatly over the news. Mrs. Flint made her usual manifestations of Christian feeling, by saying, "I'm glad of it. I hope he'll never get him again. I like to see people paid back in their own coin. I reckon Linda's children will have to pay for it. I should be glad to see them in the speculator's hands again, for I'm tired of seeing those little niggers march about the streets."

Chapter 27. New Destination for the Children

Mrs. Flint proclaimed her intention of informing Mrs. Sands who was the father of my children. She likewise proposed to tell her what an artful[2] devil I was; that I had made a great deal of trouble in her family; that when Mr. Sands was at the north, she didn't doubt I had followed him in disguise, and persuaded William to run away. She had some reason to entertain such an idea; for I had written from the north, from time to time, and I dated my letters from various places. Many of them fell into Dr. Flint's hands, as I expected they would; and he must have come to the conclusion that I travelled about a good deal. He kept a close watch over my children, thinking they would eventually lead to my detection.

A new and unexpected trial was in store for me. One day, when Mr. Sands and his wife were walking in the street, they met Benny. The lady took a fancy to him and exclaimed, "What a pretty little negro! Whom does he belong to?"

---

1 *pecuniary embarrassments* Financial difficulties.
2 *artful* Conniving.

Benny did not hear the answer; but he came home very indignant with the stranger lady, because she had called him a negro. A few days afterwards, Mr. Sands called on my grandmother, and told her he wanted her to take the children to his house. He said he had informed his wife of his relation to them, and told her they were motherless; and she wanted to see them.

When he had gone, my grandmother came and asked what I would do. The question seemed a mockery. What *could* I do? They were Mr. Sands's slaves, and their mother was a slave, whom he had represented to be dead. Perhaps he thought I was. I was too much pained and puzzled to come to any decision; and the children were carried without my knowledge.

Mrs. Sands had a sister from Illinois staying with her. This lady, who had no children of her own, was so much pleased with Ellen, that she offered to adopt her, and bring her up as she would a daughter. Mrs. Sands wanted to take Benjamin. When grandmother reported this to me, I was tried almost beyond endurance. Was this all I was to gain by what I had suffered for the sake of having my children free? True, the prospect *seemed* fair; but I knew too well how lightly slaveholders held such "parental relations." If pecuniary troubles should come, or if the new wife required more money than could conveniently be spared, my children might be thought of as a convenient means of raising funds. I had no trust in thee, O Slavery! Never should I know peace till my children were emancipated with all due formalities of law.

I was too proud to ask Mr. Sands to do anything for my own benefit; but I could bring myself to become a supplicant for my children. I resolved to remind him of the promise he had made me, and to throw myself upon his honor for the performance of it. I persuaded my grandmother to go to him, and tell him I was not dead, and that I earnestly entreated him to keep the promise he had made me; that I had heard of the recent proposals concerning my children, and did not feel easy to accept them; that he had promised to emancipate them, and it was time for him to redeem his pledge. I know there was some risk in thus betraying that I was in the vicinity; but what will not a mother do for her children? He received the message with surprise, and said, "The children are free. I have never intended to claim them as slaves. Linda may decide their fate. In my opinion, they had better be sent to the north. I don't think they are quite safe here. Dr. Flint boasts that they are still in his power. He says they were his daughter's property, and as she was not of age when they were sold, the contract is not legally binding."

So, then, after all I had endured for their sakes, my poor children were between two fires; between my old master and their new master! And I was powerless. There was no protecting arm of the law for me to invoke. Mr. Sands proposed that Ellen should go, for the present, to some of his relatives, who had removed to Brooklyn, Long Island. It was promised that she should be well taken care of, and sent to school. I consented to it, as the best arrangement I could make for her. My grandmother, of course, negotiated it all; and Mrs. Sands knew of no other person in the transaction. She proposed that they should take Ellen with them to Washington and keep her till they had a good chance of sending her, with friends, to Brooklyn. She had an infant daughter. I had a glimpse of it, as the nurse passed with it in her arms. It was not a pleasant thought to me, that the bondwoman's child should tend her free-born sister; but there was no alternative. Ellen was made ready for the journey. O, how it tried my heart to send her away, so young, alone, among strangers! Without a mother's love to shelter her from the storms of life; almost without memory of a mother! I doubted whether she and Benny would have for me the natural affection that children feel for a parent. I thought to myself that I might perhaps never see my daughter again, and I had a great desire that she should look upon me, before she went, that she might take my image with her in her memory. It seemed to me cruel to have her brought to my dungeon. It was sorrow enough for her young heart to know that her mother was a victim of slavery, without seeing the wretched hiding place to which it had driven her. I begged permission to pass the last night in one of the open chambers, with my little girl. They thought I was crazy to think of trusting such a young child with my perilous secret. I told them I had watched her character, and I felt sure she would not betray me; that I was determined to have an interview, and if they would not facilitate it, I would take my own way to obtain it. They remonstrated against the rashness of such a proceeding; but finding they could not change my purpose, they yielded. I slipped through the trapdoor into the storeroom, and my uncle kept watch at the gate, while I passed into the piazza and went upstairs, to the room I used to occupy. It was more than five years since I had seen it; and how the memories crowded on me! There I had taken shelter when my mistress drove me from her house; there came my old tyrant, to mock, insult, and curse me; there my children were first laid in my arms; there I had watched over them, each day with a deeper and sadder love; there I had knelt to God, in anguish of heart, to forgive the wrong I had done. How vividly it all came back! And after this long, gloomy interval, I stood there such a wreck!

In the midst of these meditations, I heard footsteps on the stairs. The door opened, and my uncle Phillip came in, leading Ellen by the hand. I put my arms round her, and said, "Ellen, my dear child, I am your mother." She drew back a little, and looked at me; then, with sweet confidence, she laid her cheek against mine, and I folded her to the heart that had been so long desolated. She was the first to speak. Raising her head, she said, inquiringly, "You really are my mother?" I told her I really was; that during all the long time she had not seen me, I had loved her most tenderly; and that now she was going away,

I wanted to see her and talk with her, that she might remember me. With a sob in her voice, she said, "I'm glad you've come to see me; but why didn't you ever come before? Benny and I have wanted so much to see you! He remembers you, and sometimes he tells me about you. Why didn't you come home when Dr. Flint went to bring you?"

I answered, "I couldn't come before, dear. But now that I am with you, tell me whether you like to go away." "I don't know," said she, crying. "Grand-mother says I ought not to cry; that I am going to a good place, where I can learn to read and write, and that by and by I can write her a letter. But I shan't have Benny, or grandmother, or uncle Phillip, or anybody to love me. Can't you go with me? O, *do* go, dear mother!"

I told her I couldn't go now, but sometime I would come to her, and then she and Benny and I would live together, and have happy times. She wanted to run and bring Benny to see me now. I told her he was going to the north, before long, with uncle Phillip, and then I would come to see him before he went away. I asked if she would like to have me stay all night and sleep with her. "O, yes," she replied. Then, turning to her uncle, she said, pleadingly, "*May* I stay? Please, uncle! She is my own mother." He laid his hand on her head, and said, solemnly, "Ellen, this is the secret you have promised grand-mother never to tell. If you ever speak of it to anybody, they will never let you see your grandmother again, and your mother can never come to Brooklyn." "Uncle," she replied, "I will never tell." He told her she might stay with me; and when he had gone, I took her in my arms and told her I was a slave, and that was the reason she must never say she had seen me. I exhorted her to be a good child, to try to please the people where she was going, and that God would raise her up friends. I told her to say her prayers, and remember always to pray for her poor mother, and that God would permit us to meet again. She wept, and I did not check her tears. Perhaps she would never again have a chance to pour her tears into a mother's bosom. All night she nestled in my arms, and I had no inclination to slumber. The moments were too precious to lose any of them. Once, when I thought she was asleep, I kissed her forehead softly, and she said, "I am not asleep, dear mother."

Before dawn they came to take me back to my den. I drew aside the window curtain, to take a last look of my child. The moonlight shone on her face, and I bent over her, as I had done years before, that wretched night when I ran away. I hugged her close to my throbbing heart; and tears, too sad for such young eyes to shed, flowed down her cheeks, as she gave her last kiss, and whispered in my ear, "Mother, I will never tell." And she never did.

When I got back to my den, I threw myself on the bed and wept there alone in the darkness. It seemed as if my heart would burst. When the time for Ellen's departure drew nigh, I could hear neighbors and friends saying to her,

"Goodbye, Ellen. I hope your poor mother will find you out. *Won't* you be glad to see her!" She replied, "Yes, ma'am"; and they little dreamed of the weighty secret that weighed down her young heart. She was an affectionate child, but naturally very reserved, except with those she loved, and I felt secure that my secret would be safe with her. I heard the gate close after her, with such feelings as only a slave mother can experience. During the day my meditations were very sad. Sometimes I feared I had been very selfish not to give up all claim to her, and let her go to Illinois, to be adopted by Mrs. Sands's sister. It was my experience of slavery that decided me against it. I feared that circumstances might arise that would cause her to be sent back. I felt confident that I should go to New York myself; and then I should be able to watch over her, and in some degree protect her.

Dr. Flint's family knew nothing of the proposed arrangement till after Ellen was gone, and the news displeased them greatly. Mrs. Flint called on Mrs. Sands's sister to inquire into the matter. She expressed her opinion very freely as to the respect Mr. Sands showed for his wife, and for his own character, in acknowledging those "young niggers." And as for sending Ellen away, she pronounced it to be just as much stealing as it would be for him to come and take a piece of furniture out of her parlor. She said her daughter was not of age to sign the bill of sale, and the children were her property; and when she became of age, or was married, she could take them, wherever she could lay hands on them.

Miss Emily Flint, the little girl to whom I had been bequeathed, was now in her sixteenth year. Her mother considered it all right and honorable for her, or her future husband, to steal my children; but she did not understand how anybody could hold up their heads in respectable society, after they had purchased their own children, as Mr. Sands had done. Dr. Flint said very little. Perhaps he thought that Benny would be less likely to be sent away if he kept quiet. One of my letters, that fell into his hands, was dated from Canada; and he seldom spoke of me now. This state of things enabled me to slip down into the storeroom more frequently, where I could stand upright and move my limbs more freely.

Days, weeks, and months passed, and there came no news of Ellen. I sent a letter to Brooklyn, written in my grandmother's name, to inquire whether she had arrived there. Answer was returned that she had not. I wrote to her in Washington; but no notice was taken of it. There was one person there, who ought to have had some sympathy with the anxiety of the child's friends at home; but the links of such relations as he had formed with me, are easily broken and cast away as rubbish. Yet how protectively and persuasively he once talked to the poor, helpless slave girl! And how entirely I trusted him! But now suspicions darkened my mind. Was my child dead, or had they deceived me, and sold her?

If the secret memoirs of many members of Congress should be published, curious details would be unfolded. I once saw a letter from a member of Congress to a slave, who was the mother of six of his children. He wrote to request that she would send her children away from the great house before his return, as he expected to be accompanied by friends. The woman could not read, and was obliged to employ another to read the letter. The existence of the colored children did not trouble this gentleman, it was only the fear that friends might recognize in their features a resemblance to him.

At the end of six months, a letter came to my grandmother, from Brooklyn. It was written by a young lady in the family, and announced that Ellen had just arrived. It contained the following message from her: "I do try to do just as you told me to, and I pray for you every night and morning." I understood that these words were meant for me; and they were a balsam to my heart. The writer closed her letter by saying, "Ellen is a nice little girl, and we shall like to have to have her with us. My cousin, Mr. Sands, has given her to me, to be my little waiting maid. I shall send her to school, and I hope someday she will write to you yourself." This letter perplexed and troubled me. Had my child's father merely placed her there till she was old enough to support herself? Or had he given her to his cousin, as a piece of property? If the last idea was correct, his cousin might return to the south at any time, and hold Ellen as a slave. I tried to put away from me the painful thought that such a foul wrong could have been done to us. I said to myself, "Surely there must be *some* justice in man"; then I remembered, with a sigh, how slavery perverted all the natural feelings of the human heart. It gave me a pang to look on my light-hearted boy. He believed himself free; and to have him brought under the yoke of slavery, would be more than I could bear. How I longed to have him safely out of the reach of its power!

CHAPTER 28. AUNT NANCY

I have mentioned my great-aunt, who was a slave in Dr. Flint's family, and who had been my refuge during the shameful persecutions I suffered from him. This aunt had been married at twenty years of age; that is, as far as slaves *can* marry. She had the consent of her master and mistress, and a clergyman performed the ceremony. But it was a mere form, without any legal value. Her master or mistress could annul it any day they pleased. She had always slept on the floor in the entry, near Mrs. Flint's chamber door, that she might be within call. When she was married, she was told that she might have the use of a small room in an outhouse.[1] Her mother and her husband furnished it. He was a seafaring man, and was allowed to sleep there when he was at home. But on the wedding evening, the bride was ordered to her old post on the entry floor.

Mrs. Flint, at that time, had no children; but she was expecting to be a mother, and if she should want a drink of water in the night, what could she do without her slave to bring it? So my aunt was compelled to lie at her door, until one midnight she was forced to leave, to give premature birth to a child. In a fortnight she was required to resume her place on the entry floor, because Mrs. Flint's babe needed her attentions. She kept her station there through the summer and winter, until she had given premature birth to six children; and all the while she was employed as night-nurse to Mr. Flint's children. Finally, toiling all day, and being deprived of rest at night, completely broke down her constitution, and Dr. Flint declared it was impossible she could ever become the mother of a living child. The fear of losing so valuable a servant by death, now induced them to allow her to sleep in her little room in the outhouse, except when there was sickness in the family. She afterwards had two feeble babes, one of whom died in a few days, and the other in four weeks. I well remember her patient sorrow as she held the last dead baby in her arms. "I wish it could have lived," she said; "it is not the will of God that any of my children should live. But I will try to be fit to meet their little spirits in heaven."

Aunt Nancy was housekeeper and waiting-maid in Dr. Flint's family. Indeed, she was the *factotum*[2] of the household. Nothing went on well without her. She was my mother's twin sister, and, as far as was in her power, she supplied a mother's place to us orphans. I slept with her all the time I lived in my old master's house, and the bond between us was very strong. When my friends tried to discourage me from running away, she always encouraged me. When they thought I had better return and ask my master's pardon, because there was no possibility of escape, she sent me word never to yield. She said if I persevered I might, perhaps, gain the freedom of my children; and even if I perished in doing it, that was better than to leave them to groan under the same persecutions that had blighted my own life. After I was shut up in my dark cell, she stole away, whenever she could, to bring me the news and say something cheering. How often did I kneel down to listen to her words of consolation, whispered through a crack! "I am old, and have not long to live," she used to say; "and I could die happy if I could only see you and the children free. You must pray to God, Linda, as I do for you, that he will lead you out of this darkness." I would beg her not to worry herself on my account;

---

1   *outhouse*   Smaller building outside of the main house.
2   *factotum*   Servant (in this case, an enslaved servant) who undertakes all manner of tasks in the household.

that there was an end of all the suffering sooner or later, and that whether I lived in chains or in freedom, I should always remember her as the good friend who had been the comfort of my life. A word from her always strengthened me; and not me only. The whole family relied upon her judgment, and were guided by her advice.

I had been in my cell six years when my grandmother was summoned to the bedside of this, her last remaining daughter. She was very ill, and they said she would die. Grandmother had not entered Dr. Flint's house for several years. They had treated her cruelly, but she thought nothing of that now. She was grateful for permission to watch by the deathbed of her child. They had always been devoted to each other; and now they sat looking into each other's eyes, longing to speak of the secret that had weighed so much on them both. My aunt had been stricken with paralysis. She lived two days, and the last day she was speechless. Before she lost the power of utterance, she told her mother not to grieve if she could not speak to her, that she would try to hold up her hand, to let her know that all was well with her. Even the hard-heartened doctor was a little softened when he saw the dying woman try to smile on the aged mother, who was kneeling by her side. His eyes moistened for a moment, as he said she had always been a faithful servant, and they should never be able to supply her place. Mrs. Flint took to her bed, quite overcome by the shock. While my grandmother sat alone with the dead, the doctor came in, leading his youngest son, who had always been a great pet with aunt Nancy, and was much attached to her. "Martha," said he, "aunt Nancy loved this child, and when he comes where you are, I hope you will be kind to him, for her sake." She replied, "Your wife was my foster-child, Dr. Flint, the foster-sister of my poor Nancy, and you little know me if you think I can feel anything but good will for her children."

"I wish the past could be forgotten, and that we might never think of it," said he; "and that Linda would come to supply her aunt's place. She would be worth more to us than all the money that could be paid for her. I wish it for your sake also, Martha. Now that Nancy is taken away from you, she would be a great comfort to your old age."

He knew he was touching a tender chord. Almost choking with grief, my grandmother replied, "It was not I that drove Linda away. My grandchildren are gone; and of my nine children only one is left. God help me!"

To me, the death of this kind relative was an inexpressible sorrow. I knew that she had been slowly murdered; and I felt that my troubles had helped to finish the work. After I heard of her illness, I listened constantly to hear what news was brought from the great house; and the thought that I could not go to her made me utterly miserable. At last, as uncle Phillip came into the house, I heard someone inquire, "How is she?" and he answered, "She is dead." My little cell seemed whirling round, and I knew nothing more till I opened my eyes and found uncle Phillip bending over me. I had no need to ask any questions. He whispered, "Linda, she died happy." I could not weep. My fixed gaze troubled him. "Don't look *so*," he said. "Don't add to my poor mother's trouble. Remember how much she has to bear, and that we ought to do all we can to comfort her." Ah, yes, that blessed old grandmother, who for seventy-three years had borne the pelting storms of a slave-mother's life. She did indeed need consolation!

Mrs. Flint had rendered her poor foster-sister childless, apparently without any compunction; and with cruel selfishness had ruined her health by years of incessant, unrequited toil, and broken rest. But now she became very sentimental. I suppose she thought it would be a beautiful illustration of the attachment existing between slaveholder and slave, if the body of her old worn-out servant was buried at her feet. She sent for the clergyman and asked if he had any objection to burying aunt Nancy in the doctor's family burial place. No colored person had ever been allowed interment in the white people's burying-ground, and the minister knew that all the deceased of our family reposed together in the old graveyard of the slaves. He therefore replied, "I have no objection to complying with your wish; but perhaps aunt Nancy's mother may have some choice as to where her remains shall be deposited."

It had never occurred to Mrs. Flint that slaves could have any feelings. When my grandmother was consulted, she at once said she wanted Nancy to lie with all the rest of her family, and where her own old body would be buried. Mrs. Flint graciously complied with her wish, though she said it was painful to her to have Nancy buried away from *her*. She might have added with touching pathos, "I was so long *used* to sleep with her lying near me, on the entry floor."

My uncle Phillip asked permission to bury his sister at his own expense; and slaveholders are always ready to grant *such* favors to slaves and their relatives. The arrangements were very plain, but perfectly respectable. She was buried on the Sabbath, and Mrs. Flint's minister read the funeral service. There was a large concourse of colored people, bond and free, and a few white persons who had always been friendly to our family. Dr. Flint's carriage was in the procession; and when the body was deposited in its humble resting place, the mistress dropped a tear, and returned to her carriage, probably thinking she had performed her duty nobly.

It was talked of by the slaves as a mighty grand funeral. Northern travellers, passing through the place, might have described this tribute of respect to the humble dead as a beautiful feature in the "patriarchal institution";[1] a touching proof of the attachment between slaveholders and their servants; and tender-hearted Mrs. Flint would have confirmed this impression, with handkerchief at her eyes. *We* could have told them a different story. We could have given them a chapter of wrongs and sufferings, that would have touched their hearts, if they *had* any hearts to feel for the colored people. We could have told them how the poor old slave-mother had toiled, year after year, to earn eight hundred dollars to buy her son Phillip's right to his own earnings; and how that same Phillip paid the expenses of the funeral, which they regarded as doing so much credit to the master. We could also have told them of a poor, blighted young creature, shut up in a living grave for years, to avoid the tortures that would be inflicted on her, if she ventured to come out and look on the face of her departed friend.

All this, and much more, I thought of, as I sat at my loophole, waiting for the family to return from the grave; sometimes weeping, sometimes falling asleep, dreaming strange dreams of the dead and the living.

It was sad to witness the grief of my bereaved grandmother. She had always been strong to bear, and now, as ever, religious faith supported her. But her dark life had become still darker, and age and trouble were leaving deep traces on her withered face. She had four places to knock for me to come to the trapdoor, and each place had a different meaning. She now came oftener than she had done, and talked to me of her dead daughter, while tears trickled slowly down her furrowed cheeks. I said all I could to comfort her; but it was a sad reflection, that instead of being able to help her, I was a constant source of anxiety and trouble. The poor old back was fitted to its burden.[2] It bent under it, but did not break.

Chapter 29. Preparations for Escape

I hardly expect that the reader will credit me, when I affirm that I lived in that little dismal hole, almost deprived of light and air, and with no space to move my limbs, for nearly seven years. But it is a fact; and to me a sad one, even now; for my body still suffers from the effects of that long imprisonment, to say nothing of my soul. Members of my family, now living in New York and Boston, can testify to the truth of what I say.

Countless were the nights that I sat late at the little loophole scarcely large enough to give me a glimpse of one twinkling star. There, I heard the patrols

---

1 *patriarchal institution* I.e., an institution in which slaveowners are perceived as benevolent, fatherly figures.
2 *back ... burden* Reference to a popular proverb: "God fits the back to the burden" (i.e., God gives strength to those who bear the heaviest burdens).

and slave-hunters conferring together about the capture of runaways, well knowing how rejoiced they would be to catch me.

Season after season, year after year, I peeped at my children's faces, and heard their sweet voices, with a heart yearning all the while to say, "Your mother is here." Sometimes it appeared to me as if ages had rolled away since I entered upon that gloomy, monotonous existence. At times, I was stupefied and listless; at other times I became very impatient to know when these dark years would end, and I should again be allowed to feel the sunshine, and breathe the pure air.

After Ellen left us, this feeling increased. Mr. Sands had agreed that Benny might go to the north whenever his uncle Phillip could go with him; and I was anxious to be there also, to watch over my children, and protect them so far as I was able. Moreover, I was likely to be drowned out of my den, if I remained much longer; for the slight roof was getting badly out of repair, and uncle Phillip was afraid to remove the shingles, lest someone should get a glimpse of me. When storms occurred in the night, they spread mats and bits of carpet, which in the morning appeared have been laid out to dry; but to cover the roof in the daytime might have attracted attention. Consequently, my clothes and bedding were often drenched; a process by which the pains and aches in my cramped and stiffened limbs were greatly increased. I revolved various plans of escape in my mind, which I sometimes imparted to my grandmother, when she came to whisper with me at the trap-door. The kind-hearted old woman had an intense sympathy for runaways. She had known too much of the cruelties inflicted on those who were captured. Her memory always flew back at once to the sufferings of her bright and handsome son, Benjamin, the youngest and dearest of her flock. So, whenever I alluded to the subject, she would groan out, "O, don't think of it, child. You'll break my heart." I had no good old aunt Nancy now to encourage me; but my brother William and my children were continually beckoning me to the north.

And now I must go back a few months in my story. I have stated that the first of January was the time for selling slaves, or leasing them out to new masters. If time were counted by heart-throbs, the poor slaves might reckon years of suffering during that festival so joyous to the free. On the New Year's day preceding my aunt's death, one of my friends, named Fanny, was to be sold at auction to pay her master's debts. My thoughts were with her during all the day, and at night I anxiously inquired what had been her fate. I was told that she had been sold to one master, and her four little girls to another master, far distant; that she had escaped from her purchaser, and was not to be found. Her mother was the old Aggie I have spoken of. She lived in a small tenement belonging to my grandmother, and built on the same lot with her own house. Her dwelling was searched and watched, and that brought the patrols so near me that I was obliged to keep very close in my den. The hunters were somehow eluded; and not long afterwards Benny accidentally caught sight of Fanny in her mother's hut. He told his grandmother, who charged him never to speak of it, explaining to him the frightful consequences; and he never betrayed the trust. Aggie little dreamed that my grandmother knew where her daughter was concealed, and that the stooping form of her old neighbor was bending under a similar burden of anxiety and fear; but these dangerous secrets deepened the sympathy between the two old persecuted mothers.

My friend Fanny and I remained many weeks hidden within call of each other; but she was unconscious of the fact. I longed to have her share my den, which seemed a more secure retreat than her own; but I had brought so much trouble on my grandmother, that it seemed wrong to ask her to incur greater risks. My restlessness increased. I had lived too long in bodily pain and anguish of spirit. Always I was in dread that by some accident, or some contrivance, slavery would succeed in snatching my children from me. This thought drove me nearly frantic, and I determined to steer for the North Star at all hazards. At this crisis, Providence opened an unexpected way for me to escape. My friend Peter came one evening, and asked to speak with me. "Your day has come, Linda," said he. "I have found a chance for you to go to the Free States. You have a fortnight to decide." The news seemed too good to be true; but Peter explained his arrangements, and told me all that was necessary was for me to say I would go. I was going to answer him with a joyful yes, when the thought of Benny came to my mind. I told him the temptation was exceedingly strong, but I was terribly afraid of Dr. Flint's alleged power over my child, and that I could not go and leave him behind. Peter remonstrated earnestly. He said such a good chance might never occur again; that Benny was free, and could be sent to me; and that for the sake of my children's welfare I ought not to hesitate a moment. I told him I would consult with uncle Phillip. My uncle rejoiced in the plan, and bade me to go by all means. He promised, if his life was spared, that he would either bring or send my son to me as soon as I reached a place of safety. I resolved to go, but thought nothing had better be said to my grandmother till very near the time of departure. But my uncle thought she would feel it more keenly if I left her so suddenly. "I will reason with her," said he, "and convince her how necessary it is, not only for your sake, but for hers also. You cannot be blind to the fact that she is sinking under her burdens." I was not blind to it. I knew that my concealment was an ever-present source of anxiety, and that the older she grew the more nervously fearful she was of discovery. My uncle talked with her, and finally succeeded in persuading her that it was absolutely necessary for me to seize the chance so unexpectedly offered.

The anticipation of being a free woman proved almost too much for my weak frame. The excitement stimulated me, and at the same time bewildered me. I made busy preparations for my journey, and for my son to follow me. I resolved to have an interview with him before I went, that I might give him cautions and advice, and tell him how anxiously I should be waiting for him at the north. Grandmother stole up to me as often as possible to whisper words of counsel. She insisted upon my writing to Dr. Flint, as soon as I arrived in the Free States, and asking him to sell me to her. She said she would sacrifice her house, and all she had in the world, for the sake of having me safe with my children in any part of the world. If she could only live to know *that* she could die in peace. I promised the dear old faithful friend that I would write to her as soon as I arrived, and put the letter in a safe way to reach her; but in my own mind I resolved that not another cent of her hard earnings should be spent to pay rapacious slaveholders for what they called their property. And even if I had not been unwilling to buy what I had already a right to possess, common humanity would have prevented me from accepting the generous offer, at the expense of turning my aged relative out of house and home, when she was trembling on the brink of the grave.

I was to escape in a vessel; but I forbear to mention any further particulars. I was in readiness, but the vessel was unexpectedly detained several days. Meantime, news came to town of a most horrible murder committed on a fugitive slave, named James. Charity, the mother of this unfortunate young man, had been an old acquaintance of ours. I have told the shocking particulars of his death, in my description of some of the neighboring slaveholders. My grandmother, always nervously sensitive about runaways, was terribly frightened. She felt sure that a similar fate awaited me, if I did not desist from my enterprise. She sobbed, and groaned, and entreated me not to go. Her excessive fear was somewhat contagious, and my heart was not proof against her extreme agony. I was grievously disappointed, but I promised to relinquish my project.

When my friend Peter was apprised of this, he was disappointed and vexed. He said, that judging from our past experience, it would be a long time before I had such another chance to throw away. I told him it need not be thrown away; that I had a friend concealed nearby, who would be glad enough to take the place that had been provided for me. I told him about poor Fanny, and the kind-hearted, noble fellow, who never turned his back upon anybody in distress, white or black, expressed his readiness to help her. Aggie was much surprised when she found that we knew her secret. She was rejoiced to hear of such a chance for Fanny, and arrangements were made for her to go on board the vessel the next night. They both supposed that I had long been at the north, therefore my name was not mentioned in the transaction. Fanny was carried on board at the appointed time, and stowed away in a very small cabin. This accommodation had been purchased at a price that would pay for a voyage to England. But when one proposes to go to fine old England, they stop to calculate whether they can afford the cost of the pleasure; while in making a bargain to escape from slavery, the trembling victim is ready to say, "Take all I have, only don't betray me!"

The next morning I peeped through my loophole, and saw that it was dark and cloudy. At night I received news that the wind was ahead,[1] and the vessel had not sailed. I was exceedingly anxious about Fanny, and Peter too, who was running a tremendous risk at my instigation. Next day the wind and weather remained the same. Poor Fanny had been half dead with fright when they carried her on board, and I could readily imagine how she must be suffering now. Grandmother came often to my den, to say how thankful she was I did not go. On the third morning she rapped for me to come down to the storeroom. The poor old sufferer was breaking down under her weight of trouble. She was easily flurried now. I found her in a nervous, excited state, but I was not aware that she had forgotten to lock the door behind her, as usual. She was exceedingly worried about the detention of the vessel. She was afraid all would be discovered, and then Fanny, and Peter, and I, would all be tortured to death, and Phillip should be utterly ruined, and her house would be torn down. Poor Peter! If he should die such a horrible death as the poor slave James had lately done, and all for his kindness in trying to help me, how dreadful it would be for us all! Alas, the thought was familiar to me, and had sent many a sharp pang through my heart. I tried to suppress my own anxiety, and speak soothingly to her. She brought in some allusion to aunt Nancy, the dear daughter she had recently buried, and then she lost all control of herself. As she stood there, trembling and sobbing, a voice from the piazza called out, "Whar is you, aunt Marthy?" Grandmother was startled, and in her agitation opened the door, without thinking of me. In stepped Jenny, the mischievous housemaid, who had tried to enter my room, when I was concealed in the house of my white benefactress. "I's bin huntin ebery whar for you, aunt Marthy," said she. "My missis wants you to send her some crackers." I had slunk down behind a barrel, which entirely screened me, but I imagined that Jenny was looking directly at the spot, and my heart beat violently. My grandmother immediately thought what she had done, and went out quickly with Jenny to count the crackers locking the door behind her. She returned to me, in a few minutes, the perfect picture of despair. "Poor child!" she exclaimed, "my carelessness has ruined you. The boat ain't gone yet. Get ready immediately,

---

1   *wind was ahead* I.e., there was a head wind, making it difficult to sail.

and go with Fanny. I ain't got another word to say against it now; for there's no telling what may happen this day."

Uncle Phillip was sent for, and he agreed with his mother in thinking that Jenny would inform Dr. Flint in less than twenty-four hours. He advised getting me on board the boat, if possible; if not, I had better keep very still in my den, where they could not find me without tearing the house down. He said it would not do for him to move in the matter, because suspicion would be immediately excited; but he promised to communicate with Peter. I felt reluctant to apply to him again, having implicated him too much already; but there seemed to be no alternative. Vexed as Peter had been by my indecision, he was true to his generous nature, and said at once that he would do his best to help me, trusting I should show myself a stronger woman this time.

He immediately proceeded to the wharf, and found that the wind had shifted, and the vessel was slowly beating downstream. On some pretext of urgent necessity, he offered two boatmen a dollar apiece to catch up with her. He was of lighter complexion than the boatmen he hired, and when the captain saw them coming so rapidly, he thought officers were pursuing his vessel in search of the runaway slave he had on board. They hoisted sails, but the boat gained upon them, and the indefatigable Peter sprang on board.

The captain at once recognized him. Peter asked him to go below, to speak about a bad bill he had given him. When he told his errand, the captain replied, "Why, the woman's here already; and I've put her where you or the devil would have a tough job to find her."

"But it is another woman I want to bring," said Peter. "She is in great distress, too, and you shall be paid anything within reason, if you'll stop and take her."

"What's her name?" inquired the captain.

"Linda," he replied.

"That's the name of the woman already here," rejoined the captain. "By George! I believe you mean to betray me."

"O!" exclaimed Peter, "God knows I wouldn't harm a hair of your head. I am too grateful to you. But there really is another woman in great danger. Do have the humanity to stop and take her!"

After a while they came to an understanding. Fanny, not dreaming I was anywhere about in that region, had assumed my name, though she called herself Johnson. "Linda is a common name," said Peter, "and the woman I want to bring is Linda Brent."

The captain agreed to wait at a certain place till evening, being handsomely paid for his detention.

Of course, the day was an anxious one for us all. But we concluded that if Jenny had seen me, she would be too wise to let her mistress know of it;

and that she probably would not get a chance to see Dr. Flint's family till evening, for I knew very well what were the rules in that household. I afterwards believed that she did not see me; for nothing ever came of it, and she was one of those base characters that would have jumped to betray a suffering fellow being for the sake of thirty pieces of silver.[1]

I made all my arrangements to go on board as soon as it was dusk. The intervening time I resolved to spend with my son. I had not spoken to him for seven years, though I had been under the same roof, and seen him every day, when I was well enough to sit at the loophole. I did not dare to venture beyond the storeroom; so they brought him there, and locked us up together, in a place concealed from the piazza door. It was an agitating interview for both of us. After we had talked and wept together for a little while, he said, "Mother, I'm glad you're going away. I wish I could go with you. I knew you was here; and I have been so afraid they would come and catch you!"

I was greatly surprised, and asked him how he had found it out.

He replied, "I was standing under the eaves, one day, before Ellen went away, and I heard somebody cough up over the wood shed. I don't know what made me think it was you, but I did think so. I missed Ellen, the night before she went away; and grandmother brought her back into the room in the night; and I thought maybe she'd been to see *you*, before she went, for I heard grandmother whisper to her, 'Now go to sleep; and remember never to tell.'"

I asked him if he ever mentioned his suspicions to his sister. He said he never did; but after he heard the cough, if he saw her playing with other children on that side of the house, he always tried to coax her round to the other side, for fear they would hear me cough, too. He said he had kept a close lookout for Dr. Flint, and if he saw him speak to a constable, or a patrol, he always told grandmother. I now recollected that I had seen him manifest uneasiness, when people were on that side of the house, and I had at the time been puzzled to conjecture a motive for his actions. Such prudence may seem extraordinary in a boy of twelve years, but slaves, being surrounded by mysteries, deceptions, and dangers, early learn to be suspicious and watchful, and prematurely cautious and cunning. He had never asked a question of grandmother, or uncle Phillip, and I had often heard him chime in with other children, when they spoke of my being at the north.

I told him I was now really going to the Free States; and if he was a good, honest boy, and a loving child to his dear old grandmother, the Lord would bless him, and bring him to me, and we and Ellen would live together. He began to tell me that grandmother had not eaten anything all day. While he

---

1   *thirty pieces of silver*   Before the Last Supper, Judas Iscariot betrays Jesus for thirty silver coins (see Matthew 26.15).

was speaking, the door was unlocked, and she came in with a small bag of money, which she wanted me to take. I begged her to keep a part of it, at least, to pay for Benny's being sent to the north; but she insisted, while her tears were falling fast, that I should take the whole. "You may be sick among strangers," she said, "and they would send you to the poorhouse to die." Ah, that good grandmother!

For the last time I went up to my nook. Its desolate appearance no longer chilled me, for the light of hope had risen in my soul. Yet, even with the blessed prospect of freedom before me, I felt very sad at leaving forever that old homestead, where I had been sheltered so long by the dear old grandmother; where I had dreamed my first young dream of love; and where, after that had faded away, my children came to twine themselves so closely round my desolate heart. As the hour approached for me to leave, I again descended to the storeroom. My grandmother and Benny were there. She took me by the hand, and said, "Linda, let us pray." We knelt down together, with my child pressed to my heart, and my other arm round the faithful, loving old friend I was about to leave forever. On no other occasion has it ever been my lot to listen to so fervent a supplication for mercy and protection. It thrilled through my heart, and inspired me with trust in God.

Peter was waiting for me in the street. I was soon by his side, faint in body, but strong of purpose. I did not look back upon the old place, though I felt that I should never see it again.

Chapter 30. Northward Bound

I never could tell how we reached the wharf. My brain was all of a whirl, and my limbs tottered under me. At an appointed place we met my uncle Phillip, who had started before us on a different route, that he might reach the wharf first, and give us timely warning if there was any danger. A rowboat was in readiness. As I was about to step in, I felt something pull me gently, and turning round I saw Benny, looking pale and anxious. He whispered in my ear, "I've been peeping into the doctor's window, and he's at home. Goodbye, mother. Don't cry; I'll come." He hastened away. I clasped the hand of my good uncle, to whom I owed so much, and of Peter, the brave, generous friend who had volunteered to run such terrible risks to secure my safety. To this day I remember how bright his face beamed with joy, when he told me he had discovered a safe method for me to escape. Yet that intelligent, enterprising, noble-hearted man was a chattel! liable, by the laws of a country that calls itself civilized, to be sold with horses and pigs! We parted in silence. Our hearts were all too full for words!

Swiftly the boat glided over the water. After a while, one of the sailors said, "Don't be down-hearted, madam. We will take you safely to your husband, in ——." At first I could not imagine what he meant; but I had presence of mind to think that it probably referred to something the captain had told him; so I thanked him, and said I hoped we should have pleasant weather.

When I entered the vessel the captain came forward to meet me. He was an elderly man, with a pleasant countenance. He showed me to a little box of a cabin, where sat my friend Fanny. She started as if she had seen a spectre. She gazed on me in utter astonishment, and exclaimed, "Linda, can this be *you*? or is it your ghost?" When we were locked in each other's arms, my overwrought feelings could no longer be restrained. My sobs reached the ears of the captain, who came and very kindly reminded us, that for his safety, as well as our own, it would be prudent for us not to attract any attention. He said that when there was a sail in sight he wished us to keep below; but at other times, he had no objection to our being on deck. He assured us that he would keep a good lookout, and if we acted prudently, he thought we should be in no danger. He had represented us as women going to meet our husbands in ——. We thanked him, and promised to observe carefully all the directions he gave us.

Fanny and I now talked by ourselves, low and quietly, in our little cabin. She told me of the sufferings she had gone through in making her escape, and of her terrors while she was concealed in her mother's house. Above all, she dwelt on the agony of separation from all her children on that dreadful auction day. She could scarcely credit me, when I told her of the place where I had passed nearly seven years. "We have the same sorrows," said I. "No," replied she, "you are going to see your children soon, and there is no hope that I shall ever even hear from mine."

The vessel was soon under way, but we made slow progress. The wind was against us. I should not have cared for this, if we had been out of sight of the town; but until there were miles of water between us and our enemies, we were filled with constant apprehension that the constables would come on board. Neither could I feel quite at ease with the captain and his men. I was an entire stranger to that class of people, and I had heard that sailors were rough, and sometimes cruel. We were so completely in their power, that if they were bad men, our situation would be dreadful. Now that the captain was paid for our passage, might he not be tempted to make more money by giving us up to those who claimed us as property? I was naturally of a confiding disposition, but slavery had made me suspicious of everybody. Fanny did not share my distrust of the captain or his men. She said she was afraid at first, but she had been on board three days while the vessel lay in the dock, and nobody had betrayed her, or treated her otherwise than kindly.

The captain soon came to advise us to go on deck for fresh air. His friendly and respectful manner, combined with Fanny's testimony, reassured me, and we went with him. He placed us in a comfortable seat, and occasionally entered into conversations. He told us he was a Southerner by birth, and had spent the greater part of his life in the Slave States, and that he had recently lost a brother who traded in slaves. "But," said he, "it is a pitiable and degrading business, and I always felt ashamed to acknowledge my brother in connection with it." As we passed Snaky Swamp, he pointed to it, and said, "There is a slave territory that defies all the laws." I thought of the terrible days I had spent there, and though it was not called Dismal Swamp,[1] it made me feel very dismal as I looked at it.

I shall never forget that night. The balmy air of spring was so refreshing! And how shall I describe my sensations when we were fairly sailing on Chesapeake Bay? O, the beautiful sunshine! the exhilarating breeze! and I could enjoy them without fear or restraint. I had never realized what grand things air and sunlight are till I had been deprived of them.

Ten days after we left land we were approaching Philadelphia. The captain said we should arrive there in the night, but he thought we had better wait till morning, and go on shore in broad daylight, as the best way to avoid suspicion.

I replied, "You know best. But will you stay on board and protect us?"

He saw that I was suspicious, and he said he was sorry, now that he had brought us to the end of our voyage, to find I had so little confidence in him. Ah, if he had ever been a slave he would have known how difficult it was to trust a white man. He assured us that we might sleep through the night without fear; that he would take care we were not left unprotected. Be it said to the honor of this captain, Southerner as he was, that if Fanny and I had been white ladies, and our passage lawfully engaged, he could not have treated us more respectfully. My intelligent friend, Peter, had rightly estimated the character of the man to whose honor he had intrusted us.

The next morning I was on deck as soon as the day dawned. I called Fanny to see the sunrise, for the first time in our lives, on free soil; for such I *then* believed it to be. We watched the reddening sky, and saw the great orb come up slowly out of the water, as it seemed. Soon the waves began to sparkle, and everything caught the beautiful glow. Before us lay the city of strangers. We looked at each other, and the eyes of both were moistened with tears. We had escaped from slavery, and we supposed ourselves to be safe from the hunters.

---

1   *Dismal Swamp*   The Great Dismal Swamp extends across much of southeastern Virginia and northeastern North Carolina. As was the case with swamps in other areas of the South, it was a refuge for many people who had escaped slavery.

But we were alone in the world, and we had left dear ties behind us; ties cruelly sundered by the demon Slavery.

Chapter 31. Incidents in Philadelphia

I had heard that the poor slave had many friends at the north. I trusted we should find some of them. Meantime, we would take it for granted that all were friends, till they proved to the contrary. I sought out the kind captain, thanked him for his attentions, and told him I should never cease to be grateful for the service he had rendered us. I gave him a message to the friends I had left at home, and he promised to deliver it. We were placed in a rowboat, and in about fifteen minutes were landed on a wood wharf in Philadelphia. As I stood looking round, the friendly captain touched me on the shoulder, and said, "There is a respectable-looking colored man behind you. I will speak to him about the New York trains, and tell him you wish to go directly on." I thanked him, and asked him to direct me to some shops where I could buy gloves and veils. He did so, and said he would talk with the colored man till I returned. I made what haste I could. Constant exercise on board the vessel, and frequent rubbing with salt water, had nearly restored the use of my limbs. The noise of the great city confused me, but I found the shops, and bought some double veils and gloves for Fanny and myself. The shopman told me they were so many levies.[1] I had never heard the word before, but I did not tell him so. I thought if he knew I was a stranger he might ask me where I came from. I gave him a gold piece, and when he returned the change, I counted it, and found out how much a levy was. I made my way back to the wharf, where the captain introduced me to the colored man, as the Rev. Jeremiah Durham, minister of Bethel church.[2] He took me by the hand, as if I had been an old friend. He told us we were too late for the morning cars to New York, and must wait until the evening, or the next morning. He invited me to go home with him, assuring me that his wife would give me a cordial welcome; and for my friend he would provide a home with one of his neighbors. I thanked him for so much kindness to strangers, and told him if I must be detained, I should like to hunt up some people who formerly went from our part of the country. Mr. Durham insisted that I should dine with him, and then he would assist me in finding my friends. The sailors came to bid us goodbye. I shook their hardy hands, with tears in my eyes. They had all been kind to us, and they had rendered us a greater service than they could possibly conceive of.

---

1   *levies* Taxes.
2   *Jeremiah ... church* Reverend Jeremiah Durham was the highly respected pastor of Mother Bethel African Methodist Episcopal Church in Philadelphia during the mid-nineteenth century.

I had never seen so large a city, or been in contact with so many people in the streets. It seemed as if those who passed looked at us with an expression of curiosity. My face was so blistered and peeled by sitting on deck, in wind and sunshine, that I thought they could not easily decide to what nation I belonged.

Mrs. Durham met me with a kindly welcome, without asking any questions. I was tired, and her friendly manner was a sweet refreshment. God bless her! I was sure that she had comforted other weary hearts, before I received her sympathy. She was surrounded by her husband and children, in a home made sacred by protecting laws. I thought of my own children and sighed.

After dinner Mr. Durham went with me in quest of the friends I had spoken of. They went from my native town, and I anticipated much pleasure in looking on familiar faces. They were not at home, and we retraced our steps through streets delightfully clean. On the way, Mr. Durham observed that I had spoken to him of a daughter I expected to meet; that he was surprised, for I looked so young he had taken me for a single woman. He was approaching a subject on which I was extremely sensitive. He would ask about my husband next, I thought, and if I answered him truly, what would he think of me? I told him I had two children, one in New York the other at the south. He asked some further questions, and I frankly told him some of the most important events of my life. It was painful for me to do it; but I would not deceive him. If he was desirous of being my friend, I thought he ought to know how far I was worthy of it. "Excuse me, if I have tried your feelings," said he. "I did not question you from idle curiosity. I wanted to understand your situation, in order to know whether I could be of any service to you, or your little girl. Your straightforward answers do you credit; but don't answer everybody so openly. It might give some heartless people a pretext for treating you with contempt."

That word *contempt* burned me like coals of fire. I replied, "God alone knows how I have suffered; and He, I trust, will forgive me. If I am permitted to have my children, I intend to be a good mother, and to live in such a manner that people cannot treat me with contempt."

"I respect your sentiments," said he. "Place your trust in God, and be governed by good principles, and you will not fail to find friends."

When we reached home, I went to my room, glad to shut out the world for a while. The words he had spoken made an indelible impression upon me. They brought up great shadows from the mournful past. In the midst of my meditations I was startled by a knock at the door. Mrs. Durham entered, her face all beaming with kindness, to say that there was an anti-slavery friend[1]

---

1   *anti-slavery friend*   While Jacobs may here be referring simply to a kindly abolitionist, it is also possible that she means a member of the Religious Society of Friends, a Christian denomination, also known

downstairs, who would like to see me. I overcame my dread of encountering strangers, and went with her. Many questions were asked concerning my experiences, and my escape from slavery; but I observed how careful they all were not to say anything that might wound my feelings. How gratifying this was, can be fully understood only by those who have been accustomed to be treated as if they were not included within the pale of human beings. The anti-slavery friend had come to inquire into my plans, and to offer assistance, if needed. Fanny was comfortably established, for the present, with a friend of Mr. Durham. The Anti-Slavery Society agreed to pay her expenses to New York. The same was offered to me but I declined to accept it; telling them that my grandmother had given me sufficient to pay my expenses to the end of my journey. We were urged to remain in Philadelphia a few days, until some suitable escort could be found for us. I gladly accepted the proposition, for I had a dread of meeting slaveholders, and some dread also of railroads. I had never entered a railroad car in my life, and it seemed to me quite an important event.

That night I sought my pillow with feelings I had never carried to it before. I verily believed myself to be a free woman. I was wakeful for a long time, and I had no sooner fallen asleep, than I was roused by fire-bells. I jumped up, and hurried on my clothes. Where I came from, everybody hastened to dress themselves on such occasions. The white people thought a great fire might be used as a good opportunity for insurrection, and that it was best to be in readiness; and the colored people were ordered out to labor in extinguishing the flames. There was but one engine in our town, and colored women and children were often required to drag it to the river's edge and fill it. Mrs. Durham's daughter slept in the same room with me, and seeing that she slept through all the din, I thought it was my duty to wake her. "What's the matter?" said she, rubbing her eyes.

"They're screaming fire in the streets, and the bells are ringing," I replied.

"What of that?" said she, drowsily. "We are used to it. We never get up, without[1] the fire is very near. What good would it do?"

I was quite surprised that it was not necessary for us to go and help fill the engine. I was an ignorant child, just beginning to learn how things went on in great cities.

At daylight, I heard women crying fresh fish, berries, radishes, and various other things. All this was new to me. I dressed myself at an early hour, and sat at the window to watch that unknown tide of life. Philadelphia seemed to be

---

as the Quakers, whose members were often referred to simply as "friends." The Quaker church was officially opposed to slavery and many of its members were active abolitionists; Philadelphia had long been known for its substantial Quaker population.

1   *without* Unless.

a wonderfully great place. At the breakfast table, my idea of going out to drag the engine was laughed over, and I joined in the mirth.

I went to see Fanny, and found her so well contented among her new friends that she was in no haste to leave. I was also very happy with my kind hostess. She had had advantages for education, and was vastly my superior. Every day, almost every hour, I was adding to my little stock of knowledge. She took me out to see the city as much as she deemed prudent. One day she took me to an artist's room, and showed me the portraits of some of her children. I had never seen any paintings of colored people before, and they seemed to me beautiful.

At the end of five days, one of Mrs. Durham's friends offered to accompany us to New York the following morning. As I held the hand of my good hostess in a parting clasp, I longed to know whether her husband had repeated to her what I had told him. I supposed he had, but she never made any allusion to it. I presume it was the delicate silence of womanly sympathy.

When Mr. Durham handed us our tickets, he said, "I am afraid you will have a disagreeable ride, but I could not procure tickets for the first-class cars."

Supposing I had not given him money enough, I offered more. "O, no," said he, "they could not be had for any money. They don't allow colored people to go in the first-class cars."

This was the first chill to my enthusiasm about the Free States. Colored people were allowed to ride in a filthy box, behind white people, at the south, but there they were not required to pay for the privilege. It made me sad to find how the north aped the customs of slavery.

We were stowed away in a large, rough car,[1] with windows on each side, too high for us to look out without standing up. It was crowded with people, apparently of all nations. There were plenty of beds and cradles, containing screaming and kicking babies. Every other man had a cigar or pipe in his mouth, and jugs of whiskey were handed round freely. The fumes of the whiskey and the dense tobacco smoke were sickening to my senses, and my mind was equally nauseated by the coarse jokes and ribald songs around me. It was a very disagreeable ride. Since that time there has been some improvement in these matters.

Chapter 32. The Meeting of Mother and Daughter

When we arrived in New York, I was half crazed by the crowd of coachmen calling out, "Carriage, ma'am?" We bargained with one to take us to Sullivan Street for twelve shillings. A burly Irishman stepped up and said, "I'll tak' ye for sax shillings." The reduction of half the price was an object to us, and

---

1 *car* Railway car.

we asked if he could take us right away. "Troth an I will, ladies," he replied. I noticed that the hackmen smiled at each other, and I inquired whether his conveyance was decent. "Yes, it's dacent it is, marm. Devil a bit would I be after takin' ladies in a cab that was not dacent." We gave him our checks.[1] He went for the baggage, and soon reappeared, saying, "This way, if you plase, ladies." We followed, and found our trunks on a truck, and we were invited to take our seats on them. We told him that was not what we bargained for, and he must take the trunks off. He swore they should not be touched till we had paid him six shillings. In our situation it was not prudent to attract attention, and I was about to pay him what he required, when a man nearby shook his head for me not to do it. After a great ado we got rid of the Irishman, and had our trunks fastened on a hack.[2] We had been recommended to a boarding-house in Sullivan Street, and thither we drove. There Fanny and I separated. The Anti-Slavery Society provided a home for her, and I afterwards heard of her in prosperous circumstances. I sent for an old friend from my part of the country, who had for some time been doing business in New York. He came immediately. I told him I wanted to go to my daughter, and asked him to aid me in procuring an interview.

I cautioned him not to let it be known to the family that I had just arrived from the south, because they supposed I had been at the north seven years. He told me there was a colored woman in Brooklyn who came from the same town I did, and I had better go to her house, and have my daughter meet me there. I accepted the proposition thankfully, and he agreed to escort me to Brooklyn. We crossed Fulton ferry, went up Myrtle Avenue, and stopped at the house he designated. I was just about to enter, when two girls passed. My friend called my attention to them. I turned, and recognized in the eldest, Sarah, the daughter of a woman who used to live with my grandmother, but who had left the south years ago. Surprised and rejoiced at this unexpected meeting, I threw my arms round her, and inquired concerning her mother.

"You take no notice of the other girl," said my friend. I turned, and there stood my Ellen! I pressed her to my heart, then held her away from me to take a look at her. She had changed a good deal in the two years since I parted from her. Signs of neglect could be discerned by eyes less observing than a mother's. My friend invited us all to go into the house; but Ellen said she had been sent of an errand, which she would do as quickly as possible, and go home and ask Mrs. Hobbs to let her come and see me. It was agreed that I should send for her the next day. Her companion, Sarah, hastened to tell her mother of my arrival. When I entered the house, I found the mistress of it absent,

---

1   *checks* Tickets for their baggage.
2   *hack*   I.e., hackney carriage, a horse-drawn carriage available for hire.

and I waited for her return. Before I saw her, I heard her saying, "Where is Linda Brent? I used to know her father and mother." Soon Sarah came with her mother. So there was quite a company of us, all from my grandmother's neighborhood. These friends gathered round me and questioned me eagerly. They laughed, they cried, and they shouted. They thanked God that I had got away from my persecutors and was safe on Long Island. It was a day of great excitement. How different from the silent days I had passed in my dreary den!

The next morning was Sunday. My first waking thoughts were occupied with the note I was to send to Mrs. Hobbs, the lady with whom Ellen lived. That I had recently come into that vicinity was evident; otherwise I should have sooner inquired for my daughter. It would not do to let them know I had just arrived from the south, for that would involve the suspicion of my having been harbored there, and might bring trouble, if not ruin, on several people.

I like a straightforward course, and am always reluctant to resort to subterfuges. So far as my ways have been crooked, I charge them all upon slavery. It was that system of violence and wrong which now left me no alternative but to enact a falsehood. I began my note by stating that I had recently arrived from Canada, and was very desirous to have my daughter come to see me. She came and brought a message from Mrs. Hobbs, inviting me to her house, and assuring me that I need not have any fears. The conversation I had with my child did not leave my mind at ease. When I asked if she was well treated, she answered yes; but there was no heartiness in the tone, and it seemed to me that she said it from an unwillingness to have me troubled on her account. Before she left me, she asked very earnestly, "Mother, when will you take me to live with you?" It made me sad to think that I could not give her a home till I went to work and earned the means; and that might take me a long time. When she was placed with Mrs. Hobbs, the agreement was that she should be sent to school. She had been there two years, and was now nine years old, and she scarcely knew her letters. There was no excuse for this, for there were good public schools in Brooklyn, to which she could have been sent without expense.

She stayed with me till dark, and I went home with her. I was received in a friendly manner by the family, and all agreed in saying that Ellen was a useful, good girl. Mrs. Hobbs looked me coolly in the face, and said, "I suppose you know that my cousin, Mr. Sands, has *given* her to my eldest daughter. She will make a nice waiting-maid for her when she grows up." I did not answer a word. How *could* she, who knew by experience the strength of a mother's love, and who was perfectly aware of the relation Mr. Sands bore to my children—how *could* she look me in the face, while she thrust such a dagger into my heart?

I was no longer surprised that they had kept her in such a state of ignorance. Mr. Hobbs had formerly been wealthy, but he had failed, and afterwards obtained a subordinate situation in the Custom House. Perhaps they expected to return to the south some day; and Ellen's knowledge was quite sufficient for a slave's condition. I was impatient to go to work and earn money, that I might change the uncertain position of my children. Mr. Sands had not kept his promise to emancipate them. I had also been deceived about Ellen. What security had I with regard to Benjamin? I felt that I had none.

I returned to my friend's house in an uneasy state of mind. In order to protect my children, it was necessary that I should own myself. I called myself free, and sometimes felt so; but I knew I was insecure. I sat down that night and wrote a civil letter to Dr. Flint, asking him to state the lowest terms on which he would sell me; and as I belonged by law to his daughter, I wrote to her also, making a similar request.

Since my arrival at the north I had not been unmindful of my dear brother William. I had made diligent inquiries for him, and having heard of him in Boston, I went thither. When I arrived there, I found he had gone to New Bedford. I wrote to that place, and was informed he had gone on a whaling voyage, and would not return for some months. I went back to New York to get employment near Ellen. I received an answer from Dr. Flint, which gave me no encouragement. He advised me to return and submit myself to my rightful owners, and then any request I might make would be granted. I lent this letter to a friend, who lost it; otherwise I would present a copy to my readers.

CHAPTER 33. A HOME FOUND

My greatest anxiety now was to obtain employment. My health was greatly improved, though my limbs continued to trouble me with swelling whenever I walked much. The greatest difficulty in my way was, that those who employed strangers required a recommendation; and in my peculiar position, I could, of course, obtain no certificates from the families I had so faithfully served.

One day an acquaintance told me of a lady who wanted a nurse for her babe, and I immediately applied for the situation. The lady told me she preferred to have one who had been a mother, and accustomed to the care of infants. I told her I had nursed two babes of my own. She asked me many questions, but, to my great relief, did not require a recommendation from my former employers. She told me she was an English woman, and that was a pleasant circumstance to me, because I had heard they had less prejudice against color than Americans entertained. It was agreed that we should try each other for a week. The trial proved satisfactory to both parties, and I was engaged for a month.

The heavenly Father had been most merciful to me in leading me to this place. Mrs. Bruce was a kind and gentle lady, and proved a true and sympathizing friend. Before the stipulated month expired, the necessity of passing up and down stairs frequently, caused my limbs to swell so painfully, that I became unable to perform my duties. Many ladies would have thoughtlessly discharged me; but Mrs. Bruce made arrangements to save me steps, and employed a physician to attend upon me. I had not yet told her that I was a fugitive slave. She noticed that I was often sad, and kindly inquired the cause. I spoke of being separated from my children, and from relatives who were dear to me; but I did not mention the constant feeling of insecurity which oppressed my spirits. I longed for someone to confide in; but I had been so deceived by white people, that I had lost all confidence in them. If they spoke kind words to me, I thought it was for some selfish purpose. I had entered this family with the distrustful feelings I had brought with me out of slavery; but ere six months had passed, I found that the gentle deportment of Mrs. Bruce and the smiles of her lovely babe were thawing my chilled heart. My narrow mind also began to expand under the influences of her intelligent conversation, and the opportunities for reading, which were gladly allowed me whenever I had leisure from my duties. I gradually became more energetic and more cheerful.

The old feeling of insecurity, especially with regard to my children, often threw its dark shadow across my sunshine. Mrs. Bruce offered me a home for Ellen; but pleasant as it would have been, I did not dare to accept it, for fear of offending the Hobbs family. Their knowledge of my precarious situation placed me in their power; and I felt that it was important for me to keep on the right side of them, till, by dint of labor and economy, I could make a home for my children. I was far from feeling satisfied with Ellen's situation. She was not well cared for. She sometimes came to New York to visit me; but she generally brought a request from Mrs. Hobbs that I would buy her a pair of shoes, or some article of clothing. This was accompanied by a promise of payment when Mr. Hobbs's salary at the Custom House became due; but somehow or other the pay-day never came. Thus many dollars of my earnings were expended to keep my child comfortably clothed. That, however, was a slight trouble, compared with the fear that their pecuniary embarrassments might induce them to sell my precious young daughter. I knew they were in constant communication with Southerners, and had frequent opportunities to do it. I have stated that when Dr. Flint put Ellen in jail, at two years old, she had an inflammation of the eyes, occasioned by measles. This disease still troubled her; and kind Mrs. Bruce proposed that she should come to New York for a while, to be under the care of Dr. Elliott, a well known oculist. It did not occur to me that there was anything improper in a mother's making such a request; but Mrs. Hobbs was very angry, and refused to let her go. Situated as I was, it was not politic to insist upon it. I made no complaint, but I longed to be entirely free to act a mother's part towards my children. The next time I went over to Brooklyn, Mrs. Hobbs, as if to apologize for her anger, told me she had employed her own physician to attend to Ellen's eyes, and that she had refused my request because she did not consider it safe to trust her in New York. I accepted the explanation in silence; but she had told me that my child *belonged* to her daughter, and I suspected that her real motive was a fear of my conveying her property away from her. Perhaps I did her injustice; but my knowledge of Southerners made it difficult for me to feel otherwise.

Sweet and bitter were mixed in the cup of my life, and I was thankful that it had ceased to be entirely bitter. I loved Mrs. Bruce's babe. When it laughed and crowed in my face, and twined its little tender arms confidingly about my neck, it made me think of the time when Benny and Ellen were babies, and my wounded heart was soothed. One bright morning, as I stood at the window, tossing baby in my arms, my attention was attracted by a young man in sailor's dress, who was closely observing every house as he passed. I looked at him earnestly. Could it be my brother William? It *must* be he—and yet, how changed! I placed the baby safely, flew down stairs, opened the front door, beckoned to the sailor, and in less than a minute I was clasped in my brother's arms. How much we had to tell each other! How we laughed, and how we cried, over each other's adventures! I took him to Brooklyn, and again saw him with Ellen, the dear child whom he had loved and tended so carefully, while I was shut up in my miserable den. He stayed in New York a week. His old feelings of affection for me and Ellen were as lively as ever. There are no bonds so strong as those which are formed by suffering together.

CHAPTER 34. THE OLD ENEMY AGAIN

My young mistress, Miss Emily Flint, did not return any answer to my letter requesting her to consent to my being sold. But after a while, I received a reply, which purported to be written by her younger brother. In order rightly to enjoy the contents of this letter, the reader must bear in mind that the Flint family supposed I had been at the north many years. They had no idea that I knew of the doctor's three excursions to New York in search of me; that I had heard his voice, when he came to borrow five hundred dollars for that purpose; and that I had seen him pass on his way to the steamboat. Neither were they aware that all the particulars of aunt Nancy's death and burial were conveyed to me at the time they occurred. I have kept the letter, of which I herewith subjoin a copy:

Your letter to sister was received a few days ago. I gather from it that you are desirous of returning to your native place, among your friends and relatives. We were all gratified with the contents of your letter; and let me assure you that if any members of the family have had any feeling of resentment towards you, they feel it no longer. We all sympathize with you in your unfortunate condition, and are ready to do all in our power to make you contented and happy. It is difficult for you to return home as a free person. If you were purchased by your grandmother, it is doubtful whether you would be permitted to remain, although it would be lawful for you to do so. If a servant should be allowed to purchase herself, after absenting herself so long from her owners, and return free, it would have an injurious effect. From your letter, I think your situation must be hard and uncomfortable. Come home. You have it in your power to be reinstated in our affections. We would receive you with open arms and tears of joy. You need not apprehend any unkind treatment, as we have not put ourselves to any trouble or expense to get you. Had we done so, perhaps we should feel otherwise. You know my sister was always attached to you, and that you were never treated as a slave. You were never put to hard work, nor exposed to field labor. On the contrary, you were taken into the house, and treated as one of us, and almost as free; and we, at least, felt that you were above disgracing yourself by running away. Believing you may be induced to come home voluntarily has induced me to write for my sister. The family will be rejoiced to see you; and your poor old grandmother expressed a great desire to have you come, when she heard your letter read. In her old age she needs the consolation of having her children round her. Doubtless you have heard of the death of your aunt. She was a faithful servant, and a faithful member of the Episcopal church. In her Christian life she taught us how to live—and, O, too high the price of knowledge, she taught us how to die! Could you have seen us round her death bed, with her mother, all mingling our tears in one common stream, you would have thought the same heartfelt tie existed between a master and his servant, as between a mother and her child. But this subject is too painful to dwell upon. I must bring my letter to a close. If you are contented to stay away from your old grandmother, your child, and the friends who love you, stay where you are. We shall never trouble ourselves to apprehend you. But should you prefer to come home, we will do all that we can to make you happy. If you do not wish to remain in the family, I know that father, by our persuasion, will be induced to let you be purchased by any person you may choose in our community. You will please answer this as soon as possible, and let us know your decision. Sister sends much love to you. In the meantime believe me your sincere friend and well wisher.

This letter was signed by Emily's brother, who was as yet a mere lad. I knew, by the style, that it was not written by a person of his age, and though the writing was disguised, I had been made too unhappy by it, in former years, not to recognize at once the hand of Dr. Flint. O, the hypocrisy of slaveholders! Did the old fox suppose I was goose enough to go into such a trap? Verily, he relied too much on "the stupidity of the African race." I did not return the family of Flints any thanks for their cordial invitation—a remissness for which I was, no doubt, charged with base ingratitude.

Not long afterwards I received a letter from one of my friends at the south, informing me that Dr. Flint was about to visit the north. The letter had been delayed, and I supposed he might be already on the way. Mrs. Bruce did not know I was a fugitive. I told her that important business called me to Boston, where my brother then was, and asked permission to bring a friend to supply my place as nurse, for a fortnight. I started on my journey immediately; and as soon as I arrived, I wrote to my grandmother that if Benny came, he must be sent to Boston. I knew she was only waiting for a good chance to send him north, and, fortunately, she had the legal power to do so, without asking leave of anybody. She was a free woman; and when my children were purchased, Mr. Sands preferred to have the bill of sale drawn up in her name. It was conjectured that he advanced the money, but it was not known. At the south, a gentleman may have a shoal[1] of colored children without any disgrace; but if he is known to purchase them, with the view of setting them free, the example is thought to be dangerous to their "peculiar institution," and he becomes unpopular.

There was a good opportunity to send Benny in a vessel coming directly to New York. He was put on board with a letter to a friend, who was requested to see him off to Boston. Early one morning, there was a loud rap at my door, and in rushed Benjamin, all out of breath. "O mother!" he exclaimed, "here I am! I run all the way; and I come all alone. How d'you do?"

O reader, can you imagine my joy? No, you cannot, unless you have been a slave mother. Benjamin rattled away as fast as his tongue could go. "Mother, why don't you bring Ellen here? I went over to Brooklyn to see her, and she felt very bad when I bid her goodbye. She said, 'O Ben, I wish I was going too.' I thought she'd know ever so much; but she don't know so much as I do; for I can read, and she can't. And, mother, I lost all my clothes coming. What can I do to get some more? I 'spose free boys can get along here at the north as well as white boys."

I did not like to tell the sanguine, happy little fellow how much he was mistaken. I took him to a tailor, and procured a change of clothes. The rest of the day was spent in mutual asking and answering of questions, with the wish constantly repeated that the good old grandmother was with us, and frequent

---

1   *shoal*   Flock of birds, or a group of many fish or porpoises swimming together (used figuratively here).

injunctions from Benny to write to her immediately, and be sure to tell her everything about his voyage, and his journey to Boston.

Dr. Flint made his visit to New York, and made every exertion to call upon me, and invite me to return with him; but not being able to ascertain where I was, his hospitable intentions were frustrated, and the affectionate family, who were waiting for me with "open arms," were doomed to disappointment.

As soon as I knew he was safely at home, I placed Benjamin in the care of my brother William, and returned to Mrs. Bruce. There I remained through the winter and spring, endeavoring to perform my duties faithfully, and finding a good degree of happiness in the attractions of baby Mary, the considerate kindness of her excellent mother, and occasional interviews with my darling daughter.

But when summer came, the old feeling of insecurity haunted me. It was necessary for me to take little Mary out daily, for exercise and fresh air, and the city was swarming with Southerners, some of whom might recognize me. Hot weather brings out snakes and slaveholders, and I like one class of the venomous creatures as little as I do the other. What a comfort it is, to be free to *say* so!

Chapter 35. Prejudice against Color

It was a relief to my mind to see preparations for leaving the city. We went to Albany in the steamboat *Knickerbocker*. When the gong sounded for tea, Mrs. Bruce said, "Linda, it is late, and you and baby had better come to the table with me." I replied, "I know it is time baby had her supper, but I had rather not go with you, if you please. I am afraid of being insulted." "O no, not if you are with *me*," she said. I saw several white nurses go with their ladies, and I ventured to do the same. We were at the extreme end of the table. I was no sooner seated, than a gruff voice said, "Get up! You know you are not allowed to sit here." I looked up, and, to my astonishment and indignation, saw that the speaker was a colored man. If his office required him to enforce the by-laws of the boat, he might, at least, have done it politely. I replied, "I shall not get up, unless the captain comes and takes me up." No cup of tea was offered me, but Mrs. Bruce handed me hers and called for another. I looked to see whether the other nurses were treated in a similar manner. They were all properly waited on.

Next morning, when we stopped at Troy for breakfast, everybody was making a rush for the table. Mrs. Bruce said, "Take my arm, Linda, and we'll go in together." The landlord[1] heard her, and said, "Madam, will you allow your nurse and baby to take breakfast with my family?" I knew this was to be

---

1 *landlord* The owner of the inn where the group from the steamboat breakfasted.

attributed to my complexion; but he spoke courteously, and therefore I did not mind it.

At Saratoga we found the United States Hotel crowded, and Mr. Bruce took one of the cottages belonging to the hotel. I had thought, with gladness, of going to the quiet of the country, where I should meet few people, but here I found myself in the midst of a swarm of Southerners. I looked round me with fear and trembling, dreading to see someone who would recognize me. I was rejoiced to find that we were to stay but a short time.

We soon returned to New York, to make arrangements for spending the remainder of the summer at Rockaway.[1] While the laundress was putting the clothes in order, I took an opportunity to go over to Brooklyn to see Ellen. I met her going to a grocery store, and the first words she said, were, "O, mother, don't go to Mrs. Hobbs's. Her brother, Mr. Thorne, has come from the south, and maybe he'll tell where you are." I accepted the warning. I told her I was going away with Mrs. Bruce the next day, and would try to see her when I came back.

Being in servitude to the Anglo-Saxon race,[2] I was not put into a "Jim Crow car,"[3] on our way to Rockaway, neither was I invited to ride through the streets on the top of trunks in a truck; but everywhere I found the same manifestations of that cruel prejudice, which so discourages the feelings, and represses the energies of the colored people. We reached Rockaway before dark, and put up at the Pavilion—a large hotel, beautifully situated by the seaside—a great resort of the fashionable world. Thirty or forty nurses were there, of a great variety of nations. Some of the ladies had colored waiting-maids and coachmen, but I was the only nurse tinged with the blood of Africa. When the tea bell rang, I took little Mary and followed the other nurses. Supper was served in a long hall. A young man, who had the ordering of things, took the circuit of the table two or three times, and finally pointed me to a seat at the lower end of it. As there was but one chair, I sat down and took the child in my lap. Whereupon the young man came to me and said, in the blandest manner possible, "Will you please to seat the little girl in the chair, and stand behind it and feed her? After they have done, you will be shown to the kitchen, where you will have a good supper."

This was the climax! I found it hard to preserve my self-control, when I looked round, and saw women who were nurses, as I was, and only one shade

---

1 *Rockaway* Rockaway Beach was a popular summer holiday destination for wealthy New Yorkers in the nineteenth century; the Long Island Railroad carried passengers there from New York City.

2 *Anglo-Saxon race* I.e., white people. The term "Anglo-Saxon" is now associated with modern white supremacy groups and is to be avoided; in Jacobs's day, it was a neutral descriptive term for white people, particularly people of British descent.

3 *Jim Crow car* Segregated railway car.

lighter in complexion, eyeing me with a defiant look, as if my presence were a contamination. However, I said nothing. I quietly took the child in my arms, went to our room, and refused to go to the table again. Mr. Bruce ordered meals to be sent to the room for little Mary and I. This answered[1] for a few days; but the waiters of the establishment were white, and they soon began to complain, saying they were not hired to wait on negroes. The landlord requested Mr. Bruce to send me down to my meals, because his servants rebelled against bringing them up, and the colored servants of other boarders were dissatisfied because all were not treated alike.

My answer was that the colored servants ought to be dissatisfied with *themselves*, for not having too much self-respect to submit to such treatment; that there was no difference in the price of board for colored and white servants, and there was no justification for difference of treatment. I stayed a month after this, and finding I was resolved to stand up for my rights, they concluded to treat me well. Let every colored man and woman do this, and eventually we shall cease to be trampled under foot by our oppressors.

CHAPTER 36. THE HAIR-BREADTH ESCAPE

After we returned to New York, I took the earliest opportunity to go and see Ellen. I asked to have her called downstairs; for I supposed Mrs. Hobbs's southern brother might still be there, and I was desirous to avoid seeing him, if possible. But Mrs. Hobbs came to the kitchen, and insisted on my going upstairs. "My brother wants to see you," said she, "and he is sorry you seem to shun him. He knows you are living in New York. He told me to say to you that he owes thanks to good old aunt Martha for too many little acts of kindness for him to be base enough to betray her grandchild."

This Mr. Thorne had become poor and reckless long before he left the south, and such persons had much rather go to one of the faithful old slaves to borrow a dollar, or get a good dinner, than to go to one whom they consider an equal. It was such acts of kindness as these for which he professed to feel grateful to my grandmother. I wished he had kept at a distance, but as he was here, and knew where I was, I concluded there was nothing to be gained by trying to avoid him; on the contrary, it might be the means of exciting his ill will. I followed his sister upstairs. He met me in a very friendly manner, congratulated me on my escape from slavery, and hoped I had a good place, where I felt happy.

I continued to visit Ellen as often as I could. She, good thoughtful child, never forgot my hazardous situation, but always kept a vigilant lookout for

---

1 *answered* Sufficed.

my safety. She never made any complaint about her own inconveniences and troubles; but a mother's observing eye easily perceived that she was not happy. On the occasion of one of my visits I found her unusually serious. When I asked her what was the matter, she said nothing was the matter. But I insisted upon knowing what made her look so very grave. Finally, I ascertained that she felt troubled about the dissipation that was continually going on in the house. She was sent to the store very often for rum and brandy, and she felt ashamed to ask for it so often, and Mr. Hobbs and Mr. Thorne drank a great deal, and their hands trembled so that they had to call her to pour out the liquor for them. "But for all that," said she, "Mr. Hobbs is good to me, and I can't help liking him. I feel sorry for him." I tried to comfort her, by telling her that I had laid up a hundred dollars, and that before long I hoped to be able to give her and Benjamin a home, and send them to school. She was always desirous not to add to my troubles more than she could help, and I did not discover till years afterwards that Mr. Thorne's intemperance was not the only annoyance she suffered from him. Though he professed too much gratitude to my grandmother to injure any of her descendants, he had poured vile language into the ears of her innocent great-grandchild.

I usually went to Brooklyn to spend Sunday afternoon. One Sunday, I found Ellen anxiously waiting for me near the house. "O, mother," said she, "I've been waiting for you this long time. I'm afraid Mr. Thorne has written to tell Dr. Flint where you are. Make haste and come in. Mrs. Hobbs will tell you all about it!"

The story was soon told. While the children were playing in the grape-vine arbor, the day before, Mr. Thorne came out with a letter in his hand, which he tore up and scattered about. Ellen was sweeping the yard at the time, and having her mind full of suspicions of him, she picked up the pieces and carried them to the children, saying, "I wonder who Mr. Thorne has been writing to."

"I'm sure I don't know, and don't care," replied the oldest of the children; "and I don't see how it concerns you."

"But it does concern me," replied Ellen; "for I'm afraid he's been writing to the south about my mother."

They laughed at her, and called her a silly thing, but good-naturedly put the fragments of writing together, in order to read them to her. They were no sooner arranged, than the little girl exclaimed, "I declare, Ellen, I believe you are right."

The contents of Mr. Thorne's letter, as nearly as I can remember, were as follows: "I have seen your slave, Linda, and conversed with her. She can be taken very easily, if you manage prudently. There are enough of us here to swear to her identity as your property. I am a patriot, a lover of my country, and I do this as an act of justice to the laws." He concluded by informing the doctor of the street and number where I lived. The children carried the pieces to Mrs. Hobbs, who immediately went to her brother's room for an explanation. He was not to be found. The servants said they saw him go out with a letter in his hand, and they supposed he had gone to the post office. The natural inference was, that he had sent to Dr. Flint a copy of those fragments. When he returned, his sister accused him of it, and he did not deny the charge. He went immediately to his room, and the next morning he was missing. He had gone over to New York, before any of the family were astir.

It was evident that I had no time to lose; and I hastened back to the city with a heavy heart. Again I was to be torn from a comfortable home, and all my plans for the welfare of my children were to be frustrated by that demon Slavery! I now regretted that I never told Mrs. Bruce my story. I had not concealed it merely on account of being a fugitive; that would have made her anxious, but it would have excited sympathy in her kind heart. I valued her good opinion, and I was afraid of losing it, if I told her all the particulars of my sad story. But now I felt that it was necessary for her to know how I was situated. I had once left her abruptly, without explaining the reason, and it would not be proper to do it again. I went home resolved to tell her in the morning. But the sadness of my face attracted her attention, and, in answer to her kind inquiries, I poured out my full heart to her, before bedtime. She listened with true womanly sympathy, and told me she would do all she could to protect me. How my heart blessed her!

Early the next morning, Judge Vanderpool and Lawyer Hopper were consulted. They said I had better leave the city at once, as the risk would be great if the case came to trial. Mrs. Bruce took me in a carriage to the house of one of her friends, where she assured me I should be safe until my brother could arrive, which would be in a few days. In the interval my thoughts were much occupied with Ellen. She was mine by birth, and she was also mine by Southern law, since my grandmother held the bill of sale that made her so. I did not feel that she was safe unless I had her with me. Mrs. Hobbs, who felt badly about her brother's treachery, yielded to my entreaties, on condition that she should return in ten days. I avoided making any promise. She came to me clad in very thin garments, all outgrown, and with a school satchel on her arm, containing a few articles. It was late in October, and I knew the child must suffer; and not daring to go out in the streets to purchase anything, I took off my own flannel skirt and converted it into one for her. Kind Mrs. Bruce came to bid me goodbye, and when she saw that I had taken off my clothing for my child, the tears came to her eyes. She said, "Wait for me, Linda," and went out. She soon returned with a nice warm shawl and hood for Ellen. Truly, of such souls as hers are the kingdom of heaven.

My brother reached New York on Wednesday. Lawyer Hopper advised us to go to Boston by the Stonington route, as there was less Southern travel in that direction. Mrs. Bruce directed her servants to tell all inquirers that I formerly lived there, but had gone from the city.

We reached the steamboat *Rhode Island* in safety. That boat employed colored hands, but I knew that colored passengers were not admitted to the cabin. I was very desirous for the seclusion of the cabin, not only on account of exposure to the night air, but also to avoid observation. Lawyer Hopper was waiting on board for us. He spoke to the stewardess, and asked, as a particular favor, that she would treat us well. He said to me, "Go and speak to the captain yourself by and by. Take your little girl with you, and I am sure that he will not let her sleep on deck." With these kind words and a shake of the hand he departed.

The boat was soon on her way, bearing me rapidly from the friendly home where I had hoped to find security and rest. My brother had left me to purchase the tickets, thinking that I might have better success than he would. When the stewardess came to me, I paid what she asked, and she gave me three tickets with clipped corners. In the most unsophisticated manner I said, "You have made a mistake; I asked you for cabin tickets. I cannot possibly consent to sleep on deck with my little daughter." She assured me there was no mistake. She said on some of the routes colored people were allowed to sleep in the cabin, but not on this route, which was much travelled by the wealthy. I asked her to show me to the captain's office, and she said she would after tea. When the time came, I took Ellen by the hand and went to the captain, politely requesting him to change our tickets, as we should be very uncomfortable on deck. He said it was contrary to their custom, but he would see that we had berths below; he would also try to obtain comfortable seats for us in the cars; of that he was not certain, but he would speak to the conductor about it, when the boat arrived. I thanked him, and returned to the ladies' cabin. He came afterwards and told me that the conductor of the cars was on board, that he had spoken to him, and he had promised to take care of us. I was very much surprised at receiving so much kindness. I don't know whether the pleasing face of my little girl had won his heart, or whether the stewardess inferred from Lawyer Hopper's manner that I was a fugitive, and had pleaded with him in my behalf.

When the boat arrived at Stonington, the conductor kept his promise, and showed us to seats in the first car, nearest the engine. He asked us to take seats next the door, but as he passed through, we ventured to move on toward the other end of the car. No incivility was offered us, and we reached Boston in safety.

The day after my arrival was one of the happiest of my life. I felt as if I was beyond the reach of the bloodhounds; and, for the first time during many years, I had both my children together with me. They greatly enjoyed their reunion, and laughed and chatted merrily. I watched them with a swelling heart. Their every motion delighted me.

I could not feel safe in New York, and I accepted the offer of a friend, that we should share expenses and keep house together. I represented to Mrs. Hobbs that Ellen must have some schooling, and must remain with me for that purpose. She felt ashamed of being unable to read or spell at her age, so instead of sending her to school with Benny, I instructed her myself till she was fitted to enter an intermediate school. The winter passed pleasantly, while I was busy with my needle, and my children with their books.

CHAPTER 37. A VISIT TO ENGLAND

In the spring, sad news came to me. Mrs. Bruce was dead. Never again, in this world, should I see her gentle face, or hear her sympathizing voice. I had lost an excellent friend, and little Mary had lost a tender mother. Mr. Bruce wished the child to visit some of her mother's relatives in England, and he was desirous that I should take charge of her. The little motherless one was accustomed to me, and attached to me, and I thought she would be happier in my care than in that of a stranger. I could also earn more in this way than I could by my needle.[1] So I put Benny to a trade, and left Ellen to remain in the house with my friend and go to school.

We sailed from New York, and arrived in Liverpool after a pleasant voyage of twelve days. We proceeded directly to London, and took lodgings at the Adelaide Hotel. The supper seemed to me less luxurious than those I had seen in American hotels; but my situation was indescribably more pleasant. For the first time in my life I was in a place where I was treated according to my deportment, without reference to my complexion. I felt as if a great millstone had been lifted from my breast. Ensconced in a pleasant room, with my dear little charge, I laid my head on my pillow, for the first time, with the delightful consciousness of pure, unadulterated freedom.

As I had constant care of the child, I had little opportunity to see the wonders of that great city; but I watched the tide of life that flowed through the streets, and found it a strange contrast to the stagnation in our Southern towns. Mr. Bruce took his little daughter to spend some days with friends in Oxford Crescent, and of course it was necessary for me to accompany her. I

---

1   *by my needle*   I.e., by taking paid sewing commissions, one of the few respectable occupations available
    to single women at the time.

had heard much of the systematic method of English education, and I was very desirous that my dear Mary should steer straight in the midst of so much propriety. I closely observed her little playmates and their nurses, being ready to take any lessons in the science of good management. The children were more rosy than American children, but I did not see that they differed materially in other respects. They were like all children—sometimes docile and sometimes wayward.

We next went to Steventon, in Berkshire. It was a small town, said to be the poorest in the county. I saw men working in the fields for six shillings, and seven shillings, a week, and women for sixpence, and sevenpence, a day, out of which they boarded themselves. Of course they lived in the most primitive manner; it could not be otherwise, where a woman's wages for an entire day were not sufficient to buy a pound of meat. They paid very low rents, and their clothes were made of the cheapest fabrics, though much better than could have been procured in the United States for the same money. I had heard much about the oppression of the poor in Europe. The people I saw around me were, many of them, among the poorest poor. But when I visited them in their little thatched cottages, I felt that the condition of even the meanest and most ignorant among them was vastly superior to the condition of the most favored slaves in America. They labored hard; but they were not ordered out to toil while the stars were in the sky, and driven and slashed by an overseer, through heat and cold, till the stars shone out again. Their homes were very humble; but they were protected by law. No insolent patrols could come, in the dead of night, and flog them at their pleasure. The father, when he closed his cottage door, felt safe with his family around him. No master or overseer could come and take from him his wife, or his daughter. They must separate to earn their living; but the parents knew where their children were going, and could communicate with them by letters. The relations of husband and wife, parent and child, were too sacred for the richest noble in the land to violate with impunity. Much was being done to enlighten these poor people. Schools were established among them, and benevolent societies were active in efforts to ameliorate their condition. There was no law forbidding them to learn to read and write; and if they helped each other in spelling out the Bible, they were in no danger of thirty-nine lashes, as was the case with myself and poor, pious, old uncle Fred. I repeat that the most ignorant and the most destitute of these peasants was a thousand fold better off than the most pampered American slave.

I do not deny that the poor are oppressed in Europe. I am not disposed to paint their condition so rose-colored as the Hon. Miss Murray[1] paints the condition of the slaves in the United States. A small portion of *my* experience would enable her to read her own pages with anointed eyes.[2] If she were to lay aside her title, and, instead of visiting among the fashionable, become domesticated, as a poor governess, on some plantation in Louisiana or Alabama, she would see and hear things that would make her tell quite a different story.

My visit to England is a memorable event in my life, from the fact of my having there received strong religious impressions. The contemptuous manner in which the communion had been administered to colored people, in my native place; the church membership of Dr. Flint, and others like him; and the buying and selling of slaves, by professed ministers of the gospel, had given me a prejudice against the Episcopal church. The whole service seemed to me a mockery and a sham. But my home in Steventon was in the family of a clergyman, who was a true disciple of Jesus. The beauty of his daily life inspired me with faith in the gentleness of Christian professions. Grace entered my heart, and I knelt at the communion table, I trust, in true humility of soul.

I remained abroad ten months, which was much longer than I had anticipated. During all that time, I never saw the slightest symptom of prejudice against color. Indeed, I entirely forgot it, till the time came for us to return to America.

Chapter 38. Renewed Invitations to Go South

We had a tedious winter passage,[3] and from the distance specters seemed to rise up on the shores of the United States. It is a sad feeling to be afraid of one's native country. We arrived in New York safely, and I hastened to Boston to look after my children. I found Ellen well, and improving at her school; but Benny was not there to welcome me. He had been left at a good place to learn a trade, and for several months everything worked well. He was liked by the master, and was a favorite with his fellow apprentices; but one day they accidentally discovered a fact they had never before suspected—that he was colored! This at once transformed him into a different being. Some of the apprentices were Americans, others American-born Irish; and it was offensive to their dignity to

---

1 *Hon. Miss Murray* Reference to Amelia Matilda Murray (1795–1884), a British writer whose *Letters from the United States, Cuba, and Canada* (1856) defended slavery. The book was mainly denounced in England, and Murray was required to resign from her position as Queen Victoria's Maid of Honour.

2 *anointed eyes* I.e., eyes that had been blind but could now see. The reference is to John 9.1–11, in which Christ anoints the eyes of a blind man and restores his sight: "He [the formerly blind man] answered and said, A man that is called Jesus made clay, and anointed mine eyes, and said unto me, Go to the pool of Siloam, and wash, and I went and washed, and I received sight" (John 9.11).

3 *passage* Journey across the Atlantic by ship.

have a "nigger" among them, after they had been told that he *was* a "nigger." They began by treating him with silent scorn, and finding that he returned the same, they resorted to insults and abuse. He was too spirited a boy to stand that, and he went off. Being desirous to do something to support himself, and having no one to advise him, he shipped for a whaling voyage. When I received these tidings I shed many tears, and bitterly reproached myself for having left him so long. But I had done it for the best, and now all I could do was to pray to the heavenly Father to guide and protect him.

Not long after my return, I received the following letter from Miss Emily Flint, now Mrs. Dodge:

In this you will recognize the hand of your friend and mistress. Having heard that you had gone with a family to Europe, I have waited to hear of your return to write to you. I should have answered the letter you wrote to me long since, but as I could not then act independently of my father, I knew there could be nothing done satisfactory to you. There were persons here who were willing to buy you and run the risk of getting you. To this I would not consent. I have always been attached to you, and would not like to see you the slave of another, or have unkind treatment. I am married now, and can protect you. My husband expects to move to Virginia this spring, where we think of settling. I am very anxious that you should come and live with me. If you are not willing to come, you may purchase yourself; but I should prefer having you live with me. If you come, you may, if you like, spend a month with your grandmother and friends, then come to me in Norfolk, Virginia. Think this over, and write as soon as possible, and let me know the conclusion. Hoping that your children are well, I remain you[r] friend and mistress.

Of course I did not write to return thanks for this cordial invitation. I felt insulted to be thought stupid enough to be caught by such professions.

"Come up into my parlor," said the spider to the fly;
"'Tis the prettiest little parlor that ever you did spy."[1]

It was plain that Dr. Flint's family were apprised of my movements, since they knew of my voyage to Europe. I expected to have further trouble from them; but having eluded them thus far, I hoped to be as successful in future. The money I had earned, I was desirous to devote to the education of my children, and to secure a home for them. It seemed not only hard, but unjust,

---

1   *Come up ... did spy*   These are the first two lines of the poem "The Spider and the Fly" (1829) by the English poet Mary Howitt. In it, the spider tries to lure and deceive the fly into its web by using "wily flattering words."

to pay for myself. I could not possibly regard myself as a piece of property. Moreover, I had worked many years without wages, and during that time had been obliged to depend on my grandmother for many comforts in food and clothing. My children certainly belonged to me; but though Dr. Flint had incurred no expense for their support, he had received a large sum of money for them. I knew the law would decide that I was his property, and would probably still give his daughter a claim to my children; but I regarded such laws as the regulations of robbers, who had no rights that I was bound to respect.

The Fugitive Slave Law[1] had not then passed. The judges of Massachusetts had not then stooped under chains to enter her courts of justice, so called. I knew my old master was rather skittish of Massachusetts. I relied on her love of freedom, and felt safe on her soil. I am now aware that I honored the old Commonwealth[2] beyond her deserts.

CHAPTER 39. THE CONFESSION

For two years my daughter and I supported ourselves comfortably in Boston. At the end of that time, my brother William offered to send Ellen to a boarding school. It required a great effort for me to consent to part with her, for I had few near ties, and it was her presence that made my two little rooms seem home-like. But my judgment prevailed over my selfish feelings. I made preparations for her departure. During the two years we had lived together I had often resolved to tell her something about her father; but I had never been able to muster sufficient courage. I had a shrinking dread of diminishing my child's love. I knew she must have curiosity on the subject, but she had never asked a question. She was always very careful not to say anything to remind me of my troubles. Now that she was going from me, I thought if I should die before she returned, she might hear my story from someone who did not understand the palliating circumstances; and that if she were entirely ignorant on the subject, her sensitive nature might receive a rude shock.

When we retired for the night, she said, "Mother, it is very hard to leave you alone. I am almost sorry I am going, though I do want to improve myself. But you will write to me often; won't you, mother?"

I did not throw my arms round her. I did not answer her. But in a calm, solemn way, for it cost me great effort, I said, "Listen to me, Ellen; I have

---

1   *Fugitive Slave Law*   Enacted by U.S. Congress in 1850, this law mandated the hiring of officials and issuing of warrants for hunting down and arresting fugitives. $10 rewards were given for the return of fugitives, and $5 for the capture of freed blacks. Penalties for hindering this process were substantially increased.

2   *the old Commonwealth*   I.e., the Commonwealth of Massachusetts.

something to tell you!" I recounted my early sufferings in slavery, and told her how nearly they had crushed me. I began to tell her how they had driven me into a great sin, when she clasped me in her arms, and exclaimed, "O, don't, mother! Please don't tell me anymore."

I said, "But, my child, I want you to know about your father."

"I know all about it, mother," she replied; "I am nothing to my father, and he is nothing to me. All my love is for you. I was with him five months in Washington, and he never cared for me. He never spoke to me as he did to his little Fanny. I knew all the time he was my father, for Fanny's nurse told me so; but she said I must never tell anybody, and I never did. I used to wish he would take me in his arms and kiss me, as he did Fanny; or that he would sometimes smile at me, as he did at her. I thought if he was my own father, he ought to love me. I was a little girl then, and didn't know any better. But now I never think anything about my father. All my love is for you." She hugged me closer as she spoke, and I thanked God that the knowledge I had so much dreaded to impart had not diminished the affection of my child. I had not the slightest idea she knew that portion of my history. If I had, I should have spoken to her long before; for my pent-up feelings had often longed to pour themselves out to someone I could trust. But I loved the dear girl better for the delicacy she had manifested towards her unfortunate mother.

The next morning, she and her uncle started on their journey to the village in New York, where she was to be placed at school. It seemed as if all the sunshine had gone away. My little room was dreadfully lonely. I was thankful when a message came from a lady, accustomed to employ me, requesting me to come and sew in her family for several weeks. On my return, I found a letter from brother William. He thought of opening an anti-slavery reading room in Rochester, and combining with it the sale of some books and stationery; and he wanted me to unite with him. We tried it, but it was not successful. We found warm anti-slavery friends there, but the feeling was not general enough to support such an establishment. I passed nearly a year in the family of Isaac and Amy Post, practical believers in the Christian doctrine of human brotherhood. They measured a man's worth by his character, not by his complexion. The memory of those beloved and honored friends will remain with me to my latest hour.

CHAPTER 40. THE FUGITIVE SLAVE LAW

My brother, being disappointed in his project, concluded to go to California; and it was agreed that Benjamin should go with him. Ellen liked her school, and was a great favorite there. They did not know her history, and she did not tell it, because she had no desire to make capital out of their sympathy. But when it was accidentally discovered that her mother was a fugitive slave, every method was used to increase her advantages and diminish her expenses.

I was alone again. It was necessary for me to be earning money, and I preferred that it should be among those who knew me. On my return from Rochester, I called at the house of Mr. Bruce, to see Mary, the darling little babe that had thawed my heart, when it was freezing into a cheerless distrust of all my fellow-beings. She was growing a tall girl now, but I loved her always. Mr. Bruce had married again, and it was proposed that I should become nurse to a new infant. I had but one hesitation, and that was my feeling of insecurity in New York, now greatly increased by the passage of the Fugitive Slave Law. However, I resolved to try the experiment. I was again fortunate in my employer. The new Mrs. Bruce was an American, brought up under aristocratic influences and still living in the midst of them; but if she had any prejudice against color, I was never made aware of it; and as for the system of slavery, she had a most hearty dislike of it. No sophistry of Southerners could blind her to its enormity. She was a person of excellent principles and a noble heart. To me, from that hour to the present, she has been a true and sympathizing friend. Blessings be with her and hers!

About the time that I reentered the Bruce family, an event occurred of disastrous import to the colored people. The slave Hamlin,[1] the first fugitive that came under the new law, was given up by the bloodhounds of the north to the bloodhounds of the south. It was the beginning of a reign of terror to the colored population. The great city rushed on in its whirl of excitement, taking no note of the "short and simple annals of the poor."[2] But while fashionables were listening to the thrilling voice of Jenny Lind[3] in Metropolitan Hall, the thrilling voices of poor hunted colored people went up, in an agony of supplication, to the Lord, from Zion's church. Many families, who had lived in the city for twenty years, fled from it now. Many a poor washerwoman, who, by hard labor, had made herself a comfortable home, was obliged to sacrifice her furniture, bid a hurried farewell to friends, and seek her fortune among strangers in Canada. Many a wife discovered a secret she had never known

---

1 *Hamlin* James Hamlet was the first victim of the Fugitive Slave Act; he was arrested in Manhattan and sent to Baltimore in 1850. Hamlet insisted he was a free man, but a Mary Brown of Maryland succeeded in having the law seize hold of him, separating him from his wife and two children. Hamlet was then brought to the Baltimore slave market, where he was bought by his home community in Williamsburgh, Brooklyn for eight hundred dollars, after which he was able to return to his family and his job.

2 *short ... poor* Quotation is from line 32 of Thomas Gray's "Elegy Written in a Country Churchyard" (1751). The line refers to main life events—births, deaths, marriages, and christenings—that are recorded in parish registers.

3 *Jenny Lind* Renowned Swedish opera singer who, from 1850 to 1852, toured the United States. The excitement surrounding her concerts came to be referred to as "Lind Mania."

before—that her husband was a fugitive, and must leave her to ensure his own safety. Worse still, many a husband discovered that his wife had fled from slavery years ago, and as "the child follows the condition of its mother," the children of his love were liable to be seized and carried into slavery. Everywhere, in those humble homes, there was consternation and anguish. But what cared the legislators of the "dominant race" for the blood they were crushing out of trampled hearts?

When my brother William spent his last evening with me, before he went to California, we talked nearly all the time of the distress brought on our oppressed people by the passage of this iniquitous law; and never had I seen him manifest such bitterness of spirit, such stern hostility to our oppressors. He was himself free from the operation of the law; for he did not run from any Slaveholding State, being brought into the Free States by his master. But I was subject to it; and so were hundreds of intelligent and industrious people all around us. I seldom ventured into the streets; and when it was necessary to do an errand for Mrs. Bruce, or any of the family, I went as much as possible through back streets and by-ways. What a disgrace to a city calling itself free, that inhabitants, guiltless of offence, and seeking to perform their duties conscientiously, should be condemned to live in such incessant fear, and have nowhere to turn for protection! This state of things, of course, gave rise to many impromptu vigilance committees. Every colored person, and every friend of their persecuted race, kept their eyes wide open. Every evening I examined the newspapers carefully, to see what Southerners had put up at the hotels. I did this for my own sake, thinking my young mistress and her husband might be among the list; I wished also to give information to others, if necessary; for if many were "running to and fro," I resolved that "knowledge should be increased."[1]

This brings up one of my Southern reminiscences, which I will here briefly relate. I was somewhat acquainted with a slave named Luke, who belonged to a wealthy man in our vicinity. His master died, leaving a son and daughter heirs to his large fortune. In the division of the slaves, Luke was included in the son's portion. This young man became a prey to the vices growing out of the "patriarchal institution," and when he went to the north, to complete his education, he carried his vices with him. He was brought home, deprived of the use of his limbs, by excessive dissipation. Luke was appointed to wait upon his bed-ridden master, whose despotic habits were greatly increased by exasperation at his own helplessness. He kept a cowhide beside him, and, for

---

1   *running ... increased*   These quotations are both from Daniel 12.4, where the prophet Daniel is finishing a description of what was revealed to him about the end of the world: "But thou, O Daniel, shut up the words, and seal the book, even to the time of the end: many shall run to and fro, and knowledge shall be increased."

the most trivial occurrence, he would order his attendant to bare his back, and kneel beside the couch, while he whipped him till his strength was exhausted. Some days he was not allowed to wear anything but his shirt, in order to be in readiness to be flogged. A day seldom passed without his receiving more or less blows. If the slightest resistance was offered, the town constable was sent for to execute the punishment, and Luke learned from experience how much more the constable's strong arm was to be dreaded than the comparatively feeble one of his master. The arm of his tyrant grew weak, and was finally palsied;[1] and then the constable's services were in constant requisition. The fact that he was entirely dependent on Luke's care, and was obliged to be tended like an infant, instead of inspiring any gratitude or compassion towards his poor slave, seemed only to increase his irritability and cruelty. As he lay there on his bed, a mere disgraced wreck of manhood, he took into his head the strangest freaks of despotism; and if Luke hesitated to submit to his orders, the constable was immediately sent for. Some of these freaks were of a nature too filthy to be repeated. When I fled from the house of bondage, I left poor Luke still chained to the bedside of this cruel and disgusting wretch.

One day, when I had been requested to do an errand for Mrs. Bruce, I was hurrying through back streets, as usual, when I saw a young man approaching, whose face was familiar to me. As he came nearer, I recognized Luke. I always rejoiced to see or hear of anyone who had escaped from the black pit; but, remembering this poor fellow's extreme hardships, I was peculiarly glad to see him on Northern soil, though I no longer called it *free* soil. I well remembered what a desolate feeling it was to be alone among strangers, and I went up to him and greeted him cordially. At first, he did not know me; but when I mentioned my name, he remembered all about me. I told him of the Fugitive Slave Law, and asked him if he did not know that New York was a city of kidnappers.

He replied, "De risk ain't so bad for me, as 'tis fur you. 'Cause I runned away from de speculator,[2] and you runned away from de massa. Dem speculators vont spen dar money to come here fur a runaway, if dey ain't sartin sure to put dar hans right on him. An I tell you I's tuk good car 'bout dat. I had too hard times down dar, to let 'em ketch dis nigger."

He then told me of the advice he had received, and the plans he had laid. I asked if he had money enough to take him to Canada. "'Pend upon it, I hab," he replied. "I tuk car fur dat. I'd bin workin all my days fur dem cussed whites, an got no pay but kicks and cuffs. So I tought dis nigger had a right to money nuff to bring him to de Free States. Massa Henry he lib till ebery body vish

---

1   *palsied*   Affected by tremors and paralysis; rendered incapable.
2   *speculator*   Interregional slave trader.

him dead; an ven he did die, I knowed de debbil would hab him, an vouldn't vant him to bring his money 'long too. So I tuk some of his bills, and put 'em in de pocket of his ole trousers. An ven he was buried, dis nigger ask fur dem ole trousers, an dey gub 'em to me." With a low, chuckling laugh, he added, "You see I didn't *steal* it; dey *gub* it to me. I tell you, I had mighty hard time to keep de speculator from findin it; but he didn't git it."

This is a fair specimen of how the moral sense is educated by slavery. When a man has his wages stolen from him, year after year, and the laws sanction and enforce the theft, how can he be expected to have more regard to honesty than has the man who robs him? I have become somewhat enlightened, but I confess that I agree with poor, ignorant, much-abused Luke, in thinking he had a *right* to that money, as a portion of his unpaid wages. He went to Canada forthwith, and I have not since heard from him.

All that winter I lived in a state of anxiety. When I took the children out to breathe the air, I closely observed the countenances of all I met. I dreaded the approach of summer, when snakes and slaveholders make their appearance. I was, in fact, a slave in New York, as subject to slave laws as I had been in a Slave State. Strange incongruity in a State called free!

Spring returned, and I received warning from the south that Dr. Flint knew of my return to my old place, and was making preparations to have me caught. I learned afterwards that my dress, and that of Mrs. Bruce's children, had been described to him by some of the Northern tools, which slaveholders employ for their base purposes, and then indulge in sneers at their cupidity and mean servility.

I immediately informed Mrs. Bruce of my danger, and she took prompt measures for my safety. My place as nurse could not be supplied immediately, and this generous, sympathizing lady proposed that I should carry her baby away. It was a comfort to me to have the child with me; for the heart is reluctant to be torn away from every object it loves. But how few mothers would have consented to have one of their own babes become a fugitive, for the sake of a poor, hunted nurse, on whom the legislators of the country had let loose the bloodhounds! When I spoke of the sacrifice she was making, in depriving herself of her dear baby, she replied, "It is better for you to have baby with you, Linda; for if they get on your track, they will be obliged to bring the child to me; and then, if there is a possibility of saving you, you shall be saved."

This lady had a very wealthy relative, a benevolent gentleman in many respects, but aristocratic and pro-slavery. He remonstrated with her for harboring a fugitive slave; told her she was violating the laws of her country; and asked her if she was aware of the penalty. She replied, "I am very well aware of it. It is imprisonment and one thousand dollars fine. Shame on my country that it *is* so! I am ready to incur the penalty. I will go to the state's prison, rather than have any poor victim torn from *my* house, to be carried back to slavery."

The noble heart! The brave heart! The tears are in my eyes while I write of her. May the God of the helpless reward her for her sympathy with my persecuted people!

I was sent into New England, where I was sheltered by the wife of a senator, whom I shall always hold in grateful remembrance. This honorable gentleman would not have voted for the Fugitive Slave Law, as did the senator in "Uncle Tom's Cabin";[1] on the contrary, he was strongly opposed to it; but he was enough under its influence to be afraid of having me remain in his house many hours. So I was sent into the country, where I remained a month with the baby. When it was supposed that Dr. Flint's emissaries had lost track of me, and given up the pursuit for the present, I returned to New York.

CHAPTER 41. FREE AT LAST

Mrs. Bruce, and every member of her family, were exceedingly kind to me. I was thankful for the blessings of my lot, yet I could not always wear a cheerful countenance. I was doing harm to no one; on the contrary, I was doing all the good I could in my small way; yet I could never go out to breathe God's free air without trepidation at my heart. This seemed hard; and I could not think it was a right state of things in any civilized country.

From time to time I received news from my good old grandmother. She could not write; but she employed others to write for her. The following is an extract from one of her last letters:

"Dear Daughter: I cannot hope to see you again on earth; but I pray to God to unite us above, where pain will no more rack this feeble body of mine; where sorrow and parting from my children will be no more. God has promised these things if we are faithful unto the end. My age and feeble health deprive me of going to church now; but God is with me here at home. Thank your brother for his kindness. Give much love to him, and tell him to remember the Creator in the days of his youth, and strive to meet me in the Father's kingdom. Love to Ellen and Benjamin. Don't neglect him. Tell him for me, to be a good boy. Strive, my child, to train them for God's children. May he protect and provide for you, is the prayer of your loving old mother."

These letters both cheered and saddened me. I was always glad to have tidings from the kind, faithful old friend of my unhappy youth; but her messages

---

1   *senator in "Uncle Tom's Cabin"*   In Harriet Beecher Stowe's novel *Uncle Tom's Cabin*, a state law prohibiting people from helping enslaved fugitives is signed by Senator Bird; Mrs. Bird, however, opposes the law, and ultimately convinces her husband to provide shelter and aid to the fugitive Eliza, one of the novel's protagonists.

of love made my heart yearn to see her before she died, and I mourned over the fact that it was impossible. Some months after I returned from my flight to New England, I received a letter from her, in which she wrote, "Dr. Flint is dead. He has left a distressed family. Poor old man! I hope he made his peace with God."

I remembered how he had defrauded my grandmother of the hard earnings she had loaned; how he had tried to cheat her out of the freedom her mistress had promised her, and how he had persecuted her children; and I thought to myself that she was a better Christian than I was, if she could entirely forgive him. I cannot say, with truth, that the news of my old master's death softened my feelings towards him. There are wrongs which even the grave does not bury. The man was odious to me while he lived, and his memory is odious now.

His departure from this world did not diminish my danger. He had threatened my grandmother that his heirs should hold me in slavery after he was gone; that I never should be free so long as a child of his survived. As for Mrs. Flint, I had seen her in deeper afflictions than I supposed the loss of her husband would be, for she had buried several children; yet I never saw any signs of softening in her heart. The doctor had died in embarrassed circumstances, and had little to will to his heirs, except such property as he was unable to grasp. I was well aware what I had to expect from the family of Flints; and my fears were confirmed by a letter from the south, warning me to be on my guard, because Mrs. Flint openly declared that her daughter could not afford to lose so valuable a slave as I was.

I kept close watch of the newspapers for arrivals; but one Saturday night, being much occupied, I forgot to examine the Evening Express as usual. I went down into the parlor for it, early in the morning, and found the boy about to kindle a fire with it. I took it from him and examined the list of arrivals. Reader, if you have never been a slave, you cannot imagine the acute sensation of suffering at my heart, when I read the names of Mr. and Mrs. Dodge,[1] at a hotel in Courtland Street. It was a third-rate hotel, and that circumstance convinced me of the truth of what I had heard, that they were short of funds and had need of my value, as *they* valued me; and that was by dollars and cents. I hastened with the paper to Mrs. Bruce. Her heart and hand were always open to everyone in distress, and she always warmly sympathized with mine. It was impossible to tell how near the enemy was. He might have passed and repassed the house while we were sleeping. He might at that moment be waiting to pounce upon me if I ventured out of doors. I had never seen the husband of my young mistress, and therefore I could not distinguish him

---

1   *Mr. and Mrs. Dodge*   Dr. Flint's daughter and her husband.

from any other stranger. A carriage was hastily ordered; and, closely veiled, I followed Mrs. Bruce, taking the baby again with me into exile. After various turnings and crossings and returnings, the carriage stopped at the house of one of Mrs. Bruce's friends, where I was kindly received. Mrs. Bruce returned immediately, to instruct the domestics what to say if any one came to inquire for me.

It was lucky for me that the evening paper was not burned up before I had a chance to examine the list of arrivals. It was not long after Mrs. Bruce's return to her house, before several people came to inquire for me. One inquired for me, another asked for my daughter Ellen, and another said he had a letter from my grandmother, which he was requested to deliver in person.

They were told, "She *has* lived here, but she has left."

"How long ago?"

"I don't know, sir."

"Do you know where she went?"

"I do not, sir." And the door was closed.

This Mr. Dodge, who claimed me as his property, was originally a Yankee peddler in the south; then he became a merchant, and finally a slaveholder. He managed to get introduced into what was called the first society, and married Miss Emily Flint. A quarrel arose between him and her brother, and the brother cowhided him. This led to a family feud, and he proposed to remove to Virginia. Dr. Flint left him no property, and his own means had become circumscribed, while a wife and children depended upon him for support. Under these circumstances, it was very natural that he should make an effort to put me into his pocket.

I had a colored friend, a man from my native place, in whom I had the most implicit confidence. I sent for him, and told him that Mr. and Mrs. Dodge had arrived in New York. I proposed that he should call upon them to make inquiries about his friends at the south, with whom Dr. Flint's family were well acquainted. He thought there was no impropriety in his doing so, and he consented. He went to the hotel, and knocked at the door of Mr. Dodge's room, which was opened by the gentleman himself, who gruffly inquired, "What brought you here? How came you to know I was in the city?"

"Your arrival was published in the evening papers, sir; and I called to ask Mrs. Dodge about my friends at home. I didn't suppose it would give any offence."

"Where's that negro girl, that belongs to my wife?"

"What girl, sir?"

"You know well enough. I mean Linda, that ran away from Dr. Flint's plantation, some years ago. I dare say you've seen her, and know where she is."

"Yes, sir, I've seen her, and know where she is. She is out of your reach, sir."

"Tell me where she is, or bring her to me, and I will give her a chance to buy her freedom."

"I don't think it would be of any use, sir. I have heard her say she would go to the ends of the earth, rather than pay any man or woman for her freedom, because she thinks she has a right to it. Besides, she couldn't do it, if she would, for she has spent her earnings to educate her children."

This made Mr. Dodge very angry, and some high words passed between them. My friend was afraid to come where I was; but in the course of the day I received a note from him. I supposed they had not come from the south, in the winter, for a pleasure excursion; and now the nature of their business was very plain.

Mrs. Bruce came to me and entreated me to leave the city the next morning. She said her house was watched, and it was possible that some clue to me might be obtained. I refused to take her advice. She pleaded with an earnest tenderness, that ought to have moved me; but I was in a bitter, disheartened mood. I was weary of flying from pillar to post.[1] I had been chased during half my life, and it seemed as if the chase was never to end. There I sat, in that great city, guiltless of crime, yet not daring to worship God in any of the churches. I heard the bells ringing for afternoon service, and, with contemptuous sarcasm, I said, "Will the preachers take for their text, 'Proclaim liberty to the captive, and the opening' of prison doors to them that are bound'?[2] or will they preach from the text, 'Do unto others as ye would they should do unto you'?[3] Oppressed Poles and Hungarians could find a safe refuge in that city; John Mitchell was free to proclaim in the City Hall his desire for "a plantation well stocked with slaves";[4] but there I sat, an oppressed American, not daring to show my face. God forgive the black and bitter thoughts I indulged on that Sabbath day! The Scripture says, "Oppression makes even a wise man mad";[5] and I was not wise.

I had been told that Mr. Dodge said his wife had never signed away her right to my children, and if he could not get me, he would take them. This it was, more than anything else, that roused such a tempest in my soul. Benjamin

---

1   *flying ... post*   Futile traveling from place to place.
2   *Proclaim ... bound*   See Isaiah 61.1: "The Spirit of the Lord God is upon me; because the Lord hath anointed me to preach good tidings unto the meek; he hath sent me to bind up the brokenhearted, to proclaim liberty to the captives, and the opening of the prison to them that are bound."
3   *Do unto others ... unto you*   See Matthew 7.12: "Therefore all things whatsoever ye would that men should do to you, do ye even so to them: for this is the law and the prophets."
4   *John Mitchell ... stocked with slaves*   John Mitchel was an Irish activist and journalist who escaped to America in 1853, where he became a proslavery Southern secessionist. In 1854 he claimed that he would like to have "a good plantation well-stocked with healthy negroes in Alabama."
5   *Oppression ... mad*   See Ecclesiastes 7.7: "Surely oppression maketh a wise man mad; and a gift destroyeth the heart."

was with his uncle William in California, but my innocent young daughter had come to spend a vacation with me. I thought of what I had suffered in slavery at her age, and my heart was like a tiger's when a hunter tries to seize her young.

Dear Mrs. Bruce! I seem to see the expression of her face, as she turned away discouraged by my obstinate mood. Finding her expostulations unavailing, she sent Ellen to entreat me. When ten o'clock in the evening arrived and Ellen had not returned, this watchful and unwearied friend became anxious. She came to us in a carriage, bringing a well-filled trunk for my journey— trusting that by this time I would listen to reason. I yielded to her, as I ought to have done before.

The next day, baby and I set out in a heavy snow storm, bound for New England again. I received letters from the City of Iniquity,[1] addressed to me under an assumed name. In a few days one came from Mrs. Bruce, informing me that my new master was still searching for me, and that she intended to put an end to this persecution by buying my freedom. I felt grateful for the kindness that prompted this offer, but the idea was not so pleasant to me as might have been expected. The more my mind had become enlightened, the more difficult it was for me to consider myself an article of property; and to pay money to those who had so grievously oppressed me seemed like taking from my sufferings the glory of triumph. I wrote to Mrs. Bruce, thanking her, but saying that being sold from one owner to another seemed too much like slavery; that such a great obligation could not be easily cancelled; and that I preferred to go to my brother in California.

Without my knowledge, Mrs. Bruce employed a gentleman in New York to enter into negotiations with Mr. Dodge. He proposed to pay three hundred dollars down, if Mr. Dodge would sell me, and enter into obligations to relinquish all claim to me or my children forever after. He who called himself my master said he scorned so small an offer for such a valuable servant. The gentleman replied, "You can do as you choose, sir. If you reject this offer you will never get anything; for the woman has friends who will convey her and her children out of the country."

Mr. Dodge concluded that "half a loaf was better than no bread," and he agreed to the proffered terms. By the next mail I received this brief letter from Mrs. Bruce: "I am rejoiced to tell you that the money for your freedom has been paid to Mr. Dodge. Come home tomorrow. I long to see you and my sweet babe."

---

1   *City of Iniquity*   See Habakkuk 2.12: "Woe to him that buildeth a town with blood, and stablisheth a city by iniquity!"

My brain reeled as I read these lines. A gentleman near me said, "It's true; I have seen the bill of sale." "The bill of sale!" Those words struck me like a blow. So I was *sold* at last! A human being *sold* in the free city of New York! The bill of sale is on record, and future generations will learn from it that women were articles of traffic in New York, late in the nineteenth century of the Christian religion. It may hereafter prove a useful document to antiquaries, who are seeking to measure the progress of civilization in the United States. I well know the value of that bit of paper; but much as I love freedom, I do not like to look upon it. I am deeply grateful to the generous friend who procured it, but I despise the miscreant who demanded payment for what never rightfully belonged to him or his.

I had objected to having my freedom bought, yet I must confess that when it was done I felt as if a heavy load had been lifted from my weary shoulders. When I rode home in the cars I was no longer afraid to unveil my face and look at people as they passed. I should have been glad to have met Daniel Dodge himself; to have had him seen me and known me, that he might have mourned over the untoward circumstances which compelled him to sell me for three hundred dollars.

When I reached home, the arms of my benefactress were thrown round me, and our tears mingled. As soon as she could speak, she said, "O Linda, I'm so glad it's all over! You wrote to me as if you thought you were going to be transferred from one owner to another. But I did not buy you for your services. I should have done just the same, if you had been going to sail for California tomorrow. I should, at least, have the satisfaction of knowing that you left me a free woman."

My heart was exceedingly full. I remembered how my poor father had tried to buy me, when I was a small child, and how he had been disappointed. I hoped his spirit was rejoicing over me now. I remembered how my good old grandmother had laid up her earnings to purchase me in later years, and how often her plans had been frustrated. How that faithful, loving old heart would leap for joy, if she could look on me and my children now that we were free! My relatives had been foiled in all their efforts, but God had raised me up a friend among strangers, who had bestowed on me the precious, long-desired boon. Friend! It is a common word, often lightly used. Like other good and beautiful things, it may be tarnished by careless handling; but when I speak of Mrs. Bruce as my friend, the word is sacred.

My grandmother lived to rejoice in my freedom; but not long after, a letter came with a black seal. She had gone "where the wicked cease from troubling, and the weary are at rest."[1]

Time passed on, and a paper came to me from the south, containing an obituary notice of my uncle Phillip. It was the only case I ever knew of such an honor conferred upon a colored person. It was written by one of his friends, and contained these words: "Now that death has laid him low, they call him a good man and a useful citizen; but what are eulogies to the black man, when the world has faded from his vision? It does not require man's praise to obtain rest in God's kingdom." So they called a colored man a *citizen*! Strange words to be uttered in that region!

Reader, my story ends with freedom; not in the usual way, with marriage. I and my children are now free! We are as free from the power of slaveholders as are the white people of the north; and though that, according to my ideas, is not saying a great deal, it is a vast improvement in *my* condition. The dream of my life is not yet realized. I do not sit with my children in a home of my own. I still long for a hearthstone of my own, however humble. I wish it for my children's sake far more than for my own. But God so orders circumstances as to keep me with my friend Mrs. Bruce. Love, duty, gratitude, also bind me to her side. It is a privilege to serve her who pities my oppressed people, and who has bestowed the inestimable boon of freedom on me and my children.

It has been painful to me, in many ways, to recall the dreary years I passed in bondage. I would gladly forget them if I could. Yet the retrospection is not altogether without solace; for with those gloomy recollections come tender memories of my good old grandmother, like light, fleecy clouds floating over a dark and troubled sea.

---

1   *where the wicked ... at rest*   See Job 3.17: "There the wicked cease from troubling; and there the weary be at rest."

APPENDIX

The following statement is from Amy Post,[1] a member of the Society of Friends in the State of New York, well known and highly respected by friends of the poor and the oppressed. As has been already stated, in the preceding pages, the author of this volume spent some time under her hospitable roof.
L.M.C.[2]

The author of this book is my highly-esteemed friend. If its readers knew her as I know her, they could not fail to be deeply interested in her story. She was a beloved inmate of our family nearly the whole of the year 1849. She was introduced to us by her affectionate and conscientious brother, who had previously related to us some of the almost incredible events in his sister's life. I immediately became much interested in Linda, for her appearance was prepossessing, and her deportment indicated remarkable delicacy of feeling and purity of thought.

As we became acquainted, she related to me, from time to time some of the incidents in her bitter experiences as a slave-woman. Though impelled by a natural craving for human sympathy, she passed through a baptism of suffering, even in recounting her trials to me, in private confidential conversations. The burden of these memories lay heavily upon her spirit—naturally virtuous and refined. I repeatedly urged her to consent to the publication of her narrative; for I felt that it would arouse people to a more earnest work for the disenthralment of millions still remaining in that soul-crushing condition, which was so unendurable to her. But her sensitive spirit shrank from publicity. She said, "You know a woman can whisper her cruel wrongs in the ear of a dear friend much easier than she can record them for the world to read." Even in talking with me, she wept so much, and seemed to suffer such mental agony, that I felt her story was too sacred to be drawn from her by inquisitive questions, and I left her free to tell as much, or as little, as she chose. Still, I urged upon her the duty of publishing her experience, for the sake of the good it might do; and, at last, she undertook the task.

Having been a slave so large a portion of her life, she is unlearned; she is obliged to earn her living by her own labor, and she has worked untiringly to procure education for her children; several times she has been obliged to leave her employments, in order to fly from the man-hunters and woman-hunters of our land; but she pressed through all these obstacles and overcame them. After the labors of the day were over, she traced secretly and wearily, by the midnight lamp, a truthful record of her eventful life.

---

1 *Amy Post* Amy Kirby Post (1802–89) was a prominent abolitionist and women's rights activist. She was brought up a Quaker, but later left the religion so that she could collaborate with activists outside the faith.
2 *L.M.C.* Lydia Maria Child.

This Empire State is a shabby place of refuge for the oppressed; but here, through anxiety, turmoil, and despair, the freedom of Linda and her children was finally secured, by the exertions of a generous friend. She was grateful for the boon; but the idea of having been *bought* was always galling to a spirit that could never acknowledge itself to be a chattel. She wrote to us thus, soon after the event: "I thank you for your kind expressions in regard to my freedom; but the freedom I had before the money was paid was dearer to me. God gave me *that* freedom; but man put God's image in the scales with the paltry sum of three hundred dollars. I served for my liberty as faithfully as Jacob served for Rachel.[1] At the end, he had large possessions;[2] but I was robbed of my victory; I was obliged to resign my crown,[3] to rid myself of a tyrant."

Her story, as written by herself, cannot fail to interest the reader. It is a sad illustration of the condition of this country, which boasts of its civilization, while it sanctions laws and customs which make the experiences of the present more strange than any fictions of the past.

AMY POST
ROCHESTER, N.Y., Oct. 30th, 1859

The following is from a man who is now a highly respectable colored citizen of Boston.
L.M.C.

This narrative contains some incidents so extraordinary, that, doubtless, many persons, under whose eyes it may chance to fall, will be ready to believe that it is colored highly, to serve a special purpose. But, however it may be regarded by the incredulous, I know that it is full of living truths. I have been well acquainted with the author from my boyhood. The circumstances recounted in her history are perfectly familiar to me. I knew of her treatment from her master; of the imprisonment of her children; of their sale and redemption; of her seven years' concealment; and of her subsequent escape to the North. I am now a resident of Boston, and am a living witness to the truth of this interesting narrative.

GEORGE W. LOWTHER[4]
—1856

---

1 *Jacob ... Rachel* In the biblical Book of Genesis, Jacob falls in love with Rachel, the daughter of Laban; he serves Laban for seven years in exchange for Rachel. See Genesis 29.
2 *he ... possessions* Jacob prospered, having many children and gathering wealth and possessions (see Genesis 30–33).
3 *crown* I.e., freedom.
4 GEORGE W. LOWTHER Abolitionist, barber, and Massachusetts State Representative (1878–80), born into slavery in Edenton, North Carolina.

Fugitive Slave Advertisement for Harriet Jacobs

The following advertisement was placed by Dr. James Norcom in the *American Beacon* on 4 July 1835; in it, he offers a $100 dollar reward for the return of his "servant girl," Harriet Jacobs.

$100 REWARD

WILL be given for the apprehension and delivery of my Servant Girl HARRIET. She is a light mulatto, 21 years of age, about 5 feet 4 inches high, of a thick and corpulent habit, having on her head a thick covering of black hair that curls naturally, but which can be easily combed straight. She speaks easily and fluently, and has an agreeable carriage and address. Being a good seamstress, she has been accustomed to dress well, has a variety of very fine clothes, made in the prevailing fashion, and will probably appear, if abroad, tricked out in gay and fashionable finery. As this girl absconded from the plantation of my son without any known cause or provocation, it is probable she designs to transport herself to the North.

The above reward, with all reasonable charges, will be given for apprehending her, or securing her in any prison or jail within the U. States.

All persons are hereby forewarned against harboring or entertaining her, or being in any way instrumental in her escape, under the most rigorous penalties of the law.

JAMES NORCOM.

Edenton, N. C. June 30

The "Peculiar Circumstances" of Slavery

Jacobs's career as a writer began with her anonymous "Letter from a Fugitive Slave," which was printed in the *New York Daily Tribune* in 1853. She was responding to a well-publicized conflict that took place in 1853 between two powerful women: the Duchess of Sutherland, a British aristocrat who had helped organize an effective and well-supported petition against slavery (it is known as the "Stafford House Address" or the "Address to the Christian Women of America") and Julia Tyler, who had been First Lady of the United States from 1841 to 1845. Tyler penned a defense of slavery in response to the British petition, entitled "To the Duchess of Sutherland and the Ladies of England" (also known as "The Women of England versus the Women of America").

The "Stafford House Address" was originally drafted by the Earl of Shaftesbury, who had read Harriet Beecher Stowe's *Uncle Tom's Cabin* (1852) and was moved by it to political action. He then asked the Duchess of Sutherland, a close friend of Queen Victoria and an influential socialite, to join his effort, and she helped gather signatures for the petition from over half a million English women. As a "feminine" petition, it avoided political questions and protested specifically against the domestic evils of slavery (in particular, the fact that the system separated families). The full set of signatures was presented in twenty-six volumes to Harriet Beecher Stowe on 7 May 1853, when Stowe was in England on a visit. The petition was quickly published in United States newspapers, and Julia Tyler wrote her response, which was widely printed and praised; she declared that the separation of families was a "rare occurrence" attended by "peculiar circumstances"—a claim that spurred Jacobs to write a passionate, eloquent rebuttal, in which she explicates just how pervasive and destructive the practice of family separation was in the Southern slave states.

from Anthony Ashley Cooper, 7th Earl of Shaftesbury, with Harriet Sutherland-Leveson-Gower, Duchess of Sutherland, "The Affectionate and Christian Address of Many Thousands of Women of Great Britain and Ireland to Their Sisters the Women of the United States of America" (1853)

A common origin, a common faith, and, we sincerely, believe, a common cause, urge us, at the present moment, to address you on the subject of that system of negro slavery which still prevails so extensively, and, even under kindly disposed masters, with such frightful results, in many of the vast regions of the Western world.

We will not dwell on the ordinary topics—on the progress of civilization, on the advance of freedom everywhere, on the rights and requirements of the nineteenth century; but we appeal to you very seriously to reflect and to ask counsel of God how far such a state of things is in accordance with his Holy Word, the inalienable rights of immortal souls, and the pure and merciful spirit of the Christian religion. We do not shut our eyes to the difficulties, nay, the dangers, that might beset the immediate abolition of that long-established system. We see and admit the necessity of preparation for so great an event; but, in speaking of indispensable preliminaries, we cannot be silent on those laws of your country which, in direct contravention of God's own law, "instituted in the time of man's innocency,"[1] deny in effect to the slave the sanctity of marriage, with all its joys, rights, and obligations; which separate, at the will of the master, the wife from the husband and the children from the parents. Nor can we be silent on that awful system which either by statute or by custom interdicts to any race of man or any portion of the human family education in the truths of the gospel and the ordinances of Christianity. A remedy applied to these two evils alone would commence the amelioration of their sad condition. We appeal to you, then, as sisters, as wives, and as mothers, to raise your voices to your fellow citizens and your prayers to God for the removal of this affliction and disgrace from the Christian world.

We do not say these things in a spirit of self-complacency, as though our nation were free from the guilt it perceives in others.

We acknowledge with grief and shame our heavy share in this great sin. We acknowledge that our forefathers introduced, nay, compelled the adoption of slavery in those mighty colonies. We humbly confess it before Almighty God; and it is because we so deeply feel and so unfeignedly avow our own complicity that we now venture to implore your aid to wipe away our common crime and our common dishonor. ...

from Julia Tyler, "To the Duchess of Sutherland and the Ladies of England," *Southern Literary Messenger* (February 1853)

... I must, moreover, in all frankness, declare to you, that the women of the South especially have not received your address in the kindest spirit. They regard it as entirely incompatible with all confidence in or consideration for them, to invoke the interposition of the women of what are called the Free States in a matter with which they have no more to do than have yourselves, and whose interference in the question can produce no other effect than to

---

1 *instituted ... innocency* Phrase from the marriage service in the Anglican *Book of Common Prayer* (1549).

excite disturbance and agitation and ill will, and possibly in the end, a total annihilation of kind feeling between geographical sections. It is the province of the women of the Southern States to preside over the domestic economy[1] of the estates and plantations of their husbands; it is emphatically their province to visit the sick, and attend to the comfort of all the labourers upon such estates; and it is felt to be but a poor compliment to the women of the South to suppose it necessary to introduce other superintendence than their own over the condition of their dependents and servants. ... Governments and countries which are now looked upon as stars of the first magnitude will ere long, if the United States roll on in their present orbit, be secondary and tertiary in the political hemisphere. This is quite as thoroughly known by us as by you, women of England, and therefore you should not be in the slightest degree surprised at the suspicion with which your address is regarded by all the thinking women, not only of the South, but of the whole Union. We know that there is but one subject on which there is a possibility of wrecking the bark[2] of this Union—a possibility, however, which I trust is very remote—and to that very subject you have given your attention[.] ... Yes, you are altogether correct in ascribing whatever there is of immorality or crime, in the present condition of the Southern States, to your own England. ... It will be a very, very difficult matter to furnish us with satisfactory reasons for this great and sudden conversion of a whole people, after losing the American market, on the subject of the slave trade—and we women of the United States must ever receive with suspicion all interference in our domestic affairs on the part of the noble ladies of England, or any portion of her inhabitants. Such interference implies either a want of proper and becoming conduct on our part in the management of our negroes, or it seeks to enlist the sympathies of the world against us. ... In morals we believe ourselves quite your equals, and therefore it sounds harshly in our ears to be admonished by you of our sins, real or imaginary. There is a proud heart in the American breast, which rebels against all assumption on the part of others, although they may wear ducal coronets or be considered the stars of fashions in foreign courts. ... If you wish a suggestion as to the suitable occupation of your idle hours, I will point you to the true field of your philanthropy—the unsupplied wants of your own people of England. ... Go, my good Duchess of Sutherland, on an embassy of mercy to the poor, the stricken, the hungry and the naked of your own land—cast in their laps the superflux of your enormous wealth; a single jewel from your hair, a single gem from your dress, would relieve many a poor woman of England who is now cold and shivering and destitute. ... The negro of the South

---

1 *domestic economy* I.e., management of the domestic sphere.
2 *bark* Ship.

lives sumptuously in comparison with the 100,000 of the white population of London. He is clothed warmly in winter, and has his meat twice daily without stint of bread. ... Believe me that the human heart is quite as susceptible with us as with you. Moralists and dealers in fiction may artfully overdraw and give false colouring, as they are licensed to do; but be not deceived into the belief that the heart of man or woman, on this side of the Atlantic, is either more obdurate or cruel than on yours. There is no reason, then, why you should leave your fellow subjects in misery at home in order to take your seat by the side of the black man on the plantations of America. Even if you are horror-stricken at the highly coloured picture of human distress incident to the separation of husband and wife and parents and children under our system of negro slavery—a thing, by the way, of rare occurrence among us, and then attended by peculiar circumstances—you have no occasion to leave your own land for a similar, and still harsher and more unjust exercise of authority. ...

from Harriet Jacobs, "Letter from a Fugitive Slave," *New York Daily Tribune* **(21 June 1853)**

LETTER FROM A FUGITIVE SLAVE. Slaves Sold under Peculiar Circumstances[1]

[We publish the subjoined communication exactly as written by the author, with the exception of corrections in punctuation and spelling, and the omission of one or two passages.—Ed.][2]

SIR: Having carefully read your paper for some months I became very much interested in some of the articles and comments written on Mrs. Tyler's Reply to the Ladies of England. Being a slave myself, I could not have felt otherwise. Would that I could write an article worthy of notice in your columns. As I never enjoyed the advantages of an education, therefore I could not study the arts of reading and writing, yet poor as it may be, I had rather give it from my own hand, than have it said that I employed others to do it for me. The truth can never be told so well through the second and third person as from yourself. But I am straying from the question. As Mrs. Tyler and

---

1 *Peculiar Circumstances* Jacobs is here picking up on a phrase from Julia Tyler's letter, in which she describes the splitting up of enslaved families as being driven by "peculiar circumstances" (see above). The adjective "peculiar," when used in the context of slavery, carried a specific meaning in the United States at this point in history. Slavery was often referred to by slaveholders in the South as "our peculiar institution," a euphemism that came to be used by abolitionists, too, though with them it was used ironically (they recognized it as a cowardly expression invented by those who profited from slavery but didn't want to name it).

2 *We ... Ed.* Editorial note from the *New York Daily Tribune*.

her friend Bhains were so far used up,[1] that he could not explain what those peculiar circumstances were, let one whose peculiar sufferings justifies her in explaining it for Mrs. Tyler.

I was born a slave, reared in the Southern hot-bed until I was the mother of two children, sold at the early age of two and four years old. I have been hunted through all of the Northern States, but no, I will not tell you of my own suffering—no, it would harrow up my soul, and defeat the object that I wish to pursue. Enough—the dregs of that bitter cup[2] have been my bounty for many years.

And as this is the first time that I ever took my pen in hand to make such an attempt, you will not say that it is fiction, for had I the inclination I have neither the brain or talent to write it. But to this very peculiar circumstance under which slaves are sold.

My mother was held as property by a maiden lady; when she married my younger sister[3] was in her fourteenth year, whom they took into the family. She was as gentle as she was beautiful. Innocent and guileless child, the light of our desolate hearth! But oh, my heart bleeds to tell you of the misery and degradation she was forced to suffer in slavery. The monster who owned her had no humanity in his soul. The most sincere affection that his heart was capable of, could not make him faithful to his beautiful and wealthy bride the short time of three months, but every stratagem was used to seduce my sister. Mortified and tormented beyond endurance, this child came and threw herself on her mother's bosom, the only place where she could seek refuge from her persecutor; and yet she could not protect her child that she bore into the world. On that bosom with bitter tears she told her troubles, and entreated her mother to save her. And oh, Christian mothers! you that have daughters of your own, can you think of your sable sisters without offering a prayer to that God who created all in their behalf! My poor mother, naturally high-spirited, smarting under what she considered as the wrongs and outrages which her child had to bear, sought her master, entreating him to spare her child. Nothing could exceed his rage at this what he called impertinence. My mother was dragged to jail, there remained twenty-five days, with Negro traders to come in as they liked to examine her, as she was offered for sale. My sister was told that she must yield, or never expect to see her mother again. There were three younger children; on no other condition could she be restored to them, without the sacrifice of one. That child gave herself up to her master's bidding,

---

1   *so far used up*   I.e., they had exhausted their words.
2   *dregs ... bitter cup*   See Alexander Pope's translation of the *Iliad* (1715–20), book 22, line 85: "The bitter dregs of fortune's cup to drain."
3   *my younger sister*   Jacobs is not known to have had a sister, but some elements of the following account parallel events in Jacobs's autobiography in her *Incidents in the Life of a Slave Girl.*

to save one that was dearer to her than life itself. And can you, Christian, find it in your heart to despise her? Ah, no! not even Mrs. Tyler; for though we believe that the vanity of a name would lead her to bestow her hand where her heart could never go with it,[1] yet, with all her faults and follies, she is nothing more than a woman. For if her domestic hearth is surrounded with slaves,[2] ere long before this she has opened her eyes to the evils of slavery, and that the mistress as well as the slave must submit to the indignities and vices imposed on them by their lords of body and soul. But to one of those peculiar circumstances.

At fifteen, my sister held to her bosom an innocent offspring of her guilt and misery. In this way she dragged a miserable existence of two years, between the fires of her mistress's jealousy and her master's brutal passion. At seventeen, she gave birth to another helpless infant, heir to all the evils of slavery.[3] Thus life and its sufferings was meted out to her until her twenty-first year. Sorrow and suffering has made its ravages upon her—she was less the object to be desired by the fiend who had crushed her to the earth; and as her children grew, they bore too strong a resemblance to him who desired to give them no other inheritance save Chains and Handcuffs, and in the dead hour of the night, when this young, deserted mother lay with her little ones clinging around her, little dreaming of the dark and inhuman plot that would be carried out into execution before another dawn, and when the sun rose on God's beautiful earth, that broken-hearted mother was far on her way to the capital of Virginia.[4] That day should have refused her light to so disgraceful and inhuman an act in your boasted country of Liberty. Yet, reader, it is true, those two helpless children were the sons of one of your sainted Members in Congress;[5] that agonized mother, his victim and slave. And where she now is God only knows, who has kept a record on high of all that she has suffered on earth.

And, you would exclaim, Could not the master have been more merciful to his children? God is merciful to all of his children, but it is seldom that a slaveholder has any mercy for his slave child. And you will believe it when I tell you that mother and her children were sold to make room for another sister,

---

1   *Mrs. Tyler ... with it*   Reference to Julia Tyler's having married John Tyler, the former President, even though he was thirty years her senior.

2   *if her ... slaves*   Julia Tyler and her husband held over sixty enslaved people at Sherwood Forest, their plantation in Virginia.

3   *heir ... slavery*   From 1662 onwards, slavery law in Britain and America followed the doctrine that children followed the status of their mothers (i.e., any children born to enslaved women would be themselves enslaved).

4   *on her way ... Virginia*   I.e., she was separated from her children and sent to be sold at the slave market in Richmond, Virginia.

5   *one of ... Congress*   Jacobs's two children, Joseph and Louisa, were both fathered by Samuel Sawyer, who became a Member of Congress for North Carolina's 1st District in 1837.

who was now the age of that mother when she entered the family. And this selling appeased the mistress's wrath, and satisfied her desire for revenge, and made the path more smooth for her young rival at first. For there is a strong rivalry between a handsome mulatto girl and a jealous and faded mistress, and her liege lord sadly neglects his wife or doubles his attentions, to save him being suspected by his wife. Would you not think that Southern Women had cause to despise that Slavery which forces them to bear so much deception practiced by their husbands? Yet all this is true, for a slaveholder seldom takes a white mistress, for she is an expensive commodity, not as submissive as he would like to have her, but more apt to be tyrannical; and when his passion seeks another object, he must leave her in quiet possession of all the gewgaws[1] that she has sold herself for. But not so with his poor slave victim, that he has robbed of everything that can make life desirable; she must be torn from the little that is left to bind her to life, and sold by her seducer and master, caring not where, so that it puts him in possession of enough to purchase another victim. And such are the peculiar circumstances of American Slavery—of all the evils in God's sight the most to be abhorred.

Perhaps while I am writing this you too, dear Emily, may be on your way to the Mississippi River,[2] for those peculiar circumstances occur every day in the midst of my poor oppressed fellow-creatures in bondage. And oh ye Christians, while your arms are extended to receive the oppressed of all nations, while you exert every power of your soul to assist them to raise funds, put weapons in their hands, tell them to return to their own country to slay every foe until they break the accursed yoke from off their necks,[3] not buying and selling; this they never do under any circumstances.

And because one friend of a slave has dared to tell of their wrongs you would annihilate her.[4] But in Uncle Tom's Cabin she has not told the half. Would that I had one spark from her store house of genius and talent I would tell you of my own sufferings—I would tell you of wrongs that Hungary has never inflicted, nor England ever dreamed of[5] in this free country where all

---

1 *gewgaws* Trinkets.

2 *Emily ... Mississippi River* Likely a reference to the character of Emmeline in *Uncle Tom's Cabin* (1852), a beautiful, fifteen-year-old girl whom the cruel plantation owner Legree enslaves for sex. To be "on her way" to the Mississippi River would be to be on her way to be sold at auction.

3 *the accursed ... necks* In the Bible, the yoke appears frequently as an image of enslavement, or oppression. See, for example, Genesis 27.40 and Jeremiah 28.11.

4 *her* I.e., Harriet Beecher Stowe, author of the novel *Uncle Tom's Cabin* (1852).

5 *Hungary has never inflicted* Hungary was sympathetically perceived by Americans as a country suffering under imperial yoke, particularly after the Hungarian Revolution of 1848 was suppressed by both the Austro-Hungarian and Russian empires. Americans were interested in the fate of Hungary and its struggle for freedom, partly because, in 1851, Hungarian revolutionary leader Lajos Kossuth came to the United States for political asylum, at the invitation of the United States Congress; *nor England ever dreamed of* In sections excluded from the above selection of Julia Tyler's letter, she accuses England

nations fly for liberty, equal rights and protection under your stripes and stars. It should be stripes[1] and scars, for they go along with Mrs. Tyler's peculiar circumstances, of which I have told you only one.

A FUGITIVE SLAVE.

---

of what she considered to be worse crimes than slavery, particularly their treatment of the Irish people (the Irish Famine, in which the devastating effects of a potato blight were worsened by British colonial policies and laissez-faire capitalism, took place between 1845 and 1852).

1   *stripes*   In this context, lash marks left on the skin by a whip.

Jacobs Free School, Founded by Harriet Jacobs, 1864. A small "x" inscribed onto the photo indicates where Harriet Jacobs is standing.

from *The Narratives of Fugitive Slaves in Canada* (1856)

The only collection ever compiled of first-hand interviews of black people who had escaped slavery by taking the Underground Railroad to Canada, *The Narratives of Fugitive Slaves in Canada* was published in 1856 by the Massachusetts abolitionist Benjamin Drew (1812–1903). The book—the full title of which is *A North-Side View of Slavery. The Refugee: or the Narratives of Fugitive Slaves in Canada*—was partially a response to *A South-Side View of Slavery* (1855), a book by Drew's fellow white Massachusetts writer Nehemiah Adams that described the supposed moral and religious benefits that enslavement conferred on African Americans and criticized the abolition movement's ostensible radicalism. In order to rebut Adams's arguments, Drew traveled widely in Canada West (the present-day Canadian province of Ontario), interviewing some of the thousands of escapees from slavery who had settled there and recording their accounts of their lives in slavery, their journeys to freedom, and their experiences in Canada.

Note on the Text

The excerpts from *The Narratives of Fugitive Slaves in Canada* presented here are based on the text of the book's 1856 first edition. Spelling and punctuation have been modernized in accordance with the practices of this anthology.

⌘ ⌘ ⌘

WILLIAM JOHNSON

I look upon slavery as I do upon a deadly poison. The slaves are not contented nor happy in their lot. Neither on the farm where I was in Virginia, nor in the neighborhood were the slaves satisfied. The man I belonged to did not give us enough to eat. My feet were frostbitten on my way North, but I would rather have died on the way than to go back.

It would not do to stop at all about our work—if the people should try to get a little rest, there would be a cracking spell amongst them.[1] I have had to go through a great deal of affliction; I have been compelled to work when I

---

1   *there would ... amongst them*   I.e., they would be beaten severely.

was sick. I used to have rheumatism,[1] and could not always do so much work as those who were well—then I would sometimes be whipped. I have never seen a runaway that wanted to go back—I have never heard of one.

I knew a very smart young man—he was a fellow-servant of mine, who had recently professed religion[2]—who was tied up by a quick-tempered overseer, and whipped terribly. He died not long after, and the people there believed it was because of the whipping. Some of the slaves told the owner, but he did not discharge the overseer. He will have to meet it at the day of judgment.

I had grown up quite large, before I thought anything about liberty. The fear of being sold South[3] had more influence in inducing me to leave than any other thing. Master used to say, that if we didn't suit him, he would put us in his pocket quick—meaning he would sell us. He never gave me a great coat[4] in his life—he said he knew he ought to do it, but that he couldn't get ahead far enough. His son had a child by a colored woman, and he would have sold it—his own grandchild—if the other folks hadn't opposed it.

I have found good friends in Canada, but have been able to do no work on account of my frozen feet—I lost two toes from my right foot. My determination is to go to work as soon as I am able. I have been about among the colored people in St. Catharines[5] considerably, and have found them industrious and frugal. No person has offered me any liquor since I have been here: I have seen no colored person use it. I have been trying to learn to read since I came here, and I know a great many fugitives who are trying to learn.

HARRIET TUBMAN[6]

I grew up like a neglected weed—ignorant of liberty, having no experience of it. Then I was not happy or contented: every time I saw a white man, I was afraid of being carried away. I had two sisters carried away in a chain-gang—

---

1   rheumatism   Term for a class of disorders affecting the joints, such as arthritis.
2   professed religion   Publicly embraced Christianity.
3   The fear ... South   Conditions for enslaved people in the Deep South, where most large-scale cotton cultivation took place, were generally much worse than in the more northerly slave states; consequently, enslaved people in "Upper South" states such as Virginia greatly feared being sold to new enslavers in the Deep South.
4   great coat   Long, warm overcoat.
5   St. Catharines   Town in what is now the Canadian province of Ontario, not far from the U.S. border, that became a center of abolitionist activity and a place of refuge and settlement for enslaved people who took the Underground Railroad to Canada. By the mid-1850s, about 800 black people lived there, out of a total population of approximately 6,000.
6   HARRIET TUBMAN   African American abolitionist and activist (c. 1822–1913) who was one of the most famous "conductors" on the Underground Railroad. After herself escaping from slavery in Maryland in 1849, she guided first her family and then numerous other enslaved people to freedom, for which she became known as "Moses." Tubman lived in St. Catharines from 1851 to 1858.

one of them left two children. We were always uneasy. Now I've been free, I know what a dreadful condition slavery is. I have seen hundreds of escaped slaves, but I never saw one who was willing to go back and be a slave. I have no opportunity to see my friends in my native land. We would rather stay in our native land, if we could be as free there as we are here. I think slavery is the next thing to hell. If a person would send another into bondage, he would, it appears to me, be bad enough to send him into hell, if he could.

HARRIET TUBMAN.

Harriet Tubman as she appeared during the Civil War, in which she served as a scout and spy for the U.S. Army. Tubman guided federal troops on an 1863 raid on plantations along the Combahee River in South Carolina, an action in which more than 750 enslaved people were freed. This image was printed as a frontispiece to *Scenes in the Life of Harriet Tubman* (1869).

John W. Lindsey

[Mr. Lindsey reached St. Catharines in an entirely destitute condition. He is now reputed to be worth from eight to ten thousand dollars, acquired by industry and economy.[1]]

I was born free. At the age of seven, I was kidnapped by S— G—, and carried to West Tennessee. When I was about twenty-five years old, I went to a man who had been Postmaster General, and asked him if he would do anything toward restoring my freedom, as I had been kidnapped wrongfully, and was unlawfully detained by Mr.—. He answered, that "Mr. G— had settled all that," and advised me to "Go home and be a good boy." Finding that I was to get no assistance from any quarter, and that justice was refused me, I resolved to free myself. I was whiter then than I am now, for it was twenty-one years ago, and I worked under cover[2] at blacksmithing. A person across the street could not tell whether I were a white or a colored man. Whether I was pursued or not I am unable to say. I walked by day and rested at night.

I passed people working in the fields, and once I heard one ask another, "Do you think that is a white man?" I took no notice of this, and walked on. At one time I met a man on horseback who stopped and talked with me. I spoke so familiarly of this great man and of that great man, and talked in so important a way, that he did not dare ask me if I were a slave! At one place, I was somewhat afraid of pursuit, and there seemed to be some suspicions entertained in regard to me. I walked away from the town on the bank of the river and prayed to the Lord for deliverance. Just then a steamboat came along—she was bound for Pittsburgh. I got a passage on board. The cook, who was a very black man, asked me "if I was free?" I told him that I had heard of a man in Maryland who got rich by minding his own business, and that he would find it for his own interest to attend to his own affairs. However, I found little difficulty in reaching the frontier and crossing the line.[3]

I have travelled in Maryland, Virginia, Kentucky, and Tennessee. If a man says slavery is a good institution, he might as well say there is no God—only

---

1   *industry and economy* I.e., hard work and careful management of his finances.
2   *under cover* In the shade, out of the sun.
3   *line* I.e., the Mason–Dixon Line: the southern border of Pennsylvania, which during this period formed the symbolic and literal boundary between slave states and free states.

a devil. Slavery is like the bottomless pit.[1] You hear people say to the negro, "Why don't you accomplish something?" You see the colored men, their faces scarred and wrinkled, and almost deprived of intelligence in some cases—their manliness crushed out; stooping, awkward in gait, kept in entire ignorance. Now, to ask them why they don't do some great thing, is like tying a man or weakening him by medicine, and then saying, "Why don't you go and do that piece of work, or plant that field with wheat and corn?" Slavery is mean.[2] The slaveholders want their slaves for pocket-money. The slaves are their right hand to do their work.

from WILLIAM GROSE

... I intended to stay in my native country, but I saw so many mean-looking men, that I did not dare to stay. I found a friend who helped me on the way to Canada, which I reached in 1851.

I served twenty-five years in slavery, and about five I have been free. I feel now like a man, while before I felt more as though I were but a brute. When in the United States, if a white man spoke to me, I would feel frightened, whether I were in the right or wrong; but now it is quite a different thing—if a white man speaks to me, I can look him right in the eyes—if he were to insult me, I could give him an answer. I have the rights and privileges of any other man. I am now living with my wife and children, and doing very well. When I lie down at night, I do not feel afraid of oversleeping, so that my employer might jump on me if he pleased. I am a true British subject, and I have a vote every year as much as any other man. I often used to wonder in the United States, when I saw carriages going round for voters, why they never asked me to vote. But I have since found out the reason—I know they were using my vote[3] instead of my using it—now I use it myself. Now I feel like a man, and I wish to God that all my fellow-creatures could feel the same freedom that I feel. I am not prejudiced against all the white race in the United States—it is only the portion that sustain the cursed laws of slavery.

---

1   *the bottomless pit*   Hell. See Revelation 20.1–3: "And I saw an angel come down from heaven, having the key of the bottomless pit and a great chain in his hand. And he laid hold on the dragon, that old serpent, which is the Devil, and Satan, and bound him a thousand years, And cast him into the bottomless pit."

2   *mean*   Miserly, selfish.

3   *they were ... vote*   Reference to the so-called "Three-Fifths Clause" (Article 1, Section 2, Clause 3) of the U.S. Constitution, according to which states' representation in Congress was based on "the whole Number of free Persons" plus "three fifths of all other Persons," i.e., enslaved people. Because enslaved people were not allowed to vote, this clause artificially inflated the slave states' share of congressional representatives and presidential electoral votes—in effect, it used what would otherwise have been a share of the votes of enslaved people to secure more political power for their enslavers.

Here's something I want to say to the colored people in the United States: You think you are free there, but you are very much mistaken: if you wish to be free men, I hope you will all come to Canada as soon as possible. There is plenty of land here, and schools to educate your children. I have no education myself, but I don't intend to let my children come up as I did. I have but two, and instead of making servants out of them, I'll give them a good education, which I could not do in the southern portion of the United States. True, they were not slaves there, but I could not have given them any education.

I have been through both Upper and Lower Canada,[1] and I have found the colored people keeping stores, farming, etc., and doing well. I have made more money since I came here, than I made in the United States. I know several colored people who have become wealthy by industry—owning horses and carriages—one who was a fellow-servant of mine, now owns two span[2] of horses, and two as fine carriages as there are on the bank. As a general thing, the colored people are more sober and industrious than in the States: there they feel when they have money, that they cannot make what use they would like of it, they are so kept down, so looked down upon. Here they have something to do with their money, and put it to a good purpose.

I am employed in the Clifton House, at the Falls.[3]

from WILLIAM A. HALL

... The overseer tied me to a tree, and flogged me with the whip. Afterwards he said he would stake me down, and give me a farewell whipping, that I would always remember. While he was eating supper, I got off my shoe, and slipped off a chain and ran: I ran, I suppose, some six hundred yards: then hearing a dog, which alarmed me, I climbed a hill, where I sat down to rest. Then I heard a shouting, hallooing, for dogs to hunt me up. I tried to understand, and made out they were after me. I went through the woods to a road on a ridge. I came to a guide-board—in order to read it, I pulled it up, and read it in the moonlight, and found I was going wrong—turned about and went back, travelling all night: lay by

---

1   *Upper and Lower Canada*   British colonies in what is today the nation of Canada, formed in 1791 when what had been the single Province of Quebec was divided in two. Upper Canada corresponded to the southern portion of the present-day province of Ontario, while Lower Canada covered much of what is now the province of Quebec. The two provinces were reunited into a single province, the Province of Canada, in 1841, but often continued to be thought of separately.

2   *two span*   Two pairs of horses harnessed together. Usually, both horses in a span are of similar size and color.

3   *Clifton House ... Falls*   The Clifton Hotel, built in 1833, was one of the first luxury hotels on the Canadian side of Niagara Falls.

all day, travelled at night till I came where Duck River and Tennessee[1] come together. Here I found I was wrong—went back to a road that led down Tennessee River,[2] the way I wanted to go. ... I got something to eat, and went on down the river, and travelled until Saturday night at ten, living on green corn and watermelons. Then I came to a house where an old colored man gave me a supper: another kept me with him three days. My clothes were now very dirty: I got some soap of a woman, and went to a wash-place, and washed my clothes and dried them. A heavy rain came on at daybreak, and I went down to the river for a canoe—found none—and went back for the day, got some bread, and at night went on down the river; but there were so many roads, I could not make out how to go. I laid all day in a corn field. At night I found a canoe, 12 feet long, and travelled down the river several days, to its mouth. There I got on an island, the river being low. I took my canoe across a tongue of land—a sand-bar—into the Ohio, which I crossed into Illinois. I travelled three nights, not daring to travel days, until I came to Golconda,[3] which I recognized by a description I had given on a previous attempt—for this last time when I got away was my fourth effort. I went on to three forks in the road, took the left, travelled through the night, and lay by. At two, I ventured to go on, the road not being travelled much. But it seemed to go too far west: I struck through the woods, and went on till so tired I could walk no further. I got into a tobacco-pen, and stayed till morning. Then I went through the woods, and came to where a fire had been burning—I kindled it up, roasted a lot of corn, then travelled on about three miles completely lost. I now came to a house, and revolved in my mind some hours whether to go or not, to ask. At last I ventured, and asked the road—got the information—reached Marion:[4] got bewildered, and went wrong again, and travelled back for Golconda, but I was set right by some children. At dark I went on, and at daybreak got to Frankfort—13 miles all night long, being weak from want of food. A few miles further on I found an old friend, who was backward about letting me in, having been troubled at night by white children. At last he let me in, and gave me some food, which I much needed. The next night he gave me as much as I could carry with me.

I went on to within five miles of Mount Vernon.[5] At 4 A.M., I lay down, and slept till about noon. I got up and tried to walk, but every time I tried to

---

1 *Duck River and Tennessee* Rivers in the state of Tennessee that meet in the west-central region of the state.

2 *down Tennessee River* The Tennessee River, in this region, flows north through Tennessee and Kentucky to join the Ohio, so by traveling down it, Hall would be heading north.

3 *Golconda* Town in southern Illinois, on the Ohio River.

4 *Marion* City in southern Illinois, some ways north of Golconda.

5 *Mount Vernon* City in south-central Illinois, some ways north again from Marion.

stoop under the bushes, I would fall down. I was close to a house, but did not dare to go to it; so I laid there and was sick—vomited, and wanted water very bad. At night I was so badly off that I was obliged to go to the house for water. The man gave me some, and said, "Are you a runaway?" I said, "No—I am walking away." "Where do you live?" "I live here now." "Are you a free man?" "Why should I be here, if I am not a free man? This is a free country." "Where do you live, anyhow?" "I live here, don't you understand me?" "You are a free man, are you?" "Don't you see he is a free man, who walks in a free country?" "Show me your pass—I s'pose you've got one." "Do you suppose men need a pass in a free country? this is a free country." "I suppose you run away—a good many fugitives go through here, and do mischief." Said I, "I am doing no mischief—I am a man peaceable, going about my own business; when I am doing mischief, persecute me—while I am peaceable, let no man trouble me." Said he, "I'll go with you to Mount Vernon." "You may go, if you have a mind to: I am going, if it is the Lord's will that I shall get there. Good evening"; and I started out of the gate. He said, "Stop!" Said I, "Man, don't bother me—I'm sick, and don't feel like being bothered." I kept on: he followed me—"Stop, or I'll make you stop!" "Man, didn't I tell you I was sick, and don't want to be bothered." I kept on—he picked up a little maul at a wood-pile, and came with me, his little son following, to see what was going on.

He walked a mile and a quarter with me, to a neighbor of his—called— there came out three men. He stated to them, "Here's a runaway going to Mount Vernon: I think it would be right to go with him." I made no reply. He said, "We'll go in with him, and if he be correct, we'll not injure him—we'll not do him no harm, nohow." I stood consulting with myself, whether to fight or run; I concluded to run first, and fight afterward. I ran a hundred yards: one ran after me to the edge of the woods, and turned back. I sat down to rest—say an hour. They had gone on ahead of me on horses. I took a back track, and found another road which led to Mount Vernon, which I did not reach until daybreak, although he said 't was only five miles. I hastened on very quick through town, and so got off the track again: but I found a colored friend who harbored me three days, and fulfilled the Scriptures in one sense to perfection. I was hungry, and he fed me; thirsty, and he gave me drink; weary, and he ministered to my necessities; sick, and he cared for me till I got relieved:[1] he took me on his own beast, and carried me ten miles, and his wife gave me food for four days' travel. His name was Y——. I travelled on three nights, and every morning found myself close to a town. One was a large one.

---

1 *fulfilled ... relieved* See Matthew 25.35–40, in which Jesus describes how people who practice hospitality, charity, and mercy will be rewarded at the Last Judgment: "For I was an hungered, and ye gave me meat: I was thirsty, and ye gave me drink: I was a stranger, and ye took me in[.] ... Inasmuch as ye have done it unto one of the least of these my brethren, ye have done it unto me."

I got into it early—I was scared, for people was stirring—but I got through it by turning to my right, which led me thirty miles out of my way. I was trying to get to Springfield.[1] Then I went on to Taylorville. I lay out all day, two miles out, and while there, a man came riding on horseback within two feet of me. I thought he would see me, but he wheeled his horse, and away he went. At dark I got up and started on. It rained heavily. I went on to the town. I could discover nothing—the ground was black, the sky was cloudy. I travelled a while by the lights in the windows; at last ventured to ask the way, and got a direction for Springfield. After the rain the wind blew cold; I was chilled: I went into a calf-lot, and scared up the calves, and lay where they had been lying, to warm myself. It was dark yet. I stayed there half an hour, trying to get warm, then got up, and travelled on till daybreak. It being in a prairie, I had to travel very fast to get a place to hide myself. I came to a drain between two plantations, and got into it to hide. At sundown I went on, and reached Springfield, as near as I could guess, at 3 o'clock. I got into a stable, and lay on some boards in the loft.

When I awoke, the sun was up, and people were feeding horses in the stable. I found there was no chance to get out, without being discovered, and I went down and told them that I was a stranger, knowing no one there; that I was out until late, and so went into the stable. I asked them if there was any harm. They said "No." I thanked them and pursued my way. I walked out a little and found a friend who gave me breakfast. Then I was taken sick, and could not get a step from there for ten days: then I could walk a little, and had to start.

I took directions for Bloomington[2]—but the directions were wrong, and I got thirty miles out of my way again: so that when I reached Bloomington, I was too tired to go another step. I begged for a carriage, and if they had not got one, the Lord only knows what would have happened. I was conveyed to Ottawa,[3] where I found an abolitionist who helped me to Chicago. From about the middle of August to the middle of November, I dwelt in no house except in Springfield, sick—had no bed till I got to Bloomington. In February, I cut wood in Indiana—I went to Wisconsin, and staid till harvest was over; then came to a particular friend, who offered me books. I had no money for books: he gave me a Testament, and gave me good instruction. I had worn out two Testaments in slavery, carrying them with me trying to get some instruction to carry me through life. "Now," said he, "square up your business, and go to the lake,[4] for there are men here now, even here where you are living, who

---

1   *Springfield*   Illinois's state capital, located in the center of the state.
2   *Bloomington*   Illinois city to the north of Springfield.
3   *Ottawa*   City in northern Illinois.
4   *the lake*   I.e., Lake Superior, or the Great Lakes more generally.

would betray you for half a dollar if they knew where your master is. Cross the lake: get into Canada." I thanked him for the book, which I have now; settled up and came to Canada.

I like Canada. If the United States were as free as Canada, I would still prefer to live here. I can do as much toward a living here in three days, as there in six.

—1856

William Wells Brown
c. 1814 – 1884

William Wells Brown was a charismatic writer, orator, and leader in the antislavery cause. His literary and artistic work spans a wide variety of genres, including speeches, drawings, biography, drama, travel-writing, history, memoir, and the novel. Unlike fellow abolitionists Frederick Douglass and William Lloyd Garrison, who primarily appealed to men, Brown cultivated a diverse, predominantly female audience, making use of a wide array of dramatic conventions and rhetorical strategies to bring his arguments home to his auditors and readers. He spoke more directly than most men about the particular evils of slavery for women, as well as about the importance of female education. Popular and respected in his own time, Brown is now considered one of the foremost black writers of the nineteenth century; as Henry Louis Gates Jr. writes, "It is difficult to imagine any one of his contemporaries who contributed as much or as richly to so many genres as did William Wells Brown."

Brown was born in 1814 near Lexington, Kentucky; his mother, Elizabeth, was an enslaved woman, and his father was a white plantation owner, George W. Higgins. Elizabeth and all six of her children were enslaved by Dr. John Young (a relative of Higgins). When Brown was two years old, Young moved Elizabeth and her children to Missouri, where one of Brown's earliest traumatic memories included seeing his mother whipped for being a few minutes late for work. When Brown was a small boy, the Youngs adopted a nephew named William; they then changed Brown's first name to "Sandford," so there would be no confusing the young children (Brown had a light complexion). In 1827, when Brown was thirteen, Dr. Young moved to St. Louis, taking Elizabeth and Brown with him, but leaving four of Brown's siblings behind on the plantation. Over the next five years, Young made money by renting Brown's labor out to those willing to purchase it. He was thus subjected to an even wider range of the horrors of slavery: one of the men to whom Brown was leased, a vicious drunk, beat his workers and then suffocated them in a shed full of smoke, while another, a slave trader, gave Brown the heartbreaking task of preparing enslaved people for auction. There were, however, some positive experiences. For six months, Brown worked for a newspaper editor, the well-known abolitionist Elijah P. Lovejoy, whom Brown describes as "a very good man, and decidedly the best master that I had ever had." In the offices of Lovejoy's paper, the *St. Louis Times*, Brown wrote that he received "what little learning [he] obtained while in slavery," though this happier period ended when he was severely beaten by a white man who was furious that Brown had defended the office from a thieving gang of white boys. Brown also worked on Mississippi steamboats at this time; the experience of moving from place to place and seeing how others lived gave him an expanded sense of future possibility and solidified his determination to one day make an escape.

In 1833, Young decided to sell Brown and his sister, threatening to divide further the already scattered family. Determined not to be separated from his mother, Brown convinced her to escape with him. They were captured after eleven days, and Brown's mother was sold and sent to the Deep South, which often meant exposure to even harder labor, disease, and early death. Filled with remorse and grief, Brown was sold first to a tailor, Samuel Willi, for $500, and then to Enoch Price, a steamboat merchant, for $700. In January 1834, while aboard one of Price's steamboats that had stopped in Cincinnati, Brown escaped and met a Quaker named Wells Brown, who sheltered, fed, and clothed him. At this time, William rejected the name given him by his enslavers ("Sandford"), took back his original first name, and adopted the names of his benefactor, becoming William Wells Brown.

Once in the north, Brown worked several jobs to support himself, but his main source of income for the next nine years was from working seasonally on steamships on the Great Lakes. In 1834, he married Elizabeth Schooner, with whom he had two daughters, Clarissa and Josephine. He also launched himself into an intense program of self-education, while at the same time committing himself politically to the abolitionist cause. In 1836 the family moved to Buffalo, where Brown helped transport freedom-seeking enslaved people to Canada, as well as sheltering them in his home. Brown also began giving antislavery speeches; by 1843, he had quit his job stewarding ships and committed to working full-time as a traveling lecturer for the Western New York Anti-Slavery Society. He helped organize the 1843 National Convention of Colored Citizens in Buffalo, where he met fellow-abolitionist and keynote speaker Frederick Douglass, with whom he was to have a meaningful, if sometimes fraught, professional relationship. It was also in this momentous year that Brown published his first piece of writing, a letter to the editor in the *National Anti-Slavery Standard* arguing that abolition should be primarily a persuasive movement that would in time lead to a moral and political rejection of the institution.

Brown gained a national reputation as a gifted speaker and drew crowds of people to hear his lectures. As one reviewer in 1861 put it, Brown was a speaker of "unequalled attractive powers." Over time, Brown became more and more inventive in his presentations; in fact, it is more accurate to think of his lectures as examples of performance art, moving seamlessly between exhortation, storytelling, song, and panoramas of magic lantern slides. Some of his more famous speeches include *Lecture Delivered before the Female Anti-Slavery Society of Salem* (1847), *Speech Delivered in Croydon, England* (1849), and *St. Domingo: Its Revolutions and Its Patriots* (1854). Brown's dedication to the lecture circuit had a cost, however—his absences from home further deteriorated an already difficult relationship with his wife, leading to separation in 1847.

After the separation, Brown moved with his daughters to Boston, the national hub of antislavery activity and publication, where he started writing in earnest. His *Narrative of William W. Brown, A Fugitive Slave, Written by Himself* was published in 1847; the book proved popular, running to nine editions within the next three years. In *Narrative*, Brown uses a controlled, understated narrative voice to describe the dramatic and horrific incidents of his life in slavery, creating an ironic juxtaposition between the events described and the voice of description. This polished irony was a rhetorical tool Brown would use again and again to engage his largely white audience's sympathy without alienating them. Brown's portrayal of resistance in his *Narrative* also highlights the importance of outwitting the enslaver and the slave system, a different strategy from the more physical resistance exemplified in Douglass's famous *Narrative*, which had been published two years earlier, in 1845.

In 1849, Brown traveled to Europe; the passing of the Fugitive Slave Law in 1850 made it unsafe to return to the United States, so Brown settled in England for the next five years, supporting himself by his lecturing. Brown also continued his education, reading widely and studying French, German, and Latin. He published four more books during this time abroad, including a travel narrative entitled *Three Years in Europe: or, Places I Have Seen and People I Have Met* (1852) and *Clotel, or The President's Daughter* (1853), his first and only novel. Upon publication, *Clotel* received a somewhat lackluster response, perhaps because it followed soon after Harriet Beecher Stowe's *Uncle Tom's Cabin* (1852), which had been a huge sensation the previous year (the impact of *Uncle Tom's Cabin* on the abolitionist movement was a key inspiration for Brown to try his own hand at novel-writing). *Clotel*'s story is grounded on rumors, prevalent at the time, that children were born to Thomas Jefferson and his enslaved servant Sally Hemings—rumors that have since been substantiated by DNA evidence. The novel thus exposes the narrow confines of what "freedom" meant for one of the authors of the Declaration of Independence, with Jefferson's hypocrisy serving as a microcosm for the larger hypocrisy of a free democracy built upon slavery. By focusing on the fate of a young African American woman, Brown also emphasized the particular dangers and suffering that women endured within this system.

For many years, critics saw *Clotel* as a work that tried to include too many elements and plot events into one literary space. But more recently, readers have celebrated the novel as a literary example of Brown's work as a performance artist, in which the crowding together of incident, song, poems, news clippings, and melodrama act together to attract and at times overwhelm the senses, leading to cathartic release. Critics are still unpacking the complex mixture of pleasure and discomfort that Brown elicits in this novel, even as he simultaneously makes vivid the horrors and hypocrisy of slavery; as critic Geoffrey Sanborn writes, "In [*Clotel*], anti-racism, still so often stereotyped and resisted as a joyless reformism, is capable of providing windfalls of psychic pleasure."

Brown returned to America with his daughters in 1854, after his freedom had been purchased by the British abolitionist Ellen Richardson. By this time, Brown's politics had become more radical, leaving behind the passivist ideals of Garrisonian abolitionism to support active—even violent—resistance to slavery. He began to write plays, including *Experience; or, How to Give a Northern Man a Backbone* in 1856, which he often performed at meetings and lectures, and *The Escape; or, A Leap for Freedom. A Drama in Five Acts* in 1858. Drawing heavily on Brown's own history, *The Escape* is noteworthy for its incisive exploration of moral hypocrisy and for its depiction of the increasing social tensions running up to the Civil War.

In 1860, Brown married again, and during the war he continued to write, focusing on histories and biographies aimed at celebrating the vital place of black people in America's past, present, and future. His historical works include *The Black Man; His Antecedents, His Genius, and His Achievements* (1862), *The Negro in the American Rebellion: His Heroism and His Fidelity* (1867), and *The Rising Son; or, The Antecedents and Advancement of the Colored Race* (1873). In his last autobiographical book, *My Southern Home: Or, The South and Its People* (1880), Brown records memories of his youth and also his impressions from a trip South in 1879–80, with particular attention on the deteriorating conditions for African Americans as the promise of Reconstruction faded; the book is considered an important precursor to W.E.B. Du Bois's *The Souls of Black Folk* (1903). Brown died in 1884, at the age of seventy, in Chelsea, Massachusetts.

For much of the twentieth century, Brown's work and legacy faded into the background, particularly when compared to his more famous colleague Frederick Douglass. Some of his strengths—his strategy of speaking particularly to women and of women, and his savviness in creating political performance art—run counter to the formalist aesthetics that determined literary fame in previous decades. Brown's rhetorical strategies are now, however, increasingly admired, as is his vast body of work, which touches on many subjects of contemporary scholarly interest, including racial identity, the literature of sentimentality, melodrama, minstrelsy, narrative fragmentation, and theatricality.

Note on the Text

The text presented here is based on the version of Brown's *Narrative* that appeared as a preface to the first edition of *Clotel* (1853). Spelling and punctuation have been modernized in accordance with the practices of this anthology.

⌘ ⌘ ⌘

from *The Narrative of the Life and Escape of William Wells Brown*

William Wells Brown, the subject of this narrative, was born a slave in Lexington, Kentucky, not far from the residence of the late Hon. Henry Clay.[1] His mother was the slave of Doctor John Young. His father was a slaveholder, and, besides being a near relation of his master, was connected with the Wicklief family, one of the oldest, wealthiest, and most aristocratic of the Kentucky planters. Dr. Young was the owner of forty or fifty slaves, whose chief employment was in cultivating tobacco, hemp, corn, and flax. The Doctor removed from Lexington, when William was five or six years old, to the state of Missouri, and commenced farming in a beautiful and fertile valley, within a mile of the Missouri river.

Here the slaves were put to work under a harsh and cruel overseer named Cook. A finer situation for a farm could not have been selected in the state. With climate favourable to agriculture, and soil rich, the products[2] came in abundance. At an early age William was separated from his mother, she being worked in the field, and he as a servant in his master's medical department.[3] When about ten years of age, the young slave's feelings were much hurt at hearing the cries of his mother, while being flogged by the negro driver for being a few minutes behind the other hands in reaching the field. He heard her cry, "Oh, pray! oh, pray! oh, pray!" These are the words which slaves generally utter when imploring mercy at the hands of their oppressors. The son heard it, though he was some way off. He heard the crack of the whip and the groans of his poor mother. The cold chill ran over him, and he wept aloud; but he was a slave like his mother, and could render her no assistance. He was taught by the most bitter experience, that nothing could be more heart-rending than to see a dear and beloved mother or sister tortured by unfeeling men, and to hear her cries, and not be able to render the least aid. When William was twelve years of age, his master left his farm and took up his residence near St. Louis. The Doctor having more hands than he wanted for his own use, William was let out to a Mr. Freeland, an innkeeper. Here the young slave found himself in the hands of a most cruel and heartless master. Freeland was one of the real chivalry[4] of the South; besides being himself a slaveholder, he was a

---

1   *Hon. Henry Clay*   Prominent political figure (1777–1852).
2   *products*   I.e., produce, crops.
3   *department*   Business.
4   *chivalry*   Aristocratic class governed by elaborate rules of civility and etiquette—applied sarcastically here to Freeland.

horse-racer, cock-fighter,[1] gambler, and, to crown the whole, an inveterate drunkard. What else but bad treatment could be expected from such a character? After enduring the tyrannical and inhuman usage of this man for five or six months, William resolved to stand it no longer, and therefore ran away, like other slaves who leave their masters, owing to severe treatment; and not knowing where to flee, the young fugitive went into the forest, a few miles from St. Louis. He had been in the woods but a short time, when he heard the barking and howling of dogs, and was soon satisfied that he was pursued by the negro dogs;[2] and, aware of their ferocious nature, the fugitive climbed a tree, to save himself from being torn to pieces. The hounds were soon at the trunk of the tree, and remained there, howling and barking, until those in whose charge they were came up. The slave was ordered down, tied, and taken home. Immediately on his arrival there, he was, as he expected, tied up in the smokehouse, and whipped till Freeland was satisfied, and then smoked with tobacco stems. This the slaveholder called "Virginia play." After being well whipped and smoked, he was again set to work. William remained with this monster a few months longer, and was then let out to Elijah P. Lovejoy, who years after became the editor of an abolition newspaper, and was murdered at Alton, Illinois, by a mob of slaveholders from the adjoining state of Missouri. The system of letting out slaves is one among the worst of the evils of slavery. The man who hires a slave, looks upon him in the same light as does the man who hires a horse for a limited period; he feels no interest in him, only to get the worth of his money. Not so with the man who owns the slave; he regards him as so much property, of which care should be taken. After being let out to a steamer as an under-steward, William was hired by James Walker, a slave-trader. Here the subject of our memoir was made superintendent of the gangs of slaves that were taken to the New Orleans market. In this capacity, William had opportunities, far greater than most slaves, of acquiring knowledge of the different phases of the "peculiar institution."[3] Walker was a negro speculator, who was amassing a fortune by trading in the bones, blood, and nerves, of God's children. ... Between fifty and sixty slaves were chained together, put on board a steamboat bound for New Orleans, and started on the voyage. New and strange scenes began to inspire the young slave with the hope of escaping to a land of freedom. There was in the boat a large room on the lower deck in which the slaves were kept, men and women promiscuously,[4] all chained two

---

1   cock-fighter   Person who trains roosters to engage in cockfighting, a cruel form of entertainment that is now illegal throughout the United States.

2   negro dogs   I.e., dogs trained to track enslaved people attempting to escape.

3   peculiar institution   Euphemistic term for slavery, first coined by Southern enslavers in the 1820s; Northern abolitionists began to use it ironically in their attacks on slavery in the 1830s.

4   promiscuously   Randomly, indiscriminately.

and two together, not even leaving the poor slaves the privilege of choosing their partners. …

At the end of the week they arrived at New Orleans, the place of their destination. Here the slaves were placed in a negro pen, where those who wished to purchase could call and examine them. The negro pen is a small yard surrounded by buildings, from fifteen to twenty feet wide, with the exception of a large gate with iron bars. The slaves are kept in the buildings during the night, and turned into the pen during the day. After the best of the gang were sold off, the balance was taken to the Exchange coffee-house auction-rooms, and sold at public auction. After the sale of the last slave, William and Mr. Walker left New Orleans for St. Louis.

After they had been at St. Louis a few weeks another cargo of human flesh was made up. There were amongst the lot several old men and women, some of whom had grey locks. On their way down to New Orleans William had to prepare the old slaves for market. He was ordered to shave off the old men's whiskers, and to pluck out the grey hairs where they were not too numerous; where they were, he coloured them with a preparation of blacking with a blacking brush. After having gone through the blacking process, they looked ten or fifteen years younger. William, though not well skilled in the use of scissors and razor, performed the office of the barber tolerably. After the sale of this gang of negroes they returned to St. Louis, and a second cargo was made up. In this lot was a woman who had a child at the breast, yet was compelled to travel through the interior of the country on foot with the other slaves. In a published memoir of his life, William says, "The child cried during the most of the day, which displeased Mr. Walker, and he told the mother that if her child did not stop crying, he would stop its mouth. After a long and weary journey under a burning sun, we put up for the night at a country inn. The following morning, just as they were about to start, the child again commenced crying. Walker stepped up to her and told her to give the child to him. The mother tremblingly obeyed. He took the child by one arm, as anyone would a cat by the leg, and walked into the house where they had been staying, and said to the lady, 'Madam, I will make you a present of this little nigger; it keeps making such a noise that I can't bear it.' 'Thank you, sir,' said the lady. The mother, as soon as she saw that her child was to be left, ran up to Mr. Walker, and falling on her knees, begged of him in an agony of despair, to let her have her child. She clung round his legs so closely, that for some time he could not kick her off; and she cried, 'O my child, my child. Master, do let me have my dear, dear child. Oh! do, do. I will stop its crying, and love you for ever if you will only let me have my child again.' But her prayers were not heeded, they passed on, and the mother was separated from her child forever." …

Some time after this, Walker bought a woman who had a blind child; it being considered worthless, it was given to the trader by the former owner of the woman on the score of humanity, he saying that he wished to keep mother and child together. At first Walker declined taking the child, saying that it would be too much trouble, but the mother wishing to have her boy with her, begged him to take it, promising to carry it the whole distance in her arms. Consequently he took the child, and the gang started on their route to the nearest steamboat landing, which was above one hundred miles. As might have been expected, the woman was unable to carry the boy and keep up with the rest of the gang. They put up at night at a small town, and the next morning, when about to start, Walker took the little boy from its mother and sold it to the innkeeper for the small sum of one dollar. The poor woman was so frantic at the idea of being separated from her only child, that it seemed impossible to get her to leave it. Not until the chains were put upon her limbs, and she fastened to the other slaves, could they get her to leave the spot. By main force this slave mother was compelled to go on and leave her child behind. Some days after, a lady from one of the free states was travelling the same road and put up at the same inn: she saw the child the morning after her arrival, and heard its history from one of the slaves, which was confirmed by the innkeeper's wife. ...

Nothing was more grievous to the sensitive feelings of William, than seeing the separation of families by the slave-trader: husbands taken from their wives, and mothers from their children, without the least appearance of feeling on the part of those who separated them. ...

At the expiration of the period of his hiring with Walker, William returned to his master, rejoiced to have escaped an employment as much against his own feelings as it was repugnant to human nature. But this joy was of short duration. The Doctor wanted money, and resolved to sell William's sister and two brothers. The mother had been previously sold to a gentleman residing in the city of St. Louis. William's master now informed him that he intended to sell him, and, as he was his own nephew, he gave him the privilege of finding someone to purchase him who would treat him better than if he was sold on the auction block. William tried to make some arrangement by which he could purchase his own freedom, but the old Doctor would hear nothing of the kind. If there is one thing more revolting in the trade of human flesh than another, it is the selling of one's own blood relations.

He accordingly set out for the city in search of a new master. ...

William had been in the city now two days, and as he was to be absent for only a week, it was well that he should make the best use of his time if he intended to escape. In conversing with his mother, he found her unwilling to make the attempt to reach the land of liberty, but she advised him by all means to get there himself if he possibly could. She said, as all her children were in slavery, she did not wish to leave them; but he loved his mother so intensely, that he could not think of leaving without her. He consequently used all his simple eloquence to induce her to fly with him, and at last he prevailed. They consequently fixed upon the next night as the time for their departure. The time at length arrived, and they left the city just as the clock struck nine. Having found a boat, they crossed the river in it. Whose boat it was he did not know; neither did he care: when it had served his purpose, he turned it adrift, and when he saw it last, it was going at a good speed down the river. After walking in the main road as fast as they could all night, when the morning came they made for the woods, and remained there during the day, but when night came again, they proceeded on their journey with nothing but the North Star to guide them. They continued to travel by night, and to bury themselves in the silent solitudes of the forest by day. Hunger and fatigue could not stop them, for the prospect of freedom at the end of the journey nerved them up. The very thought of leaving slavery, with its democratic whips, republican chains, and bloodhounds, caused the hearts of the weary fugitives to leap with joy. After travelling ten nights and hiding in the woods during the day for fear of being arrested and taken back, they thought they might with safety go the rest of their way by daylight. In nearly all the free states there are men who make a business of catching runaway slaves and returning them to their owners for the reward that may be offered; some of these were on the alert for William and his mother, for they had already seen the runaways advertised in the St. Louis newspapers.

All at once they heard the click of a horse's hoof, and looking back saw three men on horseback galloping towards them. They soon came up, and demanded them to stop. The three men dismounted, arrested them on a warrant, and showed them a handbill, offering two hundred dollars for their apprehension and delivery to Dr. Young and Isaac Mansfield in St. Louis.

While they were reading the handbill, William's mother looked him in the face, and burst into tears. "A cold chill ran over me," says he, "and such a sensation I never experienced before, and I trust I never shall again." They took out a rope and tied him, and they were taken back to the house of the individual who appeared to be the leader. They then had something given them to eat, and were separated. Each of them was watched over by two men during the night. The religious characteristic of the American slaveholder soon manifested itself, as before the family retired to rest they were all called together to attend prayers; and the very man who, but a few hours before, had arrested poor panting, fugitive slaves, now read a chapter from the Bible and offered a prayer to God; as if that benignant and omnipotent One consecrated the infernal act he had just committed.

The next morning they were chained and handcuffed, and started back to St. Louis. A journey of three days brought the fugitives again to the place they had left twelve days previously with the hope that they would never return. They were put in prison to await the orders of their owners. When a slave attempts to escape and fails, he feels sure of either being severely punished, or sold to the negro traders and taken to the far south, there to be worked up on a cotton, sugar, or rice plantation. This William and his mother dreaded. While they were in suspense as to what would be their fate, news came to them that the mother had been sold to a slave speculator. William was soon sold to a merchant residing in the city, and removed to his new owner's dwelling. In a few days the gang of slaves, of which William's mother was one, were taken on board a steamer to be carried to the New Orleans market. The young slave obtained permission from his new owner to go and take a last farewell of his mother. He went to the boat, and found her there, chained to another woman, and the whole number of slaves, amounting to some fifty or sixty, chained in the same manner. As the son approached his mother she moved not, neither did she weep; her emotions were too deep for tears. William approached her, threw his arms around her neck, kissed her, fell upon his knees begging her forgiveness, for he thought he was to blame for her sad condition, and if he had not persuaded her to accompany him she might not have been in chains then.

She remained for some time apparently unimpressionable, tearless, sighless, but in the innermost depths of her heart moved mighty passions. William says, "She finally raised her head, looked me in the face, and such a look none but an angel can give, and said, 'My dear son, you are not to blame for my being here. You have done nothing more nor less than your duty. Do not, I pray you, weep for me; I cannot last long upon a cotton plantation. I feel that my heavenly Master will soon call me home, and then I shall be out of the hands of the slaveholders.' I could hear no more—my heart struggled to free itself from the human form. In a moment she saw Mr. Mansfield, her master, coming toward that part of the boat, and she whispered in my ear, 'My child, we must soon part to meet no more on this side of the grave. You have ever said that you would not die a slave; that you would be a freeman. Now try to get your liberty! You will soon have no one to look after but yourself.' and just as she whispered the last sentence into my ear, Mansfield came up to me, and with an oath said, 'Leave here this instant; you have been the means of my losing one hundred dollars to get this wench back'—at the same time kicking me with a heavy pair of boots. As I left her she gave one shriek, saying, 'God be with you!' It was the last time that I saw her, and the last word I heard her utter. …"

Having been for some time employed as a servant in an hotel, and being of a very active turn, William's new owner resolved to let him out on board a steamboat. Consequently the young slave was hired out to the steamer *St. Louis*, and soon after sold to Captain Enoch Price, the owner of that boat. Here he was destined to remain but a short period, as Mrs. Price wanted a carriage-driver, and had set her heart upon William for that purpose.

Scarcely three months had elapsed from the time that William became the property of Captain Price, ere that gentleman's family took a pleasure trip to New Orleans, and William accompanied them. From New Orleans the family proceeded to Louisville. The hope of escape again dawned upon the slave's mind, and the trials of the past were lost in hopes for the future. The love of liberty, which had been burning in his bosom for years, and which at times had been well nigh extinguished, was now resuscitated. Hopes nurtured in childhood, and strengthened as manhood dawned, now spread their sails to the gales of his imagination. At night, when all around was peaceful, and in the mystic presence of the everlasting starlight, he would walk the steamer's decks, meditating on his happy prospects, and summoning up gloomy reminiscences of the dear hearts he was leaving behind him. When not thinking of the future his mind would dwell on the past. The love of a dear mother, a dear and affectionate sister, and three brothers yet living, caused him to shed many tears. If he could only be assured of their being dead, he would have been comparatively happy; but he saw in imagination his mother in the cotton-field, followed by a monster taskmaster, and no one to speak a consoling word to her. He beheld his sister in the hands of the slavedriver, compelled to submit to his cruelty, or, what was unutterably worse, his lust; but still he was far away from them, and could not do anything for them if he remained in slavery; consequently he resolved, and consecrated the resolve with a prayer, that he would start on the first opportunity.

That opportunity soon presented itself. When the boat got to the wharf where it had to stay for some time, at the first convenient moment Brown made towards the woods, where he remained until night-time. He dared not walk during the day, even in the state of Ohio; he had seen so much of the perfidy of white men, and resolved, if possible, not to get into their hands. After darkness covered the world,[1] he emerged from his hiding-place; but he did not know east from west, or north from south; clouds hid the North Star from his view. In this desolate condition he remained for some hours, when the clouds rolled away, and his friend, with its shining face—the North Star—welcomed his sight. True as the needle to the pole he obeyed its attractive beauty, and walked on till daylight dawned.

---

1   *After ... world*   See Isaiah 60.2: "For, behold, the darkness shall cover the earth, and gross darkness the people: but the Lord shall arise upon thee, and his glory shall be seen upon thee."

It was winter-time; the day on which he started was the 1st of January, and, as it might be expected, it was intensely cold; he had no overcoat, no food, no friend, save the North Star, and the God which made it. How ardently must the love of freedom burn in the poor slave's bosom, when he will pass through so many difficulties, and even look death in the face, in winning his birthright, freedom. But what crushed the poor slave's heart in his flight most was, not the want of food or clothing, but the thought that every white man was his deadly enemy. Even in the free states the prejudice against colour is so strong, that there appears to exist a deadly antagonism between the white and coloured races.

William in his flight carried a tinder-box with him, and when he got very cold he would gather together dry leaves and stubble and make a fire, or certainly he would have perished. He was determined to enter into no house, fearing that he might meet a betrayer.

It must have been a picture which would have inspired an artist, to see the fugitive roasting the ears of corn that he found or took from barns during the night, at solitary fires in the deep solitudes of woods. ...

Through cold and hunger, William was now ill, and he could go no further. The poor fugitive resolved to seek protection, and accordingly hid himself in the woods near the road, until some one should pass. Soon a traveller came along, but the slave dared not speak. A few moments more and a second passed, the fugitive attempted to speak, but fear deprived him of voice. A third made his appearance. He wore a broad-brimmed hat and a long coat, and was evidently walking only for exercise. William scanned him well, and though not much skilled in physiognomy,[1] he concluded he was the man. William approached him, and asked him if he knew anyone who would help him, as he was sick? The gentleman asked whether he was not a slave. The poor slave hesitated; but, on being told that he had nothing to fear, he answered, "Yes." The gentleman told him he was in a pro-slaving neighbourhood, but, if he would wait a little, he would go and get a covered wagon, and convey him to his house. After he had gone, the fugitive meditated whether he should stay or not, being apprehensive that the broad-brimmed gentleman had gone for someone to assist him: he however concluded to remain.

After waiting about an hour—an hour big with fate to him—he saw the covered wagon making its appearance, and no one on it but the person he before accosted. Trembling with hope and fear, he entered the wagon, and was carried to the person's house. When he got there, he still halted between two opinions, whether he should enter or take to his heels; but he soon decided after seeing the glowing face of the wife. He saw something in her that bid him welcome, something that told him he would not be betrayed.

---

1   *physiognomy*   Study of a person's facial features to determine his or her character.

He soon found that he was under the shed of a Quaker, and a Quaker of the George Fox stamp.[1] He had heard of Quakers and their kindness; but was not prepared to meet with such hospitality as now greeted him. He saw nothing but kind looks, and heard nothing but tender words. He began to feel the pulsations of a new existence. White men always scorned him, but now a white benevolent woman felt glad to wait on him; it was a revolution in his experience. The table was loaded with good things, but he could not eat. If he were allowed the privilege of sitting in the kitchen, he thought he could do justice to the viands. The surprise being over his appetite soon returned. ...

The kind Quaker, who so hospitably entertained William, was called Wells Brown. He remained with him about a fortnight, during which time he was well fed and clothed. Before leaving, the Quaker asked him what was his name besides William? The fugitive told him he had no other. "Well," said he, "then must have another name. Since thee has got out of slavery, thee has become a man, and men always have two names."

William told him that as he was the first man to extend the hand of friendship to him, he would give him the privilege of naming him.

"If I name thee," said he, "I shall call thee Wells Brown, like myself."

"But," said he, "I am not willing to lose my name of William. It was taken from me once against my will,[2] and I am not willing to part with it on any terms."

"Then," said the benevolent man, "I will call thee William Wells Brown."

"So be it," said William Wells Brown, and he has been known by this name ever since.

After giving the newly-christened freeman "a name," the Quaker gave him something to aid him to get "a local habitation." So, after giving him some money, Brown again started for Canada. In four days he reached a public-house, and went in to warm himself. He soon found that he was not out of the reach of his enemies. While warming himself, he heard some men in an adjoining bar-room talking about some runaway slaves. He thought it was time to be off, and, suiting the action to the thought, he was soon in the woods out of sight. When night came, he returned to the road and walked on; and so, for two days and two nights, till he was faint and ready to perish of hunger.

---

1 *Quaker ... George Fox stamp* The Quakers (formally known as the Society of Friends) are a Protestant sect that was and is committed to pacifism, equality of the sexes, and the antislavery cause. They typically sought to avoid worldly vanities, adhering to customs of plain dress and using an old-fashioned diction. George Fox was an English preacher (1624–91) and founder of the Quaker movement; Fox was critical of slavery, and while visiting Barbados in 1671 argued that enslaved people should be freed after a given number of years, and that Christ had sacrificed himself for people of all races.

2 *It was taken ... will* When Brown was a small boy, the couple who enslaved him—the Youngs— adopted a nephew named William; they then decided that Brown's first name would be changed to "Sandford," so there would be no confusing the children.

In this condition he arrived in the town of Cleveland, Ohio, on the banks of Lake Erie, where he determined to remain until the spring of the year, and then to try and reach Canada. Here he was compelled to work merely for his food. "Having lived in that way," said he in a speech at a public meeting in Exeter Hall, "for some weeks, I obtained a job, for which I received a shilling. This was not only the only shilling I had, but it was the first I had received after obtaining my freedom, and that shilling made me feel, indeed, as if I had a considerable stock in hand. What to do with my shilling I did not know. I would not put it into the bankers' hands, because, if they would have received it, I would not trust them. I would not lend it out, because I was afraid I should not get it back again. I carried the shilling in my pocket for some time, and finally resolved to lay it out; and after considerable thinking upon the subject, I laid out 6d.[1] for a spelling-book, and the other 6d. for sugar candy or barley sugar. Well, now, you will all say that the one 6d. for the spelling-book was well laid out; and I am of opinion that the other was well laid out too; for the family in which I worked for my bread had two little boys, who attended the school every day, and I wanted to convert them into teachers; so I thought that nothing would act like a charm so much as a little barley sugar. The first day I got my book and stock in trade, I put the book into my bosom, and went to saw wood in the wood-house on a very cold day. One of the boys, a little after four o'clock, passed through the wood-house with a bag of books. I called to him, and I said to him, 'Johnny, do you see this?' taking a stick of barley sugar from my pocket and showing it to him. Says he, 'Yes; give me a taste of it.' Said I, 'I have got a spelling book too,' and I showed that to him. 'Now,' said I, 'if you come to me in my room, and teach me my A, B, C, I will give you a whole stick.' 'Very well,' said he, 'I will; but let me taste it.' 'No; I can't.' 'Let me have it now.' Well, I thought I had better give him a little taste, until the right time came; and I marked the barley sugar about a quarter of an inch down, and told him to bite that far and no farther. He made a grab, and bit half the stick, and ran off laughing. I put the other piece in my pocket, and after a little while the other boy, little David, came through the wood-house with his books. I said nothing about the barley sugar, or my wish to get education. I knew the other lad would communicate the news to him. In a little while he returned, and said, 'Bill, John says you have got some barley sugar.' [']Well,' I said, 'what of that?' 'He said you gave him some; give me a little taste.' 'Well, if you come tonight and help me to learn my letters, I will give you a whole stick.' 'Yes; but let me taste it.' 'Ah! but you want to bite it.' 'No, I don't, but just let me taste it.' Well, I thought I had better show it to him. 'Now,' said he, 'let me touch my tongue against it.' I thought then that I

---

1   6d.   Six pence (i.e., six pennies).

had better give him a taste, but I would not trust him so far as I trusted John; so I called him to me, and got his head under my arm, and took him by the chin, and told him to hold out his tongue; and as he did so, I drew the barley sugar over very lightly. He said, 'That's very nice; just draw it over again.' 'I could stand here and let you draw it across my tongue all day.' The night came on; the two boys came out of their room up into the attic where I was lodging, and there they commenced teaching me the letters of the alphabet. We all laid down upon the floor, covered with the same blanket; and first one would teach me a letter, and then the other, and I would pass the barley sugar from one side to the other. I kept those two boys on my sixpenny worth of barley sugar for about three weeks. Of course I did not let them know how much I had. I first dealt it out to them a quarter of a stick at a time. I worked along in that way, and before I left that place where I was working for my bread, I got so that I could spell. I had a book that had the word baker in it, and the boys used to think that when they got so far as that, they were getting on pretty well. I had often passed by the school-house, and stood and listened at the window to hear them spell, and I knew that when they could spell baker they thought something of themselves; and I was glad when I got that far. Before I left that place I could read. Finally, from that I went on until I could write. How do you suppose I first commenced writing? for you will understand that up to the present time I never spent a day in school in my life, for I had no money to pay for schooling, so that I had to get my learning first from one and then from another. I carried a piece of chalk in my pocket, and whenever I met a boy I would stop him and take out my chalk and get at a board fence and then commence. First I made some flourishes with no meaning, and called a boy up, and said, 'Do you see that? Can you beat that writing?' Said he, 'That's not writing.' Well, I wanted to get so as to write my own name. I had got out of slavery with only one name. While escaping, I received the hospitality of a very good man, who had spared part of his name to me, and finally my name got pretty long, and I wanted to be able to write it. 'Now, what do you call that?' said the boy, looking at my flourishes. I said, 'Is not that William Wells Brown?' 'Give me the chalk,' says he, and he wrote out in large letters 'William Wells Brown,' and I marked up the fence for nearly a quarter of a mile, trying to copy, till I got so that I could write my name. Then I went on with my chalking, and, in fact, all board fences within half a mile of where I lived were marked over with some kind of figures I had made, in trying to learn how to write. I next obtained an arithmetic, and then a grammar, and I stand here tonight, without having had a day's schooling in my life." Such were some of the efforts made by a fugitive slave to obtain for himself an education. ...
—1853

Frederick Douglass
1818 – 1895

Author of the most powerfully written and most widely read slave narrative of the antebellum era, Frederick Douglass became the foremost voice in the abolitionist movement, and, following the Civil War, one of the foremost critics of the horrors of the new "Jim Crow" system of oppression. He spoke up too against the oppression of women and against all forms of prejudice and inequality, and he spoke up consistently in favor of speaking up—in favor of resistance. "Power concedes nothing without a demand," he famously wrote. "It never did and it never will." He occupies a unique place in American literature, American history, and American political thought.

Douglass was born Frederick Augustus Washington Bailey in Talbot County, Maryland. A degree of mystery surrounds the circumstances of Douglass's birth; like many enslaved people, he was denied full knowledge of his parentage or date of birth. He inherited the enslavement of his mother, Harriet Bailey, but his father was almost certainly a white man, quite likely his enslaver, Aaron Anthony (though other possibilities have been suggested). Douglass came to accept a tentative birth year of 1817; however, we now know that he was born in February 1818.

In 1826 Douglass was acquired by the slaveholder Thomas Auld, and was sent to live in Baltimore with Auld's brother and sister-in-law. In 1833 Douglass was removed from his situation in Baltimore and forced to work on Thomas Auld's plantation. Emboldened by his growing consciousness of slavery's injustice, Douglass grew increasingly rebellious, and was sent to work for a man named Edward Covey, locally famous as a so-called slave-breaker. Douglass attempted escape twice. In 1836 he was part of a failed plot organized by several enslaved companions, and was briefly jailed for his participation. Two years later, Douglass's second attempt was successful. Douglass left unexplained in the first and second versions of his autobiography any of the details of this escape, on the grounds—as he explains in Chapter 11—that telling the story would probably cause "difficulties" for those who helped him and "would most undoubtedly induce greater vigilance on the part of slaveholders"; it is only the third and final version—the 1881 *Life and Times of Frederick Douglass*—that includes the story of his escape.

Douglass presents the escape very largely as a solo endeavor; as we now know, he was in fact aided by several people—very much including the free black woman Anna Murray, to whom he had become engaged shortly before the escape. It was largely from Anna that Douglass obtained the funds that enabled him to travel from slavery in Baltimore to freedom in New York on 3 September 1838. Anna made the same trip a week later, and on 15 September the two were married in the home of David Ruggles, a black grocer and printer who led an organization devoted to assisting fugitive slaves. It was Ruggles who suggested that Frederick Bailey change his name—as was often done by those wishing to minimize the chances of being captured and returned to bondage. For a few days Douglass called himself Frederick Johnson, and it was under that name that he and Anna were married.

Ruggles also suggested that the couple move to New Bedford, Massachusetts, a community more friendly than was New York to fugitives who had been enslaved, and one where he felt Douglass would be able to find employment. There the Douglasses stayed initially at the home of an abolitionist named Nathan Johnson—evidently one of many Johnsons in New Bedford. Feeling that another name was necessary to distinguish himself from the other Johnsons, Frederick asked Nathan Johnson to suggest a new name; according to the narrative, it was Johnson who suggested the name under which Douglass would become famous.

In the North Douglass found a land of remarkable prosperity but also of profound contradiction; though an ordinary white laborer might enjoy a more luxurious existence and higher education level than an upper-class southern slaveholder, a free black citizen could expect continual discrimination from employers, church congregations, and other groups. Eventually Douglass—whose religious conversion experiences are given more emphasis in his two later memoirs—found employment as a licensed preacher in the African Methodist Episcopal Zion Church. Douglass also became a regular reader of the *Liberator*, an antislavery newspaper founded by leading white abolitionist William Lloyd Garrison. Douglass began attending antislavery meetings, where he soon began to share his own story and to make a local name for himself. In August 1841 he delivered his first formal speech before an antislavery audience in Nantucket. His moving story and evident oratorical talents caught Garrison's attention; Douglass became a valued contributor to the *Liberator*, and was appointed to a paid position with the Massachusetts Anti-Slavery Society not long thereafter.

Over the following years Douglass traveled widely and delivered speech after speech to audiences throughout the Northern states; he came to occupy a central place in the abolitionist movement. When the famous philosopher and orator Ralph Waldo Emerson was invited to deliver a major speech on slavery in August 1844, for example, Frederick Douglass was among the three others rounding out the program. People everywhere found something extraordinary about him. Nathaniel P. Rogers, editor of the *Herald of Freedom* abolitionist newspaper, described in 1843 the effect of Douglass's words when the speaker was in full flight as "sterner, darker, deeper" than oratory or eloquence. "It was the volcanic outbreak of human nature, long pent up in slavery and at last bursting its imprisonment. It was the storm of insurrection."

Douglass's celebrated status also often made him a target; he endured egg- and brick-throwing and, in Pennsylvania in 1843, a mob attack resulted in a permanent injury to his right hand. Even those who ostensibly supported Douglass's goals were often unable or unwilling to reconcile the distinguished and eloquent speaker they saw with the enslaved life he described, and insisted that his story must have been falsified. (Douglass averred in the second version of his autobiography that "prejudice against color is stronger in the north than [in the] south; it hangs around my neck like a heavy weight.")

Emboldened rather than intimidated by the challenges to his story, Douglass began work on an autobiography in which he would provide factual details to corroborate his claims. Written in the space of just a few months beginning in December 1844, *Narrative of the Life of Frederick Douglass, an American Slave. Written by Himself,* was published in the spring of 1845 by the Anti-Slavery Office in Boston. The book was welcomed with enthusiasm in the abolitionist press; most notably, the *New York Tribune* on 10 June 1845 printed on its front page a long and highly favorable review (written by Margaret Fuller), along with a substantial excerpt from the book. By contrast, the *New York Herald* accorded it only a few words—"a neatly printed volume, which abolitionists may find interesting"—and most mainstream newspapers in northern states ignored it altogether. (In most southern states the dissemination of such works was strictly prohibited; a *Richmond Enquirer* article from April 1849 details a case in which a preacher named Jarvis C. Bacon was prosecuted for having circulated copies of Douglass's *Narrative* and another antislavery publication.)

By the 1840s the slave narrative was a well-established literary genre; in America alone at least ten such volumes were published between 1830 and 1845. Douglass's *Narrative* closely follows the conventions of the genre in several respects. The inclusion of a prefatory address by a white activist attesting to the book's authorship; the repeated assertions, near the beginning of the text, of un-hyperbolic truthfulness; the visceral descriptions of whippings, auction blocks, and other gruesome realities of enslaved life—all these are typical of the genre. Yet from the beginning Douglass's work was recognized as extraordinary in the quality of its writing and the depth of feeling it conveys; Fuller was not alone in finding the *Narrative* to be "glowing with ... life and fertile in invention," "more simple, true, coherent, and warm with genuine feeling" than any other work of its kind. Writing in the 1860s, black abolitionist William Wells Brown reminisced that "the narrative of [Douglass's] life ... gave a new impetus to the black man's literature. All other stories of fugitive slaves faded away before the beautifully written, highly descriptive, and thrilling memoir of Frederick Douglass." Within less than four months the *Narrative* had sold almost 5,000 copies, and by 1850 some 30,000 copies had been printed.

The book's broad readership and Douglass's increasing fame, however, did nothing to alter his legal status. With the threat of discovery and capture by fugitive-slave hunters in mind, Douglass embarked in late 1845 on a lecture tour of Great Britain—a tour that broadened Douglass's readership and led to several European editions of his *Narrative*. While he was abroad a group of English friends purchased his manumission for a sum of £150; Douglass returned to the United States a legally free man in 1847, and moved with his family to Rochester, New York.

That same year Douglass established a new antislavery weekly newspaper, *The North Star* (a collaboration with the free-born black abolitionist Martin Delany). The ideals emblazoned on its masthead—"Right is of no Sex—Truth is of no Color—God is the Father of us all, and we are all Brethren"—may seem unexceptionable today, but in 1847 they were revolutionary on several fronts. Douglass struggled to build a readership (in 1851 he merged *The North Star* with another weekly to form *Frederick Douglass' Paper*, and in 1858 he began to publish monthly rather than weekly), but he managed in one form or another to keep publishing a newspaper until 1863, and each issue is believed to have had several thousand readers.

William Lloyd Garrison did not entirely welcome the competition with his *Liberator*. By 1851, Douglass and Garrison had reached a formal parting of the ways, with issues of principle having come to separate the two. Garrison was an uncompromising believer in "immediatism"—the doctrine that slavery should be abolished immediately rather than gradually—but he remained reluctant to countenance the use of force to overcome the evils of slavery; Douglass, by contrast, was more and more strongly convinced that the use of force in certain circumstances was entirely justified. Douglass's revised and expanded 1855 autobiography, *My Bondage and My Freedom*, puts forward even more powerfully than the *Narrative* the case for forceful resistance to such evils as slavery. (A passage from the 1855 autobiography is provided for comparison in this anthology.)

Douglass had also begun to feel a desire to distance himself from the sometimes patronizing guidance of white abolitionists such as Garrison; his declared goal in founding *The North Star* had been to provide "a printing-press and paper, permanently established, under the complete control and direction of the immediate victims of slavery and oppression." Increasingly, questions about the appropriate means of resisting oppression became matters not only of the moral imperatives involved, but also matters of character formation; like Emerson, Douglass took the idea of self-reliance very much to heart. As early as 1848, in an essay entitled "What Are the Colored People Doing for Themselves?," Douglass had written against "that lazy, mean, and cowardly spirit that robs us of all self-reliance, and teaches us to depend upon others for the accomplishment of that which we should achieve with our own hands." For Douglass, the principle of self-reliance had a special resonance for African Americans.

In many of Douglass's writings, self-reliance (and self-fashioning) appears to be heavily gendered; "manhood" is given a central place. But Douglass was also involved in the fight for women's rights. In 1848 he spoke at both the Rochester and the Seneca Falls Women's Rights Conventions. One of Douglass's most celebrated speeches, commonly titled "What to the Slave Is the Fourth of July?," was given at an Independence Day event hosted by the Rochester Ladies' Anti-Slavery Society. During this period, then, Douglass saw activism on behalf of African Americans and activism for women's rights as connected causes. "When the true history of the antislavery cause shall be written," he wrote, "woman will occupy a large space in its pages, for the cause of the slave has been peculiarly a woman's cause." In the wake of the Civil War, however, there was for some years a significant rift between Douglass and leading campaigners for women's rights such as Elizabeth Cady Stanton and Susan B. Anthony, as debate intensified over the 1868 Fourteenth Amendment (affirming citizenship for all people born in the United States, regardless of color, but affirming the right to vote only for *male* citizens) and the 1870 Fifteenth Amendment (affirming that the right to vote was not to "be denied ... on account of race"). Anthony and Stanton were among those who opposed the Fifteenth Amendment; they saw no reason why the vote should be granted to black men before it had been granted to white women. Douglass, on the other hand, was outspoken in his belief that the former was a more urgent imperative than the latter. (Throughout the controversy, the voices of black women activists such as Frances Harper and Mary Ann Shadd Cary were too seldom heard.)

In addition to his autobiographical writings, Douglass published hundreds of speeches and essays—and one novella, *The Heroic Slave* (1852). After the Civil War he became a prominent member of the Republican Party (which remained for many decades after Lincoln's death a party sympathetic to and supportive of African Americans). He received several government appointments, including United States Marshall for the District of Columbia and Minister (ambassador) to Haiti. In 1884, two years after Anna Murray-Douglass's death, he married Helen Pitts, a college-educated activist who had been working with Douglass in the office of the Recorder of Deeds. That she was white and he black led to accusations of betrayal and to her estrangement from several members of her family, but the two weathered the storm, and their marriage was a happy one.

Douglass lived for thirty years after the end of the Civil War, received many honors, and continued to speak out powerfully on a wide variety of topics. But in the years following the Compromise of 1877 and the rebirth of legalized oppression in the Southern states, the tide was running against Douglass. His eloquence could do little to stop the spread of revisionist versions of the Civil War that downplayed the centrality of slavery to the struggle and framed the Confederacy as a noble "lost cause." As the years went by the slave narrative genre received less and less attention. Douglass's final great act of self-fashioning—his 1881 *Life and Times of Frederick Douglass*—sold poorly. By 1900 such writing had been nearly forgotten by mainstream white America. That year saw the publication of *A Literary History of America* by Harvard Professor of English Barrett Wendell; Wendell's eighteen-page chapter on the literature of the antislavery movement makes no mention whatsoever of Douglass—or of any other African American author. Douglass remained more consistently renowned among black readers in the late nineteenth and early twentieth centuries. He was honored in a long elegy by popular African American poet Paul Laurence Dunbar upon his death in 1895, and in 1899 was the subject of a biography written by black novelist Charles Chesnutt for the popular series Beacon Biographies of Eminent Americans; in 1906 Booker T. Washington wrote, "No negro can read and study the life of Frederick Douglass without deriving from it courage to look up and forward."

Nevertheless, in the first half of the twentieth century Douglass's *Narrative* went out of print. Not until 1960 did Harvard University Press bring out a new edition of the work—and even then with some timidity, the editor suggesting in his introduction that "perhaps Douglass seemed to protest too much in making slavery out as a 'soul-killing' institution." Only in the twenty-first century has Douglass come once again to be acknowledged without apology or equivocation as a uniquely towering presence, of enduring importance to America.

Note on the Texts

The texts of the works presented here are based on their first published editions—*Narrative of the Life of Frederick Douglass* (1845) and *My Bondage and My Freedom* (1855)—except in the case of *Life and Times of Frederick Douglass*, for which the anthology reproduces the text of the expanded 1893 edition. Spelling and punctuation have been modernized in accordance with the practices of this anthology.

⌘ ⌘ ⌘

Narrative of the Life of Frederick Douglass, an American Slave. Written by Himself

PREFACE[1]

In the month of August, 1841, I attended an anti-slavery convention in Nantucket, at which it was my happiness to become acquainted with Frederick Douglass, the writer of the following Narrative. He was a stranger to nearly every member of that body; but, having recently made his escape from the southern prison-house of bondage, and feeling his curiosity excited to ascertain the principles and measures of the abolitionists—of whom he had heard a somewhat vague description while he was a slave—he was induced to give his attendance, on the occasion alluded to, though at that time a resident in New Bedford.[2]

Fortunate, most fortunate occurrence!—fortunate for the millions of his manacled brethren, yet panting for deliverance from their awful thraldom!—fortunate for the cause of negro emancipation, and of universal liberty!—fortunate for the land of his birth, which he has already done so much to save and bless!—fortunate for a large circle of friends and acquaintances, whose sympathy and affection he has strongly secured by the many sufferings he has endured, by his virtuous traits of character, by his ever-abiding remembrance of those who are in bonds, as being bound with them!—fortunate for the multitudes, in various parts of our republic, whose minds he has enlightened on the subject of slavery, and who have been melted to tears by his pathos, or roused to virtuous indignation by his stirring eloquence against the enslavers of men!—fortunate for himself, as it at once brought him into the field of public usefulness, "gave the world assurance of a MAN,"[3] quickened the slumbering energies of his soul, and consecrated him to the great work of breaking the rod of the oppressor, and letting the oppressed go free!

I shall never forget his first speech at the convention—the extraordinary emotion it excited in my own mind—the powerful impression it created upon a crowded auditory, completely taken by surprise—the applause which followed from the beginning to the end of his felicitous remarks. I think I never

---

1 *PREFACE*   Written by prominent white abolitionist William Lloyd Garrison (1805–79). It was common practice for the slave narratives of black authors to be prefaced by white authors, whose testimonials were thought to authenticate the text. This practice was not followed with Douglass's two subsequent autobiographies.

2 *New Bedford*   Douglass settled in New Bedford, Massachusetts with his wife after his self-emancipation in 1838.

3 *gave the world ... a MAN*   See Shakespeare's *Hamlet* 3.4.72.

hated slavery so intensely as at that moment; certainly, my perception of the enormous outrage which is inflicted by it, on the godlike nature of its victims, was rendered far more clear than ever. There stood one, in physical proportion and stature commanding and exact—in intellect richly endowed—in natural eloquence a prodigy—in soul manifestly "created but a little lower than the angels"[1]—yet a slave, ay, a fugitive slave—trembling for his safety, hardly daring to believe that on the American soil, a single white person could be found who would befriend him at all hazards, for the love of God and humanity! Capable of high attainments as an intellectual and moral being—needing nothing but a comparatively small amount of cultivation to make him an ornament to society and a blessing to his race—by the law of the land, by the voice of the people, by the terms of the slave code, he was only a piece of property, a beast of burden, a chattel[2] personal, nevertheless!

A beloved friend[3] from New Bedford prevailed on Mr. DOUGLASS to address the convention: He came forward to the platform with a hesitancy and embarrassment, necessarily the attendants of a sensitive mind in such a novel position. After apologizing for his ignorance, and reminding the audience that slavery was a poor school for the human intellect and heart, he proceeded to narrate some of the facts in his own history as a slave, and in the course of his speech gave utterance to many noble thoughts and thrilling reflections. As soon as he had taken his seat, filled with hope and admiration, I rose, and declared that PATRICK HENRY,[4] of revolutionary fame, never made a speech more eloquent in the cause of liberty, than the one we had just listened to from the lips of that hunted fugitive. So I believed at that time—such is my belief now. I reminded the audience of the peril which surrounded this self-emancipated young man at the North—even in Massachusetts, on the soil of the Pilgrim Fathers, among the descendants of revolutionary sires;[5] and I appealed to them, whether they would ever allow him to be carried back into slavery—law or no law, constitution or no constitution. The response was unanimous and in thunder-tones—"NO!" "Will you succor and protect

---

1 *created but ... the angels* See Psalm 8.5: "For thou hast made him [humankind] a little lower than the angels"; and Hebrews 2.7: "But we see Jesus, who was made a little lower than the angels."

2 *chattel* Property.

3 *A beloved friend* William C. Coffin, prominent white abolitionist in and around New Bedford and a supporter of Douglass.

4 *PATRICK HENRY* American revolutionary orator (1736–99), famous for the speech in which he proclaimed: "Forbid it, Almighty God! I know not what course others may take; but as for me, give me liberty or give me death!"

5 *Pilgrim Fathers ... revolutionary sires* "Pilgrim Fathers" refers to the English colonists who arrived in Plymouth, Massachusetts in 1620; *revolutionary sires* Ancestors who participated in the American Revolution.

him as a brother-man—a resident of the old Bay State?"[1] "YES!" shouted the whole mass, with an energy so startling, that the ruthless tyrants south of Mason and Dixon's line[2] might almost have heard the mighty burst of feeling, and recognized it as the pledge of an invincible determination, on the part of those who gave it, never to betray him that wanders, but to hide the outcast, and firmly to abide the consequences.

It was at once deeply impressed upon my mind, that, if Mr. DOUGLASS could be persuaded to consecrate his time and talents to the promotion of the anti-slavery enterprise, a powerful impetus would be given to it, and a stunning blow at the same time inflicted on northern prejudice against a colored complexion. I therefore endeavored to instil hope and courage into his mind, in order that he might dare to engage in a vocation so anomalous and responsible for a person in his situation; and I was seconded in this effort by warm-hearted friends, especially by the late General Agent of the Massachusetts Anti-Slavery Society, Mr. JOHN A. COLLINS,[3] whose judgment in this instance entirely coincided with my own. At first, he could give no encouragement; with unfeigned diffidence, he expressed his conviction that he was not adequate to the performance of so great a task; the path marked out was wholly an untrodden one; he was sincerely apprehensive that he should do more harm than good. After much deliberation, however, he consented to make a trial; and ever since that period, he has acted as a lecturing agent, under the auspices either of the American or the Massachusetts Anti-Slavery Society.[4] In labors he has been most abundant; and his success in combating prejudice, in gaining proselytes, in agitating the public mind, has far surpassed the most sanguine expectations that were raised at the commencement of his brilliant career. He has borne himself with gentleness and meekness, yet with true manliness of character. As a public speaker, he excels in pathos, wit, comparison, imitation, strength of reasoning, and fluency of language. There is in him that union of head and heart, which is indispensable to an enlightenment of the heads and a winning of the hearts of others. May his strength continue to be equal to his day! May he continue to "grow in grace, and in the knowledge of God,"[5] that

---

1 *old Bay State*   Massachusetts.

2 *Mason and Dixon's line*   Drawn in the 1760s by English surveyors Charles Mason and Jeremiah Dixon, the Mason-Dixon line separated parts of Pennsylvania and Delaware from parts of Maryland and Virginia; it came to signify the border between the American North and South, and thereby the literal and symbolic border between the free states and the slave states.

3 *JOHN A. COLLINS*   White antislavery activist (1810–79).

4 *American or … Society*   The Massachusetts Anti-Slavery Society was an auxiliary of the American Anti-Slavery Society; both were associated with William Lloyd Garrison.

5 *grow in grace … of God*   See 2 Peter 3.18: "But grow in grace, and in the knowledge of our Lord and Saviour Jesus Christ."

he may be increasingly serviceable in the cause of bleeding humanity, whether at home or abroad!

It is certainly a very remarkable fact, that one of the most efficient advocates of the slave population, now before the public, is a fugitive slave, in the person of FREDERICK DOUGLASS; and that the free colored population of the United States are as ably represented by one of their own number, in the person of CHARLES LENOX REMOND,[1] whose eloquent appeals have extorted the highest applause of multitudes on both sides of the Atlantic. Let the calumniators[2] of the colored race despise themselves for their baseness and illiberality of spirit, and henceforth cease to talk of the natural inferiority of those who require nothing but time and opportunity to attain to the highest point of human excellence.

It may, perhaps, be fairly questioned, whether any other portion of the population of the earth could have endured the privations, sufferings and horrors of slavery, without having become more degraded in the scale of humanity than the slaves of African descent. Nothing has been left undone to cripple their intellects, darken their minds, debase their moral nature, obliterate all traces of their relationship to mankind; and yet how wonderfully they have sustained the mighty load of a most frightful bondage, under which they have been groaning for centuries! To illustrate the effect of slavery on the white man—to show that he has no powers of endurance, in such a condition, superior to those of his black brother—DANIEL O'CONNELL,[3] the distinguished advocate of universal emancipation, and the mightiest champion of prostrate but not conquered Ireland, relates the following anecdote in a speech delivered by him in the Conciliation Hall, Dublin, before the Loyal National Repeal Association,[4] March 31, 1845. "No matter," said Mr. O'CONNELL, "under what specious term it may disguise itself, slavery is still hideous. It has a natural, an inevitable tendency to brutalize every noble faculty of man. An American sailor, who was cast away on the shore of Africa, where he was kept in slavery for three years, was, at the expiration of that period, found to be imbruted and stultified—he had lost all reasoning power; and having forgotten his native language, could only utter some savage gibberish between Arabic and English, which nobody could understand, and which even he himself found difficulty

---

1 CHARLES LENOX REMOND Free-born African American abolitionist from Salem, Massachusetts (1810–73), a close friend of Douglass after whom Douglass named his youngest son.
2 calumniators Slanderers.
3 DANIEL O'CONNELL Irish politician (1775–1847) who fought to obtain equal rights for Catholics (a goal that was partially achieved with the so-called "Catholic Emancipation" of 1829) and to obtain for Ireland a degree of independence from English rule.
4 Repeal Association Founded by O'Connell to call for repeal of the 1800 Acts of Union (which had abolished the Irish Parliament in order to bring Ireland under the direct control of Britain).

in pronouncing. So much for the humanizing influence of THE DOMESTIC INSTITUTION!" Admitting this to have been an extraordinary case of mental deterioration, it proves at least that the white slave can sink as low in the scale of humanity as the black one.

Mr. DOUGLASS has very properly chosen to write his own Narrative, in his own style, and according to the best of his ability, rather than to employ someone else. It is, therefore, entirely his own production; and, considering how long and dark was the career he had to run as a slave—how few have been his opportunities to improve his mind since he broke his iron fetters—it is, in my judgment, highly creditable to his head and heart. He who can peruse it without a tearful eye, a heaving breast, an afflicted spirit—without being filled with an unutterable abhorrence of slavery and all its abettors, and animated with a determination to seek the immediate overthrow of that execrable system—without trembling for the fate of this country in the hands of a righteous God, who is ever on the side of the oppressed, and whose arm is not shortened that it cannot save—must have a flinty heart, and be qualified to act the part of a trafficker "in slaves and the souls of men."[1] I am confident that it is essentially true in all its statements; that nothing has been set down in malice, nothing exaggerated, nothing drawn from the imagination; that it comes short of the reality, rather than overstates a single fact in regard to SLAVERY AS IT IS.[2] The experience of FREDERICK DOUGLASS, as a slave, was not a peculiar one; his lot was not especially a hard one; his case may be regarded as a very fair specimen of the treatment of slaves in Maryland, in which State it is conceded that they are better fed and less cruelly treated than in Georgia, Alabama, or Louisiana. Many have suffered incomparably more, while very few on the plantations have suffered less, than himself. Yet how deplorable was his situation! what terrible chastisements were inflicted upon his person! what still more shocking outrages were perpetrated upon his mind! with all his noble powers and sublime aspirations, how like a brute was he treated, even by those professing to have the same mind in them that was in Christ Jesus! to what dreadful liabilities was he continually subjected! how destitute of friendly counsel and aid, even in his greatest extremities! how heavy was the midnight of woe which shrouded in blackness the last ray of hope, and filled the future with terror and gloom! what longings after freedom took possession of his breast, and how his misery augmented, in proportion as he grew reflective and intelligent—thus demonstrating that a happy slave is an extinct man! how he thought, reasoned, felt, under the lash of the driver, with the chains upon his

---

1   *in slaves ... souls of men*   See Revelation 18.13.
2   *SLAVERY AS IT IS*   Allusion to white abolitionist Theodore Dwight Weld's influential 1839 antislavery book *American Slavery as It Is: A Testimony of a Thousand Witnesses.*

limbs! what perils he encountered in his endeavors to escape from his horrible doom! and how signal have been his deliverance and preservation in the midst of a nation of pitiless enemies!

This Narrative contains many affecting incidents, many passages of great eloquence and power; but I think the most thrilling one of them all is the description DOUGLASS gives of his feelings, as he stood soliloquizing respecting his fate, and the chances of his one day being a freeman, on the banks of the Chesapeake Bay—viewing the receding vessels as they flew with their white wings before the breeze, and apostrophizing[1] them as animated by the living spirit of freedom. Who can read that passage, and be insensible to its pathos and sublimity? Compressed into it is a whole Alexandrian library[2] of thought, feeling, and sentiment—all that can, all that need be urged, in the form of expostulation, entreaty, rebuke, against that crime of crimes—making man the property of his fellow-man! O, how accursed is that system, which entombs the godlike mind of man, defaces the divine image, reduces those who by creation were crowned with glory and honor to a level with four-footed beasts, and exalts the dealer in human flesh above all that is called God! Why should its existence be prolonged one hour? Is it not evil, only evil, and that continually? What does its presence imply but the absence of all fear of God, all regard for man, on the part of the people of the United States? Heaven speed its eternal overthrow!

So profoundly ignorant of the nature of slavery are many persons, that they are stubbornly incredulous whenever they read or listen to any recital of the cruelties which are daily inflicted on its victims. They do not deny that the slaves are held as property; but that terrible fact seems to convey to their minds no idea of injustice, exposure to outrage, or savage barbarity. Tell them of cruel scourgings, of mutilations and brandings, of scenes of pollution and blood, of the banishment of all light and knowledge, and they affect to be greatly indignant at such enormous exaggerations, such wholesale misstatements, such abominable libels on the character of the southern planters! As if all these direful outrages were not the natural results of slavery! As if it were less cruel to reduce a human being to the condition of a thing, than to give him a severe flagellation, or to deprive him of necessary food and clothing! As if whips, chains, thumb-screws, paddles, blood-hounds, overseers, drivers, patrols, were not all indispensable to keep the slaves down, and to give protection to their ruthless oppressors! As if, when the marriage institution is abolished, concubinage, adultery, and incest, must not necessarily abound; when all the rights of humanity are annihilated, any barrier remains to protect

---

1 *apostrophizing* Addressing inanimate objects directly in a poetic fashion.
2 *Alexandrian library* Renowned ancient library located in Alexandria, Egypt.

the victim from the fury of the spoiler; when absolute power is assumed over life and liberty, it will not be wielded with destructive sway! Skeptics of this character abound in society. In some few instances, their incredulity arises from a want of reflection; but, generally, it indicates a hatred of the light, a desire to shield slavery from the assaults of its foes, a contempt of the colored race, whether bond or free. Such will try to discredit the shocking tales of slaveholding cruelty which are recorded in this truthful Narrative; but they will labor in vain. Mr. DOUGLASS has frankly disclosed the place of his birth, the names of those who claimed ownership in his body and soul, and the names also of those who committed the crimes which he has alleged against them. His statements, therefore, may easily be disproved, if they are untrue.

In the course of his Narrative, he relates two instances of murderous cruelty—in one of which a planter deliberately shot a slave belonging to a neighboring plantation, who had unintentionally gotten within his lordly domain in quest of fish; and in the other, an overseer blew out the brains of a slave who had fled to a stream of water to escape a bloody scourging. Mr. DOUGLASS states that in neither of these instances was any thing done by way of legal arrest or judicial investigation. *The Baltimore American*, of March 17, 1845, relates a similar case of atrocity, perpetrated with similar impunity—as follows: "Shooting a slave.—We learn, upon the authority of a letter from Charles County, Maryland, received by a gentleman of this city, that a young man, named Matthews, a nephew of General Matthews, and whose father, it is believed, holds an office at Washington, killed one of the slaves upon his father's farm by shooting him. The letter states that young Matthews had been left in charge of the farm; that he gave an order to the servant, which was disobeyed, when he proceeded to the house, obtained a gun, and, returning, shot the servant. He immediately, the letter continues, fled to his father's residence, where he still remains unmolested." Let it never be forgotten, that no slaveholder or overseer can be convicted of any outrage perpetrated on the person of a slave, however diabolical it may be, on the testimony of colored witnesses, whether bond or free. By the slave code, they are adjudged to be as incompetent to testify against a white man, as though they were indeed a part of the brute creation. Hence, there is no legal protection in fact, whatever there may be in form, for the slave population; and any amount of cruelty may be inflicted on them with impunity. Is it possible for the human mind to conceive of a more horrible state of society?

The effect of a religious profession on the conduct of southern masters is vividly described in the following Narrative, and shown to be anything but salutary. In the nature of the case, it must be in the highest degree pernicious. The testimony of Mr. DOUGLASS, on this point, is sustained by a cloud of witnesses, whose veracity is unimpeachable. "A slaveholder's profession of

Christianity is a palpable imposture. He is a felon of the highest grade. He is a man-stealer. It is of no importance what you put in the other scale."

Reader! are you with the man-stealers in sympathy and purpose, or on the side of their down-trodden victims? If with the former, then are you the foe of God and man. If with the latter, what are you prepared to do and dare in their behalf? Be faithful, be vigilant, be untiring in your efforts to break every yoke, and let the oppressed go free. Come what may—cost what it may—inscribe on the banner which you unfurl to the breeze, as your religious and political motto—"NO COMPROMISE WITH SLAVERY! NO UNION WITH SLAVEHOLDERS!"

WM. LLOYD GARRISON.

BOSTON, May 1, 1845.

LETTER FROM WENDELL PHILLIPS,[1] ESQ

BOSTON, April 22, 1845

My Dear Friend

You remember the old fable of "The Man and the Lion,"[2] where the lion complained that he should not be so misrepresented "when the lions wrote history."

I am glad the time has come when the "lions write history." We have been left long enough to gather the character of slavery from the involuntary evidence of the masters. One might, indeed, rest sufficiently satisfied with what, it is evident, must be, in general, the results of such a relation, without seeking farther to find whether they have followed in every instance. Indeed, those who stare at the half-peck of corn a week, and love to count the lashes on the slave's back, are seldom the "stuff" out of which reformers and abolitionists are to be made. I remember that, in 1838, many were waiting for the results of the West India experiment,[3] before they could come into our ranks. Those "results" have come long ago; but, alas! few of that number have come with them, as converts. A man must be disposed to judge of emancipation by other

---

1   WENDELL PHILLIPS   Massachusetts-based abolitionist and social activist (1811–84).

2   The Man and the Lion   Allusion to one of Aesop's Fables, in which a man gestures towards a sculpture of a male figure conquering a lion as evidence of human superiority; the lion counters that if lions could sculpt, they would be the ones depicted as victorious. Tradition has long held that the Greek storyteller Aesop was himself enslaved.

3   West India experiment   Referring to the British West Indies Emancipation Act that formally abolished slavery in the British West Indies. It was enacted in 1833, and began to take effect a year later, but its provisions were for a phased abolition; until at least 1838 many previously enslaved people were still bound to their former enslavers as apprentices.

tests than whether it has increased the produce of sugar—and to hate slavery for other reasons than because it starves men and whips women—before he is ready to lay the first stone of his anti-slavery life.

I was glad to learn, in your story, how early the most neglected of God's children waken to a sense of their rights, and of the injustice done them. Experience is a keen teacher; and long before you had mastered your A B C, or knew where the "white sails" of the Chesapeake were bound, you began, I see, to gauge the wretchedness of the slave, not by his hunger and want, not by his lashes and toil, but by the cruel and blighting death which gathers over his soul.

In connection with this, there is one circumstance which makes your recollections peculiarly valuable, and renders your early insight the more remarkable. You come from that part of the country where we are told slavery appears with its fairest features. Let us hear, then, what it is at its best estate—gaze on its bright side, if it has one; and then imagination may task her powers to add dark lines to the picture, as she travels southward to that (for the colored man) Valley of the Shadow of Death,[1] where the Mississippi sweeps along.

Again, we have known you long, and can put the most entire confidence in your truth, candor, and sincerity. Everyone who has heard you speak has felt, and, I am confident, every one who reads your book will feel, persuaded that you give them a fair specimen of the whole truth. No one-sided portrait—no wholesale complaints—but strict justice done, whenever individual kindliness has neutralized, for a moment, the deadly system with which it was strangely allied. You have been with us, too, some years, and can fairly compare the twilight of rights, which your race enjoy at the North, with that "noon of night" under which they labor south of Mason and Dixon's line. Tell us whether, after all, the half-free colored man of Massachusetts is worse off than the pampered slave of the rice swamps!

In reading your life, no one can say that we have unfairly picked out some rare specimens of cruelty. We know that the bitter drops, which even you have drained from the cup, are no incidental aggravations, no individual ills, but such as must mingle always and necessarily in the lot of every slave. They are the essential ingredients, not the occasional results, of the system.

After all, I shall read your book with trembling for you. Some years ago, when you were beginning to tell me your real name and birthplace, you may remember I stopped you, and preferred to remain ignorant of all. With the exception of a vague description, so I continued, till the other day, when you read me your memoirs. I hardly knew, at the time, whether to thank you or

---

1 *Valley of the Shadow of Death* See Psalms 23.4.

not for the sight of them, when I reflected that it was still dangerous, in Massachusetts, for honest men to tell their names! They say the fathers, in 1776, signed the Declaration of Independence with the halter about their necks. You, too, publish your declaration of freedom with danger compassing you around. In all the broad lands which the Constitution of the United States overshadows, there is no single spot—however narrow or desolate—where a fugitive slave can plant himself and say, "I am safe." The whole armory of Northern Law has no shield for you. I am free to say that, in your place, I should throw the MS.[1] into the fire.

You, perhaps, may tell your story in safety, endeared as you are to so many warm hearts by rare gifts, and a still rarer devotion of them to the service of others. But it will be owing only to your labors, and the fearless efforts of those who, trampling the laws and Constitution of the country under their feet, are determined that they will "hide the outcast,"[2] and that their hearths shall be, spite of the law, an asylum for the oppressed, if, some time or other, the humblest may stand in our streets, and bear witness in safety against the cruelties of which he has been the victim.

Yet it is sad to think, that these very throbbing hearts which welcome your story, and form your best safeguard in telling it, are all beating contrary to the "statute in such case made and provided." Go on, my dear friend, till you, and those who, like you, have been saved, so as by fire, from the dark prison-house, shall stereotype these free, illegal pulses into statutes; and New England, cutting loose from a blood-stained Union, shall glory in being the house of refuge for the oppressed—till we no longer merely "hide the outcast," or make a merit of standing idly by while he is hunted in our midst; but, consecrating anew the soil of the Pilgrims as an asylum for the oppressed, proclaim our welcome to the slave so loudly, that the tones shall reach every hut in the Carolinas, and make the broken-hearted bondman leap up at the thought of old Massachusetts.

God speed the day!

Till then, and ever,

Yours truly,

WENDELL PHILLIPS

---

1   *MS.*   Manuscript.
2   *hide the outcast*   See Isaiah 16.3.

I was born in Tuckahoe, near Hillsborough, and about twelve miles from Easton, in Talbot county, Maryland. I have no accurate knowledge of my age, never having seen any authentic record containing it. By far the larger part of the slaves know as little of their ages as horses know of theirs, and it is the wish of most masters within my knowledge to keep their slaves thus ignorant. I do not remember to have ever met a slave who could tell of his birthday. They seldom come nearer to it than planting-time, harvest-time, cherry-time, spring-time, or fall-time. A want of information concerning my own was a source of unhappiness to me even during childhood. The white children could tell their ages. I could not tell why I ought to be deprived of the same privilege. I was not allowed to make any inquiries of my master concerning it. He deemed all such inquiries on the part of a slave improper and impertinent, and evidence of a restless spirit. The nearest estimate I can give makes me now between twenty-seven and twenty-eight years of age. I come to this, from hearing my master say, some time during 1835, I was about seventeen years old.[1]

My mother was named Harriet Bailey. She was the daughter of Isaac and Betsey Bailey, both colored, and quite dark. My mother was of a darker complexion than either my grandmother or grandfather.

My father was a white man. He was admitted to be such by all I ever heard speak of my parentage. The opinion was also whispered that my master was my father; but of the correctness of this opinion, I know nothing; the means of knowing was withheld from me. My mother and I were separated when I was but an infant—before I knew her as my mother. It is a common custom, in the part of Maryland from which I ran away, to part children from their mothers at a very early age. Frequently, before the child has reached its twelfth month, its mother is taken from it, and hired out on some farm a considerable distance off, and the child is placed under the care of an old woman, too old for field labor. For what this separation is done, I do not know, unless it be to hinder the development of the child's affection toward its mother, and to blunt and destroy the natural affection of the mother for the child. This is the inevitable result.

I never saw my mother, to know her as such, more than four or five times in my life; and each of these times was very short in duration, and at night. She was hired by a Mr. Stewart,[2] who lived about twelve miles from my home.

---

1 *I have no accurate knowledge ... years old* Records made available after Douglass's death reveal that he was born in February 1818 (though the exact date remains unknown).

2 *hired by a Mr. Stewart* I.e., her owner hired her out to a Mr. Stewart; the transaction would not have involved Douglass's mother being paid.

She made her journeys to see me in the night, travelling the whole distance on foot, after the performance of her day's work. She was a field hand, and a whipping is the penalty of not being in the field at sunrise, unless a slave has special permission from his or her master to the contrary—a permission which they seldom get, and one that gives to him that gives it the proud name of being a kind master. I do not recollect of ever seeing my mother by the light of day. She was with me in the night. She would lie down with me, and get me to sleep, but long before I waked she was gone. Very little communication ever took place between us. Death soon ended what little we could have while she lived, and with it her hardships and suffering. She died when I was about seven years old, on one of my master's farms, near Lee's Mill. I was not allowed to be present during her illness, at her death, or burial. She was gone long before I knew anything about it. Never having enjoyed, to any considerable extent, her soothing presence, her tender and watchful care, I received the tidings of her death with much the same emotions I should have probably felt at the death of a stranger.

Called thus suddenly away, she left me without the slightest intimation of who my father was. The whisper that my master was my father, may or may not be true; and, true or false, it is of but little consequence to my purpose whilst the fact remains, in all its glaring odiousness, that slaveholders have ordained, and by law established, that the children of slave women shall in all cases follow the condition of their mothers; and this is done too obviously to administer to their own lusts, and make a gratification of their wicked desires profitable as well as pleasurable; for by this cunning arrangement, the slaveholder, in cases not a few, sustains to his slaves the double relation of master and father.

I know of such cases; and it is worthy of remark that such slaves invariably suffer greater hardships, and have more to contend with, than others. They are, in the first place, a constant offence to their mistress. She is ever disposed to find fault with them; they can seldom do anything to please her; she is never better pleased than when she sees them under the lash, especially when she suspects her husband of showing to his mulatto children favors which he withholds from his black slaves. The master is frequently compelled to sell this class of his slaves, out of deference to the feelings of his white wife; and, cruel as the deed may strike anyone to be, for a man to sell his own children to human flesh-mongers, it is often the dictate of humanity for him to do so; for, unless he does this, he must not only whip them himself, but must stand by and see one white son tie up his brother, of but few shades darker complexion than himself, and ply the gory lash to his naked back; and if he lisp one word of disapproval, it is set down to his parental partiality, and only makes a bad matter worse, both for himself and the slave whom he would protect and defend.

Every year brings with it multitudes of this class of slaves. It was doubtless in consequence of a knowledge of this fact, that one great statesman of the south predicted the downfall of slavery by the inevitable laws of population. Whether this prophecy is ever fulfilled or not, it is nevertheless plain that a very different-looking class of people are springing up at the south, and are now held in slavery, from those originally brought to this country from Africa; and if their increase do no other good, it will do away the force of the argument, that God cursed Ham, and therefore American slavery is right.[1] If the lineal descendants of Ham are alone to be scripturally enslaved, it is certain that slavery at the south must soon become unscriptural; for thousands are ushered into the world, annually, who, like myself, owe their existence to white fathers, and those fathers most frequently their own masters.

I have had two masters. My first master's name was Anthony. I do not remember his first name. He was generally called Captain Anthony—a title which, I presume, he acquired by sailing a craft on the Chesapeake Bay. He was not considered a rich slaveholder. He owned two or three farms, and about thirty slaves. His farms and slaves were under the care of an overseer. The overseer's name was Plummer. Mr. Plummer was a miserable drunkard, a profane swearer, and a savage monster. He always went armed with a cowskin[2] and a heavy cudgel. I have known him to cut and slash the women's heads so horribly, that even master would be enraged at his cruelty, and would threaten to whip him if he did not mind himself. Master, however, was not a humane slaveholder. It required extraordinary barbarity on the part of an overseer to affect him. He was a cruel man, hardened by a long life of slaveholding. He would at times seem to take great pleasure in whipping a slave. I have often been awakened at the dawn of day by the most heart-rending shrieks of an own aunt of mine, whom he used to tie up to a joist, and whip upon her naked back till she was literally covered with blood. No words, no tears, no prayers, from his gory victim, seemed to move his iron heart from its bloody purpose. The louder she screamed, the harder he whipped; and where the blood ran fastest, there he whipped longest. He would whip her to make her scream, and whip her to make her hush; and not until overcome by fatigue, would he cease to swing the blood-clotted cowskin. I remember the first time I ever witnessed this horrible exhibition. I was quite a child, but I well remember it. I never shall forget it whilst I remember anything. It was the first of a long series

---

1 *God cursed Ham ... is right* Some proslavery apologists claimed that a biblical justification for slavery could be found in Genesis 9.25, in which God curses Canaan, the son of Ham, declaring that "a servant of servants shall he be unto his brethren."

2 *cowskin* Whip made from cowhide.

of such outrages, of which I was doomed to be a witness and a participant. It struck me with awful force. It was the blood-stained gate, the entrance to the hell of slavery, through which I was about to pass. It was a most terrible spectacle. I wish I could commit to paper the feelings with which I beheld it.

This occurrence took place very soon after I went to live with my old master, and under the following circumstances. Aunt Hester went out one night—where or for what I do not know—and happened to be absent when my master desired her presence. He had ordered her not to go out evenings, and warned her that she must never let him catch her in company with a young man, who was paying attention to her, belonging to Colonel Lloyd. The young man's name was Ned Roberts, generally called Lloyd's Ned. Why master was so careful of her, may be safely left to conjecture. She was a woman of noble form, and of graceful proportions, having very few equals, and fewer superiors, in personal appearance, among the colored or white women of our neighborhood.

Aunt Hester had not only disobeyed his orders in going out, but had been found in company with Lloyd's Ned; which circumstance, I found, from what he said while whipping her, was the chief offence. Had he been a man of pure morals himself, he might have been thought interested in protecting the innocence of my aunt; but those who knew him will not suspect him of any such virtue. Before he commenced whipping Aunt Hester, he took her into the kitchen, and stripped her from neck to waist, leaving her neck, shoulders, and back, entirely naked. He then told her to cross her hands, calling her at the same time a d——d b——h. After crossing her hands, he tied them with a strong rope, and led her to a stool under a large hook in the joist, put in for the purpose. He made her get upon the stool, and tied her hands to the hook. She now stood fair for his infernal purpose. Her arms were stretched up at their full length, so that she stood upon the ends of her toes. He then said to her, "Now, you d——d b——h, I'll learn[1] you how to disobey my orders!" and after rolling up his sleeves, he commenced to lay on the heavy cowskin, and soon the warm, red blood (amid heart-rending shrieks from her, and horrid oaths from him) came dripping to the floor. I was so terrified and horror-stricken at the sight, that I hid myself in a closet, and dared not venture out till long after the bloody transaction was over. I expected it would be my turn next. It was all new to me. I had never seen anything like it before. I had always lived with my grandmother on the outskirts of the plantation, where she was put to raise the children of the younger women. I had therefore been, until now, out of the way of the bloody scenes that often occurred on the plantation.

---

1   *learn*   Teach.

CHAPTER 2

My master's family consisted of two sons, Andrew and Richard; one daughter, Lucretia, and her husband, Captain Thomas Auld. They lived in one house, upon the home plantation of Colonel Edward Lloyd. My master was Colonel Lloyd's clerk and superintendent. He was what might be called the overseer of the overseers. I spent two years of childhood on this plantation in my old master's family. It was here that I witnessed the bloody transaction recorded in the first chapter; and as I received my first impressions of slavery on this plantation, I will give some description of it, and of slavery as it there existed. The plantation is about twelve miles north of Easton, in Talbot county, and is situated on the border of Miles River. The principal products raised upon it were tobacco, corn, and wheat. These were raised in great abundance; so that, with the products of this and the other farms belonging to him, he was able to keep in almost constant employment a large sloop,[1] in carrying them to market at Baltimore. This sloop was named Sally Lloyd, in honor of one of the colonel's daughters. My master's son-in-law, Captain Auld, was master of the vessel; she was otherwise manned by the colonel's own slaves. Their names were Peter, Isaac, Rich, and Jake. These were esteemed very highly by the other slaves, and looked upon as the privileged ones of the plantation; for it was no small affair, in the eyes of the slaves, to be allowed to see Baltimore.

Colonel Lloyd kept from three to four hundred slaves on his home plantation, and owned a large number more on the neighboring farms belonging to him. The names of the farms nearest to the home plantation were Wye Town and New Design. "Wye Town" was under the overseership of a man named Noah Willis. New Design was under the overseership of a Mr. Townsend. The overseers of these, and all the rest of the farms, numbering over twenty, received advice and direction from the managers of the home plantation. This was the great business place. It was the seat of government for the whole twenty farms. All disputes among the overseers were settled here. If a slave was convicted of any high misdemeanor, became unmanageable, or evinced a determination to run away, he was brought immediately here, severely whipped, put on board the sloop, carried to Baltimore, and sold to Austin Woolfolk, or some other slave-trader, as a warning to the slaves remaining.

Here, too, the slaves of all the other farms received their monthly allowance of food, and their yearly clothing. The men and women slaves received, as their monthly allowance of food, eight pounds of pork, or its equivalent in fish, and one bushel of corn meal. Their yearly clothing consisted of two coarse linen shirts, one pair of linen trousers, like the shirts, one jacket, one pair of trousers

---

1 *sloop* Small, single-masted sailing vessel.

for winter, made of coarse negro cloth,[1] one pair of stockings, and one pair of shoes; the whole of which could not have cost more than seven dollars. The allowance of the slave children was given to their mothers, or the old women having the care of them. The children unable to work in the field had neither shoes, stockings, jackets, nor trousers, given to them; their clothing consisted of two coarse linen shirts per year. When these failed them, they went naked until the next allowance-day. Children from seven to ten years old, of both sexes, almost naked, might be seen at all seasons of the year.

There were no beds given the slaves, unless one coarse blanket be considered such, and none but the men and women had these. This, however, is not considered a very great privation. They find less difficulty from the want of beds, than from the want of time to sleep; for when their day's work in the field is done, the most of them having their washing, mending, and cooking to do, and having few or none of the ordinary facilities for doing either of these, very many of their sleeping hours are consumed in preparing for the field the coming day; and when this is done, old and young, male and female, married and single, drop down side by side, on one common bed—the cold, damp floor—each covering himself or herself with their miserable blankets; and here they sleep till they are summoned to the field by the driver's horn. At the sound of this, all must rise, and be off to the field. There must be no halting; everyone must be at his or her post; and woe betides them who hear not this morning summons to the field; for if they are not awakened by the sense of hearing, they are by the sense of feeling: no age nor sex finds any favor. Mr. Severe, the overseer, used to stand by the door of the quarter, armed with a large hickory stick[2] and heavy cowskin, ready to whip anyone who was so unfortunate as not to hear, or, from any other cause, was prevented from being ready to start for the field at the sound of the horn.

Mr. Severe was rightly named: he was a cruel man. I have seen him whip a woman, causing the blood to run half an hour at the time; and this, too, in the midst of her crying children, pleading for their mother's release. He seemed to take pleasure in manifesting his fiendish barbarity. Added to his cruelty, he was a profane swearer. It was enough to chill the blood and stiffen the hair of an ordinary man to hear him talk. Scarce a sentence escaped him but that was commenced or concluded by some horrid oath. The field was the place to witness his cruelty and profanity. His presence made it both the field of blood and of blasphemy. From the rising till the going down of the sun, he was cursing, raving, cutting, and slashing among the slaves of the field, in the

---

1 *negro cloth* General term referring to the poor-quality fabric used to make clothing for enslaved people.
2 *hickory stick* Made from the tough wood of the hickory tree.

most frightful manner. His career was short. He died very soon after I went to Colonel Lloyd's; and he died as he lived, uttering, with his dying groans, bitter curses and horrid oaths. His death was regarded by the slaves as the result of a merciful providence.

Mr. Severe's place was filled by a Mr. Hopkins. He was a very different man. He was less cruel, less profane, and made less noise, than Mr. Severe. His course was characterized by no extraordinary demonstrations of cruelty. He whipped, but seemed to take no pleasure in it. He was called by the slaves a good overseer.

The home plantation of Colonel Lloyd wore the appearance of a country village. All the mechanical operations for all the farms were performed here. The shoemaking and mending, the blacksmithing, cartwrighting, coopering,[1] weaving, and grain-grinding, were all performed by the slaves on the home plantation. The whole place wore a business-like aspect very unlike the neighboring farms. The number of houses, too, conspired to give it advantage over the neighboring farms. It was called by the slaves the Great House Farm. Few privileges were esteemed higher, by the slaves of the out-farms, than that of being selected to do errands at the Great House Farm. It was associated in their minds with greatness. A representative could not be prouder of his election to a seat in the American Congress, than a slave on one of the out-farms would be of his election to do errands at the Great House Farm. They regarded it as evidence of great confidence reposed in them by their overseers; and it was on this account, as well as a constant desire to be out of the field from under the driver's lash, that they esteemed it a high privilege, one worth careful living for. He was called the smartest and most trusty fellow, who had this honor conferred upon him the most frequently. The competitors for this office sought as diligently to please their overseers, as the office-seekers in the political parties seek to please and deceive the people. The same traits of character might be seen in Colonel Lloyd's slaves, as are seen in the slaves of the political parties.

The slaves selected to go to the Great House Farm, for the monthly allowance for themselves and their fellow-slaves, were peculiarly enthusiastic. While on their way, they would make the dense old woods, for miles around, reverberate with their wild songs, revealing at once the highest joy and the deepest sadness. They would compose and sing as they went along, consulting neither time nor tune. The thought that came up, came out—if not in the word, in the sound; and as frequently in the one as in the other. They would sometimes sing the most pathetic sentiment in the most rapturous tone, and the most rapturous sentiment in the most pathetic tone. Into all of their songs

---

1   *cartwrighting*   Carpentry;   *coopering*   Making of wooden casks, barrels, and other vessels for storing goods.

they would manage to weave something of the Great House Farm. Especially would they do this, when leaving home. They would then sing most exultingly the following words:

"I am going away to the Great House Farm!
O, yea! O, yea! O!"

This they would sing, as a chorus, to words which to many would seem unmeaning jargon, but which, nevertheless, were full of meaning to themselves. I have sometimes thought that the mere hearing of those songs would do more to impress some minds with the horrible character of slavery, than the reading of whole volumes of philosophy on the subject could do.

I did not, when a slave, understand the deep meaning of those rude and apparently incoherent songs. I was myself within the circle; so that I neither saw nor heard as those without might see and hear. They told a tale of woe which was then altogether beyond my feeble comprehension; they were tones loud, long, and deep; they breathed the prayer and complaint of souls boiling over with the bitterest anguish. Every tone was a testimony against slavery, and a prayer to God for deliverance from chains. The hearing of those wild notes always depressed my spirit, and filled me with ineffable sadness. I have frequently found myself in tears while hearing them. The mere recurrence to those songs, even now, afflicts me; and while I am writing these lines, an expression of feeling has already found its way down my cheek. To those songs I trace my first glimmering conception of the dehumanizing character of slavery. I can never get rid of that conception. Those songs still follow me, to deepen my hatred of slavery, and quicken my sympathies for my brethren in bonds. If any one wishes to be impressed with the soul-killing effects of slavery, let him go to Colonel Lloyd's plantation, and, on allowance-day, place himself in the deep pine woods, and there let him, in silence, analyze the sounds that shall pass through the chambers of his soul—and if he is not thus impressed, it will only be because "there is no flesh in his obdurate heart."[1]

---

1 *there is ... obdurate heart* Douglass is quoting from an approximately 50-line passage dealing with slavery (sometimes printed as if it were a separate poem, and given the title "Slavery") that appears in Book 2 of English poet William Cowper's long poem *The Task* (1785). It reads in part as follows:

My soul is sick, with every day's report
Of wrong and outrage with which earth is filled.
There is no flesh in man's obdurate heart ...;
He finds his fellow guilty of a skin
Not colored like his own[.] ...

In America as well as in Britain, editions of Cowper's poetic works remained very widely read well into the second half of the nineteenth century, often outselling poets such as Milton and Wordsworth; it is likely that many of Douglass's readers would have been familiar with this quotation.

I have often been utterly astonished, since I came to the north, to find persons who could speak of the singing, among slaves, as evidence of their contentment and happiness. It is impossible to conceive of a greater mistake. Slaves sing most when they are most unhappy. The songs of the slave represent the sorrows of his heart; and he is relieved by them, only as an aching heart is relieved by its tears. At least, such is my experience. I have often sung to drown my sorrow, but seldom to express my happiness. Crying for joy, and singing for joy, were alike uncommon to me while in the jaws of slavery. The singing of a man cast away upon a desolate island might be as appropriately considered as evidence of contentment and happiness, as the singing of a slave; the songs of the one and of the other are prompted by the same emotion.

CHAPTER 3

Colonel Lloyd kept a large and finely cultivated garden, which afforded almost constant employment for four men, besides the chief gardener (Mr. M'Durmond). This garden was probably the greatest attraction of the place. During the summer months, people came from far and near—from Baltimore, Easton, and Annapolis—to see it. It abounded in fruits of almost every description, from the hardy apple of the north to the delicate orange of the south. This garden was not the least source of trouble on the plantation. Its excellent fruit was quite a temptation to the hungry swarms of boys, as well as the older slaves, belonging to the colonel, few of whom had the virtue or the vice to resist it. Scarcely a day passed, during the summer, but that some slave had to take the lash for stealing fruit. The colonel had to resort to all kinds of stratagems to keep his slaves out of the garden. The last and most successful one was that of tarring his fence all around; after which, if a slave was caught with any tar upon his person, it was deemed sufficient proof that he had either been into the garden, or had tried to get in. In either case, he was severely whipped by the chief gardener. This plan worked well; the slaves became as fearful of tar as of the lash. They seemed to realize the impossibility of touching tar without being defiled.

The colonel also kept a splendid riding equipage. His stable and carriage-house presented the appearance of some of our large city livery[1] establishments. His horses were of the finest form and noblest blood. His carriage-house contained three splendid coaches, three or four gigs, besides dearborns and barouches[2] of the most fashionable style.

---

1 *livery* Stable.
2 *gigs* Light two-wheeled, one-horse carriages; *dearborns* Light four-wheeled carriages; *barouches* Heavier, four-wheeled carriages, considered quite luxurious.

This establishment was under the care of two slaves—old Barney and young Barney—father and son. To attend to this establishment was their sole work. But it was by no means an easy employment; for in nothing was Colonel Lloyd more particular than in the management of his horses. The slightest inattention to these was unpardonable, and was visited upon those, under whose care they were placed, with the severest punishment; no excuse could shield them, if the colonel only suspected any want of attention to his horses—a supposition which he frequently indulged, and one which, of course, made the office of old and young Barney a very trying one. They never knew when they were safe from punishment. They were frequently whipped when least deserving, and escaped whipping when most deserving it. Everything depended upon the looks of the horses, and the state of Colonel Lloyd's own mind when his horses were brought to him for use. If a horse did not move fast enough, or hold his head high enough, it was owing to some fault of his keepers. It was painful to stand near the stable-door, and hear the various complaints against the keepers when a horse was taken out for use. "This horse has not had proper attention. He has not been sufficiently rubbed and curried, or he has not been properly fed; his food was too wet or too dry; he got it too soon or too late; he was too hot or too cold; he had too much hay, and not enough of grain; or he had too much grain, and not enough of hay; instead of old Barney's attending to the horse, he had very improperly left it to his son." To all these complaints, no matter how unjust, the slave must answer never a word. Colonel Lloyd could not brook any contradiction from a slave. When he spoke, a slave must stand, listen, and tremble; and such was literally the case. I have seen Colonel Lloyd make old Barney, a man between fifty and sixty years of age, uncover his bald head, kneel down upon the cold, damp ground, and receive upon his naked and toil-worn shoulders more than thirty lashes at the time. Colonel Lloyd had three sons—Edward, Murray, and Daniel—and three sons-in-law, Mr. Winder, Mr. Nicholson, and Mr. Lowndes. All of these lived at the Great House Farm, and enjoyed the luxury of whipping the servants when they pleased, from old Barney down to William Wilkes, the coach-driver. I have seen Winder make one of the house-servants stand off from him a suitable distance to be touched with the end of his whip, and at every stroke raise great ridges upon his back.

To describe the wealth of Colonel Lloyd would be almost equal to describing the riches of Job.[1] He kept from ten to fifteen house-servants. He was said to own a thousand slaves, and I think this estimate quite within the truth. Colonel Lloyd owned so many that he did not know them when he saw them;

---

1   *riches of Job*   The biblical figure Job is best known for the brutal test of faith he is put under by God, but prior to these events he is described as wealthy and prosperous.

nor did all the slaves of the out-farms know him. It is reported of him, that, while riding along the road one day, he met a colored man, and addressed him in the usual manner of speaking to colored people on the public highways of the south: "Well, boy, whom do you belong to?" "To Colonel Lloyd," replied the slave. "Well, does the colonel treat you well?" "No, sir," was the ready reply. "What, does he work you too hard?" "Yes, sir." "Well, don't he give you enough to eat?" "Yes, sir, he gives me enough, such as it is."

The colonel, after ascertaining where the slave belonged, rode on; the man also went on about his business, not dreaming that he had been conversing with his master. He thought, said, and heard nothing more of the matter, until two or three weeks afterwards. The poor man was then informed by his overseer that, for having found fault with his master, he was now to be sold to a Georgia trader. He was immediately chained and handcuffed; and thus, without a moment's warning, he was snatched away, and forever sundered, from his family and friends, by a hand more unrelenting than death. This is the penalty of telling the truth, of telling the simple truth, in answer to a series of plain questions.

It is partly in consequence of such facts, that slaves, when inquired of as to their condition and the character of their masters, almost universally say they are contented, and that their masters are kind. The slaveholders have been known to send in spies among their slaves, to ascertain their views and feelings in regard to their condition. The frequency of this has had the effect to establish among the slaves the maxim, that a still tongue makes a wise head. They suppress the truth rather than take the consequences of telling it, and in so doing prove themselves a part of the human family. If they have anything to say of their masters, it is generally in their masters' favor, especially when speaking to an untried man. I have been frequently asked, when a slave, if I had a kind master, and do not remember ever to have given a negative answer; nor did I, in pursuing this course, consider myself as uttering what was absolutely false; for I always measured the kindness of my master by the standard of kindness set up among slaveholders around us. Moreover, slaves are like other people, and imbibe prejudices quite common to others. They think their own better than that of others. Many, under the influence of this prejudice, think their own masters are better than the masters of other slaves; and this, too, in some cases, when the very reverse is true. Indeed, it is not uncommon for slaves even to fall out and quarrel among themselves about the relative goodness of their masters, each contending for the superior goodness of his own over that of the others. At the very same time, they mutually execrate their masters when viewed separately. It was so on our plantation. When Colonel Lloyd's slaves met the slaves of Jacob Jepson, they seldom parted without a quarrel about their masters; Colonel Lloyd's slaves contending that he was the richest, and Mr. Jepson's slaves that he was the smartest, and most of a man. Colonel Lloyd's slaves would boast his ability to buy and sell Jacob Jepson. Mr. Jepson's slaves would boast his ability to whip Colonel Lloyd. These quarrels would almost always end in a fight between the parties, and those that whipped were supposed to have gained the point at issue. They seemed to think that the greatness of their masters was transferable to themselves. It was considered as being bad enough to be a slave; but to be a poor man's slave was deemed a disgrace indeed!

CHAPTER 4

Mr. Hopkins remained but a short time in the office of overseer. Why his career was so short, I do not know, but suppose he lacked the necessary severity to suit Colonel Lloyd. Mr. Hopkins was succeeded by Mr. Austin Gore, a man possessing, in an eminent degree, all those traits of character indispensable to what is called a first-rate overseer. Mr. Gore had served Colonel Lloyd, in the capacity of overseer, upon one of the out-farms, and had shown himself worthy of the high station of overseer upon the home or Great House Farm.

Mr. Gore was proud, ambitious, and persevering. He was artful, cruel, and obdurate. He was just the man for such a place, and it was just the place for such a man. It afforded scope for the full exercise of all his powers, and he seemed to be perfectly at home in it. He was one of those who could torture the slightest look, word, or gesture, on the part of the slave, into impudence, and would treat it accordingly. There must be no answering back to him; no explanation was allowed a slave, showing himself to have been wrongfully accused. Mr. Gore acted fully up to the maxim laid down by slaveholders, "It is better that a dozen slaves should suffer under the lash, than that the overseer should be convicted, in the presence of the slaves, of having been at fault." No matter how innocent a slave might be—it availed him nothing, when accused by Mr. Gore of any misdemeanor. To be accused was to be convicted, and to be convicted was to be punished; the one always following the other with immutable certainty. To escape punishment was to escape accusation; and few slaves had the fortune to do either, under the overseership of Mr. Gore. He was just proud enough to demand the most debasing homage of the slave, and quite servile enough to crouch, himself, at the feet of the master. He was ambitious enough to be contented with nothing short of the highest rank of overseers, and persevering enough to reach the height of his ambition. He was cruel enough to inflict the severest punishment, artful enough to descend to the lowest trickery, and obdurate enough to be insensible to the voice of a reproving conscience. He was, of all the overseers, the most dreaded by the slaves. His presence was painful; his eye flashed confusion; and seldom was his sharp, shrill voice heard, without producing horror and trembling in their ranks.

Mr. Gore was a grave man, and, though a young man, he indulged in no jokes, said no funny words, seldom smiled. His words were in perfect keeping with his looks, and his looks were in perfect keeping with his words. Overseers will sometimes indulge in a witty word, even with the slaves; not so with Mr. Gore. He spoke but to command, and commanded but to be obeyed; he dealt sparingly with his words, and bountifully with his whip, never using the former where the latter would answer as well. When he whipped, he seemed to do so from a sense of duty, and feared no consequences. He did nothing reluctantly, no matter how disagreeable; always at his post, never inconsistent. He never promised but to fulfil. He was, in a word, a man of the most inflexible firmness and stone-like coolness.

His savage barbarity was equalled only by the consummate coolness with which he committed the grossest and most savage deeds upon the slaves under his charge. Mr. Gore once undertook to whip one of Colonel Lloyd's slaves, by the name of Demby. He had given Demby but few stripes,[1] when, to get rid of the scourging, he ran and plunged himself into a creek, and stood there at the depth of his shoulders, refusing to come out. Mr. Gore told him that he would give him three calls, and that, if he did not come out at the third call, he would shoot him. The first call was given. Demby made no response, but stood his ground. The second and third calls were given with the same result. Mr. Gore then, without consultation or deliberation with anyone, not even giving Demby an additional call, raised his musket to his face, taking deadly aim at his standing victim, and in an instant poor Demby was no more. His mangled body sank out of sight, and blood and brains marked the water where he had stood.

A thrill of horror flashed through every soul upon the plantation, excepting Mr. Gore. He alone seemed cool and collected. He was asked by Colonel Lloyd and my old master, why he resorted to this extraordinary expedient. His reply was (as well as I can remember) that Demby had become unmanageable. He was setting a dangerous example to the other slaves—one which, if suffered to pass without some such demonstration on his part, would finally lead to the total subversion of all rule and order upon the plantation. He argued that if one slave refused to be corrected, and escaped with his life, the other slaves would soon copy the example; the result of which would be, the freedom of the slaves, and the enslavement of the whites. Mr. Gore's defence was satisfactory. He was continued in his station as overseer upon the home plantation. His fame as an overseer went abroad. His horrid crime was not

---

1 *stripes* I.e., lash-marks.

even submitted to judicial investigation. It was committed in the presence of slaves, and they of course could neither institute a suit, nor testify against him; and thus the guilty perpetrator of one of the bloodiest and most foul murders goes unwhipped of justice, and uncensured by the community in which he lives. Mr. Gore lived in St. Michael's, Talbot county, Maryland, when I left there; and if he is still alive, he very probably lives there now; and if so, he is now, as he was then, as highly esteemed and as much respected as though his guilty soul had not been stained with his brother's blood.

I speak advisedly when I say this—that killing a slave, or any colored person, in Talbot county, Maryland, is not treated as a crime, either by the courts or the community. Mr. Thomas Lanman, of St. Michael's, killed two slaves, one of whom he killed with a hatchet, by knocking his brains out. He used to boast of the commission of the awful and bloody deed. I have heard him do so laughingly, saying, among other things, that he was the only benefactor of his country in the company, and that when others would do as much as he had done, we should be relieved of "the d——d niggers."

The wife of Mr. Giles Hicks, living but a short distance from where I used to live, murdered my wife's cousin, a young girl between fifteen and sixteen years of age, mangling her person in the most horrible manner, breaking her nose and breastbone with a stick, so that the poor girl expired in a few hours afterward. She was immediately buried, but had not been in her untimely grave but a few hours before she was taken up and examined by the coroner, who decided that she had come to her death by severe beating. The offence for which this girl was thus murdered was this: She had been set that night to mind Mrs. Hicks's baby, and during the night she fell asleep, and the baby cried. She, having lost her rest for several nights previous, did not hear the crying. They were both in the room with Mrs. Hicks. Mrs. Hicks, finding the girl slow to move, jumped from her bed, seized an oak stick of wood by the fireplace, and with it broke the girl's nose and breastbone, and thus ended her life. I will not say that this most horrid murder produced no sensation in the community. It did produce sensation, but not enough to bring the murderess to punishment. There was a warrant issued for her arrest, but it was never served. Thus she escaped not only punishment, but even the pain of being arraigned before a court for her horrid crime.

Whilst I am detailing bloody deeds which took place during my stay on Colonel Lloyd's plantation, I will briefly narrate another, which occurred about the same time as the murder of Demby by Mr. Gore.

Colonel Lloyd's slaves were in the habit of spending a part of their nights and Sundays in fishing for oysters, and in this way made up the deficiency of their scanty allowance. An old man belonging to Colonel Lloyd, while thus engaged, happened to get beyond the limits of Colonel Lloyd's, and on the premises of Mr. Beal Bondly. At this trespass, Mr. Bondly took offence, and with his musket came down to the shore, and blew its deadly contents into the poor old man.

Mr. Bondly came over to see Colonel Lloyd the next day, whether to pay him for his property, or to justify himself in what he had done, I know not. At any rate, this whole fiendish transaction was soon hushed up. There was very little said about it at all, and nothing done. It was a common saying, even among little white boys, that it was worth a half-cent to kill a "nigger," and a half-cent to bury one.

CHAPTER 5

As to my own treatment while I lived on Colonel Lloyd's plantation, it was very similar to that of the other slave children. I was not old enough to work in the field, and there being little else than field work to do, I had a great deal of leisure time. The most I had to do was to drive up the cows at evening, keep the fowls out of the garden, keep the front yard clean, and run of errands for my old master's daughter, Mrs. Lucretia Auld. The most of my leisure time I spent in helping Master Daniel Lloyd in finding his birds, after he had shot them. My connection with Master Daniel was of some advantage to me. He became quite attached to me, and was a sort of protector of me. He would not allow the older boys to impose upon me, and would divide his cakes with me.

I was seldom whipped by my old master, and suffered little from anything else than hunger and cold. I suffered much from hunger, but much more from cold. In hottest summer and coldest winter, I was kept almost naked—no shoes, no stockings, no jacket, no trousers, nothing on but a coarse tow linen[1] shirt, reaching only to my knees. I had no bed. I must have perished with cold, but that, the coldest nights, I used to steal a bag which was used for carrying corn to the mill. I would crawl into this bag, and there sleep on the cold, damp, clay floor, with my head in and feet out. My feet have been so cracked with the frost, that the pen with which I am writing might be laid in the gashes.

We were not regularly allowanced. Our food was coarse corn meal boiled. This was called mush. It was put into a large wooden tray or trough, and set down upon the ground. The children were then called, like so many pigs, and like so many pigs they would come and devour the mush; some with oyster-shells, others with pieces of shingle, some with naked hands, and none with

---

1   *tow linen*   Material made from shorter, unworked strands of flax fibers, resulting in a coarser cloth than
    regular linen.

spoons. He that ate fastest got most; he that was strongest secured the best place; and few left the trough satisfied.

I was probably between seven and eight years old when I left Colonel Lloyd's plantation. I left it with joy. I shall never forget the ecstasy with which I received the intelligence that my old master (Anthony) had determined to let me go to Baltimore, to live with Mr. Hugh Auld, brother to my old master's son-in-law, Captain Thomas Auld. I received this information about three days before my departure. They were three of the happiest days I ever enjoyed. I spent the most part of all these three days in the creek, washing off the plantation scurf, and preparing myself for my departure.

The pride of appearance which this would indicate was not my own. I spent the time in washing, not so much because I wished to, but because Mrs. Lucretia had told me I must get all the dead skin off my feet and knees before I could go to Baltimore; for the people in Baltimore were very cleanly, and would laugh at me if I looked dirty. Besides, she was going to give me a pair of trousers, which I should not put on unless I got all the dirt off me. The thought of owning a pair of trousers was great indeed! It was almost a sufficient motive, not only to make me take off what would be called by pig-drovers the mange, but the skin itself. I went at it in good earnest, working for the first time with the hope of reward.

The ties that ordinarily bind children to their homes were all suspended in my case. I found no severe trial in my departure. My home was charmless; it was not home to me; on parting from it, I could not feel that I was leaving anything which I could have enjoyed by staying. My mother was dead, my grandmother lived far off, so that I seldom saw her. I had two sisters and one brother, that lived in the same house with me; but the early separation of us from our mother had well nigh blotted the fact of our relationship from our memories. I looked for home elsewhere, and was confident of finding none which I should relish less than the one which I was leaving. If, however, I found in my new home hardship, hunger, whipping, and nakedness, I had the consolation that I should not have escaped any one of them by staying. Having already had more than a taste of them in the house of my old master, and having endured them there, I very naturally inferred my ability to endure them elsewhere, and especially at Baltimore; for I had something of the feeling about Baltimore that is expressed in the proverb, that "being hanged in England is preferable to dying a natural death in Ireland." I had the strongest desire to see Baltimore. Cousin Tom, though not fluent in speech, had inspired me with that desire by his eloquent description of the place. I could never point out anything at the Great House, no matter how beautiful or powerful, but that he had seen something at Baltimore far exceeding, both in beauty and strength, the object which I pointed out to him. Even the Great House itself, with all its pictures, was far inferior to many buildings in Baltimore. So strong was my desire, that I thought a gratification of it would fully compensate for whatever loss of comforts I should sustain by the exchange. I left without a regret, and with the highest hopes of future happiness.

We sailed out of Miles River for Baltimore on a Saturday morning. I remember only the day of the week, for at that time I had no knowledge of the days of the month, nor the months of the year. On setting sail, I walked aft, and gave to Colonel Lloyd's plantation what I hoped would be the last look. I then placed myself in the bows of the sloop, and there spent the remainder of the day in looking ahead, interesting myself in what was in the distance rather than in things near by or behind.

In the afternoon of that day, we reached Annapolis, the capital of the State. We stopped but a few moments, so that I had no time to go on shore. It was the first large town that I had ever seen, and though it would look small compared with some of our New England factory villages, I thought it a wonderful place for its size—more imposing even than the Great House Farm!

We arrived at Baltimore early on Sunday morning, landing at Smith's Wharf, not far from Bowley's Wharf. We had on board the sloop a large flock of sheep; and after aiding in driving them to the slaughterhouse of Mr. Curtis on Louden Slater's Hill, I was conducted by Rich, one of the hands belonging on board of the sloop, to my new home in Alliciana Street, near Mr. Gardner's shipyard, on Fells Point.

Mr. and Mrs. Auld were both at home, and met me at the door with their little son Thomas, to take care of whom I had been given. And here I saw what I had never seen before; it was a white face beaming with the most kindly emotions; it was the face of my new mistress, Sophia Auld. I wish I could describe the rapture that flashed through my soul as I beheld it. It was a new and strange sight to me, brightening up my pathway with the light of happiness. Little Thomas was told, there was his Freddy—and I was told to take care of little Thomas; and thus I entered upon the duties of my new home with the most cheering prospect ahead.

I look upon my departure from Colonel Lloyd's plantation as one of the most interesting events of my life. It is possible, and even quite probable, that but for the mere circumstance of being removed from that plantation to Baltimore, I should have today, instead of being here seated by my own table, in the enjoyment of freedom and the happiness of home, writing this Narrative, been confined in the galling chains of slavery. Going to live at Baltimore laid the foundation, and opened the gateway, to all my subsequent prosperity. I have ever regarded it as the first plain manifestation of that kind providence which has ever since attended me, and marked my life with so many favors. I regarded the selection of myself as being somewhat remarkable. There were a number of slave children that might have been sent from the plantation to Baltimore. There were those younger, those older, and those of the same age. I was chosen from among them all, and was the first, last, and only choice.

I may be deemed superstitious, and even egotistical, in regarding this event as a special interposition of divine Providence in my favor. But I should be false to the earliest sentiments of my soul, if I suppressed the opinion. I prefer to be true to myself, even at the hazard of incurring the ridicule of others, rather than to be false, and incur my own abhorrence. From my earliest recollection, I date the entertainment of a deep conviction that slavery would not always be able to hold me within its foul embrace; and in the darkest hours of my career in slavery, this living word of faith and spirit of hope departed not from me, but remained like ministering angels to cheer me through the gloom. This good spirit was from God, and to him I offer thanksgiving and praise.

CHAPTER 6

My new mistress proved to be all she appeared when I first met her at the door—a woman of the kindest heart and finest feelings. She had never had a slave under her control previously to myself, and prior to her marriage she had been dependent upon her own industry for a living. She was by trade a weaver; and by constant application to her business, she had been in a good degree preserved from the blighting and dehumanizing effects of slavery. I was utterly astonished at her goodness. I scarcely knew how to behave towards her. She was entirely unlike any other white woman I had ever seen. I could not approach her as I was accustomed to approach other white ladies. My early instruction was all out of place. The crouching servility, usually so acceptable a quality in a slave, did not answer when manifested toward her. Her favor was not gained by it; she seemed to be disturbed by it. She did not deem it impudent or unmannerly for a slave to look her in the face. The meanest slave was put fully at ease in her presence, and none left without feeling better for having seen her. Her face was made of heavenly smiles, and her voice of tranquil music.

But, alas! this kind heart had but a short time to remain such. The fatal poison of irresponsible power was already in her hands, and soon commenced its infernal work. That cheerful eye, under the influence of slavery, soon became red with rage; that voice, made all of sweet accord, changed to one of harsh and horrid discord; and that angelic face gave place to that of a demon.

Very soon after I went to live with Mr. and Mrs. Auld, she very kindly commenced to teach me the A, B, C. After I had learned this, she assisted me in learning to spell words of three or four letters. Just at this point of my progress, Mr. Auld found out what was going on, and at once forbade Mrs.

Auld to instruct me further, telling her, among other things, that it was unlawful, as well as unsafe, to teach a slave to read. To use his own words, further, he said, "If you give a nigger an inch, he will take an ell.¹ A nigger should know nothing but to obey his master—to do as he is told to do. Learning would spoil the best nigger in the world. Now," said he, "if you teach that nigger (speaking of myself) how to read, there would be no keeping him. It would forever unfit him to be a slave. He would at once become unmanageable, and of no value to his master. As to himself, it could do him no good, but a great deal of harm. It would make him discontented and unhappy." These words sank deep into my heart, stirred up sentiments within that lay slumbering, and called into existence an entirely new train of thought. It was a new and special revelation, explaining dark and mysterious things, with which my youthful understanding had struggled, but struggled in vain. I now understood what had been to me a most perplexing difficulty—to wit, the white man's power to enslave the black man. It was a grand achievement, and I prized it highly. From that moment, I understood the pathway from slavery to freedom. It was just what I wanted, and I got it at a time when I the least expected it. Whilst I was saddened by the thought of losing the aid of my kind mistress, I was gladdened by the invaluable instruction which, by the merest accident, I had gained from my master. Though conscious of the difficulty of learning without a teacher, I set out with high hope, and a fixed purpose, at whatever cost of trouble, to learn how to read. The very decided manner with which he spoke, and strove to impress his wife with the evil consequences of giving me instruction, served to convince me that he was deeply sensible of the truths he was uttering. It gave me the best assurance that I might rely with the utmost confidence on the results which, he said, would flow from teaching me to read. What he most dreaded, that I most desired. What he most loved, that I most hated. That which to him was a great evil, to be carefully shunned, was to me a great good, to be diligently sought; and the argument which he so warmly urged, against my learning to read, only served to inspire me with a desire and determination to learn. In learning to read, I owe almost as much to the bitter opposition of my master, as to the kindly aid of my mistress. I acknowledge the benefit of both.

I had resided but a short time in Baltimore before I observed a marked difference, in the treatment of slaves, from that which I had witnessed in the country. A city slave is almost a freeman, compared with a slave on the plantation. He is much better fed and clothed, and enjoys privileges altogether unknown to the slave on the plantation. There is a vestige of decency, a sense of shame, that does much to curb and check those outbreaks of atrocious

---

1   *an ell*   Approximately 45 inches.

cruelty so commonly enacted upon the plantation. He is a desperate slave-holder, who will shock the humanity of his non-slaveholding neighbors with the cries of his lacerated slave. Few are willing to incur the odium attaching to the reputation of being a cruel master; and above all things, they would not be known as not giving a slave enough to eat. Every city slaveholder is anxious to have it known of him, that he feeds his slaves well; and it is due to them to say, that most of them do give their slaves enough to eat. There are, however, some painful exceptions to this rule. Directly opposite to us, on Philpot Street, lived Mr. Thomas Hamilton. He owned two slaves. Their names were Henrietta and Mary. Henrietta was about twenty-two years of age, Mary was about fourteen; and of all the mangled and emaciated creatures I ever looked upon, these two were the most so. His heart must be harder than stone, that could look upon these unmoved. The head, neck, and shoulders of Mary were literally cut to pieces. I have frequently felt her head, and found it nearly covered with festering sores, caused by the lash of her cruel mistress. I do not know that her master ever whipped her, but I have been an eye-witness to the cruelty of Mrs. Hamilton. I used to be in Mr. Hamilton's house nearly every day. Mrs. Hamilton used to sit in a large chair in the middle of the room, with a heavy cowskin always by her side, and scarce an hour passed during the day but was marked by the blood of one of these slaves. The girls seldom passed her without her saying, "Move faster, you black gip!" at the same time giving them a blow with the cowskin over the head or shoulders, often drawing the blood. She would then say, "Take that, you black gip!" continuing, "If you don't move faster, I'll move you!" Added to the cruel lashings to which these slaves were subjected, they were kept nearly half-starved. They seldom knew what it was to eat a full meal. I have seen Mary contending with the pigs for the offal thrown into the street. So much was Mary kicked and cut to pieces, that she was oftener called "pecked" than by her name.

CHAPTER 7

I lived in Master Hugh's family about seven years. During this time, I succeeded in learning to read and write. In accomplishing this, I was compelled to resort to various stratagems. I had no regular teacher. My mistress, who had kindly commenced to instruct me, had, in compliance with the advice and direction of her husband, not only ceased to instruct, but had set her face against my being instructed by anyone else. It is due, however, to my mistress to say of her, that she did not adopt this course of treatment immediately. She at first lacked the depravity indispensable to shutting me up in mental darkness. It was at least necessary for her to have some training in the exercise of irresponsible power, to make her equal to the task of treating me as though I were a brute.

My mistress was, as I have said, a kind and tender-hearted woman; and in the simplicity of her soul she commenced, when I first went to live with her, to treat me as she supposed one human being ought to treat another. In entering upon the duties of a slaveholder, she did not seem to perceive that I sustained to her the relation of a mere chattel, and that for her to treat me as a human being was not only wrong, but dangerously so. Slavery proved as injurious to her as it did to me. When I went there, she was a pious, warm, and tender-hearted woman. There was no sorrow or suffering for which she had not a tear. She had bread for the hungry, clothes for the naked, and comfort for every mourner that came within her reach. Slavery soon proved its ability to divest her of these heavenly qualities. Under its influence, the tender heart became stone, and the lamblike disposition gave way to one of tiger-like fierceness. The first step in her downward course was in her ceasing to instruct me. She now commenced to practise her husband's precepts. She finally became even more violent in her opposition than her husband himself. She was not satisfied with simply doing as well as he had commanded; she seemed anxious to do better. Nothing seemed to make her more angry than to see me with a newspaper. She seemed to think that here lay the danger. I have had her rush at me with a face made all up of fury, and snatch from me a newspaper, in a manner that fully revealed her apprehension. She was an apt woman; and a little experience soon demonstrated, to her satisfaction, that education and slavery were incompatible with each other.

From this time I was most narrowly[1] watched. If I was in a separate room any considerable length of time, I was sure to be suspected of having a book, and was at once called to give an account of myself. All this, however, was too late. The first step had been taken. Mistress, in teaching me the alphabet, had given me the inch, and no precaution could prevent me from taking the ell.

The plan which I adopted, and the one by which I was most successful, was that of making friends of all the little white boys whom I met in the street. As many of these as I could, I converted into teachers. With their kindly aid, obtained at different times and in different places, I finally succeeded in learning to read. When I was sent of errands, I always took my book with me, and by going one part of my errand quickly, I found time to get a lesson before my return. I used also to carry bread with me, enough of which was always in the house, and to which I was always welcome; for I was much better off in this regard than many of the poor white children in our neighborhood. This bread I used to bestow upon the hungry little urchins, who, in return, would

---

1 *narrowly* Closely.

give me that more valuable bread of knowledge. I am strongly tempted to give the names of two or three of those little boys, as a testimonial of the gratitude and affection I bear them; but prudence forbids—not that it would injure me, but it might embarrass them; for it is almost an unpardonable offence to teach slaves to read in this Christian country. It is enough to say of the dear little fellows, that they lived on Philpot Street, very near Durgin and Bailey's shipyard. I used to talk this matter of slavery over with them. I would sometimes say to them, I wished I could be as free as they would be when they got to be men. "You will be free as soon as you are twenty-one, but I am a slave for life! Have not I as good a right to be free as you have?" These words used to trouble them; they would express for me the liveliest sympathy, and console me with the hope that something would occur by which I might be free.

I was now about twelve years old, and the thought of being a slave for life began to bear heavily upon my heart. Just about this time, I got hold of a book entitled "The Columbian Orator."[1] Every opportunity I got, I used to read this book. Among much of other interesting matter, I found in it a dialogue between a master and his slave. The slave was represented as having run away from his master three times. The dialogue represented the conversation which took place between them, when the slave was retaken the third time. In this dialogue, the whole argument in behalf of slavery was brought forward by the master, all of which was disposed of by the slave. The slave was made to say some very smart as well as impressive things in reply to his master—things which had the desired though unexpected effect; for the conversation resulted in the voluntary emancipation of the slave on the part of the master.

In the same book, I met with one of Sheridan's[2] mighty speeches on and in behalf of Catholic emancipation. These were choice documents to me. I read them over and over again with unabated interest. They gave tongue to interesting thoughts of my own soul, which had frequently flashed through my mind, and died away for want of utterance. The moral which I gained from the dialogue was the power of truth over the conscience of even a slaveholder. What I got from Sheridan was a bold denunciation of slavery, and a powerful vindication of human rights. The reading of these documents enabled me to utter my thoughts, and to meet the arguments brought forward to sustain

---

1 *The Columbian Orator* Anthology of speeches and essays collected by New England educator Caleb Bingham (1757–1817), popular as a schoolbook.

2 *Sheridan* Douglass is misremembering here. Richard Brinsley Sheridan (1751–1816) was an Irish poet, playwright, and politician; a short parliamentary speech by Sheridan is included in the contents of the *Orator*, but it bears little resemblance to what Douglass describes here. The text to which he likely meant to refer is the speech for Catholic Emancipation given by United Irishman Arthur O'Connor in 1795, which directly follows the "Dialogue between a Master and Slave." (This speech is often further misidentified as having been given by Daniel O'Connell.)

slavery; but while they relieved me of one difficulty, they brought on another even more painful than the one of which I was relieved. The more I read, the more I was led to abhor and detest my enslavers. I could regard them in no other light than a band of successful robbers, who had left their homes, and gone to Africa, and stolen us from our homes, and in a strange land reduced us to slavery. I loathed them as being the meanest as well as the most wicked of men. As I read and contemplated the subject, behold! that very discontentment which Master Hugh had predicted would follow my learning to read had already come, to torment and sting my soul to unutterable anguish. As I writhed under it, I would at times feel that learning to read had been a curse rather than a blessing. It had given me a view of my wretched condition, without the remedy. It opened my eyes to the horrible pit, but to no ladder upon which to get out. In moments of agony, I envied my fellow-slaves for their stupidity. I have often wished myself a beast. I preferred the condition of the meanest reptile to my own. Anything, no matter what, to get rid of thinking! It was this everlasting thinking of my condition that tormented me. There was no getting rid of it. It was pressed upon me by every object within sight or hearing, animate or inanimate. The silver trump of freedom had roused my soul to eternal wakefulness. Freedom now appeared, to disappear no more forever. It was heard in every sound, and seen in everything. It was ever present to torment me with a sense of my wretched condition. I saw nothing without seeing it, I heard nothing without hearing it, and felt nothing without feeling it. It looked from every star, it smiled in every calm, breathed in every wind, and moved in every storm.

I often found myself regretting my own existence, and wishing myself dead; and but for the hope of being free, I have no doubt but that I should have killed myself, or done something for which I should have been killed. While in this state of mind, I was eager to hear anyone speak of slavery. I was a ready listener. Every little while, I could hear something about the abolitionists. It was some time before I found what the word meant. It was always used in such connections as to make it an interesting word to me. If a slave ran away and succeeded in getting clear, or if a slave killed his master, set fire to a barn, or did anything very wrong in the mind of a slaveholder, it was spoken of as the fruit of abolition. Hearing the word in this connection very often, I set about learning what it meant. The dictionary afforded me little or no help. I found it was "the act of abolishing"; but then I did not know what was to be abolished. Here I was perplexed. I did not dare to ask anyone about its meaning, for I was satisfied that it was something they wanted me to know very little about. After a patient waiting, I got one of our city papers, containing an account of the number of petitions from the north, praying for the abolition of slavery in the District of Columbia, and of the slave trade between the States. From this time I understood the words abolition and abolitionist, and always drew near when that word was spoken, expecting to hear something of importance to myself and fellow-slaves. The light broke in upon me by degrees. I went one day down on the wharf of Mr. Waters; and seeing two Irishmen unloading a scow of stone, I went, unasked, and helped them. When we had finished, one of them came to me and asked me if I were a slave. I told him I was. He asked, "Are ye a slave for life?" I told him that I was. The good Irishman seemed to be deeply affected by the statement. He said to the other that it was a pity so fine a little fellow as myself should be a slave for life. He said it was a shame to hold me. They both advised me to run away to the north; that I should find friends there, and that I should be free. I pretended not to be interested in what they said, and treated them as if I did not understand them; for I feared they might be treacherous. White men have been known to encourage slaves to escape, and then, to get the reward, catch them and return them to their masters. I was afraid that these seemingly good men might use me so; but I nevertheless remembered their advice, and from that time I resolved to run away. I looked forward to a time at which it would be safe for me to escape. I was too young to think of doing so immediately; besides, I wished to learn how to write, as I might have occasion to write my own pass. I consoled myself with the hope that I should one day find a good chance. Meanwhile, I would learn to write.

The idea as to how I might learn to write was suggested to me by being in Durgin and Bailey's shipyard, and frequently seeing the ship carpenters, after hewing, and getting a piece of timber ready for use, write on the timber the name of that part of the ship for which it was intended. When a piece of timber was intended for the larboard[1] side, it would be marked thus—"L." When a piece was for the starboard side, it would be marked thus—"S." A piece for the larboard side forward, would be marked thus—"L. F." When a piece was for starboard side forward, it would be marked thus—"S. F." For larboard aft, it would be marked thus—"L. A." For starboard aft, it would be marked thus—"S. A." I soon learned the names of these letters, and for what they were intended when placed upon a piece of timber in the ship-yard. I immediately commenced copying them, and in a short time was able to make the four letters named. After that, when I met with any boy who I knew could write, I would tell him I could write as well as he. The next word would be, "I don't believe you. Let me see you try it." I would then make the letters which I had been so fortunate as to learn, and ask him to beat that. In this way I got a good many lessons in writing, which it is quite possible I should never have gotten in any other way. During this time, my copy-book was the board fence, brick wall, and pavement; my pen and ink was a lump of chalk.

---

1 *larboard* Left (or "port") side of a ship; the right side is referred to as the "starboard."

With these, I learned mainly how to write. I then commenced and continued copying the italics in Webster's Spelling Book,[1] until I could make them all without looking on the book. By this time, my little Master Thomas had gone to school, and learned how to write, and had written over a number of copy-books. These had been brought home, and shown to some of our near neighbors, and then laid aside. My mistress used to go to class meeting at the Wilk Street meeting house every Monday afternoon, and leave me to take care of the house. When left thus, I used to spend the time in writing in the spaces left in Master Thomas's copy-book, copying what he had written. I continued to do this until I could write a hand very similar to that of Master Thomas. Thus, after a long, tedious effort for years, I finally succeeded in learning how to write.

CHAPTER 8

In a very short time after I went to live at Baltimore, my old master's youngest son Richard died; and in about three years and six months after his death, my old master, Captain Anthony, died, leaving only his son, Andrew, and daughter, Lucretia, to share his estate. He died while on a visit to see his daughter at Hillsborough. Cut off thus unexpectedly, he left no will as to the disposal of his property. It was therefore necessary to have a valuation of the property, that it might be equally divided between Mrs. Lucretia and Master Andrew. I was immediately sent for, to be valued with the other property. Here again my feelings rose up in detestation of slavery. I had now a new conception of my degraded condition. Prior to this, I had become, if not insensible to my lot, at least partly so. I left Baltimore with a young heart overborne with sadness, and a soul full of apprehension. I took passage with Captain Rowe, in the schooner Wild Cat, and, after a sail of about twenty-four hours, I found myself near the place of my birth. I had now been absent from it almost, if not quite, five years. I, however, remembered the place very well. I was only about five years old when I left it, to go and live with my old master on Colonel Lloyd's plantation; so that I was now between ten and eleven years old.

We were all ranked together at the valuation. Men and women, old and young, married and single, were ranked with horses, sheep, and swine. There were horses and men, cattle and women, pigs and children, all holding the same rank in the scale of being, and were all subjected to the same narrow examination. Silvery-headed age and sprightly youth, maids and matrons, had

---

1 *Webster's Spelling Book* Refers to *The American Spelling Book* by American educator Noah Webster (1758–1843); first published in 1783, the book was a steady bestseller into the second half of the nineteenth century.

to undergo the same indelicate inspection. At this moment, I saw more clearly than ever the brutalizing effects of slavery upon both slave and slaveholder.

After the valuation, then came the division. I have no language to express the high excitement and deep anxiety which were felt among us poor slaves during this time. Our fate for life was now to be decided. We had no more voice in that decision than the brutes among whom we were ranked. A single word from the white men was enough—against all our wishes, prayers, and entreaties—to sunder forever the dearest friends, dearest kindred, and strongest ties known to human beings. In addition to the pain of separation, there was the horrid dread of falling into the hands of Master Andrew. He was known to us all as being a most cruel wretch—a common drunkard, who had, by his reckless mismanagement and profligate dissipation, already wasted a large portion of his father's property. We all felt that we might as well be sold at once to the Georgia traders, as to pass into his hands; for we knew that that would be our inevitable condition—a condition held by us all in the utmost horror and dread.

I suffered more anxiety than most of my fellow-slaves. I had known what it was to be kindly treated; they had known nothing of the kind. They had seen little or nothing of the world. They were in very deed men and women of sorrow, and acquainted with grief. Their backs had been made familiar with the bloody lash, so that they had become callous; mine was yet tender; for while at Baltimore I got few whippings, and few slaves could boast of a kinder master and mistress than myself; and the thought of passing out of their hands into those of Master Andrew—a man who, but a few days before, to give me a sample of his bloody disposition, took my little brother by the throat, threw him on the ground, and with the heel of his boot stamped upon his head till the blood gushed from his nose and ears—was well calculated to make me anxious as to my fate. After he had committed this savage outrage upon my brother, he turned to me, and said that was the way he meant to serve me one of these days—meaning, I suppose, when I came into his possession.

Thanks to a kind Providence, I fell to the portion of Mrs. Lucretia, and was sent immediately back to Baltimore, to live again in the family of Master Hugh. Their joy at my return equalled their sorrow at my departure. It was a glad day to me. I had escaped a worse than lion's jaws. I was absent from Baltimore, for the purpose of valuation and division, just about one month, and it seemed to have been six.

Very soon after my return to Baltimore, my mistress, Lucretia, died, leaving her husband and one child, Amanda; and in a very short time after her death, Master Andrew died. Now all the property of my old master, slaves included, was in the hands of strangers—strangers who had had nothing to do with accumulating it. Not a slave was left free. All remained slaves, from the youngest to the oldest. If any one thing in my experience, more than another, served to deepen my conviction of the infernal character of slavery, and to fill me with unutterable loathing of slaveholders, it was their base ingratitude to my poor old grandmother. She had served my old master faithfully from youth to old age. She had been the source of all his wealth; she had peopled his plantation with slaves; she had become a great grandmother in his service. She had rocked him in infancy, attended him in childhood, served him through life, and at his death wiped from his icy brow the cold death-sweat, and closed his eyes forever. She was nevertheless left a slave—a slave for life—a slave in the hands of strangers; and in their hands she saw her children, her grandchildren, and her great-grandchildren, divided, like so many sheep, without being gratified with the small privilege of a single word, as to their or her own destiny. And, to cap the climax of their base ingratitude and fiendish barbarity, my grandmother, who was now very old, having outlived my old master and all his children, having seen the beginning and end of all of them, and her present owners finding she was of but little value, her frame already racked with the pains of old age, and complete helplessness fast stealing over her once active limbs, they took her to the woods, built her a little hut, put up a little mud-chimney, and then made her welcome to the privilege of supporting herself there in perfect loneliness; thus virtually turning her out to die! If my poor old grandmother now lives, she lives to suffer in utter loneliness; she lives to remember and mourn over the loss of children, the loss of grandchildren, and the loss of great-grandchildren. They are, in the language of the slave's poet, Whittier,[1]

> Gone, gone, sold and gone
> To the rice swamp dank and lone,
> Where the slave-whip ceaseless swings,
> Where the noisome insect stings,
> Where the fever-demon strews
> Poison with the falling dews,
> Where the sickly sunbeams glare
> Through the hot and misty air:—
> Gone, gone, sold and gone
> To the rice swamp dank and lone,
> From Virginia hills and waters—
> Woe is me, my stolen daughters!

---

1 *the slave's poet, Whittier* John Greenleaf Whittier (1807–92), white Quaker poet and abolitionist who was associated with William Lloyd Garrison. The quotation is from "The Farewell of a Virginia Slave Mother to Her Daughters Sold into Southern Bondage."

The hearth is desolate. The children, the unconscious children, who once sang and danced in her presence, are gone. She gropes her way, in the darkness of age, for a drink of water. Instead of the voices of her children, she hears by day the moans of the dove, and by night the screams of the hideous owl. All is gloom. The grave is at the door. And now, when weighed down by the pains and aches of old age, when the head inclines to the feet, when the beginning and ending of human existence meet, and helpless infancy and painful old age combine together—at this time, this most needful time, the time for the exercise of that tenderness and affection which children only can exercise towards a declining parent—my poor old grandmother, the devoted mother of twelve children, is left all alone, in yonder little hut, before a few dim embers. She stands—she sits—she staggers—she falls—she groans—she dies—and there are none of her children or grandchildren present, to wipe from her wrinkled brow the cold sweat of death, or to place beneath the sod her fallen remains. Will not a righteous God visit for these things?[1]

In about two years after the death of Mrs. Lucretia, Master Thomas married his second wife. Her name was Rowena Hamilton. She was the eldest daughter of Mr. William Hamilton. Master now lived in St. Michael's. Not long after his marriage, a misunderstanding took place between himself and Master Hugh; and as a means of punishing his brother, he took me from him to live with himself at St. Michael's. Here I underwent another most painful separation. It, however, was not so severe as the one I dreaded at the division of property; for, during this interval, a great change had taken place in Master Hugh and his once kind and affectionate wife. The influence of brandy upon him, and of slavery upon her, had effected a disastrous change in the characters of both; so that, as far as they were concerned, I thought I had little to lose by the change. But it was not to them that I was attached. It was to those little Baltimore boys that I felt the strongest attachment. I had received many good lessons from them, and was still receiving them, and the thought of leaving them was painful indeed. I was leaving, too, without the hope of ever being allowed to return. Master Thomas had said he would never let me return again. The barrier betwixt himself and brother he considered impassable.

I then had to regret that I did not at least make the attempt to carry out my resolution to run away; for the chances of success are tenfold greater from the city than from the country.

I sailed from Baltimore for St. Michael's in the sloop Amanda, Captain Edward Dodson. On my passage, I paid particular attention to the direction which the steamboats took to go to Philadelphia. I found, instead of going

---

1 *Will not ... these things?* See Jeremiah 5.29: "Shall I not visit for these things? saith the Lord: shall not my soul be avenged on such a nation as this?"

down, on reaching North Point they went up the bay, in a north-easterly direction. I deemed this knowledge of the utmost importance. My determination to run away was again revived. I resolved to wait only so long as the offering of a favorable opportunity. When that came, I was determined to be off.

CHAPTER 9

I have now reached a period of my life when I can give dates. I left Baltimore, and went to live with Master Thomas Auld, at St. Michael's, in March, 1832. It was now more than seven years since I lived with him in the family of my old master, on Colonel Lloyd's plantation. We of course were now almost entire strangers to each other. He was to me a new master, and I to him a new slave. I was ignorant of his temper and disposition; he was equally so of mine. A very short time, however, brought us into full acquaintance with each other. I was made acquainted with his wife not less than with himself. They were well matched, being equally mean[1] and cruel. I was now, for the first time during a space of more than seven years, made to feel the painful gnawings of hunger—a something which I had not experienced before since I left Colonel Lloyd's plantation. It went hard enough with me then, when I could look back to no period at which I had enjoyed a sufficiency. It was tenfold harder after living in Master Hugh's family, where I had always had enough to eat, and of that which was good. I have said Master Thomas was a mean man. He was so. Not to give a slave enough to eat, is regarded as the most aggravated development of meanness even among slaveholders. The rule is, no matter how coarse the food, only let there be enough of it. This is the theory; and in the part of Maryland from which I came, it is the general practice—though there are many exceptions. Master Thomas gave us enough of neither coarse nor fine food. There were four slaves of us in the kitchen—my sister Eliza, my aunt Priscilla, Henny, and myself; and we were allowed less than a half of a bushel of corn-meal per week, and very little else, either in the shape of meat or vegetables. It was not enough for us to subsist upon. We were therefore reduced to the wretched necessity of living at the expense of our neighbors. This we did by begging and stealing, whichever came handy in the time of need, the one being considered as legitimate as the other. A great many times have we poor creatures been nearly perishing with hunger, when food in abundance lay mouldering in the safe and smoke-house,[2] and our pious mistress was aware of the fact; and yet that mistress and her husband would kneel every morning, and pray that God would bless them in basket and store![3]

---

1 *mean* Lowly and undignified; also, miserly.
2 *safe and smoke-house* Storage-places for meat.
3 *bless ... store* See Deuteronomy 28.5: "Blessed shall be thy basket and thy store."

Bad as all slaveholders are, we seldom meet one destitute of every element of character commanding respect. My master was one of this rare sort. I do not know of one single noble act ever performed by him. The leading trait in his character was meanness; and if there were any other element in his nature, it was made subject to this. He was mean; and, like most other mean men, he lacked the ability to conceal his meanness. Captain Auld was not born a slaveholder. He had been a poor man, master only of a Bay craft. He came into possession of all his slaves by marriage; and of all men, adopted slaveholders are the worst. He was cruel, but cowardly. He commanded without firmness. In the enforcement of his rules, he was at times rigid, and at times lax. At times, he spoke to his slaves with the firmness of Napoleon and the fury of a demon; at other times, he might well be mistaken for an inquirer who had lost his way. He did nothing of himself. He might have passed for a lion, but for his ears. In all things noble which he attempted, his own meanness shone most conspicuous. His airs, words, and actions, were the airs, words, and actions of born slaveholders, and, being assumed, were awkward enough. He was not even a good imitator. He possessed all the disposition to deceive, but wanted the power. Having no resources within himself, he was compelled to be the copyist of many, and being such, he was forever the victim of inconsistency; and of consequence he was an object of contempt, and was held as such even by his slaves. The luxury of having slaves of his own to wait upon him was something new and unprepared for. He was a slaveholder without the ability to hold slaves. He found himself incapable of managing his slaves either by force, fear, or fraud. We seldom called him "master"; we generally called him "Captain Auld," and were hardly disposed to title him at all. I doubt not that our conduct had much to do with making him appear awkward, and of consequence fretful. Our want of reverence for him must have perplexed him greatly. He wished to have us call him master, but lacked the firmness necessary to command us to do so. His wife used to insist upon our calling him so, but to no purpose. In August, 1832, my master attended a Methodist camp-meeting[1] held in the Bay-side, Talbot county, and there experienced religion. I indulged a faint hope that his conversion would lead him to emancipate his slaves, and that, if he did not do this, it would, at any rate, make him more kind and humane. I was disappointed in both these respects. It neither made him to be humane to his slaves, nor to emancipate them. If it had any effect on his character, it made him more cruel and hateful in all his ways; for I believe him to have been a much worse man after his conversion than before. Prior to his conversion, he relied upon his own depravity to shield and sustain him in his savage barbarity; but after his conversion, he found religious sanction

---

1   *camp-meeting* Outdoor meeting.

and support for his slaveholding cruelty. He made the greatest pretensions to piety. His house was the house of prayer. He prayed morning, noon, and night. He very soon distinguished himself among his brethren, and was soon made a class-leader and exhorter. His activity in revivals was great, and he proved himself an instrument in the hands of the church in converting many souls. His house was the preachers' home. They used to take great pleasure in coming there to put up; for while he starved us, he stuffed them. We have had three or four preachers there at a time. The names of those who used to come most frequently while I lived there, were Mr. Storks, Mr. Ewery, Mr. Humphry, and Mr. Hickey. I have also seen Mr. George Cookman[1] at our house. We slaves loved Mr. Cookman. We believed him to be a good man. We thought him instrumental in getting Mr. Samuel Harrison, a very rich slaveholder, to emancipate his slaves; and by some means got the impression that he was laboring to effect the emancipation of all the slaves. When he was at our house, we were sure to be called in to prayers. When the others were there, we were sometimes called in and sometimes not. Mr. Cookman took more notice of us than either of the other ministers. He could not come among us without betraying his sympathy for us, and, stupid as we were, we had the sagacity to see it.

While I lived with my master in St. Michael's, there was a white young man, a Mr. Wilson, who proposed to keep a Sabbath school for the instruction of such slaves as might be disposed to learn to read the New Testament. We met but three times, when Mr. West and Mr. Fairbanks, both class-leaders, with many others, came upon us with sticks and other missiles, drove us off, and forbade us to meet again. Thus ended our little Sabbath school in the pious town of St. Michael's.

I have said my master found religious sanction for his cruelty. As an example, I will state one of many facts going to prove the charge. I have seen him tie up a lame young woman, and whip her with a heavy cowskin upon her naked shoulders, causing the warm red blood to drip; and, in justification of the bloody deed, he would quote this passage of Scripture—"He that knoweth his master's will, and doeth it not, shall be beaten with many stripes."[2]

Master would keep this lacerated young woman tied up in this horrid situation four or five hours at a time. I have known him to tie her up early in the morning, and whip her before breakfast; leave her, go to his store, return at dinner, and whip her again, cutting her in the places already made raw with his cruel lash. The secret of master's cruelty toward "Henny" is found in the

---

1 *Mr. George Cookman* Methodist minister (1800–41) who served as Chaplain to the Senate and promoted emancipation.

2 *He that knoweth ... many stripes* See Luke 12.47.

fact of her being almost helpless. When quite a child, she fell into the fire, and burned herself horribly. Her hands were so burnt that she never got the use of them. She could do very little but bear heavy burdens. She was to master a bill of expense; and as he was a mean man, she was a constant offence to him. He seemed desirous of getting the poor girl out of existence. He gave her away once to his sister; but, being a poor gift, she was not disposed to keep her. Finally, my benevolent master, to use his own words, "set her adrift to take care of herself." Here was a recently-converted man, holding on upon the mother, and at the same time turning out her helpless child, to starve and die! Master Thomas was one of the many pious slaveholders who hold slaves for the very charitable purpose of taking care of them.

My master and myself had quite a number of differences. He found me unsuitable to his purpose. My city life, he said, had had a very pernicious effect upon me. It had almost ruined me for every good purpose, and fitted me for everything which was bad. One of my greatest faults was that of letting his horse run away, and go down to his father-in-law's farm, which was about five miles from St. Michael's. I would then have to go after it. My reason for this kind of carelessness, or carefulness, was, that I could always get something to eat when I went there. Master William Hamilton, my master's father-in-law, always gave his slaves enough to eat. I never left there hungry, no matter how great the need of my speedy return. Master Thomas at length said he would stand it no longer. I had lived with him nine months, during which time he had given me a number of severe whippings, all to no good purpose. He resolved to put me out, as he said, to be broken; and, for this purpose, he let me for one year to a man named Edward Covey. Mr. Covey was a poor man, a farm-renter. He rented the place upon which he lived, as also the hands with which he tilled it. Mr. Covey had acquired a very high reputation for breaking young slaves, and this reputation was of immense value to him. It enabled him to get his farm tilled with much less expense to himself than he could have had it done without such a reputation. Some slaveholders thought it not much loss to allow Mr. Covey to have their slaves one year, for the sake of the training to which they were subjected, without any other compensation. He could hire young help with great ease, in consequence of this reputation. Added to the natural good qualities of Mr. Covey, he was a professor of religion—a pious soul—a member and a class-leader in the Methodist church. All of this added weight to his reputation as a "nigger-breaker." I was aware of all the facts, having been made acquainted with them by a young man who had lived there. I nevertheless made the change gladly; for I was sure of getting enough to eat, which is not the smallest consideration to a hungry man.

CHAPTER 10

I had left Master Thomas's house, and went to live with Mr. Covey, on the 1st of January, 1833. I was now, for the first time in my life, a field hand. In my new employment, I found myself even more awkward than a country boy appeared to be in a large city. I had been at my new home but one week before Mr. Covey gave me a very severe whipping, cutting my back, causing the blood to run, and raising ridges on my flesh as large as my little finger. The details of this affair are as follows: Mr. Covey sent me, very early in the morning of one of our coldest days in the month of January, to the woods, to get a load of wood. He gave me a team of unbroken oxen. He told me which was the in-hand ox, and which the off-hand one.[1] He then tied the end of a large rope around the horns of the in-hand ox, and gave me the other end of it, and told me, if the oxen started to run, that I must hold on upon the rope. I had never driven oxen before, and of course I was very awkward. I, however, succeeded in getting to the edge of the woods with little difficulty; but I had got a very few rods into the woods, when the oxen took fright, and started full tilt, carrying the cart against trees, and over stumps, in the most frightful manner. I expected every moment that my brains would be dashed out against the trees. After running thus for a considerable distance, they finally upset the cart, dashing it with great force against a tree, and threw themselves into a dense thicket. How I escaped death, I do not know. There I was, entirely alone, in a thick wood, in a place new to me. My cart was upset and shattered, my oxen were entangled among the young trees, and there was none to help me. After a long spell of effort, I succeeded in getting my cart righted, my oxen disentangled, and again yoked to the cart. I now proceeded with my team to the place where I had, the day before, been chopping wood, and loaded my cart pretty heavily, thinking in this way to tame my oxen. I then proceeded on my way home. I had now consumed one half of the day. I got out of the woods safely, and now felt out of danger. I stopped my oxen to open the woods gate; and just as I did so, before I could get hold of my ox-rope, the oxen again started, rushed through the gate, catching it between the wheel and the body of the cart, tearing it to pieces, and coming within a few inches of crushing me against the gate-post. Thus twice, in one short day, I escaped death by the merest chance. On my return, I told Mr. Covey what had happened, and how it happened. He ordered me to return to the woods again immediately. I did so, and he followed on after me. Just as I got into the woods, he came up and told me to stop my cart, and that he would teach me how to trifle away my time, and break gates. He then went to a large gum-tree, and with his axe cut

---

1 *in-hand ox ... off-hand one* Oxen on the right- and left-hand sides of a pair, respectively.

three large switches, and, after trimming them up neatly with his pocketknife, he ordered me to take off my clothes. I made him no answer, but stood with my clothes on. He repeated his order. I still made him no answer, nor did I move to strip myself. Upon this he rushed at me with the fierceness of a tiger, tore off my clothes, and lashed me till he had worn out his switches, cutting me so savagely as to leave the marks visible for a long time after. This whipping was the first of a number just like it, and for similar offences.

I lived with Mr. Covey one year. During the first six months, of that year, scarce a week passed without his whipping me. I was seldom free from a sore back. My awkwardness was almost always his excuse for whipping me. We were worked fully up to the point of endurance. Long before day we were up, our horses fed, and by the first approach of day we were off to the field with our hoes and ploughing teams. Mr. Covey gave us enough to eat, but scarce time to eat it. We were often less than five minutes taking our meals. We were often in the field from the first approach of day till its last lingering ray had left us; and at saving-fodder time, midnight often caught us in the field binding blades.[1]

Covey would be out with us. The way he used to stand it, was this. He would spend the most of his afternoons in bed. He would then come out fresh in the evening, ready to urge us on with his words, example, and frequently with the whip. Mr. Covey was one of the few slaveholders who could and did work with his hands. He was a hard-working man. He knew by himself just what a man or a boy could do. There was no deceiving him. His work went on in his absence almost as well as in his presence; and he had the faculty of making us feel that he was ever present with us. This he did by surprising us. He seldom approached the spot where we were at work openly, if he could do it secretly. He always aimed at taking us by surprise. Such was his cunning, that we used to call him, among ourselves, "the snake." When we were at work in the cornfield, he would sometimes crawl on his hands and knees to avoid detection, and all at once he would rise nearly in our midst, and scream out, "Ha, ha! Come, come! Dash on, dash on!" This being his mode of attack, it was never safe to stop a single minute. His comings were like a thief in the night. He appeared to us as being ever at hand. He was under every tree, behind every stump, in every bush, and at every window, on the plantation. He would sometimes mount his horse, as if bound to St. Michael's, a distance of seven miles, and in half an hour afterwards you would see him coiled up in the corner of the wood-fence, watching every motion of the slaves. He would, for this purpose, leave his horse tied up in the woods. Again, he would sometimes walk up to us, and give us orders as though he was upon the point

---

1 *saving-fodder time* Harvest time; *binding blades* Binding wheat sheaves.

of starting on a long journey, turn his back upon us, and make as though he was going to the house to get ready; and, before he would get half way thither, he would turn short and crawl into a fence-corner, or behind some tree, and there watch us till the going down of the sun.

Mr. Covey's *forte*[1] consisted in his power to deceive. His life was devoted to planning and perpetrating the grossest deceptions. Everything he possessed in the shape of learning or religion, he made conform to his disposition to deceive. He seemed to think himself equal to deceiving the Almighty. He would make a short prayer in the morning, and a long prayer at night; and, strange as it may seem, few men would at times appear more devotional than he. The exercises of his family devotions were always commenced with singing; and, as he was a very poor singer himself, the duty of raising the hymn generally came upon me. He would read his hymn, and nod at me to commence. I would at times do so; at others, I would not. My non-compliance would almost always produce much confusion. To show himself independent of me, he would start and stagger through with his hymn in the most discordant manner. In this state of mind, he prayed with more than ordinary spirit. Poor man! such was his disposition, and success at deceiving, I do verily believe that he sometimes deceived himself into the solemn belief, that he was a sincere worshipper of the most high God; and this, too, at a time when he may be said to have been guilty of compelling his woman slave to commit the sin of adultery. The facts in the case are these: Mr. Covey was a poor man; he was just commencing in life; he was only able to buy one slave; and, shocking as is the fact, he bought her, as he said, for a breeder. This woman was named Caroline. Mr. Covey bought her from Mr. Thomas Lowe, about six miles from St. Michael's. She was a large, able-bodied woman, about twenty years old. She had already given birth to one child, which proved her to be just what he wanted. After buying her, he hired a married man of Mr. Samuel Harrison, to live with him one year; and him he used to fasten up with her every night! The result was, that, at the end of the year, the miserable woman gave birth to twins. At this result Mr. Covey seemed to be highly pleased, both with the man and the wretched woman. Such was his joy, and that of his wife, that nothing they could do for Caroline during her confinement was too good, or too hard, to be done. The children were regarded as being quite an addition to his wealth.

If at any one time of my life more than another, I was made to drink the bitterest dregs of slavery, that time was during the first six months of my stay with Mr. Covey. We were worked in all weathers. It was never too hot or too cold; it could never rain, blow, hail, or snow, too hard for us to work in the field. Work, work, work, was scarcely more the order of the day than of the

---

1 *forte* Italian: strength; particular ability.

night. The longest days were too short for him, and the shortest nights too long for him. I was somewhat unmanageable when I first went there, but a few months of this discipline tamed me. Mr. Covey succeeded in breaking me. I was broken in body, soul, and spirit. My natural elasticity was crushed, my intellect languished, the disposition to read departed, the cheerful spark that lingered about my eye died; the dark night of slavery closed in upon me; and behold a man transformed into a brute!

Sunday was my only leisure time. I spent this in a sort of beast-like stupor, between sleep and wake, under some large tree. At times I would rise up, a flash of energetic freedom would dart through my soul, accompanied with a faint beam of hope, that flickered for a moment, and then vanished. I sank down again, mourning over my wretched condition. I was sometimes prompted to take my life, and that of Covey, but was prevented by a combination of hope and fear. My sufferings on this plantation seem now like a dream rather than a stern reality.

Our house stood within a few rods of the Chesapeake Bay, whose broad bosom was ever white with sails from every quarter of the habitable globe. Those beautiful vessels, robed in purest white, so delightful to the eye of free-men, were to me so many shrouded ghosts, to terrify and torment me with thoughts of my wretched condition. I have often, in the deep stillness of a summer's Sabbath, stood all alone upon the lofty banks of that noble bay, and traced, with saddened heart and tearful eye, the countless number of sails moving off to the mighty ocean. The sight of these always affected me power-fully. My thoughts would compel utterance; and there, with no audience but the Almighty, I would pour out my soul's complaint, in my rude way, with an apostrophe[1] to the moving multitude of ships:

"You are loosed from your moorings, and are free; I am fast in my chains, and am a slave! You move merrily before the gentle gale, and I sadly before the bloody whip! You are freedom's swift-winged angels, that fly round the world; I am confined in bands of iron! O that I were free! O, that I were on one of your gallant decks, and under your protecting wing! Alas! betwixt me and you, the turbid waters roll. Go on, go on. O that I could also go! Could I but swim! If I could fly! O, why was I born a man, of whom to make a brute! The glad ship is gone; she hides in the dim distance. I am left in the hottest hell of unending slavery. O God, save me! God, deliver me! Let me be free! Is there any God? Why am I a slave? I will run away. I will not stand it. Get caught, or get clear, I'll try it. I had as well die with ague as the fever.[2] I have only one

---

1   *apostrophe*   Exclamatory speech made either to one or more people who are unable to respond (whether because they are not present or because they are not alive) or to one or more inanimate objects.

2   *ague ... fever*   The point here is that there is little difference between the two; "ague" was a term given to a range of infectious maladies for which a high fever was a key symptom.

life to lose. I had as well be killed running as die standing. Only think of it; one hundred miles straight north, and I am free! Try it? Yes! God helping me, I will. It cannot be that I shall live and die a slave. I will take to the water. This very bay shall yet bear me into freedom. The steamboats steered in a north-east course from North Point. I will do the same; and when I get to the head of the bay, I will turn my canoe adrift, and walk straight through Delaware into Pennsylvania. When I get there, I shall not be required to have a pass; I can travel without being disturbed. Let but the first opportunity offer, and, come what will, I am off. Meanwhile, I will try to bear up under the yoke. I am not the only slave in the world. Why should I fret? I can bear as much as any of them. Besides, I am but a boy, and all boys are bound to someone. It may be that my misery in slavery will only increase my happiness when I get free. There is a better day coming."

Thus I used to think, and thus I used to speak to myself; goaded almost to madness at one moment, and at the next reconciling myself to my wretched lot.

I have already intimated that my condition was much worse, during the first six months of my stay at Mr. Covey's, than in the last six. The circumstances leading to the change in Mr. Covey's course toward me form an epoch in my humble history. You have seen how a man was made a slave; you shall see how a slave was made a man. On one of the hottest days of the month of August, 1833, Bill Smith, William Hughes, a slave named Eli, and myself, were engaged in fanning wheat.[1] Hughes was clearing the fanned wheat from before the fan. Eli was turning, Smith was feeding, and I was carrying wheat to the fan. The work was simple, requiring strength rather than intellect; yet, to one entirely unused to such work, it came very hard. About three o'clock of that day, I broke down; my strength failed me; I was seized with a violent aching of the head, attended with extreme dizziness; I trembled in every limb. Finding what was coming, I nerved myself up, feeling it would never do to stop work. I stood as long as I could stagger to the hopper with grain. When I could stand no longer, I fell, and felt as if held down by an immense weight. The fan of course stopped; every one had his own work to do; and no one could do the work of the other, and have his own go on at the same time.

Mr. Covey was at the house, about one hundred yards from the treading-yard where we were fanning. On hearing the fan stop, he left immediately, and came to the spot where we were. He hastily inquired what the matter was. Bill answered that I was sick, and there was no one to bring wheat to the fan. I had by this time crawled away under the side of the post and rail-fence by which the yard was enclosed, hoping to find relief by getting out of the sun. He then

---

1   *fanning wheat*   Separating chaff from the wheat by means of a large fanning mill.

asked where I was. He was told by one of the hands. He came to the spot, and, after looking at me awhile, asked me what was the matter. I told him as well as I could, for I scarce had strength to speak. He then gave me a savage kick in the side, and told me to get up. I tried to do so, but fell back in the attempt. He gave me another kick, and again told me to rise. I again tried, and succeeded in gaining my feet; but, stooping to get the tub with which I was feeding the fan, I again staggered and fell. While down in this situation, Mr. Covey took up the hickory slat with which Hughes had been striking off the half-bushel measure, and with it gave me a heavy blow upon the head, making a large wound, and the blood ran freely; and with this again told me to get up. I made no effort to comply, having now made up my mind to let him do his worst. In a short time after receiving this blow, my head grew better. Mr. Covey had now left me to my fate. At this moment I resolved, for the first time, to go to my master, enter a complaint, and ask his protection. In order to [do] this, I must that afternoon walk seven miles; and this, under the circumstances, was truly a severe undertaking. I was exceedingly feeble; made so as much by the kicks and blows which I received, as by the severe fit of sickness to which I had been subjected. I, however, watched my chance, while Covey was looking in an opposite direction, and started for St. Michael's. I succeeded in getting a considerable distance on my way to the woods, when Covey discovered me, and called after me to come back, threatening what he would do if I did not come. I disregarded both his calls and his threats, and made my way to the woods as fast as my feeble state would allow; and thinking I might be overhauled by him if I kept the road, I walked through the woods, keeping far enough from the road to avoid detection, and near enough to prevent losing my way. I had not gone far before my little strength again failed me. I could go no farther. I fell down, and lay for a considerable time. The blood was yet oozing from the wound on my head. For a time I thought I should bleed to death; and think now that I should have done so, but that the blood so matted my hair as to stop the wound. After lying there about three quarters of an hour, I nerved myself up again, and started on my way, through bogs and briers, barefooted and bareheaded, tearing my feet sometimes at nearly every step; and after a journey of about seven miles, occupying some five hours to perform it, I arrived at master's store. I then presented an appearance enough to affect any but a heart of iron. From the crown of my head to my feet, I was covered with blood. My hair was all clotted with dust and blood; my shirt was stiff with blood. I suppose I looked like a man who had escaped a den of wild beasts, and barely escaped them. In this state I appeared before my master, humbly entreating him to interpose his authority for my protection. I told him all the circumstances as well as I could, and it seemed, as I spoke, at times to affect him. He would then walk the floor, and seek to justify Covey by saying he expected I deserved it. He asked me what I wanted. I told him, to let me get a new home; that as sure as I lived with Mr. Covey again, I should live with but to die with him; that Covey would surely kill me; he was in a fair way for it. Master Thomas ridiculed the idea that there was any danger of Mr. Covey's killing me, and said that he knew Mr. Covey; that he was a good man, and that he could not think of taking me from him; that, should he do so, he would lose the whole year's wages; that I belonged to Mr. Covey for one year, and that I must go back to him, come what might; and that I must not trouble him with any more stories, or that he would himself get hold of me. After threatening me thus, he gave me a very large dose of salts,[1] telling me that I might remain in St. Michael's that night (it being quite late), but that I must be off back to Mr. Covey's early in the morning; and that if I did not, he would get hold of me, which meant that he would whip me. I remained all night, and, according to his orders, I started off to Covey's in the morning (Saturday morning), wearied in body and broken in spirit. I got no supper that night, or breakfast that morning. I reached Covey's about nine o'clock; and just as I was getting over the fence that divided Mrs. Kemp's fields from ours, out ran Covey with his cowskin, to give me another whipping. Before he could reach me, I succeeded in getting to the cornfield; and as the corn was very high, it afforded me the means of hiding. He seemed very angry, and searched for me a long time. My behavior was altogether unaccountable. He finally gave up the chase, thinking, I suppose, that I must come home for something to eat; he would give himself no further trouble in looking for me. I spent that day mostly in the woods, having the alternative before me—to go home and be whipped to death, or stay in the woods and be starved to death. That night, I fell in with Sandy Jenkins, a slave with whom I was somewhat acquainted. Sandy had a free wife[2] who lived about four miles from Mr. Covey's; and it being Saturday, he was on his way to see her. I told him my circumstances, and he very kindly invited me to go home with him. I went home with him, and talked this whole matter over, and got his advice as to what course it was best for me to pursue. I found Sandy an old adviser. He told me, with great solemnity, I must go back to Covey; but that before I went, I must go with him into another part of the woods, where there was a certain root, which, if I would take some of it with me, carrying it always on my right side, would render it impossible for Mr. Covey, or any other white man, to whip me. He said he had carried it for years; and since he had done so, he had never received a blow, and never expected to while he carried it. I at first rejected the idea, that the simple

---

1   *large dose of salts*   I.e., smelling salts, comprising a mixture of carbonate of ammonia and other scented components, used to restore people from spells of fainting or dizziness.

2   *a free wife*   Because slavery often resulted in spouses being sold to different slaveowners, it sometimes occurred that one would be granted their freedom while the other remained enslaved.

carrying of a root in my pocket would have any such effect as he had said, and was not disposed to take it; but Sandy impressed the necessity with much earnestness, telling me it could do no harm, if it did no good. To please him, I at length took the root, and, according to his direction, carried it upon my right side. This was Sunday morning. I immediately started for home; and upon entering the yard gate, out came Mr. Covey on his way to meeting. He spoke to me very kindly, bade me drive the pigs from a lot near by, and passed on towards the church. Now, this singular conduct of Mr. Covey really made me begin to think that there was something in the root which Sandy had given me; and had it been on any other day than Sunday, I could have attributed the conduct to no other cause than the influence of that root; and as it was, I was half inclined to think the root to be something more than I at first had taken it to be. All went well till Monday morning. On this morning, the virtue of the root was fully tested. Long before daylight, I was called to go and rub, curry,[1] and feed, the horses. I obeyed, and was glad to obey. But whilst thus engaged, whilst in the act of throwing down some blades from the loft, Mr. Covey entered the stable with a long rope; and just as I was half out of the loft, he caught hold of my legs, and was about tying me. As soon as I found what he was up to, I gave a sudden spring, and as I did so, he holding to my legs, I was brought sprawling on the stable floor. Mr. Covey seemed now to think he had me, and could do what he pleased; but at this moment—from whence came the spirit I don't know—I resolved to fight; and, suiting my action to the resolution, I seized Covey hard by the throat; and as I did so, I rose. He held on to me, and I to him. My resistance was so entirely unexpected that Covey seemed taken all aback. He trembled like a leaf. This gave me assurance, and I held him uneasy, causing the blood to run where I touched him with the ends of my fingers. Mr. Covey soon called out to Hughes for help. Hughes came, and, while Covey held me, attempted to tie my right hand. While he was in the act of doing so, I watched my chance, and gave him a heavy kick close under the ribs. This kick fairly sickened Hughes, so that he left me in the hands of Mr. Covey. This kick had the effect of not only weakening Hughes, but Covey also. When he saw Hughes bending over with pain, his courage quailed. He asked me if I meant to persist in my resistance. I told him I did, come what might; that he had used me like a brute for six months, and that I was determined to be used so no longer. With that, he strove to drag me to a stick that was lying just out of the stable door. He meant to knock me down. But just as he was leaning over to get the stick, I seized him with both hands by his collar, and brought him by a sudden snatch to the ground. By this time, Bill came. Covey called upon him for assistance. Bill wanted to know what he

---

1   *curry* Brush.

could do. Covey said, "Take hold of him, take hold of him!" Bill said his master hired him out to work, and not to help to whip me; so he left Covey and myself to fight our own battle out. We were at it for nearly two hours. Covey at length let me go, puffing and blowing at a great rate, saying that if I had not resisted, he would not have whipped me half so much. The truth was, that he had not whipped me at all. I considered him as getting entirely the worst end of the bargain; for he had drawn no blood from me, but I had from him. The whole six months afterwards, that I spent with Mr. Covey, he never laid the weight of his finger upon me in anger. He would occasionally say, he didn't want to get hold of me again. "No," thought I, "you need not; for you will come off worse than you did before."

This battle with Mr. Covey was the turning-point in my career as a slave. It rekindled the few expiring embers of freedom, and revived within me a sense of my own manhood. It recalled the departed self-confidence, and inspired me again with a determination to be free. The gratification afforded by the triumph was a full compensation for whatever else might follow, even death itself. He only can understand the deep satisfaction which I experienced, who has himself repelled by force the bloody arm of slavery. I felt as I never felt before. It was a glorious resurrection, from the tomb of slavery, to the heaven of freedom. My long-crushed spirit rose, cowardice departed, bold defiance took its place; and I now resolved that, however long I might remain a slave in form, the day had passed forever when I could be a slave in fact. I did not hesitate to let it be known of me, that the white man who expected to succeed in whipping, must also succeed in killing me.

From this time I was never again what might be called fairly whipped, though I remained a slave four years afterwards. I had several fights, but was never whipped.

It was for a long time a matter of surprise to me why Mr. Covey did not immediately have me taken by the constable to the whipping-post, and there regularly whipped for the crime of raising my hand against a white man in defence of myself. And the only explanation I can now think of does not entirely satisfy me; but such as it is, I will give it. Mr. Covey enjoyed the most unbounded reputation for being a first-rate overseer and negro-breaker. It was of considerable importance to him. That reputation was at stake; and had he sent me—a boy about sixteen years old—to the public whipping-post, his reputation would have been lost; so, to save his reputation, he suffered me to go unpunished.

My term of actual service to Mr. Edward Covey ended on Christmas day, 1833. The days between Christmas and New Year's Day are allowed as holidays; and, accordingly, we were not required to perform any labor, more than to feed and take care of the stock. This time we regarded as our own, by the grace of our masters; and we therefore used or abused it nearly as we pleased. Those of us who had families at a distance, were generally allowed to spend the whole six days in their society. This time, however, was spent in various ways. The staid, sober, thinking and industrious ones of our number would employ themselves in making corn-brooms, mats, horse-collars, and baskets; and another class of us would spend the time in hunting opossums, hares, and coons. But by far the larger part engaged in such sports and merriments as playing ball, wrestling, running foot-races, fiddling, dancing, and drinking whisky; and this latter mode of spending the time was by far the most agreeable to the feelings of our masters. A slave who would work during the holidays was considered by our masters as scarcely deserving them. He was regarded as one who rejected the favor of his master. It was deemed a disgrace not to get drunk at Christmas; and he was regarded as lazy indeed, who had not provided himself with the necessary means, during the year, to get whisky enough to last him through Christmas.

From what I know of the effect of these holidays upon the slave, I believe them to be among the most effective means in the hands of the slaveholder in keeping down the spirit of insurrection. Were the slaveholders at once to abandon this practice, I have not the slightest doubt it would lead to an immediate insurrection among the slaves. These holidays serve as conductors, or safety-valves, to carry off the rebellious spirit of enslaved humanity. But for these, the slave would be forced up to the wildest desperation; and woe betide the slaveholder, the day he ventures to remove or hinder the operation of those conductors! I warn him that, in such an event, a spirit will go forth in their midst, more to be dreaded than the most appalling earthquake.

The holidays are part and parcel of the gross fraud, wrong, and inhumanity of slavery. They are professedly a custom established by the benevolence of the slaveholders; but I undertake to say, it is the result of selfishness, and one of the grossest frauds committed upon the down-trodden slave. They do not give the slaves this time because they would not like to have their work during its continuance, but because they know it would be unsafe to deprive them of it. This will be seen by the fact, that the slaveholders like to have their slaves spend those days just in such a manner as to make them as glad of their ending as of their beginning. Their object seems to be, to disgust their slaves with freedom, by plunging them into the lowest depths of dissipation. For instance, the slaveholders not only like to see the slave drink of his own accord, but will adopt various plans to make him drunk. One plan is, to make bets on their slaves, as to who can drink the most whisky without getting drunk; and in this way they succeed in getting whole multitudes to drink to excess. Thus, when the slave asks for virtuous freedom, the cunning slaveholder, knowing his ignorance, cheats him with a dose of vicious dissipation, artfully labelled with the name of liberty. The most of us used to drink it down, and the result was just what might be supposed; many of us were led to think that there was little to choose between liberty and slavery. We felt, and very properly too, that we had almost as well be slaves to man as to rum. So, when the holidays ended, we staggered up from the filth of our wallowing, took a long breath, and marched to the field—feeling, upon the whole, rather glad to go, from what our master had deceived us into a belief was freedom, back to the arms of slavery.

I have said that this mode of treatment is a part of the whole system of fraud and inhumanity of slavery. It is so. The mode here adopted to disgust the slave with freedom, by allowing him to see only the abuse of it, is carried out in other things. For instance, a slave loves molasses; he steals some. His master, in many cases, goes off to town, and buys a large quantity; he returns, takes his whip, and commands the slave to eat the molasses, until the poor fellow is made sick at the very mention of it. The same mode is sometimes adopted to make the slaves refrain from asking for more food than their regular allow- . ance. A slave runs through his allowance, and applies for more. His master is enraged at him; but, not willing to send him off without food, gives him more than is necessary, and compels him to eat it within a given time. Then, if he complains that he cannot eat it, he is said to be satisfied neither full nor fasting, and is whipped for being hard to please! I have an abundance of such illustrations of the same principle, drawn from my own observation, but think the cases I have cited sufficient. The practice is a very common one.

On the first of January, 1834, I left Mr. Covey, and went to live with Mr. William Freeland, who lived about three miles from St. Michael's. I soon found Mr. Freeland a very different man from Mr. Covey. Though not rich, he was what would be called an educated southern gentleman. Mr. Covey, as I have shown, was a well-trained negro-breaker and slave-driver. The former (slaveholder though he was) seemed to possess some regard for honor, some reverence for justice, and some respect for humanity. The latter seemed totally insensible to all such sentiments. Mr. Freeland had many of the faults peculiar to slaveholders, such as being very passionate and fretful; but I must do him the justice to say, that he was exceedingly free from those degrading vices to which Mr. Covey was constantly addicted. The one was open and frank, and we always knew where to find him. The other was a most artful deceiver, and could be understood only by such as were skilful enough to detect his cunningly-devised frauds. Another advantage I gained in my new master was, he made no pretensions to, or profession of, religion; and this, in my opinion, was truly a great advantage. I assert most unhesitatingly, that the religion of the south is a mere covering for the most horrid crimes—a justifier of the most appalling barbarity—a sanctifier of the most hateful frauds—and a dark shelter under, which the darkest, foulest, grossest, and most infernal deeds of slaveholders find the strongest protection. Were I to be again reduced to the chains of slavery, next to that enslavement, I should regard being the slave of a religious master the greatest calamity that could befall me. For of all slaveholders with whom I have ever met, religious slaveholders are the worst. I have ever found them the meanest and basest, the most cruel and cowardly, of all others. It was my unhappy lot not only to belong to a religious slaveholder, but to live in a community of such religionists. Very near Mr. Freeland lived the Rev. Daniel Weeden, and in the same neighborhood lived the Rev. Rigby Hopkins. These were members and ministers in the Reformed Methodist Church. Mr. Weeden owned, among others, a woman slave, whose name I have forgotten. This woman's back, for weeks, was kept literally raw, made so by the lash of this merciless, religious wretch. He used to hire hands. His maxim was, Behave well or behave ill, it is the duty of a master occasionally to whip a slave, to remind him of his master's authority. Such was his theory, and such his practice.

Mr. Hopkins was even worse than Mr. Weeden. His chief boast was his ability to manage slaves. The peculiar feature of his government was that of whipping slaves in advance of deserving it. He always managed to have one or more of his slaves to whip every Monday morning. He did this to alarm their fears, and strike terror into those who escaped. His plan was to whip for the smallest offences, to prevent the commission of large ones. Mr. Hopkins could always find some excuse for whipping a slave. It would astonish one, unaccustomed to a slaveholding life, to see with what wonderful ease a slaveholder can find things, of which to make occasion to whip a slave. A mere look, word, or motion—a mistake, accident, or want of power—are all matters for which a slave may be whipped at any time. Does a slave look dissatisfied? It is said, he has the devil in him, and it must be whipped out. Does he speak loudly when spoken to by his master? Then he is getting high-minded, and should be taken down a button-hole lower. Does he forget to pull off his hat at the approach of a white person? Then he is wanting in reverence, and should be whipped for it. Does he ever venture to vindicate his conduct, when censured for it? Then he is guilty of impudence—one of the greatest crimes of which a slave can be guilty. Does he ever venture to suggest a different mode of doing things from that pointed out by his master? He is indeed presumptuous, and getting above himself; and nothing less than a flogging will do for him. Does he, while ploughing, break a plough—or, while hoeing, break a hoe? It is owing to his carelessness, and for it a slave must always be whipped. Mr. Hopkins could always find something of this sort to justify the use of the lash, and he seldom failed to embrace such opportunities. There was not a man in the whole county, with whom the slaves who had the getting their own home, would not prefer to live, rather than with this Rev. Mr. Hopkins. And yet there was not a man anywhere round, who made higher professions of religion, or was more active in revivals—more attentive to the class, love-feast, prayer and preaching meetings, or more devotional in his family—that prayed earlier, later, louder, and longer—than this same reverend slave-driver, Rigby Hopkins.

But to return to Mr. Freeland, and to my experience while in his employment. He, like Mr. Covey, gave us enough to eat; but, unlike Mr. Covey, he also gave us sufficient time to take our meals. He worked us hard, but always between sunrise and sunset. He required a good deal of work to be done, but gave us good tools with which to work. His farm was large, but he employed hands enough to work it, and with ease, compared with many of his neighbors. My treatment, while in his employment, was heavenly, compared with what I experienced at the hands of Mr. Edward Covey.

Mr. Freeland was himself the owner of but two slaves. Their names were Henry Harris and John Harris. The rest of his hands he hired. These consisted of myself, Sandy Jenkins,[1] and Handy Caldwell. Henry and John were quite intelligent, and in a very little while after I went there, I succeeded in creating in them a strong desire to learn how to read. This desire soon sprang up in the others also. They very soon mustered up some old spelling-books, and nothing would do but that I must keep a Sabbath school. I agreed to do so, and accordingly devoted my Sundays to teaching these my loved fellow-slaves how to read. Neither of them knew his letters when I went there. Some of the slaves of the neighboring farms found what was going on, and also availed themselves of this little opportunity to learn to read. It was understood, among all who came, that there must be as little display about it as possible. It was necessary to keep our religious masters at St. Michael's unacquainted with the fact, that, instead of spending the Sabbath in wrestling, boxing, and drinking whisky, we were trying to learn how to read the will of God; for they had much rather see us engaged in those degrading sports, than to see us behaving like intellectual, moral, and accountable beings. My blood boils as I think of the bloody manner in which Messrs. Wright Fairbanks and Garrison West, both class-leaders, in connection with many others, rushed in upon us with sticks and stones, and broke up our virtuous little Sabbath school, at St. Michael's—all calling themselves Christians! humble followers of the Lord Jesus Christ! But I am again digressing.

---

1   [Douglass's note]   This is the same man who gave me the roots to prevent my being whipped by Mr. Covey. He was "a clever soul." We used frequently to talk about the fight with Covey, and as often as we did so, he would claim my success as the result of the roots which he gave me. This superstition is very common among the more ignorant slaves. A slave seldom dies but that his death is attributed to trickery.

I held my Sabbath school at the house of a free colored man, whose name I deem it imprudent to mention; for should it be known, it might embarrass him greatly, though the crime of holding the school was committed ten years ago. I had at one time over forty scholars, and those of the right sort, ardently desiring to learn. They were of all ages, though mostly men and women. I look back to those Sundays with an amount of pleasure not to be expressed. They were great days to my soul. The work of instructing my dear fellow-slaves was the sweetest engagement with which I was ever blessed. We loved each other, and to leave them at the close of the Sabbath was a severe cross indeed. When I think that these precious souls are today shut up in the prison-house of slavery, my feelings overcome me, and I am almost ready to ask, "Does a righteous God govern the universe? and for what does he hold the thunders in his right hand, if not to smite the oppressor, and deliver the spoiled out of the hand of the spoiler?"[1] These dear souls came not to Sabbath school because it was popular to do so, nor did I teach them because it was reputable to be thus engaged. Every moment they spent in that school, they were liable to be taken up, and given thirty-nine lashes. They came because they wished to learn. Their minds had been starved by their cruel masters. They had been shut up in mental darkness. I taught them, because it was the delight of my soul to be doing something that looked like bettering the condition of my race. I kept up my school nearly the whole year I lived with Mr. Freeland; and, beside my Sabbath school, I devoted three evenings in the week, during the winter, to teaching the slaves at home. And I have the happiness to know, that several of those who came to Sabbath school learned how to read; and that one, at least, is now free through my agency.

The year passed off smoothly. It seemed only about half as long as the year which preceded it. I went through it without receiving a single blow. I will give Mr. Freeland the credit of being the best master I ever had, till I became my own master. For the ease with which I passed the year, I was, however, somewhat indebted to the society of my fellow-slaves. They were noble souls; they not only possessed loving hearts, but brave ones. We were linked and interlinked with each other. I loved them with a love stronger than anything I have experienced since. It is sometimes said that we slaves do not love and confide in each other. In answer to this assertion, I can say, I never loved any or confided in any people more than my fellow-slaves, and especially those with whom I lived at Mr. Freeland's. I believe we would have died for each other. We never undertook to do anything, of any importance, without a mutual consultation. We never moved separately. We were one; and as much so by

---

1 *Does a righteous ... the spoiler* These lines contain allusions to several biblical passages, including Exodus 15 and Isaiah 33.1.

our tempers and dispositions, as by the mutual hardships to which we were necessarily subjected by our condition as slaves.

At the close of the year 1834, Mr. Freeland again hired me of my master, for the year 1835. But, by this time, I began to want to live upon free land as well as with Freeland; and I was no longer content, therefore, to live with him or any other slaveholder. I began, with the commencement of the year, to prepare myself for a final struggle, which should decide my fate one way or the other. My tendency was upward. I was fast approaching manhood, and year after year had passed, and I was still a slave. These thoughts roused me—I must do something. I therefore resolved that 1835 should not pass without witnessing an attempt, on my part, to secure my liberty. But I was not willing to cherish this determination alone. My fellow-slaves were dear to me. I was anxious to have them participate with me in this, my life-giving determination. I therefore, though with great prudence, commenced early to ascertain their views and feelings in regard to their condition, and to imbue their minds with thoughts of freedom. I bent myself to devising ways and means for our escape, and meanwhile strove, on all fitting occasions, to impress them with the gross fraud and inhumanity of slavery. I went first to Henry, next to John, then to the others. I found, in them all, warm hearts and noble spirits. They were ready to hear, and ready to act when a feasible plan should be proposed. This was what I wanted. I talked to them of our want of manhood, if we submitted to our enslavement without at least one noble effort to be free. We met often, and consulted frequently, and told our hopes and fears, recounted the difficulties, real and imagined, which we should be called on to meet. At times we were almost disposed to give up, and try to content ourselves with our wretched lot; at others, we were firm and unbending in our determination to go. Whenever we suggested any plan, there was shrinking—the odds were fearful. Our path was beset with the greatest obstacles; and if we succeeded in gaining the end of it, our right to be free was yet questionable—we were yet liable to be returned to bondage. We could see no spot, this side of the ocean, where we could be free. We knew nothing about Canada. Our knowledge of the north did not extend farther than New York; and to go there, and be forever harassed with the frightful liability of being returned to slavery—with the certainty of being treated tenfold worse than before—the thought was truly a horrible one, and one which it was not easy to overcome. The case sometimes stood thus: At every gate through which we were to pass, we saw a watchman—at every ferry a guard—on every bridge a sentinel—and in every wood a patrol. We were hemmed in upon every side. Here were the difficulties, real or imagined—the good to be sought, and the evil to be shunned. On the one hand, there stood slavery, a stern reality, glaring frightfully upon us—its robes already crimsoned with the blood of millions, and even now feasting itself greedily upon our own flesh. On the other hand, away back in the dim distance, under the flickering light of the north star, behind some craggy hill or snow-covered mountain, stood a doubtful freedom—half frozen—beckoning us to come and share its hospitality. This in itself was sometimes enough to stagger us; but when we permitted ourselves to survey the road, we were frequently appalled. Upon either side we saw grim death, assuming the most horrid shapes. Now it was starvation, causing us to eat our own flesh; now we were contending with the waves, and were drowned; now we were overtaken, and torn to pieces by the fangs of the terrible bloodhound. We were stung by scorpions, chased by wild beasts, bitten by snakes, and finally, after having nearly reached the desired spot—after swimming rivers, encountering wild beasts, sleeping in the woods, suffering hunger and nakedness—we were overtaken by our pursuers, and, in our resistance, we were shot dead upon the spot! I say, this picture sometimes appalled us, and made us

> rather bear those ills we had,
> Than fly to others, that we knew not of.[1]

In coming to a fixed determination to run away, we did more than Patrick Henry, when he resolved upon liberty or death. With us it was a doubtful liberty at most, and almost certain death if we failed. For my part, I should prefer death to hopeless bondage.

Sandy, one of our number, gave up the notion, but still encouraged us. Our company then consisted of Henry Harris, John Harris, Henry Bailey, Charles Roberts, and myself. Henry Bailey was my uncle, and belonged to my master. Charles married my aunt: he belonged to my master's father-in-law, Mr. William Hamilton.

The plan we finally concluded upon was, to get a large canoe belonging to Mr. Hamilton, and upon the Saturday night previous to Easter holidays, paddle directly up the Chesapeake Bay. On our arrival at the head of the bay, a distance of seventy or eighty miles from where we lived, it was our purpose to turn our canoe adrift, and follow the guidance of the north star till we got beyond the limits of Maryland. Our reason for taking the water route was, that we were less liable to be suspected as runaways; we hoped to be regarded as fishermen; whereas, if we should take the land route, we should be subjected to interruptions of almost every kind. Anyone having a white face, and being so disposed, could stop us, and subject us to examination.

The week before our intended start, I wrote several protections, one for each of us. As well as I can remember, they were in the following words, to wit:

---

1 *rather bear ... knew not of* See Shakespeare's *Hamlet* 3.1.89–90.

This is to certify that I, the undersigned, have given the bearer, my servant, full liberty to go to Baltimore, and spend the Easter holidays. Written with mine own hand, &c., 1835.
WILLIAM HAMILTON,
   Near St. Michael's, in Talbot county, Maryland

We were not going to Baltimore; but, in going up the bay, we went toward Baltimore, and these protections were only intended to protect us while on the bay.

As the time drew near for our departure, our anxiety became more and more intense. It was truly a matter of life and death with us. The strength of our determination was about to be fully tested. At this time, I was very active in explaining every difficulty, removing every doubt, dispelling every fear, and inspiring all with the firmness indispensable to success in our undertaking; assuring them that half was gained the instant we made the move; we had talked long enough; we were now ready to move; if not now, we never should be; and if we did not intend to move now, we had as well fold our arms, sit down, and acknowledge ourselves fit only to be slaves. This, none of us were prepared to acknowledge. Every man stood firm; and at our last meeting, we pledged ourselves afresh, in the most solemn manner, that, at the time appointed, we would certainly start in pursuit of freedom. This was in the middle of the week, at the end of which we were to be off. We went, as usual, to our several fields of labor, but with bosoms highly agitated with thoughts of our truly hazardous undertaking. We tried to conceal our feelings as much as possible; and I think we succeeded very well.

After a painful waiting, the Saturday morning, whose night was to witness our departure, came. I hailed it with joy, bring what of sadness it might. Friday night was a sleepless one for me. I probably felt more anxious than the rest, because I was, by common consent, at the head of the whole affair. The responsibility of success or failure lay heavily upon me. The glory of the one, and the confusion of the other, were alike mine. The first two hours of that morning were such as I never experienced before, and hope never to again. Early in the morning, we went, as usual, to the field. We were spreading manure; and all at once, while thus engaged, I was overwhelmed with an indescribable feeling, in the fulness of which I turned to Sandy, who was near by, and said, "We are betrayed!" "Well," said he, "that thought has this moment struck me." We said no more. I was never more certain of anything.

The horn was blown as usual, and we went up from the field to the house for breakfast. I went for the form, more than for want of anything to eat that morning. Just as I got to the house, in looking out at the lane gate, I saw four white men, with two colored men. The white men were on horseback, and the colored ones were walking behind, as if tied. I watched them a few moments till they got up to our lane gate. Here they halted, and tied the colored men to the gate-post. I was not yet certain as to what the matter was. In a few moments, in rode Mr. Hamilton, with a speed betokening great excitement. He came to the door, and inquired if Master William was in. He was told he was at the barn. Mr. Hamilton, without dismounting, rode up to the barn with extraordinary speed. In a few moments, he and Mr. Freeland returned to the house. By this time, the three constables rode up, and in great haste dismounted, tied their horses, and met Master William and Mr. Hamilton returning from the barn; and after talking awhile, they all walked up to the kitchen door. There was no one in the kitchen but myself and John. Henry and Sandy were up at the barn. Mr. Freeland put his head in at the door, and called me by name, saying, there were some gentlemen at the door who wished to see me. I stepped to the door, and inquired what they wanted. They at once seized me, and, without giving me any satisfaction, tied me—lashing my hands closely together. I insisted upon knowing what the matter was. They at length said, that they had learned I had been in a "scrape," and that I was to be examined before my master; and if their information proved false, I should not be hurt.

In a few moments, they succeeded in tying John. They then turned to Henry, who had by this time returned, and commanded him to cross his hands. "I won't!" said Henry, in a firm tone, indicating his readiness to meet the consequences of his refusal. "Won't you?" said Tom Graham, the constable. "No, I won't!" said Henry, in a still stronger tone. With this, two of the constables pulled out their shining pistols, and swore, by their Creator, that they would make him cross his hands or kill him. Each cocked his pistol, and, with fingers on the trigger, walked up to Henry, saying, at the same time, if he did not cross his hands, they would blow his damned heart out. "Shoot me, shoot me!" said Henry; "you can't kill me but once. Shoot, shoot—and be damned! I won't be tied!" This he said in a tone of loud defiance; and at the same time, with a motion as quick as lightning, he with one single stroke dashed the pistols from the hand of each constable. As he did this, all hands fell upon him, and, after beating him some time, they finally overpowered him, and got him tied.

During the scuffle, I managed, I know not how, to get my pass out, and, without being discovered, put it into the fire. We were all now tied; and just as we were to leave for Easton jail, Betsy Freeland, mother of William Freeland, came to the door with her hands full of biscuits, and divided them between Henry and John. She then delivered herself of a speech, to the following effect: addressing herself to me, she said, "You devil! You yellow devil! it was you that put it into the heads of Henry and John to run away. But for you, you long-legged mulatto devil! Henry nor John would never have thought of such a thing." I made no reply, and was immediately hurried off towards St. Michael's. Just a moment previous to the scuffle with Henry, Mr. Hamilton suggested the propriety of making a search for the protections which he had understood Frederick had written for himself and the rest. But, just at the moment he was about carrying his proposal into effect, his aid was needed in helping to tie Henry; and the excitement attending the scuffle caused them either to forget, or to deem it unsafe, under the circumstances, to search. So we were not yet convicted of the intention to run away.

When we got about half way to St. Michael's, while the constables having us in charge were looking ahead, Henry inquired of me what he should do with his pass. I told him to eat it with his biscuit, and own nothing; and we passed the word around, "Own nothing"; and "Own nothing!" said we all. Our confidence in each other was unshaken. We were resolved to succeed or fail together, after the calamity had befallen us as much as before. We were now prepared for anything. We were to be dragged that morning fifteen miles behind horses, and then to be placed in the Easton jail. When we reached St. Michael's, we underwent a sort of examination. We all denied that we ever intended to run away. We did this more to bring out the evidence against us, than from any hope of getting clear of being sold; for, as I have said, we were ready for that. The fact was, we cared but little where we went, so we went together. Our greatest concern was about separation. We dreaded that more than anything this side of death. We found the evidence against us to be the testimony of one person; our master would not tell who it was; but we came to a unanimous decision among ourselves as to who their informant was. We were sent off to the jail at Easton. When we got there, we were delivered up to the sheriff, Mr. Joseph Graham, and by him placed in jail. Henry, John, and myself, were placed in one room together—Charles, and Henry Bailey, in another. Their object in separating us was to hinder concert.

We had been in jail scarcely twenty minutes, when a swarm of slave traders, and agents for slave traders, flocked into jail to look at us, and to ascertain if we were for sale. Such a set of beings I never saw before! I felt myself surrounded by so many fiends from perdition.[1] A band of pirates never looked more like their father, the devil. They laughed and grinned over us, saying, "Ah, my boys! we have got you, haven't we?" And after taunting us in various ways, they one by one went into an examination of us, with intent to ascertain our value. They would impudently ask us if we would not like to have them for our masters. We would make them no answer, and leave them to find out as best they could. Then they would curse and swear at us, telling us that they could take the devil out of us in a very little while, if we were only in their hands.

---

1   *perdition* Hell.

While in jail, we found ourselves in much more comfortable quarters than we expected when we went there. We did not get much to eat, nor that which was very good; but we had a good clean room, from the windows of which we could see what was going on in the street, which was very much better than though we had been placed in one of the dark, damp cells. Upon the whole, we got along very well, so far as the jail and its keeper were concerned. Immediately after the holidays were over, contrary to all our expectations, Mr. Hamilton and Mr. Freeland came up to Easton, and took Charles, the two Henrys, and John, out of jail, and carried them home, leaving me alone. I regarded this separation as a final one. It caused me more pain than anything else in the whole transaction. I was ready for anything rather than separation. I supposed that they had consulted together, and had decided that, as I was the whole cause of the intention of the others to run away, it was hard to make the innocent suffer with the guilty; and that they had, therefore, concluded to take the others home, and sell me, as a warning to the others that remained. It is due to the noble Henry to say, he seemed almost as reluctant at leaving the prison as at leaving home to come to the prison. But we knew we should, in all probability, be separated, if we were sold; and since he was in their hands, he concluded to go peaceably home.

I was now left to my fate. I was all alone, and within the walls of a stone prison. But a few days before, and I was full of hope. I expected to have been safe in a land of freedom; but now I was covered with gloom, sunk down to the utmost despair. I thought the possibility of freedom was gone. I was kept in this way about one week, at the end of which, Captain Auld, my master, to my surprise and utter astonishment, came up, and took me out, with the intention of sending me, with a gentleman of his acquaintance, into Alabama. But, from some cause or other, he did not send me to Alabama, but concluded to send me back to Baltimore, to live again with his brother Hugh, and to learn a trade.

Thus, after an absence of three years and one month, I was once more permitted to return to my old home at Baltimore. My master sent me away, because there existed against me a very great prejudice in the community, and he feared I might be killed.

In a few weeks after I went to Baltimore, Master Hugh hired me to Mr. William Gardner, an extensive ship-builder, on Fells Point. I was put there to learn how to caulk.[1] It, however, proved a very unfavorable place for the accomplishment of this object. Mr. Gardner was engaged that spring in building two large man-of-war brigs, professedly for the Mexican government. The vessels were to be launched in the July of that year, and in failure

---

1   *caulk*   Seal the wooden seams of a boat against leakage with oakum and melted tar.

thereof, Mr. Gardner was to lose a considerable sum; so that when I entered, all was hurry. There was no time to learn anything. Every man had to do that which he knew how to do. In entering the shipyard, my orders from Mr. Gardner were, to do whatever the carpenters commanded me to do. This was placing me at the beck and call of about seventy-five men. I was to regard all these as masters. Their word was to be my law. My situation was a most trying one. At times I needed a dozen pair of hands. I was called a dozen ways in the space of a single minute. Three or four voices would strike my ear at the same moment. It was—"Fred., come help me to cant[1] this timber here."—"Fred., come carry this timber yonder."—"Fred., bring that roller here."—"Fred., go get a fresh can of water."—"Fred., come help saw off the end of this timber."—"Fred., go quick, and get the crowbar."—"Fred., hold on the end of this fall."[2]—"Fred., go to the blacksmith's shop, and get a new punch."—"Hurra, Fred! run and bring me a cold chisel."—"I say, Fred., bear a hand, and get up a fire as quick as lightning under that steam-box."—"Halloo, nigger! come, turn this grindstone."—"Come, come! move, move! and bowse[3] this timber forward."—"I say, darky, blast your eyes, why don't you heat up some pitch?"—"Halloo! halloo! halloo!" (Three voices at the same time.) "Come here!—Go there!—Hold on where you are! Damn you, if you move, I'll knock your brains out!"

This was my school for eight months; and I might have remained there longer, but for a most horrid fight I had with four of the white apprentices, in which my left eye was nearly knocked out, and I was horribly mangled in other respects. The facts in the case were these: Until a very little while after I went there, white and black ship-carpenters worked side by side, and no one seemed to see any impropriety in it. All hands seemed to be very well satisfied. Many of the black carpenters were freemen. Things seemed to be going on very well. All at once, the white carpenters knocked off, and said they would not work with free colored workmen. Their reason for this, as alleged, was, that if free colored carpenters were encouraged, they would soon take the trade into their own hands, and poor white men would be thrown out of employment. They therefore felt called upon at once to put a stop to it. And, taking advantage of Mr. Gardner's necessities, they broke off, swearing they would work no longer, unless he would discharge his black carpenters. Now, though this did not extend to me in form, it did reach me in fact. My fellow-apprentices very soon began to feel it degrading to them to work with me. They began to put on airs, and talk about the "niggers" taking the country,

---

1 *cant* Smoothen a sharp angle.
2 *fall* Free end of a rope used for hauling.
3 *bowse* Haul.

saying we all ought to be killed; and, being encouraged by the journeymen, they commenced making my condition as hard as they could, by hectoring me around, and sometimes striking me. I, of course, kept the vow I made after the fight with Mr. Covey, and struck back again, regardless of consequences; and while I kept them from combining, I succeeded very well; for I could whip the whole of them, taking them separately. They, however, at length combined, and came upon me, armed with sticks, stones, and heavy handspikes. One came in front with a half brick. There was one at each side of me, and one behind me. While I was attending to those in front, and on either side, the one behind ran up with the handspike, and struck me a heavy blow upon the head. It stunned me. I fell, and with this they all ran upon me, and fell to beating me with their fists. I let them lay on for a while, gathering strength. In an instant, I gave a sudden surge, and rose to my hands and knees. Just as I did that, one of their number gave me, with his heavy boot, a powerful kick in the left eye. My eyeball seemed to have burst. When they saw my eye closed, and badly swollen, they left me. With this I seized the handspike, and for a time pursued them. But here the carpenters interfered, and I thought I might as well give it up. It was impossible to stand my hand against so many. All this took place in sight of not less than fifty white ship-carpenters, and not one interposed a friendly word; but some cried, "Kill the damned nigger! Kill him! kill him! He struck a white person." I found my only chance for life was in flight. I succeeded in getting away without an additional blow, and barely so; for to strike a white man is death by Lynch law[1]—and that was the law in Mr. Gardner's shipyard; nor is there much of any other out of Mr. Gardner's shipyard.

I went directly home, and told the story of my wrongs to Master Hugh; and I am happy to say of him, irreligious as he was, his conduct was heavenly, compared with that of his brother Thomas under similar circumstances. He listened attentively to my narration of the circumstances leading to the savage outrage, and gave many proofs of his strong indignation at it. The heart of my once overkind mistress was again melted into pity. My puffed-out eye and blood-covered face moved her to tears. She took a chair by me, washed the blood from my face, and, with a mother's tenderness, bound up my head, covering the wounded eye with a lean piece of fresh beef. It was almost compensation for my suffering to witness, once more, a manifestation of kindness from this, my once affectionate old mistress. Master Hugh was very much enraged. He gave expression to his feelings by pouring out curses upon the heads of

---

1   *is death by Lynch law*   Will lead inevitably to being lynched (i.e., killed by a vigilante mob falsely claiming to be administering justice). Though some lynchings targeted Jews and other minorities, the vast majority were racially motivated murders of black persons by white mobs; the practice became increasingly widespread following the end of Reconstruction in 1877, and remained common throughout the early decades of the twentieth century, during the Jim Crow era of segregation.

those who did the deed. As soon as I got a little the better of my bruises, he took me with him to Esquire Watson's, on Bond Street, to see what could be done about the matter. Mr. Watson inquired who saw the assault committed. Master Hugh told him it was done in Mr. Gardner's ship-yard at midday, where there were a large company of men at work. "As to that," he said, "the deed was done, and there was no question as to who did it." His answer was, he could do nothing in the case, unless some white man would come forward and testify. He could issue no warrant on my word. If I had been killed in the presence of a thousand colored people, their testimony combined would have been insufficient to have arrested one of the murderers. Master Hugh, for once, was compelled to say this state of things was too bad. Of course, it was impossible to get any white man to volunteer his testimony in my behalf, and against the white young men. Even those who may have sympathized with me were not prepared to do this. It required a degree of courage unknown to them to do so; for just at that time, the slightest manifestation of humanity toward a colored person was denounced as abolitionism, and that name subjected its bearer to frightful liabilities. The watchwords of the bloody-minded in that region, and in those days, were, "Damn the abolitionists!" and "Damn the niggers!" There was nothing done, and probably nothing would have been done if I had been killed. Such was, and such remains, the state of things in the Christian city of Baltimore.

Master Hugh, finding he could get no redress, refused to let me go back again to Mr. Gardner. He kept me himself, and his wife dressed my wound till I was again restored to health. He then took me into the ship-yard of which he was foreman, in the employment of Mr. Walter Price. There I was immediately set to calking, and very soon learned the art of using my mallet and irons. In the course of one year from the time I left Mr. Gardner's, I was able to command the highest wages given to the most experienced caulkers. I was now of some importance to my master. I was bringing him from six to seven dollars per week. I sometimes brought him nine dollars per week: my wages were a dollar and a half a day. After learning how to caulk, I sought my own employment, made my own contracts, and collected the money which I earned. My pathway became much more smooth than before; my condition was now much more comfortable. When I could get no calking to do, I did nothing. During these leisure times, those old notions about freedom would steal over me again. When in Mr. Gardner's employment, I was kept in such a perpetual whirl of excitement, I could think of nothing, scarcely, but my life; and in thinking of my life, I almost forgot my liberty. I have observed this in my experience of slavery—that whenever my condition was improved, instead of its increasing my contentment, it only increased my desire to be free, and set me to thinking of plans to gain my freedom. I have found that, to make a contented slave, it is necessary to make a thoughtless one. It is necessary to darken his moral and mental vision, and, as far as possible, to annihilate the power of reason. He must be able to detect no inconsistencies in slavery; he must be made to feel that slavery is right; and he can be brought to that only when he ceases to be a man.

I was now getting, as I have said, one dollar and fifty cents per day. I contracted for it; I earned it; it was paid to me; it was rightfully my own; yet, upon each returning Saturday night, I was compelled to deliver every cent of that money to Master Hugh. And why? Not because he earned it—not because he had any hand in earning it—not because I owed it to him—nor because he possessed the slightest shadow of a right to it; but solely because he had the power to compel me to give it up. The right of the grim-visaged pirate upon the high seas is exactly the same.

CHAPTER II

I now come to that part of my life during which I planned, and finally succeeded in making, my escape from slavery. But before narrating any of the peculiar circumstances, I deem it proper to make known my intention not to state all the facts connected with the transaction. My reasons for pursuing this course may be understood from the following: First, were I to give a minute statement of all the facts, it is not only possible, but quite probable, that others would thereby be involved in the most embarrassing difficulties. Secondly, such a statement would most undoubtedly induce greater vigilance on the part of slaveholders than has existed heretofore among them; which would, of course, be the means of guarding a door whereby some dear brother bondsman might escape his galling chains. I deeply regret the necessity that impels me to suppress anything of importance connected with my experience in slavery. It would afford me great pleasure indeed, as well as materially add to the interest of my narrative, were I at liberty to gratify a curiosity, which I know exists in the minds of many, by an accurate statement of all the facts pertaining to my most fortunate escape. But I must deprive myself of this pleasure, and the curious of the gratification which such a statement would afford. I would allow myself to suffer under the greatest imputations which evil-minded men might suggest, rather than exculpate myself, and thereby run the hazard of closing the slightest avenue by which a brother slave might clear himself of the chains and fetters of slavery.

I have never approved of the very public manner in which some of our western friends have conducted what they call the underground railroad,[1] but

---

1   *underground railroad*   Secret network of people and safe-houses by means of which many enslaved persons escaped to the North.

which I think, by their open declarations, has been made most emphatically the upper-ground railroad. I honor those good men and women for their noble daring, and applaud them for willingly subjecting themselves to bloody persecution, by openly avowing their participation in the escape of slaves. I, however, can see very little good resulting from such a course, either to themselves or the slaves escaping; while, upon the other hand, I see and feel assured that those open declarations are a positive evil to the slaves remaining, who are seeking to escape. They do nothing towards enlightening the slave, whilst they do much towards enlightening the master. They stimulate him to greater watchfulness, and enhance his power to capture his slave. We owe something to the slave south of the line as well as to those north of it; and in aiding the latter on their way to freedom, we should be careful to do nothing which would be likely to hinder the former from escaping from slavery. I would keep the merciless slaveholder profoundly ignorant of the means of flight adopted by the slave. I would leave him to imagine himself surrounded by myriads of invisible tormentors, ever ready to snatch from his infernal grasp his trembling prey. Let him be left to feel his way in the dark; let darkness commensurate with his crime hover over him; and let him feel that at every step he takes, in pursuit of the flying bondman, he is running the frightful risk of having his hot brains dashed out by an invisible agency. Let us render the tyrant no aid; let us not hold the light by which he can trace the footprints of our flying brother. But enough of this. I will now proceed to the statement of those facts, connected with my escape, for which I am alone responsible, and for which no one can be made to suffer but myself.

In the early part of the year 1838, I became quite restless. I could see no reason why I should, at the end of each week, pour the reward of my toil into the purse of my master. When I carried to him my weekly wages, he would, after counting the money, look me in the face with a robber-like fierceness, and ask, "Is this all?" He was satisfied with nothing less than the last cent. He would, however, when I made him six dollars, sometimes give me six cents, to encourage me. It had the opposite effect. I regarded it as a sort of admission of my right to the whole. The fact that he gave me any part of my wages was proof, to my mind, that he believed me entitled to the whole of them. I always felt worse for having received anything; for I feared that the giving me a few cents would ease his conscience, and make him feel himself to be a pretty honorable sort of robber. My discontent grew upon me. I was ever on the look-out for means of escape; and, finding no direct means, I determined to try to hire my time, with a view of getting money with which to make my escape. In the spring of 1838, when Master Thomas came to Baltimore to purchase his spring goods, I got an opportunity, and applied to him to allow me to hire my time. He unhesitatingly refused my request, and told me this was another stratagem by which to escape. He told me I could go nowhere but that he could get me; and that, in the event of my running away, he should spare no pains in his efforts to catch me. He exhorted me to content myself, and be obedient. He told me, if I would be happy, I must lay out no plans for the future. He said, if I behaved myself properly, he would take care of me. Indeed, he advised me to complete thoughtlessness of the future, and taught me to depend solely upon him for happiness. He seemed to see fully the pressing necessity of setting aside my intellectual nature, in order to contentment in slavery. But in spite of him, and even in spite of myself, I continued to think, and to think about the injustice of my enslavement, and the means of escape.

About two months after this, I applied to Master Hugh for the privilege of hiring my time. He was not acquainted with the fact that I had applied to Master Thomas, and had been refused. He too, at first, seemed disposed to refuse; but, after some reflection, he granted me the privilege, and proposed the following terms: I was to be allowed all my time, make all contracts with those for whom I worked, and find my own employment; and, in return for this liberty, I was to pay him three dollars at the end of each week; find myself in calking tools, and in board and clothing. My board was two dollars and a half per week. This, with the wear and tear of clothing and calking tools, made my regular expenses about six dollars per week. This amount I was compelled to make up, or relinquish the privilege of hiring my time. Rain or shine, work or no work, at the end of each week the money must be forthcoming, or I must give up my privilege. This arrangement, it will be perceived, was decidedly in my master's favor. It relieved him of all need of looking after me. His money was sure. He received all the benefits of slaveholding without its evils; while I endured all the evils of a slave, and suffered all the care and anxiety of a freeman. I found it a hard bargain. But, hard as it was, I thought it better than the old mode of getting along. It was a step towards freedom to be allowed to bear the responsibilities of a freeman, and I was determined to hold on upon it. I bent myself to the work of making money. I was ready to work at night as well as day, and by the most untiring perseverance and industry, I made enough to meet my expenses, and lay up a little money every week. I went on thus from May till August. Master Hugh then refused to allow me to hire my time longer. The ground for his refusal was a failure on my part, one Saturday night, to pay him for my week's time. This failure was occasioned by my attending a camp meeting about ten miles from Baltimore. During the week, I had entered into an engagement with a number of young friends to start from Baltimore to the camp ground early Saturday evening; and being detained by my employer, I was unable to get down to Master Hugh's without disappointing the company. I knew that Master Hugh was in no special need of the money that night. I therefore decided to go to camp meeting, and upon my return pay him the three dollars. I stayed at the camp meeting one day longer than I intended when I left. But as soon as I returned, I called upon him to pay him what he considered his due. I found him very angry; he could scarce restrain his wrath. He said he had a great mind to give me a severe whipping. He wished to know how I dared to go out of the city without asking his permission. I told him I hired my time and while I paid him the price which he asked for it, I did not know that I was bound to ask him when and where I should go. This reply troubled him; and, after reflecting a few moments, he turned to me, and said I should hire my time no longer; that the next thing he should know of, I would be running away. Upon the same plea, he told me to bring my tools and clothing home forthwith. I did so; but instead of seeking work, as I had been accustomed to do previously to hiring my time, I spent the whole week without the performance of a single stroke of work. I did this in retaliation. Saturday night, he called upon me as usual for my week's wages. I told him I had no wages; I had done no work that week. Here we were upon the point of coming to blows. He raved, and swore his determination to get hold of me. I did not allow myself a single word; but was resolved, if he laid the weight of his hand upon me, it should be blow for blow. He did not strike me, but told me that he would find me in constant employment in future. I thought the matter over during the next day, Sunday, and finally resolved upon the third day of September, as the day upon which I would make a second attempt to secure my freedom. I now had three weeks during which to prepare for my journey. Early on Monday morning, before Master Hugh had time to make any engagement for me, I went out and got employment of Mr. Butler, at his ship-yard near the drawbridge, upon what is called the City Block, thus making it unnecessary for him to seek employment for me. At the end of the week, I brought him between eight and nine dollars. He seemed very well pleased, and asked why I did not do the same the week before. He little knew what my plans were. My object in working steadily was to remove any suspicion he might entertain of my intent to run away; and in this I succeeded admirably. I suppose he thought I was never better satisfied with my condition than at the very time during which I was planning my escape. The second week passed, and again I carried him my full wages; and so well pleased was he, that he gave me twenty-five cents (quite a large sum for a slaveholder to give a slave), and bade me to make a good use of it. I told him I would.

Things went on without very smoothly indeed, but within there was trouble.[1] It is impossible for me to describe my feelings as the time of my contemplated start drew near. I had a number of warmhearted friends in

---

[1] *within there was trouble* I felt troubled within myself.

Baltimore—friends that I loved almost as I did my life—and the thought of being separated from them forever was painful beyond expression. It is my opinion that thousands would escape from slavery, who now remain, but for the strong cords of affection that bind them to their friends. The thought of leaving my friends was decidedly the most painful thought with which I had to contend. The love of them was my tender point, and shook my decision more than all things else. Besides the pain of separation, the dread and apprehension of a failure exceeded what I had experienced at my first attempt. The appalling defeat I then sustained returned to torment me. I felt assured that, if I failed in this attempt, my case would be a hopeless one—it would seal my fate as a slave forever. I could not hope to get off with anything less than the severest punishment, and being placed beyond the means of escape. It required no very vivid imagination to depict the most frightful scenes through which I should have to pass, in case I failed. The wretchedness of slavery, and the blessedness of freedom, were perpetually before me. It was life and death with me. But I remained firm, and, according to my resolution, on the third day of September, 1838, I left my chains, and succeeded in reaching New York without the slightest interruption of any kind. How I did so—what means I adopted, what direction I travelled, and by what mode of conveyance—I must leave unexplained, for the reasons before mentioned.

I have been frequently asked how I felt when I found myself in a free State. I have never been able to answer the question with any satisfaction to myself. It was a moment of the highest excitement I ever experienced. I suppose I felt as one may imagine the unarmed mariner to feel when he is rescued by a friendly man-of-war[1] from the pursuit of a pirate. In writing to a dear friend, immediately after my arrival at New York, I said I felt like one who had escaped a den of hungry lions. This state of mind, however, very soon subsided; and I was again seized with a feeling of great insecurity and loneliness. I was yet liable to be taken back, and subjected to all the tortures of slavery.[2] This in itself was enough to damp the ardor of my enthusiasm. But the loneliness overcame me. There I was in the midst of thousands, and yet a perfect stranger; without home and without friends, in the midst of thousands of my own brethren—children of a common Father, and yet I dared not to unfold to any one of them my sad condition. I was afraid to speak to anyone for fear of speaking to the wrong one, and thereby falling into the hands of money-loving kidnappers, whose business it was to lie in wait for the panting fugitive, as the ferocious beasts of the forest lie in wait for their prey. The motto which I

---

1   *man-of-war*   Large warship.
2   *I was yet liable … tortures of slavery*   When an enslaved person escaped, under the provisions of the Fugitive Slave Act of 1793 a slaveholder was guaranteed the right to seek out, capture, and return that person to enslavement. (Later, the Fugitive Slave Act of 1850 made these provisions even harsher.)

adopted when I started from slavery was this—"Trust no man!" I saw in every white man an enemy, and in almost every colored man cause for distrust. It was a most painful situation; and, to understand it, one must needs experience it, or imagine himself in similar circumstances. Let him be a fugitive slave in a strange land—a land given up to be the hunting-ground for slaveholders—whose inhabitants are legalized kidnappers—where he is every moment subjected to the terrible liability of being seized upon by his fellowmen, as the hideous crocodile seizes upon his prey!—I say, let him place himself in my situation—without home or friends—without money or credit—wanting[1] shelter, and no one to give it—wanting bread, and no money to buy it—and at the same time let him feel that he is pursued by merciless men-hunters, and in total darkness as to what to do, where to go, or where to stay—perfectly helpless both as to the means of defence and means of escape—in the midst of plenty, yet suffering the terrible gnawings of hunger—in the midst of houses, yet having no home—among fellow-men, yet feeling as if in the midst of wild beasts, whose greediness to swallow up the trembling and half-famished fugitive is only equalled by that with which the monsters of the deep swallow up the helpless fish upon which they subsist—I say, let him be placed in this most trying situation—the situation in which I was placed—then, and not till then, will he fully appreciate the hardships of, and know how to sympathize with, the toil-worn and whip-scarred fugitive slave.

Thank Heaven, I remained but a short time in this distressed situation. I was relieved from it by the humane hand of Mr. David Ruggles,[2] whose vigilance, kindness, and perseverance, I shall never forget. I am glad of an opportunity to express, as far as words can, the love and gratitude I bear him. Mr. Ruggles is now afflicted with blindness, and is himself in need of the same kind offices which he was once so forward in the performance of toward others. I had been in New York but a few days, when Mr. Ruggles sought me out, and very kindly took me to his boarding-house at the corner of Church and Lespenard Streets. Mr. Ruggles was then very deeply engaged in the memorable Darg case,[3] as well as attending to a number of other fugitive slaves, devising ways and means for their successful escape; and, though watched and hemmed in on almost every side, he seemed to be more than a match for his enemies.

Very soon after I went to Mr. Ruggles, he wished to know of me where I wanted to go; as he deemed it unsafe for me to remain in New York. I told him I was a caulker, and should like to go where I could get work. I thought

---

1   *wanting*   Lacking.
2   *Mr. David Ruggles*   Free-born black abolitionist from Connecticut (1810–49), who aided fugitives via the Underground Railroad.
3   *Darg case*   In 1838, Ruggles had been involved in assisting the enslaved man Thomas Hughes in escaping from the enslaver John P. Darg, for which involvement Ruggles was briefly imprisoned.

of going to Canada; but he decided against it, and in favor of my going to New Bedford, thinking I should be able to get work there at my trade. At this time, Anna,[1] my intended wife, came on; for I wrote to her immediately after my arrival at New York (notwithstanding my homeless, houseless, and helpless condition), informing her of my successful flight, and wishing her to come on forthwith. In a few days after her arrival, Mr. Ruggles called in the Rev. J.W.C. Pennington,[2] who, in the presence of Mr. Ruggles, Mrs. Michaels, and two or three others, performed the marriage ceremony, and gave us a certificate, of which the following is an exact copy:

This may certify, that I joined together in holy matrimony Frederick John-son[3] and Anna Murray, as man and wife, in the presence of Mr. David Ruggles and Mrs. Michaels.

JAMES W.C. PENNINGTON
New York, Sept. 15, 1838

Upon receiving this certificate, and a five-dollar bill from Mr. Ruggles, I shouldered one part of our baggage, and Anna took up the other, and we set out forthwith to take passage on board of the steamboat John W. Richmond for Newport, on our way to New Bedford. Mr. Ruggles gave me a letter to a Mr. Shaw in Newport, and told me, in case my money did not serve me to New Bedford, to stop in Newport and obtain further assistance; but upon our arrival at Newport, we were so anxious to get to a place of safety, that, notwithstanding we lacked the necessary money to pay our fare, we decided to take seats in the stage,[4] and promise to pay when we got to New Bedford. We were encouraged to do this by two excellent gentlemen, residents of New Bedford, whose names I afterward ascertained to be Joseph Ricketson and William C. Taber. They seemed at once to understand our circumstances, and gave us such assurance of their friendliness as put us fully at ease in their presence. It was good indeed to meet with such friends, at such a time. Upon reaching New Bedford, we were directed to the house of Mr. Nathan Johnson, by whom we were kindly received, and hospitably provided for. Both Mr. and Mrs. Johnson took a deep and lively interest in our welfare. They proved themselves quite worthy of the name of abolitionists. When the stage-driver found us unable to pay our fare, he held on upon our baggage as security for the debt. I had but to mention the fact to Mr. Johnson, and he forthwith advanced the money.

---

1   [Douglass's note]   She was free.
2   *J.W.C. Pennington*   Formerly enslaved abolitionist and minister (1807–70).
3   [Douglass's note]   I had changed my name from Frederick *Bailey* to that of *Johnson*.
4   *stage*   Stagecoach.

We now began to feel a degree of safety, and to prepare ourselves for the duties and responsibilities of a life of freedom. On the morning after our arrival at New Bedford, while at the breakfast-table, the question arose as to what name I should be called by. The name given me by my mother was, "Frederick Augustus Washington Bailey." I, however, had dispensed with the two middle names long before I left Maryland so that I was generally known by the name of "Frederick Bailey." I started from Baltimore bearing the name of "Stanley." When I got to New York, I again changed my name to "Frederick Johnson," and thought that would be the last change. But when I got to New Bedford, I found it necessary again to change my name. The reason of this necessity was, that there were so many Johnsons in New Bedford, it was already quite difficult to distinguish between them. I gave Mr. Johnson the privilege of choosing me a name, but told him he must not take from me the name of "Frederick." I must hold on to that, to preserve a sense of my identity. Mr. Johnson had just been reading the "Lady of the Lake,"[1] and at once suggested that my name be "Douglass." From that time until now I have been called "Frederick Douglass"; and as I am more widely known by that name than by either of the others, I shall continue to use it as my own.

I was quite disappointed at the general appearance of things in New Bedford. The impression which I had received respecting the character and condition of the people of the north, I found to be singularly erroneous. I had very strangely supposed, while in slavery, that few of the comforts, and scarcely any of the luxuries, of life were enjoyed at the north, compared with what were enjoyed by the slaveholders of the south. I probably came to this conclusion from the fact that northern people owned no slaves. I supposed that they were about upon a level with the non-slaveholding population of the south. I knew they were exceedingly poor, and I had been accustomed to regard their poverty as the necessary consequence of their being non-slaveholders. I had somehow imbibed the opinion that, in the absence of slaves, there could be no wealth, and very little refinement. And upon coming to the north, I expected to meet with a rough, hard-handed, and uncultivated population, living in the most Spartan-like[2] simplicity, knowing nothing of the ease, luxury, pomp, and grandeur of southern slaveholders. Such being my conjectures, anyone acquainted with the appearance of New Bedford may very readily infer how palpably I must have seen my mistake.

---

1 *Lady of the Lake* Narrative poem by Scottish author Sir Walter Scott (1771–1832). Two of the main characters are James Douglas, an exiled former mentor of King James V of Scotland, and Douglas's daughter Ellen Douglas.

2 *Spartan-like* Resembling the Spartans, who were known for their militaristic self-discipline and material plainness of living.

In the afternoon of the day when I reached New Bedford, I visited the wharves, to take a view of the shipping. Here I found myself surrounded with the strongest proofs of wealth. Lying at the wharves, and riding in the steam, I saw many ships of the finest model, in the best order, and of the largest size. Upon the right and left, I was walled in by granite warehouses of the widest dimensions, stowed to their utmost capacity with the necessaries and comforts of life. Added to this, almost everybody seemed to be at work, but noiselessly so, compared with what I had been accustomed to in Baltimore. There were no loud songs heard from those engaged in loading and unloading ships. I heard no deep oaths or horrid curses on the laborer. I saw no whipping of men; but all seemed to go smoothly on. Every man appeared to understand his work, and went at it with a sober, yet cheerful earnestness, which betokened the deep interest which he felt in what he was doing, as well as a sense of his own dignity as a man. To me this looked exceedingly strange. From the wharves I strolled around and over the town, gazing with wonder and admiration at the splendid churches, beautiful dwellings, and finely-cultivated gardens; evincing an amount of wealth, comfort, taste, and refinement, such as I had never seen in any part of slaveholding Maryland.

Everything looked clean, new, and beautiful. I saw few or no dilapidated houses, with poverty-stricken inmates; no half-naked children and barefooted women, such as I had been accustomed to see in Hillsborough, Easton, St. Michael's, and Baltimore. The people looked more able, stronger, healthier, and happier, than those of Maryland. I was for once made glad by a view of extreme wealth, without being saddened by seeing extreme poverty. But the most astonishing as well as the most interesting thing to me was the condition of the colored people, a great many of whom, like myself, had escaped thither as a refuge from the hunters of men. I found many, who had not been seven years out of their chains, living in finer houses, and evidently enjoying more of the comforts of life, than the average slaveholders in Maryland. I will venture to assert, that my friend Mr. Nathan Johnson (of whom I can say with a grateful heart, "I was hungry, and he gave me meat; I was thirsty, and he gave me drink; I was a stranger, and he took me in"[1]) lived in a neater house; dined at a better table; took, paid for, and read, more newspapers; better understood the moral, religious, and political character of the nation—than nine tenths of the slaveholders in Talbot county, Maryland. Yet Mr. Johnson was a working man. His hands were hardened by toil, and not his alone, but those also of Mrs. Johnson. I found the colored people much more spirited than I had supposed they would be. I found among them a determination to protect each other from the blood-thirsty kidnapper, at all hazards. Soon after my arrival, I was

---

1   *I was hungry ... took me in*   See Matthew 25.35.

told of a circumstance which illustrated their spirit. A colored man and a fugitive slave were on unfriendly terms. The former was heard to threaten the latter with informing his master of his whereabouts. Straightway a meeting was called among the colored people, under the stereotyped[1] notice, "Business of importance!" The betrayer was invited to attend. The people came at the appointed hour, and organized the meeting by appointing a very religious old gentleman as president, who, I believe, made a prayer, after which he addressed the meeting as follows: "Friends, we have got him here, and I would recommend that you young men just take him outside the door, and kill him!" With this, a number of them bolted at him; but they were intercepted by some more timid than themselves, and the betrayer escaped their vengeance, and has not been seen in New Bedford since. I believe there have been no more such threats, and should there be hereafter, I doubt not that death would be the consequence.

I found employment, the third day after my arrival, in stowing a sloop with a load of oil.[2] It was new, dirty, and hard work for me; but I went at it with a glad heart and a willing hand. I was now my own master. It was a happy moment, the rapture of which can be understood only by those who have been slaves. It was the first work, the reward of which was to be entirely my own. There was no Master Hugh standing ready, the moment I earned the money, to rob me of it. I worked that day with a pleasure I had never before experienced. I was at work for myself and newly-married wife. It was to me the starting-point of a new existence. When I got through with that job, I went in pursuit of a job of caulking; but such was the strength of prejudice against color, among the white caulkers, that they refused to work with me, and of course I could get no employment.[3] Finding my trade of no immediate benefit, I threw off my caulking habiliments, and prepared myself to do any kind of work I could get to do. Mr. Johnson kindly let me have his wood-horse and saw, and I very soon found myself a plenty of work. There was no work too hard—none too dirty. I was ready to saw wood, shovel coal, carry wood, sweep the chimney, or roll oil casks—all of which I did for nearly three years in New Bedford, before I became known to the anti-slavery world.

In about four months after I went to New Bedford, there came a young man to me, and inquired if I did not wish to take the "Liberator."[4] I told him I did; but, just having made my escape from slavery, I remarked that I was

---

1 *stereotyped* Printed. (Stereotyping was a then-new method of printing identical copies using metal plates.)
2 *stowing a sloop with a load of oil* Loading casks of whale oil onto a cargo sailing ship.
3 [Douglass's note] I am told that colored persons can now get employment at caulking in New Bedford—a result of anti-slavery effort.
4 *take* Subscribe to; *the "Liberator"* Radical abolitionist newspaper established in 1831 and published by William Lloyd Garrison.

unable to pay for it then. I, however, finally became a subscriber to it. The paper came, and I read it from week to week with such feelings as it would be quite idle for me to attempt to describe. The paper became my meat and my drink. My soul was set all on fire. Its sympathy for my brethren in bonds—its scathing denunciations of slaveholders—its faithful exposures of slavery—and its powerful attacks upon the upholders of the institution—sent a thrill of joy through my soul, such as I had never felt before!

I had not long been a reader of the "Liberator" before I got a pretty correct idea of the principles, measures, and spirit of the anti-slavery reform. I took right hold of the cause. I could do but little; but what I could, I did with a joyful heart, and never felt happier than when in an anti-slavery meeting. I seldom had much to say at the meetings, because what I wanted to say was said so much better by others. But, while attending an anti-slavery convention at Nantucket, on the 11th of August, 1841, I felt strongly moved to speak, and was at the same time much urged to do so by Mr. William C. Coffin, a gentleman who had heard me speak in the colored people's meeting at New Bedford.[1] It was a severe cross, and I took it up reluctantly. The truth was, I felt myself a slave, and the idea of speaking to white people weighed me down. I spoke but a few moments, when I felt a degree of freedom, and said what I desired with considerable ease. From that time until now, I have been engaged in pleading the cause of my brethren—with what success, and with what devotion, I leave those acquainted with my labors to decide.

APPENDIX

I find, since reading over the foregoing Narrative, that I have, in several instances, spoken in such a tone and manner, respecting religion, as may possibly lead those unacquainted with my religious views to suppose me an opponent of all religion. To remove the liability of such misapprehension, I deem it proper to append the following brief explanation. What I have said respecting and against religion, I mean strictly to apply to the slaveholding religion of this land, and with no possible reference to Christianity proper; for, between the Christianity of this land, and the Christianity of Christ, I recognize the widest possible difference—so wide, that to receive the one as good, pure, and holy, is of necessity to reject the other as bad, corrupt, and wicked. To be the friend of the one, is of necessity to be the enemy of the other. I love the pure, peaceable, and impartial Christianity of Christ: I therefore hate the corrupt, slaveholding, women-whipping, cradle-plundering, partial and hypocritical

---

1   colored people's ... New Bedford   I.e., at the meeting of the African Methodist Episcopal Zion Church, where Douglass had begun preaching in 1839.

Christianity of this land. Indeed, I can see no reason, but the most deceitful one, for calling the religion of this land Christianity. I look upon it as the climax of all misnomers, the boldest of all frauds, and the grossest of all libels. Never was there a clearer case of "stealing the livery of the court of heaven to serve the devil in."[1] I am filled with unutterable loathing when I contemplate the religious pomp and show, together with the horrible inconsistencies, which everywhere surround me. We have men-stealers for ministers, women-whippers for missionaries, and cradle-plunderers for church members. The man who wields the blood-clotted cowskin during the week fills the pulpit on Sunday, and claims to be a minister of the meek and lowly Jesus. The man who robs me of my earnings at the end of each week meets me as a class-leader on Sunday morning, to show me the way of life, and the path of salvation. He who sells my sister, for purposes of prostitution, stands forth as the pious advocate of purity. He who proclaims it a religious duty to read the Bible denies me the right of learning to read the name of the God who made me. He who is the religious advocate of marriage robs whole millions of its sacred influence, and leaves them to the ravages of wholesale pollution. The warm defender of the sacredness of the family relation is the same that scatters whole families—sundering husbands and wives, parents and children, sisters and brothers—leaving the hut vacant, and the hearth desolate. We see the thief preaching against theft, and the adulterer against adultery. We have men sold to build churches, women sold to support the gospel, and babes sold to purchase Bibles for the Poor Heathen! All For The Glory Of God And The Good Of Souls! The slave auctioneer's bell and the church-going bell chime in with each other, and the bitter cries of the heart-broken slave are drowned in the religious shouts of his pious master. Revivals of religion and revivals in the slave-trade go hand in hand together. The slave prison and the church stand near each other. The clanking of fetters and the rattling of chains in the prison, and the pious psalm and solemn prayer in the church, may be heard at the same time. The dealers in the bodies and souls of men erect their stand in the presence of the pulpit, and they mutually help each other. The dealer gives his blood-stained gold to support the pulpit, and the pulpit, in return, covers his infernal business with the garb of Christianity. Here we have religion and robbery the allies of each other—devils dressed in angels' robes, and hell presenting the semblance of paradise.

Just God! and these are they,
Who minister at thine altar, God of right!

---

1   *stealing the livery … devil in*   From Book 8 of Scottish poet Robert Pollok's popular poem *The Course of Time* (1827).

Men who their hands, with prayer and blessing, lay
    On Israel's ark of light.[1]
What! preach, and kidnap men?
    Give thanks, and rob thy own afflicted poor?
Talk of thy glorious liberty, and then
    Bolt hard the captive's door?
What! servants of thy own
    Merciful Son, who came to seek and save
The homeless and the outcast, fettering down
    The tasked and plundered slave!
Pilate and Herod[2] friends!
    Chief priests and rulers, as of old, combine!
Just God and holy! is that church which lends
    Strength to the spoiler thine?[3]

The Christianity of America is a Christianity, of whose votaries it may be as truly said, as it was of the ancient scribes and Pharisees,[4] "They bind heavy burdens, and grievous to be borne, and lay them on men's shoulders, but they themselves will not move them with one of their fingers. All their works they do for to be seen of men. They love the uppermost rooms at feasts, and the chief seats in the synagogues, ... and to be called of men, Rabbi, Rabbi. But woe unto you, scribes and Pharisees, hypocrites! for ye shut up the kingdom of heaven against men; for ye neither go in yourselves, neither suffer ye them that are entering to go in. Ye devour widows' houses, and for a pretence make long prayers; therefore ye shall receive the greater damnation. Ye compass sea and land to make one proselyte, and when he is made, ye make him twofold more the child of hell than yourselves. Woe unto you, scribes and Pharisees, hypocrites! for ye pay tithe of mint, and anise, and cumin, and have omitted the weightier matters of the law, judgment, mercy, and faith; these ought ye to have done, and not to leave the other undone. Ye blind guides! which strain at a gnat, and swallow a camel. Woe unto you, scribes and Pharisees, hypocrites! for ye make clean the outside of the cup and of the platter; but within, they are full of extortion and excess. Woe unto you, scribes

---

1   *Israel's ark of light* I.e., the Ark of the Covenant, containing the two stone tablets upon which the Ten Commandments were written, and thus symbolizing religious law as a whole.

2   *Pilate and Herod* Pontius Pilate, the Roman ruler who approved Jesus' crucifixion; and the Galilean ruler Herod Antipas, who was involved in the executions both of John the Baptist and Jesus.

3   *Just God ... spoiler thine?* The above comprises the first four stanzas of John Greenleaf Whittier's poem "Clerical Oppressors" (1835).

4   *ancient scribes and Pharisees* The scribes were professional scholars of religious law, while the Pharisees were a sect whose members insisted on strict adherence to oral and written religious laws; the lines that follow are taken from Matthew 23.4–28, wherein Jesus denounces the scribes and Pharisees for hypocrisy.

and Pharisees, hypocrites! for ye are like unto whited sepulchres, which indeed appear beautiful outward, but are within full of dead men's bones, and of all uncleanness. Even so ye also outwardly appear righteous unto men, but within ye are full of hypocrisy and iniquity."

Dark and terrible as is this picture, I hold it to be strictly true of the overwhelming mass of professed Christians in America. They strain at a gnat, and swallow a camel. Could anything be more true of our churches? They would be shocked at the proposition of fellowshipping a sheep-stealer; and at the same time they hug to their communion a man-stealer, and brand me with being an infidel, if I find fault with them for it. They attend with Pharisaical strictness to the outward forms of religion, and at the same time neglect the weightier matters of the law, judgment, mercy, and faith. They are always ready to sacrifice, but seldom to show mercy. They are they who are represented as professing to love God whom they have not seen, whilst they hate their brother whom they have seen. They love the heathen on the other side of the globe. They can pray for him, pay money to have the Bible put into his hand, and missionaries to instruct him; while they despise and totally neglect the heathen at their own doors.

Such is, very briefly, my view of the religion of this land; and to avoid any misunderstanding, growing out of the use of general terms, I mean by the religion of this land, that which is revealed in the words, deeds, and actions, of those bodies, north and south, calling themselves Christian churches, and yet in union with slaveholders. It is against religion, as presented by these bodies, that I have felt it my duty to testify.

I conclude these remarks by copying the following portrait of the religion of the south (which is, by communion and fellowship, the religion of the north), which I soberly affirm is "true to the life," and without caricature or the slightest exaggeration. It is said to have been drawn, several years before the present anti-slavery agitation began, by a northern Methodist preacher, who, while residing at the south, had an opportunity to see slaveholding morals, manners, and piety, with his own eyes. "Shall I not visit for these things? saith the Lord. Shall not my soul be avenged on such a nation as this?"[1]

A PARODY

Come, saints and sinners, hear me tell
How pious priests whip Jack and Nell,
And women buy and children sell,

---

1 *Shall I not ... as this?* See Jeremiah 5.9. The identity of the preacher to whom Douglass refers is unknown; the following poem, which parodies the popular Southern hymn "Heavenly Union," seems to have been written by Douglass himself.

And preach all sinners down to hell,
　　And sing of heavenly union.

They'll bleat and baa, dona like goats,
Gorge down black sheep, and strain at motes,
Array their backs in fine black coats,
Then seize their negroes by their throats,
　　And choke, for heavenly union.

They'll church you if you sip a dram,
And damn you if you steal a lamb;
Yet rob old Tony, Doll, and Sam,
Of human rights, and bread and ham;
　　Kidnapper's heavenly union.

They'll talk loudly of Christ's reward,
And bind his image with a cord,
And scold, and swing the lash abhorred,
And sell their brother in the Lord
　　To handcuffed heavenly union.

They'll read and sing a sacred song,
And make a prayer both loud and long,
And teach the right and do the wrong,
Hailing the brother, sister throng,
　　With words of heavenly union.

We wonder how such saints can sing,
Or praise the Lord upon the wing,
Who roar, and scold, and whip, and sting,
And to their slaves and mammon cling,
　　In guilty conscience union.

They'll raise tobacco, corn, and rye,
And drive, and thieve, and cheat, and lie,
And lay up treasures in the sky,
By making switch and cowskin fly,
　　In hope of heavenly union.

They'll crack old Tony on the skull,
And preach and roar like Bashan bull,[1]
Or braying ass, of mischief full,

1　*Bashan bull*　Strong bull mentioned in Psalm 22.12–13.

Then seize old Jacob by the wool,
    And pull for heavenly union.

A roaring, ranting, sleek man-thief,
Who lived on mutton, veal, and beef,
Yet never would afford relief
To needy, sable sons of grief,
    Was big with heavenly union.

"Love not the world," the preacher said,
And winked his eye, and shook his head;
He seized on Tom, and Dick, and Ned,
Cut short their meat, and clothes, and bread,
    Yet still loved heavenly union.

Another preacher whining spoke
Of One whose heart for sinners broke:
He tied old Nanny to an oak,
And drew the blood at every stroke,
    And prayed for heavenly union.

Two others oped their iron jaws,
And waved their children-stealing paws;
There sat the children in gewgaws;[1]
By stinting negroes' backs and maws,
    They kept up heavenly union.

All good from Jack another takes,
And entertains their flirts and rakes[2]
Who dress as sleek as glossy snakes,
And cram their mouths with sweetened cakes;
    And this goes down for union.

Sincerely and earnestly hoping that this little book may do something toward throwing light on the American slave system, and hastening the glad day of deliverance to the millions of my brethren in bonds—faithfully relying upon the power of truth, love, and justice, for my success in my humble efforts—and solemnly pledging my self anew to the sacred cause—I subscribe myself,

FREDERICK DOUGLASS
LYNN, Mass., April 28, 1845

—1845

---

1 *gewgaws* Ornamental or showy clothing.
2 *rakes* Licentious or immoral men.

from *My Bondage and My Freedom*

This excerpt from Douglass's expanded 1855 autobiography provides an interesting point of comparison with the account provided in Chapter 10 of the *Narrative*.

CHAPTER 17
THE LAST FLOGGING

Sleep itself does not always come to the relief of the weary in body, and the broken in spirit; especially when past troubles only foreshadow coming disasters. The last hope had been extinguished. My master, who I did not venture to hope would protect me as *a man*, had even now refused to protect me as *his property*; and had cast me back, covered with reproaches and bruises, into the hands of a stranger to that mercy which was the soul of the religion he professed. May the reader never spend such a night as that allotted to me, previous to the morning which was to herald my return to the den of horrors from which I had made a temporary escape.

I remained all night—sleep I did not—at St. Michael's;[1] and in the morning (Saturday) I started off, according to the order of Master Thomas, feeling that I had no friend on earth, and doubting if I had one in heaven. I reached Covey's about nine o'clock; and just as I stepped into the field, before I had reached the house, Covey, true to his snakish habits, darted out at me from a fence corner, in which he had secreted himself, for the purpose of securing me. He was amply provided with a cowskin[2] and a rope; and he evidently intended to *tie me up*, and to wreak his vengeance on me to the fullest extent. I should have been an easy prey, had he succeeded in getting his hands upon me, for I had taken no refreshment since noon on Friday; and this, together with the pelting, excitement, and the loss of blood, had reduced my strength. I, however, darted back into the woods, before the ferocious hound could get hold of me, and buried myself in a thicket, where he lost sight of me. The corn-field afforded me cover, in getting to the woods. But for the tall corn, Covey would have overtaken me, and made me his captive. He seemed very much chagrined that he did not catch me, and gave up the chase, very reluctantly; for I could see his angry movements, toward the house from which he had sallied, on his foray.

---

1   *St. Michael's*   Town in Maryland, home of Thomas Auld.
2   *cowskin*   Whip made from cowhide.

Well, now I am clear of Covey, and of his wrathful lash, for the present. I am in the wood, buried in its somber gloom, and hushed in its solemn silence; hid from all human eyes; shut in with nature and nature's God, and absent from all human contrivances. Here was a good place to pray; to pray for help for deliverance—a prayer I had often made before. But how could I pray? Covey could pray—Capt. Auld could pray—I would fain[1] pray; but doubts (arising partly from my own neglect of the means of grace, and partly from the sham religion which everywhere prevailed, cast in my mind a doubt upon all religion, and led me to the conviction that prayers were unavailing and delusive) prevented my embracing the opportunity, as a religious one. Life, in itself, had almost become burdensome to me. All my outward relations were against me; I must stay here and starve (I was already hungry), or go home to Covey's, and have my flesh torn to pieces, and my spirit humbled under the cruel lash of Covey. This was the painful alternative presented to me. The day was long and irksome. My physical condition was deplorable. I was weak, from the toils of the previous day, and from the want of food and rest; and had been so little concerned about my appearance, that I had not yet washed the blood from my garments. I was an object of horror, even to myself. Life, in Baltimore, when most oppressive, was a paradise to this. What had I done, what had my parents done, that such a life as this should be mine? That day, in the woods, I would have exchanged my manhood for the brutehood of an ox.

Night came. I was still in the woods, unresolved what to do. Hunger had not yet pinched me to the point of going home, and I laid myself down in the leaves to rest; for I had been watching for hunters all day, but not being molested during the day, I expected no disturbance during the night. I had come to the conclusion that Covey relied upon hunger to drive me home; and in this I was quite correct—the facts showed that he had made no effort to catch me, since morning.

During the night, I heard the step of a man in the woods. He was coming toward the place where I lay. A person lying still has the advantage over one walking in the woods, in the day time, and this advantage is much greater at night. I was not able to engage in a physical struggle, and I had recourse to the common resort of the weak. I hid myself in the leaves to prevent discovery. But, as the night rambler in the woods drew nearer, I found him to be a *friend*, not an enemy; it was a slave of Mr. William Groomes, of Easton, a kind hearted fellow, named "Sandy." Sandy lived with Mr. Kemp that year, about four miles from St. Michael's. He, like myself, had been hired out by the year; but, unlike myself, had not been hired out to be broken. Sandy was

---

1 *fain* Like to.

the husband of a free woman, who lived in the lower part of "*Pot-pie Neck*,"[1] and he was now on his way through the woods, to see her, and to spend the Sabbath with her.

As soon as I had ascertained that the disturber of my solitude was not an enemy, but the good-hearted Sandy—a man as famous among the slaves of the neighborhood for his good nature, as for his good sense—I came out from my hiding place, and made myself known to him. I explained the circumstances of the past two days, which had driven me to the woods, and he deeply compassionated my distress. It was a bold thing for him to shelter me, and I could not ask him to do so; for, had I been found in his hut, he would have suffered the penalty of thirty-nine lashes on his bare back, if not something worse. But, Sandy was too generous to permit the fear of punishment to prevent his relieving a brother bondman from hunger and exposure; and, therefore, on his own motion, I accompanied him to his home, or rather to the home of his wife—for the house and lot were hers. His wife was called up—for it was now about midnight—a fire was made, some Indian meal was soon mixed with salt and water, and an ash cake[2] was baked in a hurry to relieve my hunger. Sandy's wife was not behind him in kindness—both seemed to esteem it a privilege to succor me; for, although I was hated by Covey and by my master, I was loved by the colored people, because *they* thought I was hated for my knowledge, and persecuted because I was feared. I was the *only* slave *now* in that region who could read and write. There had been one other man, belonging to Mr. Hugh Hamilton, who could read (his name was "Jim"), but he, poor fellow, had, shortly after my coming into the neighborhood, been sold off to the far south. I saw Jim ironed,[3] in the cart, to be carried to Easton for sale—pinioned[4] like a yearling for the slaughter. My knowledge was now the pride of my brother slaves; and, no doubt, Sandy felt something of the general interest in me on that account. The supper was soon ready, and though I have feasted since, with honorables, lord mayors and aldermen, over the sea, my supper on ash cake and cold water, with Sandy, was the meal, of all my life, most sweet to my taste, and now most vivid in my memory.

Supper over, Sandy and I went into a discussion of what was *possible* for me, under the perils and hardships which now overshadowed my path. The question was, must I go back to Covey, or must I now attempt to run away? Upon a careful survey, the latter was found to be impossible; for I was on a narrow neck of land, every avenue from which would bring me in sight of pursuers. There was the Chesapeake Bay to the right, and "Pot-pie" River to the left, and

---

1 *Pot-pie Neck*   Local name for a section of the Tilghman peninsula in Talbot County, Maryland.
2 *Indian meal*   I.e., cornmeal;   *ash cake*   Plain flatbread baked on hot ashes.
3 *ironed*   I.e., bound in iron cuffs or chains.
4 *pinioned*   Having his arms and legs bound.

St. Michael's and its neighborhood occupying the only space through which there was any retreat.

I found Sandy an old adviser. He was not only a religious man, but he professed to believe in a system for which I have no name. He was a genuine African, and had inherited some of the so called magical powers, said to be possessed by African and eastern nations. He told me that he could help me; that, in those very woods, there was an herb, which in the morning might be found, possessing all the powers required for my protection (I put his thoughts in my own language); and that, if I would take his advice, he would procure me the root of the herb of which he spoke. He told me further, that if I would take that root and wear it on my right side, it would be impossible for Covey to strike me a blow; that with this root about my person, no white man could whip me. He said he had carried it for years, and that he had fully tested its virtues. He had never received a blow from a slaveholder since he carried it; and he never expected to receive one, for he always meant to carry that root as a protection. He knew Covey well, for Mrs. Covey was the daughter of Mr. Kemp; and he (Sandy) had heard of the barbarous treatment to which I was subjected, and he wanted to do something for me.

Now all this talk about the root, was, to me, very absurd and ridiculous, if not positively sinful. I at first rejected the idea that the simple carrying a root on my right side (a root, by the way, over which I walked every time I went into the woods), could possess any such magic power as he ascribed to it, and I was, therefore, not disposed to cumber my pocket with it. I had a positive aversion to all pretenders to "*divination*." It was beneath one of my intelligence to countenance such dealings with the devil, as this power implied. But, with all my learning—it was really precious little—Sandy was more than a match for me. "My book learning," he said, "had not kept Covey off me" (a powerful argument just then), and he entreated me, with flashing eyes, to try this. If it did me no good, it could do me no harm, and it would cost me nothing, anyway. Sandy was so earnest, and so confident of the good qualities of this weed, that, to please him, rather than from any conviction of its excellence, I was induced to take it. He had been to me the good Samaritan,[1] and had, almost providentially, found me, and helped me when I could not help myself; how did I know but that the hand of the Lord was in it? With thoughts of this sort, I took the roots from Sandy, and put them in my right hand pocket.

This was, of course, Sunday morning. Sandy now urged me to go home, with all speed, and to walk up bravely to the house, as though nothing had

---

1 *good Samaritan* See Luke 10.33, in which Jesus tells a parable of a man who is beaten and left for dead by thieves, but is rescued and nursed back to health by a Samaritan. (The Samaritans are an ethnoreligious group who are often looked down upon by the Jews in the Bible.)

happened. I saw in Sandy too deep an insight into human nature, with all his superstition, not to have some respect for his advice; and perhaps, too, a slight gleam or shadow of his superstition had fallen upon me. At any rate, I started off toward Covey's, as directed by Sandy. Having, the previous night, poured my griefs into Sandy's ears, and got him enlisted in my behalf, having made his wife a sharer in my sorrows, and having, also, become well refreshed by sleep and food, I moved off, quite courageously, toward the much dreaded Covey's. Singularly enough, just as I entered his yard gate, I met him and his wife, dressed in their Sunday best—looking as smiling as angels—on their way to church. The manner of Covey astonished me. There was something really benignant in his countenance. He spoke to me as never before; told me that the pigs had got into the lot, and he wished me to drive them out; inquired how I was, and seemed an altered man. This extraordinary conduct of Covey, really made me begin to think that Sandy's herb had more virtue in it than I, in my pride, had been willing to allow; and, had the day been other than Sunday, I should have attributed Covey's altered manner solely to the magic power of the root. I suspected, however, that the *Sabbath*, and not the *root*, was the real explanation of Covey's manner. His religion hindered him from breaking the Sabbath, but not from breaking my skin. He had more respect for the *day* than for the *man*, for whom the day was mercifully given; for while he would cut and slash my body during the week, he would not hesitate, on Sunday, to teach me the value of my soul, or the way of life and salvation by Jesus Christ.

All went well with me till Monday morning; and then, whether the root had lost its virtue, or whether my tormentor had gone deeper into the black art than myself (as was sometimes said of him), or whether he had obtained a special indulgence, for his faithful Sabbath day's worship, it is not necessary for me to know, or to inform the reader; but, this much I *may* say—the pious and benignant smile which graced Covey's face on *Sunday*, wholly disappeared on *Monday*. Long before daylight, I was called up to go and feed, rub, and curry[1] the horses. I obeyed the call, and I would have so obeyed it, had it been made at an earlier hour, for I had brought my mind to a firm resolve, during that Sunday's reflection, viz:[2] to obey every order, however unreasonable, if it were possible, and, if Mr. Covey should then undertake to beat me, to defend and protect myself to the best of my ability. My religious views on the subject of resisting my master, had suffered a serious shock, by the savage persecution to which I had been subjected, and my hands were no longer tied by my religion. Master Thomas's indifference had severed the last link. I had

---

1   *curry*   Brush.
2   *viz*   Abbreviation for the Latin videlicet, meaning "namely" or "that is to say."

now to this extent "backslidden" from this point in the slave's religious creed; and I soon had occasion to make my fallen state known to my Sunday-pious brother, Covey.

Whilst I was obeying his order to feed and get the horses ready for the field, and when in the act of going up the stable loft for the purpose of throwing down some blades, Covey sneaked into the stable, in his peculiar snake-like way, and seizing me suddenly by the leg, he brought me to the stable floor, giving my newly mended body a fearful jar. I now forgot my *roots*, and remembered my pledge to *stand up in my own defense*. The brute was endeavoring skillfully to get a slip-knot on my legs, before I could draw up my feet. As soon as I found what he was up to, I gave a sudden spring (my two day's rest had been of much service to me), and by that means, no doubt, he was able to bring me to the floor so heavily. He was defeated in his plan of tying me. While down, he seemed to think he had me very securely in his power. He little thought he was—as the rowdies say—"in" for a "rough and tumble" fight; but such was the fact. Whence came the daring spirit necessary to grapple with a man who, eight-and-forty hours before, could, with his slightest word, have made me tremble like a leaf in a storm, I do not know; at any rate, *I was resolved to fight*, and, what was better still, I was actually hard at it. The fighting madness had come upon me, and I found my strong fingers firmly attached to the throat of my cowardly tormentor; as heedless of consequences, at the moment, as though we stood as equals before the law. The very color of the man was forgotten. I felt as supple as a cat, and was ready for the snakish creature at every turn. Every blow of his was parried, though I dealt no blows in turn. I was strictly on the *defensive*, preventing him from injuring me, rather than trying to injure him. I flung him on the ground several times, when he meant to have hurled me there. I held him so firmly by the throat, that his blood followed my nails. He held me, and I held him.

All was fair, thus far, and the contest was about equal. My resistance was entirely unexpected, and Covey was taken all aback by it, for he trembled in every limb. "*Are you going to resist*, you scoundrel?" said he. To which, I returned a polite "*yes sir*"; steadily gazing my interrogator in the eye, to meet the first approach or dawning of the blow, which I expected my answer would call forth. But, the conflict did not long remain thus equal. Covey soon cried out lustily for help; not that I was obtaining any marked advantage over him, or was injuring him, but because he was gaining none over me, and was not able, single handed, to conquer me. He called for his cousin Hughes, to come to his assistance, and now the scene was changed. I was compelled to give blows, as well as to parry them; and, since I was, in any case, to suffer for resistance, I felt (as the musty proverb goes) that "I might as well be hanged for an old sheep as a lamb." I was still *defensive* toward Covey, but *aggressive* toward Hughes; and, at the first approach of the latter, I dealt a blow, in my desperation, which fairly sickened my youthful assailant. He went off, bending over with pain, and manifesting no disposition to come within my reach again. The poor fellow was in the act of trying to catch and tie my right hand, and while flattering himself with success, I gave him the kick which sent him staggering away in pain, at the same time that I held Covey with a firm hand.

Taken completely by surprise, Covey seemed to have lost his usual strength and coolness. He was frightened, and stood puffing and blowing, seemingly unable to command words or blows. When he saw that poor Hughes was standing half bent with pain—his courage quite gone—the cowardly tyrant asked if I "meant to persist in my resistance." I told him "I *did mean to resist, come what might*"; that I had been by him treated like a *brute*, during the last six months; and that I should stand it *no longer*. With that, he gave me a shake, and attempted to drag me toward a stick of wood, that was lying just outside the stable door. He meant to knock me down with it; but, just as he leaned over to get the stick, I seized him with both hands by the collar, and, with a vigorous and sudden snatch, I brought my assailant harmlessly, his full length, on the *not over* clean ground—for we were now in the cow yard. He had selected the place for the fight, and it was but right that he should have all the advantages of his own selection.

By this time, Bill, the hired man, came home. He had been to Mr. Hemsley's, to spend the Sunday with his nominal wife, and was coming home on Monday morning, to go to work. Covey and I had been skirmishing from before daybreak, till now, that the sun was almost shooting his beams over the eastern woods, and we were still at it. I could not see where the matter was to terminate. He evidently was afraid to let me go, lest I should again make off to the woods; otherwise, he would probably have obtained arms from the house, to frighten me. Holding me, Covey called upon Bill for assistance. The scene here, had something comic about it. "Bill," who knew *precisely* what Covey wished him to do, affected ignorance, and pretended he did not know what to do. "What shall I do, Mr. Covey," said Bill. "Take hold of him—take hold of him!" said Covey. With a toss of his head, peculiar to Bill, he said, "indeed, Mr. Covey, I want to go to work." "*This is* your work," said Covey; "take hold of him." Bill replied, with spirit, "My master hired me here, to work, and *not* to help you whip Frederick." It was now my turn to speak. "Bill," said I, "don't put your hands on me." To which he replied, "MY GOD! Frederick, I aint goin' to tech ye," and Bill walked off, leaving Covey and myself to settle our matters as best we might.

But, my present advantage was threatened when I saw Caroline (the slave-woman of Covey) coming to the cow yard to milk, for she was a powerful woman, and could have mastered me very easily, exhausted as I now was.

As soon as she came into the yard, Covey attempted to rally her to his aid. Strangely—and, I may add, fortunately—Caroline was in no humor to take a hand in any such sport. We were all in open rebellion, that morning. Caroline answered the command of her master to "*take hold of me*," precisely as Bill had answered, but in *her*, it was at greater peril so to answer; she was the slave of Covey, and he could do what he pleased with her. It was *not* so with Bill, and Bill knew it. Samuel Harris, to whom Bill belonged, did not allow his slaves to be beaten, unless they were guilty of some crime which the law would punish. But, poor Caroline, like myself, was at the mercy of the merciless Covey; nor did she escape the dire effects of her refusal. He gave her several sharp blows.

Covey at length (two hours had elapsed) gave up the contest. Letting me go, he said—puffing and blowing at a great rate—"now, you scoundrel, go to your work; I would not have whipped you half so much as I have had you not resisted." The fact was, *he had not whipped me at all.* He had not, in all the scuffle, drawn a single drop of blood from me. I had drawn blood from him; and, even without this satisfaction, I should have been victorious, because my aim had not been to injure him, but to prevent his injuring me.

During the whole six months that I lived with Covey, after this transaction, he never laid on me the weight of his finger in anger. He would, occasionally, say he did not want to have to get hold of me again—a declaration which I had no difficulty in believing; and I had a secret feeling, which answered, "you need not wish to get hold of me again, for you will be likely to come off worse in a second fight than you did in the first."

Well, my dear reader, this battle with Mr. Covey—undignified as it was, and as I fear my narration of it is—was the turning point in my "*life as a slave.*" It rekindled in my breast the smouldering embers of liberty; it brought up my Baltimore dreams, and revived a sense of my own manhood. I was a changed being after that fight. I was *nothing* before; I WAS A MAN NOW. It recalled to life my crushed self-respect and my self-confidence, and inspired me with a renewed determination to be A FREEMAN. A man, without force, is without the essential dignity of humanity. Human nature is so constituted, that it cannot *honor* a helpless man, although it can *pity* him; and even this it cannot do long, if the signs of power do not arise.

He only can understand the effect of this combat on my spirit, who has himself incurred something, hazarded something, in repelling the unjust and cruel aggressions of a tyrant. Covey was a tyrant, and a cowardly one, withal. After resisting him, I felt as I had never felt before. It was a resurrection from the dark and pestiferous tomb of slavery, to the heaven of comparative freedom. I was no longer a servile coward, trembling under the frown of a brother worm of the dust, but, my long-cowed spirit was roused to an attitude of manly independence. I had reached the point, at which I was *not afraid to die.*

This spirit made me a freeman in *fact*, while I remained a slave in *form*. When a slave cannot be flogged he is more than half free. He has a domain as broad as his own manly heart to defend, and he is really "*a power on earth.*"[1] While slaves prefer their lives, with flogging, to instant death, they will always find Christians enough, like unto Covey, to accommodate that preference. From this time, until that of my escape from slavery, I was never fairly whipped. Several attempts were made to whip me, but they were always unsuccessful. Bruises I did get, as I shall hereafter inform the reader; but the case I have been describing, was the end of the brutification to which slavery had subjected me.

The reader will be glad to know why, after I had so grievously offended Mr. Covey, he did not have me taken in hand by the authorities; indeed, why the law of Maryland, which assigns hanging to the slave who resists his master, was not put in force against me; at any rate, why I was not taken up, as is usual in such cases, and publicly whipped, for an example to other slaves, and as a means of deterring me from committing the same offense again. I confess, that the easy manner in which I got off, was, for a long time, a surprise to me, and I cannot, even now, fully explain the cause.

The only explanation I can venture to suggest, is the fact, that Covey was, probably, ashamed to have it known and confessed that he had been mastered by a boy of sixteen. Mr. Covey enjoyed the unbounded and very valuable reputation, of being a first rate overseer and *negro breaker*. By means of this reputation, he was able to procure his hands for *very trifling* compensation, and with very great ease. His interest and his pride mutually suggested the wisdom of passing the matter by, in silence. The story that he had undertaken to whip a lad, and had been resisted, was, of itself, sufficient to damage him; for his bearing should, in the estimation of slaveholders, be of that imperial order that should make such an occurrence *impossible*. I judge from these circumstances, that Covey deemed it best to give me the go-by. It is, perhaps, not altogether creditable to my natural temper, that, after this conflict with Mr. Covey, I did, at times, purposely aim to provoke him to an attack, by refusing to keep with the other hands in the field, but I could never bully him to another battle. I had made up my mind to do him serious damage, if he ever again attempted to lay violent hands on me.

"Hereditary bondmen, know ye not
Who would be free, themselves must strike the blow?"[2]
—1855

---

1 *a power on earth*   See Mark 2.10 and Matthew 9.6: "the Son of man hath power on earth to forgive sins."

2 *Hereditary bondmen … strike the blow*   From English poet Lord Byron's *Childe Harold's Pilgrimage* 2.76 (1812–18). Douglass frequently used this quotation in his speeches.

from *Life and Times of Frederick Douglass*

In the first and second versions of his autobiography, Douglass had left unexplained any of the details of his escape from slavery, on the grounds—as he explains in Chapter 11 of the *Narrative*—that telling the story would probably cause "difficulties" for those who helped him and "would most undoubtedly induce greater vigilance on the part of slaveholders." It was only in 1881, sixteen years after the passing of the Thirteenth Amendment, that Douglass decided it would be safe to tell the story of his escape in greater detail than had ever been revealed to the reading public before. This material from Douglass's third and final autobiography, *Life and Times of Frederick Douglass*, is included below, reproducing text from the revised and expanded 1893 edition.

from PART I

from CHAPTER 20
APPRENTICESHIP LIFE

... [A]fter three years spent in the country, roughing it in the field, and experiencing all sorts of hardships, I was again permitted to return to Baltimore, the very place of all others, short of a free State, where I most desired to live. The three years spent in the country had made some difference in me, and in the household of Master Hugh. "Little Tommy" was no longer little Tommy, and I was not the slender lad who had left the Eastern Shore just three years before. The loving relations between Master Tommy and myself were broken up. He was no longer dependent on me for protection, but felt himself a *man*, and had other and more suitable associates. In childhood he had considered me scarcely inferior to himself—certainly quite as good as any other boy with whom he played; but the time had come when his *friend* must be his slave. So we were cold to each other, and parted. It was a sad thing to me, that, loving each other as we had done, we must now take different roads. To him a thousand avenues were open. Education had made him acquainted with all the treasures of the world and liberty had flung open the gates thereunto; but I who had attended him seven years; who had watched over him with the care of a big brother, fighting his battles in the street and shielding him from harm to an extent which induced his mother to say, "Oh, Tommy is always safe when he is with Freddy"—I must be confined to a single condition. He had grown and become a *man*: I, though grown to the stature of manhood, must all my life remain a minor—a mere boy. Thomas Auld, junior, obtained a situation on board the brig *Tweed*, and went to sea. I have since heard of his death.

There were few persons to whom I was more sincerely attached than to him. Very soon after I went to Baltimore to live, Master Hugh succeeded in getting me hired to Mr. William Gardiner,[1] an extensive ship-builder on Fells Point. ... At the end of eight months Master Hugh refused longer to allow me to remain with Gardiner. The circumstance which led to this refusal was the committing of an outrage upon me, by the white apprentices of the ship-yard. The fight was a desperate one, and I came out of it shockingly mangled. I was cut and bruised in sundry places, and my left eye was nearly knocked out of its socket. The facts which led to this brutal outrage upon me illustrate a phase of slavery which was destined to become an important element in the overthrow of the slave system, and I may therefore state them with some minuteness. That phase was this—the conflict of slavery with the interests of white mechanics and laborers. In the country this conflict was not so apparent; but in cities, such as Baltimore, Richmond, New Orleans, Mobile, etc., it was seen pretty clearly. The slaveholders, with a craftiness peculiar to themselves, by encouraging the enmity of the poor laboring white man against the blacks, succeeded in making the said white man almost as much a slave as the black slave himself. The difference between the white slave and the black slave was this: the latter belonged to one slaveholder, while the former belonged to the slaveholders collectively. The white slave had taken from him by indirection what the black slave had taken from him directly and without ceremony. Both were plundered, and by the same plunderers. The slave was robbed by his master of all his earnings, above what was required for his bare physical necessities, and the white laboring man was robbed by the slave system of the just results of his labor, because he was flung into competition with a class of laborers who worked without wages. The slaveholders blinded them to this competition by keeping alive their prejudice against the slaves as *men*—not against them as *slaves*. They appealed to their pride, often denouncing emancipation as tending to place the white working man on an equality with negroes, and by this means they succeeded in drawing off the minds of the poor whites from the real fact, that by the rich slave-master they were already regarded as but a single remove from equality with the slave. The impression was cunningly made that slavery was the only power that could prevent the laboring white man from falling to the level of the slave's poverty and degradation. To make this enmity deep and broad between the slave and the poor white man, the latter was allowed to abuse and whip the former without hindrance. But, as I have said, this state of affairs prevailed *mostly* in the country. In the city of Baltimore there were not unfrequent murmurs that educating slaves to be mechanics might, in the end, give slave-masters power to dispense altogether with the

---

1   *William Gardiner* Spelled "Gardner" in Douglass's *Narrative* (1845).

services of the poor white man. But with characteristic dread of offending the slaveholders, these poor white mechanics in Mr. Gardiner's ship-yard, instead of applying the natural, honest remedy for the apprehended evil, and object- ing at once to work there by the side of slaves, made a cowardly attack upon the free colored mechanics, saying they were eating the bread which should be eaten by American freemen, and swearing that they, the mechanics, would not work with them. The feeling was *really* against having their labor brought into competition with that of the colored freeman, and aimed to prevent him from serving himself, in the evening of life, with the trade with which he had served his master, during the more vigorous portion of his days. Had they succeeded in driving the black freemen out of the ship-yard, they would have determined also upon the removal of the black slaves. The feeling was, about this time, very bitter toward all colored people in Baltimore (1836), and they—free and slave—suffered all manner of insult and wrong.

... In the conflict which ended my stay at Mr. Gardiner's I was beset by four of them [white laborers] at once—Ned North, Ned Hayes, Bill Stewart, and Tom Humphreys. Two of them were as large as myself, and they came near killing me, in broad daylight. One came in front, armed with a brick; there was one at each side and one behind, and they closed up all around me. I was struck on all sides; and while I was attending to those in front I received a blow on my head from behind, dealt with a heavy hand-spike. I was completely stunned by the blow, and fell heavily on the ground among the timbers. Taking advantage of my fall they rushed upon me and began to pound me with their fists. With a view of gaining strength, I let them lay on for awhile after I came to myself. They had done me little damage, so far; but finally getting tired of that sport I gave a sudden surge, and despite their weight I rose to my hands and knees. Just as I did this one of their number planted a blow with his boot in my left eye, which for a time seemed to have burst my eye-ball. When they saw my eye completely closed, my face covered with blood, and I staggering under the stunning blows they had given me, they left me. As soon as I gathered strength I picked up the hand-spike and madly enough attempted to pursue them; but here the carpenters interfered and compelled me to give up my pursuit. It was impossible to stand against so many.

Dear reader, you can hardly believe the statement, but it is true and there- fore I write it down; that no fewer than fifty white men stood by and saw this brutal and shameful outrage committed, and not a man of them all interposed a single word of mercy. There were four against one, and that one's face was beaten and battered most horribly, and no one said, "that is enough"; but some cried out, "Kill him! kill him! kill the d——n nigger! knock his brains out! he struck a white person!" I mention this inhuman outcry to show the character of the men and the spirit of the times at Gardiner's ship-yard; and, indeed, in Baltimore generally, in 1836. As I look back to this period, I am almost amazed that I was not murdered outright, so murderous was the spirit which prevailed there. On two other occasions while there I came near losing my life. On one of these, I was driving bolts in the hold through the keelson, with Hayes. In its course the bolt bent. Hayes cursed me and said that it was my blow which bent the bolt. I denied this and charged it upon him. In a fit of rage he seized an adze and darted toward me. I met him with a maul and parried his blow, or I should have lost my life.

After the united attack of North, Stewart, Hayes, and Humphreys, finding that the carpenters were as bitter toward me as the apprentices, and that the latter were probably set on by the former, I found my only chance for life was in flight. I succeeded in getting away without an additional blow. To strike a white man was death by lynch law, in Gardiner's ship-yard; nor was there much of any other law toward the colored people at that time in any other part of Maryland.

After making my escape from the ship-yard I went straight home and related my story to Master Hugh; and to his credit I say it, that his conduct, though he was not a religious man, was every way more humane than that of his brother Thomas, when I went to him in a somewhat similar plight, from the hands of his "Brother Edward Covey."[1] Master Hugh listened attentively to my narration of the circumstances leading to the ruffianly assault, and gave many evidences of his strong indignation at what was done. He was a rough but manly-hearted fellow, and at this time his best nature showed itself.

The heart of my once kind mistress Sophia was again melted in pity towards me. My puffed-out eye and my scarred and blood-covered face moved the dear lady to tears. She kindly drew a chair by me, and with friendly and consoling words, she took water and washed the blood from my face. No mother's hand could have been more tender than hers. She bound up my head and covered my wounded eye with a lean piece of fresh beef. It was almost compensation for all I suffered, that it occasioned the manifestation once more of the originally characteristic kindness of my mistress. Her affectionate heart was not yet dead, though much hardened by time and circumstances.

As for Master Hugh, he was furious, and gave expression to his feelings in the forms of speech usual in that locality. He poured curses on the whole of the ship-yard company, and swore that he would have satisfaction. His indignation was really strong and healthy; but unfortunately it resulted from

---

1 *Brother Edward Covey* In his first *Narrative*, Douglass describes his time working under the brutal overseer Edward Covey, which results in a violent confrontation in which Douglass overcomes him; Douglass continues to live with Covey for several months after this incident, but is never physically abused by him again.

the thought that his rights of property, in my person, had not been respected, more than from any sense of the outrage perpetrated upon me as a *man*. I had reason to think this from the fact that he could, himself, beat and mangle when it suited him to do so.

Bent on having satisfaction, as he said, just as soon as I got a little the better of my bruises Master Hugh took me to Esquire Watson's office on Bond Street, Fells Point, with a view to procuring the arrest of those who had assaulted me. He gave to the magistrate an account of the outrage as I had related it to him, and seemed to expect that a warrant would at once be issued for the arrest of the lawless ruffians. Mr. Watson heard all that he had to say, then coolly inquired, "Mr. Auld, who saw this assault of which you speak?" "It was done, sir, in the presence of a ship-yard full of hands." "Sir," said Mr. Watson, "I am sorry, but I cannot move in this matter, except upon the oath of white witnesses." "But here's the boy; look at his head and face," said the excited Master Hugh; "*they* show *what* has been done." But Watson insisted that he was not authorized to do anything, unless white witnesses of the transaction would come forward and testify to what had taken place. He could issue no warrant, on my word, against white persons, and if I had been killed in the presence of a *thousand blacks*, their testimony combined would have been insufficient to condemn a single murderer. Master Hugh was compelled to say, for once, that this state of things was *too* bad, and he left the office of the magistrate disgusted.

Of course it was impossible to get any white man to testify against my assailants. The carpenters saw what was done; but the actors were but the agents of their malice, and did only what the carpenters sanctioned. They had cried with one accord, "Kill the nigger! kill the nigger!" Even those who may have pitied me, if any such were among them, lacked the moral courage to volunteer their evidence. The slightest show of sympathy or justice toward a person of color was denounced as abolitionism; and the name of abolitionist subjected its hearer to frightful liabilities. "D——n abolitionists," and "kill the niggers," were the watch-words of the foul-mouthed ruffians of those days. Nothing was done, and probably would not have been, had I been killed in the affray. The laws and the morals of the Christian city of Baltimore afforded no protection to the sable[1] denizens of that city.

Master Hugh, on finding that he could get no redress for the cruel wrong, withdrew me from the employment of Mr. Gardiner and took me into his own family, Mrs. Auld kindly taking care of me and dressing my wounds until they were healed and I was ready to go to work again.

---

1 *sable* I.e., dark-skinned.

While I was on the Eastern Shore, Master Hugh had met with reverses which overthrew his business and had given up ship-building in his own yard, on the City Block, and was now acting as foreman of Mr. Walter Price. The best that he could do for me was to take me into Mr. Price's yard, and afford me the facilities there for completing the trade which I began to learn at Gardiner's. Here I rapidly became expert in the use of caulkers'[1] tools, and in the course of a single year, I was able to command the highest wages paid to journeymen caulkers in Baltimore.

The reader will observe that I was now of some pecuniary value to my master. During the busy season I was bringing six and seven dollars per week. I have sometimes brought him as much as nine dollars a week, for wages were a dollar and a half per day.

After learning to caulk, I sought my own employment, made my own contracts, and collected my own earnings—giving Master Hugh no trouble in any part of the transactions to which I was a party.

Here, then, were better days for the Eastern Shore *slave*. I was free from the vexatious assaults of the apprentices at Gardiner's; free from the perils of plantation life and once more in favorable condition to increase my little stock of education, which had been at a dead stand since my removal from Baltimore. I had on the Eastern Shore been only a teacher, when in company with other slaves, but now there were colored persons here who could instruct me. Many of the young caulkers could read, write, and cipher. Some of them had high notions about mental improvement, and the free ones on Fells Point organized what they called the "East Baltimore Mental Improvement Society." To this society, notwithstanding it was intended that only free persons should attach themselves, I was admitted, and was several times assigned a prominent part in its debates. I owe much to the society of these young men.

The reader already knows enough of the *ill* effects of good treatment on a slave to anticipate what was now the case in my improved condition. It was not long before I began to show signs of disquiet with slavery, and to look around for means to get out of it by the shortest route. I was living among *freemen*, and was in all respects equal to them by nature and attainments. *Why should I be a slave?* There was *no* reason why I should be the thrall of any man. Besides, I was now getting, as I have said, a dollar and fifty cents per day. I contracted for it, worked for it, collected it; it was paid to me, and it was *rightfully* my own; and yet upon every returning Saturday night, this money—my own hard earnings, every cent of it—was demanded of me and taken from me by Master Hugh. He did not earn it; he had no hand in earning it; why, then should he have it? I owed him nothing. He had given me no schooling,

---

1 *caulkers* Workers who seal the wooden seams of a boat against leakage with oakum and melted tar.

and I had received from him only my food and raiment; and for these, my services were supposed to pay from the first. The right to take my earnings was the right of the robber. He had the power to compel me to give him the fruits of my labor, and this *power* was his only right in the case. I became more and more dissatisfied with this state of things, and in so becoming I only gave proof of the same human nature which every reader of this chapter in my life—slaveholder, or non-slaveholder—is conscious of possessing.

To make a contented slave, you must make a thoughtless one. It is necessary to darken his moral and mental vision, and, as far as possible, to annihilate his power of reason. He must be able to detect no inconsistencies in slavery. The man who takes his earnings must be able to convince him that he has a perfect right to do so. It must not depend upon mere force: the slave must know no higher law than his master's will. The whole relationship must not only demonstrate to his mind its necessity, but its absolute rightfulness. If there be one crevice through which a single drop can fall, it will certainly rust off the slave's chain.

from SECOND PART

CHAPTER I
ESCAPE FROM SLAVERY

In the first narrative of my experience in slavery, written nearly forty years ago, and in various writings since, I have given the public what I considered very good reasons for withholding the manner of my escape. In substance these reasons were, first, that such publication at any time during the existence of slavery might be used by the master against the slave, and prevent the future escape of any who might adopt the same means that I did. The second reason was, if possible, still more binding to silence—for publication of details would certainly have put in peril the persons and property of those who assisted. Murder itself was not more sternly and certainly punished in the State of Maryland than was the aiding and abetting the escape of a slave. Many colored men, for no other crime than that of giving aid to a fugitive slave, have, like Charles T. Torrey,[1] perished in prison. The abolition of slavery in my native State[2] and throughout the country, and the lapse of time, render the caution hitherto observed no longer necessary. But, even since the abolition of slavery, I have sometimes thought it well enough to baffle curiosity by saying that

---

1 *Charles T. Torrey* Influential white abolitionist and one of the first operators of the Underground Railroad, who was jailed for his activities in 1846 and died there of tuberculosis a few months thereafter. Approximately four hundred enslaved people were freed due to his direct efforts.
2 *my native State* Maryland.

while slavery existed there were good reasons for not telling the manner of my escape, and since slavery had ceased to exist there was no reason for telling it. I shall now, however, cease to avail myself of this formula, and, as far as I can, endeavor to satisfy this very natural curiosity. I should perhaps have yielded to that feeling sooner, had there been anything very heroic or thrilling in the incidents connected with my escape, for I am sorry to say I have nothing of that sort to tell; and yet the courage that could risk betrayal and the bravery which was ready to encounter death if need be, in pursuit of freedom, were essential features in the undertaking. My success was due to address rather than to courage; to good luck rather than to bravery. My means of escape were provided for me by the very men who were making laws to hold and bind me more securely in slavery. It was the custom in the State of Maryland to require of the free colored people to have what were called free papers. This instrument they were required to renew very often, and by charging a fee for this writing, considerable sums from time to time were collected by the State. In these papers the name, age, color, height and form of the free man were described, together with any scars or other marks upon his person which could assist in his identification. This device of slaveholding ingenuity, like other devices of wickedness, in some measure defeated itself—since more than one man could be found to answer the same general description. Hence many slaves could escape by personating the owner of one set of papers; and this was often done as follows: A slave nearly or sufficiently answering the descrip-tion set forth in the papers, would borrow or hire them till he could by their means escape to a free state, and then, by mail or otherwise, return them to the owner. The operation was a hazardous one for the lender as well as for the borrower. A failure on the part of the fugitive to send back the papers would imperil his benefactor, and the discovery of the papers in possession of the wrong man would imperil both the fugitive and his friend. It was therefore an act of supreme trust on the part of a freeman of color thus to put in jeopardy his own liberty that another might be free. It was, however, not unfrequently bravely done, and was seldom discovered. I was not so fortunate as to suf-ficiently resemble any of my free acquaintances as to answer the description of their papers. But I had one friend—a sailor—who owned a sailor's protection, which answered somewhat the purpose of free papers—describing his person and certifying to the fact that he was a free American sailor. The instrument had at its head the American eagle, which at once gave it the appearance of an authorized document. This protection did not, when in my hands, describe its bearer very accurately. Indeed, it called for a man much darker than myself, and close examination of it would have caused my arrest at the start. In order to avoid this fatal scrutiny on the part of the railroad official, I had arranged with Isaac Rolls, a hackman,[1] to bring my baggage to the train just on the moment of starting, and jumped upon the car myself when the train was already in motion. Had I gone into the station and offered to purchase a ticket, I should have been instantly and carefully examined, and undoubtedly arrested. In choosing this plan upon which to act, I considered the jostle of the train, and the natural haste of the conductor in a train crowded with passengers, and relied upon my skill and address[2] in playing the sailor as described in my protection, to do the rest. One element in my favor was the kind feeling which prevailed in Baltimore and other seaports at the time, towards "those who go down to the sea in ships."[3] "Free trade and sailors' rights"[4] expressed the sentiment of the country just then. In my clothing I was rigged out in sailor style. I had on a red shirt and a tarpaulin hat and black cravat, tied in sailor fashion, carelessly and loosely about my neck. My knowledge of ships and sailor's talk came much to my assistance, for I knew a ship from stem to stern, and from keelson to cross-trees, and could talk sailor like an "old salt." On sped the train, and I was well on the way to Havre de Grace before the conductor came into the negro car to collect tickets and examine the papers of his black passengers. This was a critical moment in the drama. My whole future depended upon the decision of this conductor. Agitated I was while this ceremony was proceeding, but still, externally at least, I was apparently calm and self-possessed. He went on with his duty—examining several colored passengers before reaching me. He was somewhat harsh in tone and peremptory in manner until he reached me, when, strangely enough, and to my surprise and relief, his whole manner changed. Seeing that I did not readily produce my free papers, as the other colored persons in the car had done, he said to me in a friendly contrast with that observed towards the others: "I suppose you have your free papers?" To which I answered: "No, sir; I never carry my free papers to sea with me." "But you have something to show that you are a free man, have you not?" "Yes, sir," I answered; "I have a paper with the American eagle on it, that will carry me round the world." With this I drew from my deep sailor's pocket my seaman's protection, as before described. The merest glance at the paper satisfied him, and he took my fare and went on about his business. This moment of time was one of the most anxious I ever experienced. Had the conductor looked closely at the paper, he could not have failed to discover that it called for a very different looking person from myself, and in

1 *hackman* Person hired to drive carriages and transport goods.
2 *address* Manner of speaking, deportment.
3 *those who ... in ships* See Psalm 107.23–24: "They that go down to the sea in ships, that do business in great waters; These see the works of the Lord, and his wonders in the deep."
4 *Free trade and sailors' rights* Well-known slogan of the War of 1812, written upon a flag flown by Captain David Porter.

that case it would have been his duty to arrest me on the instant and send me back to Baltimore from the first station. When he left me with the assurance that I was all right, though much relieved, I realized that I was still in great danger: I was still in Maryland, and subject to arrest at any moment. I saw on the train several persons who would have known me in any other clothes, and I feared they might recognize me, even in my sailor "rig," and report me to the conductor, who would then subject me to a closer examination, which I knew well would be fatal to me.

Though I was not a murderer fleeing from justice, I felt, perhaps, quite as miserable as such a criminal. The train was moving at a very high rate of speed for that time of railroad travel, but to my anxious mind, it was moving far too slowly. Minutes were hours, and hours were days during this part of my flight. After Maryland I was to pass through Delaware—another slave State, where slave-catchers generally awaited their prey, for it was not in the interior of the State, but on its borders, that these human hounds were most vigilant and active. The border lines between slavery and freedom were the dangerous ones, for the fugitives. The heart of no fox or deer, with hungry hounds on his trail, in full chase, could have beaten more anxiously or noisily than did mine from the time I left Baltimore till I reached Philadelphia. The passage of the Susquehanna River at Havre de Grace was at that time made by ferry-boat, on board of which I met a young colored man by the name of Nichols, who came very near betraying me. He was a "hand" on the boat, but instead of minding his business, he insisted upon knowing me, and asking me dangerous questions as to where I was going, and when I was coming back, etc. I got away from my old and inconvenient acquaintance as soon as I could decently do so, and went to another part of the boat. Once across the river I encountered a new danger. Only a few days before I had been at work on a revenue cutter,[1] in Mr. Price's ship-yard, under the care of Captain McGowan. On the meeting at this point of the two trains, the one going south stopped on the track just opposite to the one going north, and it so happened that this Captain McGowan sat at a window where he could see me very distinctly, and would certainly have recognized me had he looked at me but for a second. Fortunately, in the hurry of the moment, he did not see me, and the trains soon passed each other on their respective ways. But this was not the only hair-breadth escape. A German blacksmith, whom I knew well, was on the train with me, and looked at me very intently, as if he thought he had seen me somewhere before in his travels. I really believe he knew me, but had no heart to betray me. At any rate he saw me escaping and held his peace.

---

1 *revenue cutter* Vessel built for customs officers, whose purpose is to guard the coast and catch smugglers.

The last point of imminent danger, and the one I dreaded most, was Wilmington. Here we left the train and took the steamboat for Philadelphia. In making the change I again apprehended arrest, but no one disturbed me, and I was soon on the broad and beautiful Delaware, speeding away to the Quaker City.¹ On reaching Philadelphia in the afternoon I inquired of a colored man how I could get on to New York? He directed me to the Willow Street depot, and thither I went, taking the train that night. I reached New York Tuesday morning, having completed the journey in less than twenty-four hours. Such is briefly the manner of my escape from slavery—and the end of my experience as a slave. Other chapters will tell the story of my life as a freeman.

from CHAPTER 11
SECESSION AND WAR

THE BLACK MAN AT THE WHITE HOUSE²

My efforts to secure just and fair treatment for the colored soldiers did not stop at letters and speeches. At the suggestion of my friend, Major Stearns,³ ... I was induced to go to Washington and lay the complaints of my people before President Lincoln and the Secretary of War;⁴ and to urge upon them such action as should secure to the colored troops then fighting for the country a reasonable degree of fair play. I need not say that at the time I undertook this mission it required much more nerve than a similar one would require now. The distance then between the black man and the white American citizen⁵ was immeasurable. I was an ex-slave, identified with a despised race, and yet I was to meet the most exalted person in this great republic. It was altogether an unwelcome duty, and one from which I would gladly have been excused. I could not know what kind of a reception would be accorded me. I might be told to go home and mind my business, and leave such questions as I had come to discuss to be managed by the men wisely chosen by the American people to deal with them. Or I might be refused an interview altogether. Nevertheless, I

---

1   *the Quaker City*   I.e., Philadelphia, which has strong historical connections to the Quakers, having been founded by Quaker leader William Penn (1644–1718).

2   In August 1863, Douglass met with Abraham Lincoln at the White House to petition for the equal treatment of black soldiers in the U.S. Army. He recounted the story of that meeting both in speeches and in his final autobiography in 1881.

3   *Major Stearns*   George Luther Stearns (1809–67), white abolitionist who worked during the Civil War as a recruiter of black soldiers for the U.S. Army.

4   *Secretary of War*   Edwin Stanton (1814–69).

5   *the black ... American citizen*   Douglass's wording here alludes to the 1857 Supreme Court ruling (*Dred Scott v. Sanford*) determining that no black person, whether free or enslaved, could be considered a U.S. citizen.

felt bound to go, and my acquaintance with Senators Charles Sumner, Henry Wilson, Samuel Pomeroy, Secretary Salmon P. Chase, Secretary William H. Seward, and Assistant Secretary of War Charles A. Dana[1] encouraged me to hope at least for a civil reception. My confidence was fully justified in the result. I shall never forget my first interview with this great man. I was accompanied to the executive mansion and introduced to President Lincoln by Senator Pomeroy. The room in which he received visitors was the one now used by the President's secretaries. I entered it with a moderate estimate of my own consequence, and yet there I was to talk with, and even to advise, the head man of a great nation. Happily for me, there was no vain pomp and ceremony about him. I was never more quickly or more completely put at ease in the presence of a great man than in that of Abraham Lincoln. He was seated, when I entered, in a low arm-chair with his feet extended on the floor, surrounded by a large number of documents and several busy secretaries. The room bore the marks of business, and the persons in it, the President included, appeared to be much over-worked and tired. Long lines of care were already deeply written on Mr. Lincoln's brow, and his strong face, full of earnestness, lighted up as soon as my name was mentioned. As I approached and was introduced to him he arose and extended his hand, and bade me welcome. I at once felt myself in the presence of an honest man—one whom I could love, honor, and trust without reserve or doubt. Proceeding to tell him who I was and what I was doing, he promptly, but kindly, stopped me, saying, "I know who you are, Mr. Douglass; Mr. Seward has told me all about you. Sit down. I am glad to see you." I then told him the object of my visit: that I was assisting to raise colored troops; that several months before I had been very successful in getting men to enlist, but that now it was not easy to induce the colored men to enter the service, because there was a feeling among them that the government did not, in several respects, deal fairly with them. Mr. Lincoln asked me to state particulars. I replied that there were three particulars which I wished to bring to his attention. First, that colored soldiers ought to receive the same wages as those paid to white soldiers. Second, that colored soldiers ought to receive the same protection when taken prisoners, and be exchanged as readily and on the same terms as any other prisoners, and if Jefferson Davis should shoot or hang colored soldiers in cold blood the United States government should, without delay, retaliate in kind and degree upon Confederate prisoners in its hands. Third, when colored soldiers, seeking the "bubble reputation at the cannon's mouth,"[2] performed great and uncommon service on the battlefield, they

---

1   *Senators ... Dana*   Various significant Republican Party members and abolitionists.

2   *seeking ... mouth*   See Shakespeare's *As You Like It*: "Seeking the bubble reputation / Even in the cannon's mouth" (2.7.159–60).

should be rewarded by distinction and promotion precisely as white soldiers are rewarded for like services.

Mr. Lincoln listened with patience and silence to all I had to say. He was serious and even troubled by what I had said and by what he had evidently before thought upon the same points. He, by his silent listening not less than by his earnest reply to my words, impressed me with the solid gravity of his character.

He began by saying that the employment of colored troops at all was a great gain to the colored people; that the measure could not have been successfully adopted at the beginning of the war; that the wisdom of making colored men soldiers was still doubted; that their enlistment was a serious offense to popular prejudice; that they had larger motives for being soldiers than white men; that they ought to be willing to enter the service upon any condition; that the fact that they were not to receive the same pay as white soldiers seemed a necessary concession to smooth the way to their employment at all as soldiers; but that ultimately they would receive the same. On the second point, in respect to equal protection, he said the case was more difficult. Retaliation was a terrible remedy, and one which it was very difficult to apply; that, if once begun, there was no telling where it would end; that if he could get hold of the Confederate soldiers who had been guilty of treating colored soldiers as felons he could easily retaliate, but the thought of hanging men for a crime perpetrated by others was revolting to his feelings. He thought that the rebels themselves would stop such barbarous warfare; that less evil would be done if retaliation were not resorted to and that he had already received information that colored soldiers were being treated as prisoners of war. In all this I saw the tender heart of the man rather than the stern warrior and commander-in-chief of the American army and navy, and, while I could not agree with him, I could but respect his humane spirit.

On the third point he appeared to have less difficulty, though he did not absolutely commit himself. He simply said that he would sign any commission to colored soldiers whom his Secretary of War should commend to him. Though I was not entirely satisfied with his views, I was so well satisfied with the man and with the educating tendency of the conflict that I determined to go on with the recruiting.

From the President I went to see Secretary Stanton. The manner of no two men could be more widely different. I was introduced by Assistant Secretary Dana, whom I had known many years before at "Brook Farm," Mass.,[1] and afterward as managing editor of the New York *Tribune*. Every line in Mr.

---

1   *many years ... Mass.*   Assistant Secretary of War Charles A. Dana lived between 1841 and 1846 at the Transcendentalist utopian community Brook Farm.

Stanton's face told me that my communication with him must be brief, clear, and to the point; that he might turn his back upon me as a bore at any moment; that politeness was not one of his weaknesses. His first glance was that of a man who says: "Well, what do you want? I have no time to waste upon you or anybody else, and I shall waste none. Speak quick, or I shall leave you." The man and the place seemed alike busy. Seeing I had no time to lose, I hastily went over the ground I had gone over to President Lincoln. As I ended I was surprised by seeing a changed man before me. Contempt and suspicion and brusqueness had all disappeared from his face and manner, and for a few minutes he made the best defense that I had then heard from anybody of the treatment of colored soldiers by the government. I was not satisfied, yet I left in the full belief that the true course to the black man's freedom and citizenship was over the battlefield, and that my business was to get every black man I could into the Union armies. Both the President and Secretary of War assured me that justice would ultimately be done my race, and I gave full faith and credit to their promise. On assuring Mr. Stanton of my willingness to take a commission, he said he would make me assistant adjutant to General Thomas,[1] who was then recruiting and organizing troops in the Mississippi valley. He asked me how soon I could be ready. I told him in two weeks, and that my commission might be sent to me at Rochester. For some reason, however, my commission never came. The government, I fear, was still clinging to the idea that positions of honor in the service should be occupied by white men, and that it would not do to inaugurate just then the Policy of perfect equality. I wrote to the department for my commission, but was simply told to report to General Thomas. This was so different from what I expected and from what I had been promised that I wrote to Secretary Stanton that I would report to General Thomas on receipt of my commission, but it did not come, and I did not go to the Mississippi valley as I had fondly hoped. I knew too much of camp life and the value of shoulder straps in the army to go into the service without some visible mark of my rank. I have no doubt that Mr. Stanton in the moment of our meeting meant all he said, but thinking the matter over he felt that the time had not then come for a step so radical and aggressive. Meanwhile my three sons were in the service, Lewis and Charles ... in the Massachusetts regiments, and Frederick recruiting colored troops in the Mississippi valley.

—1881, 1893

---

1 *General Thomas* U.S. Army general George Henry Thomas (1816–70).

In Context

Responses to Frederick Douglass's *Narrative*

Margaret Fuller, Review of *Narrative of the Life of Frederick Douglass, an American Slave*, from *The New York Tribune* (10 June 1845)

Douglass's *Narrative* was welcomed with enthusiasm in the abolitionist press; most notably, the *New York Tribune* on 10 June 1845 printed on its front page a long and highly favorable review written by prominent feminist and Transcendentalist Margaret Fuller. Like many of her contemporaries, Fuller saw parallels between the fight for women's rights and the fight for racial equality, which she saw as linked by a "natural following out of principles." Yet the extent of Fuller's support for abolitionism as a movement has also been the source of substantial disagreement among readers, even among her contemporaries. According to English sociologist Harriet Martineau, Fuller regarded "the anti-slavery subject as simply a low and disagreeable one, which should be left to unrefined persons to manage, while others were occupied with higher things" (*Harriet Martineau's Autobiography*, 1877). Martineau continued: "The difference between us was that while [Fuller] was living and moving in an ideal world ... she looked down upon persons who acted instead of talking finely, and devoted their fortunes, their peace, their repose, and their very lives to the preservation of the principles of the republic." Whether entirely fair or not, the same criticism could have been made of numerous Transcendentalists in the 1830s and 40s, including Ralph Waldo Emerson and Henry David Thoreau—both of whom became ardent abolitionists in the years leading up to the Civil War. Fuller herself died in a shipwreck in 1850, leaving forever unanswered the question of whether or not she would have immersed herself deeper into the antislavery movement later in life.

Frederick Douglass has been for some time a prominent member of the Abolition party. He is said to be an excellent speaker—can speak from a thorough personal experience—and has upon the audience, beside, the influence of a strong character and uncommon talents. In the book before us he has put into the story of his life the thoughts, the feelings and the adventures that have been so affecting through the living voice; nor are they less so from the printed page. He has had the courage to name the persons, times and places, thus exposing himself to obvious danger, and setting the seal on his deep convictions as to the religious need of speaking the whole truth. Considered merely as a narrative, we have never read one more simple, true, coherent, and warm with genuine feeling. It is an excellent piece of writing, and on that score to be prized as a specimen of the powers of the Black Race, which Prejudice persists in disputing. We prize highly all evidence of this kind, and it is becoming more abundant. The Cross of the Legion of Honor has just been conferred in France on Dumas and Soulié,[1] both celebrated in the paths of light literature. Dumas, whose father was a General in the French Army, is a Mulatto; Soulié, a Quadroon.[2] He went from New-Orleans, where, though to the eye a white man, yet, as known to have African blood in his veins, he could never have enjoyed the privileges due to a human being. Leaving the Land of Freedom, he found himself free to develop the powers that God had given.

Two wise and candid thinkers—the Scotchman, Kinment,[3] prematurely lost to this country, of which he was so faithful and generous a student, and the late Dr. Channing[4]—both thought that the African Race had in them a peculiar element, which, if it could be assimilated with those imported among us from Europe, would give to genius a development, and to the energies of character a balance and harmony beyond what has been seen heretofore in the history of the world. Such an element is indicated in their lowest estate by a talent for melody, a ready skill at imitation and adaptation, an almost indestructible elasticity of nature. It is to be remarked in the writings both of Soulié and Dumas, full of faults but glowing with plastic life and fertile in invention. The same torrid energy and saccharine fulness may be felt in the writings of this Douglass, though his life being one of action or resistance, was less favorable to *such* powers than one of a more joyous flow might have been.

The book is prefaced by two communications—one from Garrison, and one from Wendell Phillips[.] That from the former is in his usual over emphatic style. His motives and his course have been noble and generous. We look upon him with high respect, but he has indulged in violent invective and denunciation till he has spoiled the temper of his mind. Like a man who has been in the habit of screaming himself hoarse to make the deaf hear,

---

1   *Dumas and Soulié*   Alexandre Dumas (1802–70) and Frédéric Soulié (1800–47), widely read French novelists; Dumas's paternal grandmother, Marie-Cessette Dumas, was an enslaved woman of African descent who lived in the French colony of Saint-Domingue (present-day Haiti).

2   *Mulatto ... Quadroon*   Terms commonly used in the nineteenth century to classify individuals of mixed racial background; while "mulatto" generally meant a person with one white parent and one parent of African descent, and "quadroon" a person with one grandparent of African descent, the terms were often used rather loosely and might refer more to a person's physical appearance than to his or her actual known ancestry. Persons who were known to have African ancestry or who appeared mixed-race often had more limited social and legal opportunities than those who could "pass" for a white person.

3   *Kinment*   Alexander Kinmont (1799–1838), Scottish philosopher and educator who taught in Cincinnati for several years.

4   *Dr. Channing*   William Ellery Channing (1780–1842), American Unitarian preacher who became an abolitionist late in life (but nevertheless maintained a rather paternalistic form of racism in his writings).

he can no longer pitch his voice on a key agreeable to common ears. Mr. Phillips's remarks are equally decided, without this exaggeration in the tone. Douglass himself seems very just and temperate[.] We feel that his view, even of those who have injured him most, may be relied upon. He knows how to allow for motives and influences. Upon the subject of Religion, he speaks with great force, and not more than our own sympathies can respond to. The inconsistencies of Slaveholding professors of religion[1] cry to Heaven. We are not disposed to detest, or refuse communion with them. Their blindness is but one form of that prevalent fallacy which substitutes a creed for a faith, a ritual for a life. We have seen too much of this system of atonement not to know that those who adopt it often began with good intentions, and are, at any rate, in their mistakes worthy of the deepest pity. But that is no reason why the truth should not be uttered, trumpet-tongued, about the thing. "Bring no more vain oblations"; sermons must daily be preached anew on that text. Kings, five hundred years ago, built churches with the spoils of war; clergymen today command slaves to obey a Gospel which they will not allow them to read, and call themselves Christians amid the curses of their fellow men. The world ought to get on a little faster than that, if there be really any principle of improvement in it. The Kingdom of Heaven may not at the beginning have dropped seed larger than a mustard-seed, but even from that we had a right to expect a fuller growth than can be believed to exist,[2] when we read such a book as this of Douglass. Unspeakably affecting is the fact that he never saw his mother at all by daylight. ...

Copies of the work may be had of W.H. Graham, Tribune Buildings. Price, 50 cents.

A.C.C. Thompson, "TO THE PUBLIC. FALSEHOOD REFUTED," from *The Delaware Republican*, reprinted in *The Liberator* (12 December 1845)

It was common practice for antislavery publications to reprint in their pages articles in support of slavery—in order to refute their claims. Thus was this piece, originally from *The Delaware Republican*, reprinted in *The Liberator*, the abolitionist paper run by Douglass's friend and supporter, William Lloyd Garrison.

---

1 *professors of religion* I.e., those who profess, or pretend, to embrace religious values.
2 *The Kingdom of Heaven … to exist* See Matthew 13.31–32: "The kingdom of heaven is like to a grain of mustard seed, which a man took, and sowed in his field: Which indeed is the least of all seeds: but when it is grown, it is the greatest among herbs, and becometh a tree, so that the birds of the air come and lodge in the branches thereof."

It is with considerable regret that I find myself measurably compelled to appear before the public; but my attention has lately been arrested by a pamphlet which has been freely circulated in Wilmington and elsewhere, with the following superscription: *Extract from a Narrative of Frederick Douglass, an American Slave, written by himself.*

And although I am aware that no sensible, unprejudiced person will credit such a ridiculous publication, which bears the glaring impress of falsehood on every page, yet I deem it expedient that I should give the public some information respecting the validity of this narrative, because I was for many years a citizen of the section of country where the scenes of the above mentioned narrative are laid; and am intimately acquainted with most of the gentlemen whose characters are so shamefully traduced; and I am also aware, that the Narrative was not written by the professed author, but from statements of this runaway slave, some evil designed[1] person or persons have composed this catalogue of lies to excite the indignation of the public opinion against the slaveholders of the South; and have even attempted to plunge their venomous fangs in the vitals of the church.

I shall, therefore, briefly notice some of the most glaring falsehoods contained in the aforesaid Narrative, and give a true representation of the character of those gentlemen, who have been censured in such an uncharitable manner, as murderers, hypocrites, and everything else that is vile.

I indulge no animosity against the fabricators and circulators of the Narrative, neither do I know them; but I positively declare the whole to be a bucket of falsehoods, from beginning to end.

1st. The identity of the author. About eight years ago, I knew this recreant[2] slave by the name of Frederick Bailey (instead of Douglass). He then lived with Mr. Edward Covy, and was an unlearned, and rather an ordinary negro, and [I] am confident he was not capable of writing the Narrative alluded to; for none but an educated man, and one who had some knowledge of the rules of grammar, could write so correctly. Although, to make the imposition at all creditable, the composer has labored to write it in as plain a style as possible: consequently, the detection of this first falsehood proves the whole production to be notoriously untrue.

Again. "It is a common custom in the part of Maryland from which I ran away, to separate children from their mothers at a very early age."[3]

This also I know to be false. There is no such custom prevalent in that section of the country; but, on the contrary, the children are raised with their

---

1   *evil designed*   I.e., with evil intentions.
2   *recreant*   Disobedient.
3   *It is … early age*   Quotation from Douglass's *Narrative*.

mothers, and generally live with them in the same house, except in some few instances where the mother is hired out as a cook or laborer in some other family.

The gentlemen whose names are so prominently set forth in the said Narrative are Col. Edward Lloyd, Capt. Anthony, Austin Gore, Thomas Lamdin (not Lanman), Giles Hicks, Thomas Auld, and Edward Covy. Most of these persons I am intimately acquainted with and shall give a brief sketch of their characters as follows:

Col. Edward Lloyd was one of the most wealthy and respectable planters in the State of Maryland. He was at one time the Governor of the State, and for several years, a member of the Legislature. He owned several thousand acres of land, and between 4 and 500 slaves. He died before I had much knowledge of him; but I know that he was a kind and charitable man, and in every respect an honorable and worthy citizen.

Most of the same slaves are now owned by his three sons, and they manage their servants in the same manner as did their father; and I know there are no such barbarities committed on their plantations.

Could it be possible that charitable feeling men could murder human beings, with as little remorse of conscience, as the narrative of this infamous libel wishes to make us believe; and that the laws of Maryland, which operate *alike upon black and white*, bond or free, could permit such foul murders to pass unnoticed? No! it is impossible; and every sensible man knows that these false accusations are the ebullition of an unchristian prejudice.

Captain Anthony and Giles Hicks, I know but little of. The accused murderer, Mr. Gore, is a respectable citizen, living near St. Michaels, and I believe a worthy member of the Methodist Episcopal Church; he was formerly an overseer for Col. Lloyd, and at this time, all who know him, think him anything but a murderer.

Thomas Lamdin, who, it is said (in the Narrative), boasted so frequently of his murders, is at this time an honest school teacher in the District where I formerly lived; and all the harm that can be said of him is, that he is too good-natured and harmless to injure any person but himself.

Capt. Thomas Auld, whose hypocritical meanness is so strongly depicted in the aforesaid Narrative, was for many years a respectable merchant in the town of St. Michaels, and an honorable and worthy member of the Methodist E. Church, and only notable for his integrity and irreproachable Christian character. He is now retired from the turmoil of a mercantile life, and engaged in the worthy occupation of tilling the soil, little dreaming of the foul accusations that are circulated against him.

Edward Covy, the renowned "negro breaker," is also a plain, honest farmer, and a tried and faithful member of the Methodist E. Church. Mr. Covy lived for several years on a farm adjoining my father's, at which time this runaway negro lived with him, and I am well aware that no such bloody tragedy as is recorded in that lying Narrative ever occurred on Mr. Covy's farm. All that can be said of Mr. Covy is that he is a good Christian, and a hard working man, and makes everyone around him work and treats them well. By his honest industry, he has purchased a fine farm, and is now reaping the reward of his labor.

Such are the characters of the men whom the imposers of this dirty Narrative have so uncharitably traduced, and by blending these false accusations with the Methodist religion of the South, they wish to lacerate her already bleeding wounds.

I was raised among slaves, and have also owned them, and am well aware that the slaves live better and fare better in many respects than the free blacks.

Yet, I am positively opposed to slavery, for I know it is a great evil; but *the evil falls not upon the slave,* but on the owner.

Intrigue and false accusations will never liberate the slave of the South; but, on the contrary, every such attempt will only forge for them new and stronger fetters.

Let the tender-hearted philanthropists of the North speak truth and love towards their southern brethren, and make a liberal application of their gold for the removing the blacks from the country, and their chance of success will be more flattering.

I have given a true representation of the persons connected with the aforesaid Narrative, and I respectfully submit the facts to the judgment of an impartial public.

A.C.C. THOMPSON

No. 101 Market-st. Wilmington, Del.

☞ This attempt to invalidate the Narrative of Frederick Douglass, only confirms its correctness, as Mr. Thompson admits everything but the cruelty described by Douglass—and on that point the latter speaks from experience and knowledge.

Frederick Douglass, "Reply to Mr. A.C.C. Thompson," *The Liberator* (27 February 1846)

To the Editor of the Liberator

DEAR FRIEND—For the sake of our righteous cause, I was delighted to see, by an extract copied into the *Liberator* of 12th Dec. 1845, from *The Delaware Republican,* that Mr. A.C.C. Thompson, No. 101, Market-street,

Wilmington, has undertaken to invalidate my testimony against the slave-holders, whose names I have made prominent in the narrative of my experience while in slavery.

Slaveholders and slave-traders never betray greater indiscretion, than when they venture to defend themselves, or their system of plunder, in any other community than a slaveholding one. Slavery has its own standard of morality, humanity, justice, and Christianity. Tried by that standard, it is a system of the greatest kindness to the slave—sanctioned by the purest morality—in perfect agreement with justice—and, of course, not inconsistent with Christianity. But, tried by any other, it is doomed to condemnation. The naked relation of master and slave is one of those monsters of darkness, to whom the light of truth is death! The wise ones among the slaveholders know this, and they studiously avoid doing anything, which, in their judgment, tends to elicit truth. They seem fully to understand, that their safety is in their silence. They may have learned this wisdom from Junius, who counselled his opponent, Sir William Draper, when defending Lord Granby,[1] never to attract attention to a character, which would only pass without condemnation, when it passed without observation.

I am now almost too far away[2] to answer this attempted refutation by Mr. Thompson. I fear his article will be forgotten, before you get my reply. I, however, think the whole thing worth reviving, as it is seldom we have so good a case for dissection. In any country but the United States, I might hope to get a hearing[3] through the columns of the paper in which I was attacked. But this would be inconsistent with American usage and magnanimity. It would be folly to expect such a hearing. They might possibly advertise me as a runaway slave, and share the reward of my apprehension; but on no other conditions would they allow my reply a place in their columns.

In this, however, I may judge the "Republican" harshly. It may be that, having admitted Mr. Thompson's article, the editor will think it but fair—negro though I am—to allow my reply an insertion.

---

1   *Junius ... Lord Granby*   "Junius" was the pseudonym of a writer of anonymous letters to the London newspaper *Public Advertiser* in 1769–72, which aimed to publicly expose various failures of the British government at that time. In particular, Douglass refers to an instance in which military officer William Draper attempted to defend Member of Parliament John Manners, Lord Granby, from accusations of heavy drinking and unscrupulousness leveled by Junius, only to inadvertently confirm those accusations through his defense.

2   *I am ... far away*   Douglass was living in the United Kingdom (which then included both Britain and all of Ireland) at this time, in part to avoid capture by people who hunted fugitives from slavery.

3   *get a hearing*   I.e., have his reply to Thompson's article published in the same paper where Thompson's article appeared.

In replying to Mr. Thompson, I shall proceed as I usually do in preaching the slaveholder's sermon,—dividing the subject under two general heads, as follows:

1st. The statement of Mr. Thompson, in confirmation of the truth of my narrative.

2ndly. His denials of its truthfulness.

Under the first, I beg Mr. Thompson to accept my thanks for his full, free and unsolicited testimony, in regard to my identity. There now need be no doubt on that point, however much there might have been before. Your testimony, Mr. Thompson, has settled the question forever. I give you the fullest credit for the deed, saying nothing of the motive. But for you, sir, the pro-slavery people in the North might have persisted, with some show of reason, in representing me as being an imposter—a free negro who had never been south of Mason & Dixon's line—one whom the abolitionists, acting on the jesuitical principle, that the end justifies the means, had educated and sent forth to attract attention to their faltering cause. I am greatly indebted to you, sir, for silencing those truly prejudicial insinuations. I wish I could make you understand the amount of service you have done me. You have completely tripped up the heels of your pro-slavery friends, and laid them flat at my feet. You have done a piece of anti-slavery work, which no anti-slavery man could do. Our cautious and truth-loving people in New England would never have believed this testimony, in proof of my identity, had it been borne by an abolitionist. Not that they really think an abolitionist capable of bearing false witness intentionally; but such persons are thought fanatical, and to look at everything through a distorted medium. They will believe you—they will believe a slaveholder. They have, somehow or other, imbibed (and, I confess, strangely enough) the idea that persons such as yourself are dispassionate, impartial and disinterested, and therefore capable of giving a fair representation of things connected with slavery. Now, under these circumstances, your testimony is of the utmost importance. It will serve to give effect to my exposures of slavery, both at home and abroad. I hope I shall not administer to your vanity when I tell you that you seem to have been raised up for this purpose! I came to this land with the highest testimonials from some of the most intelligent and distinguished abolitionists in the United States; yet some here have entertained and expressed doubt as to whether I have ever been a slave. You may easily imagine the perplexing and embarrassing nature of my situation, and how anxious I must have been to be relieved from it. You, sir, have relieved me. I now stand before both the American and British public, endorsed by you as being just what I have ever represented myself to be—to wit, an *American slave.*

You say, "I knew this recreant slave by the name of Frederick Bailey (instead of Douglass)." Yes, that was my name; and, leaving out the term recreant, which savors a little of bitterness, your testimony is direct and perfect—just what I have long wanted. But you are not yet satisfied. You seem determined to bear the most ample testimony in my favor. You say you knew me when I lived with Mr. Covey. "And with most of the persons" mentioned in my narrative, "you are intimately acquainted." This is excellent. Then Mr. Edward Covey is not a creature of my imagination, but really did, and may yet exist.

You thus brush away the miserable insinuation of my northern pro-slavery enemies, that I have used fictitious not real names. You say—"Col. Lloyd was a wealthy planter. Mr. Gore was once an overseer for Col. Lloyd, but is now living near St. Michael's, is respected and [you] believe he is a member of the Methodist Episcopal Church. Mr. Thomas Auld is an honorable and worthy member of the Methodist Episcopal Church. Mr. Covey, too, is a member of the Methodist church, and all that can be said of him is, that he is a good Christian," &c. &c. Do allow me, once more, to thank you for this triumphant vindication of the truth of my statements; and to show you how highly I value your testimony, I will inform you that I am now publishing a second edition of my narrative in this country,[1] having already disposed of the first. I will insert your article with my reply as an appendix to the edition now in progress. If you find any fault with my frequent thanks, you may find some excuse for me in the fact, that I have serious fears that you will be but poorly thanked by those whose characters you have felt it your duty to defend. I am almost certain they will regard you as running before you were sent, and as having spoken when you should have been silent. Under these trying circumstances, it is evidently the duty of those interested in your welfare to extend to you such words of consolation as may ease, if not remove, the pain of your sad disappointment! But enough of this.

Now, then, to the second part—or your denials. You are confident I did not write the book; and the reason of your confidence is, that when you knew me, I was an unlearned and rather an ordinary negro. Well, I have to admit I was rather an ordinary negro when you knew me, and I do not claim to be a very extraordinary one now. But you knew me under very unfavorable circumstances. It was when I lived with Mr. Covey, the negro-breaker, *and member of the Methodist Church.* I had just been living with master Thomas Auld, where I had been reduced by hunger. Master Thomas did not allow me enough to eat. Well, when I lived with Mr. Covey, I was driven so hard, and whipped so often, that my soul was crushed and my spirits broken. I was a mere wreck. The degradation to which I was then subjected, as I now look back to it, seems

---

1 *this country* I.e., the United Kingdom.

more like a dream than a horrible reality. I can scarcely realize how I ever passed through it, without quite losing all my moral and intellectual energies. I can easily understand that you sincerely doubt if I wrote the narrative; for if any one had told me, seven years ago, I should ever be able to write such an one, I should have doubted as strongly as you now do. You must not judge me now by what I then was—a change of circumstances has made a surprising change in age. Frederick Douglass, the *freeman*, is a very different person from Frederick Bailey,[1] the *slave*. I feel myself almost a new man—freedom has given me new life. I fancy you would scarcely know me. I think I have altered very much in my general appearance, and know I have in my manners. You remember when I used to meet you on the road to St. Michael's, or near Mr. Covey's lane gate, I hardly dared to lift my head, and look up at you. If I should meet you now, amid the free hills of old Scotland, where the ancient "black Douglass"[2] once met his foes, I presume I might summon sufficient fortitude to look you full in the face; and were you to attempt to make a slave of me, it is possible you might find me almost as disagreeable a subject, as was the Douglass to whom I have just referred. Of one thing, I am certain—you would see *a great change* in me!

I trust I have now explained away your reason for thinking I did not write the narrative in question.

You next deny the existence of such cruelty in Maryland as I reveal in my narrative; and ask, with truly marvellous simplicity, "could it be possible that charitable, feeling men could murder human beings with as little remorse as the narrative of this infamous libeller would make us believe; and that the laws of Maryland, which operate alike upon black and white, bond and free, could permit such foul murders to pass unnoticed?" "No," you say, "it is impossible." I am not to determine what charitable, feeling men can do; but, to show what Maryland slaveholders actually do, their charitable feeling is to be determined by their deeds, and not their deeds by their charitable feelings. The cowskin[3] makes as deep a gash in my flesh, when wielded by a professed saint, as it does when wielded by an open sinner. The deadly musket does as fatal execution when its trigger is pulled by Austin Gore, the Christian, as when the same is done by Beal Bondly,[4] the infidel. The best way to ascertain what those charitable, feeling men can do, will be to point you to the laws made by them, and which you say operate alike upon the white and the black, the bond and the

---

1 [Douglass's note] My former name.
2 *black Douglass* Douglass's chosen namesake, a character from Walter Scott's loosely historical poem "The Lady of the Lake" (1810). The historical "black Douglas" was James Douglas, Lord of Douglas (c. 1286–1330), an important leader in the fight for Scottish independence.
3 *cowskin* Whip made of cowhide.
4 *Austin Gore ... Beal Bondly* Cruel enslavers mentioned in Douglass's *Narrative*.

free. By consulting the statute laws of Maryland, you will find the following: "Any slave for rambling in the night, or riding horses in the day time without leave, or running away, may be punished by whipping, cropping,[1] branding in the cheek, or otherwise—not rendering him unfit for labor."—p. 337.

Then another: "Any slave convicted of petty treason, murder, or wilful burning of dwelling-houses, may be sentenced to have the right hand cut off, to be hanged in the usual way—his head severed from his body—the body divided into four quarters, and the head and quarters set up in the most public place where such act was committed."—Page 190.

Now, Mr. Thompson, when you consider with what ease a slave may be convicted of any one or all of these crimes, how bloody and atrocious do those laws appear! Yet, sir, they are but the breath of those pious and charitable feeling men, whom you would defend. I am sure I have recorded in my narrative, nothing so revoltingly cruel, murderous, and infernal, as may be found in your own statute book.

You say that the laws of Maryland operate alike upon the white and black, the bond and free. If you mean by this, that the parties named are all equally protected by law, you perpetrate a falsehood as big as that told by President Polk in his inaugural address.[2] It is a notorious fact, even on this side the Atlantic, that a black man cannot testify against a white in any court in Maryland, or any other slave State. If you do not know this, you are more than ordinarily ignorant, and are to be pitied rather than censured. I will not say "that the detection of this falsehood proves all you have said to be false"—for I wish to avail myself of your testimony, in regard to my identity—but I will say, you have made yourself very liable to suspicion.

I will close these remarks by saying, your positive opposition to slavery is fully explained, and will be well understood by anti-slavery men, when you say the evil of the system does not fall upon the slave, but the slaveholder. This is like saying that the evil of being burnt is not felt by the person burnt, but by him who kindles up the fire about him.

FREDERICK DOUGLASS
Perth, (Scotland,) 27th Jan. 1846

---

1 *cropping* Cutting off one's ears.
2 *President Polk ... inaugural address* Douglass is likely referring to the following statement made by President James Polk in his inaugural address of March 1845: "All distinctions of birth or rank have been abolished. All citizens, whether native or adopted, are placed upon terms of precise equality. All are entitled to equal rights and equal protection." Polk was a slaveholder throughout most of his adult life.

from *To My Old Master*

Douglass published this as an open letter in the 8 September 1848 issue of the *North Star*; the letter was reprinted in William Lloyd Garrison's abolitionist newspaper *The Liberator* two weeks later, and Douglass also included it, with minor revisions, in the appendices to his second autobiography, *My Bondage and My Freedom* (1855).

THOMAS AULD—SIR:

... I have often thought I should like to explain to you the grounds upon which I have justified myself in running away from you. I am almost ashamed to do so now, for by this time you may have discovered them yourself. I will, however, glance at them. When yet but a child about six years old, I imbibed the determination to run away. The very first mental effort that I now remember on my part, was an attempt to solve the mystery, Why am I a slave? and with this question my youthful mind was troubled for many days, pressing upon me more heavily at times than others. When I saw the slave-driver whip a slave-woman, cut the blood out of her neck, and heard her piteous cries, I went away into the corner of the fence, wept and pondered over this mystery. I had, through some medium, I know not what, got some idea of God, the Creator of all mankind, the black and the white, and that he had made the blacks to serve the whites as slaves. How he could do this and be *good*, I could not tell. I was not satisfied with this theory, which made God responsible for slavery, for it pained me greatly, and I have wept over it long and often. At one time, your first wife, Mrs. Lucretia, heard me singing and saw me shedding tears, and asked of me the matter, but I was afraid to tell her. I was puzzled with this question, till one night, while sitting in the kitchen, I heard some of the old slaves talking of their parents having been stolen from Africa by white men, and were sold here as slaves. The whole mystery was solved at once. Very soon after this, my aunt Jinny and uncle Noah ran away, and the great noise made about it by your father-in-law, made me for the first time acquainted with the fact, that there were free States as well as slave States. From that time, I resolved that I would someday run away. The morality of the act, I dispose of as follows: I am myself; you are yourself; we are two distinct persons, equal persons. What you are I am. You are a man, so am I. God created both, and made us separate beings. I am not by nature bound to you, or you to me. Nature does not make your existence depend upon me, or mine to depend upon yours. I cannot walk upon your legs, or you upon mine. I cannot breathe for you, or you for me; I must breathe for myself, and you for yourself. We are distinct persons, and are each equally provided with faculties necessary to our individual existence. In leaving you, I took nothing but what belonged to me, and in no way lessened your means of obtaining an *honest* living. Your faculties remained yours, and mine became useful to their rightful owner. I therefore see no wrong in any part of the transaction. It is true, I went off secretly, but that was more your fault than mine. Had I let you into the secret, you would have defeated the enterprise entirely; but for this, I should have been really glad to have made you acquainted with my intention to leave.

You may perhaps want to know how I like my present condition. I am free to say, I greatly prefer it to that which I occupied in Maryland. I am, however, by no means prejudiced against that State as such. Its geography, climate, fertility, and products, are such as to make it a very desirable abode for any man; and but for the existence of slavery there, it is not impossible that I might again take up my abode in that State. It is not that I love Maryland less, but freedom more.[1] You will be surprised to learn that people at the North labor under the strange delusion that if the slaves were emancipated at the South, they would all flock to the North. So far from this being the case, in that event, you would see many old and familiar faces back again at the South. The fact is, there are few here who would not return to the South in the event of emancipation. We want to live in the land of our birth, and to lay our bones by the side of our fathers'; and nothing short of an intense love of personal freedom keeps us from the South. For the sake of this, most of us would live on a crust of bread and a cup of cold water.

Since I left you, I have had a rich experience. I have occupied stations which I never dreamed of when a slave. Three out of the ten years since I left you, I spent as a common laborer on the wharves of New Bedford, Massachusetts. It was there I earned my first free dollar. It was mine. I could spend it as I pleased. I could buy hams or herring with it, without asking any odds of anybody. That was a precious dollar to me. You remember when I used to make seven or eight, and even nine dollars a week in Baltimore, you would take every cent of it from me every Saturday night, saying that I belonged to you, and my earnings also. I never liked this conduct on your part—to say the best, I thought it a little mean.[2] I would not have served you so. But let that pass. I was a little awkward about counting money in New Bedford. I like to have betrayed myself several times. I caught myself saying phip,[3] for four pence; and one time a man actually charged me with being a runaway, whereupon I was silly enough to become one by running away from him, for

---

1 *not that ... freedom more*   See Shakespeare's *Julius Caesar* 3.2.21–24: "If then that friend demand why Brutus rose against Caesar, this is my answer: not that I loved Caesar less, but that I loved Rome more."
2 *mean*   Ungenerous; ignoble.
3 *phip*   Maryland slang for a four-pence coin.

I was greatly afraid he might adopt measures to get me again into slavery, a condition I then dreaded more than death.

I soon, however, learned to count money as well as to make it, and got on swimmingly. I married soon after leaving you:[1] in fact, I was engaged to be married before I left you; and instead of finding my companion a burden, she was truly a helpmeet. She went to live—at service, and I to work on the wharf, and though we toiled hard the first winter, we never lived more happily. After remaining in New Bedford for three years, I met with Wm. Lloyd Garrison,[2] a person of whom you have *possibly* heard, as he is pretty generally known among slaveholders. He put it into my head that I might make myself service-able to the cause of the slave by devoting a portion of my time to telling my own sorrows, and those of other slaves which had come under my observation. This was the commencement of a higher state of existence than any to which I had ever aspired. I was thrown into society the most pure, enlightened and benevolent that the country affords. Among these, I have never forgotten you, but have invariably made you the topic of conversation—thus giving you all the notoriety I could do. I need not tell you that the opinion formed of you in these circles, is far from being favorable. They have little respect for your honesty, and less for your religion.

But I was going on to relate to you something of my interesting experience. I had not long enjoyed the excellent society to which I have referred, before the light of its excellence exerted a beneficial influence on my mind and heart. Much of my early dislike of white persons was removed, and their manners, habits and customs, so entirely unlike what I have been used to in the kitchen-quarters on the plantations of the South, fairly charmed me, and gave me a strong disrelish for the coarse and degrading customs of my former condition. I therefore made an effort so to improve my mind and deportment, as to be somewhat fitted to the station to which I seemed almost Providentially called. The transition from degradation to respectability was indeed great, and to get from one to the other without carrying some marks of one's former condition, is truly a difficult matter. I would not have you think that I am now entirely clear of all plantation peculiarities, but my friends here, while they entertain the strongest dislike to them, regard me with that charity to which my past life somewhat entitles me, so that my condition in this respect is exceedingly pleasant. So far as my domestic affairs are concerned, I can boast of as com-fortable a dwelling as your own. I have an industrious and neat companion,

---

1 *I married ... leaving you* Douglass's first wife, Anna Murray-Douglass (1813–82), was born free in Maryland, and provided Douglass with crucial aid in his self-emancipation.
2 *Wm. Lloyd Garrison* Among the most prominent white abolitionists of the era, William Lloyd Gar-rison (1805–79) founded the abolitionist newspaper *The Liberator* as well as the American Anti-Slavery Society.

and four dear children—the oldest a girl of nine years, and three fine boys, the oldest eight, the next six, and the youngest four years old. The three oldest are now going regularly to school—two can read and write, and the other can spell with tolerable correctness words of two syllables. Dear fellows! they are all in comfortable beds, and are sound asleep, perfectly secure under my own roof. There are no slaveholders here to rend my heart by snatching them from my arms, or blast a proud mother's dearest hopes by tearing them from her bosom. These dear children are ours—not to work up into rice, sugar, and tobacco, but to watch over, regard, and protect, and to rear them up in the nurture and admonition of the gospel—to train them up in the paths of wisdom and virtue, and, as far as we can, to make them useful to the world and to themselves. Oh! sir, a slaveholder never appears to me so completely an agent of hell, as when I think of and look upon my dear children. It is then that my feelings rise above my control. I meant to have said more with respect to my own prosperity and happiness, but thoughts and feelings which this recital has quickened, unfits me to proceed further in that direction. The grim horrors of slavery rise in all their ghastly terror before me, the wails of millions pierce my heart, and chill my blood. I remember the chain, the gag, the bloody whip, the deathlike gloom overshadowing the broke spirit of the fettered bondman, the appalling liability of his being torn away from wife and children and sold like a beast in the market. Say not this is a picture of fancy.[1] You well know that I wear stripes[2] on my back inflicted by your direction; and that you, while we were brothers in the same church, caused this right hand, with which I am now penning this letter, to be closely tied to my left, and my person dragged at the pistol's mouth, fifteen miles, from the Bay side to Easton, to be sold like a beast in the market, for the alleged crime of intending to escape from your possession. All this and more you remember, and know to be perfectly true, not only of yourself, but of nearly all of the slaveholders around you.

At this moment, you are probably the guilty holder of at least three of my own dear sisters, and my only brother in bondage. These you regard as your property. They are recorded on your ledger, or perhaps have been sold to human flesh mongers, with a view to filling your own ever-hungry purse. Sir, I desire to know how and where these dear sisters are. Have you sold them? or are they still in your possession? What has become of them? are they living or dead? And my dear old grandmother, whom you turned out like an old horse, to die in the woods—is she still alive? Write and let me know all about them. If my grandmother be still alive, she is of no service to you, for by this time

---

1 *fancy* Imagination; a fiction.
2 *stripes* I.e., scars from having been whipped.

she must be nearly eighty years old—too old to be cared for by one to whom she has ceased to be of service; send her to me at Rochester,[1] or bring her to Philadelphia,[2] and it shall be the crowning happiness of my life to take care of her in her old age. Oh! she was to me a mother, and a father, so far as hard toil for my comfort could make her such. Send me my grandmother! that I may watch over and take care of her in her old age. And my sisters, let me know all about them. I would write to them, and learn all I want to know of them, without disturbing you in any way, but that, through your unrighteous conduct, they have been entirely deprived of the power to read and write. You have kept them in utter ignorance, and have therefore robbed them of the sweet enjoyments of writing or receiving letters from absent friends and relatives. Your wickedness and cruelty committed in this respect on your fellow-creatures, are greater than all the stripes you have laid upon my back, or theirs. It is an outrage upon the soul—a war upon the immortal spirit, and one for which you must give account at the bar of our common Father and Creator.

The responsibility which you have assumed in this regard is truly awful—and how you could stagger under it these many years is marvellous. Your mind must have become darkened, your heart hardened, your conscience seared and petrified, or you would have long since thrown off the accursed load and sought relief at the hands of a sin forgiving God. How, let me ask, would you look upon me, were I some dark night in company with a band of hardened villains, to enter the precincts of your own elegant dwelling and seize the person of your own lovely daughter Amanda, and carry her off from your family, friends, and all the loved ones of her youth—make her my slave—compel her to work, and I take her wages—place her name on my ledger as property—disregard her personal rights—fetter the powers of her immortal soul by denying her the right and privilege of learning to read and write—feed her coarsely—clothe her scantily, and whip her on the naked back occasionally; more and still more horrible, leave her unprotected—a degraded victim to the brutal lust of fiendish overseers who would pollute, blight, and blast her fair soul—rob her of all dignity—destroy her virtue, and annihilate all in her person the graces that adorn the character of virtuous womanhood? I ask how would you regard me, if such were my conduct? Oh! the vocabulary of the damned would not afford a word sufficiently infernal, to express your idea of my God-provoking wickedness. Yet sir, your treatment of my beloved sisters is in all essential points, precisely like the case I have now supposed. Damning

---

1   *Rochester* The home of Douglass and his family, in New York.
2   *Philadelphia* One of Douglass's first stops on his way to freedom, Philadelphia was largely populated by Quakers, who generally opposed slavery. (Though Pennsylvania was the first state to pass an act abolishing slavery in 1780, its gradual nature meant that there were still people living enslaved in the state well into the early nineteenth century.)

as would be such a deed on my part, it would be no more so than that which you have committed against me and my sisters.

I will now bring this letter to a close; you shall hear from me again unless you let me hear from you. I intend to make use of you as a weapon with which to assail the system of slavery—as a means of concentrating public attention on the system, and deepening the horror of trafficking in the souls and bodies of men. I shall make use of you as a means of exposing the character of the American church and clergy—and as a means of bringing this guilty nation with yourself to repentance. In doing this I entertain no malice towards you personally. There is no roof under which you would be more safe than mine, and there is nothing in my house which you might need for your comfort, which I would not readily grant. Indeed, I should esteem it a privilege, to set you an example as to how mankind ought to treat each other.

I am your fellow man but not your slave,

FREDERICK DOUGLASS

P.S. I send a copy of the paper containing this letter, to save postage.—F.D.

—1848

Photographs of Frederick Douglass

Frederick Douglass was a great proponent of the new art of photography. He saw it as a fundamentally democratic medium as well as a crucial tool in the fight to end slavery and racial discrimination. Douglass used photography as a means to assert greater control over his public image as a black man, sitting for at least 160 distinct portraits over the course of his life (as identified by John Stauffer, Zoe Trodd, and Celeste-Marie Bernier in their 2015 *Picturing Frederick Douglass*). By contrast, there are only 126 photographs of Abraham Lincoln known to exist, and only 127 of Walt Whitman.

Daguerreotype taken c. 1841, artist unknown. This is the first known photograph of Douglass.

Daguerreotype taken in July or August 1843, two years before the publication of Douglass's *Narrative*, artist unknown.

Daguerreotype taken in May 1848 by Edward White Gallery.

Daguerreotype taken c. 1853, two years before the publication of Douglass's second autobiography, *My Bondage and My Freedom*. Artist unknown.

Engraving of a photograph taken by John Howe Kent on 3 November 1882, used as the frontispiece to Douglass's revised third autobiography, *The Life and Times of Frederick Douglass* (1893).

Photograph taken on 31 October 1894 by Phineas C. Headley Jr. and James E. Reed, a few months before Douglass's death. Douglass very rarely smiled in his photographs.

Portrait of Douglass seated with his second wife, Helen Pitts (right). Helen's sister, Eva Pitts, stands in the center. Taken c. 1884, shortly after their marriage, artist unknown.

Engraving used as the frontispiece to the first edition of Douglass's 1845 *Narrative*, artist unknown.

Cover of an 1847 anti-abolitionist pamphlet reprinting one of Douglass's speeches. The pamphlet described Douglass as a "presumptive negro" and as a "runaway slave from Baltimore," despite the fact that he had been manumitted some months before.

William and Ellen Craft
1824 – 1900 and 1826 – 1891

Speaking at an abolitionist event held in honor of William and Ellen Craft in 1849, the antislavery orator Wendell Phillips proclaimed, "We would look in vain through the most trying times of our Revolutionary history for an incident of courage and noble daring to equal that of the escape of William and Ellen Craft; and future historians and poets would tell this story as one of the most thrilling of the nation's annals." Over the five days leading up to Christmas in 1848, the Crafts journeyed from enslavement in Georgia to freedom in Pennsylvania by means of a ploy that immediately made them famous for its ingenuity, bravery, and provocativeness: the mixed-race Ellen successfully posed as a white male planter seeking medical treatment in the North, while her husband William acted the part of an enslaved man accompanying his "master" on the journey. The Crafts' escape made them antislavery celebrities, and their story was told and retold, by themselves and others, many times over the ensuing decade, culminating in their 1860 book, *Running a Thousand Miles for Freedom.* This book, now one of the most extensively studied slave narratives, provides a gripping account of the Crafts' journey to freedom, together with an incisive portrayal of how race, gender, class, and physical ability and disability intersected in mid-nineteenth-century America.

The Crafts were both born into slavery in central Georgia. Ellen was the daughter of a biracial enslaved woman, Maria, and her married enslaver, James Smith; however, Ellen's fair skin led many observers to think that she was one of Smith's legitimate children. As a result, Smith's wife developed an enmity towards Ellen and gave her away to her half-sister as a wedding present at the age of eleven, separating Ellen from her mother; she was enslaved as a ladies' maid for the newlyweds. William was similarly separated from his family when his parents and sister were sold off to different enslavers during his youth, after which he was sold himself; his new enslaver apprenticed him to a cabinetmaker. William and Ellen married in 1846 and staged their escape two years later. *Running a Thousand Miles for*

Freedom credits the bulk of their escape plan to William, although it ascribes to Ellen the idea of wearing bandages on her face and arm to avoid recognition of either her true gender or her inability to write (because enslaved people were forbidden to learn to read or write, neither of the Crafts were literate at the time of their escape). However, another version of the genesis of their escape—the 1856 *Biography of an American Bondsman*, a life story of the Crafts' friend and promoter William Wells Brown, published by his daughter Josephine—describes Ellen as coming up with the entire plan. In any case, the escape's success depended largely on Ellen's performance as a white male enslaver, for which Brown hailed her as "truly a heroine."

After the Crafts' arrival in the North, news of their escape quickly brought them to the attention of Brown, a prominent abolitionist who introduced the Crafts to the antislavery lecture circuit. In Brown's company, the Crafts spoke at more than sixty locations in the first four months of 1849, recounting their escape and presenting it as further evidence for the evil of the institution they had fled. Typically, Brown and William Craft did most of the lecturing, but Ellen also spoke, sometimes even adopting her persona as "William Johnson," the identity she had assumed during their escape. When Ellen did not appear at one of these lectures, the audience was reported to have expressed "considerable disappointment." The Crafts eventually settled in Boston, where they achieved another one of their goals in escaping: a formal Christian marriage. (Marriages between enslaved people were not legally recognized in slave states.) After the passage of the 1850 Fugitive Slave Act, though, Ellen's former enslaver sent bounty hunters after them. White and black abolitionists and Boston's black community rallied to protect the Crafts and foil their would-be apprehenders. However, when the U.S. President himself authorized the use of military force, if necessary, to re-enslave the Crafts, they decided to leave the country altogether and move to England.

In Britain, the Crafts again lectured widely—once more in the company of Brown—and drew crowds in the thousands. As in the U.S., Ellen was the primary draw: to audiences that, despite their antislavery commitments, were still steeped in white supremacy, the idea of a "white" woman being enslaved was particularly provocative and an especially potent sign of slavery's perversity. As one abolitionist ruefully noted, "To think of such a woman being held as a piece of property, subject to be traded off to the highest bidder (while it is no worse or wickeder than when done to the blackest woman that ever was) does yet stir a community brought up in prejudice against color a thousand times more deeply than could be effected in different circumstances." The Crafts also pursued their own educations, learning to read and write as students at the Ockham School in Surrey, and started a family, eventually having five children. Later, William acted as an agent for British companies seeking to establish trading relations in West Africa. The couple publicly challenged the anti-black racism they encountered in Britain while continuing to protest American slavery: they staged a demonstration at the American section of the London Great Exhibition in 1851, and Ellen contested rumors spread by proslavery newspapers that they regretted their flight to England, writing that "I had much rather starve in England, a free woman, than be a slave for the best man that ever breathed upon the American continent."

The Crafts' ongoing antislavery agitation culminated with *Running a Thousand Miles for Freedom*, published in London in 1860. Because the book is narrated in William's voice, critics have often identified William as its sole author, even suggesting that it stifles Ellen. More recently, however, a consensus has developed that Ellen played an integral part with her husband in the book's composition, based on several pieces of evidence: the book's narration of incidents in which only Ellen was involved; its origins in the Crafts' lectures, in which Ellen also appeared and participated; and Ellen's well-documented outspokenness on issues of race and slavery. In addition, scholars have shown that William Wells Brown, to whom the Crafts sent a draft of the book, added material that amounts to at least a quarter and as much as half of the published text (much of it either plagiarized or quoted with attribution). *Running a Thousand Miles for Freedom* is thus widely understood to be a collaborative effort—a fact that is echoed in the narrative itself, in which collaboration is of central thematic importance. The book stresses marital and familial partnership both through the direct example of the Crafts themselves, whose marital teamwork enables them to escape, and through its pervasive emphasis on slavery's threat to such bonds. Besides this focus on marital collaboration, the book commands interest for its analysis of the racial, gender, and class ideologies of pre-Civil War America, which it accomplishes largely through its account of the Crafts' successful transgressions of the supposedly stable identity boundaries on which these ideologies were based. By the time *Running a Thousand Miles for Freedom* appeared, the couple's story was familiar on both sides of the Atlantic, but the book still went through two editions in as many years and was saluted by reviewers for—as the London *National Magazine* put it—"illustrat[ing] in the most striking and remarkable manner the abominable character of American slavery."

The Civil War, and the abolition of slavery that resulted from it, enabled the Crafts to return to America. They settled back in Georgia, where they bought a plantation and, in 1873, founded an agricultural school for formerly enslaved children and adults. This project experienced a severe setback in 1876, when William was accused of misappropriating some of the school's funds; he sued for libel but lost, and the school closed soon after. The Crafts also suffered from the racist terrorism with which white Southerners resisted

Reconstruction and reasserted white supremacy. Nevertheless, they soldiered on until Ellen's death in 1891. William followed her in 1900.

Even before the publication of *Running a Thousand Miles for Freedom*, the story of the Crafts' escape had already had a significant impact on American literature. Their escape formed the basis for Lydia Maria Child's play *The Stars and Stripes: A Melo-Drama* (1853) and William Wells Brown's novel *Clotel* (1853), widely considered to be the first novel published by an African American. The Crafts' published narrative helped engender a new surge of interest in them in the twentieth century: the black poet and playwright Georgia Douglas Johnson wrote *William and Ellen Craft: A Play in One Act* in 1935, and two years later, the African American historian Carter Godwin Woodson inaugurated his pioneering *Negro History Bulletin* with an article about the Crafts. More recent artistic retellings of the Crafts' story include the 2004 off-Broadway opera *Ellen Craft*, as well as community reenactments of their marriage and escape that have been staged in places from New York City to Macon, Georgia. *Running a Thousand Miles for Freedom* also continues to garner increasing scholarly attention, as critics debate its incorporation of Ellen's voice and perspective, as well as its portrayal of not just race, gender, and class, but also disability.

Note on the Text

The excerpts from *Running a Thousand Miles for Freedom* presented here are based on the first published edition of the book. Some British spellings have been retained from this first published edition; otherwise, spelling and punctuation have been modernized in accordance with the practices of this anthology.

⌘ ⌘ ⌘

from *Running a Thousand Miles for Freedom*

from PART I

"God gave us only over beast, fish, fowl,
Dominion absolute; that right we hold
By his donation. But man over man
He made not lord; such title to himself
Reserving, human left from human free."

MILTON[1]

My wife and myself were born in different towns in the State of Georgia, which is one of the principal slave States. It is true, our condition as slaves was not by any means the worst; but the mere idea that we were held as chattels,[2] and deprived of all legal rights—the thought that we had to give up our hard earnings to a tyrant, to enable him to live in idleness and luxury—the thought that we could not call the bones and sinews that God gave us our own: but above all, the fact that another man had the power to tear from our cradle the new-born babe and sell it in the shambles[3] like a brute, and then scourge us if we dared to lift a finger to save it from such a fate, haunted us for years.

But in December, 1848, a plan suggested itself that proved quite successful, and in eight days after it was first thought of we were free from the horrible trammels of slavery, rejoicing and praising God in the glorious sunshine of liberty.

My wife's first master was her father, and her mother his slave, and the latter is still the slave of his widow.

Notwithstanding my wife being of African extraction on her mother's side, she is almost white—in fact, she is so nearly so that the tyrannical old lady to whom she first belonged became so annoyed, at finding her frequently mistaken for a child of the family, that she gave her when eleven years of age to a daughter, as a wedding present. This separated my wife from her mother, and also from several other dear friends. But the incessant cruelty of her old mistress made the change of owners or treatment so desirable, that she did not grumble much at this cruel separation. ...

[The portion of the book omitted here recounts William and Ellen's backgrounds and early life up to their marriage in 1846.]

---

1   *God ... MILTON*   From *Paradise Lost* (1674), 12.67–71, by the English poet John Milton.
2   *chattels*   Property or possessions; the word originally meant "cattle."
3   *shambles*   Meat-market.

... [A]fter puzzling our brains for years, we were reluctantly driven to the sad conclusion, that it was almost impossible to escape from slavery in Georgia, and travel 1,000 miles across the slave States. We therefore resolved to get the consent of our owners, be married, settle down in slavery, and endeavour to make ourselves as comfortable as possible under that system; but at the same time ever to keep our dim eyes steadily fixed upon the glimmering hope of liberty, and earnestly pray God mercifully to assist us to escape from our unjust thraldom.

We were married, and prayed and toiled on till December, 1848, at which time (as I have stated) a plan suggested itself[.] ...

Knowing that slaveholders have the privilege of taking their slaves to any part of the country they think proper, it occurred to me that, as my wife was nearly white, I might get her to disguise herself as an invalid gentleman, and assume to be my master, while I could attend as his slave, and that in this manner we might effect our escape. After I thought of the plan, I suggested it to my wife, but at first she shrank from the idea. She thought it was almost impossible for her to assume that disguise, and travel a distance of 1,000 miles across the slave States. However, on the other hand, she also thought of her condition. She saw that the laws under which we lived did not recognize her to be a woman, but a mere chattel, to be bought and sold, or otherwise dealt with as her owner might see fit. Therefore the more she contemplated her helpless condition, the more anxious she was to escape from it. So she said, "I think it is almost too much for us to undertake; however, I feel that God is on our side, and with his assistance, notwithstanding all the difficulties, we shall be able to succeed. Therefore, if you will purchase the disguise, I will try to carry out the plan."

But after I concluded[1] to purchase the disguise, I was afraid to go to any one to ask him to sell me the articles. It is unlawful in Georgia for a white man to trade with slaves without the master's consent. But, notwithstanding this, many persons will sell a slave any article that he can get the money to buy. Not that they sympathize with the slave, but merely because his testimony is not admitted in court against a free white person.[2]

Therefore, with little difficulty I went to different parts of the town, at odd times, and purchased things piece by piece (except the trowsers which she found necessary to make) and took them home to the house where my wife resided. She being a ladies' maid, and a favourite slave in the family, was allowed a little room to herself; and amongst other pieces of furniture

---

1   *concluded* Resolved.
2   *Not that ... white person* I.e., the white person selling goods to an enslaved person does not fear breaking the law, because the enslaved person cannot testify against a white person in court.

which I had made in my overtime,[1] was a chest of drawers; so when I took the articles home, she locked them up carefully in these drawers. No one about the premises knew that she had anything of the kind. So when we fancied we had everything ready the time was fixed for the flight. But we knew it would not do to start off without first getting our master's[2] consent to be away for a few days. Had we left without this, they would soon have had us back into slavery, and probably we should never have got another fair opportunity of even attempting to escape.

Some of the best slaveholders will sometimes give their favourite slaves a few days' holiday at Christmas time; so, after no little amount of perseverance on my wife's part, she obtained a pass from her mistress, allowing her to be away for a few days. The cabinet-maker with whom I worked gave me a similar paper, but said that he needed my services very much, and wished me to return as soon as the time granted was up. I thanked him kindly; but somehow I have not been able to make it convenient to return yet; and, as the free air of good old England[3] agrees so well with my wife and our dear little ones, as well as with myself, it is not at all likely we shall return at present to the "peculiar institution"[4] of chains and stripes.[5] ...

... [A]t first, we were highly delighted at the idea of having gained permission to be absent for a few days; but when the thought flashed across my wife's mind, that it was customary for travellers to register their names in the visitors' book at hotels, as well as in the clearance or Custom-house book at Charleston, South Carolina—it made our spirits droop within us.

So, while sitting in our little room upon the verge of despair, all at once my wife raised her head, and with a smile upon her face, which was a moment before bathed in tears, said, "I think I have it!" I asked what it was. She said, "I think I can make a poultice[6] and bind up my right hand in a sling, and with propriety ask the officers to register my name for me." I thought that would do.

---

1 *overtime* I.e., time spent working on his own volition, over and above his regular working hours.
2 *our master* Ellen's enslaver, Robert Collins, had also paid half the purchase price for William when William's first enslaver sold him to pay off gambling debts.
3 *free ... England* Paraphrase of and reference to a passage from *The Task* (1785), a book-length poem by the English poet and abolitionist William Cowper: "Slaves cannot breathe in England; if their lungs / Receive our air, that moment they are free, / They touch our country and their shackles fall" (2.40–42). The Crafts quote these lines as the epigraph on the title page of *Running a Thousand Miles for Freedom*.
4 *peculiar institution* Euphemistic term for slavery, first coined by Southern enslavers in the 1820s; Northern abolitionists began to use it ironically in their attacks on slavery in the 1830s.
5 *stripes* Lashes.
6 *poultice* Soft, moist substance applied to the skin for medicinal purposes by means of a bandage or dressing.

It then occurred to her that the smoothness of her face might betray her; so she decided to make another poultice, and put it in a white handkerchief to be worn under the chin, up the cheeks, and to tie over the head. This nearly hid the expression of the countenance, as well as the beardless chin.

The poultice is left off in the engraving, because the likeness could not have been taken well with it on.

My wife, knowing that she would be thrown a good deal into the company of gentlemen, fancied that she could get on better if she had something to go over the eyes; so I went to a shop and bought a pair of green spectacles.[1] This was in the evening.

Ellen Craft in the disguise she wore during the Crafts' escape, as pictured in an engraving in the first edition of *Running a Thousand Miles for Freedom*.

We sat up all night discussing the plan, and making preparations. Just before the time arrived, in the morning, for us to leave, I cut off my wife's hair square at the back of the head, and got her to dress in the disguise and stand out on the floor. I found that she made a most respectable looking gentleman.

My wife had no ambition whatever to assume this disguise, and would not have done so had it been possible to have obtained our liberty by more simple means; but we knew it was not customary in the South for ladies to travel with male servants; and therefore, notwithstanding my wife's fair complexion, it would have been a very difficult task for her to have come off as a free white lady, with me as her slave; in fact, her not being able to write would have made this quite impossible. We knew that no public conveyance would take us, or any other slave, as a passenger, without our master's consent. This consent could never be obtained to pass into a free State. My wife's being muffled in

---

1 *green spectacles* Tinted glasses.

the poultices, etc., furnished a plausible excuse for avoiding general conversation, of which most Yankee[1] travellers are passionately fond. ...

When the time had arrived for us to start, we blew out the lights, knelt down, and prayed to our Heavenly Father mercifully to assist us, as he did his people of old, to escape from cruel bondage; and we shall ever feel that God heard and answered our prayer. Had we not been sustained by a kind, and I sometimes think special, providence, we could never have overcome the mountainous difficulties which I am now about to describe.

After this we rose and stood for a few moments in breathless silence—we were afraid that someone might have been about the cottage listening and watching our movements. So I took my wife by the hand, stepped softly to the door, raised the latch, drew it open, and peeped out. Though there were trees all around the house, yet the foliage scarcely moved; in fact, everything appeared to be as still as death. I then whispered to my wife, "Come, my dear, let us make a desperate leap for liberty!" But poor thing, she shrank back, in a state of trepidation. I turned and asked what was the matter; she made no reply, but burst into violent sobs, and threw her head upon my breast. This appeared to touch my very heart, it caused me to enter into her feelings more fully than ever. We both saw the many mountainous difficulties that rose one after the other before our view, and knew far too well what our sad fate would have been, were we caught and forced back into our slavish den. Therefore on my wife's fully realizing the solemn fact that we had to take our lives, as it were, in our hands, and contest every inch of the thousand miles of slave territory over which we had to pass, it made her heart almost sink within her, and, had I known them at that time, I would have repeated the following encouraging lines, which may not be out of place here—

> "The hill, though high, I covet to ascend,
> The *difficulty will not me offend*;[2]
> For I perceive the way to life lies here:
> Come, pluck up heart, let's neither faint nor fear;
> Better, though difficult, the right way to go,
> Than wrong, though easy, where the end is woe."[3]

---

1   *Yankee*   In common American usage, this term refers specifically to New Englanders, or later to Northerners in general; however, the Crafts here use it in its British sense as a synonym for "American."
2   *offend*   Cause to stumble; impede.
3   *The hill ... woe*   From *The Pilgrim's Progress* (1678), by the English writer and preacher John Bunyan. Bunyan's work, to which the Crafts' book refers several other times, is an allegorical narrative in which a character named "Christian" undertakes a difficult journey from the City of Destruction to the Celestial City.

However, the sobbing was soon over, and after a few moments of silent prayer she recovered her self-possession, and said, "Come, William, it is getting late, so now let us venture upon our perilous journey."

We then opened the door, and stepped as softly out as "moonlight upon the water."[1] I locked the door with my own key, which I now have before me, and tiptoed across the yard into the street. I say tiptoed, because we were like persons near a tottering avalanche, afraid to move, or even breathe freely, for fear the sleeping tyrants should be aroused, and come down upon us with double vengeance, for daring to attempt to escape in the manner which we contemplated.

We shook hands, said farewell, and started in different directions for the railway station. I took the nearest possible way to the train, for fear I should be recognized by someone, and got into the negro car in which I knew I should have to ride; but my *master* (as I will now call my wife) took a longer way round, and only arrived there with the bulk of the passengers. He obtained a ticket for himself and one for his slave to Savannah,[2] the first port, which was about two hundred miles off. ...

[The Crafts journey by train to Savannah, in the course of which Ellen has a brief scare when she notices a friend of her enslaver's family in the same car as her; however, he does not recognize her and she successfully feigns deafness when he attempts to engage her in conversation. At Savannah, the Crafts board a steamer for Charleston, South Carolina, where Ellen is advised by fellow passengers not to bring an enslaved person with her to the North.]

On my master [i.e., Ellen] entering the cabin he found at the breakfast-table a young southern military officer, with whom he had travelled some distance the previous day.

After passing the usual compliments the conversation turned upon the old subject—niggers.[3]

The officer, who was also travelling with a man-servant, said to my master, "You will excuse me, Sir, for saying I think you are very likely to spoil your boy

---

1 *moonlight ... water* From the short story "Titbottom's Spectacles" (1854), by the writer and abolitionist George William Curtis. In the story, this phrase occurs in a passage describing the "vague reveries of sweet possibility" a character engages in. Curtis knew of the Crafts and may have met them; after the Civil War, he advertised for funds for the agricultural school the Crafts founded in Georgia.

2 *Savannah* Seaport on Georgia's Atlantic coast that had been a major destination for slave ships during the transatlantic slave trade. Charleston, South Carolina, to which the Crafts sail from Savannah, was another major slave trade port: forty percent of the enslaved Africans taken to the U.S. during the transatlantic slave trade were brought there.

3 *niggers* By the nineteenth century, as the context here suggests, this word had firmly established itself in white American vernacular as an emphatically pejorative alternative to the then-more neutral term "negro."

by saying 'thank you' to him. I assure you, sir, nothing spoils a slave so soon as saying, 'thank you' and 'if you please' to him. The only way to make a nigger toe the mark, and to keep him in his place, is to storm at him like thunder, and keep him trembling like a leaf. Don't you see, when I speak to my Ned, he darts like lightning; and if he didn't I'd skin him."

Just then the poor dejected slave came in, and the officer swore at him fearfully, merely to teach my master what he called the proper way to treat me.

After he had gone out to get his master's luggage ready, the officer said, "That is the way to speak to them. If every nigger was drilled in this manner, they would be as humble as dogs, and never dare to run away."

The gentleman urged my master not to go to the North for the restoration of his health, but to visit the Warm Springs in Arkansas.

My master said, he thought the air of Philadelphia would suit his complaint best; and, not only so, he thought he could get better advice there.

The boat had now reached the wharf. The officer wished my master a safe and pleasant journey, and left the saloon. ...

[In Charleston, Ellen checks into a hotel, where William replaces her poultices.]

... I then ordered dinner, and took my master's boots out to polish them. While doing so I entered into conversation with one of the slaves. I may state here, that on the sea-coast of South Carolina and Georgia the slaves speak worse English than in any other part of the country. This is owing to the frequent importation, or smuggling in, of Africans, who mingle with the natives. Consequently the language cannot properly be called English or African, but a corruption of the two.[1]

The shrewd son of African parents to whom I referred said to me, "Say, brudder, way you come from, and which side you goin day wid dat ar little don up buckra" (white man)?

I replied, "To Philadelphia."

"What!" he exclaimed, with astonishment, "to Philumadelphy?"

"Yes," I said.

"By squash! I wish I was going wid you! I hears um say dat dare's no slaves way over in dem parts; is um so?"

I quietly said, "I have heard the same thing."

---

1 *on the sea-coast ... the two* Gullah, a creole language combining English with elements from several African languages, was the main language spoken in the nineteenth century by the African American population of coastal South Carolina and Georgia (also known as the Gullah) but was stigmatized, especially by white Americans, as an ignorant corruption of English. While its use has declined since the nineteenth century, the language survives in the area today.

"Well," continued he, as he threw down the boot and brush, and, placing his hands in his pockets, strutted across the floor with an air of independence— "Gorra Mighty, dem is de parts for Pompey; and I hope when you get dare you will stay, and nebber follow dat buckra back to dis hot quarter no more, let him be eber so good."

I thanked him; and just as I took the boots up and started off, he caught my hand between his two, and gave it a hearty shake, and, with tears streaming down his cheeks, said:

"God bless you, broder, and may de Lord be wid you. When you gets de freedom, and sitin under your own wine and fig-tree,[1] don't forget to pray for poor Pompey."

I was afraid to say much to him, but I shall never forget his earnest request, nor fail to do what little I can to release the millions of unhappy bondmen, of whom he was one. ...

When we left Macon, it was our intention to take a steamer at Charleston through to Philadelphia; but on arriving there we found that the vessels did not run during the winter, and I have no doubt it was well for us they did not; for on the very last voyage the steamer made that we intended to go by, a fugitive was discovered secreted on board, and sent back to slavery. However, as we had also heard of the Overland Mail Route, we were all right. So I ordered a fly[2] to the door, had the luggage placed on; we got in, and drove down to the Custom-house Office, which was near the wharf where we had to obtain tickets, to take a steamer for Wilmington, North Carolina. When we reached the building, I helped my master into the office, which was crowded with passengers. He asked for a ticket for himself and one for his slave to Philadelphia. This caused the principal officer—a very mean-looking, cheese-coloured fellow, who was sitting there—to look up at us very suspiciously, and in a fierce tone of voice he said to me, "Boy, do you belong to that gentleman?" I quickly replied, "Yes, sir" (which was quite correct). The tickets were handed out, and as my master was paying for them the chief man said to him, "I wish you to register your name here, sir, and also the name of your nigger, and pay a dollar duty on him."

My master paid the dollar, and pointing to the hand that was in the poultice, requested the officer to register his name for him. This seemed to offend the "high-bred" South Carolinian. He jumped up, shaking his head; and,

---

1   sitin ... fig-tree   The phrase "sitting under the vine and the fig-tree" is used several times in the Hebrew Bible (the Old Testament) to describe an ideal state of life, especially that which is prophesied to pertain in the Kingdom of God. See, for example, Micah 4.4: "they shall sit every man under his vine and under his fig-tree, and none shall make them afraid: for the mouth of the Lord of hosts hath spoken it."
2   fly   Type of carriage.

cramming his hands almost through the bottom of his trousers pockets, with a slave-bullying air, said, "I shan't do it."

This attracted the attention of all the passengers. Just then the young military officer with whom my master travelled and conversed on the steamer from Savannah stepped in, somewhat the worse for brandy; he shook hands with my master, and pretended to know all about him. He said, "I know his kin (friends) like a book"; and as the officer was known in Charleston, and was going to stop there with friends, the recognition was very much in my master's favour.

The captain of the steamer, a good-looking, jovial fellow, seeing that the gentleman appeared to know my master, and perhaps not wishing to lose us as passengers, said in an off-hand sailor-like manner, "I will register the gentleman's name, and take the responsibility upon myself." He asked my master's name. He said, "William Johnson." The names were put down, I think, "Mr. Johnson and slave." The captain said, "It's all right now, Mr. Johnson." He thanked him kindly, and the young officer begged my master to go with him, and have something to drink and a cigar; but as he had not acquired these accomplishments, he excused himself, and we went on board and came off to Wilmington, North Carolina. When the gentleman finds out his mistake, he will, I have no doubt, be careful in future not to pretend to have an intimate acquaintance with an entire stranger. During the voyage the captain said, "It was rather sharp shooting this morning, Mr. Johnson. It was not out of any disrespect to you, sir; but they make it a rule to be very strict at Charleston. I have known families to be detained there with their slaves till reliable information could be received respecting them. If they were not very careful, any d——d abolitionist might take off a lot of valuable niggers."

My master said, "I suppose so," and thanked him again for helping him over the difficulty. ...

[From Wilmington, the Crafts travel by rail to Richmond, Virginia; from there to Washington, D.C., and from there to Baltimore, Maryland.]

We left our cottage on Wednesday morning, the 21st of December, 1848, and arrived at Baltimore, Saturday evening, the 24th (Christmas Eve). Baltimore was the last slave port of any note at which we stopped.

On arriving there we felt more anxious than ever, because we knew not what that last dark night would bring forth. It is true we were near the goal, but our poor hearts were still as if tossed at sea; and, as there was another great and dangerous bar to pass, we were afraid our liberties would be wrecked, and, like the ill-fated *Royal Charter*,[1] go down for ever just off the place we longed to reach.

They are particularly watchful at Baltimore to prevent slaves from escaping into Pennsylvania, which is a free State. After I had seen my master into one of the best carriages, and was just about to step into mine, an officer, a full-blooded Yankee of the lower order, saw me. He came quickly up, and, tapping me on the shoulder, said in his unmistakable native twang, together with no little display of his authority, "Where are you going, boy?" "To Philadelphia, sir," I humbly replied. "Well, what are you going there for?" "I am travelling with my master, who is in the next carriage, sir." "Well, I calculate you had better get him out; and be mighty quick about it, because the train will soon be starting. It is against my rules to let any man take a slave past here, unless he can satisfy them in the office that he has a right to take him along."

The officer then passed on and left me standing upon the platform, with my anxious heart apparently palpitating in the throat. At first I scarcely knew which way to turn. But it soon occurred to me that the good God, who had been with us thus far, would not forsake us at the eleventh hour. So with renewed hope I stepped into my master's carriage, to inform him of the difficulty. I found him sitting at the farther end, quite alone. As soon as he looked up and saw me, he smiled. I also tried to wear a cheerful countenance, in order to break the shock of the sad news. I knew what made him smile. He was aware that if we were fortunate we should reach our destination at five o'clock the next morning, and this made it the more painful to communicate what the officer had said; but, as there was no time to lose, I went up to him and asked him how he felt. He said "Much better," and that he thanked God we were getting on so nicely. I then said we were not getting on quite so well as we had anticipated. He anxiously and quickly asked what was the matter. I told him. He started as if struck by lightning, and exclaimed, "Good Heavens! William, is it possible that we are, after all, doomed to hopeless bondage?" I could say nothing, my heart was too full to speak, for at first I did not know what to do. However we knew it would never do to turn back to the "City of Destruction," like Bunyan's Mistrust and Timorous, because they saw lions in the narrow way after ascending the hill Difficulty; but press on, like noble Christian and Hopeful, to the great city in which dwelt a few "shining ones."[2]

---

1   *Royal Charter*   Ship wrecked off the British coast, with great loss of life, near the end of its voyage from Melbourne, Australia, to Liverpool in October 1859.

2   *However ... "shining ones"*   Another reference to Bunyan's *Pilgrim's Progress*. In Bunyan's narrative, the allegorical protagonist Christian is accompanied on his journey from the City of Destruction by another pilgrim, Hopeful; they are hindered by characters named Mistrust and Timorous (representing the doubts and fears that obstruct Christian faith), who try to persuade them to turn back, but are assisted by "shining ones" (i.e., angels) from the Celestial City, their destination.

So, after a few moments, I did all I could to encourage my companion, and we stepped out and made for the office; but how or where my master obtained sufficient courage to face the tyrants who had power to blast all we held dear, heaven only knows! Queen Elizabeth could not have been more terror-stricken, on being forced to land at the traitors' gate leading to the Tower,[1] than we were on entering that office. We felt that our very existence was at stake, and that we must either sink or swim. But, as God was our present and mighty helper in this as well as in all former trials, we were able to keep our heads up and press forwards.

On entering the room we found the principal man, to whom my master said, "Do you wish to see me, sir?" "Yes," said this eagle-eyed officer; and he added, "It is against our rules, sir, to allow any person to take a slave out of Baltimore into Philadelphia, unless he can satisfy us that he has a right to take him along." "Why is that?" asked my master, with more firmness than could be expected. "Because, sir," continued he, in a voice and manner that almost chilled our blood, "if we should suffer any gentleman to take a slave past here into Philadelphia; and should the gentleman with whom the slave might be travelling turn out not to be his rightful owner; and should the proper master come and prove that his slave escaped on our road, we shall have him to pay for; and, therefore, we cannot let any slave pass here without receiving security to show, and to satisfy us, that it is all right."

This conversation attracted the attention of the large number of bustling passengers. After the officer had finished, a few of them said, "Chit, chit, chit"; not because they thought we were slaves endeavouring to escape, but merely because they thought my master was a slaveholder and invalid gentleman, and therefore it was wrong to detain him. The officer, observing that the passengers sympathised with my master, asked him if he was not acquainted with some gentleman in Baltimore that he could get to endorse for him, to show that I was his property, and that he had a right to take me off. He said, "No"; and added, "I bought tickets in Charleston to pass us through to Philadelphia, and therefore you have no right to detain us here." "Well, sir," said the man, indignantly, "right or no right, we shan't let you go." These sharp words fell upon our anxious hearts like the crack of doom,[2] and made us feel that hope only smiles to deceive.

---

1 *Queen Elizabeth ... the Tower* Before ascending the throne in 1558, Queen Elizabeth I of England was imprisoned in the Tower of London, a notorious castle and prison, for allegedly supporting a rebellion against her sister, Queen Mary I.

2 *crack of doom* Traditional phrase describing the blast of trumpets that will supposedly herald the end of the world and the Last Judgment.

For a few moments perfect silence prevailed. My master looked at me, and I at him, but neither of us dared to speak a word, for fear of making some blunder that would tend to our detection. We knew that the officers had power to throw us into prison, and if they had done so we must have been detected and driven back, like the vilest felons, to a life of slavery, which we dreaded far more than sudden death.

We felt as though we had come into deep waters and were about being overwhelmed, and that the slightest mistake would clip asunder the last brittle thread of hope by which we were suspended, and let us down for ever into the dark and horrible pit of misery and degradation from which we were straining every nerve to escape. While our hearts were crying lustily unto Him who is ever ready and able to save, the conductor of the train that we had just left stepped in. The officer asked if we came by the train with him from Washington; he said we did, and left the room. Just then the bell rang for the train to leave; and had it been the sudden shock of an earthquake it could not have given us a greater thrill. The sound of the bell caused every eye to flash with apparent interest, and to be more steadily fixed upon us than before. But, as God would have it, the officer all at once thrust his fingers through his hair, and in a state of great agitation said, "I really don't know what to do; I calculate it is all right." He then told the clerk to run and tell the conductor to "let this gentleman and slave pass"; adding, "As he is not well, it is a pity to stop him here. We will let him go." My master thanked him, and stepped out and hobbled across the platform as quickly as possible. I tumbled him unceremoniously into one of the best carriages, and leaped into mine just as the train was gliding off towards our happy destination.

We thought of this plan about four days before we left Macon; and as we had our daily employment to attend to, we only saw each other at night. So we sat up the four long nights talking over the plan and making preparations.

We had also been four days on the journey; and as we travelled night and day, we got but very limited opportunities for sleeping. I believe nothing in the world could have kept us awake so long but the intense excitement, produced by the fear of being retaken on the one hand, and the bright anticipation of liberty on the other.

We left Baltimore about eight o'clock in the evening; and not being aware of a stopping-place of any consequence between there and Philadelphia, and also knowing that if we were fortunate we should be in the latter place early the next morning, I thought I might indulge in a few minutes' sleep in the car; but I, like Bunyan's Christian in the arbour, went to sleep at the wrong time, and took too long a nap.[1] So, when the train reached Havre de Grace,[2] all the first-class passengers had to get out of the carriages and into a ferry-boat, to be ferried across the Susquehanna river, and take the train on the opposite side.

The road was constructed so as to be raised or lowered to suit the tide. So they rolled the luggage-vans on to the boat, and off on the other side; and as I was in one of the apartments adjoining a baggage-car, they considered it unnecessary to awaken me, and tumbled me over with the luggage. But when my master was asked to leave his seat, he found it very dark, and cold, and raining. He missed me for the first time on the journey. On all previous occasions, as soon as the train stopped, I was at hand to assist him. This caused many slaveholders to praise me very much: they said they had never before seen a slave so attentive to his master: and therefore my absence filled him with terror and confusion; the children of Israel could not have felt more troubled on arriving at the Red Sea.[3] So he asked the conductor if he had seen anything of his slave. The man being somewhat of an abolitionist, and believing that my master was really a slaveholder, thought he would tease him a little respecting me. So he said, "No, sir; I haven't seen anything of him for some time: I have no doubt he has run away, and is in Philadelphia, free, long before now." My master knew that there was nothing in this; so he asked the conductor if he would please to see if he could find me. The man indignantly replied, "I am no slave-hunter; and as far as I am concerned everybody must look after their own niggers." He went off and left the confused invalid to fancy whatever he felt inclined. My master at first thought I must have been kidnapped into slavery by some one, or left, or perhaps killed on the train. He also thought of stopping to see if he could hear anything of me, but he soon remembered that he had no money. That night all the money we had was consigned to my own pocket, because we thought, in case there were any pickpockets about, a slave's pocket would be the last one they would look for. However, hoping to meet me some day in a land of liberty, and as he had the tickets, he thought it best upon the whole to enter the boat and come off to Philadelphia, and endeavour to make his way alone in this cold and hollow world as best he could. The time was now up, so he went on board and came across with feelings that can be better imagined than described.

---

1 *like Bunyan's ... nap* In *Pilgrim's Progress*, while ascending the Hill of Difficulty (described above in the passage quoted as the Crafts are about to set off on their journey), Christian arrives in "a pleasant Arbour," where he falls "into a fast sleep, which detained him in that place until it was almost night. ... Now as he was sleeping, there came one to him and awaked him, saying '*Go to the ant, thou sluggard, consider her ways, and be wise*' [Proverbs 6.6], and with that Christian suddenly started up, and sped him on his way."

2 *Havre de Grace* Town in Maryland at the mouth of the Susquehanna River and the head of Chesapeake Bay; the name means "Harbor of Grace" in French.

3 *the children ... Red Sea* See Exodus 14.

After the train had got fairly on the way to Philadelphia, the guard came into my car and gave me a violent shake, and bawled out at the same time, "Boy, wake up!" I started, almost frightened out of my wits. He said, "Your master is scared half to death about you." That frightened me still more—I thought they had found him out; so I anxiously inquired what was the matter. The guard said, "He thinks you have run away from him." This made me feel quite at ease. I said, "No, sir; I am satisfied my good master doesn't think that." So off I started to see him. He had been fearfully nervous, but on seeing me he at once felt much better. He merely wished to know what had become of me.

On returning to my seat, I found the conductor and two or three other persons amusing themselves very much respecting my running away. So the guard said, "Boy, what did your master want?"[1] I replied, "He merely wished to know what had become of me." "No," said the man, "that was not it; he thought you had taken French leave,[2] for parts unknown. I never saw a fellow so badly scared about losing his slave in my life. Now," continued the guard, "let me give you a little friendly advice. When you get to Philadelphia, run away and leave that cripple, and have your liberty." "No, sir," I indifferently replied, "I can't promise to do that." "Why not?" said the conductor, evidently much surprised; "don't you want your liberty?" "Yes, sir," I replied; "but I shall never run away from such a good master as I have at present."

One of the men said to the guard, "Let him alone; I guess he will open his eyes when he gets to Philadelphia, and see things in another light." After giving me a good deal of information, which I afterwards found to be very useful, they left me alone.

I also met with a coloured gentleman on this train, who recommended me to a boarding-house that was kept by an abolitionist, where he thought I would be quite safe, if I wished to run away from my master. I thanked him kindly, but of course did not let him know who we were. Late at night, or rather early in the morning, I heard a fearful whistling of the steam-engine; so I opened the window and looked out, and saw a large number of flickering lights in the distance, and heard a passenger in the next carriage—who also had his head out of the window—say to his companion, "Wake up, old horse, we are at Philadelphia!"

The sight of those lights and that announcement made me feel almost as happy as Bunyan's Christian must have felt when he first caught sight of the

---

1 [Crafts' note] I may state here that every man slave is called boy till he is very old, then the more respectable slaveholders call him uncle. The women are all girls till they are aged, then they are called aunts. This is the reason why Mrs. Stowe calls her characters Uncle Tom, Aunt Chloe, Uncle Tiff, etc. [The Crafts refer here to *Uncle Tom's Cabin*, the bestselling 1852 antislavery novel by Harriet Beecher Stowe.]
2 *French leave* Unannounced or unsanctioned departure; escape.

cross.[1] I, like him, felt that the straps that bound the heavy burden to my back began to pop, and the load to roll off. I also looked, and looked again, for it appeared very wonderful to me how the mere sight of our first city of refuge should have all at once made my hitherto sad and heavy heart become so light and happy. As the train speeded on, I rejoiced and thanked God with all my heart and soul for his great kindness and tender mercy,[2] in watching over us, and bringing us safely through.

As soon as the train had reached the platform, before it had fairly stopped, I hurried out of my carriage to my master, whom I got at once into a cab, placed the luggage on, jumped in myself, and we drove off to the boarding-house which was so kindly recommended to me. On leaving the station, my master—or rather my wife, as I may now say—who had from the commencement of the journey borne up in a manner that much surprised us both, grasped me by the hand, and said, "Thank God, William, we are safe!" and then burst into tears, leant upon me, and wept like a child. The reaction was fearful. So when we reached the house, she was in reality so weak and faint that she could scarcely stand alone. However, I got her into the apartments that were pointed out, and there we knelt down, on this Sabbath, and Christmas Day—a day that will ever be memorable to us—and poured out our heartfelt gratitude to God, for his goodness in enabling us to overcome so many perilous difficulties, in escaping out of the jaws of the wicked.[3]

from PART 2

After my wife had a little recovered herself, she threw off the disguise and assumed her own apparel. We then stepped into the sitting-room, and asked to see the landlord. The man came in, but he seemed thunderstruck on finding a fugitive slave and his wife, instead of a "young cotton planter and his nigger." As his eyes travelled round the room, he said to me, "Where is your master?" I pointed him out. The man gravely replied, "I am not joking, I really wish to see your master." I pointed him out again, but at first he could not believe his eyes; he said "he knew that was not the gentleman that came with me."

But, after some conversation, we satisfied him that we were fugitive slaves, and had just escaped in the manner I have described. We asked him if he

---

1   *Bunyan's Christian … cross*   Relatively early in Christian's journey in *Pilgrim's Progress*, he arrives at a Cross, at the sight of which the "Burden" that he has been carrying drops off and disappears, making him "glad and lightsome."

2   *great … mercy*   "Kindness" (or "lovingkindness") and "tender mercy" are frequently paired in the Bible in reference to God's comfort, compassion, and redemption or salvation; see, for example, Psalms 40.11 and 103.4 and Colossians 3.12.

3   *in escaping … wicked*   See Job 29.17: "And I brake the jaws of the wicked, and plucked the spoil out of his teeth."

thought it would be safe for us to stop in Philadelphia. He said he thought not, but he would call in some persons who knew more about the laws than himself. He then went out, and kindly brought in several of the leading abolitionists of the city, who gave us a most hearty and friendly welcome amongst them. As it was in December, and also as we had just left a very warm climate, they advised us not to go to Canada as we had intended, but to settle at Boston in the United States. It is true that the constitution of the Republic has always guaranteed the slaveholders the right to come into any of the so-called free States, and take their fugitives back to southern Egypt.[1] But through the untiring, uncompromising, and manly efforts of Mr. Garrison, Wendell Phillips, Theodore Parker,[2] and a host of other noble abolitionists of Boston and the neighbourhood, public opinion in Massachusetts had become so much opposed to slavery and to kidnapping, that it was almost impossible for anyone to take a fugitive slave out of that State.

So we took the advice of our good Philadelphia friends, and settled at Boston. I shall have something to say about our sojourn there presently.

Among other friends we met with at Philadelphia, was Robert Purves, Esq.,[3] a well educated and wealthy coloured gentleman, who introduced us to Mr. Barkley Ivens, a member of the Society of Friends,[4] and a noble and generous-hearted farmer, who lived at some distance in the country.

This good Samaritan[5] at once invited us to go and stop quietly with his family, till my wife could somewhat recover from the fearful reaction of the past journey. We most gratefully accepted the invitation, and at the time appointed we took a steamer to a place up the Delaware river, where our new and dear friend met us with his snug little cart, and took us to his happy home. This was the first act of great and disinterested kindness we had ever received from a white person.

The gentleman was not of the fairest complexion, and therefore, as my wife was not in the room when I received the information respecting him and his

---

1   *southern Egypt*   I.e., the Southern slave states, which the Crafts here metaphorically liken to Egypt, where the Israelites were enslaved in the Bible.

2   *Mr. Garrison, Wendell Phillips, Theodore Parker*   William Lloyd Garrison (1805–79), Phillips (1811–84), and Parker (1810–60) were all leading Boston-based white abolitionists. Parker, a Unitarian minister, conducted the Crafts' formal wedding ceremony in 1850.

3   *Robert Purves, Esq.*   I.e., Robert Purvis (1810–98), a wealthy mixed-race South Carolina-born abolitionist who chose to identify as black.

4   *Society of Friends*   Formal name of the Quakers, a Christian denomination known for the strong anti-slavery commitment of many of its members.

5   *good Samaritan*   Reference to Jesus' parable of the Good Samaritan in Luke 10.25–37, which Jesus tells in answer to the question, "who is my neighbour?" In the parable, a man assaulted by thieves is ignored by members of the religious establishment but aided by a Samaritan, a member of an ethnic group viewed with suspicion by Jews at the time.

anti-slavery character, she thought of course he was a quadroon[1] like herself. But on arriving at the house, and finding out her mistake, she became more nervous and timid than ever.

As the cart came into the yard, the dear good old lady, and her three charming and affectionate daughters, all came to the door to meet us. We got out, and the gentleman said, "Go in, and make yourselves at home; I will see after the baggage." But my wife was afraid to approach them. She stopped in the yard, and said to me, "William, I thought we were coming among coloured people?" I replied, "It is all right; these are the same." "No," she said, "it is not all right, and I am not going to stop here; I have no confidence whatever in white people, they are only trying to get us back to slavery." She turned round and said, "I am going right off." The old lady then came out, with her sweet, soft, and winning smile, shook her heartily by the hand, and kindly said, "How art thou, my dear? We are all very glad to see thee and thy husband. Come in, to the fire; I dare say thou art cold and hungry after thy journey."[2]

We went in, and the young ladies asked if she would like to go upstairs and "fix" herself before tea. My wife said, "No, I thank you; I shall only stop a little while." "But where art thou going this cold night?" said Mr. Ivens, who had just stepped in. "I don't know," was the reply. "Well, then," he continued, "I think thou hadst better take off thy things and sit near the fire; tea will soon be ready." "Yes, come, Ellen," said Mrs. Ivens, "let me assist thee" (as she commenced undoing my wife's bonnet-strings) "don't be frightened, Ellen, I shall not hurt a single hair of thy head. We have heard with much pleasure of the marvellous escape of thee and thy husband, and deeply sympathise with thee in all that thou hast undergone. I don't wonder at thee, poor thing, being timid; but thou needs not fear us; we would as soon send one of our own daughters into slavery as thee; so thou mayest make thyself quite at ease!" These soft and soothing words fell like balm upon my wife's unstrung nerves, and melted her to tears; her fears and prejudices vanished, and from that day she has firmly believed that there are good and bad persons of every shade of complexion.

After seeing Sally Ann and Jacob, two coloured domestics, my wife felt quite at home. After partaking of what Mrs. Stowe's Mose and Pete[3] called a "busting supper," the ladies wished to know whether we could read. On learning we could not, they said if we liked they would teach us. To this kind

---

1 *quadroon* Term commonly used in the nineteenth century to classify a person of mixed racial background—specifically, someone with one black and three white grandparents.
2 *How art thou ... thy journey* Quakers were known for their archaic speech, which continued to include pronouns like "thee" and "thou" long after they had passed out of common spoken English.
3 *Mrs. Stowe's Mose and Pete* In Stowe's *Uncle Tom's Cabin*, Mose and Pete are the two sons of the enslaved title character.

offer, of course, there was no objection. But we looked rather knowingly at each other, as much as to say that they would have rather a hard task to cram anything into our thick and matured skulls.

However, all hands set to and quickly cleared away the tea-things, and the ladies and their good brother brought out the spelling and copy books and slates, etc., and commenced with their new and green pupils. We had, by stratagem, learned the alphabet while in slavery, but not the writing characters; and, as we had been such a time learning so little, we at first felt that it was a waste of time for any one at our ages to undertake to learn to read and write. But, as the ladies were so anxious that we should learn, and so willing to teach us, we concluded to give our whole minds to the work, and see what could be done. By so doing, at the end of the three weeks we remained with the good family we could spell and write our names quite legibly. They all begged us to stop longer; but, as we were not safe in the State of Pennsylvania, and also as we wished to commence doing something for a livelihood, we did not remain.

When the time arrived for us to leave for Boston, it was like parting with our relatives. We have since met with many very kind and hospitable friends, both in America and England; but we have never been under a roof where we were made to feel more at home, or where the inmates took a deeper interest in our well-being, than Mr. Barkley Ivens and his dear family. May God ever bless them, and preserve each one from every reverse of fortune!

We finally, as I have stated, settled at Boston, where we remained nearly two years, I employed as cabinet-maker and furniture broker,[1] and my wife at her needle; and, as our little earnings in slavery were not all spent on the journey, we were getting on very well, and would have made money, if we had not been compelled by the General Government, at the bidding of the slaveholders, to break up business, and fly from under the Stars and Stripes to save our liberties and our lives.

...

—1860

---

1 *furniture broker* Someone who sells used or second-hand furniture.

Maps

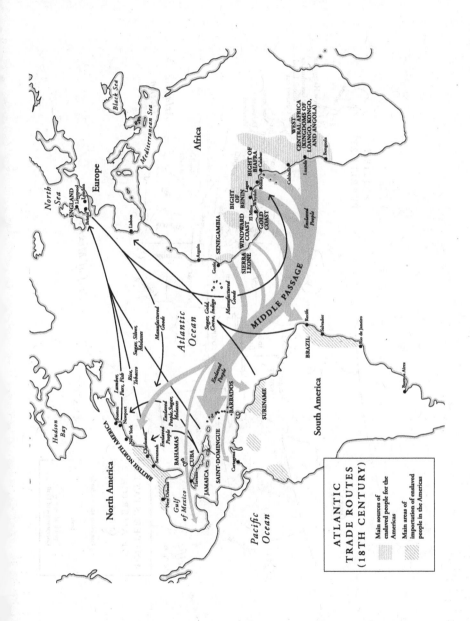

ATLANTIC
TRADE ROUTES
(18TH CENTURY)

Main sources of
enslaved people for the
Americas

Main areas of
importation of enslaved
people in the Americas

MIDDLE PASSAGE

Europe

Africa

WEST
CENTRAL AFRICA
(KINGDOMS OF
LOANGO, KONGO,
AND ANGOLA)

BIGHT
OF
BIAFRA

BIGHT
OF
BENIN

GOLD
COAST

WINDWARD
COAST

SIERRA
LEONE

SENEGAMBIA

North
Sea

ENGLAND

Atlantic
Ocean

North America

BRITISH NORTH AMERICA

Gulf
of Mexico

Hudson
Bay

BAHAMAS

CUBA

JAMAICA

SAINT-DOMINGUE

BARBADOS

SURINAME

South America

BRAZIL

Pacific
Ocean

Black Sea

Mediterranean Sea

Manufactured
Goods

Sugar, Gold,
Cocoa, Indigo

Enslaved
People

Enslaved
People

Enslaved
People

Enslaved
People, Sugar,
Molasses

Lumber,
Furs, Fish

Rice,
Tobacco

Sugar, Silver,
Molasses

Manufactured
Goods

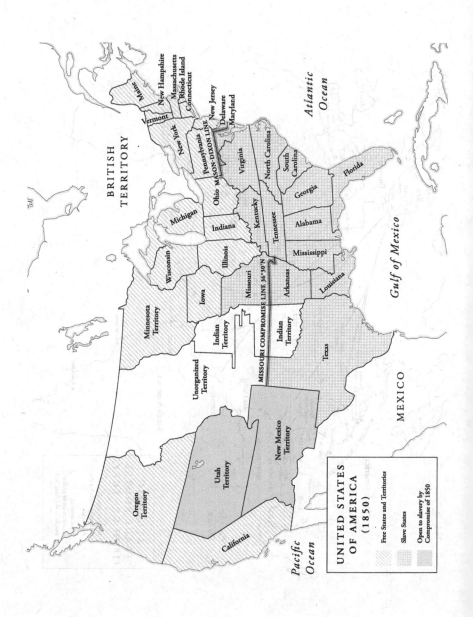

BRITISH TERRITORY

Maine

New Hampshire
Massachusetts
Rhode Island
Connecticut

Vermont

New York

New Jersey
Delaware
Maryland

Pennsylvania

MASON-DIXON LINE

Ohio

Virginia

North Carolina

South Carolina

Florida

Michigan

Indiana

Kentucky

Tennessee

Georgia

Alabama

Wisconsin

Illinois

Mississippi

Minnesota Territory

Iowa

Missouri

Arkansas

Louisiana

Indian Territory

MISSOURI COMPROMISE LINE 36°30'N

Indian Territory

Texas

Unorganized Territory

New Mexico Territory

Utah Territory

Oregon Territory

California

Atlantic Ocean

Gulf of Mexico

MEXICO

Pacific Ocean

UNITED STATES
OF AMERICA
(1850)

Free States and Territories

Slave States

Open to slavery by
Compromise of 1850

From the Publisher

A name never says it all, but the word "Broadview" expresses a good deal of the philosophy behind our company. We are open to a broad range of academic approaches and political viewpoints. We pay attention to the broad impact book publishing and book printing has in the wider world; for some years now we have used 100% recycled paper for most titles. Our publishing program is internationally oriented and broad-ranging. Our individual titles often appeal to a broad readership too; many are of interest as much to general readers as to academics and students.

Founded in 1985, Broadview remains a fully independent company owned by its shareholders—not an imprint or subsidiary of a larger multinational.

To order our books or obtain up-to-date information, please visit broadviewpress.com.

broadview press
www.broadviewpress.com

This book is made of paper from well-managed FSC® - certified
forests, recycled materials, and other controlled sources.